Vines, Grapes and Wines

For W.I.L.

Vines, Grapes and Wines

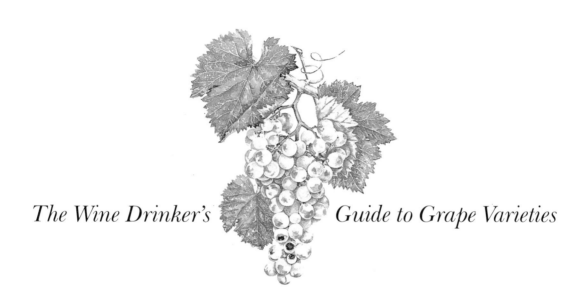

The Wine Drinker's   *Guide to Grape Varieties*

Jancis Robinson

MITCHELL BEAZLEY

Vines, Grapes and Wines by Jancis Robinson
First published in Great Britain in 1986 by Mitchell Beazley, an imprint of
Octopus Publishing Group Ltd, 2-4 Heron Quays, London E14 4JP

First published in paperback in 1992
Reprinted 1994, 1996, 1997, 2002
Copyright © Octopus Publishing Ltd 1986, 1992, 1994, 1996, 1997, 2002
Text copyright © Jancis Robinson 1986, 1992, 1994, 1996, 1997, 2002

The vine classification table on page 8 appears in Alexis Lichine's
Encyclopedia of Wines and Spirits 6th edition and is used with permission
of the publishers Cassell Ltd.

ISBN 1 85732 999 6

A CIP record for this book is available from the British Library

The author and the publisher will be grateful for any information which will assist
them in keeping future editions up to date. Although all reasonable care has been taken
in the preparation of this book, neither the publisher nor the author can
accept any liability for any consequences arising from the use thereof or from the
information contained herein.

Typeset by Servis Filmsetting Ltd., Manchester, England
Reproduction by Anglia Reproductions Ltd., Witham, England
Printed in China

Editor	Dian Taylor
Senior Designer	Paul Drayson
Cartographic Editor	Anita Wagner
Cartographic Researcher	Catherine Palmer
Copy Editors and Index	Naomi Good & Rachel Grenfell
Editorial Assistant	Liz Parks
Production	Philip Collyer
Senior Executive Editor	Chris Foulkes
Senior Executive Art Editor	Roger Walton
Grape Illustrations	Fiona Currie (Classic Varieties)
	Lesli Sternberg (Major Varieties)
	Lisa Horstmann, Wendy Brett,
	Sue Sharples (Other Varieties)
Other Illustrations	Steve Kirk
Maps	Paul Margiotta (pages 11 and 22-53)
	Mulkern Rutherford (pages 18-21)
	David Mallot (pages 198-230)
Great Vineyards	Sue Sharples

Contents

Introduction

Over the last 10 years the world's wine drinkers have been rapidly conditioned to what might be called varietal worship: respect for those wines labelled with the name of the principal grape variety from which they were made. No sooner were wine lovers in America and Australia clamouring for domestic Cabernet Sauvignon and Chardonnay, than much of the eastern European vineyard began to supply cheap versions of such grapes, the Italians smartly stepped into the international marketplace with their varietal offerings, and even the French started to slip jargon as novel as Pinot Noir and Chardonnay on to their labels to give them greater appeal to the new, variety-conscious breed of wine consumer.

Yet remarkably little has been done to explain the magical world of vine varieties to the wine drinker.

A wine's varietal make-up is crucial, a far more important influence on its flavour and character than geological wrinkle, accident of climate or craft in the cellar. The grape alone determines perhaps 90 percent of the flavour of a wine, and shapes its character by regulating the intensity, weight, acidity, longevity and potential.

It is extraordinary how little the average wine drinker, even the sophisticated one, has been able to penetrate the jungle of thousands of vine varieties. He and increasingly she may be vaguely familiar with the handful of "international" classics grown and sold from Seattle to the South Island, but that is fewer even than the nine included in this book's Classic Varieties section. The fascinating mesh of interrelationships between them and the Major Varieties that follow is a potentially revealing aspect of connoisseurship which has remained uncharted in all but the most arcane literature. And the intricacies of the distribution and often inspiring characters of the 1,000 or so further varieties described in this volume represent *terra incognita* to most of the world's most enthusiastic wine lovers.

The importance and relevance of this subject matter have been recognized and some noble attempts made to cover it, though rarely with any degree of detail. The most admirably thorough work in recent years has been Professor Pierre Galet's four-tome ampelographical work *Cépages et Vignobles de France*, published in the fifties and sixties. Even Lucie T. Morton's excellent American adaptation leaves it skewered awkwardly on a Franco-American axis with little coverage of such rich vine territories as Italy and Iberia, however.

The last major truly international work on vine varieties was published in French in 1909. Written by another Montpellier-trained viticulturist Pierre Viala (now honoured by an eponymous *Place* in Montpellier) with a colleague, Victor Vermorel, this seven-volume *Traité Général d'Ampélographie* is awe-inspiring in its scope and usefulness even today. *Vines, Grapes and Wines* is an attempt at a concise and updated version of Viala. This is the first time, to the author's knowledge at least, that a comprehensive international survey of vine varieties has been undertaken in English. It is designed specifically not for vine growers but for the wine drinker who wants to understand more about why the wines made today taste the way they do, and who wants to study just how the world's wine production is shaped by some often fairly random events and questionable decisions.

The primary aim of this book is to describe how the wine made by each grape variety tastes, why, where it is grown and how this influences that taste. The secondary aim is to allow the wine drinker to analyse and assess the varietal make-up of the world's vineyards.

THE NEED FOR A VARIETAL APPROACH

This systematic inspection of the vine types grown internationally has thrown up a worryingly high number of varieties capable of producing good-quality wines with real character which have effectively become endangered species. This applies particularly to some of the more traditional varieties of Portugal, Spain and Italy – just a few obvious examples being Arinto, Touriga Nacional, Alvarinho, Aglianico, Barbarossa, Greco – though the phenomenon is apparent in wine regions as dissimilar as Somló in Hungary, the Cape and even the Médoc. Now that the principles of selecting good plant material including, especially, clonal selection are well understood, there is an urgent need for a review and possible revival of many of these varieties before their one or two viticultural inconveniences consign them to extinction.

Another factor is probably that the earthily traditional varieties, even the top-quality ones such as Malvasia and Vermentino, tend to be in the hands of those least equipped to transform them into clean, stable, top-quality wine. Perhaps greater familiarity with such varieties on the part of the cosmopolitan wine drinker will help the better examples more firmly to stamp their identity and establish a market and, therefore, long-term future.

The increased awareness of, some might say obsession with, grape varieties in the newer wine regions has had interesting effects on winemakers as well as wine drinkers. The fortunes of the proudly traditional vignerons of Gascony, for instance, have taken a distinct turn for the better since someone drew their attention to the fact that the Californians were doing rather clever things with their brandy variety Colombard, which transformed it into extremely appetizing table wine. The eventual result has been the very toothsome Colombard Vin de Pays de Côtes de Gascogne.

By looking in more detail at the grape varieties available to the modern winemaker, and how they respond to different conditions and treatments throughout the world, the wine drinker will be able to understand better not only what *is* offered, but also what should and could be offered. Vine growers are extremely conservative, as one might expect of farmers who have to invest in a crop for 30 years at a stretch. (This is one area in which the larger wine companies, able to formulate long-term strategy and take the concomitant risks on a corporate basis, are much better placed than the individual vine farmer.) With greater understanding of the varieties available, it will be seen that the wines currently vaunted on the international market represent a tiny fraction of the exciting possibilities ahead.

HOW THE BOOK WORKS

The map section at the beginning of this book is self-explanatory; the categorization of specific grape varieties that follows is not. It starts with a detailed study of nine Classic vine varieties, chosen for such distinction on the basis of their quantitative as well as qualitative importance. Each of these vine types is fairly widely distributed across the wine world, and is capable of producing truly great wine, even if, as in the case of Chenin Blanc, the great majority of its produce is much more ordinary.

After this come the Major varieties, which include the most important members of the multifarious Muscat family, chosen because they are associated with the best-known names on the international wine market. Viognier is perhaps the most contentious member of this group, but has been included because of the stature of Condrieu and Château-Grillet.

The principal name chosen for any variety in this book traces it back as closely as possible to its origins. Thus references to the Grenache of the Midi and Provence will be found under Garnacha; the Muscadet grape is called Melon de Bourgogne; and the Ugni Blanc now so quantitatively important to the French *vignoble* is doggedly referred to as Trebbiano to underline its provenance. Galet's principal names and spellings have been followed for French varieties and authorities of similar standing have been sought for other countries.

The rest of the vine types are divided into red-wine and white-wine varieties, because this is a guide for wine drinkers rather than grape spotters. This means that dark grape varieties such as Gewürztraminer, Schönburger and some of the Muscats which are habitually used to produce white wine are listed in the "white" section. The red-fleshed Teinturiers are clearly marked as such and rated "dark". Of course, different-hued mutations are known for almost every grape variety. That elusive plant true Pinot is notorious in this respect, as is Veltliner. It is quite possible to find grapes which should technically be classified "light", "dark" and "grey" on the same plant or even, in some cases, on the same bunch.

Where a different coloured mutation has established a discernible identity and considerable influence for itself, such as Garnacha Blanca, Pinot Blanc and Merlot Blanc, separate entries can be found in the appropriate section.

These red and white sections of Other vine types are split into obvious geographical divisions. Each variety is listed under that region or country which currently has the greatest area planted with it. And, within each combination of colour and country or region, the varieties are listed in decreasing order of quantitative importance wherever this is documented. Macabeo, for instance, appears under Spain because Spanish plantings outnumber French hectares planted with it by seven to one, and it is listed second under Spanish white varieties because Airén is the only other white variety to cover a greater area of Spanish vineyard land. All of these statistical decisions are only as good as the statistics on which they are based, of course, and every effort has been made to use the most recent available. This means as long ago as 1979 in the case of most of France, unfortunately, but even the now rather dated official agricultural census is a sterling feat of precision compared to most of the Mediterranean countries and Portugal, which few vineyard statisticians appear to have visited for several decades.

SOME RELATIONSHIPS – FACTS AND FALLACIES

This lack of familiarity with some of the world's most ramified national groupings of vine varieties has led to widespread acceptance of many an error. Ampelography, the science of vine description, has only recently been refined and codified, notably by Galet, to make identification internationally possible. The leaves and shoots, being that part of the vine available for study for the longest period of the year, either growing or dried in the winter, are chosen as the most useful raw material for a series of very detailed measurements. When taken together with the all-important hairiness of the growing tip, shoot tip and eventual leaf, the systematic description of shoot, cane, buds, flowers, cluster, berries and seeds makes up the equivalent of a fingerprint for each vine variety.

Thus an experienced ampelographer can tell when a "Cabernet Franc" is really a Merlot, as is often the case in California; when Western Australia's "Sémillon" and a Victorian plantation of "Chardonnay" are in fact Chenin Blanc, as the invited French ampelographer Paul Truel found in 1976; and when two grape varieties popularly held to be related, as Chardonnay and Pinot Noir were for so long, are not.

Portugal and Spain are perhaps richest in disproved hypotheses of vine relationships, many of them backed up by very pretty historical fable. Contrary to accepted folklore, no ampelographical connection can be found between Riesling and Sercial (Cerceal), Arinto or Pedro Ximénez, for instance. There are no Pinot Noir genes in any known Douro variety, and the German red Portugieser appears unrelated to any Portuguese vine, though a tiny parcel of Portugieser cuttings is now cultivated in the Douro for observation purposes.

Another obvious example of common misapprehension is the supposition that the Limberger of Austria, often known as Blaufränkisch in German-speaking countries, Kékfrankos in Hungary and other Slav variations on that "blue French" theme in eastern Europe, is related to or identical with Gamay. The Beaujolais grape is, in fact, very unusual among those associated with internationally famous wines in that it is hardly found outside its native region – and not at all outside its native country, despite the California habit of using its name so liberally for a pair of quite unrelated (though admittedly French) varieties.

The value clearly attached to certain vine names in some areas has exacerbated initial confusion. Pinot is an obvious example, its name being applied liberally not only to the Pinots Blanc and Gris related to Pinot Noir, but also erroneously to Chardonnay and the likes of Pineau d'Aunis, Pineau de la Loire (Chenin Blanc) and Pinot de Romans (Durif). The same is true in Italy of Malvasia, often used in synonyms of varieties quite unrelated to the great Greek original. In France, too, there are several Malvoisies with genealogical connections closer to, for example, Pinot Gris than Malvasia. Auxerrois meanwhile is the name of the Alsace partner of Pinot Blanc as well as the Cahors synonym for Malbec and therefore just as confusing, though compared with Italy, France's vine nomenclature looks a model of clarity.

All sorts of fascinating facts, interesting anomalies and intriguing mysteries are spotlit when the vine world rather than the wine world is studied. Few of the world's wine drinkers, for instance, would guess that the vine variety covering the largest vineyard area by far is the white Airén of La Mancha. Nor would many realize that the robust Bastardo of Portugal, the Trousseau of the Jura and California's Gray Riesling are so closely related.

Examination of the viticultural characteristics of each variety raises further questions about their geographical distribution. The late-ripening Chenin Blanc seems a perverse choice for a region as northerly as the Loire, while the astringent Carignan, particularly the poor clones of Carignan so commonly planted throughout the Midi, seems with hindsight to have been a questionable variety to promulgate in a region which can only afford to make early-maturing wines. In Italy, Verdicchio is extraordinarily well entrenched on the east coast, covering perhaps three times the area of France's total plantings of Cabernet Sauvignon; yet it yields so grudgingly that the objective observer is forced to wonder at its popularity.

By now most possible genealogical links between the world's known vine varieties have been established, but there remain some enigmatic areas, notably around the ampelographically uncharted eastern Mediterranean. It is well known that many Italian varieties, indeed many of the better Italian varieties, are Greek in origin. It could be extremely useful to Greek vineyards, which have an uncertain future, to establish, for instance, which of the vines they currently nurture are Aglianico and Grechetto. And absolute proof is needed for the attractive and just about convincing theory that the Ribolla of Friuli is the Rebula of Yugoslavia is the Robola of the Greek island of Cephalonia. Could Portugal's Rabo de Ovelho be Hungary's Juhfark? The names have the same literal translation; the vines and resultant wines seem very similar; there are cultural links

between the two countries. Could Viognier, the mystery vine of the northern Rhône, be related to the eponymous vine of the Dalmatian island of Vugava? Why did the South Americans latch so enthusiastically on to the Torrontes of Galicia from among the thousands of Spanish vine types available to them? Perhaps this book will promote an interest and exchange of information so that a future edition could answer all these questions.

THE VINE FAMILY

Only the *Vitis* genus of plants, belonging to the *Ampelidaceae* family, is of relevance to wine drinkers, even though four of the other nine genera of *Ampelidaceae* yield grapes of a sort. This table shows how the best-known of the different species of the *Vitis* genus, or vine family, are classified.

SUB-GENUS *EUVITES*

American Species

Temperate Regions: Eastern zone

Vitis labrusca	*Vitis aestivalis*
Vitis lincecunici	*Vitis bicolor*

Temperate Regions: Central zone

Vitis riparia	*Vitis rupestris*
Vitis rubra	*Vitis monticola*
Vitis berlandieri	*Vitis cordifolia*
Vitis candicans	*Vitis cinerea*

Temperate Regions: Western zone

Vitis Californica	*Vitis Arizonica*

Torrid Regions: Florida and the Bahamas

Vitis coriacea	*Vitis gigas*

Torrid Regions: Tropical and Equatorial zones

Vitis Bourgoeana	*Vitis Cariboea*

Eastern Asian Species (incomplete)

Temperate Regions

Vitis amurensis	(Japan, Mongolia, Sakhalin Is.)
Vitis coignetiae	(Japan, Sakhalin Is., Korea)
Vitis Thunbergii	(Japan, Korea, Formosa, Southwest China)
Vitis flexuosa	(Korea, Japan, India, Nepal, Cochin-China)
Vitis Romaneti	(China)
Vitis Piasezkii	(China)
Vitis armata	(China)
Vitis Wilsonae	(China)
Vitis rutilans	(China)
Vitis Pagnucii	(China)
Vitis pentagona	(China)
Vitis Romanetia	(China)
Vitis Davidii	(China)

Sub-Tropical Regions

Vitis Retordi	(Tonkin)
Vitis Balansaeana	(Tonkin)
Vitis lanata	(India, Nepal, Dekkan, Southern China, Burma)
Vitis pedicellata	(Himalayan Mountains)

European and East and Central Asian Species

Vitis vinifera

SUB-GENUS *MUSCADINIAE*

North American Species

Vitis rotundifolia
Vitis Munsoniana
Vitis Popenoei

Furthermore, remarkably few of the 40-odd species of that *Vitis* genus, divided by botanists into the *Euvites* and *Muscadiniae* subgenera, yield grapes worth turning into wine. Indeed, one species alone, *Vitis vinifera*, the only one native to Europe and Central Asia, is responsible for 99.998 percent of the world's wine production.

There are other species of some relevance to the wine drinker, either as rootstocks, progenitors of hybrids or as direct producers of wine in their own right:

Vitis amurensis Named after the Amur river which forms the Sino-Siberian frontier, this species is notable for its resistance to cold, as one might expect. The Russians and now the Germans are experimenting with hybrids of *amurensis* and *vinifera*. Although officially barred from using them for quality wine production in Germany, Professor Helmut Becker of Geisenheim is delighted with their performance in trials, and they could be of great use in England and New Zealand.

Vitis labrusca Edward Hyams postulates that this native of New England and Canada was the vine spotted in his "Vinland" by Leif Ericsson in 1001. It was certainly the first American vine to be identified, in 1763, and has the dubious privilege of being suspected of bringing phylloxera to Europe in the nineteenth century. In fact, its phylloxera resistance is not reckoned high enough to make it useful as a rootstock in Europe and it is known to wine drinkers chiefly in all-*labrusca* varieties such as the Concord of New York State and Isabella of the USSR and Madeira, or as a parent of hybrids such as Baco Blanc, Catawba and Delaware. The wines it and most of its hybrids produce are notorious for their overpowering "foxy" flavour.

Vitis riparia The "river bank" species is another American vine but notable for its resistance to phylloxera and, therefore, much used for breeding phylloxera-resistant rootstocks. It and its hybrid descendants such as Baco Noir ripen extremely early so are useful in cold climates.

Vitis rupestris This is one of the few species whose name appears in a varietal name, Rupestris St George or Rupestris du Lot, its most famous incarnation, for it is of importance almost solely as a rootstock.

Vitis berlandieri This American vine has good resistance to both phylloxera and lime chlorosis and only its difficulties in rooting have stopped it directly playing a role as *vinifera* rootstock. It has to be hybridized instead.

Vitis aestivalis Quite a number of hybrids, with *labrusca* and *rupestris* chiefly, have been successful, mainly because of the good disease resistance and high yield of *aestivalis*. It is not sufficiently resistant to phylloxera to yield good rootstock material on its own.

Vitis cinerea This native of the American Midwest and southern states is encountered as progenitor of Black Spanish and Herbemont (now eliminated from French vineyards), bred from *aestivalis-cinerea-vinifera*.

Vitis rotundifolia is the species to which Scuppernong belongs; it is one of the few Muscadine vines, all of them native to the Gulf of Mexico, which is grown commercially.

Others occasionally involved, however obliquely, with winemaking are *Vitis candicans* and *Vitis monticola*.

THE SPREAD OF VITIS VINIFERA

Vitis vinifera is distinguished by having in general much smaller berries, thicker shoots and more deeply indented leaves, usually orbicular, than the American wild vines, most of whose varieties are capable of producing only dark berries.

This European wine-producing species of vine evolved from the primitive *labrusca*-like wild vines long before even man evolved from less sophisticated mammals. It is still possible to find wild vines that are at different points between these two stages in evolution. The Leningrad botanist A. M. Negrul was able to deduce from his observations of such plants around the Black Sea in the thirties that *Vitis vinifera* evolved from the vines of eastern Asia and that, therefore, all *vinifera* varieties have some eastern genes lurking in their make-up.

Like man, the vine – and *Vitis vinifera* in particular – has a remarkable ability to adapt itself to the conditions in which it finds itself. More than most other sorts of fruit, *vinifera* vines are very heterozygous, which means that their genes, already numerous, can be dealt and recombined as easily as if they were a pack of cards.

Unlike wild vines which would naturally be a mixture of fruitless males and irregularly fecund females, *Vitis vinifera* has evolved as a reliably fruitful hermaphrodite. This means that it can propagate itself vegetatively rather than sexually, and bud mutation, resulting in new clones and new varieties, is very common. In addition, some varieties such as Pinot are particularly easily mutable. The number of genes, together with the ease with which they can be permutated and the wide variety of different conditions in which the *vinifera* vine has been asked to thrive, help to explain why there are quite so many different varieties of *vinifera* and why wine is so fascinatingly varied.

Varieties as such had already been identified by the ancient Greeks. The Romans were able to distinguish and name several, some of which we can still enjoy today in one of our most direct links with the past. In support of Negrul's work, some of the varieties known to the Romans were specifically Asian, and are still grown in China. See pages 20–21 for more on the evolution and distribution of wine grape varieties in the last two millennia.

The botanical jumble of early history was gradually transformed into an ordered selection of vine types, usually suited to their particular environment. If, like everything else, grape varieties are the product of natural evolution, they still fail to take on relevant identity until we take notice of them and give them a name. Our forefathers did not suddenly discover Pinot Noir. It slowly developed a recognizable identity and that identity was eventually recognized and distinguished with a name.

The authors of *General Viticulture*, the most recent bible on the subject and a product of the University of California at Davis, suggest that as many as 8,000 different grape varieties may have been named and described at some point, although this includes wild varieties as well as all those ever used for table grape and raisin production. They qualify this daunting number by pointing out that only "about 20 percent of them may be growing somewhere in vineyards, gardens, and variety collections". The 1,000 vine varieties described in this book are believed to constitute all those relevant to the wine drinker today.

It is quite clear that, while some varieties have evolved by adaptation and mutation, others have been lost forever by a combination of natural selection and man's insouciance. And it is probably true, too, that a certain proportion of the world's vine growers simply do not know exactly which grape varieties, often bizarrely assorted, are growing in their vineyards.

PHYLLOXERA VASTATRIX – THE SECOND COMING?

Even before a vine can metaphorically set down its roots in this brief introduction, the great vine blight of the last century must be considered. Like any other plant, the vine is prey to all sorts of insects. There is the grape berry moth, the grape leaf hopper, the grape rust mite, grape mealy bug, grape blossom midge, and that couple who sound straight out of a tragic opera, cochylis and eudemis. But far worse than any of these is phylloxera, which has been more far-reaching and long term in its effects than any other agricultural disaster.

Following closely on the heels of the eclipsing oidium, the fungus disease that ravaged the vineyards of Europe in the mid-nineteenth century, the phylloxera insect reached France in 1860. Until then phylloxera had been confined to the eastern United States, and *vinifera* vines, unlike American vines which had presumably been exposed to it for centuries, had developed no resistance to it whatsoever. (This probably explains the failure of those such as Thomas Jefferson who had tried to plant ungrafted *vinifera* vines in the eastern United States.) Phylloxera, like oidium, was first observed in Britain, almost certainly borne to Hammersmith and to Europe's vineyards via botanical specimens. The Victorians were avid collectors and classifiers of nature and there was much international traffic in plant material, blithely unhindered by quarantine requirements.

Phylloxera had a wonderful European *grande bouffe*, munching its way through *vinifera* roots and injecting a poisonous saliva into them. Whole vineyard areas were gradually destroyed and, thanks to the international trade in *vinifera* vine cuttings, phylloxera eventually blighted wine production all over Europe, in South Africa, Australia, New Zealand and even California – by then planted with *vinifera* – by the turn of the century.

To this day, the only known effective control of phylloxera's fatal predations on vine roots (although there are treatments suitable for leaf galls) is to graft cuttings of *vinifera* on to phylloxera-resistant rootstocks. This is common practice in all of Europe except where the soil is protected by sand, a medium apparently impenetrable by phylloxera. In many of the newer wine regions, however, grafting is far from *de rigueur*, being much more expensive

than just taking a chance, and this sort of vineyard Russian roulette has had perhaps predictably worrying results.

Infestations of phylloxera have recently been identified, so far on a limited scale only, in California, New Zealand and even England. And Australian vineyards, worryingly, are still 90 percent ungrafted. Phylloxera spreads not only through the soil but also on vineyard tools and machinery (mechanical harvesters posing a new threat), by foot and, in the winged stage of its complex 18-stage life cycle, by flying through the air. Dangerous indeed for the wine industry's future.

Since some rootstocks condemned in one part of the world as being insufficiently resistant perform perfectly well in another, it is possible that there are different biotypes of phylloxera. This seems even more depressing, although some *vinifera* vines appear to have a certain natural resistance. Perfectly healthy phylloxera-infested Monastrell was spotted in Spain in 1984, for instance. It is worth pointing out that it is rarely phylloxera alone that kills a vine, but rather the diseases, notably fan-leaf virus, which usually attack a plant weakened by phylloxera.

VINE HEALTH AND VIRUSES

It is heart-breaking for the lover of wine to observe how poor is the health of much of the plant material used to create such a dramatic increase in wine production in the newer wine regions. South Africa, California, Australia and New Zealand – probably in that order of gravity – each has a major crisis of confidence in the quality of the vines planted with such enthusiasm over the past two decades. Superb technical conversion of substandard fruit into wine is the happy norm in all these countries.

The most common problem in each of these countries has been some sort of virus infection. Fan-leaf or *court-noué* and leaf roll are the two most common forms, though several others are well-known in specific areas of Europe. Shoot necrosis is the scourge of Apulia for instance, and it can be traced to a single vine, such is its virulence. Quite apart from making the afflicted vines produce fewer grapes of poorer quality and taking years off their productive life, viruses can also ruin a vineyard for future vine plantings unless it is fumigated. There is no practical cure for virus diseases; prophylaxis in the form of using only virus-free plant material for both cuttings and rootstocks is the only measure available.

The Californians at Davis have been the most convinced of the need for antivirus treatments of vines and have developed a bank of more than 200 varieties of certified "clean" budwood and rootstock. They instituted a programme of developing plants from cuttings found to be free of all known viruses, and have in many cases subjected them to heat treatments in an effort to eliminate any viruses so far unrecognized. These are despatched to customers all over the world and it is, therefore, easy to see how vital it is that they should be genuinely healthy, and correctly identified.

Of course, this is just one step towards vine health. All

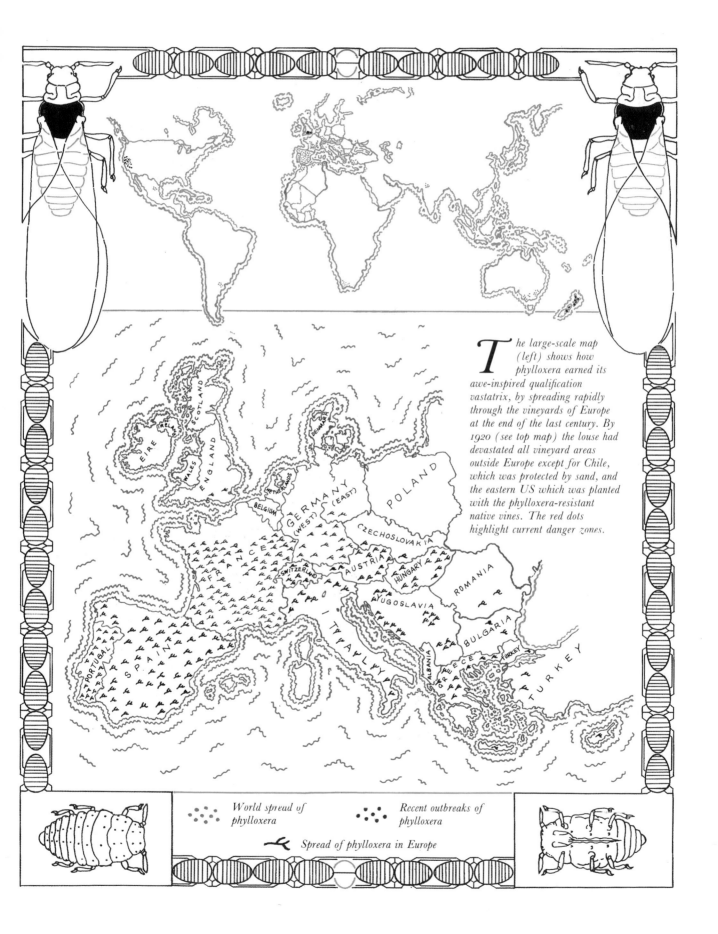

*T*he large-scale map (left) shows how phylloxera earned its awe-inspired qualification vastatrix, by spreading rapidly through the vineyards of Europe at the end of the last century. By 1920 (see top map) the louse had devastated all vineyard areas outside Europe except for Chile, which was protected by sand, and the eastern US which was planted with the phylloxera-resistant native vines. The red dots highlight current danger zones.

World spread of phylloxera

Recent outbreaks of phylloxera

Spread of phylloxera in Europe

sorts of other non-virus diseases, such as Pierce's disease, affect vines even before they are planted, as well as the host of fungus diseases and physical disorders which can attack an established vineyard.

Many believe that careful clonal selection (see below) can be demonstrated to work and is far more valuable than trying to keep one step ahead of the development of vine viruses. They feel that antivirus treatments can never offer a guarantee and may even be a waste of time. The Davis heat-treaters have already found that some of the clones used in their virus-free programme were not particularly good quality.

In countries as isolated as Australia and New Zealand quarantines are imposed on imported vine cuttings, as on any other imported plant material, which are perhaps over-stringent. They are certainly a cause of enormous frustration to the domestic winemakers trying to keep pace with consumer demand for "exotic" varietals such as Chardonnay and Sauvignon Blanc.

THE RIGHT CLONES

The importance of clonal selection is now almost universally recognized. The Germans were the most effective pioneers. California has at last acknowledged the concept, has already made progress with its Chardonnay and Trebbiano material and is hard at work on Cabernet Sauvignon. Even Bordeaux has its individual proponents of this method of breeding only from carefully selected plants (the selection apparently being most effective by simple observation rather than by complicated measurement). By 1981, nearly 3,000 registered vine clones were available, mainly from France, Italy, Germany, South Africa, Czechoslovakia, Switzerland and Austria.

Of course, a programme of clonal selection is only as good as the basis on which the selection is made. Bordeaux and Burgundy can each, sadly, provide examples of unsatisfactory selection procedures. As discussed on page 81 many Burgundian growers have chosen to plant clones designed for high yields alone, with scant regard for concomitant poor quality. Meanwhile, between 1970 and 1975 in the wake of the truly rotten 1968 vintage, the Bordelais were officially only allowed to plant a clone of Cabernet Sauvignon specially developed to resist rot but near-impossible to ripen.

The Germans have perhaps demonstrated most ably the success of clonal selection. Their average yield in the mid-fifties was 45 hectolitres per hectare, while that of the mid-seventies was 97 hectolitres per hectare. This is partly because a different pattern of more productive varieties now prevails, but also because individual clones of the old favourites Riesling and Müller-Thurgau have been selected for quantity and, they claim, quality too. If quality is measurable by must weight, no one can gainsay them. The French, of course, still argue officially that this is impossible, indeed contrary to the basic tenets of Appellation Contrôlée regulations which set lower maximum yields for the grander appellations.

While some advantages of clonal selection are obvious, it is important to keep the clonal options open. Too few clones would result in too limited a range of flavours (as has happened in regions dependent on only a few strains of yeast); and there is the scary possibility that a whole vine type could be wiped out by a single disease.

GENETIC ENGINEERING

Using work pioneered at Davis, it now looks possible that plants particularly resistant to specific diseases, pests and environmental disadvantages can be developed much faster than by cumbersome propagation in the nursery. Vine cells are artificially cultured and bombarded with the phenomenon to which resistance is required. The surviving cells are then regenerated to proper plants in this system of "mutant selection".

Yet more sophisticated gene cookery techniques are being developed although grapes, comfortingly to the wine lover, are proving a more intractable raw material than most other plant matter.

NEW VARIETIES FROM OLD

This sort of genetic manipulation could presumably be used, with intriguing results, to breed whole new families of vine varieties. Conventional methods have already yielded a host of useful, and not-so-useful, additions to the vine varietal range. The word "new", of course, is strictly relative. For all we know, half the varieties we call "classic" were bred, or at least selected, by a thoughtful vineyardist. Our knowledge is only as good as the records kept.

It is well-known, for instance, that Müller-Thurgau was bred from a Riesling and a Silvaner vine in 1882. Muscat Ottonel was developed in the Loire in 1852. Louis Bouschet was alreading working on crossing Teinturier du Cher with the local varieties of the Languedoc in the 1830s. Earlier examples of vine-breeding could doubtless be found.

The Germans, again, have been formidable in their work on crossings, bred solely from *Vitis vinifera*, as well as some hybrids in which another species of *Vitis* is involved. The leading exponent of this activity – so frenetic that the Germans ran out of names years ago – is Professor Helmut Becker of Geisenheim. A natural iconoclast, he claims to have developed several crossings and even one or two hybrids (of *vinifera* and *amurensis*) superior in every respect to Riesling. Only legal recognition and consumer education stand in their way. The hybrids are tested in England, still technically an experimental vine region in the eyes of the law, because they are so frowned upon by EEC authorities.

It is true that hybrids with *labrusca* antecedents tend to taste very odd and even offensive to many palates. There is no shortage of examples of hybrids, however, whose only fault is a certain neutrality of flavour but which can be extremely useful because they have inherited worthwhile resistance to, for example, cold weather or phylloxera. Seyval Blanc is a good example.

ROOTSTOCKS

The advent of phylloxera was good news for one group of people – nurserymen. It led to the development of an important industry in supplying suitable resistant rootstocks, though not before a number of mistakes were made. As outlined on page 9, the American species vary considerably in their resistance to phylloxera. *Vitis berlandieri* is particularly good at standing up to the pestilence, but will not root properly, so hybrids of *berlandieri* and *riparia* such as SO4 and 5BB or of *berlandieri* and *rupestris* such as 110 Richter and 99 Richter are particularly popular.

Rootstocks have to be chosen with other factors in mind, however. They must be compatible with the *vinifera* scion and the local combination of soil fertility and climate in their effect on vine vigour. If a vine is too vigorous, too much of its energy may be devoted to growing leaves rather than producing fruit. Over-vigorous rootstocks can lead to poor fruit set and, especially in cooler climates, may make the harvest date dangerously late. In New Zealand's coolish, damp and very fertile volcanic soils, for instance, extremely weak rootstocks are needed. The vigour of a *vinifera* variety can be "adjusted" as appropriate by the use of either a very vigorous or particularly weak rootstock. Particularly vigorous varieties include Sauvignon Blanc, Colombard and Grenache.

Some control of the spread of virus disease is possible with the choice of rootstock, too. Professor Denis Boubals of Bordeaux has graded the commonly used French rootstocks in their resistance to the nematodes in soil which transmit viruses. SO4, 5BB and 99R are among those particularly nematode resistant, while the popular 3309C and, particularly, 41B are very sensitive.

Very dry climates need rootstocks with good drought resistance such as 110R and 140Ru of Sicily.

Careful consideration of soil composition, especially salt content, is also part of rootstock choice. In damp soils with a high proportion of active lime, some varieties suffer seriously from mineral deficiency (especially iron) or chlorosis, unless a very resistant rootstock such as 41B is used.

The most popular rootstocks in France are 110R, SO4 and 41B. In California, Rupestris St George (du Lot), the vigorous rootstock on to which Aramon was traditionally grafted, and Aramon Rupestris Ganzin 1 (AXR1) have been widely promulgated, while 1202 Couderc is widespread in Australia and New Zealand.

SOIL AND VINE VARIETIES

The exact relationship between specific vine varieties and different soil composition is a contentious issue. Calcareous soils, those with a high lime content, are traditionally associated with Chardonnay; the happy combination of Cabernet Sauvignon with gravel is disputed by few who have tasted the Médoc *crus*. Yet there is no scientific proof of a necessary connection between quality and soil composition on a varietal basis. Indeed, there are so many delicious exceptions that they surely *disprove* any posited rule.

Although the geology and resulting soil composition must influence the character of a wine, there seems no demonstrable connection between certain compositions and certain varieties. What seems most important is the unique combination of microclimate and soil *structure* defined by each vineyard. Apparently more important than the exact cocktail of mineral elements represented in the soil is its relationship with a single element – water.

THE VINE AS EFFICIENT WINE PRODUCER

Water is just as important to the ripe grape as to man, constituting between 70 and 85 percent of the whole. It is just one of three inputs, along with sun and soil nutrients, which result in the two outputs of ripe grapes and vegetative matter in the form of leaves and shoots. The secret of transforming a barren vine stump into the most inspiring liquid possible each growing season lies in optimizing the balance between these three elements for each vine variety in each vineyard setting.

As has already been mentioned under rootstocks, the relationship between vegetative matter and fruit is the most crucial. If too many grapes are encouraged to form by lax pruning techniques, there may not be enough vegetative matter to ripen them. If too few grapes set, then there may be so much growth that all of the vine's energy is diverted into leaf production with the same net result: too few ripe grapes. Somewhere in the middle lies the perfect balance for the well-run wine factory that the grower would like every vine to be.

It follows from this that the ideal vine structure varies enormously according to the fertility of the soil, the moisture and the sunshine available to the vine. On very fertile soils, the vine left to its own devices sprouts forth like a jungle and produces only a few, poor-quality grapes. It is much easier to achieve the right balance between the elements on poor soils, as has been found so gratefully by Europeans who need the more fertile land for other crops.

NEW WAYS OF MANIPULATING VINES

The equation can be loaded. Soil nutrients can be added artificially, though fertilizer is expensive. Dry land can be irrigated, either by sprinkler or drip. The effects of sunshine can be regulated to a certain extent by summer pruning or special trellising of shoots thereby producing shade. The amount of vegetative matter produced can even be controlled nowadays by chemical plant-growth regulators. The amount of fruit produced will already have been determined by the winter prune and the flowering, but some very dedicated winemakers even snip off whole bunches during the summer if they think fruit quality is being adversely affected by quantity. And it is not unknown for some varieties to shoot forth a second crop towards the end of a protracted growing season: New Zealand's South Island Pinotage, for example.

There are two more fundamental and interrelated methods of loading the dice: vine density and trellising.

These important building blocks in vineyard design are only just being understood, and play a vital if often underestimated part in determining yield and quality.

Vine density can be well under 1,000 vines per hectare (400 per acre) in hot, dry climates, where land costs and vine bushes are low as in central Spain and southern Italy. The moisture available to the vineyard naturally limits the number of plants it can nurture. On the well-watered, poor soils of Burgundy on the other hand, many vineyards sport more than 10,000 vines per hectare – unthinkable in California where spacings of about 1,125 plants per hectare, or about 450 per acre, have been the norm.

Viticulturists all over the world are currently experimenting with different densities. Wherever irrigation is possible, as in California, closer planting is probably desirable, though many more vines than 3,000 a hectare would be extremely difficult to harvest mechanically. It would be fascinating on the other hand to see what sort of wine would result from slightly reduced vine density on some of the poorer soils of Burgundy.

Artful management of the vegetative matter by careful trellising can dramatically increase yields, without any appreciable drop in quality, claim its exponents. The Geneva Double Curtain method developed in New York State and Alain Carbonneau's Lyre system developed in Bordeaux are the two best known for low-density plantings. These three-dimensional vine frames have worked much better on fairly fertile soils than the traditional Guyot method of training the foliage on a single vertical axis. Factors include not only the quantity of vegetative matter and fruit produced, but also the shade afforded the latter by the former. It is already proven that such systems are capable of producing medium-quality wine, but some authorities argue that careful use or adaptation of these systems will finally prove that real quality can go hand in hand with quantity.

YIELDS

The yield from a hectare of vines can vary from zero, after frost or hail at the wrong time, for instance, to 50 tons of Pedro Ximénez in the hot, irrigated vineyards of Australia. One ton of fruit can produce 1,300 litres or about 1,700 bottles. The factors that influence production have been discussed above.

VINEYARD HEALTH

As grapes ripen they become attractive to birds and animals as well as to insects. The modern vine grower's anti-bird measures include homespun scarecrows, ambulant human versions thereof expected to prowl by the hour, high pitched signals, shotguns programmed to fire blanks regularly, netting of all sorts and even, in New Zealand once, a spray guaranteed to give birds stomach ache (though it has unfortunately been found, in wine, to do the same thing to humans). Animals which show a particular interest in ripe grapes include the common picnicker in France; wild boar in Penedés and Tuscany; the kangaroo in parts of Australia; and hyenas and leopards in Tanzania. One begins to see the value of Burgundy's *clos*.

More widespread is the threat posed by the fungus diseases to which some varieties are particularly prone. These vary considerably with geography and seem only loosely related to climate. In Europe, for instance, the three most important are downy mildew or peronospera, powdery mildew or oidium, and rot or botrytis which in the right conditions can be invaluable to some makers of sweet wine but which usually prohibits red-wine production if it affects more than 20 percent of the grapes. In the eastern United States downy mildew is practically unknown but the major hazard is black rot, which is now rarely (though increasingly?) found in Europe. Fungus diseases are generally much less common in the arid parts of California and Australia as most of them are encouraged by humidity, though oidium is a problem in California. Botrytis is increasingly recognized and encouraged, for sweet white-wine production, in the newer wine regions.

The traditional treatments involving chemicals which can easily be washed off leaves by rain are being replaced by systemic treatments which cure or prevent from within the plant itself. Although considerable work is being done on the development of these preparations, the fungus can often start to develop resistance to existing treatments before new ones are devised. There is hope, however, that the systemic fungicides may eventually manage to eradicate some diseases completely.

The quite considerable cost of likely treatments has to be taken into account when deciding which variety to plant.

RIPENING

Throughout this book varieties are described as early, medium or late ripening or belonging to one of the four "epochs" of ripening in relation to Chasselas, the earliest *vinifera* variety. Early-ripening grapes also include Müller-Thurgau and Chardonnay (a dream to grow), Pinot Noir, Muscat à Petits Grains, Emerald Riesling; particularly late-ripening are Nebbiolo (definitely fourth epoch), Cabernet Sauvignon and Carignan. These are broad categories describing when different varieties ripen in chronological relation to each other, but the concept of ripeness is not a scientifically finite one.

The point at which a grape starts to ripen, which the French call *veraison*, is very distinct and easily definable. The final tint of the grapes' skin begins to be substituted for the chlorophyll green of any unripe fruit; the berries start to soften; and there is a major metabolic change whereby sugar suddenly starts to be accumulated. Ripening is merely the continuum of what happens between this point and the overripe stage at which the berries stop accumulating sugar but continue to lose acid and may start to shrivel.

The point at which the grapes are ripe and must, therefore, be picked is less scientifically quantifiable. This crucial decision is often taken in the light of very detailed measurements of levels of fructose, sucrose, malic acid, tartaric acid and/or pH, but it is, ultimately, subjective. Ripeness is more in the mind of the grower rather than at a measurable point on a refractometer. And the mind of the grower will be influenced not only by local climate but also by the purpose for which the grapes will be used. Pinot Noir grapes considered ripe in Champagne would be spurned as immature on the Côte d'Or.

There are signs that local social conditioning may play a part, too. Of course, grapes ripen faster in a hot climate and the grower is quite right to pick Riesling much earlier in California than in the Mosel, and Chenin Blanc much earlier in Stellenbosch than in Vouvray. However, although in Germany Riesling is considered a late-ripening variety overall, in California it is considered an early-ripening one. Such is the fear of flabby wines here that even those varieties which keep their acids well are perhaps picked unnecessarily soon. There seems to be some leap-frogging in the ripening order of grapes when climatic conditions are changed, but it also appears to vary with local perceptions of what varieties are meant to taste like.

It is cited as an advantage to plant a whole vineyard from a single clone so that all the vines ripen simultaneously. Some of those forging new vineyard ground in Australia, however, are deliberately planting steep hillsides so that different parts of a single vineyard will have different microclimates, ripen at different rates, and the resulting wines – they believe – have more of that magical ingredient, complexity.

It is worth remembering that, because of the range of different varieties, wine styles and psyches making the picking decision, even though there are only two hemispheres and therefore only two "autumns", there is not a month in the year when grapes are not being picked somewhere. The vintage can begin as early as July in the northern hemisphere – Greece's Liatiko is an example that springs to mind. It can continue into the next calendar year, as the 1970/71 marked on some German wine labels testifies. In the hotter wine districts of the southern hemisphere meanwhile, picking in January is common-place, while New Zealanders have been known to persevere with grapes for late-harvest wines into June.

This assumes only one vintage a year, of course, but two grape harvests a year are quite common in the hot, damp vineyards of Brazil, Tanzania and the Canaries by leaving buds on the vine after the post-vintage prune. There is even a vine station in Taiwan apparently which prides itself on its four crops per annum.

──────── *LABELLING AND MARKETING* ────────

In the attempted chronological logic of this introduction, it may seem as though once the grapes have been picked, the story of wine-grape varieties is over. In a way, however, it is only just beginning.

The winemaker, of course, has enormous power in shaping just how each grape will taste when transformed into wine – though the fascinating detail of this transformation is outside the scope of this book. He also chooses, or sometimes has imposed upon him by deliveries of ready-mixed grapes, which varieties he will blend together.

Work is currently being done on establishing a scientifically determined profile of the wine made by each individual varietal. Muscat with its intense and easily recognizable flavour was chosen as guinea pig for this "flavour fingerprint", using either liquid or gas chromatography. The Australians working in this field now feel confident enough to state that the very different characters of different varietals probably stem simply from different proportions of the same substances. They reckon that as a result of this analysis they will eventually be able to maximize a wine's flavour by vineyard treatments – and even perhaps make the crop of an unpopular variety taste more like another, more marketable one.

Quite apart from this is the philosophical question of how varieties are to be presented to the consumer. Varietal or geographical labelling? The French, subsequently Italians, now Greeks and Spaniards, and eventually Portuguese have devised a system of tying one ineluctably to the other. Bourgogne Blanc on a label promises Chardonnay; if Hermitage is there, there is no need for Syrah; who needs the word Nebbiolo when Barolo is promised? And so on.

Backing out of Europe into the objectivity of a distant planet, one wonders whether this revered system has not been just a bit too restrictive. It is certainly a "smart marketing ploy" as one smart "New World" viticultural guru put it, but does it unnecessarily deny the consumer some potentially very successful combinations of variety and region – Loire Rieslings, for instance?

Meanwhile those concerned with making top-quality wines in non-traditional areas have chosen to vaunt on the label their common denominator with the vinous Old Country, the varietal. This even reached the stage in California when it was obviously considered more profitable to flaunt the name of an inferior variety than to subject a wine to the ignominy of being labelled simply "California Burgundy" or "White".

In the ideal world of this lover of wine and words, detailed varietal information would be spelt out on every label along with geographical provenance, but in a very subordinate position relative to the name of the producer – whose reputation would be the prime and often sufficient sales pitch.

It is worth noting here how much depends on a name. The classic story is that of Sauvignon Blanc which Californians were loth to buy in the early seventies. Robert Mondavi fashioned the style but, more importantly, changed the name to Fumé Blanc, and sales have soared ever since. Similarly, Gewürztraminer has all but ousted that rather stodgier term Traminer on wine labels throughout the world, while many producers of Chardonnay and even Meunier obdurately cling to the suffix "Pinot" as a sales aid.

Today the vine grower has more ability than ever before to respond to market trends, as witness the field grafting or T-budding of one variety over to another, more fashionable one in many American and Australian vineyards.

——— *THE GRAPE IN THE CRYSTAL BALL* ———

Observations of and comments on the current vine scene run through this book. There is the understandable but worryingly universal Chardonnay-mania; the puzzling passion for Sauvignon Blanc; the wonderment at so many important mis-namings; the apparent insouciance over or ignorance of how easily some of our top-quality traditional varieties could disappear. But what of the future?

It is, of course, much easier to sit at a desk making arrogant suggestions about more suitable grape varieties than it is to risk the fortunes of one's family in planting new grape varieties or uprooting in favour of better clones of established ones.

A handful of forecasts follow nevertheless.

● It seems likely that the next French vineyard census in 1989, or more probably the one after that, will show that France has found a suitable variety or varieties for inexpensive white wine production – particularly in and around the Midi.

● It seems virtually certain that hybrids and Aramon will have disappeared from the vineyards of France – though this may be just in time to see EEC authorities recognize their value and allow them in a limited way for quality-wine production in Germany. Much rationalization of grape varieties is likely here, but while Dornfelder may become a thing of the past, new *amurensis–vinifera* Riesling-like varieties will be of the moment. Good-quality Soviet varieties will be in demand.

● The varietal profile of Portugal will doubtless change out of all recognition and, who knows, intelligent vine growers in warmer winelands such as Australia may, yet again, be importing cuttings of classic varieties from port's homeland – along with cuttings of traditional Italian or Italo/Greek varieties designed for hot climates.

● And by 2001, the Californians will either have charted exactly which variety may be planted in which acre of land, in the manner of the Appellation Contrôlée laws. Or, perish the thought, they could even have been legislated into a second Prohibition.

——— *ACKNOWLEDGMENTS* ———

This book has benefited enormously from the knowledge and cooperation of the following people. Stephen Krebs, assisted by Laura Lindquist, was particularly hardworking in the vineyards of Spain, Portugal and California; Cornelia Smith-Bauer brought her formidable intellect to bear on those of Germany; Sergio di Luca, Renato Trestini and Nicolas Belfrage MW were extremely useful and necessary guides in Italy; Jorge Böhm and David Pamment were particularly illuminating about Portugal and Madeira respectively.

Each of the following has been most kind: James Ainsworth; Professor Helmut Becker; William Bolter; Nick Clarke MW; Brian Croser; Jean Delmas; Sarah Fraser; Professor Pierre Galet; Rosemary George MW; Geoffrey Godbert; Bruce Guimaraens; Robert Hardy; John Hawes; Graham Hynes; François Henry; Johnny Hugel; Jane Hunt MW; Ian Jamieson MW; John Lipitch; Catharine Manac'h; John Radford; Ramos Pinto; Paul Pontallier; Jan Read; Domaines des Salins du Midi; Peter Sichel; Dr Richard Smart; Bernard Teltscher; Rolf Temming; Paul Tholen MW; Margo Todorov; Miguel Torres; Dr Traxler; Jeremy Watson; Frank Wood.

The editorial team could not have been more tolerant and hardworking. Roger Walton with Paul Drayson has designed a book more beautiful than I deserve. Anita Wagner suffered long with both me and the intricacies of the maps. Chris Foulkes was endlessly optimistic; Dian Taylor unaccountably cheerful. Naomi Good and Rachel Grenfell suppressed the worst in me. Adrian Webster had the brilliant idea in the first place and the late James Mitchell the wisdom to act on it. Nick Lander was his usual forbearing self.

Where Grapes Grow and Why

——*Historical Vine Movements*——

This thicket of arrows showing just some of the more seminal movements of the vine vividly illustrates the trouble man has taken to furnish himself with a drink both stimulating and palatable.

The vine species native to each part of the world, such as *Vitis labrusca* of eastern America and *Vitis amurensis* of the Far East, have been growing wild for centuries. This map attempts to chart the taming of the weed, one of the first plants to be adopted and adapted by man for his own use. The very earliest dates given indicate when *Vitis vinifera* was first recorded as being cultivated in that region. As can be seen, current thinking is that this "European" species of vine originated to the south of the Black Sea in Transcaucasia. From there deliberate cultivation of the *vinifera* vine spread to the far eastern Mediterranean, including Egypt where probably the first illustrations of vine growing can still be seen. The habit spread slowly westwards through the ancient civilization of Greece and Italy, known to the Greeks as Enotria, or "Wineland". It was the Romans who introduced viticulture and vinification to France, just as Catherine de Medici is said to have introduced the notion of *haute cuisine*. No wonder the Italians feel aggrieved that they are seen as second best to France in matters gastronomic.

The first specific variety of *vinifera* to be recognized and named was a Pinot in Burgundy in 1375. Throughout the next five centuries, the varieties which had gradually established themselves as botanical entities were finally recognized and named by vine growers and wine drinkers. It was not until the late eighteenth century, for instance, that Cabernets had established an identity. The "claret" grape picked up on the Cape of Good Hope by Captain Phillips in 1788, and taken for planting in Australia, was unlikely to have been Cabernet Sauvignon as the variety was little planted in Bordeaux at that time.

The varieties which are found in some of the newer wine regions but have apparently been lost in Europe can provide valuable evidence for the little-studied subject of the history of grape varieties. Cape settlers, for instance, took vine cuttings first from Germany via the Netherlands, thus beginning a continuing but sometimes contrary practice of relying on cool-climate German wine tradition. The Huguenots then took out French vine cuttings in 1688, and we can perhaps surmise that the "Pontac" variety which can still, just, be found on the Cape must have been a precursor of Cabernet Sauvignon.

On the other side of the world but in the same hemisphere, relatively new to viticulture, some obscure 100-year-old vines still flourish in the New Zealand countryside, near an old French mission at Akaroa in the South Island. They may provide clues not only to the varieties most suitable for conditions in the South Island, but also to what was planted there by French settlers, and hence in France, in the early nineteenth century.

The vine has been transported around the world by all sorts of couriers: nomads in the earliest days; crusaders in the Middle Ages as perhaps with Furmint; merchant adventurers in the sixteenth century who dispersed Malvasia, for instance, so widely around the Mediterranean; the conquistadores and subsequently the missionaries who introduced the vine to South America, probably by planting the seeds of the raisins they took with them; and early settlers in the rest of the southern hemisphere who, sensibly, regarded vine cuttings as an essential element in a first cargo. More recently, commerce rather than pleasure and refreshment have provided primary motivation. The French settled the vine in Algeria; *vinifera* growers all over the world desperately imported American vines to ward off phylloxera; and international traffic in better quality varieties flourishes as never before wherever there is the will to produce more and more delicious wine from them.

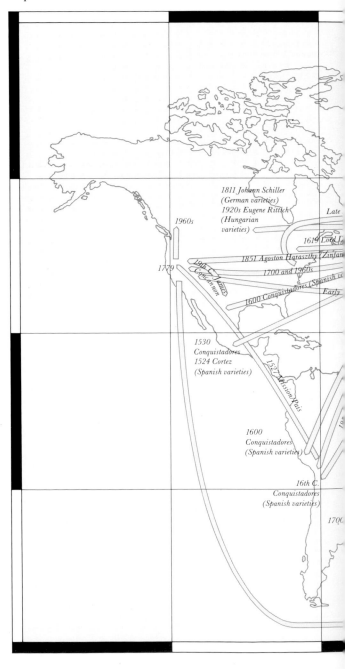

1811 Johann Schiller
(German varieties)
1920s Eugene Rittich
(Hungarian varieties)
Late
1960s
1619 Lord D.
1851 Agoston Haraszthy (Zinfan
1779
1700 and 1960s
1600 Conquistadores (Spanish va
Early
1530 Conquistadores
1524 Cortez
(Spanish varieties)
1527 Mission Pais
1600 Conquistadores
(Spanish varieties)
16th C.
Conquistadores
(Spanish varieties)
1700

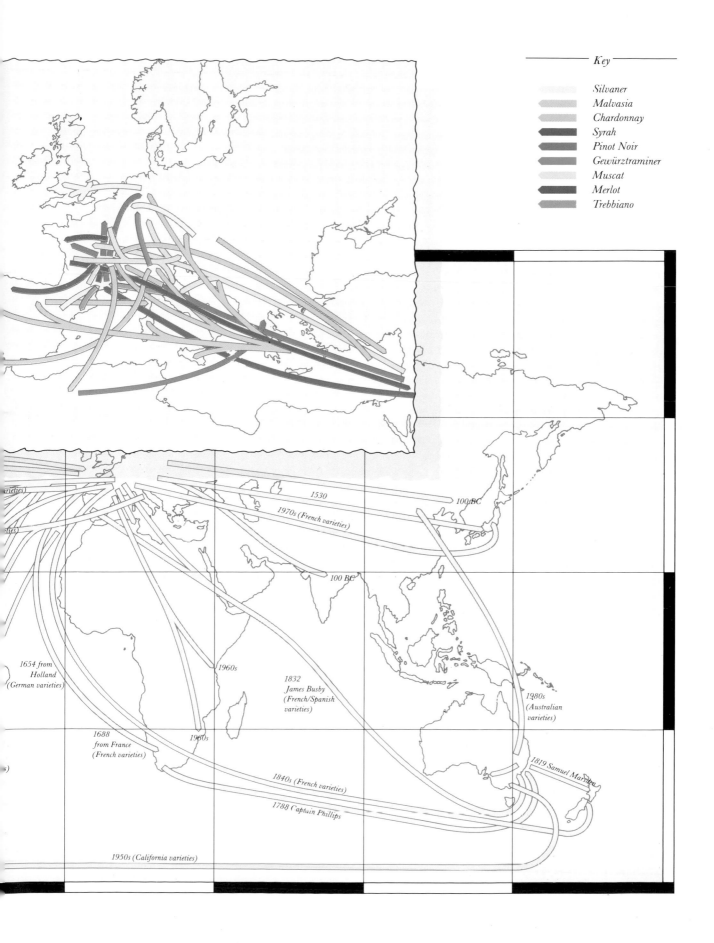

Key

Silvaner
Malvasia
Chardonnay
Syrah
Pinot Noir
Gewürztraminer
Muscat
Merlot
Trebbiano

1530

1970s (French varieties)

100 BC

100 BC

1654 from
Holland
(German varieties)

1960s

1832
James Busby
(French/Spanish
varieties)

1980s
(Australian
varieties)

1688
from France
(French varieties)

1960s

1819 Samuel Marsden

1840s (French varieties)

1788 Captain Phillips

1950s (California varieties)

World Grape Distribution

Perhaps even more illuminating than the mind-boggling record of the extent to which the classic grape varieties have been asked to travel is an analysis of those major wine regions which have decided that, on the whole, they can manage very well without imports, thank you.

Just about every single country with any aspirations to wine production has at least an experimental plot of Cabernet Sauvignon and Chardonnay. Though too minutely to be mapped, Cabernet is grown in the Peruvian desert; Chardonnay flourishes on the equator in Tanzania. Only the EEC's three most northerly wine-producing countries – Germany, Luxembourg and England – utterly reject even a trial row of Cabernet.

Some very important wine producers have little more than experimental plantings of such varieties, however. Italy is the most obvious example although, like neighbouring Slovenia, northeastern Italy grows a wide range of varieties which are French and German in origin. The number of growers with at least a few rows of such vines, especially both sorts of Cabernet and Chardonnay, is increasing all over the rest of the country; and the effervescent *spumante* industry is ever greedier for Pinots. But the great majority of Italy's wine producers still rely totally on varieties that are unknown outside Italy, and often outside their own particular region.

This isolationism is even more marked in Spain and Portugal. Spain's answer to Friuli is Penedés. In these high Catalonian vineyards, producers such as Jean León and Miguel Torres have shown just how well varieties as diverse as Cabernet Sauvignon and Gewürztraminer can perform if suitably matched to microclimate. On the other side of the country, Vega Sicilia has depended on Cabernet for at least some of its inimitable quality for decades. But well over 95 percent of Spain's exceptionally extensive vineyards continue to ignore such folderols and concentrate on native varieties.

Although covering a rather more limited area, the vineyards of Portugal are yet more introspective than those of Spain. All but a smattering are planted with a labyrinth of intricately related traditional Portuguese varieties, recently supplanted by others chosen specifically for commercial expediency.

In most of the rest of the consciously vine-growing world, there is discernible evidence of worship at the altar of at least a handful of the classic varieties illustrated on this map. All the newly emerging, potentially major forces in wine production such as the Soviet Union, China, Australia and North America have chosen to concentrate a sizeable proportion of their effort in this direction.

It is instructive, however, to look at central and eastern Europe. While northern Yugoslavia, Romania and especially Bulgaria have rapidly been planting Cabernet, Riesling, Chardonnay and the like, Austria and Hungary remain defiantly independent. Each country can boast an impressive array of very distinctive varieties, even if they sometimes overlap as one would expect from the two major national relics of the Austro-Hungarian empire. Grüner Veltliner, Zierfandler, Furmint, Hárslevelü and Juhfark are just some examples of the genuinely characterful varieties that persist in Middle Europe. The wine drinker cannot fail to be heartened by such triumphs of individual character over international fashion.

It is facile to profess a certain weariness with the world's apparent obsession with a handful of vine types. Winemakers in most of the newer locations for the classic grape varieties are still at the stage of trying to emulate the prototypes as closely as possible. The evolution of individual and exciting styles from combinations of traditional varieties and modern locations may, however, be just round the corner.

Key

▼ Cabernet Sauvignon
▼ Pinot Noir
▼ Merlot
▽ Riesling
▽ Chardonnay
▼ Sauvignon Blanc
▼ Syrah
▼ Chenin Blanc
▼ Sémillon

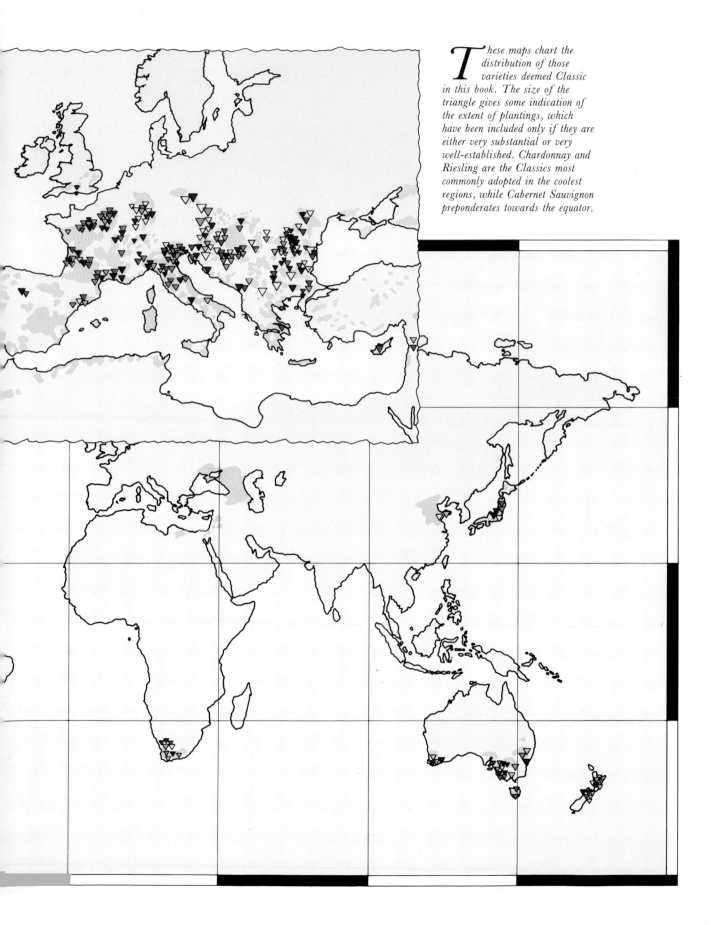

*T*hese maps chart the distribution of those varieties deemed Classic in this book. The size of the triangle gives some indication of the extent of plantings, which have been included only if they are either very substantial or very well-established. Chardonnay and Riesling are the Classics most commonly adopted in the coolest regions, while Cabernet Sauvignon preponderates towards the equator.

France

France's Minister of Agriculture tots up his stocks of vine varieties every 10 years. It is annoying to have to wait until 1989 for an update on the 1979 figures, although this slightly dated picture is very revealing.

In the 11 years before 1979 the country's total vineyard area shrank, by 22 percent, to just under one million hectares (2,500,000 acres), 681,000 (1,702,500 acres) of them planted with black grapes. Carignan and Ugni Blanc (Trebbiano) remained the two most planted varieties; although a few Carignan vines were swept away in the Midi during the seventies, a subsidized rash of new planting in the Charentes resulted in a 30 percent increase in total French vineyard planted with Ugni Blanc.

The connoisseur might well be surprised and disappointed to read down France's list of top 10 red and white varieties: Carignan, Grenache Noir, Aramon, Cinsaut, Merlot, Gamay, Cabernet Sauvignon, Cabernet Franc, Alicante Bouschet and Pinot Noir; Ugni Blanc, Sémillon, Grenache Blanc, Chardonnay, Baco Blanc, Chenin Blanc, Melon (Muscadet), Terrets Gris and Blanc, Macabeo (Maccabeu) and Sauvignon Blanc. Of the really aristocratic grapes on which France's wine reputation rests, only Merlot's total plantings top 25,000 hectares (62,500 acres).

This is a distinct improvement, however, on the recent past. The seventies saw a dramatic fall, by 50 percent, in plantings of the puny Aramon of the Midi, although Alicante Bouschet, traditionally planted alongside it to add colour, mysteriously increased – perhaps to compensate for the pulling up of 2,000 hectares (5,000 acres) or 84 percent of the various red-fleshed Gamays Teinturiers.

The real, and fundamentally gratifying, transformation in France's varietal make-up, however, concerns the hybrids. In 1968 total plantings of varieties such as Villard, Couderc, Seibel, Planet, Chambourcin and Baco were well over 200,000 hectares (500,000 acres). By 1979 they had fallen to about 50,000 hectares (125,000 acres).

Put that total together with such undesirable *viniferas* as Aramon, Grand Noir de la Calmette and Terret, and it becomes clear that as recently as 1979 they still covered as much as 125,000 hectares (312,500 acres) of France's vineyard – and that is probably about 125,000 more than most wine lovers realized.

And as in other well-established wine-producing countries there are worrying signs that some of the more obscure but still interesting traditional varieties are in serious decline. Viognier is the most obvious example, but Mondeuse, Fer, Carmenère, Petit Verdot, Tibouren and Ondenc are in danger of being forgotten as the "international" varieties Cabernet, Merlot, Syrah, Pinot Noir and Chardonnay continue to increase their hold on vineyard land within their homeland as well as abroad.

France, however, does not bow to international fashion in all respects. She remains very much a red wine country. Pinot Noir plantings are still way ahead of those of Chardonnay, and Ugni Blanc is the only white variety to figure in the country's top seven varieties overall. Even the traditional white wine regions of the southwest and the Loire have been switching towards darker hued grapes and wines, in obdurate defiance of current fashion elsewhere.

It is significant, and possibly even perceptible to some palates, that the proportion of older vines among France's three top-quality red varieties – Cabernet Sauvignon, Pinot Noir and Syrah – was very low in 1979; only 7 percent of Cabernet Sauvignon, for instance, was more than 20 years old, thanks to the severe winter of 1956, presumably. This may help to explain why, according to some authorities, great wine just does not seem so great any more.

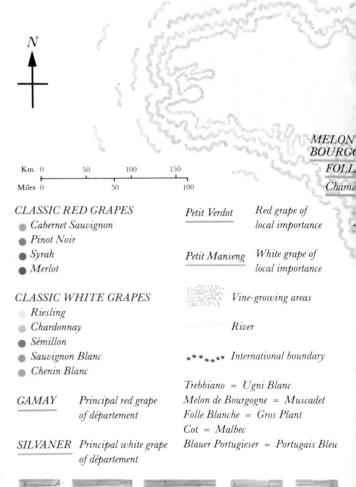

N

Km. 0   50   100   150
Miles 0   50   100

MELON
BOURG
FOLL
Cham

CLASSIC RED GRAPES		Petit Verdot	Red grape of
●	Cabernet Sauvignon		local importance
●	Pinot Noir		
●	Syrah	Petit Manseng	White grape of
●	Merlot		local importance

CLASSIC WHITE GRAPES			Vine-growing areas
○	Riesling		
○	Chardonnay		River
●	Sémillon		
●	Sauvignon Blanc	••••••	International boundary
●	Chenin Blanc		

GAMAY   Principal red grape
of *département*

SILVANER Principal white grape
of *département*

Trebbiano = Ugni Blanc
Melon de Bourgogne = Muscadet
Folle Blanche = Gros Plant
Cot = Malbec
Blauer Portugieser = Portugais Bleu

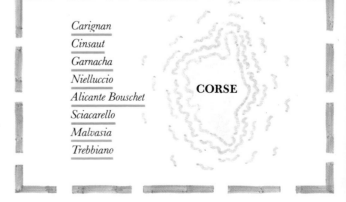

Carignan
Cinsaut
Garnacha
Nielluccio
Alicante Bouschet
Sciacarello
Malvasia
Trebbiano

CORSE

Seine

MEUNIER

Sacy

Paris

Marne

Moselle

○ SILVANER
● GEWÜRZTRAMINER

Savagnin Rosé
GEWÜRZTRAMINER
SILVANER
AUXERROIS BLANC
Chasselas

GAMAY
Arbois
Pineau d'Aunis
Plantet

Seine

César
Tressot
Sacy

•**Orléans**

Doubs

CABERNET FRANC
GROLLEAU
Plantet
Gamay
Cot

Romorantin
Rayon d'Or
Meslier St-François

Dijon •

ALIGOTE

Saône

Savagnin
Poulsard
Trousseau

BERNET FRANC
GROLLEAU
E
GAMAY
ntes *Melon de Bourgogne*

Loire

Loire

GAMAY

Jacquière
Altesse
Mondeuse Noir

Vienne

Gamay

Rhône

Piquepoul Gris

Trebbiano
Colombard

Marsanne
Viognier
Couderc Noir
Carignan

Aramon
Villard Noir
Garnacha
Cinsaut

Garnacha
Carignan
Cinsaut
Clairette Blanc

Trebbiano
Cabernet Franc
Merlot
Blanc

Muscadelle

Dordogne

Fer

CARIGNAN
ARAMON
CINSAUT
Terret Gris
Alicante Bouschet
Garnacha
Villard Blanc
Trebbiano
Clairette Blanc

Rhône

Garnacha Mourvèdre
Carignan Clairette Blanc
Cinsaut Aramon
Trebbiano Terret Noir
Aubun

Vaccarese
Muscadin
Bourboulenc

•**Nice**

Cabernet Franc
Trebbiano
Colombard
Muscadelle
Cot
Merlot Blanc
Petit Verdot
Gros Verdot
Carmenère

Trebbiano
Grapput
Ondenc

•**Bordeaux**

Lot

Mauzac Blanc
Jurançon
Villard Noir
Blauer Portugieser
Villard Blanc

CARIGNAN
ARAMON
GARNACHA
Cinsaut
Alicante Bouschet
Couderc Noir
Villard Blanc

Marseille
●

CARIGNAN
GARNACHA
CINSAUT
Aramon
Trebbiano
Aubun
Alicante Bouschet

CARIGNAN
TREBBIANO
CINSAUT
Garnacha
Aramon
Mourvèdre
Clairette Blanc
Roussanne
Alicante Bouschet
Couderc Noir
Tibouren

Trebbiano
Baco Blanc
Tannat
Colombard

l'En de l'Elh
Mérille

CARIGNAN
CINSAUT
ARAMON

Garonne

Baco Blanc
Baroque
Trebbiano

Jurançon
Jurançon Blanc
Villard Blanc
Valdiguié
Négrette

Duras

Alicante Bouschet
Garnacha
Garnacha Blanca
Mauzac Blanc
Terret Gris
Morrastel Bouschet
Villard Blanc

CARIGNAN
GARNACHA BLANCA
GARNACHA
Macabeo
Muscat of Alexandria
Muscat Blanc à Petits Grains
Carignan Blanc

Trebbiano
Clairette Blanc
Aubun
Villard Noir
Grand Noir de la Calmette
Piquepoul Noir
Aramon
Fuella

Petit Manseng
Gros Manseng
Plant de Graisse

——— *Bordeaux* ———

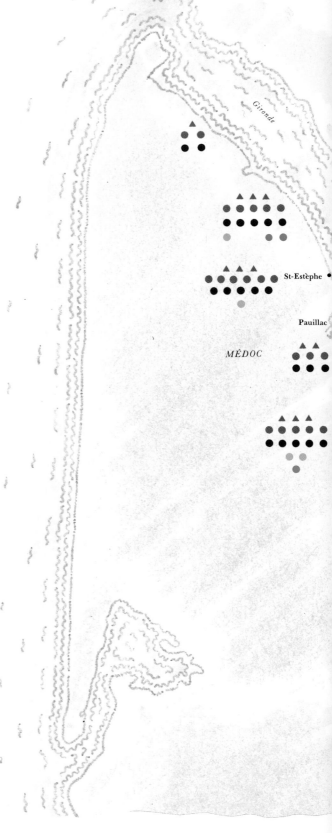

Bordeaux tends to be seen as a talisman of order and immutability, but analysis of the make-up of its vineyard throws up some surprising facts.

Cabernet Sauvignon, for instance, the vine variety regarded as Bordeaux's greatest and much-travelled ambassador, has a relatively recent history in the Gironde. While Pinot Noir was made, drunk, enjoyed and chronicled in Burgundy as early as the fourteenth century and possibly long before, Cabernet Sauvignon emerged to inject quality into the substantially white-grape vineyards of the Médoc only towards the end of the eighteenth century. Merlot was, becoming established in St-Emilion only at about the same time, and took several decades to cross the Gironde.

Today, plantings of Cabernet Sauvignon in the Gironde *département* form a much smaller proportion of the total than most connoisseurs would imagine – less than 18 percent – while Merlot covers 32 percent of available vineyard land. Only in the Médoc and southeastern half of the Entre-Deux-Mers is Cabernet Sauvignon rather than Merlot the dominant red grape variety – just. In the Médoc the split is Cabernet Sauvignon 52 percent, Cabernet Franc 8 percent and Merlot 40 percent, and in St-Emilion, Pomerol, Fronsac, Bourg and Blaye, Merlot outweighs Cabernet Sauvignon by more than five to one. Cabernet Franc is quantitatively important only in St-Emilion and Fronsac.

Currently, these three major red varieties account for nearly 90 percent of all dark grapes planted in the Gironde, and their proportions are carefully adjusted in each district within the *département* to take account of local micro-climates. There are signs of a growing realization, however, that some of the traditional, if difficult, varieties such as Petit Verdot and Carmenère could repay perseverance by providing valuable "seasoning".

Perhaps much more interesting than the relative importance of the red varieties is the role still played by various white varieties, some of them not very distinguished. The last census of the Girondin *vignoble* showed that plantings of Trebbiano or Ugni Blanc were as high as 6,500 hectares (16,250 acres), making it the second most planted white-vine variety after Sémillon, whose 16,600 hectares (41,500 acres) put it only just behind Cabernet Sauvignon in area covered. Nearly two-thirds of the Ugni Blanc area was in the Hauts de Gironde (Bourg and Blaye) bordering on the cognac vineyards of the Charentes, which are also dominated by Ugni Blanc. There were a further 2,000 hectares (5,000 acres) of vineyard producing thin, tart Ugni Blanc wine in Entre-Deux-Mers.

That other alembic-directed white variety of western France, Colombard, occupies a total Girondin area more than half as important as that of Ugni Blanc, while plantings of Merlot Blanc, not a variety of which the wine lover is taught much, covered a good 1,700 hectares (4,250 acres) of Bordeaux vineyard.

In 1979, Sauvignon plantings were only one-eighth those of Sémillon – an unexpected statistic in view of the number of Sauvignon-dominated white Bordeaux that are now available.

Although this map illustrates the state of Bordeaux viticulture as it was when last counted, indications are that there has been a substantial decrease in Sémillon plantings in Bordeaux in the last few years, typically in Entre-Deux-Mers in favour of red varieties which can be turned into wine for which there is greater market demand.

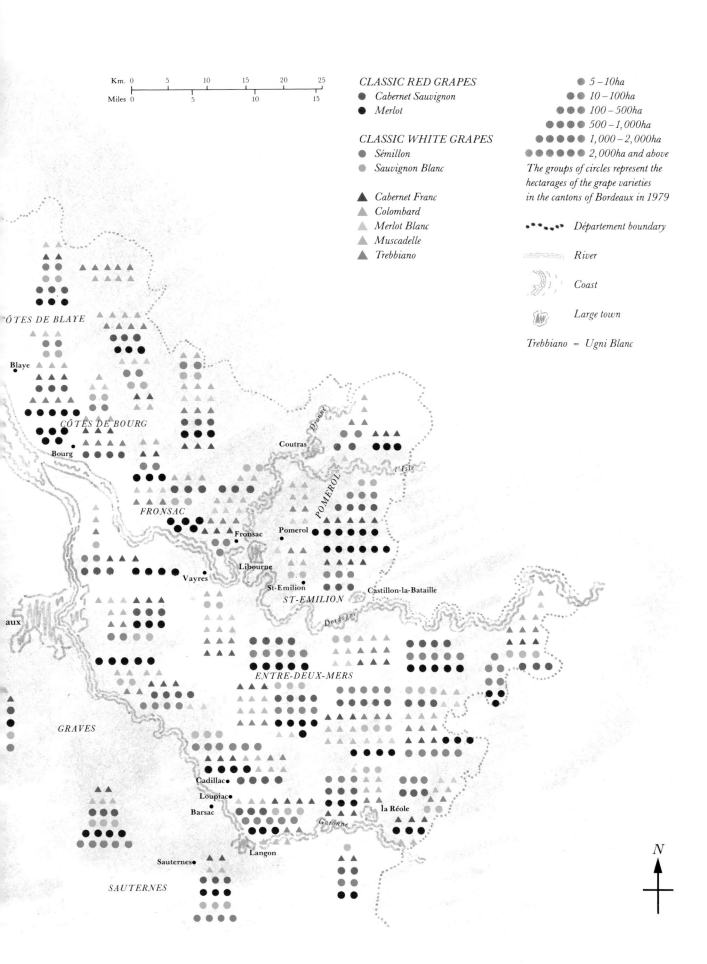

CLASSIC RED GRAPES
- *Cabernet Sauvignon*
- *Merlot*

CLASSIC WHITE GRAPES
- *Sémillon*
- *Sauvignon Blanc*

- ▲ *Cabernet Franc*
- ▲ *Colombard*
- ▲ *Merlot Blanc*
- ▲ *Muscadelle*
- ▲ *Trebbiano*

- 5 – 10ha
- 10 – 100ha
- 100 – 500ha
- 500 – 1,000ha
- 1,000 – 2,000ha
- 2,000ha and above

The groups of circles represent the hectarages of the grape varieties in the cantons of Bordeaux in 1979

- *Département boundary*
- *River*
- *Coast*
- *Large town*

Trebbiano = *Ugni Blanc*

CÔTES DE BLAYE

Blaye

CÔTES DE BOURG

Bourg

FRONSAC

Fronsac

Libourne

Vayres

St-Emilion

ST-EMILION

Coutras

Dronne

l'Isle

POMEROL

Pomerol

Castillon-la-Bataille

Dordogne

aux

GRAVES

ENTRE-DEUX-MERS

Cadillac

Loupiac

Barsac

la Réole

Garonne

Langon

Sauternes

SAUTERNES

N

Burgundy

The Burgundian is the original proponent of varietal wines, although if you said that to him he would have not a clue what you were talking about. For centuries – longer than in any other fine wine region – peasants have been making fine wines here, and they have made them, with only a few temporary hiccups, from one grape variety alone.

In Burgundy, red means Pinot Noir and white means Chardonnay. Chablis to the north is faithful to Chardonnay but on the Côte d'Or, France's most concentrated stretch of top-quality vineyard, more than seven in every 10 vines is Pinot Noir. This may surprise those makers and drinkers of wine in the newer wine regions who are so besotted with Chardonnay. It certainly helps to explain the astronomical prices of fine white burgundy.

Who can blame the Burgundians for their tenacity with Pinot Noir when they appear to have almost exclusive rights to its successful cultivation? While Chardonnay has shown itself an enthusiastic traveller and adapted well in almost every country which claims to be a wine producer, only a handful of non-Burgundian Pinot Noirs have so far shown anything like the quality deemed normal on the thin strip of vineyards from Dijon to Chagny. Devotion to Pinot Noir seems only sensible.

Some Pinot Noir plant material has been of very disappointing quality, however, with predictable results in the bottle. It took the seventies' experience of thin, overproduced red burgundy to demonstrate to the world's connoisseurs, and Burgundy's vignerons, the importance of clonal selection.

There had been hints that quality was not uppermost in every vine grower's heart ever since the *vignoble* had been so intricately parcellated after the Revolution. In the first half of this century, even those working the precious Côte d'Or vineyards were tempted by the disease resistance and high sugar levels offered by the likes of Oberlin, Plantet and Baco Noir. In 1968, these three varieties still occupied 10 percent of available Côte d'Or vineyard land, although they have been substantially grubbed up by now. Even Gamay and Aligoté have been declining in the Côte d'Or and now represent only about 10 percent of total vines.

Aligoté, Burgundy's definitely second white-vine variety, seems to be on the way out. It is being replaced by the more lucrative Chardonnay throughout Burgundy. This has been particularly obvious in the Côte Chalonnaise and the Mâconnais where Chardonnay has almost overtaken Gamay to become the most planted variety. Pinot Noir accounts for about a quarter of total vineyard land in the area between the Côte d'Or and Beaujolais proper. In the seventies much of the 1,000-odd hectares (2,500 acres) previously planted with the red-fleshed Gamays Teinturiers was replanted with Pinot Noir.

Gamays Teinturiers were never a speciality of the heartland of the Beaujolais region, which is doggedly Gamay country and presents the wine lover with as successful an illustration of matching variety to region as he will ever encounter. Is it significant that true Gamay has travelled so little and so unhappily from its base in the Beaujolais hills?

Burgundy is distinguished, if that is the right word, by its exceptionally high vine density: up to 13,000 plants per hectare now, and at one time even more.

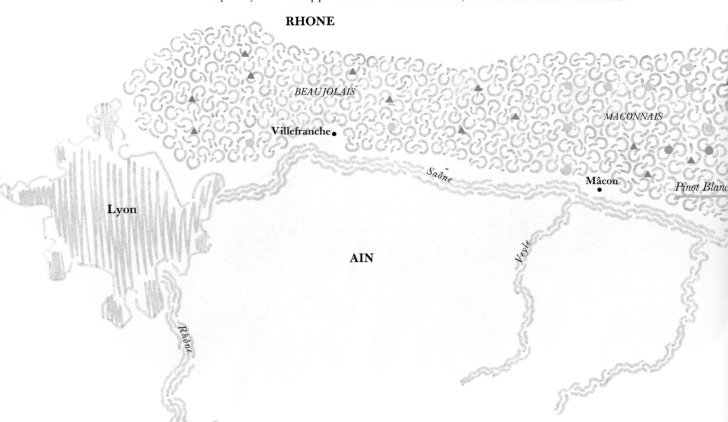

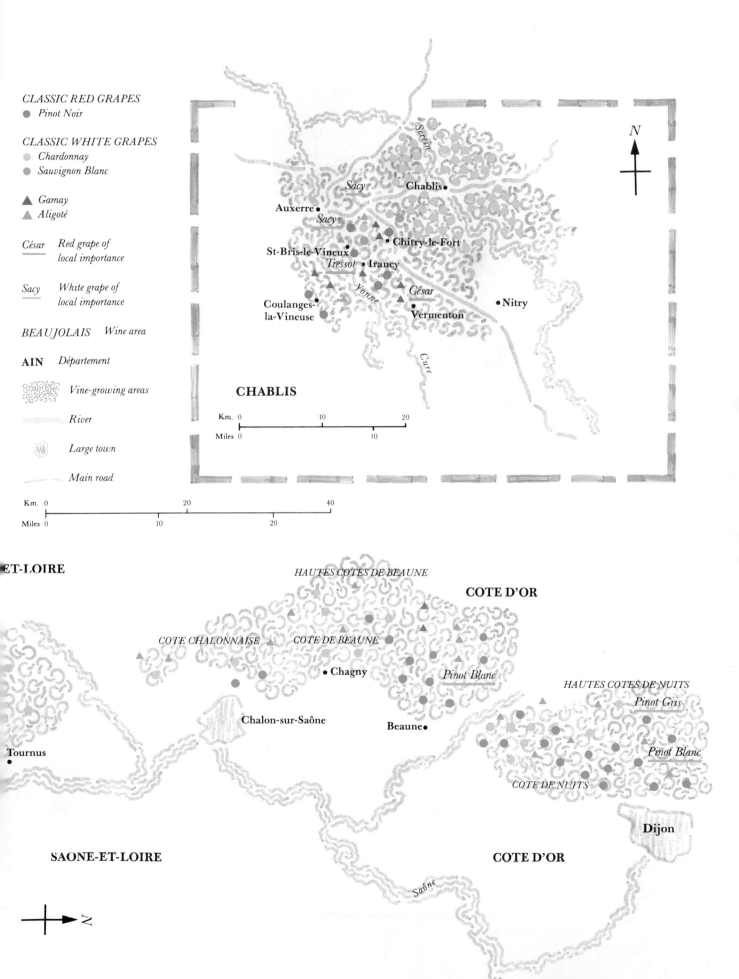

CLASSIC RED GRAPES
● *Pinot Noir*

CLASSIC WHITE GRAPES
○ *Chardonnay*
● *Sauvignon Blanc*

▲ *Gamay*
▲ *Aligoté*

César   Red grape of
        local importance

Sacy   White grape of
        local importance

BEAUJOLAIS   Wine area

AIN   *Département*

        Vine-growing areas

        River

        Large town

        Main road

CHABLIS

Km.   0   10   20
Miles 0   10

Serein
Sacy   **Chablis**
Auxerre
Sacy
Chitry-le-Fort
St-Bris-le-Vineux
Tressot   **Irancy**
César
**Coulanges-
la-Vineuse**   *Yonne*   **Vermenton**   **Nitry**
Cure

N

Km.   0   20   40
Miles 0   10   20

ET-LOIRE

HAUTES CÔTES DE BEAUNE   **COTE D'OR**

COTE CHALONNAISE   *COTE DE BEAUNE*

Chagny   *Pinot Blanc*

HAUTES CÔTES DE NUITS
Pinot Gris

Chalon-sur-Saône

Beaune   *Pinot Blanc*

Tournus

COTE DE NUITS

Dijon

SAONE-ET-LOIRE   **COTE D'OR**

Saône

N

The Loire

Even superficially, the Loire valley presents a very diverse pattern of vine plantings, from Sauvignon Blanc around the major bend in the river through Chenin Blanc, Cabernet Franc and Gamay in the middle of the seaward stretch to Muscadet or Melon de Bourgogne at the river mouth. Closer inspection reveals an even more confused picture, with unexpectedly high reliance on hybrids.

As recently as 1979, no fewer than 23 different vine varieties covered more than 100 hectares (250 acres) of Loire wine land, and only Melon covered more than 5,500 (13,750) of the Loire total of well over 60,000 hectares (150,000 acres) of vineyard. Varieties such as Grolleau, Arbois, Pineau d'Aunis and Folle Blanche, none of them exactly of great fame, are among the Loire's most popular. And, just to add further diversity, all sorts of Loire satellite regions, Haut-Poitou or St-Pourçain-sur-Sioule, for example, are now emerging as viticultural entities – usually with their very own varietal profile.

In 1979, the hybrids Plantet, Chambourcin, Villard Noir and Bacos Noir and Blanc accounted for 6,000 hectares (15,000 acres), or 10 percent of all Loire vines.

Many of these have doubtless been grubbed up in the last few years, but their continued importance illustrates well just how much very ordinary wine is made in the Loire. In most cases these hybrids have been chosen by Loire vignerons not for their resistance to winter cold, but for their resistance to or recovery from spring frost.

The change in the balance of grape varieties has provided the real drama in the Loire in the last decade or so. Although the total *vignoble* of the Loir-et-Cher *département* at the easternmost tip of the main Loire wine region has shrunk, Gamay and Sauvignon doubled their area in the seventies, at the expense of Arbois, Pineau d'Aunis, Chenin and Plantet. These plantings have firmly established the two varietals from what might be called Greater Touraine. Meanwhile plantings of Gamay in Indre-et-Loire around the town of Tours itself have actually declined; and the *département* has become yet more polarized as a producer of Chenin, around Vouvray, and Cabernet Franc in the Chinon/Bourgueil district. Grolleau is in decline here.

In Anjou country, Grolleau, mainstay of France's most-exported rosé, has been holding its own, while Cabernet

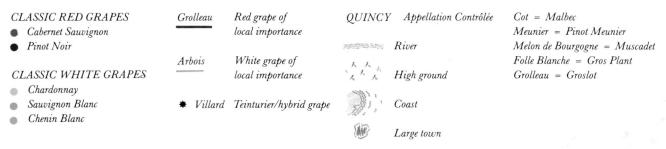

CLASSIC RED GRAPES
- Cabernet Sauvignon
- Pinot Noir

CLASSIC WHITE GRAPES
- Chardonnay
- Sauvignon Blanc
- Chenin Blanc

Grolleau — Red grape of local importance

Arbois — White grape of local importance

✻ Villard — Teinturier/hybrid grape

QUINCY — Appellation Contrôlée

〰️ River

High ground

Coast

Large town

Cot = Malbec
Meunier = Pinot Meunier
Melon de Bourgogne = Muscadet
Folle Blanche = Gros Plant
Grolleau = Groslot

N

Franc has been catching up on Chenin. Chenin Blanc remains the great mystery of the Loire valley. Delicious as the best of its produce can be, it is an inconveniently early-budding and late-ripening variety for a wine region so far from the equator. Some Chardonnay has been creeping into Anjou Blanc, to extremely good effect, though this has been too recent and too limited to figure in official statistics.

An increase in plantings of Cabernet Sauvignon was already noticeable by 1979 when there were more than 1,300 hectares (3,250 acres) in the middle of the Loire *vignoble* compared with only 400 (1,000 acres) a decade earlier. Its influence can be tasted in the reds of both Anjou and Saumur, and its success adds weight to the view that Cabernet Sauvignon could thrive much better in St-Emilion and Pomerol than most growers believe.

Around the mouth of the Loire, the Muscadet grape Melon represents one vine in every two and has been gradually increasing its importance to the detriment of the Folle Blanche or Gros Plant Nantais. All sorts of other varieties are grown on the fringes of the main Muscadet vineyard, however, including some Gamay and Cabernet Franc as well as an array of hybrids.

*I*n the cellars of the champenisateurs of Saumur, the Chenin Blanc grape is persuaded to produce some wines of the quality of France's most famous fizz, based instead on Chardonnay and Pinots.

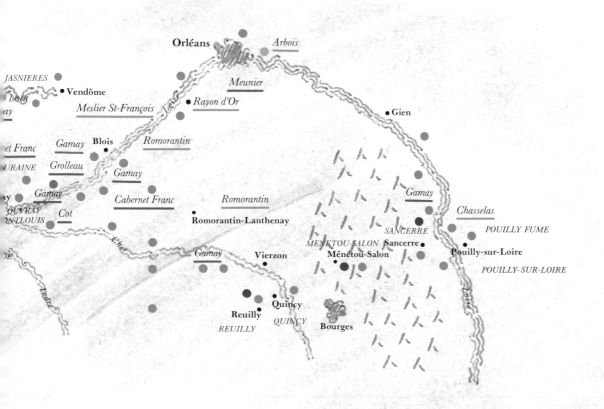

Alsace

Alsace must occupy a very special place in a work of this sort. Not only do its winemakers show more concern to get pure grape flavour into the bottle than any of their counterparts elsewhere, they have also worshipped vine varieties to the extent of being the first modern exponents of varietal labelling.

Every act in a quality-conscious Alsace wine cellar is designed to preserve natural varietal aroma; no nuance is masked by the deliberate maintenance of residual sugar. And a good bottle of wine from Alsace (good, happily, being typical) sings out its grape of inspiration on the label as well as in the glass. Alsace was the last major French wine region to join the Appellation Contrôlée party and did so with just one basic appellation to be predicated only by grape variety.

Today the region's vines are a happy combination of French and German influences, but it is worth considering that if it were still German, as it was at the turn of the century, then Müller-Thurgau (of which there is not a single vine today) would presumably reign supreme.

Although the world's connoisseurs tend to think of Alsace as a homogeneous wine region, there is a sharp viticultural distinction between the Haut-Rhin and Bas-Rhin *départements*, or between those vineyards on the flatter land north of Sélestat and the more obviously Vosgienne wineland to the south.

In the coarser soils of the vineyards of the Plaine d'Alsace in Bas-Rhin, Silvaner (Sylvaner) has been the most popular variety, but Riesling and now Pinot Blanc are fast catching up as wine consumers become disaffected with

the somewhat austere character of Silvaner (though give it an aroma and you almost have Sauvignon Blanc). Up and well into the lee of the Vosges, Gewürztraminer is quantitatively the most important vine, grown to produce sufficient of Alsace's most distinctive wine to meet the demands of visitors from across the Rhine. It is here, in the concentration of the finest, steepest sites, that by far the highest proportion of each of the region's *cépages nobles* is grown.

Although the range of varieties allowed in this relatively small wine region is wide for northern France, Alsace vine growers are backed by sufficient history so that they can match variety to site with a precision that would be the envy of many in the world's newer wine regions. Even in an area as tiny as the commune of Riquewihr (population 2,000), for instance, it is well-known that the steep, chalky

Schoenenbourg vineyard is for Riesling, the heavier soils and gentler elevation of Sporen for Gewürztraminer.

Although Pinots Gris and Noir fascinate Alsace enthusiasts, and constitute major items on the wine lists of the region's excellent restaurants, these varieties are planted in only very limited quantity – though Pinot Noir plantings have been increasing over the last few years, just as they have further along the frontier of red wine possibility in Germany.

Even in 1982 Pinot Noir plantings covered less than a third of the total area planted with Alsace's most important varieties – Gewürztraminer, Riesling, Silvaner and what is usually called Pinot Blanc.

For some reason, Alsace chooses to hide the identity of one of its most planted grape varieties. Auxerrois is rarely seen on a label, yet it constitutes nearly half the blend of many a wine sold as Pinot Blanc. Auxerrois covers for Pinot Blanc's meanness in poor years, but gets little public recognition for it, even though plantings of both Auxerrois and true Pinot Blanc have been increasing at the expense of Silvaner since 1979.

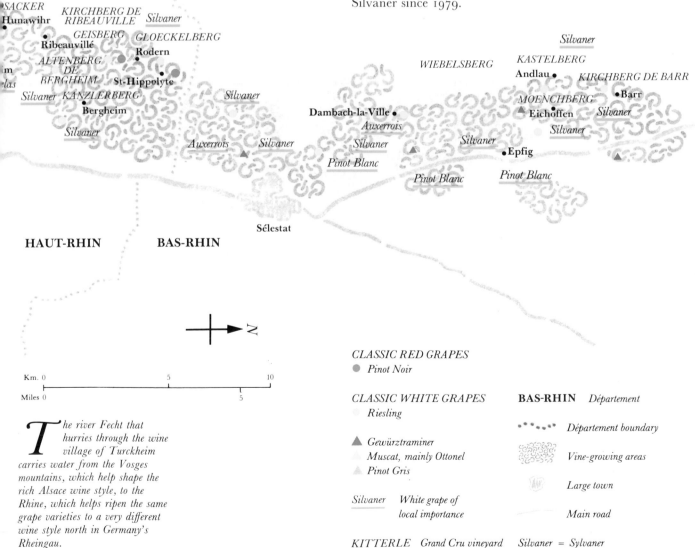

The river Fecht that hurries through the wine village of Turckheim carries water from the Vosges mountains, which help shape the rich Alsace wine style, to the Rhine, which helps ripen the same grape varieties to a very different wine style north in Germany's Rheingau.

Km. 0   5   10
Miles 0   5

HAUT-RHIN   **BAS-RHIN**

CLASSIC RED GRAPES
● *Pinot Noir*

CLASSIC WHITE GRAPES   **BAS-RHIN**   *Département*
Riesling

▲ *Gewürztraminer*   ●••••••   *Département boundary*
Muscat, mainly Ottonel
▲ *Pinot Gris*   *Vine-growing areas*

               Large town
Silvaner   *White grape of*
              local importance   *Main road*

KITTERLE   *Grand Cru vineyard*   *Silvaner = Sylvaner*

Champagne

Perhaps the most surprising fact to emerge from viticultural analysis of the Champagne region is the supremacy of Meunier, in quantitative terms at least. About 50 percent of all Champagne vineyards in the major Marne heartland shown here were planted with Meunier in 1979, while the much nobler Pinot Noir accounted for only 24 percent and Chardonnay 26 percent.

The area of Marne vineyards increased enormously in the seventies, by about a third, and this expansion has increased apace in the eighties, too. Plantings of Chardonnay increased significantly more than those of the dark grapes, as one would expect at a time when the (surely tautological?) Blanc de Blancs style came into its own, not only for champagne but also for still wine of all kinds.

The general principle on which varieties have been chosen by the vignerons of Champagne, however, is that the most capricious vine of the three, Pinot Noir, is planted wherever there is more than half a chance of its ripening properly. The Meunier is planted wherever the land is so vulnerable to spring frosts that Chardonnay would be at risk and Pinot Noir impossible. It is the only variety for the low-lying vineyards of the Vallée de la Marne and those in the Aisne *département* (not shown on this map).

The vineyards of the Aube to the south on the other hand are considerably warmer than the Marne average and 2,700 of the 3,400 hectares (6,750 of the 8,500 acres) are planted with Pinot Noir. This means that once the *encépagement* of the Aube and Aisne is included in the overall *cuvée*, the Pinot Noir's contribution increases to 30 percent, Meunier's decreases to 44 percent and Chardonnay's remains at 26 percent. Other varieties such as Petit Meslier and Arbane are there as mere smatterings.

There are subtle variations on the general principle outlined above, however. Wherever the chalk underlay of the countryside is at its most exposed, Chardonnay is the natural choice. Thus, the Côte des Blancs to the south of Epernay, the very similar Côte de Sézanne to the southwest (not shown), and the Chardonnay plantings around the northern escarpment of the Montagne de Reims are where Champagne's best white grapes are to be found.

Pinot Noir is at its greatest concentration on the southern slopes of the Montagne de Reims because that is where the vineyards enjoy maximum exposure to the sunshine and warmth. The stricture that Meunier is not allowed in the most august sites in the top *crus* is hardly needed since there is every economic incentive for growers to plant the two *cépages nobles* for which an extra franc a kilo is automatically paid.

The philosophically minded will wonder why it is these three grapes which have been chosen as ingredients for the world's most famous fizz. As has been outlined above, Pinot Noir at least is far from ideal for this climate, and Meunier has its detractors even in the region itself. Put those facts together with the difficulty of producing white wine from black grapes, and the difficulty some tasters have in distinguishing Blanc de Blancs champagnes from the more usual Blanc de Noirs et Blancs, and one sometimes wonders why Chardonnay is not more widespread in the region.

Mareuil-le-Port •

CLASSIC RED GRAPES
● *Pinot Noir*

CLASSIC WHITE GRAPES
● *Chardonnay*

▲ *Meunier*

BOUZY *Commune with average vineyard rating of 90% and above*

〜 *Boundary of Appellation Contrôlée Champagne*

Vine-growing areas

River

Woods

Large town

Main road

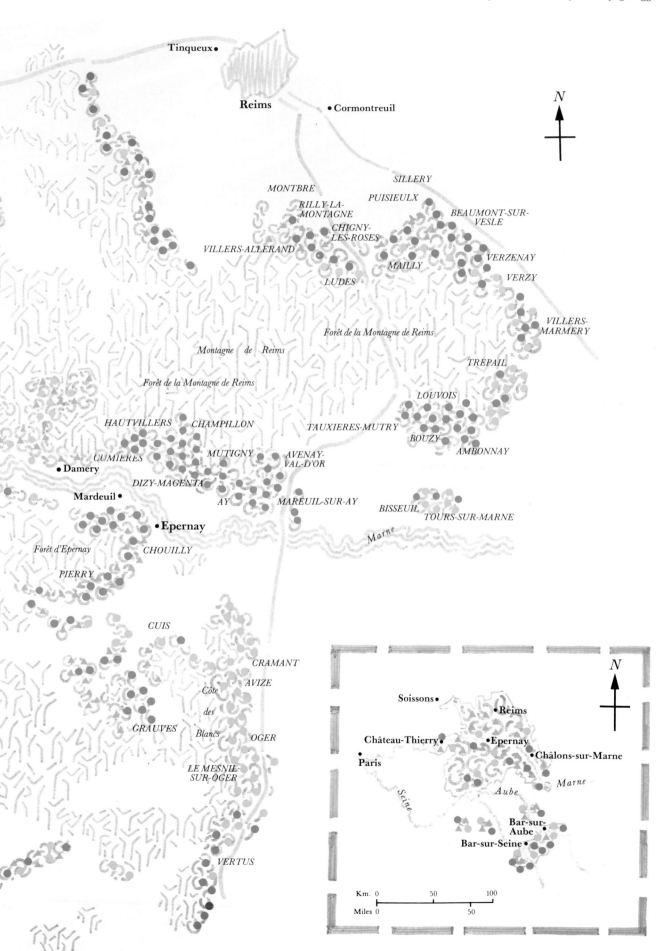

The Midi

N

Minervois
Principal Grape Distribution

A
Carignan
Syrah
Macabeo
Garnacha Blanca
Bourboulenc

B	**C**	**D**
Carignan	Carignan	Carignan
Cinsaut	Cinsaut	Cinsaut
Syrah	Syrah	Mourvèdre
Macabeo	Macabeo	Macabeo
Garnacha	Garnacha	Garnacha
Garnacha Blanca	Garnacha Blanca	Garnacha Blanca
Bourboulenc	Bourboulenc	Bourboulenc

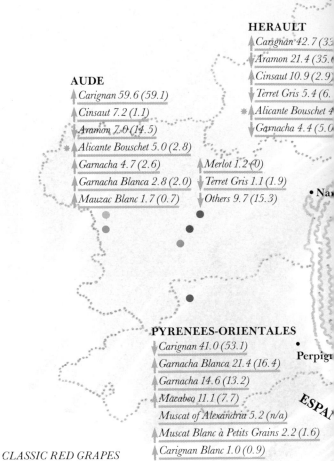

HERAULT
Carignan 42.7 (33.
Aramon 21.4 (35.
Cinsaut 10.9 (2.9)
Terret Gris 5.4 (6.
Alicante Bouschet 4
Garnacha 4.4 (5.0

AUDE
Carignan 59.6 (59.1)
Cinsaut 7.2 (1.1)
Aramon 7.0 (14.5)
Alicante Bouschet 5.0 (2.8)
Garnacha 4.7 (2.6)
Garnacha Blanca 2.8 (2.0)
Mauzac Blanc 1.7 (0.7)

Merlot 1.2 (0)
Terret Gris 1.1 (1.9)
Others 9.7 (15.3)

PYRENEES-ORIENTALES
Carignan 41.0 (53.1)
Garnacha Blanca 21.4 (16.4)
Garnacha 14.6 (13.2)
Macabeo 11.1 (7.7)
Muscat of Alexandria 5.2 (n/a)
Muscat Blanc à Petits Grains 2.2 (1.6)
Carignan Blanc 1.0 (0.9)
Others 3.5 (5.5)

CLASSIC RED GRAPES
● Cabernet Sauvignon
● Syrah
● Merlot

CLASSIC WHITE GRAPES
● Chardonnay
● Sauvignon Blanc
● Chenin Blanc

Garnacha Red grape of
                local importance

Clairette White grape of
                local importance

After each grape is the percentage
of total département plantings
for 1979 and, in brackets, 1968.

✳ Teinturier/hybrid grape

↑ Increase in planting since 1968

↓ Decrease in planting since 1968

AUDE Département

•••••••• Département boundary

〰〰 Zonal boundary

Trebbiano = Ugni Blanc
Garnacha = Grenache
Garnacha Blanca = Grenache Blanc

The Future in Minervois

Minervois is typical of a good Midi area trying to make itself even better. The map above shows which varieties, in declining order, are currently planted. The AC regulations below come into effect in 1990 and show the region's aspirations towards better quality (and less Carignan).

Red
Garnacha
Lladoner Pelut Noir } Must be at least 30% of the blend
Syrah
Mourvèdre } Must be at least 10% of the blend
Carignan
Cinsaut } Must be max. 60% of the blend
Piquepoul Noir
Terret Noir
Aspiran Noir

White
Bourboulenc
Macabeo
Garnacha Blanca } Must be at least 50% of the blend
Piquepoul Blanc
Clairette Blanc
Terret Blanc

Lladoner, or Ledoner, Pelut Noir is a Garnacha variant of Catalonian origins; Aspiran is an ancient workhorse and table grape.

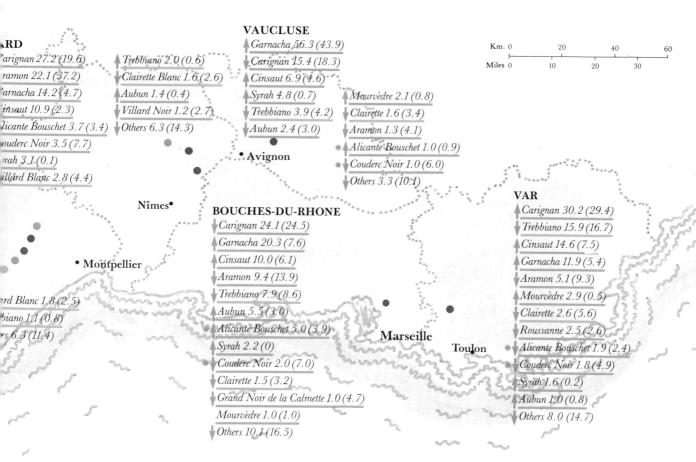

VAUCLUSE
Garnacha 56.3 (43.9)
Carignan 15.4 (18.3)
Cinsaut 6.9 (4.6)
Syrah 4.8 (0.7)
Trebbiano 3.9 (4.2)
Aubun 2.4 (3.0)

Mourvèdre 2.1 (0.8)
Clairette 1.6 (3.4)
Aramon 1.3 (4.1)
Alicante Bouschet 1.0 (0.9)
Couderc Noir 1.0 (6.0)
Others 3.3 (10.1)

RD
arignan 27.2 (19.6)
ramon 22.1 (37.2)
arnacha 14.2 (4.7)
insaut 10.9 (2.3)
licante Bouschet 3.7 (3.4)
ouderc Noir 3.5 (7.7)
rah 3.1 (0.1)
illard Blanc 2.8 (4.4)

Trebbiano 2.0 (0.6)
Clairette Blanc 1.6 (2.6)
Aubun 1.4 (0.4)
Villard Noir 1.2 (2.7)
Others 6.3 (14.3)

Nîmes

Avignon

BOUCHES-DU-RHONE
Carignan 24.1 (24.5)
Garnacha 20.3 (7.6)
Cinsaut 10.0 (6.1)
Aramon 9.4 (13.9)
Trebbiano 7.9 (8.6)
Aubun 5.5 (3.0)
Alicante Bouschet 5.0 (3.9)
Syrah 2.2 (0)
Couderc Noir 2.0 (7.0)
Clairette 1.5 (3.2)
Grand Noir de la Calmette 1.0 (4.7)
Mourvèdre 1.0 (1.0)
Others 10.1 (16.5)

Montpellier

rd Blanc 1.8 (2.5)
biano 1.1 (0.8)
s 6.3 (11.4)

Marseille

Toulon

VAR
Carignan 30.2 (29.4)
Trebbiano 15.9 (16.7)
Cinsaut 14.6 (7.5)
Garnacha 11.9 (5.4)
Aramon 5.1 (9.3)
Mourvèdre 2.9 (0.5)
Clairette 2.6 (5.6)
Roussanne 2.5 (2.6)
Alicante Bouschet 1.9 (2.4)
Couderc Noir 1.8 (4.9)
Syrah 1.6 (0.2)
Aubun 1.0 (0.8)
Others 8.0 (14.7)

Km. 0   20   40   60
Miles 0   10   20   30

Quantitatively, this is by far the most important wine region of France. Qualitatively, it is an unmitigated disaster – although things are discernibly if gradually improving.

Although this part of France is often treated as vinously homogeneous, there are very clear regional variations. In the far east, Italy encroaches slightly, *vide* Braquet and Vermentino. From the west, Spain's influence has been enormous. Carignan, also known as Cariñena, dominates the region right round as far as Châteauneuf country, where another Spanish variety, Garnacha, takes over. Macabeo, or Maccabeu, increasingly important in the far west, is none other than Rioja's Viura while Mourvèdre is of Spanish origin. Monastrell has seeped over the border into the Pyrenées-Orientales and even Tempranillo has made an impact on the vineyards of southern France, though each disappears into "Others" on the map. In the great wine wasteland of the Languedoc-Roussillon, the major influence has not been that of its neighbours but of commercial expediency. In the eighteenth century and the beginning of the nineteenth, the area planted was much smaller, producing only 15 percent of France's wine – and much of that, prophetically, went straight to the distillery. White-vine varieties dominated then: Terret, Piquepoul, Oeillade, Clairette, Muscat.

In mid-nineteenth century oidium struck the vineyards of France, wine prices rose, wine production took on a new commercial allure which was further increased by the arrival of the railways, suddenly opening up the thirsty urban markets to the north and east. The fertile plains, designed to produce common wine, were rapidly planted with the irrevocably common, high-yielding Aramon, whose colour was reinforced from the 1860s by the Bouschet family of hybrid *teinturiers*. The advent of phylloxera served only to underline the need in vignerons' eyes for high-yielding varieties. Carignan retreated to the hills.

The aftermath of this disastrous period is still with us. It took a general plunge in French wine prices, thanks to the spread of high-yielding hybrids to other French areas and the development of the Algerian *vignoble* in the twenties, to make these Midi wine farmers realize that quantity might not be all. And when that quantity was severely reduced by disease and poor weather, against which they were so much worse equipped then, life must have looked pretty bleak.

Carignan's resurgence owes much to the development of sprays against fungus disease to which the variety is so prone. It has been brought down on to the plains where the hybrids and Aramon are, at last, in retreat – although it was probably not the ideal variety to promulgate. EEC authorities, drained of resources in supporting the production of a huge surplus of poor quality wine each year by buying it for useless distillation, have been trying to change things. Financial carrots are offered for those prepared either to grub up vines on unsuitable land or replant with *cépages améliorateurs* such as Grenache, Cinsaut, Mourvèdre and Syrah – even Cabernet and Merlot in some corners.

But cultivation of vines on the flat lands of the Languedoc-Roussillon is now in its fifth generation of vignerons in some areas. They are a stubborn lot; it is easier and no less rewarding in the short term to continue to produce wine for the overworked Community still. The take-up rate for replanting is as yet low, though the next national agricultural census of 1989 may bring good news for all of us concerned with wine quality.

FRANKEN *Wine region*

  Vine-growing areas

Pinot Noir = *Blauer Spätburgunder*
Pinot Gris = *Ruländer*
Chasselas = *Weisser Gutedel*
Pinot Blanc = *Weisserburgunder*

N

Km. 0 — 20 — 40
Miles 0 — 10 — 20

AHR
MITTELRHEIN
Mosel
Koblenz
Rhein
MOSEL-SAAR-RUWER
Trier
Nahe
NAHE
Wiesbaden
RHEINGAU
Mainz
Frankfurt
RHEINHESSEN
HESSISCHE BERGSTRASSE
FRANKEN
Main
Würz...
BADEN
Mannheim
Heidelberg
Neckar
RHEINPFALZ
Saarbrücken
WÜRTTEMBERG
BADEN
FRANCE
Stuttgart
Rhein
BADEN
Freiburg
BADEN
Bodensee
Basel

Rheingau	1984	1965
Total number of hectares	2,752	3,092
Percentages of vines planted:		
Riesling	79.5	77.2
Müller-Thurgau	6.9	11.8
Pinot Noir	4.3	1.5
Silvaner	0.8	7.6
Blauer Portugieser	0.3	0.2
Others	8.2	1.7

. . . figures not available

Ahr	1984	1964
Total number of hectares	383	431
Percentages of vines planted:		
Pinot Noir	31.3	24
Blauer Portugieser	27.7	34
Riesling	17	23.7
Müller-Thurgau	14.4	16.5
Kerner	1	. . .
Others	8.6	1.8

Mosel-Saar-Ruwer	1984	1964
Total number of hectares	11,631	9,777
Percentages of vines planted:		
Riesling	56.6	79.5
Müller-Thurgau	22.6	8.9
Weisser Elbling	8.6	10.8
Kerner	4.9	. . .
Others	7.3	0.8

Mittelrhein	1984	1965
Total number of hectares	721	870
Percentages of vines planted:		
Riesling	75.5	85
Müller-Thurgau	10.5	9.5
Kerner	5.7	. . .
Silvaner	1.4	2.5
Pinot Noir	0.7	. . .
Blauer Portugieser	0.3	. . .
Others	5.9	3.0

Nahe	1984	1965
Total number of hectares	4,264	3,006
Percentages of vines planted:		
Müller-Thurgau	28	26
Riesling	21.3	29
Silvaner	15.2	40
Kerner	6.9	. . .
Blauer Portugieser	0.8	. . .
Pinot Noir	0.4	. . .
Others	27.4	5

Germany

Germany's minutely recorded vineyards are currently in an interesting state of flux. Far less than in Europe's other major wine-producing countries is grape variety dictated by local traditions and laws. The German wine grower's choice of vine type is influenced, as in that other even more marginal climate England, by the ripening potential of each site and what is most commercially viable. There is no point, for instance, in wasting an exceptionally sheltered microclimate in the Mosel on Müller-Thurgau, which will ripen almost anywhere and fetches a much lower price than Riesling.

In harmony with this natural feature of the country is Germany's unrivalled activity in vine breeding, which also helps make the country's varietal profile one of the most flexible in the world. So many products of vine procreation have been developed that one almost feels a sense of surfeit. Do they really need Hochkroner, Schlagarrebe and Tekla when they already have, and are not sure how to use, Albalonga, Domina and Tamara?

The current breeder-in-chief, Professor Helmut Becker, may find the perfect variety – Riesling without the viticultural design faults. (Indeed, he reckons he already has with several new vine types, some of them even – horror of horrors – hybrids.) But if the German public are already sated with new wine names, how is he ever to market this exciting new possibility? It has yet to be proved that any crossing other than the venerable Müller-Thurgau can withstand the breezes of fashion which sway Germany's fickle wine-buying public.

The total area of Germany's vineyard has been steadily increasing, at the rate of about 1 percent a year. The area planted with Germany's trump card of a vine variety, Riesling, is increasing just a little more slowly than that but still represents about 20 percent of total plantings.

Having supplanted the Silvaner so popular earlier this century, the bland, boring and, in some vintages, rather unaccommodating Müller-Thurgau is gradually losing its grip on the German wine industry. It is still the most planted variety but whereas in 1976 it covered 27.3 percent of Germany's vineyard, by the next exceptional vintage in 1983 this proportion had dropped to 25.8 percent.

Among white varieties, the "new" crossings (some of which actually date from before the First World War) have been the chief beneficiaries of the decline in Müller-Thurgau (the prototype German crossing) and in the traditional varieties – Silvaner, Elbling, Pinot Gris (Ruländer), Chasselas (Gutedel), Pinot Blanc (Weissburgunder) and Gewürztraminer. Scheurebe, Bacchus, Faber and, especially, the Riesling-like Kerner are all now important varieties, and varietals, in their own right. Mercifully, demand for the overpoweringly aromatic Morio-Muskat appears to have peaked.

There has also been a quiet revolution in red-wine grapes planted in Germany. Although the rather ordinary Portugieser has been losing ground, Pinot Noir or Spätburgunder is becoming perceptibly more important as the increasingly cosmopolitan German wine drinker recognizes the modishness of this variety.

And if ever there were a sign that Germany's vineyards were becoming less, how shall we say, German, then it is the recent appearance on one or two German wine labels of that very international name indeed, Chardonnay.

Rheinhessen	1984	1964
Total number of hectares	22,470	16,441
Percentages of vines planted:		
Müller-Thurgau	24.9	33.2
Silvaner	14.1	47
Scheurebe	9.6	1
Kerner	6.9	...
Riesling	5.1	6.1
Morio-Muskat	4.6	2
Blauer Portugieser	2.8	8.1
Pinot Noir	0.8	0.3
Others	31.2	2.3

Rheinpfalz	1984	1964
Total number of hectares	20,537	17,670
Percentages of vines planted:		
Müller-Thurgau	23.6	20.3
Riesling	13.4	13.6
Kerner	10.7	...
Silvaner	9.6	39.4
Morio-Muskat	8.3	3.9
Blauer Portugieser	7.4	17.7
Scheurebe	6.4	0.6
Pinot Noir	0.8	...
Gewürztraminer	...	1.1
Others	19.8	3.4

Hessische Bergstrasse	1984	1964
Total number of hectares	356	...
Percentages of vines planted:		
Riesling	52.2	...
Müller-Thurgau	18.5	...
Silvaner	8.7	...
Pinot Noir	0.6	...
Blauer Portugieser	0.3	...
Others	19.7	...

Baden	1984	1964
Total number of hectares	14,815	7,607
Percentages of vines planted:		
Müller-Thurgau	37.6	24.5
Pinot Noir	20	19.9
Pinot Gris	12.1	13.2
Chasselas	8.3	15.4
Riesling	7.6	7.1
Silvaner	3.8	8.2
Pinot Blanc	2.8	...
Blauer Portugieser	0.3	...
Others	7.5	11.7

Franken	1984	1964
Total number of hectares	4,494	2,203
Percentages of vines planted:		
Müller-Thurgau	50	31.6
Silvaner	21	55.2
Riesling	2.3	3.9
Pinot Noir	1.2	...
Blauer Portugieser	0.7	...
Perle	...	2.8
Rieslaner	...	1.2
Others	24.8	5.3

Württemberg	1984	1965
Total number of hectares	9,449	6,090
Percentages of vines planted:		
Riesling	23.2	24.8
Blauer Trollinger	22.9	29
Müller-Thurgau	10.2	6.2
Kerner	8.4	0.5
Silvaner	5.7	13.8
Blauer Portugieser	3.7	11.7
Schwarzriesling	...	4.8
Pinot Noir	3.2	1
Pinot Gris	1.1	0.6
Others	21.6	7.6

Spain & Portugal

S pain and Portugal present *terra* virtually *incognita* to the student of vine varieties. Portugal and, in a slightly smaller though very different way, Spain almost constitute viticultural islands. Only in the Minho is there any overlap between the varieties grown on the other side of the border, and Spain's influence here is arguably much less than it is on the other side of the Pyrenees.

Spain keeps most varieties to herself, which means an awesome range of different vines. Galicia alone, one of the least homogeneous vine regions admittedly, is reputed to boast more than 1,000 varieties. Officially the Spaniards admit to a national total of 600, though a mere 20 cover more than 80 percent of Spain's sprawling vineyard. Only the seven most planted are shown here, which illustrates well, by omission, just how relatively unimportant are some of those Spanish varieties which are much more internationally famous. Also by omission, the map shows how small scale are Spain's experiments with classic imports compared with her ocean of Airén in La Mancha.

Productivity here is notoriously low, mainly because of the low rainfall and low soil fertility in the major vine regions of the centre. Vines are, typically, planted sparsely and grown as low bushes without wires. Techniques have been improving, however, so that average yields have leapt from below 20 hectolitres per hectare in the early seventies to 26 in the early eighties.

Spain is, perhaps unexpectedly, much richer in white varieties than red; and her most planted grape, which makes it also the world's most planted variety, is the quite respectable white Airén. Over the last few decades there has been a discernible decrease in plantings of some of the better quality but more troublesome varieties – Rioja's Graciano is an obvious example. It is to be hoped that efforts will be made to rescue them from extinction.

This process has been set under way with some urgency in Portugal (including Madeira). Damage to traditional vine types from virus diseases has led to an upsurge in plantings of very ordinary, high-yielding varieties, many of them crossings and some of them hybrids. Only in the Douro, with its myriad and often exceptional port sorts, and in small pockets of thoughtfully husbanded vines, has quality been maintained in her vineyards.

Of the several hundred varieties in Portugal, only a handful are known outside the country. Malvasia has long been a feature of vineyards on the mainland as well as in Madeira, and, apart from that, only Palomino (Perrum), Trebbiano (Thalia), Elbling (Alva), Carignan (Pinot Evara) and Tempranillo (Tinta Roriz or Aragonez) seem to have penetrated from abroad. Portugal has its own traditional varieties well-suited to producing suitably balanced wines even in relatively hot temperatures. With any luck, the nineties will see their renaissance.

Curiously, Portugal's vines and viticultural methods were some of the best described at the end of the last century. Current information is much more difficult to come by. The map shows some of those varieties most planted in Portugal today, together with some that are thought to have particularly good potential.

Bobal — Red grape of local importance

Airén — White grape of local importance

LA MANCHA — Demarcated wine area

CATALUNA — Administrative zone

Vine-growing areas

International boundary

Coast

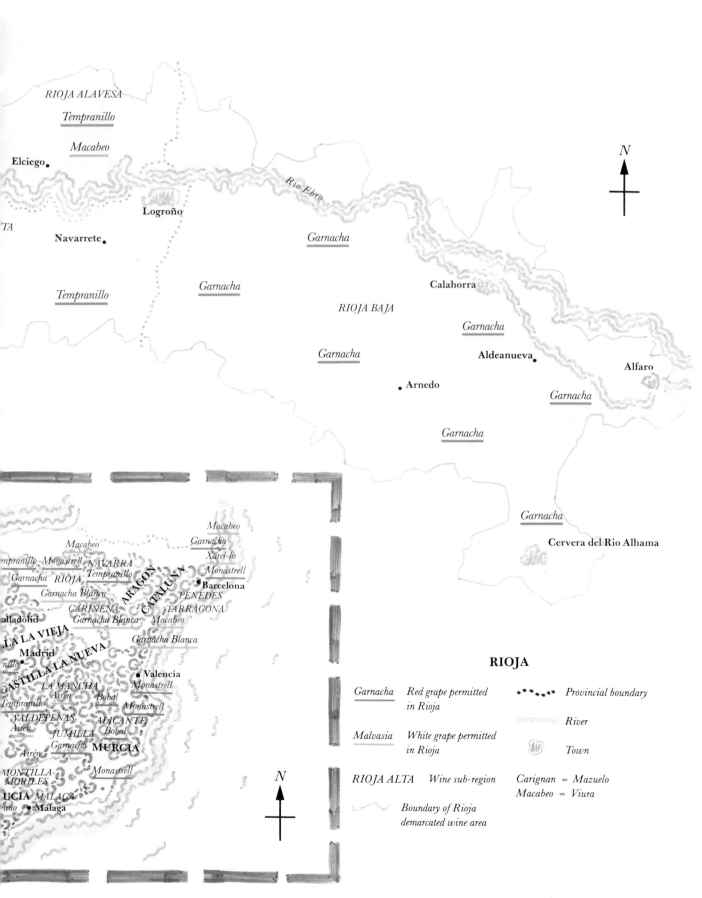

RIOJA ALAVESA

Tempranillo

Macabeo

Elciego .

Logroño

Navarrete .

Tempranillo

TA

Rio Ebro

Garnacha

Garnacha

RIOJA BAJA

Calahorra

Garnacha

Garnacha

Aldeanueva .

Alfaro

. **Arnedo**

Garnacha

Garnacha

Garnacha

Cervera del Rio Alhama

N

Macabeo

Macabeo

Garnacha

Xarel-lo

mpranillo Monastrell **NAVARRA**

Monastrell

Garnacha **RIOJA** *Tempranillo*

ARAGON

CATALUÑA

. Barcelona

Garnacha Blanca

PENEDES

CARINENA

TARRAGONA

alladolid *Garnacha Blanca* *Macabeo*

LA LA VIEJA

Garnacha Blanca

Madrid

nillo .

CASTILLA LA NUEVA

. Valencia

LA MANCHA *Monastrell*

Tempranillo *Airen* *Bobal*

Monastrell

VALDEPEÑAS **ALICANTE**

Airen *Bobal*

JUMILLA

Airen *Garnacha* **MURCIA**

MONTILLA-MORILLES *Monastrell*

UCIA *MALAGA*

nino . **Málaga**

N

RIOJA

Garnacha	Red grape permitted in Rioja	••••••	Provincial boundary
Malvasia	White grape permitted in Rioja		River
			Town
RIOJA ALTA	Wine sub-region	Carignan = Mazuelo	
	Boundary of Rioja demarcated wine area	Macabeo = Viura	

Italy

The Frescobaldis, whose Castello di Nippozzano is seen here, have been in the wine business for six centuries. In that time they have seen the local grape varieties evolve from Greek legacies, through the establishment of Tuscany's most successful indigenous varieties, to the current influx of Cabernet Sauvignon vines from France.

Divinely unquantifiable and uncharted, Italy's vineyards and more random vine plantings make difficult raw material for analysis such as this. Almost any agricultural smallholding will encompass a few vines, often still promiscuously interspersed with other crops regarded as staples by the average Italian household. The large, ordered vine plantation owned by a commercial organization is the exception, though Villa Banfi's recent remodelling of Montalcino proves the rule as never before.

There are at least approximate geographical clusterings of varieties to provide beacons for foreign travellers. Only Trebbiano and Sangiovese come anywhere near ubiquity, and in the south Bombino Bianco and Montepulciano, white and red respectively, play similar parts. Elsewhere, as with the edible, each region tends to have its very own varieties, carefully adapted to that region over the centuries. It is a sobering thought that the Etruscans knew Lambrusco as intimately as the East-siders now do.

The picture is complicated by much local confusion about variety names. Bonvino is a cheerily common synonym for a wide range of completely different varieties. Trebbiano often crops up inaccurately, too.

Most Italian varieties are just that, found in one region of Italy and only there. One or two cultural influences can nevertheless be discerned. In the south there are some, usually very good quality, varieties whose origins are clearly Greek which make one yearn to track them down in modern Greece. Aglianico is the most obvious dark variety, Greco its light equivalent. The route travelled by the Ribolla of Friuli may be different. It is certainly the same as the Rebula of northwest Yugoslavia and almost certainly the same as Cephalonia's Robola. This hints at a more land-based route from Greece to Italy.

There are instances of Franco/Italian overlap but they are surprisingly few. Asti's Brachetto is Bellet's Braquet; Savoie's Mondeuse is Friuli's Refosco (and Istria's Terrano); each may well be a memento of the influence of the House of Savoy in northern Italy in the eighteenth century.

Few essentially Italian varieties have been exported. The Californians have embraced some Piedmontese reds, and their Zinfandel is almost certainly Apulia's Primitivo. Emigrés took Muscat Blanc à Petits Grains, Bonarda, Lambrusco and Barbera to Argentina. Those who count the Italian Tyrol as Italy will agree that Germany's Trollinger counts as an Italian export (of Schiava). And if ampelographer Truel is to be believed, Tocai Friulano is Sauvignonasse or Sauvignon Vert and can be disentangled in Chile, mixed in with Sauvignon Blanc vines as "Sauvignon", and in California as "Muscadelle" if you please.

Much easier to find are the varieties we now consider international "classics" in Italy. Although Italy has not been left untouched by the craze to attempt a Margaux and Montrachet, there is nothing essentially new in this. Pinots of all hues, both Cabernets, Merlot and Chardonnay were introduced as long ago as the eighteenth century in the northeast, probably by Napoleon's revolutionaries.

There are strong links with Spain, especially in Sardinia whose Cannonau, for instance, is none other than Garnacha. Malvasia is probably even more important in Italy than in Spain and Madeira, and well represents that shrinking group of ancient and potentially great varieties which need urgent attention.

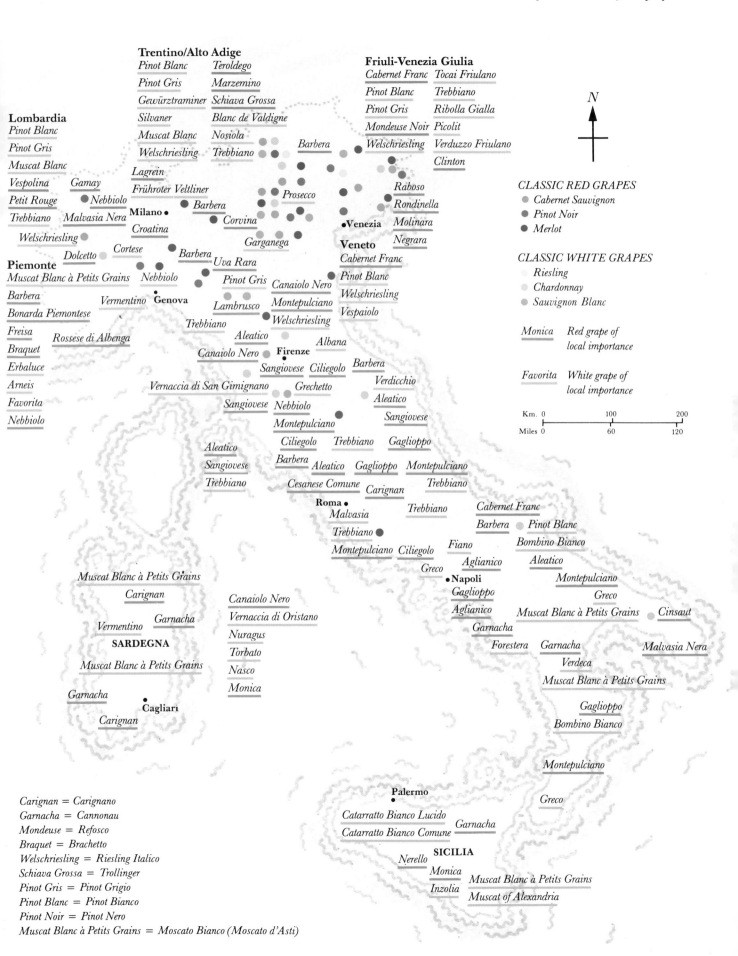

Trentino/Alto Adige
Pinot Blanc   Teroldego
Pinot Gris   Marzemino
Gewürztraminer   Schiava Grossa
Silvaner   Blanc de Valdigne
Muscat Blanc   Nosiola
Welschriesling   Trebbiano
Lagrein
Frühroter Veltliner

Friuli-Venezia Giulia
Cabernet Franc   Tocai Friulano
Pinot Blanc   Trebbiano
Pinot Gris   Ribolla Gialla
Mondeuse Noir   Picolit
Welschriesling   Verduzzo Friulano
Clinton

Lombardia
Pinot Blanc
Pinot Gris
Muscat Blanc
Vespolina   Gamay
Petit Rouge   Nebbiolo
Trebbiano   Malvasia Nera
Welschriesling

Barbera

Prosecco

Raboso
Rondinella
Molinara
Negrara

Milano
Croatina
Barbera
Corvina
Garganega

Venezia

Veneto
Cabernet Franc
Pinot Blanc
Welschriesling
Vespaiolo

Piemonte
Muscat Blanc à Petits Grains
Barbera
Bonarda Piemontese
Freisa
Braquet
Erbaluce
Arneis
Favorita
Nebbiolo

Dolcetto   Cortese
Barbera
Nebbiolo   Uva Rara
Pinot Gris

Vermentino   **Genova**
Lambrusco
Trebbiano
Aleatico
Canaiolo Nero

Canaiolo Nero
Montepulciano
Welschriesling

Albana

Firenze
Sangiovese   Ciliegolo
Vernaccia di San Gimignano   Grechetto
Sangiovese   Nebbiolo
Montepulciano
Ciliegolo   Trebbiano
Barbera   Aleatico   Gaglioppo
Cesanese Comune   Carignan

Barbera
Verdicchio
Aleatico
Sangiovese
Gaglioppo
Montepulciano
Trebbiano

Roma
Malvasia
Trebbiano
Montepulciano   Ciliegolo

Trebbiano

Fiano
Greco

Napoli
Gaglioppo
Aglianico
Garnacha
Forestera

Cabernet Franc
Barbera   Pinot Blanc
Bombino Bianco
Aleatico
Montepulciano
Greco
Muscat Blanc à Petits Grains   Cinsaut
Garnacha   Malvasia Nera
Verdeca
Muscat Blanc à Petits Grains

Gaglioppo
Bombino Bianco

Montepulciano

CLASSIC RED GRAPES
● *Cabernet Sauvignon*
● *Pinot Noir*
● *Merlot*

CLASSIC WHITE GRAPES
○ *Riesling*
○ *Chardonnay*
○ *Sauvignon Blanc*

Monica   Red grape of local importance

Favorita   White grape of local importance

Km. 0   100   200
Miles 0   60   120

Muscat Blanc à Petits Grains
Carignan
Vermentino   Garnacha
SARDEGNA
Muscat Blanc à Petits Grains
Garnacha
Carignan
Cagliari

Canaiolo Nero
Vernaccia di Oristano
Nuragus
Torbato
Nasco
Monica

Montepulciano

Greco

Palermo
Catarratto Bianco Lucido
Catarratto Bianco Comune   Garnacha
SICILIA
Nerello
Monica
Inzolia   Muscat Blanc à Petits Grains
Muscat of Alexandria

Carignan = Carignano
Garnacha = Cannonau
Mondeuse = Refosco
Braquet = Brachetto
Welschriesling = Riesling Italico
Schiava Grossa = Trollinger
Pinot Gris = Pinot Grigio
Pinot Blanc = Pinot Bianco
Pinot Noir = Pinot Nero
Muscat Blanc à Petits Grains = Moscato Bianco (Moscato d'Asti)

DDR

Pinot Blanc
Pinot Gris

Gewürztraminer
Silvaner

• **Praha**

CESKOSLOVENSKO

Portugieser
St-Laurent

Grüner Veltliner
Welschriesling

Grüner Veltliner   *Muscatel*
Welschriesling   *Furmint*
Neuburger   *Silvaner*
Muscatel

Frühroter Veltliner
St-Laurent Rotgipfler   *Müller-Thurgau*
Grüner Veltliner   *Welschriesling*
Silvaner
Gewürztraminer
Neuburger   *Pinot Blanc*

Kadarka   *Furmint*
Ezerjó

ÖSTERREICH   *Zierfandler*   • **Wien**

Welschriesling

Muscat Ottonel   *Blaufränkisch*   *Hárslevelü*   **MAGYARORSZAG**

Pinot Gris Bouvier Pinot Blanc   *Furmint*   *Pinot Gris*   • **Budapest**
Muskat-Silvaner   *Kadarka*   *Gewürztraminer*   *Kéknyelü*   *Zierfandler*
Blauer Wildbacher Blaufränkisch Portugieser   *Juhfark*   *Silvaner*   *Feteasca Alba*
Gewürztraminer   *Mézesféhr*   *Kövidinka*

Ribolla   *Welschriesling*   *Pinot Blanc*   *Kadarka*   *Welschriesling*
Gialla   *Gewürztraminer*   *Cabernet Franc*   *Muscat Ottonel*
Pinot Gris   *Pinot Blanc*   *Kövidinka*   *Banat Riesling*

Malvasia   *Pinot Gris Gewürztraminer*   *Kadarka*   *Smederevka*
Pinot Blanc   *Kraljevina*   *Plemenka*   *Welschriesling*
Zametovka   *Maraština*   *Prokupac*
Blaufränkisch   *Barbera*   **Beograd**
Mondeuse   *Plavac Mali*

Plavina   **JUGOSLAVIJA**

Maraština
Plavac Beli   *Plavac Mali*
Bogdanusa
Vugava   *Plavac Mali Zilavka*
Blatina Plavac Beli
Grk   *Vranac*
Plavina

Banat Riesling
Cabernet Fran
Kadarka
Feteasca Neag

Welschriesling
Prokupac
Blaufränkisch

Prokupac   *Plemenka*

Welschriesli
Cabernet Fr
Blaufränkisc
Proku
Smede

Prokupac   *Belan*
Plovdina   *Mona*

We
Pin
Fete
Ge
Mu

CLASSIC RED GRAPES
● *Cabernet Sauvignon*
● *Pinot Noir*
● *Merlot*

CLASSIC WHITE GRAPES
○ *Riesling*
○ *Chardonnay*
○ *Sauvignon Blanc*

Barbera   Red grape of
local importance

Silvaner   White grape of
local importance

N
Km. 0   50   100   150
Miles 0   50   100

Central Europe

What a ravaged and exotic vinescape to reduce to the confines of a double-page spread! The Soviet Union alone, with more land under vine than the French and the Italians by now, warrants at least a chapter to itself. Admittedly, the chapter would be of dubious use to the international wine drinker, but would show just how quantitatively important is a handful of vines virtually unknown in the west such as Rkatsiteli and Saperavi. It is heartening that these widely planted Soviet vines are actually capable of producing some extremely good and distinctive wine.

Like most of the countries on this map, the Soviet Union has also been dabbling in the international varieties to a greater or lesser extent. (The world's darling, Chardonnay, for instance was already well established in Georgia,

Moldavia and the Ukraine by the mid-seventies.) One end of this spectrum is represented by Bulgaria whose ethnic red varieties such as Melnik and Pamid have been subjugated to the rule of Merlot and Cabernet Sauvignon, of which Bulgaria has rather more planted than Bordeaux. The Bulgarian cap has been set firmly at non-Bulgarian customers, and very successful this vineyard *putsch* has been, too.

The other stand, determinedly isolated from the winds of varietal fashion, is represented by Hungary, home of a quiver of Magyar vines, arrow sharp in definition. Furmint is the most obvious, found all over eastern Europe in various guises and even in Savoie as Altesse. Its red equivalent, Kadarka, though most readily associated with Hungary, is actually Albanian in origin, but other Hungarian native varietals Hárslevelü, Kéknyelü, Ezerjó and Juhfark – all, curiously, white – can in their smoulderingly original ways be truly exciting and quite unlike any wine produced anywhere else.

Romania and Yugoslavia sport a blend of vines associated with eastern Europe and more international varieties. Romania is interesting in that it seems to have provided a birthplace or at least a crèche for several vines now fairly widespread such as Feteasča, Tămîioasă and perhaps even Welschriesling. And it can still field a number of other less well-distributed but potentially interesting native varieties. Yugoslavia can hardly be regarded as a single country in vine or wine terms. The north and middle are good at making cheap varietals with familiar names; the coast and south present a labyrinth of local specialities, some of them of real interest. Is there really no connection between Vugava and Viognier? There must also be much closer links than have yet been established between Macedonia's sturdy vines and those of neighbouring northern Greece.

Naturally, in this area of relatively newly created political groupings, vine variety distribution does not always correspond neatly to national frontiers. Some of the original Tokay vines now find themselves in Czechoslovakia, for instance, and Austria's wines are reflected just over its borders in Czechoslovakia, Hungary and Yugoslavia.

Austria's wines may seem to follow a pattern – of full-bodied, spicy Germanic whites and rather light, syrupy reds. But this by no means reflects a lack of individuality in the vineyard. In the many Veltliners, Neuburger, Bouvier, Rotgipfler, Zierfandler, Blauer Limberger and Zweigelt, Austria presents the ampelographer with an enthralling range of originals of which only Limberger or Blaufränkisch can be said to have travelled much.

S.S.S.R.

Cot
Tamîioasa Romaneasca
Grasa
Saperavi
Gewürztraminer
Muscat Ottonel
Rkatsiteli
Aligoté
Feteasca

ROMANIA

Feteasca Alba
Feteasca Neagra
Feteasca Regala
Neuburger
Aligoté
Feteasca Alba
Tamîioasa Romaneasca
Muscat Ottonel
Babeasca Neagra
Feteasca Regala
Grasa
Pinot Gris
Welschriesling
Muscat

Bucureşti

Tamîioasa Romaneasca
Kadarka

Dimiat
Rkatsiteli
Feteasca Alba
Rkatsiteli
Pamid
Kadarka

BÂLGARIJA

Aligoté
Dimiat
Mavrud
Gewürztraminer
Saperavi
Red Misket

bernet Franc
roka Melnishka Losa

~~~~~ *Coast*

•••••• *International boundary*

Blaufränkisch = *Kékfrankos*
= *Blauer Limberger*
Mondeuse = *Terrano* = *Refosco*
Feteascǎ Albǎ = *Leányka*
Sauvignon Blanc = *Muskat-Silvaner*

Welschriesling = *Laskiriesling*
(*Yugoslavia*)
= *Olaszriesling*
(*Hungary*)
= *Italiansky Rizling*
(*Bulgaria*)

USA: The West Coast

More than any other corner of the wine world, the West Coast of America is swept by the winds of wine-drinking fashion. The Midi peasant remains blithely oblivious to the fact that the wine he produces is not what the consumer wants to drink; Brussels will guarantee him a price for it anyway. Meanwhile, his West Coast equivalent was field-grafting his Zinfandel vines over to Sauvignon Blanc within a season of the coining of the phrase "white wine boom" in *Time* and *Newsweek* in the early eighties.

In 1974 when Robert Mondavi was making his first notable Cabernet Sauvignon Reserve, California's ratio of white-wine grapes to red was 33,600 to 58,400 hectares (84,000 to 146,000 acres). Ten years later, this had been transformed, tailored to suit the market – or rather the market of three years previously – to 79,200 and 66,000 hectares (198,000 and 165,000 acres) respectively. In other words, while the acreage of red-wine grapes had risen by a modest 13 percent, white-wine grape cultivation had more than doubled. Even as recently as the two seasons prior to 1985, 680 hectares (1,700 acres) of red-wine vines were field grafted each year to produce white wine. And just for good measure, a further 320 hectares (800 acres) of vines producing rather ordinary white wine were grafted over to superior white-wine varieties. As in so many other aspects of West Coast life, analysis and the resultant tinkering are still essential elements in wine production.

Colombard, in California given the cachet of the adjective "French", has been the great beneficiary of America's white-wine boom. It is by far the most planted grape variety, covering almost twice as much land as its nearest rival, Chenin Blanc. As recently as 1983, there were 11,200 hectares (28,000 acres) of young, not-yet-bearing Colombard to be added to the nearly 18,400 hectares (46,000 acres) of more established plants. Chardonnay is the state's third most planted white variety with 9,600 hectares (24,000 acres), and of reds only that California curiosity Zinfandel surpasses it. That Cabernet Sauvignon is California's second most planted red-wine variety shows to what extent the American public is varietal conscious.

Only slowly have American wine drinkers relinquished the talisman of the single-varietal wine, and allowed plantings of the likes of Merlot and Cabernet Franc gently to rise as the virtues of what are sometimes even referred to somewhat pompously as multivarietal wines are better understood. Few of California's connoisseurs, however, will realize that that revered Gironde antique, Petit Verdot, has been growing in their vineyards for years, albeit on a tiny scale, erroneously called Gros Manseng.

Once past the classics and obvious imports, notably from Italy and presumably encouraged by Italian immigrants, any international student of the varieties planted in California will start to be puzzled. All sorts of names, quite unheard of elsewhere, are relatively important. Products of

——CALIFORNIA VINE-GROWING AREAS AND THEIR OTHER GRAPE VARIETIES (SEE MAP)——

A MENDOCINO, LAKE
Colombard
Gewürztraminer
Trousseau Gris
Garnacha
Carignan
Valdiguié
Gamay Beaujolais
Durif
Zinfandel

B SONOMA
Gewürztraminer
Colombard
Melon de Bourgogne
Muscadelle
Durif
Carignan
Valdiguié
Gamay Beaujolais
Zinfandel

C NAPA
Colombard
Gewürztraminer
Trousseau Gris
Cabernet Franc
Gamay Beaujolais
Zinfandel
Durif
Valdiguié

D ALAMEDA, SANTA CLARA, SANTA CRUZ
Trousseau Gris

E MONTEREY, SAN BENTO
Melon de Bourgogne
Gewürztraminer
Silvaner
Colombard
Emerald Riesling
Trousseau Gris

Malvasia
Folle Blanche
Muscat Blanc à Petits Grains
Carignan
Gamay Beaujolais
Garnacha
Zinfandel
Durif
Valdiguié

F SAN LUIS OBISPO, SANTA BARBARA
Gewürztraminer
Silvaner
Durif
Zinfandel

G CENTRAL VALLEY
Monbadon
Colombard
Emerald Riesling
Flora

Malvasia
Muscat Blanc à Petits Grains
Palomino
Peverella
Trebbiano
Alicanté Bouschet
Garnacha
Barbera
Cinsaut
Carignan
Carnelian
Centurion
Valdiguié
Mission
Durif
Royalty 1390
Rubired
Ruby Cabernet
Salvador
Zinfandel
Garnacha

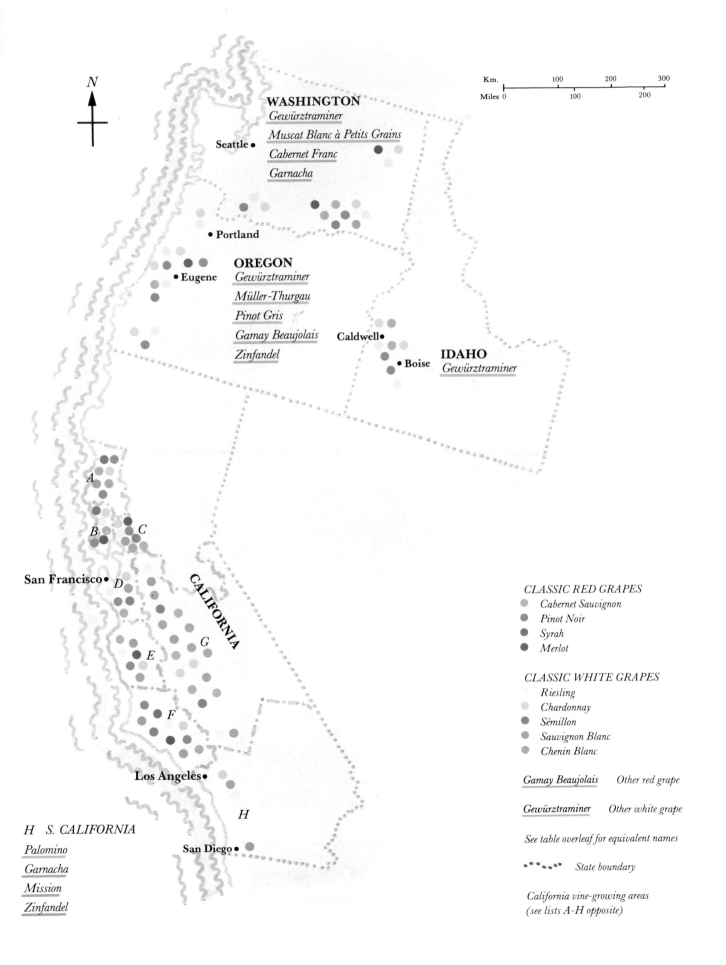

N

Km.   100   200   300
Miles 0   100   200

WASHINGTON
Gewürztraminer
Muscat Blanc à Petits Grains
Cabernet Franc
Garnacha

Seattle •

• Portland

OREGON
Gewürztraminer
Müller-Thurgau
Pinot Gris
Gamay Beaujolais
Zinfandel

• Eugene

Caldwell •
• Boise

IDAHO
Gewürztraminer

A

B   C

San Francisco •   D

CALIFORNIA

E

G

F

Los Angeles •

H

San Diego •

H   S. CALIFORNIA
Palomino
Garnacha
Mission
Zinfandel

CLASSIC RED GRAPES
   Cabernet Sauvignon
   Pinot Noir
   Syrah
   Merlot

CLASSIC WHITE GRAPES
   Riesling
   Chardonnay
   Sémillon
   Sauvignon Blanc
   Chenin Blanc

Gamay Beaujolais   *Other red grape*

Gewürztraminer   *Other white grape*

See table overleaf for equivalent names

••••••••• *State boundary*

*California vine-growing areas
(see lists A-H opposite)*

USUAL WEST COAST NAME	TRUE IDENTITY
Petite Sirah	Durif
Gamay Beaujolais	clone of Pinot Noir
Napa Gamay	Valdiguié
Pinot St George	Négrette*
Early Burgundy	Abouriou
Charbono	Corbeau
Gros Manseng	Petit Verdot
Xeres	Graciano, Morrastel
Valdepeñas	Tempranillo*
Zinfandel	Primitivo, Plavac Mali*
Pinot Blanc	Melon, Muscadet
Sauvignon Vert	Muscadelle
Savagnin Musqué	Sauvignon Blanc
Burger	Monbadon
Gray Riesling	Trousseau Gris (see also Bastardo)
	* probable

the Davis breeding programme of the fifties such as Ruby Cabernet, Carnelian and Emerald Riesling are easy to explain. Others less so. A Frenchman would be mystified by Early Burgundy, Napa Gamay, Charbono, Burger and Gray Riesling, yet all are varieties well known in France but by completely different names (see table).

The average American consumer on the other hand, supposedly so thirsty for the whole truth, so insistent on unambiguous labelling, might be surprised to learn that the vines known on the West Coast as Pinot Blanc are completely unrelated to the Pinot Blanc of Alsace and the Pinot Bianco of Italy but are, in fact, the Melon of Muscadet. Similarly, Californians have by a combination of error and tradition been taught to attach the word Gamay to two varieties quite unrelated either to each other or to the true Gamay of France, as shown in the table. Proper varietal identification seems amazingly low down the list of viticultural priorities on the West Coast.

The establishment of virus-free plant material has been the most important, and successful, aim of the official viticulturists. Clonal selection is much less advanced.

The most pressing need now is for more guidance on matching specific varieties to regions or, preferably, sites. In this respect things seem to be moving backwards rather than forwards. The Davis system of counting up degree days, labelling areas as anything from cool Region I to baking hot Region V, is still in use but recommending region types for each variety has recently been given less emphasis because some of the best wines are being made outside the Davis guidelines.

The map on this page attempts to forecast which grape varieties might ultimately show their paces most dazzlingly in which areas. The paucity of markings indicates perhaps better than words can that the systematic selection of grape varieties is still in its infancy in California. In some ways, the situation is easier in Oregon because vineyard sites are more limited, and in Washington where the wine industry is so much more contained and self-determined.

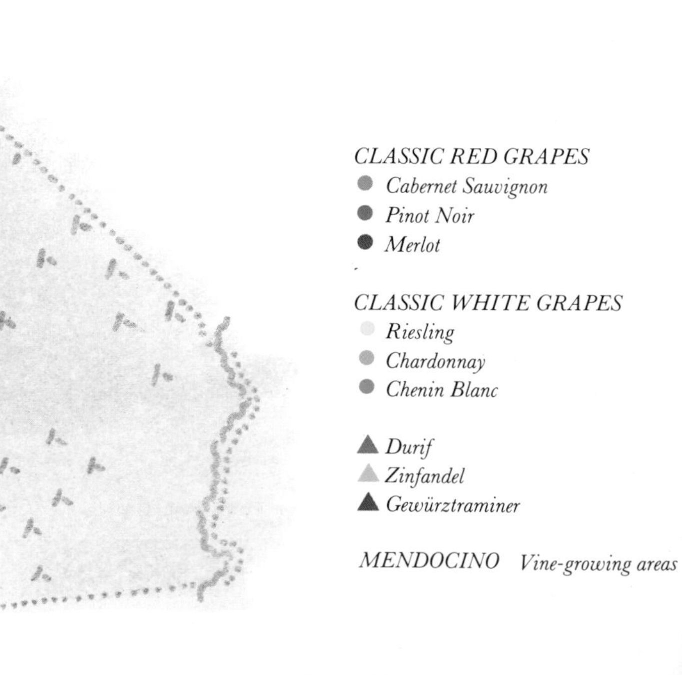

N

MENDOCINO

SONOMA NAPA

CARNEROS

San Francisco

SAN JOAQUIN

Sacramento

San Joaquin

Salinas

MONTEREY

SANTA BARBARA San Joaquin

Los Angeles

San Diego

••••• State boundary

Land over 900 metres

Durif = Petite Sirah

CLASSIC RED GRAPES
● Cabernet Sauvignon
● Pinot Noir
● Merlot

CLASSIC WHITE GRAPES
● Riesling
● Chardonnay
● Chenin Blanc

▲ Durif
▲ Zinfandel
▲ Gewürztraminer

MENDOCINO *Vine-growing areas*

South America

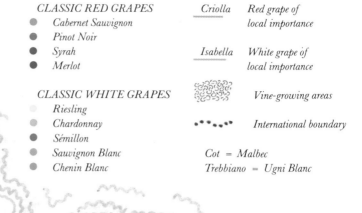

CLASSIC RED GRAPES
- Cabernet Sauvignon
- Pinot Noir
- Syrah
- Merlot

CLASSIC WHITE GRAPES
- Riesling
- Chardonnay
- Sémillon
- Sauvignon Blanc
- Chenin Blanc

Criolla — Red grape of local importance

Isabella — White grape of local importance

Vine-growing areas

International boundary

Cot = Malbec
Trebbiano = Ugni Blanc

Palomino
Mission
Tempranillo
Garnacha
Carignan
Colombard

MEXICO

Trebbiano
Ruby Cabernet
Colombard

Gamay
Pinot Gris

N

Km. 0 ... 1000 ... 3000
Miles 0 ... 500 ... 1000

COLOMBIA

PERU

BRASIL

Cot

BOLIVIA

Dutchess
Niagara
Peverella
Trebbiano
Couderc
Delaware
Concord
Herbemont

Muscat à Petit Grains
Muscat of Alexandria
Torrontes
Pedro Ximénez
Pinot Blanc
Gewürztraminer
Tocai Friulano
País
Cabernet Franc
Carignan
Cot
Petit Verdot

ARGENTINA
Muscat à Petits Grains
Pedro Ximénez
Trebbiano
Gewürztraminer
Cereza Criolla
Cot Bonarda
Tempranillo
Lambrusco
Fer Barbera
Cabernet Franc

CHILE

URUGUAY
Pinot Blanc
Isabella
Tannat
Vidiella
Barbera
Nebbiolo

South America is even less a viticultural whole than North America, and the key bit of that word is "cultural". Chile's vineyards have been shaped chiefly by the vines of Bordeaux, thanks to the mid-nineteenth century import of cuttings from France. In Argentina, the dominant influence is Italian, thanks to the emigrés after the First World War. In South American vineyards north of these two principal wine producers, the choice of vine varieties has been largely dependent on the multinational companies who have decided to exploit wine potential there: Domecq in Mexico, for instance, and Moët & Chandon and Cinzano in Brazil (though it will be some time before Brazil is weaned off the play-safe American vines it adopted for its very humid climate).

Thanks to the missionaries who followed the conquistadores, a number of grape varieties which were Spanish in origin can be found along the west coast of the Americas, but that number is surprisingly small – much smaller than the number of Italian varieties. The obscure Galician variety Torrontes has for some reason struck a chord in both Chile and Argentina, and the sherry grape Pedro Ximénez is very popular in Argentina, but they are atypical of Spanish varieties in that respect. Muscats of several sorts and hues are also widely planted in these two countries.

Although South America looks set to become an important source of classic varietals, the most planted vines by far are of distinctly coarser genetic make-up. Chile's Pais is related to California's Mission, and Argentina's Criolla Grande and Cereza are of similar stock. Their importance is declining, but together they still account for perhaps one in every three vines planted in the continent.

South Africa

Even more than California, Australia and New Zealand, South Africa has a problem in her vineyards not even hinted at by the quality of the wines produced: vine health.

Viruses present the main problem: fan-leaf, leaf roll and corky bark. The very obvious presence of these in many vineyards not only reduces yields, it also slows the process of vine propagation enormously. The vine nurseries will not release cuttings of new varieties, imported or domestically bred, until they have been subjected to extensive quarantine and clonal selection as well as to antivirus heat treatments.

Demand from South African wine drinkers and winemakers (usually quite distinct from the vine growers) for new varieties can scarcely be met. The Cape has, like every other anglophone wine market, been struck by a severe case of Chardonnaymania, closely followed by Sauvignonphilia. Yet a prominent vineyardist was moved publicly to complain as recently as 1984 that "Not a single one of the noble shy-bearing cultivars, with the exception of Cabernet Sauvignon, is readily available and a good clone of Chardonnay is virtually unobtainable."

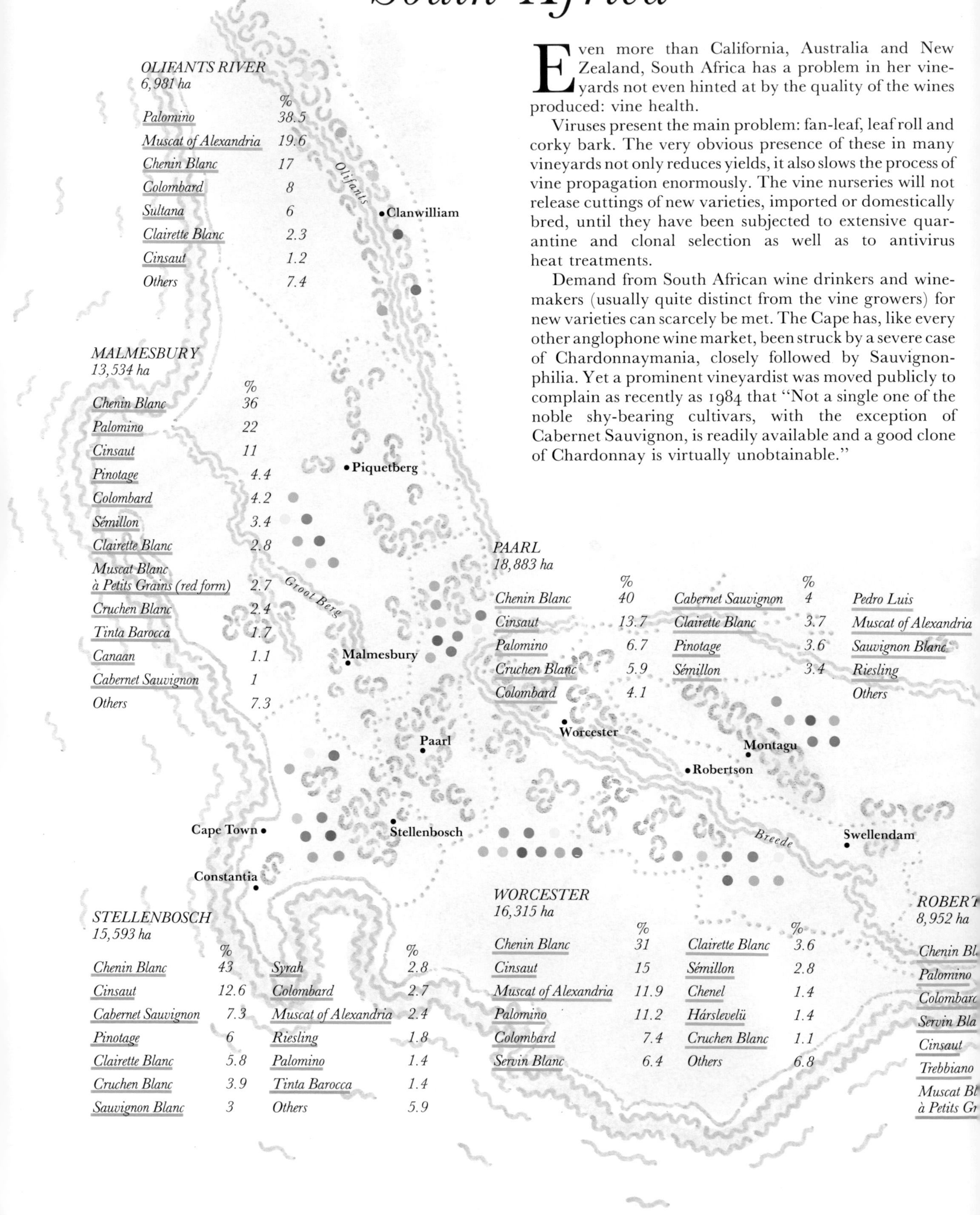

OLIFANTS RIVER
6,981 ha

	%
Palomino	38.5
Muscat of Alexandria	19.6
Chenin Blanc	17
Colombard	8
Sultana	6
Clairette Blanc	2.3
Cinsaut	1.2
Others	7.4

MALMESBURY
13,534 ha

	%
Chenin Blanc	36
Palomino	22
Cinsaut	11
Pinotage	4.4
Colombard	4.2
Sémillon	3.4
Clairette Blanc	2.8
Muscat Blanc à Petits Grains (red form)	2.7
Cruchen Blanc	2.4
Tinta Barocca	1.7
Canaan	1.1
Cabernet Sauvignon	1
Others	7.3

PAARL
18,883 ha

	%		%	
Chenin Blanc	40	Cabernet Sauvignon	4	Pedro Luis
Cinsaut	13.7	Clairette Blanc	3.7	Muscat of Alexandria
Palomino	6.7	Pinotage	3.6	Sauvignon Blanc
Cruchen Blanc	5.9	Sémillon	3.4	Riesling
Colombard	4.1			Others

STELLENBOSCH
15,593 ha

	%		%
Chenin Blanc	43	Syrah	2.8
Cinsaut	12.6	Colombard	2.7
Cabernet Sauvignon	7.3	Muscat of Alexandria	2.4
Pinotage	6	Riesling	1.8
Clairette Blanc	5.8	Palomino	1.4
Cruchen Blanc	3.9	Tinta Barocca	1.4
Sauvignon Blanc	3	Others	5.9

WORCESTER
16,315 ha

	%		%
Chenin Blanc	31	Clairette Blanc	3.6
Cinsaut	15	Sémillon	2.8
Muscat of Alexandria	11.9	Chenel	1.4
Palomino	11.2	Hárslevelü	1.4
Colombard	7.4	Cruchen Blanc	1.1
Servin Blanc	6.4	Others	6.8

ROBERT
8,952 ha

Chenin Bl
Palomino
Colombar
Servin Bla
Cinsaut
Trebbiano
Muscat Bl
à Petits Gr

Clanwilliam

Piquetberg

Malmesbury

Paarl

Worcester

Montagu

Robertson

Cape Town

Stellenbosch

Constantia

Swellendam

Olifants

Groot Berg

Breede

It seems doubtful that any transformation of Cape vineyards in the near future can be rapid for this and many other reasons, and it is not helped by a quota system that does nothing to encourage wine quality, or even vine planting in the appropriate cooler areas.

The pattern of varieties, or cultivars as they are pragmatically called in South Africa, has changed considerably over the last 20 years reflecting chiefly the Cape winemakers' mastery of cool fermented Chenin Blanc. Cinsaut, which dominated the South African vineyard in 1960, is now only the third most planted variety. Palomino peaked in the late sixties but is still in second place, while Chenin Blanc or Steen plantings have soared to account for nearly 30 percent of all Cape vines.

In some respects, South African varieties show marked similarities to those of Australia. This is hardly surprising since the Cape was the First Fleet's last port of call before landing in New South Wales, and Captain Phillips saw vine cuttings as an essential item of supplies – as well he might, having tasted the Cape's Pontac and world-famous Constantia dessert wine of the time.

Both countries are still heavily dependent on Muscat of Alexandria, known as Hanepoot in South Africa and Gordo Blanco in Australia, as well as owing much to Palomino, Sultana, Sémillon, Clairette Blanc and Cruchen Blanc, the last a grape completely obscure in its native Gascony but very much part of the South African and Australian vineyard as Cape Riesling and Clare Riesling respectively.

For social rather than climatic reasons, the South African wine industry has been inclined to take its instruction from Germany rather than from a source with the same major problem – heat; and it is only recently that the need for specifically hot-climate grape varieties has been recognized. The work currently under way in Portugal may well be of use in pointing the way to those traditional varieties able to maintain high acid levels even in high temperatures.

Although one or two crossings such as Chenel have emerged more recently, the 60-year-old Pinotage has so far constituted South Africa's only gift to the wine world. It is a little difficult to understand the logic of including any Pinot Noir genes in a variety with Cinsaut, designed for such a resolutely un-Burgundian climate.

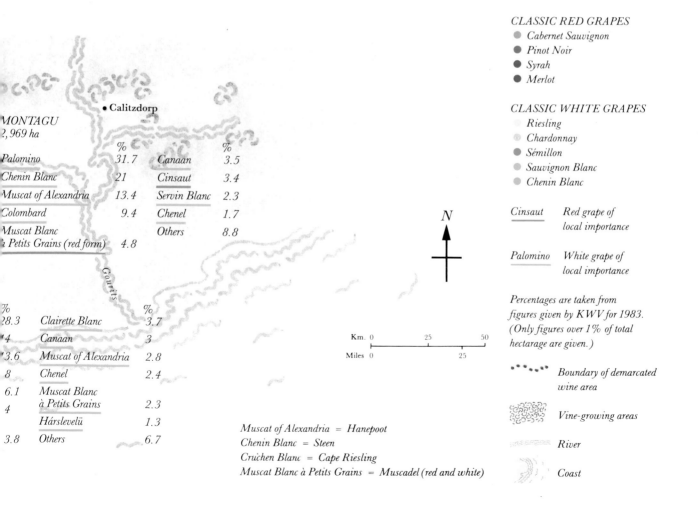

• Calitzdorp

MONTAGU
2,969 ha

	%		%
Palomino	31.7	Canaan	3.5
Chenin Blanc	21	Cinsaut	3.4
Muscat of Alexandria	13.4	Servin Blanc	2.3
Colombard	9.4	Chenel	1.7
Muscat Blanc à Petits Grains (red form)	4.8	Others	8.8

%		%
28.3	Clairette Blanc	3.7
4	Canaan	3
3.6	Muscat of Alexandria	2.8
8	Chenel	2.4
6.1	Muscat Blanc à Petits Grains	2.3
4	Hárslevelü	1.3
3.8	Others	6.7

N

Km. 0   25   50
Miles 0   25

CLASSIC RED GRAPES
● *Cabernet Sauvignon*
● *Pinot Noir*
● *Syrah*
● *Merlot*

CLASSIC WHITE GRAPES
○ *Riesling*
◐ *Chardonnay*
● *Sémillon*
◔ *Sauvignon Blanc*
◑ *Chenin Blanc*

Cinsaut   Red grape of
           local importance

Palomino   White grape of
           local importance

Percentages are taken from figures given by KWV for 1983. (Only figures over 1% of total hectarage are given.)

••••••• Boundary of demarcated
         wine area

         Vine-growing areas

         River

         Coast

Muscat of Alexandria = Hanepoot
Chenin Blanc = Steen
Cruchen Blanc = Cape Riesling
Muscat Blanc à Petits Grains = Muscadel (red and white)

── *Australia* ──

What an exciting time this is for Australian viticulture. And how exciting a place Australia is for any viticulturist. After a century of making largely soupy dessert wines in some pretty hot wine regions, the Australian vine grower is responding to the demands of the consumer for lighter, crisper wines by seeking out cooler sites for vineyards, often in tiny isolated pockets. Unlike his counterpart in Europe, he can still find huge tracts of affordable land with great potential. And unlike his counterpart in America – an inevitable comparison – he has already made great strides in matching vine variety to region and even microclimate.

South Australia, the Barossa Valley and environs in particular, can claim a fluency in Riesling rivalled only by the Germans. In the far southeast of the wine state, the marriage of Coonawarra and Cabernet Sauvignon has been happy for decades. The Hunter Valley's suitability for Syrah (Shiraz) and Sémillon was established in the last century, and some of its Cabernets and Chardonnays have been enthralling Sydney-siders for years. And in northeast Victoria, the brown version of Muscat de Frontignan (Muscat Blanc à Petits Grains) is so at home that it produces the unique Liqueur Muscats of Rutherglen.

The really extraordinary, and fortunate, aspect of Australian viticulture, however, is its preponderance of top quality vine varieties – a fact of which most Australian wine drinkers seem blithely unaware. Setting aside the huge quantities of Sultana which are absorbed by the dried fruit industry, Australia's most planted white-grape variety is Riesling. Many a German connoisseur would be deeply envious of this statistic and yet familiarity with the variety has bred something not too far from contempt in the average Australian wine drinker, now suffering from the "dry = sophisticated" dictum. Chardonnay at any price is the prevailing sentiment, and there is even a disturbing trend towards planting varieties regarded as "exotic" such as Gewürztraminer and Sauvignon Blanc in areas much too hot to allow them to develop flavour before acidity levels plummet.

This insouciance about one of the world's finest grape varieties is even more apparent in Australia's red varietal profile. More than a third of the country's dark vines is Shiraz, or the revered Syrah of the Rhône. Again, the vignerons of the Midi, who are painstakingly increasing Syrah plantings to pepper their reds with something of such high quality, would be enormously impressed. To the Australians, Shiraz is simply their everyday red, admittedly too often overproduced and carelessly vinified in high temperatures to produce rather jammy, hollow wines. If the Australian consumer could be infected with some of the reverence that the European has for Hermitage and Côte Rôtie, then Shiraz's lot, and style, might improve.

Australian vine varieties are interesting in other aspects, too. There is a strong tradition of fortified wine varieties probably imported from Spain, Portugal and France early in the last century. Muscat of Alexandria (called Gordo Blanco here) covers an area of vineyard land only slightly smaller than that planted with Rhine Riesling – although

These maps illustrate just one observer's impressions of which varieties seem to do best in which corner of the continent. They by no means reflect absolutely the current state of the Australian vine-growing art, which is dominated by the vast tracts of much hotter irrigated vineyard land. In very general terms, the cooler the region, the greater the varietal assortment which can be persuaded to produce top-quality wines there. Hence the density of blobs in the southern corner of Western Australia. Perhaps the high frequency of Chardonnay's appearance on these guide maps reflects as much the brouhaha surrounding this variety as its cheerful adaptability to climates as varied as those of the Adelaide hills and the Upper Hunter.

CLASSIC RED GRAPES
- Cabernet Sauvignon
- Pinot Noir
- Syrah

CLASSIC WHITE GRAPES
- Riesling
- Chardonnay
- Sémillon

▲ Muscat de Frontignan
▲ Muscadelle

PADTHAWAY   Vine-growing areas

〜 River

Main road

the land itself tends to be much hotter. From sherry country came Palomino, Pedro Ximénez and Cañocazo (now hardly encountered in Jerez itself). Doradillo is probably also Spanish. From Portugal came a confusing clutch of varieties whose disentanglement formed a major part of the task for the French ampelographer P. Truel when he was asked to come and make sense of the Australian vineyard in 1976. There is at least one sort of Touriga, Bonvedro, Tinta Amarella and some excellent Verdelho.

Another layer of confusion has been added by the much more recent importation of vine cuttings from California, itself somewhat uncertain as to the identity of some of its vines. Any list of Australian varieties is a confusing blend of English (the most common English word being False), French, Spanish and Portuguese littered with misleading trails and false scents. And just to keep the aspiring vine student on his toes, some of the older plantings sport patches of a quite unexpected variety. After all, Australia has been growing vines unfettered by tradition or legislation for two centuries now. It is hardly surprising that her vineyards need some unravelling.

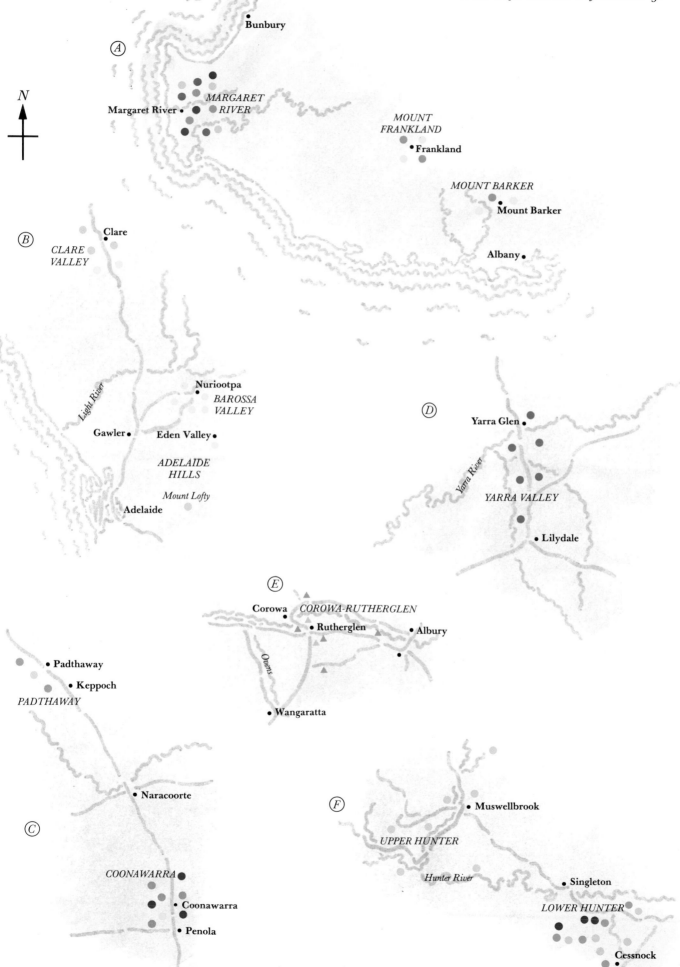

N

Ⓐ
• Bunbury

MARGARET RIVER

Margaret River •

MOUNT FRANKLAND

• Frankland

MOUNT BARKER

Mount Barker

• Albany

Ⓑ
Clare •

CLARE VALLEY

Nuriootpa •

BAROSSA VALLEY

Light River

Gawler •   Eden Valley •

ADELAIDE HILLS

Mount Lofty

Adelaide

Ⓓ
Yarra Glen •

Yarra River

YARRA VALLEY

• Lilydale

Ⓔ
Corowa •   COROWA-RUTHERGLEN

• Rutherglen   • Albury

Ovens

• Wangaratta

• Padthaway

• Keppoch

PADTHAWAY

• Naracoorte

Ⓒ
COONAWARRA

• Coonawarra

• Penola

Ⓕ
• Muswellbrook

UPPER HUNTER

Hunter River

• Singleton

LOWER HUNTER

Cessnock

New Zealand

The New Zealand wine industry, still relatively tiny, is undergoing a more radical vineyard transformation than perhaps any other, hinting at enormous potential. In 1986 a vineyard *putsch* was initiated to uproot that quarter of vineyard land planted with the least desirable grape varieties in the least suitable locations.

Since 1960 the hybrids once thought necessary for this relatively cool climate have been virtually routed by *vinifera* vines so that, for instance, Müller-Thurgau plantings increased from 60 hectares (150 acres) in 1960 to produce 45 percent of the annual vintage in 1985, when total vineyard area had reached 6,000 hectares (15,000 acres). This represented a greater domination of a national wine industry by one vine variety than anywhere else. New Zealand, like England, manages to make more exciting, vibrant Müller-Thurgau than its native Germany, but its ubiquity robs it of the respect it deserves on the North and South Islands.

Today hybrids cover less than 7 percent of New Zealand's vineyard, which is planted with only one red-wine vine for every eight white. As in Australia, current fascination is with those vines associated with dry white varietals: Sauvignon Blanc and Gewürztraminer (so much better suited to New Zealand than Australia), Chenin Blanc and, especially, Chardonnay. Curiously, Riesling has not so far performed as well in New Zealand, with its much more Germanic climate, as it has in Australia.

This may be the result of the poor health of much available plant material. New Zealand's viticultural guru Richard Smart has hit upon a novel solution for this problem, all too common in the world's newer wine regions. Early settlers, including missionaries from France, brought *vinifera* vine cuttings to New Zealand as early as 1819. Their formal cultivation was quashed by the double burden of near Prohibition and phylloxera, but they were also distributed to Maoris for domestic wine production. Smart is on the trail of descendants of these early vines planted in the wild. Their very survival guarantees their excellent health and suitability to the New Zealand climate as breeding material.

The view that New Zealand is too cool satisfactorily to ripen red grapes should be dismissed immediately. Some Cabernet/Merlot blends of such quality have emerged in the North Island, as well as a promising Pinot Noir from the world's southernmost vineyard near Christchurch, that we can hope to see an increase in plantings of red grapes here.

Volcanic activity is very recent, in some cases still visible, which means that the soil is extremely fertile and one of the major problems for vine growers is to control growth and yield. Yields are anyway forced up by the structure of the wine business which has so far left vine growing and winemaking in the hands of two distinct factions, whose aims are not always harmonious. The key to maximizing both quality and yield lies in careful trellising, of course, and this is being studied at the Te Kauwhata research station.

Because of the almost embarrassing fertility, devigorating rootstocks are needed, and work is also under way to improve the quality (and identification) of these growth regulators. Messrs Truel and Galet found that out of the dozen rootstocks established in New Zealand, five of them were incorrectly named and more discoveries of an equally illuminating nature are expected.

A high proportion of New Zealand's more interesting vineyards are planted with relatively young vines, as at Cook's Te Kauwhata site on the North Island. We can expect the wines to mature as the vines do.

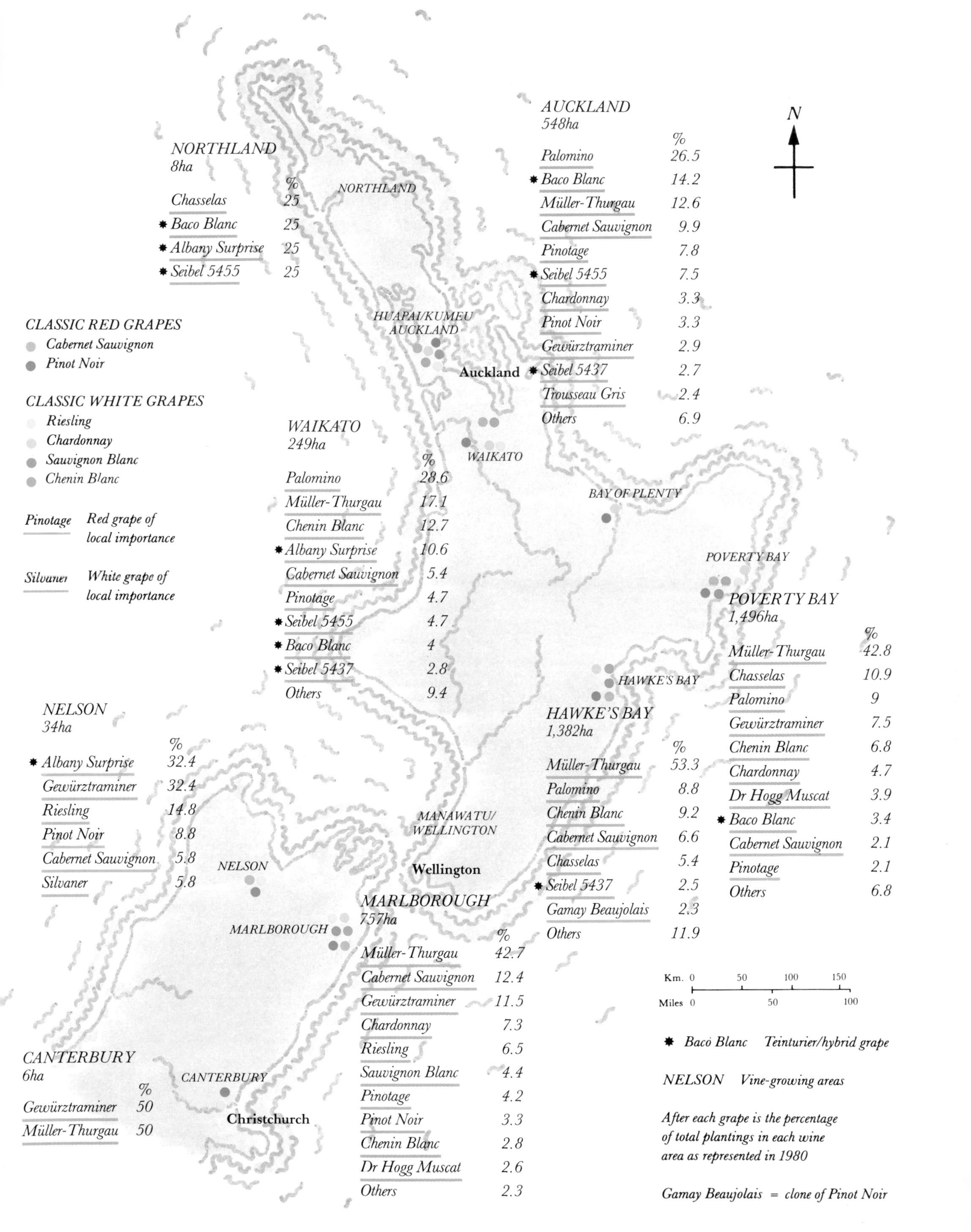

N

NORTHLAND
8ha

	%
Chasselas	25
✷ Baco Blanc	25
✷ Albany Surprise	25
✷ Seibel 5455	25

NORTHLAND

CLASSIC RED GRAPES
- Cabernet Sauvignon
- Pinot Noir

CLASSIC WHITE GRAPES
- Riesling
- Chardonnay
- Sauvignon Blanc
- Chenin Blanc

Pinotage   Red grape of
            local importance

Silvaner   White grape of
            local importance

HUAPAI/KUMEU
AUCKLAND

Auckland

AUCKLAND
548ha

	%
Palomino	26.5
✷ Baco Blanc	14.2
Müller-Thurgau	12.6
Cabernet Sauvignon	9.9
Pinotage	7.8
✷ Seibel 5455	7.5
Chardonnay	3.3
Pinot Noir	3.3
Gewürztraminer	2.9
✷ Seibel 5437	2.7
Trousseau Gris	2.4
Others	6.9

WAIKATO
249ha

WAIKATO

	%
Palomino	28.6
Müller-Thurgau	17.1
Chenin Blanc	12.7
✷ Albany Surprise	10.6
Cabernet Sauvignon	5.4
Pinotage	4.7
✷ Seibel 5455	4.7
✷ Baco Blanc	4
✷ Seibel 5437	2.8
Others	9.4

BAY OF PLENTY

POVERTY BAY

POVERTY BAY
1,496ha

	%
Müller-Thurgau	42.8
Chasselas	10.9
Palomino	9
Gewürztraminer	7.5
Chenin Blanc	6.8
Chardonnay	4.7
Dr Hogg Muscat	3.9
✷ Baco Blanc	3.4
Cabernet Sauvignon	2.1
Pinotage	2.1
Others	6.8

HAWKE'S BAY

HAWKE'S BAY
1,382ha

	%
Müller-Thurgau	53.3
Palomino	8.8
Chenin Blanc	9.2
Cabernet Sauvignon	6.6
Chasselas	5.4
✷ Seibel 5437	2.5
Gamay Beaujolais	2.3
Others	11.9

NELSON
34ha

	%
✷ Albany Surprise	32.4
Gewürztraminer	32.4
Riesling	14.8
Pinot Noir	8.8
Cabernet Sauvignon	5.8
Silvaner	5.8

NELSON

MANAWATU/
WELLINGTON

Wellington

MARLBOROUGH
757ha

MARLBOROUGH

	%
Müller-Thurgau	42.7
Cabernet Sauvignon	12.4
Gewürztraminer	11.5
Chardonnay	7.3
Riesling	6.5
Sauvignon Blanc	4.4
Pinotage	4.2
Pinot Noir	3.3
Chenin Blanc	2.8
Dr Hogg Muscat	2.6
Others	2.3

CANTERBURY
6ha

CANTERBURY

	%
Gewürztraminer	50
Müller-Thurgau	50

Christchurch

Km. 0   50   100   150

Miles 0   50   100

✷ Baco Blanc   Teinturier/hybrid grape

NELSON   Vine-growing areas

After each grape is the percentage
of total plantings in each wine
area as represented in 1980

Gamay Beaujolais = clone of Pinot Noir

Top Twenty Varieties

There will be few wine lovers who cast their eye over the table below with a knowing nod. For a start, few will be familiar with the variety in prime position. Airén, the white grape of La Mancha, rarely finds its way into the collective consciousness, or even onto the collective palate, of the world's connoisseurs. The same goes for most of the other Spanish grapes in this listing – Monastrell, Bobal and Xarel-lo – although many will be familiar with Garnacha as Grenache in France, and possibly with Macabeo either in France as Maccabeu or in Rioja as Viura.

Spanish names preponderate because the only possible way of compiling the table is on the basis of total area covered by each variety. Spain has more land under vine than any other country (although the USSR is fast catching up, hence Rkatsiteli's prominent position). Her arid conditions mean that vines are very widely spaced compared to, say, Burgundy but they do cover very impressive areas. A comparison of the number of vines planted of each variety would probably result in a rather different order, as would the equally impossible comparison of the amount of wine produced by each vine type.

Cosmopolitan wine drinkers may well be wondering where in this listing is, for instance, Pinot Noir (a mere 37,000 hectares/92,500 acres planted), Chardonnay (just 34,000 hectares/85,000 acres), Sauvignon Blanc and Müller-Thurgau (about 28,000 hectares/70,000 acres apiece). As the table clearly shows, it is the varieties which dominate in one substantial area which get top placings rather than a variety such as Cabernet Sauvignon which seems to be ubiquitous and yet nowhere covers an enormous tract of land. For this reason, also-rans which "beat" even Pinot Noir are Spain's Tempranillo and Italy's Lambrusco. It is interesting to note, however, just what a chunk of the world's vineyard is still occupied by those varieties related to the Pais of Chile, such as the Criolla of Argentina and Mission of California, as well as by the combined forces of the Muscat family.

The countries included here are all those which are major wine producers, apart from Portugal and Greece which are planted with myriad varieties virtually unknown elsewhere. Vineyards devoted to table-grape or raisin production have been excluded from the reckoning. The total area planted with some varieties may well be slightly underestimated because some of the tinier wine-producing countries have been excluded, but this would not make any substantial difference to the order of the varieties in the table. Since so few countries publish statistics on the total area planted with each grape variety, too many of the figures in this table are estimates, but the overall picture is correct, and very revealing.

■ Red grape
■ White grape

	Total area of variety, in 1,000s of hectares	Spain	USSR	Italy	France	USA	Argentina	Romania	Yugoslavia	Bulgaria	Hungary	Chile	W. Germany	S. Africa	Australia	Austria
Total vineyard area, in 1,000s of hectares		1,610	1,376	1,135	1,096	330	322	301	243	168	157	121	101	100	66	59
Airén	476	476														
Garnacha Tinta	331	240		2	78	7									4	
Rkatsiteli	267		248							19						
Trebbiano	262			130	127		3								2	
Carignan	221			2	207	8						4				
Pais/Mission/Criolla	145					1	105					39				
Cabernet Sauvignon	135		20	7	23	9	3	10	10	18	2	26		3	4	
Muscat	122	23	20	10	7	5	24	3	6	5	1	2		10	5	1
Monastrell	113	113														
Barbera	102			90		7	5									
Bobal	95	95														
Merlot	90			15	38	1	4	10	8		10	4				
Sémillon	75				23	2	6		2			35		4	3	
Riesling	66		25		2	5	1	3	3	2			19		5	1
Verdicchio	65			65												
Welschriesling	64		2	5				8	21	4	19					5
Macabeo	58	51			7											
Cot	43				5		30					8				
Xarel-lo	43	43														
Garnacha Blanca	41	25			16											

Great
Vineyards

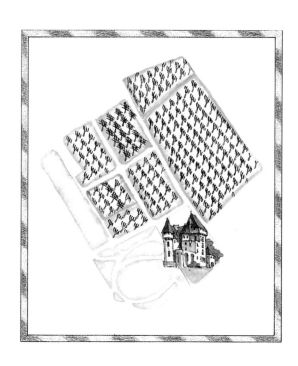

Aloxe-Corton

This particular corner of the matchless Côte d'Or has been chosen for detailed mapping because it is the only one to sport a Grand Cru appellation of both colours. Most of the top-quality land of Burgundy is pre-ordained either Pinot Noir or Chardonnay territory, but many of the growers of what might be called Greater Aloxe-Corton are unique in the choice available to them.

In the old days, this was red-wine country. There was the odd Chardonnay vine just as Aligoté flourished here and there, but basically Aloxe was known for its Corton, grand and indisputably red. The appearance of a white wine called after Emperor Charlemagne – said by some to have owned vineyards here and by others to have turned to white wine because it did not stain his beard so incriminatingly – was regarded by the grandfathers of today's vine growers as a mere gimmick.

Not much more than thirty years ago, the fields in which the now-revered Domaine Bonneau de Martray have vineyards qualifying for the white Grand Cru Corton-Charlemagne were still unplanted. Red wine was what this part of the Côte de Beaune, at its confluence with the Côte de Nuits, was all about. The first bottles labelled Corton-Charlemagne, and the all-Aligoté wine allowed to be sold as straight Charlemagne, were seen in the same light as, say, Pavillon Blanc de Château Margaux today: a perhaps interesting, but basically perverse phenomenon.

By the 1980s things have changed considerably. Far from being perverse, white wine is seen in Burgundy's most flattering light, that of maximum *rentabilité*. As the world clamours for white burgundy and often disparages its red counterpart, Chardonnay continues to encroach upon this traditional Pinot Noir territory. Yields allowed for the two Grand Cru appellations tell much of the story: 35 hectolitres per hectare for Corton Rouge, 40 hectolitres per hectare for Corton-Charlemagne and the tiny production of Corton Blanc. Taking into account the actual cropping levels and the current market price of the white wines vis à vis the reds, Chardonnay is now almost twice as profitable as Pinot Noir in this area, and gaining ground fast.

The vineyards wind round the lower slopes of the hill of Corton and their names bear only a distant relation to the wines now produced there. The red Grand Cru Corton was traditionally limited to the east-facing vineyards such as Bressandes, Clos du Roi and Renardes, as well as the tiny strip named Corton, which fell within the village boundary of Aloxe. Then along came Corton-Charlemagne and Charlemagne which could be produced from the upper vineyards on the southern slopes of the Corton hill within the Aloxe commune.

Since then demand for both red Corton and white Corton-Charlemagne has been such that the appellations have been extended into the better vineyards of neighbouring Ladoix-Serrigny and Pernand-Vergelesses respectively, as shown here. Traditionalists said that only the very top strip of Charlemagne vineyard was suitable for white wine production, but today some excellent Chardonnays are made from Pougets vineyard to be sold as Corton-Charlemagne, as they are, perhaps ironically, from the very top of the vineyard called Le Corton.

The reason why Chardonnay is so often planted in preference to Pinot Noir in those vineyards in which it is allowed is simple. As the most influential vineyard owner in Aloxe-Corton, Louis Latour, puts it: "Money is the reason. I am ashamed."

The famous Corton hill rises behind the church of Aloxe-Corton, crested by the Bois de Corton. Just below the treeline today, Chardonnay is grown to produce Corton-Charlemagne, though this is heresy to some older locals who believe the first duty of their wine is to be red.

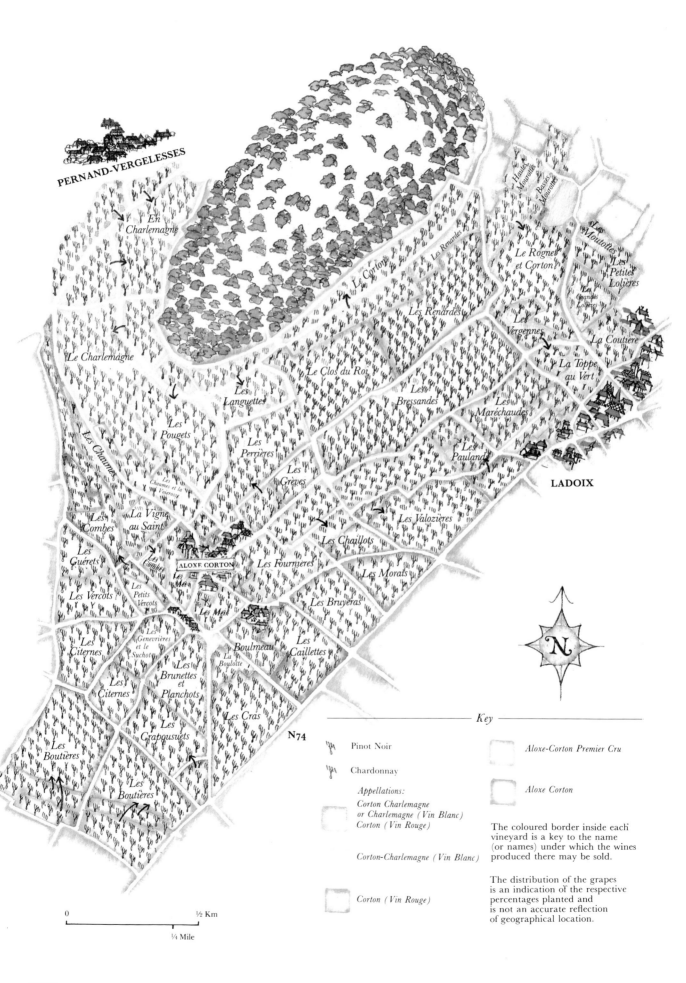

PERNAND-VERGELESSES

En Charlemagne

Le Charlemagne

Les Chaumes

Les Languettes

Les Pougets

Les Chaumes et la Voierosse

Les Perrières

Le Corton

Les Renardes

Le Clos du Roi

Les Bressandes

Les Grèves

Les Renardes

Les Maréchaudes

Les Vergennes

Le Rognet et Corton

Hautes Mourottes

Basses Mourottes

Les Mourottes

Les Petites Lolières

Les Grandes Lolières

La Coutière

La Toppe au Vert

Les Paulands

LADOIX

La Vigne au Saint

Les Combes

Les Guérets

Les Combes

ALOXE CORTON

Les Meix

Les Petits Vercots

Les Vercots

Les Genevrières et le Suchot

Les Citernes

La Boulotte

Les Meix

Boulmeau

Les Caillettes

Les Valozières

Les Chaillots

Les Fourmières

Les Morais

Les Bruyères

Les Citernes

Les Brunettes et Planchots

Les Cras

Les Grapousuets

Les Boutières

Les Boutières

N74

N

Key

Pinot Noir

Chardonnay

Appellations:
Corton Charlemagne
or Charlemagne (Vin Blanc)
Corton (Vin Rouge)

Corton-Charlemagne (Vin Blanc)

Corton (Vin Rouge)

Aloxe-Corton Premier Cru

Aloxe Corton

The coloured border inside each
vineyard is a key to the name
(or names) under which the wines
produced there may be sold.

The distribution of the grapes
is an indication of the respective
percentages planted and
is not an accurate reflection
of geographical location.

0   ½ Km

¼ Mile

Château Margaux & Château Palmer

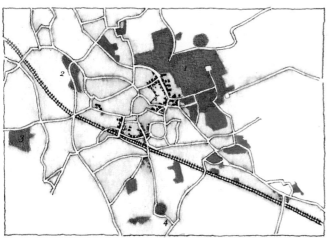

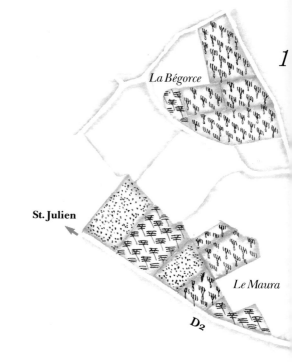

1

La Bégorce

St. Julien

Le Maura

D2

MARGAUX

Château Margaux
(pages 58–59)

Château Palmer
(pages 60–61)

Perhaps the most striking feature of this particularly intrusive examination of the vineyards of the two great, adjoining properties of the Margaux appellation is shown in the diagram above. This illustrates dramatically just how dispersed are the holdings of these by no means atypical Médoc châteaux.

Just as that other first-growth Château Latour to the north has its distant plots Pinada and Petit Batailley, so Château Margaux has acquired parcels of vineyard as distant from the château as the Vire Fougasse. Château Palmer is every bit as disjointed, as shown overleaf.

Such a lack of homogeneity comes as a surprise to many unfamiliar with the ways of the Médoc. The talisman of the single, unalterable plot of land which constitutes Château X appears to slip tantalizingly out of the wine student's grasp. Indeed, a glance at the Robert Mondavi Rutherford holdings on pages 68–69 is enough to suggest that his is closer to the traditional, if notional, Bordeaux ideal. How come, ask perceptive and persistent American visitors to the Médoc châteaux, you can say your quality is determined by your soil, if you're always adding on new bits?

It is a fair question, but not fair to assume that the bits are necessarily new. The Château Margaux estate, for instance, already included the three distant plots Vire Fougasse, Chigarail and Ninotte 200 years ago. This land must have contributed to its award of first-growth status in the famous 1855 classification of Médoc and Graves properties and, therefore, should not be scorned.

Château Palmer is a much younger property altogether. It was established by the eponymous General only in the early nineteenth century by putting together an existing property, Château de Gasq, with various other completely unrelated and distant plots of land. Proximity to the château building itself was irrelevant since he ran out of money long before he managed to build one. When in 1957

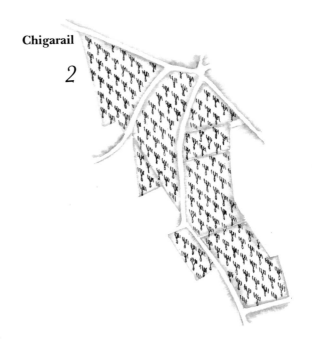

Chigarail

2

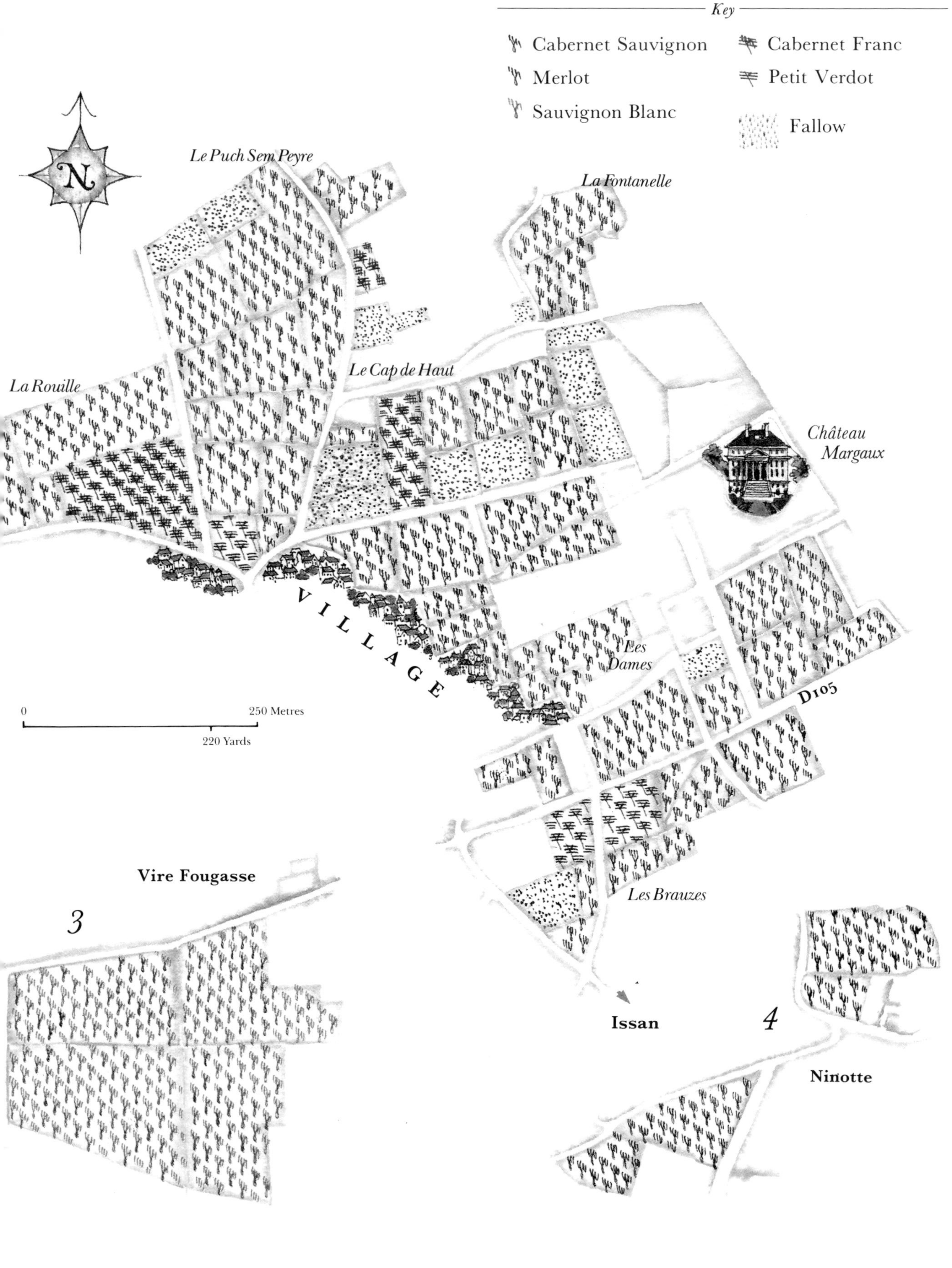

Key

🌿 Cabernet Sauvignon   🌿 Cabernet Franc

🌿 Merlot   🌿 Petit Verdot

🌿 Sauvignon Blanc   Fallow

N

Le Puch Sem Peyre

La Fontanelle

La Rouille

Le Cap de Haut

Château Margaux

V I L L A G E

Les Dames

D105

0   250 Metres

220 Yards

Vire Fougasse

3

Les Brauzes

Issan   4

Ninotte

Château Palmer acquired the vineyards of Château Desmirail, that nearby property also classified a third growth
in 1855, it seemed merely an extension of company policy.
Château Desmirail vines presumably contributed to the
fabulous Palmer '61. And when in 1981 the Château
Desmirail name was sold to the owner of Château Brane-
Cantenac, a small exchange of vines seemed only logical – if
confusing for purists.

The maps on these pages show in detail exactly which
variety is planted where on these two estates with very
similar macro- if not micro-climates. There are some
general rules in matching variety to local conditions in the
Médoc, but they are rarely as important as many observers
imagine. The patchwork of vine types looks so complicated
that one feels it must be governed by some intricate but
arcane mechanism.

The overriding motivation for planting a mix of varieties at all, however, is less to utilize the various soil types and
quirks of nature peculiar to each plot, and more to spread
the risk attached to each growing season's vicissitudes.

MARGAUX

Issan

*Château
Palmer*

Mathéau

C A N T E N A C

Key	
🌱 Cabernet Sauvignon	🌿 Cabernet Franc
🌱 Merlot	🌾 Petit Verdot
🌱 Sauvignon Blanc	⠿ Fallow

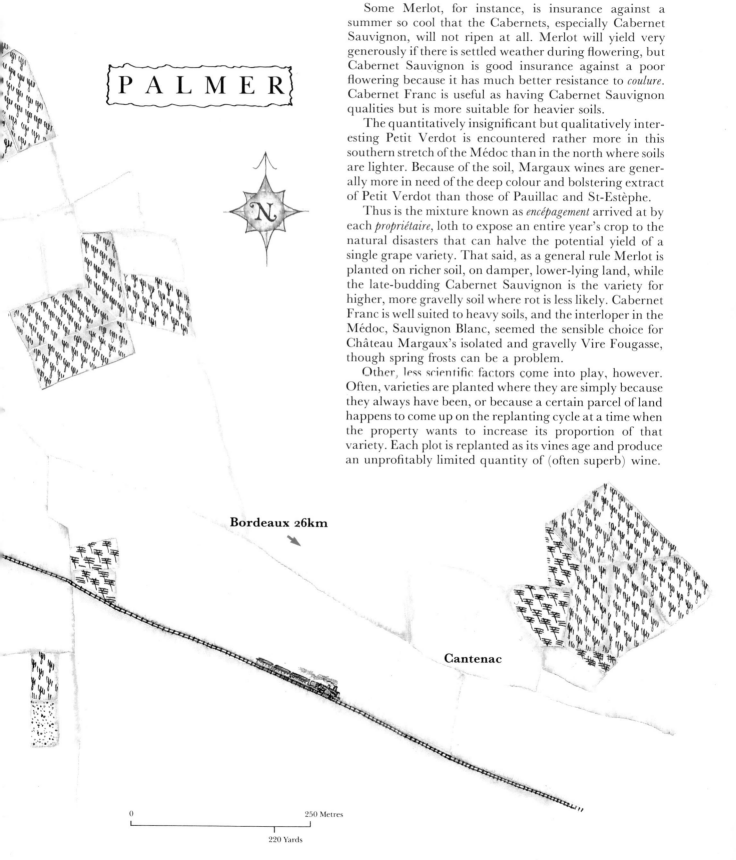

P A L M E R

Bordeaux 26km

Cantenac

0   250 Metres

220 Yards

Some Merlot, for instance, is insurance against a summer so cool that the Cabernets, especially Cabernet Sauvignon, will not ripen at all. Merlot will yield very generously if there is settled weather during flowering, but Cabernet Sauvignon is good insurance against a poor flowering because it has much better resistance to *coulure*. Cabernet Franc is useful as having Cabernet Sauvignon qualities but is more suitable for heavier soils.

The quantitatively insignificant but qualitatively interesting Petit Verdot is encountered rather more in this southern stretch of the Médoc than in the north where soils are lighter. Because of the soil, Margaux wines are generally more in need of the deep colour and bolstering extract of Petit Verdot than those of Pauillac and St-Estèphe.

Thus is the mixture known as *encépagement* arrived at by each *propriétaire*, loth to expose an entire year's crop to the natural disasters that can halve the potential yield of a single grape variety. That said, as a general rule Merlot is planted on richer soil, on damper, lower-lying land, while the late-budding Cabernet Sauvignon is the variety for higher, more gravelly soil where rot is less likely. Cabernet Franc is well suited to heavy soils, and the interloper in the Médoc, Sauvignon Blanc, seemed the sensible choice for Château Margaux's isolated and gravelly Vire Fougasse, though spring frosts can be a problem.

Other, less scientific factors come into play, however. Often, varieties are planted where they are simply because they always have been, or because a certain parcel of land happens to come up on the replanting cycle at a time when the property wants to increase its proportion of that variety. Each plot is replanted as its vines age and produce an unprofitably limited quantity of (often superb) wine.

Châteaux Haut-Brion & La Mission

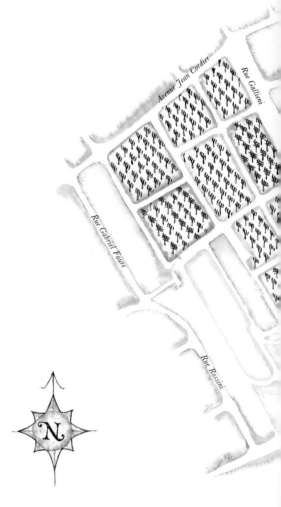

These two great, and contiguous, estates are the undisputed leaders of the Graves region, each producing both red and white wine in the unique local tradition.

The attention of the wine world has been focused on the properties since early 1984 when it was announced that, after years of rivalry, they were to come under the same ownership and direction. After disagreements among the Dewavrin-Woltners who had owned La Mission, they sold to the Mouchy-Dillon interests which had owned Haut-Brion for nearly half a century. Jean Delmas has now added La Mission's 17 hectares (42 acres) to his charge of the 44-hectare (110-acre) Haut-Brion vineyard. Haut-Brion's white wine is simply Château Haut-Brion Blanc, while La Mission produces a second wine, Château La Tour-Haut-Brion, as well as the "grand vin" rouge and the highly priced white Château Laville-Haut-Brion.

The estates are intertwined physically as well as financially as the map clearly shows. Delmas, one of Bordeaux's great exponents of the importance of clonal selection, is a firm believer in the significance of matching variety even to the different microclimates of the 71 tiny parcels of vines on the two properties.

The geology and the soil structure of the area has an influence on vine distribution. The land is fairly flat, with two small rises (too small to be hills), the larger north and east of the Château of Haut-Brion. The smaller, and higher – 31 metres – rise is to the south, underlying the two isolated vineyards of La Mission. The hills are composed of gravel: a 10-metre-thick layer of large-diameter gravel deposited in glacial times. Beneath this the subsoil is coarse sand and clay. The major soil variation is, therefore, the thickness of the gravel layer: deepest where the land is highest.

Jean Delmas is slowly altering the planting pattern of the estate in line with his findings on soil, microclimate and clonal selection. The overall balance is Haut-Brion: Cabernet Sauvignon 55 percent, Cabernet Franc 20 percent, Merlot 25 percent; La Mission and La Tour: Cabernet Sauvignon 60 percent, Cabernet Franc 5 percent, Merlot 35 percent; Laville: Sémillon 60 percent, Sauvignon Blanc 40 percent. Haut-Brion Blanc is made from roughly equal plots of the two white vines.

Merlot is generally planted on the lower, richer soils with a high proportion of clay and, therefore, warmer microclimate. Note, for example, that it is planted in the two northernmost Haut-Brion parcels, map references 40 and 44, where the land falls away. At La Mission, too, Merlot is planted on the damper, lower land to left of the track leading from the railway line.

The tight bunches of Cabernet Sauvignon would easily rot in such humidity and the variety is more suitable for the higher, poorer but well-drained very gravelly soils such as parcels 49, 52 and 56 which lie on the crest of the ridge. The white varieties for Château Haut-Brion Blanc are planted on plots within the red-vine plantation which encourages early ripening.

Its La Mission counterpart Château Laville-Haut-Brion does not exist as a separate entity. Indeed the parcels of white vines are planted in among the red, with the patches of damp land thought too heavy for good-quality red grapes given over to whites. The five white-grape parcels lie on the southern and western edges of that area of· La Mission vineyard from which most of La Tour and Laville wine comes, where the ground slopes towards the streams which bound the Haut-Brion-La Mission complex.

Cabernet Sauvignon

Merlot

Sauvignon Blanc

Sémillon

Cabernet Franc

Château Haut-Brion
Premier Grand Cru Classé

Château La Mission Haut-Brion
Grand Cru Classé

Château La Tour-Haut-Brion
Grand Cru Classé

Château Laville-Haut-Brion
Grand Cru Classé

Commune de Pessac

Commune
de Talence

Château
La Mission
Haut-Brion

0   250 Metres

220 Yards

Commune de Pessac

Commune
de Talence

*T*he map (right) acts as a key to the one on the previous page, which shows the 71 tiny plots into which the estate is divided and illustrates their planting pattern. The numbers on the key map refer to the list below, which gives the names, sizes, year planted and vines grown for each of the plots. Both map and chart are colour-coded to show which plots are devoted to which wine.

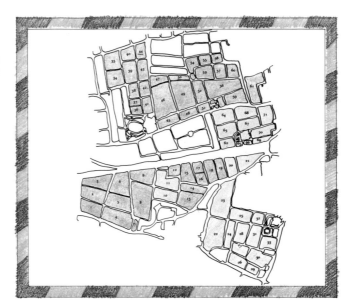

Château Haut-Brion
Premier Grand Cru Classé

Château La Mission Haut-Brion
Grand Cru Classé

Château La Tour-Haut-Brion
Grand Cru Classé

Château Laville-Haut-Brion
Grand Cru Classé

No.	PLOT NAME	PLANTED	HECTARES	VINES
1	CANDAU	1971	1ha24a10	CS
2	LA GRAVIERE SUD	1930	1ha19a78	CS
3	LA GRAVIERE NORD	1972	1ha62a49	CS
4	LA POMPE	1976	1ha99a37	M
5	LES HUITRES	1981	1ha39a95	M
6	ARCACHON	1930	1ha66a41	CS CF
7	LA MAISON		17a20	
8	BAHANS	1974	2ha78a87	CS CF
9	L'ETENDARD	1973	1ha33a75	M
10	BARON	1966	1ha20a20	M
11	LE GRAND DUCHE	1975	1ha44a20	CS
12	CARLES	1969	57a80	CS
13	POLO SUD	1981	1ha45a98	CS
14	POLO NORD	1980	80a23	CF
15	SAUVIGNONNIERE	1966	1ha11a80	CS
16	PINSON	1971	30a38	SA
17	SAPINETTE	1971	78a21	SA
18	GIAC OUEST	1980	94a42	SE
19	GIAC EST	1981	84a00	SE SA
20	HAUT PINSON	1964	86a06	CS
21	L'ENCLOS	1930	1ha21a37	CF M
22	LES MISSIONNAIRES	1934	2ha47a90	SE SA
23	BAGATELLE	1979	2ha58a66	M
24	SARGET	1943	88a56	M
25	HENRI	1938	1ha09a35	CF M
26	BAS LAVILLE OUEST	1960	93a96	SE
27	HAUT LAVILLE	1960	68a57	SE
28	SEYMOUR	1981	1ha09a55	CS
29	BAS LAVILLE EST	1979	50a97	SE
30	LES CATHOLIQUES	1979	1ha45a97	SE SA
31	LA MEDOQUINE	1985	1ha19a68	CS
32	FERNAND	1938	62a41	CF
33	LA VIEILLE	1938	90a23	CS
34	MAILLOT HAUT	1945	1ha05a57	CF CS
35	MAILLOT BAS	1930	1ha25a14	CS
36	LE JARDIN	1946	36a00	M

No.	PLOT NAME	PLANTED	HECTARES	VINES
37	CLONES	1978	47a80	CS M CF
38	LE LAPINEV	1972	59a32	M
39	TERRE ROUGE	1954	1ha18a96	CS
40	LA LEYREYRE OUEST	1957	72a40	M
41	L'ORANGERIE	1957	67a84	CF
42	HAUT LAFUE SUD	1942	62a24	CS
43	HAUT LAFUE NORD	1938	88a83	CF
44	LA PEYREYRE	1958	66a67	M
45	LE BUREAU	1958	76a73	CF
46	BAS PLANTEY SUD	1934	2ha54a40	CF M
47	BAS PLANTEY NORD	1975	71a06	M
48	LE PAVE	1958	67a76	M
49	HAUT PLANTEY SUD	1951	2ha28a55	CS
50	HAUT PLANTEY NORD	1975	47a58	CS
51	LE MOTEUR	1936	44a40	CF
52	CATALAN	1956	1ha03a30	CS
53	GUILHEM ESTEOU	1936	97a50	SE
54	LA TOURETTE	1973	72a70	CS
55	LE CHENE I	1965	59a88	CS
56	LES DOUZES	1930	2ha12a40	CS
57	DOMINIQUE OUEST	1930	30a78	CS
58	LE CHENE II	1950	39a92	SE
59	LE COLONEL	1930	1ha13a80	M
60	DOMINIQUE EST	1982	1ha32a02	M
61	TOURAILLES	1982	1ha66a00	CS CF
62	ORMIERE	1938	68a60	CS
63	LES LAZARISTES	1961	1ha13a45	CS
64	CHAI NEUF	1963	1ha22a75	M
65	PAYSAN	1961	16a35	M
66	PAYSAN	1961	18a83	M
67	CHAPELLE	1970	96a15	CS
68	PORTAIL	1975	1ha01a42	CS
69	LIGNE	1932	39a82	CF
70	MADAME	1965	95a49	CS
71	BAS PEDRON	1968	1ha10a95	CS

CS = Cab. Sauv.   M = Merlot   SA = Sauv. Blanc   SE = Sém.   CF = Cab. Franc

Nierstein

The vineyards of Nierstein represent an island of classic German wine in a sea of Liebfraumilch and other blends more suitable for milk teeth than more mature wine lovers.

Looking at the varietal and topographical profiles of the Rheinhessen region *in toto* it is easy to dismiss it as flat and bland, but it is on the Rheinfront or Rheinterrasse that the peaks of both quality and altitude are achieved. Of all Germany's 11 wine regions Rheinhessen has the lowest proportion of Riesling: under 6 percent as opposed to nearly 80 percent just across the Rhine in the Rheingau. The most planted Rheinhessen variety is Müller-Thurgau, covering a quarter of vineyard land (much interspersed with small plantings of other crops), which can be tasted in so many Liebfraumilch blends labelled Rheinhessen. However, Silvaner, Scheurebe, Bacchus, Kerner and Faber are each more important quantitatively than Riesling in the Rheinhessen, which is every bit as diverse varietally as the Rheinpfalz.

The most formidable concentration of Riesling in the Rheinhessen is to be found around the town of Nierstein (a name much prostituted). The familiar Niersteiner Gutes Domtal is the name of a sprawling Grosslage (large vineyard area) in the flat hinterland which just abuts on to the much better quality vineyards surrounding the pretty riverside town itself.

The Grosslagen which are much more properly associated with Nierstein, and with quality, are – from north to south – Rehbach, Spiegelberg and Auflangen. Their vineyards, together with those of the adjoining Ortsteil Schwabsburg, are mapped overleaf. This is partly to show the typically German system of Einzellagen, individual registered and numbered vineyards tucked away inside Grosslagen, and partly to show in detail just how the varieties planted depend on exact site specifications.

This particular slice of German vineyard illustrates more graphically than most the close correlation between incline and Riesling. (One might suppose that this is even more evident in the Mosel-Saar-Ruwer, but the problem there is that mysteriously few growers will admit to harbouring anything other than the Riesling which, according to official statistics, covers well under 60 percent of vineyard land.)

The northernmost vineyard shown on the map, the very respectable Pettenthal Einzellage in Grosslage Rehbach, provides a good example. The land rises steeply from the riverbank, up from below 100 metres to more than 150 in a short space, and all Pettenthal vines are, therefore, Riesling but for the narrow riverside ribbon which is planted with Silvaner. The explanation for this is that only the magic name Riesling can command the price necessary for such uneconomically steep vineyard land. The gradients of these particular Einzellagen at their steepest vary between a giddy 40 and 55 percent.

Germany is the only wine-producing country to be quite so preoccupied with the angle of her vineyards (the official register gives the range of slopes for each Einzellage) and a steepness suitability factor is given for each variety. In reality this is less a reflection of the inherent characteristics of each vine type than of labour costs in Germany. Steep vineyards are extremely expensive to maintain in a country with so many relatively well-paid industrial jobs on offer.

It is easy to see why this twist of the Rhine, with its steep rise of vineyards to the north and south of Nierstein, is called the Rheinterrasse (formerly the Rheinfront). The vines in the foreground, clinging to the slope of the Hölle vineyard, include Riesling to make the most of the site.

The vineyard landscaping involved in the programme of Flurbereinigung (consolidation) has already bulldozed more than half of Germany's vineyards into economic shape. Some slopes are just too steep even for this treatment, however, and it seems likely that Riesling will cling to the steepest slopes to the immediate north and west of Nierstein for many years to come.

These slopes include not only Pettenthal but also, as shown on the map, the steep inclines of Brudersberg, Hipping, Goldene Luft in Grosslage Rehbach; as well as Ölberg and Heiligenbaum in Grosslage Auflangen. In each of these sites the Riesling grapes, which need a relatively gentle climate for their long growing season, benefit from a southeastern exposure – morning sunlight – and supposedly some reflection, in Pettenthal at least, from the surface of the river Rhine. Much of the soil here is a distinctive red loam that retains the heat well and results in comparatively soft, almost spicy Rieslings without the attack or longevity of their counterparts across the river but with an aristocratically perfumed character all of their own.

Refreshingly, however, the most quality-conscious traditional Rheinhessen wine producers, of which there are several quartered in the town of Nierstein, have not limited their respect to Riesling. Silvaner was considerably more important in the first half of this century, but even today the wine produced by the Silvaner grown at the bottom of the steepest slopes, and on the surrounding flatter land, enjoys a certain reputation. The Silvaners made here, in a similar sort of way to their Franconian counterparts, are self-confidently sturdy yet racy. It is significant that the 22.5 hectares (56 acres) of choice, rich soil, where the Grosslage Auflangen meets the river and which is divided into the Kranzberg, Zehnmorgen, Bergkirche and Glöck vineyards, is planted almost exclusively with Silvaner. Only in the much more varied terrain of the Orbel and Schloss Schwabsburg vineyards further inland above the village of Schwabsburg is there a substantial mixture of the two top classic varieties of Rheinhessen, because the two vineyards encompass both steep slope and quite a bit of flatter land.

Most of the rest of the vineyard mapped here is much more even, flatter, more easy to cultivate countryside, and most growers spread the load between Silvaner and Müller-Thurgau, with the latter predominating. The clayey loam here suits either of these lesser varieties, posing no threat to the chlorosis-sensitive Silvaner.

What the map cannot show is the extent to which the growers have adopted the "new" crossings. Kerner has been a particular success in this little corner of Rheinhessen, as befits an area associated with quality. The tiny Hölle vineyard just upstream of Nierstein, for instance, is planted with a mix of Riesling and newer varieties which is much more typical of Rheinhessen as a whole than any one of the varietal options charted here.

A subsidiary but very satisfying rationalization for choosing to examine the Nierstein area in detail is to demonstrate forcibly that Rheinhessen should not be dismissed, as it so often is abroad, as capable of producing only some of Germany's least characterful wine exports.

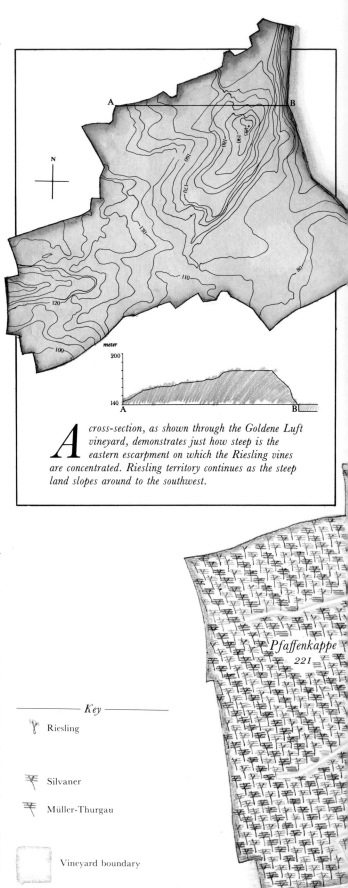

A cross-section, as shown through the Goldene Luft vineyard, demonstrates just how steep is the eastern escarpment on which the Riesling vines are concentrated. Riesling territory continues as the steep land slopes around to the southwest.

Pfaffenkappe
221

——— *Key* ———

Riesling

Silvaner

Müller-Thurgau

Vineyard boundary

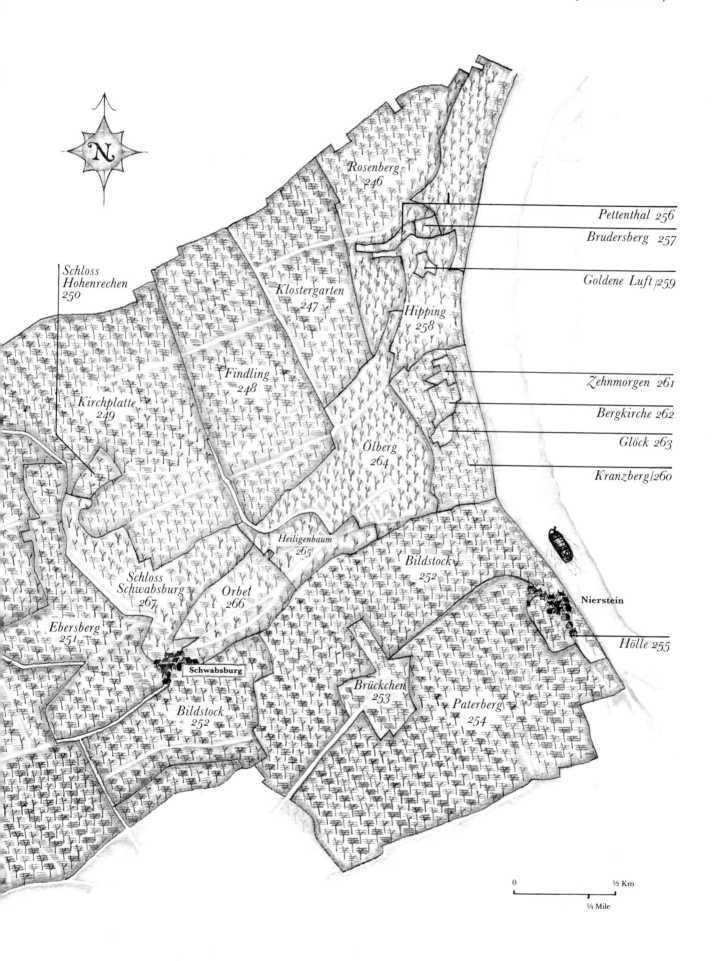

N

Rosenberg 246

Pettenthal 256

Brudersberg 257

Goldene Luft /259

Schloss Hohenrechen 250

Klostergarten 247

Hipping 258

Zehnmorgen 261

Bergkirche 262

Glöck 263

Kranzberg/260

Findling 248

Kirchplatte 249

Ölberg 264

Heiligenbaum 265

Bildstock 252

Nierstein

Schloss Schwabsburg 267

Orbel 266

Ebersberg 251

Schwabsburg

Hölle 255

Brückchen 253

Bildstock 252

Paterberg 254

0   ½ Km

¼ Mile

The Rutherford Bench

I f ever a stretch of land had a legitimate right to the title of California Médoc, this is it. As demonstrated quite clearly on this map, the Rutherford Bench is Cabernet Sauvignon country, with (among red-grape varieties) Merlot as a distinct secondary influence and Cabernet Franc also coming on strong. It is absurd, of course, to seek to draw too close a parallel with anything European; the Napa Valley stamps its own very special character on to this slice of vineyard land and the wines made from it. But what is extraordinary to the historically minded observer is

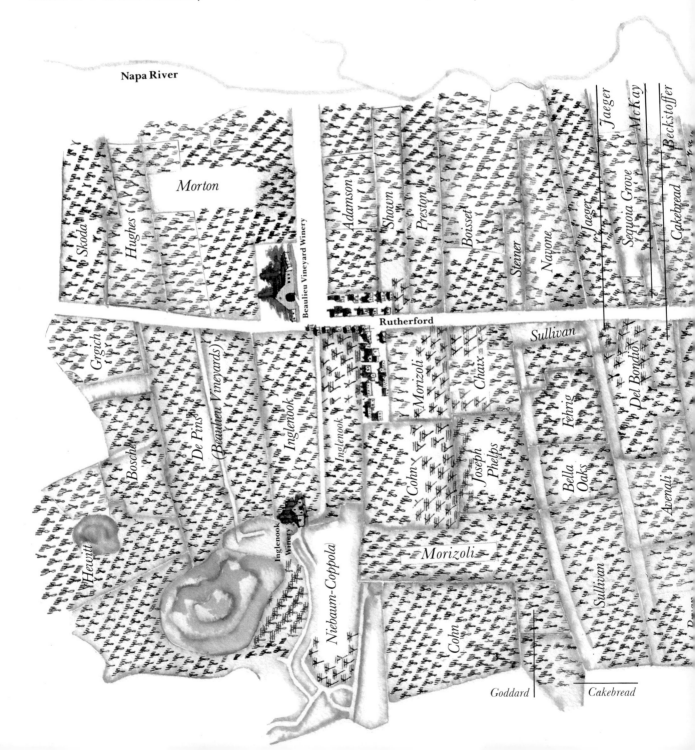

Napa River

Morton

Skoda

Hughes

Beaulieu Vineyard Winery

Adamson

Shown

Preston

Boisset

Steiner

Nayone

Jaeger

Jaeger

Sequoia Grove

McKay

Beckstoffer

Cakebread

Rutherford

Grgich

De Pins

(Beaulieu Vineyards)

Boschet

Inglenook

Inglenook

Cohn

Morizoli

Chaix

Joseph Phelps

Sullivan

Fehrig

Bella Oaks

Del Bondio

Avenali

Hewitt

Inglenook Winery

Niebaum-Coppola

Morizoli

Cohn

Sullivan

Goddard   Cakebread

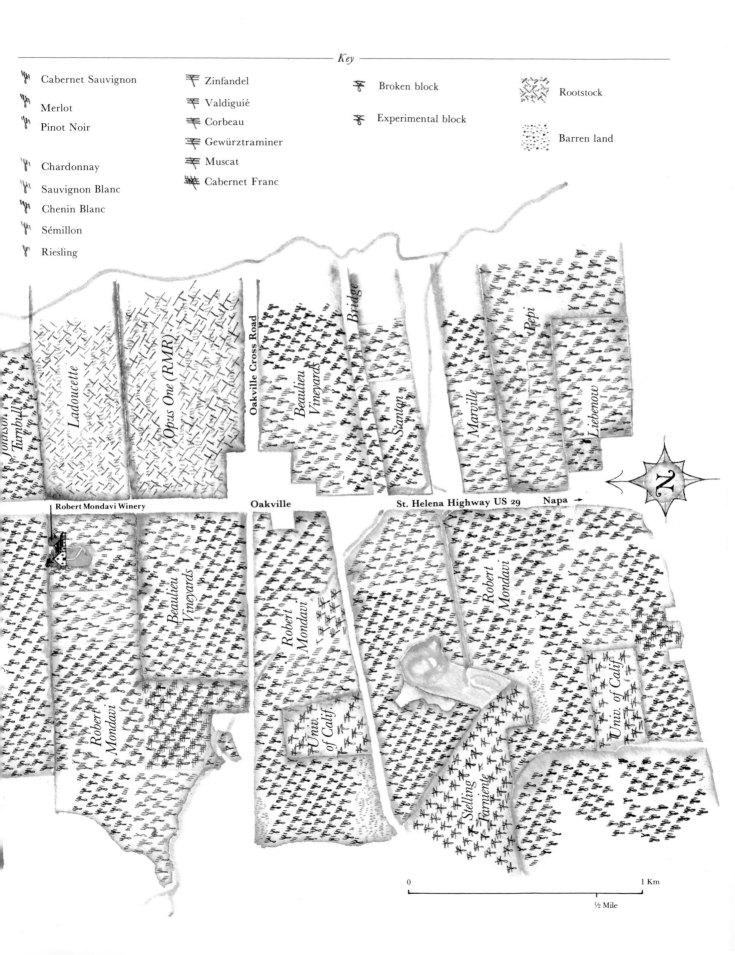

—— *Key* ——

Ψ Cabernet Sauvignon

Ψ Merlot

Ψ Pinot Noir

Ψ Chardonnay

Ψ Sauvignon Blanc

Ψ Chenin Blanc

Ψ Sémillon

Ψ Riesling

Ψ Zinfandel

Ψ Valdiguié

Ψ Corbeau

Ψ Gewürztraminer

Ψ Muscat

Ψ Cabernet Franc

Ψ Broken block

Ψ Experimental block

Rootstock

Barren land

Johnson Turnbull

Ladoucette

Opus One (RMR)

Oakville Cross Road

Beaulieu Vineyards

Bridge

Stanton

Marville

Pepi

Liebenow

Robert Mondavi Winery

Beaulieu Vineyards

Robert Mondavi

Oakville

Robert Mondavi

Univ. of Calif.

St. Helena Highway US 29   Napa →

Robert Mondavi

Stelling Tamienlè

Univ. of Calif.

0 — 1 Km

½ Mile

the extent to which the land is concentrated on a single variety despite its relatively short history.

In the twenties and early thirties the most stimulating liquid this corner of California was allowed to produce was altar wine, for which demand was exceptionally buoyant then. The California wine business proper had to start from scratch after the repeal of Prohibition in 1933, but wasted little time in producing some truly brilliant signpost Cabernet Sauvignon such as Beaulieu's Georges de Latour bottlings, of which the 1952 is probably the star.

If any Rutherford grower was still unconvinced of the wisdom of planting Cabernet Sauvignon by the early seventies, then the price asked, and received, for Heitz Martha's Vineyard from the 1966 vintage on should have convinced him. Bella Oaks, another Heitz source of top-quality Cabernet Sauvignon, is a worthy successor.

The higher land west of the St Helena Highway nudging up into the hills is prime Cabernet Sauvignon land. The closer the vineyard to the hills, the more gravelly and better-drained it will be – though few California vignerons have pushed this theory to the limit by planting much above valley floor level. Mechanization is obviously a factor here, though one would have thought the example of Martha's Vineyard tucked into the hillside might have inspired more daring sites.

Merlot, just as in the Médoc, is reserved for lower, slightly damper land with richer soils such as those vineyards between the highway and the river. Merlot's early budbreak makes it particularly sensitive to the frosts which pose a rather greater threat on this lower land, but the Californians are better equipped to deal with this sort of hazard. A valley floor peppered with sprinkler systems and wind machines is the result.

There is admittedly much more deviation from the tri-varietal norm here than in the Médoc – indeed the map shows a veritable patchwork of different grapes – but that is only to be expected in a wine region whose current working foundations have been laid so recently. (And after all, the Médoc was planted with a kaleidoscope of varieties, both red and white, not so long ago.)

Although a long way behind Cabernet Sauvignon, Chardonnay and Sauvignon Blanc are the two most popular white varieties, though one suspects that fashion has governed their location as much as any consideration of microclimate, which many a Frenchman would consider too warm for either. It is perhaps significant that the most substantial block of these two varieties is at the southern end of the map, towards the cooler Bay-influenced areas of Yountville and Carneros.

Zinfandel starts to creep into the picture at the northern end of the Rutherford Bench, where the Bay's influence is at its least and daytime temperatures are even higher.

Parcels of Chenin Blanc can be found all over the Rutherford Bench, but this probably reflects more the role of the wine as convenient all-purpose white varietal than any particular matching of the vine and microclimate.

It is interesting to note that the land used initially for the famous Mondavi-Rothschild joint-venture wine Opus One is at the southern, coolest end of the Rutherford region where climatological conditions most resemble the chillier climes to which the French partner is accustomed. Doubtless the addition of the plot of lower, warmer land opposite the Robert Mondavi winery will have an enriching effect on the eventual style of the wine.

It is impossible to ignore the importance of the name Robert Mondavi on this map or, for a European, not to marvel at the sophistication of the wine produced from this land still divided into neat pioneer blocks, an astonishing proportion of them in the hands of private growers. What a contrast to the social geography of the Médoc.

Classic
Varieties

Cabernet Sauvignon

Ah, Cabernet Sauvignon! The merest whiff of its aristocratic concentration of blackcurrants and cedarwood is enough to signal connoisseurs and blind tasters the world over that they are home.

Not to every one of them, of course. Not to a Burgundian anyway, nor to a Portuguese, nor to many a Spaniard. But to the great majority of conscious wine-drinking palates in the world today, top quality red wine is Cabernet Sauvignon. Only those with their own distinctive native grape varieties remain immune to Cabernet's charms.

Those intrigued by the genetics versus environment debate concerning people may wish to ponder the same sort of question about Cabernet Sauvignon. Do so many of us worship it because it is inherently the best red grape variety in the world, or simply because it happens to be the principal ingredient in the most widely available fine red wine, claret? Has our Anglo-Saxon partiality sprung from the grape's innate quality or have we been conditioned at least in part by our maritime and commercial connections with Bordeaux?

It would be easier to believe this last proposition were it not for Cabernet Sauvignon's quite breathtakingly dazzling performance as an international traveller. Even more than Chardonnay, and certainly more than Riesling, Syrah or Pinot Noir, Cabernet Sauvignon has blithely set down its roots all over the world. In spots as cool as New Zealand's South Island and as hot as the Bekaa Valley, Cabernet grapes have ripened to produce well-balanced, obviously "serious" wines rich in varietal character.

Cabernet Sauvignon is *the* red grape variety of Bordeaux, and in particular of those most aristocratic areas of Bordeaux, the Médoc and Graves, though it may be a comparatively recent arrival. It was only at the end of the eighteenth century when Baron Hector de Branne was building up the great wine estates that the white grapes were uprooted to be replaced by the wide variety of red grapes then commonly available. Of these, Petite and Grande Vidure were two of the most highly regarded (although not necessarily most widely planted). As early as 1736, the Abbé Bellet had included the two Vidures in the 18 black varieties and 20 whites he recorded in the *vignoble* around Cadillac. To Montesquieu's son, de Secondat, we owe the etymology of Vidure (*vigne dure*, or hard vine) and therefore its identity, the tough-wooded Cabernet. To this day, Cabernet Sauvignon is sometimes called Vidure in the Graves, and there are still those who try to find a link between it and Pliny's Biturica.

This promising plant was assiduously cultivated on the top estates of the Médoc; and acceptance of the vine's churlish yield gradually spread down the ranks until at the last French agricultural census in 1979 there were 17,200 hectares (43,000 acres) of Cabernet Sauvignon in the Gironde *département*: slightly more than Sémillon, but very much less than Merlot. The increase in recent years has been impressive: the Gironde had only 6,800 hectares (17,000 acres) in 1958. It is extraordinary what an international impact this relatively recent vine arrival has made.

The vine is admittedly delightfully easy to grow and, most importantly, to harvest. Its particularly hard wood makes it, like Riesling, a survivor in cold winters. It buds late and is therefore no fearer of spring frosts. It ripens late, which can pose problems in very wet, cool autumns – and in damp, cool soils such as those of Pomerol and St-Emilion. But the grapes are robustly resistant to the vagaries of weather towards the end of their very gradual and usefully non-critical ripening cycle; the loose bunches of thick-skinned grapes can shrug off even heavy rain, rot and the depredations of insects. Apart from Cabernet Sauvignon's susceptibility to oidium, which can be cured, it has remarkably few disadvantages *except* for its relatively low yields – and the clonal selectors are hard at work on this.

It is heartening that the winemakers of the world are sufficiently fired by the quality of the wine produced to be prepared to accept lower-than-average yields. Cabernet Sauvignon may be the world's most fashionable red varietal, but the extra cost of growing it in those newer areas, where there is some choice in the matter, is not always fully borne by the consumer. In the financial juggling involved in evolving a pricing policy, many a winery accountant is prepared to indulge Cabernet Sauvignon at the expense of a rather less regal variety.

Within France's better-quality wine regions, low yields are seen as a virtue and indeed are one of the basic tenets of Appellation Contrôlée law. It is not surprising that Cabernet Sauvignon should be embraced so warmly there; what is surprising is that it is limited to such a small area. Total French plantings may have doubled between 1968 and 1979, to nearly 23,000 hectares (57,500 acres), but three-quarters of the total is made up of Bordeaux vineyards, and even that is mainly Médoc and Graves.

Many would argue that the Cabernet Sauvignon reaches its apogee in these twin areas (and especially in the Haut-Médoc) so proud of their well-drained, gravelly soil, although significantly no 100 percent varietal wines are produced here. Château de Pez may have its 1970 varietal demonstration models, but 1970 was a very exceptional vintage, and even Mouton tempers its Cabernet Sauvignon with 10 percent Cabernet Franc and 5 percent Merlot (though in vintages such as 1984 Mouton, like many other châteaux, made an overwhelmingly Cabernet Sauvignon wine). The Bordeaux blending tradition may stem partly from the hotchpotch of different varieties which the Bordelais have inherited and are gradually refining in their vineyards. It is also soundly based on experience and hedges against the failure of any single variety.

It is widely held that although Cabernet Sauvignon,

CABERNET SAUVIGNON
Leaf
length: 133mm (5¼in)   width: 133mm (5¼in)
Grape Cluster
length: 267mm (10½in)   width: 165mm (6½in)

Cabernet Franc and Merlot can be grown on the left bank of the Gironde in the Médoc and Graves, only the latter two will thrive on the right bank in St-Emilion and Pomerol. Tradition has it that Cabernet Sauvignon is very difficult to ripen on the less temperate right bank. The attempted compulsory promulgation by the authorities of a particularly poor clone of Cabernet Sauvignon on both sides of the Gironde in the wake of rot in the sixties did nothing to make the variety more popular in St-Emilion and Pomerol. Thierry Manoncourt, more than a third of whose Château Figeac is planted with Cabernet Sauvignon, maintains that the variety ripens easily but slightly too long after Cabernet Franc to be convenient for those who need to keep a team of pickers in work without a break.

Of all grapes, the tiny, dusty blue-black berries of Cabernet Sauvignon have one of the highest proportions of pip to pulp: almost 1 to 12, according to Peynaud (as opposed to less than 1 to 25 for Sémillon). Since the pips, with the usually discarded stalks, are a grape's most important source of tannin, a 100 percent Cabernet Sauvignon wine is extremely tough. (It is also extremely deep-coloured, thanks to particularly thick, almost black grape skins.) Blending with softer grape varieties such as Merlot, Cabernet Franc and perhaps Malbec, totalling on average 30 percent of the blend, is the most obvious solution. Other varieties add complexity as well as accessibility. It is surprising how relatively few plantings of the Bordeaux "mixer" varieties are to be found in those newer wine regions so enamoured of Bordeaux's great reds that they have vast tracts planted with Cabernet Sauvignon.

Another possible measure to counteract Cabernet Sauvignon's intractability is to vinify extremely fast, as in the *macération carbonique* practised for some less exalted wines in Bordeaux now.

The third and best remedy is, quite simply, time. Cabernet Sauvignon produces wines that are slow to evolve, especially in Bordeaux where the heat is never such as to add its own voluptuousness, as it so often does in parts of California and Australia. The Bordelais consciously, or more usually unconsciously, mirroring the techniques of the great *crus classés*, make wines that are specifically designed for long ageing. Cabernet Sauvignon has, like Chardonnay, a natural affinity with oak. This is used to great advantage in Bordeaux's top properties where the assemblage of different grape varieties is matured in small, 225-litre casks – Nevers or Limousin usually – for 18 to 24 months before bottling. Not surprisingly, consummation of this marriage of fruit tannins and wood tannins takes some time: the standard Bordeaux rule has been that bottles should not be broached until they are at least into their second decade.

There are signs that even in Bordeaux some wines are being made to mature earlier than formerly (accountants in the past having been rather more lenient and less pressurized by interest rates). But claret, in which Cabernet Sauvignon is the prime ingredient, is one of the very few long-lived wines still made. Indeed, so impenetrable are some great clarets in their youth – ink-black, puckeringly astringent, searingly tart – that Cabernet Sauvignon has earned itself a reputation as the masochist's delight. As one California guide (*Pride of the Wineries*, A California Living Book [*sic*]) puts it: "Cabernet Sauvignon is a wine for people who like to sleep on the ground, play rugby, climb mountains, eat brussels sprouts and do other things in which some punishment is part of the pleasure."

The writer clearly had not succumbed to the thrall of mature claret: unrivalled complexity; appetizingly moderate alcohol level; sublime balance of fruit, oak and reductive flavours; an intellectual as well as sensual treat. Ah, Cabernet Sauvignon!

Such is its power that all over France, especially in that favoured southeastern corner called Provence, there are single-minded individuals trying to make first-growth claret in an unlikely setting. Château Vignelaure near Rians is perhaps the best-known example; Mas de Daumas Gassac in the Hérault perhaps the most obstinate.

Closer to the Gironde, Cabernet Sauvignon is grown in the Dordogne to give class to that *département's* claret-shaped reds. It is also on the increase in the Loire, where there are about 1,300 hectares (3,250 acres). The variety is especially favoured in the Anjou-Touraine where it can add colour and body to Bourgueil, Anjou and Touraine Rouge, and to one of France's best-established varietals, Cabernet d'Anjou rosé. It is also catching on as a *cépage améliorateur* in the Midi (although its lower yield makes it noticeably less popular than Merlot) and there are now several thousand hectares of the Languedoc-Roussillon vineyard luxuriating in the Cabernet Sauvignon's vigorous growth. "A touch of Cabernet" has done much to improve the quality of some of the Midi's named wines of both Vin de Pays and VDQS status. It is to be hoped that those producers persevering with quality in this area are justly rewarded, and that there is ever more EEC encouragement to others to emulate them. What price grapes grown for a Community distillery? Still too high.

It is, thankfully, quite difficult to make Cabernet Sauvignon overproduce to such an extent that its character is diluted out of all recognition. Over-fertilizing and heavy-handed irrigation are the two best ways to rob Cabernet Sauvignon of its distinguishing marks. Neither technique is practised widely in the Midi where the principal lesson to be learnt from the arrival of Cabernet Sauvignon is that a miracle can be achieved by adding just a small amount to an otherwise nondescript blend.

The California total of more than 9,000 hectares (22,500 acres) of Cabernet Sauvignon, perhaps surprisingly, increased more sedately than France's plantings of the grape during the seventies – and is dwarfed by Bulgaria's 18,000 hectares (45,000 acres). Were the American public not quite so crazy about white wine, Cabernet plantings might have been more frenzied. Those who have been canny enough to cellar away stocks of California Cabernets will doubtless reap their own reward when the pendulum swings back, and Sauvignon Blanc vines are desperately T-grafted to the newly modish red varieties.

Greatest acreages are to be found in California's coastal

wine regions, especially Napa, Sonoma and Monterey. Most Californians who understand and enjoy claret (real, honest to goodness French claret, that is) would agree that the variety seems to have found its most exhilarating setting outside Bordeaux in certain favoured sites in California, mainly in the Napa Valley. By now established classics include Heitz Martha's Vineyard (which, with its distinctively minty eucalyptus nose, has come to be regarded as California Cab essence), the more muted Beaulieu Georges de Latour Private Reserve, the much-admired Robert Mondavi Reserve, the dense Stag's Leap, and Ridge's Montebello made way south of Napa from old vines high up in the mountains above Palo Alto. There is no shortage of challengers from the ranks however, and a blind tasting of top quality California Cabernets and *cru classé* claret becomes ever more difficult.

Any California winemaker worth his salt will demand new French oak casks just like Lafite's, and will give his Cabernet Sauvignon just the same *élevage* as the wine at any well-kept *cru classé* château in the Médoc. Even if his wine were fairly distinctively Californian straight out of the fermentation vat, having been made from 100 percent Cabernet Sauvignon grapes grown on richer soil than that of Haut-Médoc, everything after this stage is geared to giving the wine a distinctly French polish.

But there is a noticeable movement among California's most quality-conscious producers away from 100 percent Cabernet Sauvignon wines. In the seventies dislike of wines labelled generically led to overenthusiasm for pure varietals (although "Claret", interestingly, was never a favourite appellation in California). California's slender acquaintance with the geographical detail of the state's wine potential seemed to leave no alternative icons to 100 percent varietal wines. When that varietal is Cabernet ripened by the California sun and matured in new French oak, the result can be a very tough wine indeed. Too often, tannin was equated to potential quality, and a lot of tannin to potentially top quality. If Cabernet Sauvignon was acknowledged California's best red varietal, how could blending with another one do anything but harm?

Happily, things are now seen much less simplistically – and blending is condoned by the labelling laws which require the wine to contain at least 75 percent of the variety specified on the label. In the eighties wines such as Joseph Phelps Insignia and, much more noisily trumpeted, the Mondavi-Rothschild joint-venture wine Opus One, have shown how successfully the Bordeaux blending recipe can be applied to California. California Cabernet Franc and Merlot may not always be what they are named (as suggested on page 96, they may in fact be Merlot and Cabernet Franc!), but the complexity and accessibility they add to the Cabernet Sauvignon is generally agreed upon. That said, it is certainly true that Cabernet Sauvignon with the fuller body and extra layer of apparent sweetness makes a much more attractive 100 percent varietal than its Bordeaux equivalent – provided the plump little number from California is not given the five-star new oak treatment, and provided it is grown in one of

*O*pus One provides the most expensive way to drink Cabernet Sauvignon outside Bordeaux, the product of a joint venture in the Napa Valley between Robert Mondavi (left) and Baron Philippe de Rothschild (right). In the first four vintages the proportion of Cabernet Sauvignon varied from 80 percent (1979) to 96 percent (1980). The balance is Cabernet Franc, although the first vintage – 1978 – had 4 percent Merlot. Cabernet ripened under the California sun tends to need less of this "softening grape" than on its home ground.

California's medium microclimates, say Region II or III. Wines such as Parducci's straight Cabernet Sauvignon prove this admirably.

In the cooler reaches of California, especially in the northern stretch of Monterey's vineyards, Cabernet Sauvignon can take on an almost unattractively herbaceous quality. Bell peppers, green olives and all sorts of things from the salad bowl are regularly found in such wines (leading to a lot of confusion as the land used for such vineyards was in fact reclaimed from a number of vegetable crops). So slowly do the grapes ripen around Gonzales that Cabernet may not be picked until late November, a full two months after Bordeaux. If everything goes right, the wine may end up with a sufficient cocktail of different elements to be genuinely interesting, but if the grapes are picked too early then Cabernet Sauvignon takes on some of the weediness of Cabernet Franc.

Certainly Pinot Noir's supremacy over Cabernet Sauvignon to the north in Oregon is a direct result of this phenomenon. "Stolid" and "one-dimensional" are other criticisms of the variety's performance for connoisseurs of Oregon's wines. The variety has adapted well, however, to the warmer, carefully irrigated growing conditions of Washington State. Even here, Cabernet Sauvignon tends to have a minty note to it (perhaps there is a direct clonal relationship with Napa Cabernets) and, so far, have been noticeably early maturing. There are strong stylistic similarities between the Cabernets of Washington State and those of northeast Italy, although the Italian versions seem to retain more of the particularly blackcurrant fruit so often associated with Médoc Cabernet Sauvignon. The variety is currently the subject of vineyard experiments all over the United States.

Australians have also been exceedingly successful with the variety, according it the serious approach so badly needed by much of their even more widely planted Shiraz. As a very general rule, top Australian Cabernets come by their marked acidity more naturally than the California equivalents, and some seem to have a more obviously blackcurrant flavour. The wine industry worked out relatively early on that it had a perfect spot for Cabernet Sauveegnon, as they call it, and that spot was Coonawarra, a curiously isolated vineyard area way down in the southeast corner of South Australia. Nearly two-thirds of all Australian Cabernet Sauvignon is grown in the state of South Australia, with about 600 hectares (1,500 acres) of Coonawarra and its overspill in Padthaway devoted to this extremely suitable red variety.

Coonawarra is one of Australia's chilliest vine-growing areas. In terms of degree-days, which measure heat and sunshine, much of Coonawarra is more temperate than Beaune or even Epernay. But Cabernet rather than Pinot prevails since it has demonstrated a very special affinity with the extraordinary soils of Coonawarra: red loam "terra rossa" and black rendzina on fossilized limestone subsoil with a high water table. The grapes need a long, leisurely growing season to ripen, and even ripening at all is critical in very cool autumns. The grapes are often not picked here

*C*abernet Sauvignon has a natural affinity with oak. On top estates in Bordeaux, as here at Château Cantemerle, it is put into new barriques for well over a year.

Few other varieties could take the extra 200 mg per litre of the wood tannin exuded by the Limousin or Nevers oak in its first year, but Cabernet Sauvignon is unique in its concentration and longevity.

till late April or May, but always bring fine colour and acid to the fermentation vat.

Such is the fragmented structure of Australia's wine industry that the fermentation vat may be hundreds of miles from Coonawarra, and the resulting wine may even be blended with another produced from grapes grown in a quite different area, possibly even a different state. Trucking refrigerated grapes or must is an established Australian practice, especially for the produce of remote Coonawarra, and some wineries even hold carefully cleaned must for weeks before fermentation. Cabernet Sauvignon is gaining ground in the Hunter Valley, traditionally the stronghold of Shiraz, in the irrigated river regions of the baking hot interior, with notable success in Western Australia, and in all sorts of odd, cool spots in Victoria. Its overall quality is extremely high. Indeed its plucky, if uninspiring, performance when roasted, fertilized and irrigated up towards yields of 100 hectolitres per hectare in Australia's less reputable wine areas provides strong evidence for the variety's inherent class. These wines lack the backbone of great wine, but many of them are clean, fruity, well-balanced and deep-tinted, with definite character.

Cabernet Sauvignon's traditional Australian blending partner is Shiraz, a concept that might send a shudder of horror down French spines, but works remarkably well here. Australian Shiraz's richer-than-Rhône style complements the leanness of Cabernet well. Australians maintain that Shiraz "fills out the middle palate" of Cabernet, although there have been some positively voluptuous 100 percent varietals, too.

A Cabernet/Shiraz blend is a distinct wine type, quite unlike either grape variety in isolation: usually full and plummy, often almost chocolatey. On the other hand, up to 40 percent of Merlot, Cabernet Franc and/or Malbec added to Cabernet Sauvignon merely softens and tames the principal variety; they are easier to dominate than Shiraz.

Much of New Zealand's Cabernet Sauvignon (like Tasmania's) suffers the twin disadvantages of an excessively cool climate: thin, herbaceous flavours and a lack of body. Cabernet Sauvignon is New Zealand's most important red grape variety by far, producing 3.5 percent of the nation's wine harvest. Not a plant of Cabernet Franc is knowingly cultivated, and yet many of New Zealand's Cabernets are more reminiscent of a slightly cooked Chinon than of a Bordeaux. There are problems with colour, too. In youth, New Zealand Cabernets are a palish crimson and then brown rapidly after only a few years in bottle. It may be partly the fault of the particular virus-indexed selection promulgated there, which crops unusually heavily. All in all, New Zealand serves more as a reminder that there are limits to Cabernet's powers rather than as proof of its genius. But wines as wonderfully complex, well-balanced and intense in hue and flavour as Coleraine Cabernet-Merlot from Te Mata show what can be done.

South African Cabernets have also been characterized by early browning, though certainly not by any lack of body. Here there is often a "burn" of alcohol, and an almost medicinal concentration, or perhaps more properly reduction, of flavour which can often be rather hollow. Acidity and tannin are marked to be sure, but the fruit can be too austere to charm, and the traditional practice of blending with Cinsaut serves only to accentuate this.

Then came the cult of the 100 percent varietal, still the most common form in which the Cape's 2,500 hectares (6,250 acres) of Cabernet Sauvignon are marketed. The variety, as cultivar, is the most stubborn yielder of any grown in South Africa, but the magic of great claret, and of the finest native products such as Cabernets from Meerlust and Rustenberg, is sufficient to fan the flames of interest in Cabernet Sauvignon. There is a heartening move towards blending with Merlot and, to a certain extent, Cabernet Franc, which can fill in the gaps around Cabernet Sauvignon's spare frame – as demonstrated by Meerlust's Rubicon blend. Cabernet Sauvignon undoubtedly has exciting potential in South Africa but, considering that it was already extolled there in the twenties, it is taking a long time to realize. Most of South Africa's Cabernet Sauvignon is grown in Paarl and Stellenbosch.

Cabernet Sauvignon has an even longer tradition in South America. It is grown in fairly tiny quantities in most of South America's wine-producing areas, including Argentina where yields of 200 hectolitres per hectare using high trellising are not unknown.

For long it has been the mainstay of Chile's highly reputable quality wine business, accounting for a quarter of all red wine production and, after the pale red local Pais, is the most important variety capable of yielding red wine. Chile's wines, of which Cabernet Sauvignon is the most successful, provide the world with an easy and interesting object lesson in the effect of ungrafted vines on flavour. Mountains and sand have protected Chile from the ravages of phylloxera, and the cuttings on which the industry is based were taken from Bordeaux in pre-oidium days. The arid summers produce grapes almost bouncing with health. Standards in the winery, sadly, do not yet match up to those in the vineyard.

Chilean Cabernet Sauvignon is certainly characterized by a very healthy, fruity, almost plummy flavour – as though there were some Malbec or Merlot planted too, as well there may be. There is a stronger suggestion of sweetness, and higher glycerol, than in any but Bordeaux's ripest vintages. As in South African Cabernets, it is easy to find a minerally, medicinal note in the wines' astringence, but the Chilean wines are much fruitier than those produced on the Cape.

The Chilean wine business has not been without its problems, all of them social, and there have been hiccups in quality. Maipo is Chilean for Médoc, Cousiño Macul for Mouton. This odd, determinedly small family concern consciously blend in Merlot and Malbec with their Cabernet Sauvignon, giving it more careful oak ageing than is customary in Chile to produce a wine that might be mistaken for a particularly rich vintage of Giscours.

The exciting and fashionable newcomer here is Miguel Torres Jr who is producing a Cabernet along classic lines in his newly built *bodega*. First vintages made for him showed the standard Chilean weakness of being rather loose-knit. He took some time to be convinced that his "Cabernet" vines were C. Sauvignon and not C. Franc. No Cabernet Franc is grown as such in Chile, but it seems likely that at least the original Bordeaux cuttings included some Cabernet Franc, either by design or accident.

Torres is one of the very few non-Chilean wine men to be on intimate terms with Chile's wine business (Paul Draper of Ridge Vineyards, California, is another). When he went prospecting in Chile in the late seventies, he had good reason to look favourably on Cabernet Sauvignon. The varietal had worked wonders for him at home in Catalonia, both in terms of performance and Torres' own reputation. In the Gault-Millau "Paris Wine Olympics" of 1979 the most publicized result was that the first vintage of his particular blend of Cabernet Sauvignon and the local Tempranillo, Torres Black Label Gran Coronas 1970, "beat" a host of more glamorous wines, notably Château Latour 1970.

Those who have tasted this robust Spanish blend, matured in American oak but pure Bordelais in structure,

*T*he vineyard of Château Latour is planted with 75 percent Cabernet Sauvignon, 10 percent each of Cabernet Franc and Merlot, with 5 percent Petit Verdot. Yields of the different varieties vary enormously from year to year and the cocktail has been devised more to hedge against natural disaster than to shape the wine's flavour.

may well understand the brouhaha. Certainly those who have tasted Jean León's chewily concentrated 100 percent Cabernet Sauvignon made in the same region and using the same unheard-of technique of training the vines on wires, will know that the variety is very comfortable with its lodgings in the middle Penedés.

Plantings of Cabernet in the Iberian peninsula are few and far between. The Bordelais who fled phylloxera across the Pyrenees may have brought their equipment and expertise with them but vine cuttings would very definitely have been unwelcome at that stage. Marqués de Riscal have a tiny patch of Cabernet Sauvignon, usually vinified separately. The low-yielding, late-ripening Cabernet would presumably be an unwelcome substitute for Tempranillo. The only very mature Cabernet vineyard of any

size is at the famous Vega Sicilia *bodega* near Valladolid, cuttings having been imported from Bordeaux in 1864. There are signs that Cabernet will eventually make its mark in the Iberian peninsula as almost everywhere else. The huge Raimat estate near Lérida in northeast Spain is being extensively planted with heat-treated noble vines, particularly Cabernet Sauvignon, from the University of California at Davis, if you please. Raimat's Abadia demonstrates ably how Cabernet Sauvignon can rub along just as nicely with American oak as with the much more expensive French oak.

Cabernet Sauvignon would also do pretty well in many Portuguese wine regions. J. M. da Fonseca's Quinta de Bacalhôa, matured in *barriques* of chestnut, hints at this, as does their juicy Camarate, made from Cabernet Sauvignon fruit blended with grapes from the much more traditional Periquita vines grown around Azeitão.

Europe's major grower of Cabernet Sauvignon, other than France, is Italy. Indeed the Italians know more about the history of their Cabernet than the French. It was introduced into Italy as long ago as 1820 by the Count of

Sambuy near Alessandria in Piedmont. It is grown today by a handful of Piedmont's most wilful modernists (Gaja will eventually stun us all with a Cabernet Sauvignon); but its most extensive plantings are in the northeast. It is not as popular as Cabernet Franc because it is not as productive and, this far south, the leaner, grassier character of Cabernet Franc is not so obvious. Extraordinarily few of the dozens of northeastern Cabernet DOCs specify either Franc or Sauvignon; and it is as difficult for the consumer to know what proportion of each variety goes into any given "Cabernet" as it is for the producer to tell him.

As with Merlot, the volume of Italian Cabernet is made from high-yielding vines grown on fertile soils on the valley floor, but it is more difficult to dilute the character of the Cabernet Sauvignon than Merlot and, although standard Friuli Cabernet may not be exciting, it is not as drearily bland as standard Merlot. Most such Cabernets are made to be drunk young, with noticeable acidity but hardly a trace of tannin. However, some Cabernets from the Colli Orientali del Friuli can age beautifully. There is a host of variations on the Cabernets/Merlot/Malbec theme from

the Veneto, with Costozza's being one of the more impressive varietal Cabernets. Capo del Monte is an intriguing mix of Cabernet with Marzemino.

There is the same problem of distinguishing the two Cabernets in the vineyards of the South Tyrol, although plantings are by no means extensive. Both Trentino and Alto Adige produce some fine Cabernets, which can take an age to ripen – both on the vine and in the bottle. Acidity and colour levels are appetizingly high, even though tannins are less noticeable than in many other Cabernets.

Cabernet is also increasingly grown in Emilia-Romagna, reviving a tradition, but nowhere is it more modish than in Tuscany where it is now being feverishly reared to produce wines as various as Carmignano, Tignanello and Sassicaia. Carmignano, a Chianti-like wine made in the hills to the northwest of Florence, is one of the very few DOCs to enshrine in law the practice of adding Cabernet Sauvignon to the Chianti grapes, notably Sangiovese. Then Antinori with their Tignanello carefully aged in *barriques* showed that it is possible to fetch a high price for a non-DOC wine of this sort, and now every

Chianti producer wants his own strongly Cabernet, highly priced *vino da tavola*. There is no doubt that just a touch of Cabernet adds immeasurable class to Sangiovese, and the DOCG laws of 1984 were specially designed to allow just this.

Sassicaia was Tuscany's first 100 percent Cabernet Sauvignon wine and such wines are now emerging from every *castello*. They too command premium prices and some of them are delicious, although they are curiously alien to an Italian setting. Anything Tuscany does, Dr Lungarotti in next-door Umbria is also bound to have done. His Cabernet Sauvignon di Miralduolo is helpfully specific, and equally well defined on the palate.

If Cabernet's sphere of influence is gently nudging down Italy's boot, so it is around the whole of the eastern Mediterranean. Greece has its Château Carras, Bordeaux by the Aegean complete with Professor Peynaud, as well as plantings at the Tsantalis winery nearby. Cabernet Sauvignon is an ingredient in Israeli reds and Turkey's Villa Doluca. Lebanon has had the miraculous Château Musar in which old Cabernet vines are blended with Cinsaut and Syrah (thus combining South African and Australian ways with Cabernet). Good heavens, even sleepy little Cyprus is starting to try out both Cabernets.

The vine also marches east. China and Japan try. Yugoslavia, Romania and, especially, Bulgaria are pinning their export hopes on Cabernet Sauvignon. In Yugoslavia, the wines tend to lack "varietal definition", that is, they are just a bit muddy, but there are some light, toothsome examples from Serbia. Hungary prefers to leave Bulls Blood to do its courting of red-wine drinkers

and plantings of Cabernet Sauvignon there are minute. Romania has quite extensive Cabernet plantings, but the wines are plodding and can seem flabby to western palates.

Most avid wooer of the western wine drinker is Bulgaria, and Cabernet Sauvignon is seen as the strongest suit. With an amazing 18,000 hectares (45,000 acres), only 5,000 hectares (12,500 acres) less than France, Cabernet Sauvignon is Bulgaria's most important red grape variety by far. Second is Merlot, with which it blends well in a Bulgarian setting. Enthusiastic mechanization is the key to Bulgaria's impressive quality:price ratio. It is difficult to find varietal Cabernet Sauvignon less expensively than in one of Bulgaria's bull-necked bottles. Quality varies, from shipment to shipment according to some wine merchants, but overall the wine drinker must award them A for effort.

"Boiled blackcurrants" is probably the least flattering but not uncommon tasting note, but even the most basic level of Bulgarian Cabernet Sauvignon has good colour and acid – especially acid. Although the wines are indisputably fruity, malic acid is more pronounced than Cabernet flavours in basic versions suggesting that early picking is a feature of the Bulgarian way with the variety. The north concentrates on Cabernet Sauvignon and wines from Svistov have been some of the cleanest and most interesting.

The Russians are not so open about their wines. Indeed while Bulgaria floods Europe with her wines, the USSR drains the EEC wine lake. Little information is released about Soviet vines, but Cabernet is certainly grown in Georgia and the brand Teliani given the treat of a year's oak ageing. The Institut Magaratch doubtless has cellars full of Lafite taste-alikes, but is keeping them to itself.

Synonyms: Petit-Cabernet, Vidure, Petite-Vidure (Graves); Bouchet, Bouche (Gironde); Petit-Bouchet (St-Emilion and Pomerol); Sauvignon Rouge (central France).	*Vigour:* Very vigorous.
	Pruning: Cane pruning; Guyot is traditional.
Soils: Will grow on a wide range of soils but performs stunningly on the well-drained gravels of the Haut-Médoc. Over-fertile soils encourage such vigorous growth that fruit setting and maturation is uneven.	*Susceptibility:* Only to oidium. Very good resistance to rot and other pests and diseases.
	Rootstocks: Fairly low vigour needed. SO4 and 3309 used extensively in Europe.
	Yield: Low.

Top quality. Very fashionable at the moment.

Pinot Noir

The Pinot Noir is a minx of a vine. Indubitably feminine alas, if not exactly female, this is an exasperating variety for growers, winemakers and wine drinkers alike. It leads us a terrible dance, tantalizing with an occasional glimpse of the riches in store for those who persevere, yet obstinately refusing to be tamed.

It is natural to draw comparisons between the great red grapes of Bordeaux and Burgundy, but the similarities are few. Whereas Cabernet Sauvignon happily packs its bags and dashes about the world, the Pinot Noir travels sullenly. So alluring is the goal of making even the faintest shadow of great red burgundy in the newer wine regions that the task has become almost a fetish with quality minded winemakers. The phrase Holy Grail crops up often in discussions about cultivating Pinot Noir outside Europe.

Cabernet Sauvignons may vary enormously in quality, but most wines made predominantly, or even partly, from the grape will exhibit its characteristic flavour and framework. Pinot Noir has no single recognizable flavour or style, unless we count its suggestion of sweetness (perhaps) and its relatively high alcohol (although in Burgundy this owes so much to chaptalization). In youth it can taste of freshly squashed raspberries in delicate Côte de Beaune wines; sun-warmed strawberries in vintages from the Côte de Nuits; ink in young Chalonnaise reds; plum jam in California; and precious little in northern Italy and eastern Europe. Mature red burgundy, on the other hand, evolves rapidly away from anything as simple as mere fruit: its bouquet of extraordinary flavours can suggest anything from violets to game, from rotten vegetables to truffles. And in terms of quality, the gap between peaks and troughs yawns far wider still for Pinot than for Cabernet.

The trouble is that, unlike the urbane Cabernet Sauvignon, Pinot Noir is hardly civilized. It may be the head of the Pinot family, but like any Pinot vine it is not genetically stable and mutates easily. Pinot Meunier just happens to be one of the better corralled mutations but the mass of different Pinots Noir, Blanc and Gris (Chardonnay is no longer charged with being a member of this dissolute clan) make an unruly mob among which direct links are difficult to trace. The Pinotscape is further obscured by the vine's tendency to degenerate – and to die young. The working life of many plants is over before their third decade, when the grower may be presented with quite a different sort of Pinot Noir for replanting. Anthony Hanson notes more than 1,000 different types or clones of Pinot Noir in his study of Burgundy; Oregon's wine ambassador David Lett notes 200, but points out that no *vinifera* is subject to more genetic variation.

The fact that Pinot Noir is such an ancient vine doubtless plays a part here. It is thought to be one of the first refinements of wild vines made by man on his route to varietal civilization, and it is certainly not difficult to see

the gypsy in Pinot Noir. If Pinot Noir as we try to know it was identified and cultivated so early in its evolution, it is not surprising that it is capricious.

A vine sounding plausibly like Pinot Noir was already being cultivated by the Allobroger tribe around the Burgundy area when the Romans invaded Gaul. The *Vitis allobrogica* (not a name to launch a thousand cases today) was described by both Pliny and Columella in the first century AD and there is further evidence that a Pinot existed in Burgundy in the fourth century. "Pinot vermeil" was already named in records of Burgundian hospitality dated 1375, presumably a reference to a vine, like Pinot Noir, whose clusters were shaped like a pine cone (not a striking distinguishing mark, it is true). No other vine variety has a name that has been in use for more than six centuries. The name remains the same, only the vine itself has changed.

Nowhere has this been more exasperatingly apparent than in Burgundy. The region is now planted – sometimes deliberately, often carelessly – with a wide variety of different clones of Pinot Noir. (It now accounts for more than 70 percent of all Côte d'Or vines while in 1968 it took up less than half the total *vignoble*.) Clonal selection became an urgent priority to fight off viruses, especially the leaf roll to which Pinot Noir is particularly susceptible. Considerations of quality were thrown to the winds. Over the last 50 years, many growers have been tempted to plant clones of Pinot Droit which are easy to cultivate because in the crowded vineyards of Burgundy they grow conveniently upright (like the California clone G.B.) and produce notably more wine than the traditional Pinot Fin or Pinot Tordu. Who can blame them? The burgundy lovers of the world have come to curse these new clones with their swollen thin-skinned berries, just as they have cursed the thin, pale wines that result from fermenting such grapes at a frantic pace. The explanation for the enormous variation in quality in red burgundies on sale today lies almost as much in the cellar as in the vineyard.

There are encouraging signs, however. The third generation of post-phylloxera vines are now maturing nicely after their early-sixties planting. The proportion of *vin sérieux* made every year on the Côte d'Or seems to be perceptibly rising. The agrochemical industry is teaching Burgundians how to cope with rot, a serious problem for Pinot Noir's compact bunches. There is large-scale experimentation with different clones from around the world, so with luck the world's wine drinkers may once again enjoy the great drink they know red burgundy can be.

The wider than usual variation in different plants makes generalizations about Pinot Noir difficult. Is Pinot Noir a thick-skinned grape high in tannin and anthocyanins? The evidence from the likes of Romanée Conti, de Vogüé and Doudet Naudin would suggest that this is so, but at least 50 percent of Côte d'Or reds are markedly pale.

It is generally agreed (although Germany is the exception) that Pinot Noir is an early budder and early ripener. It is therefore best suited to coolish, preferably marginal climates. The longer the grapes can stay on the vine before tending to raisin and *surmaturité*, the more complex the resulting wine will be. Proneness to rot makes this a risky exercise. Spring frosts are also particularly dangerous, especially as secondary growth is so sluggish, and in some years there are problems with fruit-setting. As almost everyone who has actually *chosen* to plant it expostulates from time to time, Pinot Noir is a ****** to grow.

Not surprisingly, France has the world's largest plantings of Pinot Noir: 17,000 hectares (42,500 acres) in 1979 as opposed to 12,000 hectares (30,000 acres) in 1968 (although Cabernet Sauvignon plantings increased much more rapidly from the same base in the same period). French distribution of the variety is concentrated in the northeast, with nearly half the vines in what one might call Greater Burgundy – of which two-thirds or 5,700 hectares (14,250 acres) are on the Côte d'Or – and most of the rest in the Marne and, importantly, Aube *départements* of Champagne.

Alsace has about 600 hectares (1,500 acres) making the lightish, heavily scented reds of the region, which are likely to become more substantial as longer maceration becomes a habit. The grape is also responsible for a host of other light red oddities such as Sancerre rouge and rosé, Irancy, the odd Lorraine red or *gris* and the pale reds of Savoie and Jura.

It is in Champagne, however, that Pinot Noir is used in its most bizarre form: as provider of white base wines for champenization. It is a prized ingredient in the *cuvée* for its substance and longevity. Considering how delicate a task it is to keep the Pinot juice free of tint from the skins, how much more productive Chardonnay (and Pinot Meunier) can be than Pinot Noir, and how delicious Blanc de Blancs champagne can be, it is perhaps surprising that the Champenois are still so devoted to Pinot Noir. The credo of blending is clearly strongly held in Champagne.

The ordinary champagne drinker rarely has a chance to assess the contribution made to his glass by the famous Pinot Noir of the villages on the Montagne de Reims. There is always the still Coteaux Champenois of the likes of Bouzy, produced in particularly ripe, plentiful vintages, but these heavily chaptalized light rubies seem very distant relatives of the finest fizz. Sparkling Blancs de Noirs are made but rarely, and often owe more to Pinot Meunier than to Pinot Noir. Perhaps the most extraordinary and telling wine is Bollinger's Vieilles Vignes, made in exceptional years from layered pre-phylloxera Pinot Noir stock. This is a champagne that on the nose has all the impact of a good Côte de Nuits red burgundy, on the throat the unctuous power of a very fine cough syrup.

As Spätburgunder, Pinot Noir is very important to the German wine industry. There has been a dramatic increase in plantings of this popular variety so that Germany now has more than 4,000 hectares (10,000 acres), mainly in the southern Baden and Württemberg regions, but also in the Rheingau (especially Assmannshausen), Ahr and Rheinhessen. The red-wine style apparently most appreciated by the Germans, and by most other German-speaking nations, is not always that best understood by an outsider. Spätburgunder is not one of Germany's great wine exports, which is perhaps just as well. Like that of Alsace, the German version of Pinot Noir can in many vintages be so pale it is a rosé (often with an orangey tinge), and is very noticeably short on fruit and flavour. Unlike Alsace, Germany finds it difficult to grow much stuffing for the wine; Spätburgunder is scarcely sturdier than Germany's light whites. This difficulty in fully ripening red grapes is exacerbated in the Ahr, which is Germany's most famous red-wine region but also its most northerly. A measure of sweetness is seen as a great saviour of, or at least distraction from, this weakness, and the State Domain at Assmannshausen delights many a German collector with its pink Auslesen. Such rarities, suggesting a combination of pink burgundy and a light syrup, strike the visitor as very odd.

Considering Germany inevitably involves considering productivity. The plant breeders of Geisenheim and others have even managed to coax yields of 80 hectolitres per hectare from this naturally shy-bearing grape, although vine rows have to keep their distance to guard against the

*B*ernard Theobald of Westbury in England's Thames Valley consistently mystifies his rivals with his deep-coloured Pinot Noir grown on vines trained high on the Geneva Double Curtain system.

PINOT NOIR

Leaf
length: 127mm (5in)   width: 127mm (5in)

Grape Cluster
length: 165mm (6½in)   width: 89mm (3½in)

The Germans expect their Spätburgunder, such as that produced here at Oberbergen in Baden, to be merely pink. The variety's susceptibility to botrytis means that the grapes have to be picked before pigmentation is much developed.

spread of rot as the grapes slowly ripen into autumn. This far north the Pinot Noir ripens only just before Silvaner.

It should also be mentioned that at least one grower, Bernard Theobald of Westbury, has managed to produce sizeable quantities of deep-coloured Pinot Noir in England's Thames Valley. His luxuriant Geneva Double Curtain training system, of which he is official English exponent, is doubtless one key factor.

Like Germany, northern Italy provides no shortage of examples of Pinot Noir's frequent mediocrity. There are just two peaks in the uninspiring plain south of the Alps, one of them only just south. As Blauburgunder, the variety can produce wines of real interest and finesse when grown on the higher slopes of the Alto Adige valley. Here the temperatures are sufficiently low to prolong the growing season until reasonably complex wines are produced from the 200 hectares (500 acres) or so. Structure and colour and, especially, aroma are heartening for those who despair of finding any Pinot Noir quality outside Burgundy. Most of them are best consumed young, but those who have tasted them wistfully cite memories of Josef Hofstätter's '69 and '74 as evidence that there are exceptions. Mazzon is rated the local Côte d'Or.

As Pinot Nero the variety is cultivated all over northeastern Italy. Areas include, in approximately ascending order of quality, Breganze, Trentino, Collio, Friuli and Colli Orientali del Friuli, all accorded the honour of their own DOC. Most of these wines are simple, reasonably

fruity reds, without specifically evoking any of Pinot's higher qualities. In some examples, even the colour, ever a problem for producers of Pinot Noir, is lacking.

Pinot's other high spot in Italy, Oltrepò Pavese, makes a virtue of this fault. Enormous quantities of Pinot Nero are grown here to be vinified as white wine, either for immediate sale as a toothsome, light still wine, or for the effervescent and often admirable Italian sparkling-wine industry. The application of the *metodo champenois* to Pinot is every bit as successful here as in northeastern France. It is worth considering that in 20 years' time Pinot Noir may be more useful to the wine enthusiast as provider of sparkling rather than still wine, so voracious is our collective appetite for fizz.

Only way up in the Aosta valley is the variety actually called Pinot Noir, just as it is in the French-speaking cantons of Switzerland where it is relatively important. In the Valais it constitutes perhaps two-thirds of all the important red grapes planted there and should form the base for the ubiquitous Dôle, an often doleful blend in which the Gamay ingredient and over-chaptalization predominate. It is possible, however, to find very toothsome 100 percent Pinot Noir which is like a cross between the Alsace version and a good Côte Chalonnaise wine. A *pétillant* Pinot Noir vinified *en blanc* to produce the brilliantly named Oeil de Perdrix is the delicate speciality of Neuchâtel. Pinot Noir also predominates in the red-wine vineyards around Zürich where it provides the city's much

*V*ignerons in the Hautes-
Côtes de Beaune prepare
barrels for a new crop of
Pinot Noir – the same grape as
the finest red burgundies of the
Côte d'Or, but often distinctly
inferior clones lacking the colour,
finesse, concentration and velvety
staying power that gives the
variety its allure.

appreciated Klevner. Swiss plantings of Pinot Noir total a considerable 3,000 hectares (7,500 acres).

The variety is also, not surprisingly, planted all over eastern Europe, although many examples testify to Pinot Noir's need for a temperate climate to show its distinguishing marks. Czechoslovakia could have potential. Austria has about 300 hectares (750 acres) for her curiously inky sweet reds but prefers the indigenous variety, sometimes confusingly known as Pinot St-Laurent.

As Burgundac Crni it is cultivated in the generally overheated climate of Macedonia and Serbia as well as on the Dalmatian coast. It is also planted on a relatively small scale in Romania, the USSR, Bulgaria (where most investment is firmly in Cabernet Sauvignon) and China.

Only in Hungary are any great claims made for the variety which, as Nagyburgundi, is prized as the country's finest red. Its reputation is built on the produce of three districts in the deep south: Villány, Szekszárd and Vaskút. The wines are given what might be called old oak ageing to produce "old fashioned burgundy", and can be disconcertingly sweet.

Blurred reflections of Côte d'Or's finest wines are not for the ambitious winemakers of North America and Australia. They continue to aim high, a frustrating approach with a vine as capricious as Pinot Noir. So far, Oregon and certain cooler corners of Australia have promised best. The variety suits the fiercely individualist wine producers of Oregon as well as the state's climate suits it. And Pinot Noir

has rewarded them to such an extent that, with more than 400 hectares (1,000 acres) of vineyard, it constitutes the state's most widely planted grape variety by far. While aiming at similar Brix levels of around 23°, Oregonians can extend Pinot Noir's growing season a full six nail-biting weeks past the California Pinot Noir crush. This gives complexity to the grapes and therefore to the wines and, with attractive levels of acids, tannins and anthocyanins, endows them with framework as well as flavour. Pinots from the Eyrie Vineyard have been particularly good ambassadors for this often overlooked corner of the wine world, but there are several other enterprises whose Pinot Noirs exhibit consistency of quality that many a Burgundian should envy.

California's total plantings are nearly eight times those of Oregon but the success rate is many times lower. Pinot Noir is cultivated all over the state but only the wines of Chalone, high up in the Santa Lucia Mountains above Salinas, have shown consistent style. Hopes are pinned on isolated vineyards in San Luis Obispo and Santa Barbara counties, and the foggy Carneros district just north of San Francisco Bay has been a useful source of early-picked Pinot Noir for sparkling wines. Much of Napa, Sonoma and especially Mendocino is simply too hot for the long growing season needed to produce fine still wine: picking in August is by no means exceptional in view of the variety's tendency to sunburn. There have also been problems here with Pierce's disease, and in distinguishing it from the confusingly named non-relative Pinot St George (see the entry for Negrette on page 204).

The typical California Pinot Noir is deep in colour and high in tannin and extract as a result of prolonged maceration. One wonders whether this is because the typical Californian does not expect to be able to see the bottom of his glass, however delicately tinted the grape variety is by nature. It is also very plummy, sometimes almost burnt, and often has an unnerving suggestion of overboiled cabbage about it. Were this a more attractive combination, the Californians could justifiably defend it as simply "California-style Pinot Noir". The sad fact is that in California as everywhere else in the world, no one has come up with a variation on, or even a good imitation of, the Pinot Noir theme that could compare with burgundy.

In Australia the goals are the same, the problems very similar. Total plantings are only a few hundred hectares, but only a small proportion of them seem to be in a suitably cool location. Tyrrell's international success with a 1976 Hunter Valley specimen was regarded with amusement in Australia, and the Hunter is generally regarded as only just cool enough to produce Cabernet Sauvignon, let alone

Pinot Noir. Some fine examples have been produced in Coonawarra and elsewhere in the southeastern reaches of South Australia, and there have been some very promising bottles from the Margaret River and Mount Barker districts of Western Australia and, especially, the Yarra Valley near Melbourne. Mount Mary and Yarra Yering can genuinely coax quality out of this sulker of a vine. New Zealand may be a better bet eventually and should certainly be capable of producing light, delicate Pinots in the Santenay style. So far winemakers seem preoccupied with proving the upper limit of extraction rather than settling on an optimum one.

In South Africa only Hamilton-Russell and Meerlust are trying seriously with the variety, but the name if not the style is kept to the forefront of the industry by its 5,000 hectares (12,500 acres) of Pinotage, a beefy crossing of Cinsaut and a strain of Pinot.

In South America, Chile makes the most self-confident, non-Burgundian Pinot of all: deep-coloured, chock-full of flavour and plummy fruit, but a bit short on acid. In such warm climes, Pinot Noir can ripen so much earlier than other varieties that it poses organizational problems.

Synonyms:
Pineau, Franc Pineau, Noirien (France);
Savagnin Noir, Salvagnin (Jura);
Morillon, Auvernat, Plant Doré,
Vert Doré (Champagne);
Spätburgunder, Blauburgunder, Blauer Klevner
(Germany); Klevner, Cortaillod (Switzerland);
Blauburgunder, Pignol, Pignola,
Pinot Nero (Italy);
Blauer Spätburgunder (Austria);
Burgundac Crni (Yugoslavia);
Rouci, Rouci Modre (Czechoslovakia);
Nagyburgundi (Hungary).

Soils:
Partly because of its proneness to rot,
it responds well to well-drained deepish soils,
with notable success on the calcareous soils
of Champagne.

Vigour: Moderate.

Pruning:
Cane pruning best,
with Guyot method most common in Burgundy.

Susceptibility:
Fairly susceptible to downy and powdery mildew.
Very prone to bunch or grey rot.
Leaf roll has been a major problem for vines
prior to virus indexing.

Rootstocks:
Moderate to vigorous needed.
3309C, 55B and SO4 have been used in Burgundy;
41B and 161–49 in Champagne.

Yields:
Low. This is a key factor in producing
Pinot Noir of any quality.
Yields of as little as 25 hl/ha are the norm in some
climats of the Côte d'Or.
Double this is probably the average worldwide.

Potentially top quality. Tantalizingly fashionable.

Syrah

Syrah presents a conundrum. In France where it represents less than 2 percent of all red-wine grape plantings, Syrah is worshipped. In the northern Rhône it provides wines as great as Hermitage and Côte Rôtie, indubitably the most serious contenders for a seat at the high table already occupied by top quality claret and burgundy. Throughout the Midi it is the *cépage améliorateur* par excellence. In Australia where it represents 40 percent of all red-wine grape plantings, it is largely ignored. All but a handful of Australia's more cosmopolitan winemakers treat Shiraz as though its generous distribution somehow robs it of its nobility. There is a moral here somewhere: perhaps it is that growers will always make a lot of mediocre wine in preference to a small quantity of wonderful stuff, if the option is open to them.

Although France and Australia are the only important producers of the variety today, this has not always been so. Syrah has the oldest charted geography, as well as history, of the noble grape varieties. The vine's origins are most popularly thought to be Middle Eastern. It seems too much of a coincidence that one of the world's two earliest wine-producing regions includes the city of Shiraz from which there are several plausible routes by which the vine we call Syrah could have been brought to the Rhône valley. Shiraz is in the southeast of what is now Iran and it seems eminently possible that the vine was brought to Marseilles by the Phocaeans. Greek amphorae excavated at Tain, the small town dominated by the Hermitage vineyards, is offered as clear evidence for this theory. An alternative hypothesis has the Roman legions of Probus bringing the vine north from the Egyptian vineland via Syracuse, and encouraging plantings of it in Gaul during the Roman occupation. What is certain is that the vine was already well-established in the Rhône valley by Roman times, long before it reached that vinous wilderness on the Atlantic seaboard.

The arrival of Syrah in Australia is easier to chart. It seems highly likely that it was one of the 400 cuttings foraged by James Busby on his trip to Europe in 1832. A stint in Sydney's Botanic Gardens proved it could stand the climate, and by the late 1840s notes from Sir William Macarthur's "Letters on the Vine", cleverly extracted by James Halliday in *The Hunter Valley*, included the following: "Scyras . . . An excellent grape, and promises to be at least equally as valuable for red wine as the Verdeilho is for white. This is the sort said to be chiefly cultivated on the celebrated hill of Hermitage. It is a very hardy plant, produces well, and seems to be liable to no accident or disease."

Why then is it so little grown elsewhere? It is a relatively reliable cropper, producing much bigger yields than Cabernet Sauvignon, for example, provided the weather during flowering is sufficiently warm, since Syrah is particularly sensitive to *coulure*. It is, on the other hand, resistant to most other pests and diseases and is a cinch to grow. The answer perhaps is partly that prototype Syrahs, the fine wines of the northern Rhône, are produced in such tiny quantity – the Hermitage appellation consists of a mere 152 hectares (380 acres) – that the wine drinkers of the world have been exposed to very little great Syrah.

And there is another problem: although it is much easier to grow Syrah than Cabernet Sauvignon, it is more difficult to make a great, as opposed to palatable, wine from Syrah than from Cabernet. Syrah can be just as distinctive as Cabernet. It is dry, dark, dense, tannic and matches Cabernet's cassis with burnt rubber for some, smoke and tar for others. However, it does require some effort: the grower must choose the right site and deliberately restrict his yield; the winemaker must respect the concentration of flavour, treat it to long, cool fermentation and, ideally, a decent upbringing in oak. Syrah is also much more prone than Cabernet to oxidize. Cabernet Sauvignon is to the winemaker what Syrah is to the grower. Perhaps their relative popularities also reflect the relative status of the two activities.

Like Cabernet Sauvignon and that other very tannic grape variety Nebbiolo (with which it can quite easily be confused in youth), Syrah needs time to show its greatness. Ironically, with time, a great northern Rhône Syrah starts to taste like great claret, as any who have tasted 1961 Hermitage La Chapelle will willingly testify. Certainly, the Syrah grape reared carefully anywhere in the world responds well to wood ageing, and Hermitage La Chapelle, for example, is given 18 months in Burgundian casks.

For most wine lovers, Hermitage is quintessential Syrah, Crozes-Hermitage a useful lighter version of it, Cornas and St-Joseph slightly more substantial than Crozes, and Côte-Rôtie potentially one of the most complex wines in the world with its dab of Viognier scent (see pages 180–2). Would that such wines, or their like, were available in greater quantity.

Syrah may be taking its time to spread around the world, but the last decade has seen an extraordinary expansion of its sphere of influence in France from that northern Rhône base. Total French plantings increased almost fivefold between the agricultural censuses of 1968 and 1979, to nearly 13,000 hectares (32,500 acres), thereby overtaking total Australian plantings (for perhaps the first time since the last century). Thanks largely to EEC subsidies for planting such "improver vines" in the Midi, the French total is probably well on the way towards 20,000 hectares (50,000 acres) already. There is now more Syrah planted in the Gard *département*, for instance, than in Drôme in northern Rhône, and 80 percent of all Syrah vines planted in France today are less than 15 years old.

New plantings have also been made in its traditional

*T*he hill of Hermitage, towering over the Rhône, is the source of quintessential Syrah. The steeply terraced granite slope faces due south, and is planted 80 percent with Syrah, the balance being almost all white Marsanne nowadays, although better clones of the more delicate, traditional Roussanne are being developed.

areas. Vaucluse now has as much of the variety as Drôme. Syrah had always been a splash on the well-loaded palette of the Châteauneuf-du-Pape craftsman, but it has increased its importance in recent years in the outlying appellations of the Côtes-du-Rhône. In the southern Rhône the grape has traditionally been blended (in blending vat, fermentation vat and even vineyard) with the more alcoholic Grenache and the local hotchpotch of more obscure varieties. It is not usually detectable unless it constitutes more than half of the blend, but it does provide excellent structure and longevity.

It is also making a name for itself as one of France's few varietal wines. Syrah de l'Ardèche has enjoyed a certain vogue as an inexpensive reflection of more concentrated Syrah and some Vins de Pays from further south carry the name of the variety. In the herby Provence reds, too, its impact can be tasted.

French growers distinguish between Grosse and Petite Syrah, Petite being the goody, Grosse being the Mondeuse, much more vigorous, productive and rather frowned upon. It is generally agreed that Australian Syrah is Petite Syrah (which has nothing to do with California's Petite Sirah which is the little-known Durif of the Midi).

As Shiraz (an understandable Strinisation of Macarthur's "Scyras"), Syrah is immensely important to the Australian wine industry, in quantitative terms at least. Total plantings have been declining as the gospel of off-dry whites spreads Down Under as everywhere else, but there are still about 7,000 hectares (17,500 acres), more than any grape variety other than the ignominious Sultana. It is grown all over the country, largely in New South Wales and South Australia, in different but usually relatively hot climates. Syrah is quite happy in relatively high tempera-

tures, but not so happy to be over-irrigated as a result.

Because it is so widely available and can be made to bear so profusely, Shiraz all too often plays the workhorse role. Basic red wine in Australia means Shiraz, with a measure of Grenache and even perhaps a dash of Currant. High-yielding Shiraz tastes sweet, tends to brown easily and loses its concentration. This is archetypal "hot country" red wine, with all the flavour boiled out of it. Lucky Australians to have such extensive plantings of such a noble grape; foolish them to squander it.

One area, the Hunter Valley and specifically the Lower Hunter, has sufficient quality-conscious winemakers to turn some of the valley's vast amounts of Shiraz into really "serious" wines. Admittedly the soaring temperatures and poor soils characteristic of this area combine to produce wines with a very distinctive style. Admittedly, Hunter "Hermitage", as Shiraz is still often known here, is, like Hunter Sémillon, an assault on the senses of those raised on more classical wines. And, like the Sémillons, these wines need time to show quality. Many vintages can be simply too hot, and the wines asked to mature at dangerously high temperatures so that oxidation and off-odours can be a problem. When everything goes right, however, and yields here can be as little as half a ton per acre, the wines develop an extraordinary style of their own: part richness of an almost chocolatey sort, part a mineral element that gives them a tang the locals call "sweaty saddle". Shiraz is still very much the red-wine grape of the Hunter, but Cabernet Sauvignon is currently giving it a run for its money.

Australia's most dearly loved red, the extraordinarily rich and complex Grange Hermitage, made in the Barossa Valley from local fruit, provides the model for Shiraz

SYRAH

Leaf
length: 152mm (6in)   width: 133mm (5¼in)

Grape Cluster
length: 229mm (9in)   width: 165mm (6½in)

reared in the warmer parts of South Australia. Much of this ripe Shiraz is used as blending material, indeed we owe a debt to the Australian wine industry for proving what successful if unlikely partners Shiraz and Cabernet Sauvignon can be. Claret was often "Hermitagé", or blended with Syrah, "Hermitage" in the last century but tastes and the wines were rather different then. The blend might be just a bit too austere if translated into current French, but the generous climate of the Barossa Valley and McLaren Vale round out the edges and make a Cabernet/Shiraz blend a mercifully early-maturing wine.

There is a fourth, and very promising, style of Australian Shiraz. When the variety is raised in relatively cool climates, such as Coonawarra (where optimum, but not necessarily lowest, yield is 5 tons per acre), southwestern Australia and the isolated well-tempered vineyards of Victoria, it takes on the dry peppery quality that is so appetizing in many reds of the northern Rhône. Acid and tannin levels are kept well up; these wines, much more familiar to European palates, keep their colour and age extremely well. Granite Hills and Balgownie in Victoria and Plantagenet and Cape Mentelle in Western Australia have all produced inspiring examples.

All these areas are at that finely judged limit of successful Syrah cultivation. The trouble is that Syrah does not respond well to too cool a climate. One wonders what sort of wine is produced from the Syrah cultivated on Dr Wuilloud's Swiss domain at Diolly in the Valais. Even in northern Rhône in a cool year the dry pepper and spice of the nose can seem too much for the lean, tart palate. This is the perfectly reasonable explanation of why Syrah is not grown in New Zealand or the Loire. However, it does not explain why it is so little cultivated in the vast tracts of warmer wine country in the Iberian peninsula, Italy, South America or California. The explanation may be that Syrah's qualities are not sufficiently distinct from those of the Latin native grape varieties.

A handful of California growers, persuaded by an appreciation of northern Rhône wines, have planted genuine Syrah vines. At Joseph Phelps they began planting in 1974 and ended in 1979 with clones both French and Australian in origin, between which they see very few differences. The wines have so far shown little of the concentration of which the variety is capable, but the flavour is definitely there and will presumably manifest itself as the vines mature. Phelps have found the vine responds best to hillside slopes with maximum exposure to sunshine, in short, sites most reminiscent of the northern Rhône. Others persevering with proper Syrah, as opposed to the completely unrelated Petite Sirah, include Estrella River of San Luis Obispo, Duxoup and Preston of Sonoma, McDowell Valley of Mendocino and Bonny Doon of Santa Cruz (who also share Phelps' fascination with Syrah's white waif of a sister, Viognier).

In Argentina they are just starting to experiment with an improved strain of the variety. And, despite a little local difficulty with the wind blowing away the Syrah's comparatively brittle shoots, there are several hundred hectares of it planted around Stellenbosch and Paarl in South Africa from which some varietal wine is now made. There are small but perceptible signs that Syrah may yet gain the international attention it deserves.

Synonyms:
Schiras, Sirac, Syra,
Syrac, Sirah, Petite Syrah, Hignin Noir,
Candive, Entournerein,
Antourenein Noir, Serène, Serenne, Sereine,
Serine, Marsanne Noir (France);
Shiraz (Australia and South Africa);
Balsamina (Argentina).

Soils:
Performs best on poor soil;
the rock of Hermitage is granite based.

Vigour: Vigorous.

Pruning:
Gobelet used in some northern Rhône vineyards.

Susceptibility:
Good disease resistance
although there are some rot problems.

Rootstocks:
SO4 most commonly used in the Rhône.

Yields:
Moderate (certainly more than
Cabernet Sauvignon), but reasonably low yields
are a crucial factor for quality.

Potentially top quality. Very limited popularity.

Merlot

Merlot, or more properly Merlot Noir since there is a distinctly different variety called Merlot Blanc, is one of the vine world's great underdogs. Connoisseurs who go weak at the knees at the very whisper of Pétrus would not dream of choosing a wine based on Merlot if a Cabernet alternative was offered anywhere outside this hallowed plot of Pomerol clay. And there are even those purists who, unimpressed by Château Pétrus's consistently record-breaking form in the saleroom, still see this Merlot superstar as *infra dig* because of its brazen lusciousness compared with the more austere charms of Cabernet Sauvignon.

Merlot's plus points – its fruitiness, its forwardness and its productivity – are turned to its disadvantage in the eyes of wine drinkers. All over the world, the highest red varietal pedestal is reserved for Cabernet. Almost every wine region outside France is peopled by winemakers trying to prove they can give Château Latour a run for its money, yet hardly any of them take Bordeaux's other great red grape seriously. Conveniently overlooking the century-old tradition of blending at least some Merlot and probably some Cabernet Franc and Malbec to soften the Cabernet Sauvignon (practised even at Latour), they have worshipped too long at the 100 percent varietal altar, ignoring Merlot's potential as blending material as well as its alluring character unblended. It is true that Pétrus probably owes its indubitable quality substantially to the unique ferrous clay subsoil and to the relative antiquity of the vines, but it and many other St-Emilion/Pomerol properties show just what can be achieved with these oft-despised grapes.

Viticulturally Merlot is characterized by its relatively early budding and flowering, which exposes it to the twin dangers of spring frosts and *coulure*. It also ripens comparatively early, although, being thinner skinned than the Cabernet Sauvignon to which it is inevitably compared, it is liable to rot in a wet vintage unless treated carefully and expensively with one of the new generation of sprays. Its fairly large, loose-bunched grapes are much less dustily blue than Cabernet's. They tend to be notably lower in tannins than Cabernet, higher in sugars and in warmer climates dangerously short of malic acid as well. Vinification produces a supple, well-coloured wine which can achieve great richness, as in the better Pomerols and St-Emilions, and is usually a degree or two stronger than Cabernet produced from the same vineyard. In much of Bordeaux and therefore inevitably throughout much of the world, Merlot is regarded as an ingredient in a blend, a suitable foil for Cabernet, usually Sauvignon and sometimes Franc as well.

Petit-Lafitte's *La Vigne en Bordelais* (1868) cites two explanations for the origin of the name Merlot, "little blackbird" in Bordeaux patois, although this, as when two

excuses are made for the same thing, leads one to question the plausibility of both. It is said that the Merlot is the grape that the blackbird guzzles first, and also that the bird's colour resembles that of the grapes on the Merlot vine (and not a few others, surely?).

Merlot appears to be a relatively recent variety (which doubtless also contributes to its slightly parvenu image) in that it appears in records of the Médoc only in the last century. It seems to have been relatively common on the St-Emilion/Pomerol side of the Gironde in the eighteenth century: Enjalbert cites a reference in Faurveau's subdelegate's report of 1784 to Merlot as one of the better Libournais varieties.

Its influence today is greatest by far in Bordeaux, and it is the most planted grape variety in the Gironde *département* where its 32,000 hectares (80,000 acres) make Cabernet Sauvignon's 17,200 hectares (43,000 acres) look rather small beer. Merlot plantings have been increasing dramatically both here and in Languedoc-Roussillon so that in the

The obvious distinction of fine claret has moved vine growers all over the world to import cuttings of Cabernet Sauvignon and Merlot. Thanks to a consignment way back in 1864, the Vega Sicilia vineyard is today Spain's most respected.

last French agricultural census of 1979 it covered an area of 38,000 hectares (95,000 acres), of which 5,000 hectares (12,500 acres) were planted with vines less than three years old. It was the sixth most planted grape variety of any colour in France.

Unlike Cabernet Sauvignon, Merlot is planted all over the three wine-producing *départements* of Aquitaine: Gironde, Dordogne and Lot-et-Garonne, with a total of 2,000 and 1,000 hectares (5,000 and 2,500 acres) respectively in the last two. Its productivity makes it popular with growers and it can adapt itself to a wide range of different soils and microclimates, whereas Cabernet Sauvignon can be difficult to ripen north of the Gironde.

After the severe cold of 1956, many Merlot vines were irreparably damaged; although Madame Loubat is supposed to have nursed her Pétrus *pieds* back to life herself, either by grafting young vines on to the precious old roots that survived, or by taking suckers. This setback prompted a wave of new Merlot plantings. Then in the sixties came a series of vintages ruined by rot, especially of Merlot. The authorities sought to solve this problem by allowing only Cabernet Sauvignon plantings in Bordeaux in 1970–75. Christian Moueix describes this as "that short, awful period". Unfortunately the clone they promoted was very good at withstanding rot, but not very good at ripening, thereby vindicating the many who doubt this vine's suitability for Pomerol/St-Emilion. Merlot plantings are now on the upgrade as never before, even though poor weather at flowering can still devastate the crop.

Within Aquitaine it is only in the Médoc and Graves that Merlot is required to play second fiddle to Cabernet Sauvignon. In these subregions it constitutes typically about 25 percent of the *encépagement* and is blended mainly with Cabernet Sauvignon, some Cabernet Franc and still sometimes with a bit of Petit Verdot. In St-Emilion/ Pomerol it usually dominates the blend, constituting two-thirds to Cabernet Franc's one-third. These blends vary enormously, from truly noble fruit essences down to miserably watery hints at claret. In the Entre-Deux-Mers where growers have been switching white vineyards to red, Merlot is very popular, as it is in the Bourg, Blaye and Fronsac districts.

Its character is such that it is well suited to blending with Cabernet. In basic AC Bordeaux Rouge even a fairly small amount of Cabernet Sauvignon is enough to give the wine the distinctive perfume and rather tannic structure expected of it, while Merlot makes the wine relatively easy to drink when young. It fleshes out the rather gaunt figure of the more aristocratic varietal and, like Cabernet, responds well to oak ageing. Merlot's enormous advantage or disadvantage, depending on one's point of view, is that its round fruitiness, lowish fruit tannin and apparent sweetness mean that it can be enjoyed very early in its development, much earlier than Cabernet. *Cru classé* St-Emilion may not last the three decades of a *cru classé* Médoc, but at least most of it can be enjoyed after only four or five years. Merlot obligingly provides us with that favourite of the wine writers, "a real drinking wine", and seems

expressly designed for an inflationary age. If only growers would coax fewer grapes and greater quality from it.

To the east, Merlot is a common ingredient, with the standard Bordeaux grape varieties, in Bergerac, Pécharmant, Côtes de Duras, Côtes de Buzet, and with Malbec in Cahors.

More excitingly, and more recently, Merlot has really taken hold in the troubled Languedoc-Roussillon vineyards. Of all the *cépages améliorateurs* that growers there are encouraged to plant in place of coarse, high-yielding varieties such as Aramon and Carignan, Merlot occupies a pathetic 1.2 percent of the total *vignoble*, but twice as much as either Cabernet Sauvignon or Syrah. There are another 800 hectares (2,000 acres) in the even more extensive vineyards of Hérault, and some of the wines produced from them have been encouragingly toothsome. Merlot's natural sweetness is often accentuated in these rather hotter vineyards, but many producers are clearly skilled at picking before acid levels plummet, which they are wont to do as Merlot ripens fully. Merlot is commonly blended here but varietal wines are also marketed.

Outside France, Merlot's influence is widespread but weak. The wines are often also weak, a sign of overproduction. This is particularly true of many Italian Merlots. Indeed for many wine drinkers their first witting encounter with Merlot is in the form of a cheap north Italian varietal, soft and light to the point of negligibility.

Merlot is very popular in Italy, being planted in 14 of its 20 regions, preferred to the Cabernets because it is higher yielding and perhaps because it provides a more useful contrast to the noble but chewy native Italian varieties. Italian Merlot (in which the flabby Merlot of Italian Switzerland should be included) is almost exclusively designed to be drunk young, and few keep much vitality after four years. Burton Anderson instances as evidence that Italy can produce great Merlot examples from Ruggero Veneri in Spello, Umbria; Borgo Conventi in the Collio Goriziano, Friuli; and the Campo del Lago bottling from Villa Dal Ferro in Veneto.

Merlot's greatest popularity is in the northeast, especially Grave del Friuli and Piave in the Veneto, each of which produce about 100,000 hectolitres of Merlot annually. So important is the variety in the former, indeed, that there is even a Strada del Merlot, a popular tourist wine route along the Isonzo river. DOC Merlots in Friuli-Venezia Giulia include, in approximately descending order of quality, Collio, Colli Orientali del Friuli, Isonzo, Grave del Friuli and Aquileia. In neighbouring eastern Veneto Merlot holds equal sway and is the most important variety, producing DOC wines labelled Colli Euganei, Colli Berici, Montello e Colli Asolani, Piave and, especially good and often spiced with 10 percent Cabernet, Merlot di Pramaggiore.

To the north, Merlot is the predominant grape variety in Trentino, but is fading fast in the Alto Adige where prices are too high compared with those paid for the sea of Merlot produced on the plains to the south and east. Other named Merlots come from Oltrepò Pavese, the Colli Bolognesi in

MERLOT

Leaf
length: 120mm (4½in)   width: 113mm (4¼in)

Grape Cluster
length: 200mm (7¾in)   width: 120mm (4½in)

Emilia-Romagna and Aprilia south of Rome. Merlot, like Chianti, has become an Italian brand name whose reputation has been sullied by poor and mediocre examples.

Further east Merlot has been understandably popular. It is grown substantially just over the Italo-Yugoslav border in Slovenia, down the Dalmatian coast, around Lake Ohrid, and most notably in Istria where acid levels can be kept relatively high, very necessary if its wines are not to become bloated and lifeless. Yugoslavian Merlot can be attractively plummy and, if yields were restricted further, could be one of Slovenia's better candidates for ageing.

Merlot is also grown in Hungary, notably in the northeastern Eger district. It is perversely known as Médoc Noir (perhaps a name with great prestige in Hungary, where the leading brand of cigarettes is also known as Médoc). Complementing Kékfrankos with Oporto and the native Kadarka, it has a bit part in that great international production Bulls Blood. It is most prized, however, as an oddly sweet varietal (sold as Egri Médoc Noir) which has good acid and a light, moderately fruity nose, but is difficult to imagine with food. Médoc Noir produces another highly prized wine on the southern border around Villány where summer temperatures can be very high and the wines very deeply coloured as a result.

Merlot is also planted all over Romania and, after Cabernet Sauvignon, is the second most widely planted grape variety in Bulgaria. Merlot plantings total 9,500 hectares (23,750 acres), largely in the Chirpan and Haskovo districts in the south where it can produce some very attractive, mouth-filling wines with more alluring fruit than many of the Cabernets. The clever, export-conscious Bulgarians have also been experimenting with Cabernet-Merlot blends, including the most creditable Oriahovica.

Merlot is virtually unknown in Spain and Portugal where grapes with higher natural acids tend to perform better than such potentially voluptuous specimens as Merlot. The extraordinary Vega Sicilia vineyard, on the

Merlot flourishes in outposts as diverse as Yakima Valley and Hawkes Bay but is still its richly plummy best at home, Pomerol, such as here at Château de Sales.

chilly plateau east of Valladolid, is planted with cuttings taken from the original cuttings brought from Bordeaux in the nineteenth century, and these include some Merlot. Since Vega Sicilia is Spain's most expensive and revered wine, it seems likely that Merlot could thrive in other cooler Spanish, and possibly the more maritime Portuguese, microclimates. Proof of this theory can be tasted in several J. M. da Fonseca reds from Portugal.

A little Merlot is grown under Spanish and Portuguese influence in South America, with the variety constituting 5 percent of all red wine grape plantings in Chile and a bit more than 1 percent in Argentina, but its Bordelais complements Malbec and Cabernet are much more common. This, one hopes, is because acid levels fall too dramatically towards the end of ripening in the relatively warm summers of most South American vineyards.

It is curious that Merlot has taken so little hold in the southern hemisphere. In South Africa there are perhaps a few thousand vines, but the quality of the wine they produce has not been startling and their main contribution so far seems to have been to lend verisimilitude to a blend in the image of claret. Meerlust estate probably have the most extensive plantings of Merlot for their promising Rubicon cultivar cocktail.

In Australia Merlot has great potential; many Australian Cabernets already taste as though they have been softened by Merlot, when the softening agent has been sunshine. Because of its tendency to ripen early, Merlot needs a relatively cool microclimate such as can easily be found in that great "claret" district Coonawarra in South Australia or, preferably, an even cooler location. For some time Reynella and Mildara have each produced a good Cabernet/Merlot blend, and Cullens of Western Australia have established a reputation for treating the variety with the respect it deserves. Plantings of Merlot are still very limited in Australia and, with the Australian tradition of using Shiraz instead of Merlot to soften and fill Cabernet flavours, it may be that the variety's Australian potential may never be fully realized.

New Zealanders are perhaps slightly more aware of the possibilities of Bordeaux's other grape. With its coolish climate, New Zealand may offer just the right conditions

for the grape to ripen sufficiently late to have concentrated flavours. The only problem may be Merlot's literally perennial difficulty, in cooler latitudes anyway, of uncertain flowering. Plantings are steadily increasing and the San Marino Kumeu river version has shown promise. As with all New Zealand red varietals, the problem seems to be filling the flavour gap in the middle of the mouthful, but Merlot should stand a better chance than most.

In a similarly cool climate in the northern hemisphere, where the wine industry is also in a nascent state, Oregonians have all but given up on Merlot. They have lost just too many potential grapes to uncharitable weather at flowering. They have tried it, despite Pinot Noir's more obvious success, because just to the north of Oregon, in Washington State, is one of Merlot's great footholds. (This is yet another example of how we are as wrong to bundle Oregon and Washington together as we are to consider Spain and Portugal vinous relatives.)

Chateau Ste Michelle, the Gallo of Washington State, has particularly extensive plantings of Merlot, but many other wineries produce varietal wines and Cabernet blends which show how successfully the vine can perform in the unusual climate here. The Columbia Basin, with its warm days and cool nights, is ideal for Merlot; each evening provides a break for its impetuous ripening process, and risks of poor flowering are much less than in Oregon. The wines have considerable substance, are relatively early maturing (although this may be simply because no one has experimented much with longer maceration) and provide the cosmopolitan wine drinker with a reasonably priced, "serious" red wine in quantity, which is not Cabernet.

California has embraced the varietal much less rapturously. Plantings total hardly 800 hectares (2,000 acres). Furthermore, it is doubtful whether even half of these are genuine Merlot. Christian Moueix of Château Pétrus, who would doubtless shudder to be given his trite but due title of King of Merlot, was intrigued to find, when researching possibilities for his own California wine Dominus, that much of what the Californians call Merlot is in fact Cabernet Franc – and in some cases vice versa.

The new Newton winery was established on Spring Mountain with cuttings from Moueix himself, and it turned out some impressively formidable wines of great Pomerol-like concentration when Ric Forman was making wine there. This particular combination was a reflection of Forman's early and unusual successes with the varietal at Sterling, a tradition that the new owners, Seagram, are doing their best to continue.

Duckhorn is another name which has proved that, when California attacks the Merlot question, it does so with Pomerol gusto rather than with basic St-Emilion vapidity. This diminutive winery, plumb centre in the Napa Valley, has firmly put its eggs in the Merlot basket with great success. Down in the Santa Barbara hinterland, Firestone have shown just what happens if the varietal is taken to its logical conclusion and made as full-blown and almost as sweet as can be. Perhaps sadly, for the strongly constituted anyway, they too have allowed the vogue for earlier picking to slim down this Rubens of a wine.

California Merlot can be very good: much denser than most other attempts with the variety outside Bordeaux. Provided the vines are planted somewhere sufficiently slow-ripening, and acid levels are kept well up, Merlot can be shaped into a really exciting varietal. Even more significantly for the long term, it can provide great blending material for California Cabernet – as demonstrated in various bottles of Mondavi-Rothschild Opus One or Joseph Phelps Insignia.

Synonyms: Merlau, Vitraille, Crabutet, Bigney, Sémillon Rouge (France); Médoc Noir (Hungary).	*Susceptibility:* Resistant to oidium, but prone to grey rot and downy mildew.
Soils: Can withstand damp, clayey soils much better than Cabernet.	*Rootstocks:* Low to moderate vigour. 420 A, SO4, Gloire de Riparia and 5BB are all used.
Vigour: Moderate.	*Yields:* Moderate to high. 70–80 hl/ha in SW France without difficulty.
Pruning: Medium to long canes.	

Potentially top quality. Very isolated modishness.

Riesling

Nothing testifies more eloquently to France's extraordinary chauvinism and self-confidence as a wine producer than her total disdain (outside her almost accidental Germanic enclave of Alsace) for the great grape of Germany. Riesling is so clearly one of the world's great vines, arguably that which produces the finest white wines of all. Yet, because it is the only one in this top rank that is not firmly and principally established in France, it is not allowed to be grown more than 50 kilometres (30 miles) from the German border.

Chardonnay is probably better suited to France than Riesling. Undoubtedly there are more ideal sites for the latter in Germany than in France. But the exciting Rieslings produced in widely varying climates and soils all over the world demonstrate that the vine could thrive and even dazzle in all kinds of French vineyards too. It is fascinating to ponder on the results of allowing Riesling a rather firmer foothold on French soil than the odd experimental plot at the Salins du Midi (for which special dispensation had to be sought). What a sad legacy of war and its resulting prejudices that the owner of Château Doisy-Daëne has to dissemble to the appellation authorities (although not to visiting connoisseurs) about his few rows of excellent Riesling in Barsac.

The Riesling is a wonder of a vine. Although it reflects the different soils and microclimates in which it is grown better than any other Germanic vine yet, like the Cabernet Sauvignon, it preserves its identity wherever it is grown. The Germans maintain that it loses its character completely south of the Bodensee; and it is true that when asked to set down roots in a very warm climate, it can put on too much weight to retain its allure. In the cooler, damper vineyards of New Zealand it can take on a rather grassy character. But in any decently made example of Riesling wine there is the same vibrancy, a nerviness, a much more piercing quality than is found in any "French" varietals, other than Sauvignon Blanc perhaps. So convinced was the Alsace viticultural chronicler M. J. L. Stoltz of an historical connection between the two varieties that he devoted an entire section of his 1852 *Ampélographie Rhénane* to exploring this hypothesis. Many human noses find some examples of Riesling and Sauvignon quite difficult to distinguish, both being tart and strongly aromatic, yet on the palate the former has a more complex, long-lasting impact. However sweet, and sometimes Riesling can be very sweet, there is a suggestion of flowers, honey, and perhaps spice. There should also be a length of flavour which is distinctly unusual in Sauvignon wines. And Riesling, unlike Sauvignon Blanc, has enormous ageing potential.

More than any other great grape, Riesling has suffered from prostitution of its name. The word "Riesling" has been filched for incorporation into the names of all sorts of vine, many of them mediocre. California has its Rieslings Gray and Emerald; South Africa its Cape and Paarl; Australia takes the noble name in vain to describe almost any white wine, even some of its Hunter Valley Sémillon.

The insult felt most keenly in Germany is that the widely planted, really rather ordinary and quite unrelated Welschriesling, or Italian Riesling, sullies the name of their own noble vine. They have lobbied tenaciously in Brussels to change European practice, so that this less noble vine may be known by more identifiably non-Teutonic names such as Laski and Italianski Rizling.

Even the Germans themselves are guilty of applying the magic eight-letter word too freely. Grauer Riesling and Schwarzriesling are common synonyms for Ruländer and Müllerrebe respectively, just two of many instances.

Although within Germany the varietal is simply called Riesling, the ampelographer Moog suggests that Weisser Riesling, or White Riesling, is the correct name, and there has been a trend towards these names in South Africa and California. Another common German synonym, Johannisberg Riesling (colloquially "J.R."), is still popular with Californians, although it is a mystery why they chose this one of Riesling's many geographical German synonyms. These usually developed simply because a particular place, be it Johannisberg, Hochheim or Baden's Durbach Klingelberg, was the first to be recognized for outstanding Riesling. More general but still geographical is the synonym Rheinriesling, or Rhine Riesling, which is favoured by Australians (and therefore New Zealanders). The attractively alliterative ring clearly appeals to central Europeans, too, with their Riesling Renano, Rajinski Rizling and the like – although Rheinriesling, Moselriesling and Riesling are all identical.

As one might expect, Riesling's origins, if obscure, are unquestionably German. Most authorities agree it is a descendant of a Rhineland wild vine, probably *Vitis vinifera silvestris*. The eminent historian Bassermann-Jordan can even find similarities between it and a vine described by Pliny in the first century AD. Others have the ninth-century King Louis uprooting Trollinger and Orleaner along the Rhine in favour of Riesling. Certainly its growth was recorded in 1435 in what is Germany today, at Rüsselsheim outside Frankfurt, and Hieronymus Bock notes its cultivation on the Rhine, Mosel and around Worms in 1551. The first records of Riesling monoculture, the ultimate compliment, date from 1716 at Schloss Johannisberg in the Rheingau.

The theories about how Riesling got its name are more revealing about the vine's characteristics than anything else. "Rus" means dark wood, and the Riesling is notable for its strong dark wood. The word's root may have been "Rissig" for the bark's deep grooves; "reissen" for its racy acidity; or "verrieseln" for *coulure*, or its poor flowering propensity in cool weather.

In Germany Riesling is so much the linchpin of the entire wine fabric that it is the model on which the myriad new and newish crossings are based. Almost all of them have at least some Riesling genes because, although late ripening and therefore a perennial tease, Riesling is so obviously the variety best suited to the German climate. The oldest of them all, the centenarian Müller-Thurgau, was evolved to provide Riesling characteristics in a more reliable, if dilute, form. This has proved so successful that it has overtaken total plantings of Riesling by a considerable margin. Its popularity undoubtedly owes more to expediency than quality, and purists, both in Germany and outside, are always delighted by a vintage such as 1979 which demonstrates the superiority of Riesling.

Müller-Thurgau may ripen earlier and therefore be less susceptible to autumn chill and humidity, but Riesling's wood is so strong that it can survive at much lower temperatures than Müller-Thurgau. On New Year's Day 1979, the temperature dropped suddenly, by as much as 30°C in some places, to minus 20°C. The eyes, potential provenance of that year's crop, of "soft" varieties such as Müller-Thurgau were devastated, while most Riesling vines were quite unaffected. In the Bereich Schloss Böckelheim, for instance, the 1979 Müller-Thurgau crop was 80 percent lower than in 1978, whereas the Riesling harvest was 75 percent higher. Bravo for the linchpin.

Although more than 40 successful Riesling crosses have been developed in the last hundred years, Riesling is unique among Germanic grape varieties in its ability to ripen to lusciously high Oechsle levels, without allowing acidity to slip dangerously low. Acidity averages 10–15 grams per litre, whether the ripeness is in the usual 60–80° Oechsle range, or heading over 200° for some exceptional Trockenbeerenauslesen. A crossing such as Scheurebe (Silvaner × Riesling) or the even more popular Kerner (Trollinger × Riesling) can notch up impressive ratings on the refractometer, too, but usually at the expense of the *rassig* (racy) character that gives Riesling its bite. Riesling grapes manage to retain their acidity through the long growing cycle right up to their traditionally late harvest.

Some of the most respected crossings have emerged from Geisenheim under the aegis of Dr Helmut Becker, who has been heard to claim (although not in Germany) that some of his new "crossings of crossings" are even more promising than Riesling. He instances Arnsberger × Reichensteiner, and he also has high hopes of Rotberger × Reichensteiner.

Perhaps because of a new recognition in Germany of Riesling's star quality, the decline in total area planted with the vine, which was evident in the early eighties, has been halted. There were nearly 19,000 hectares (47,500 acres) of Riesling vines in Germany in 1983, in very definite second place to Müller-Thurgau's 25,500 hectares (63,750 acres) but a long way ahead of any other variety. (Interestingly, even Germany's 19,000 hectares are not enough to make it the number one grower of Riesling. It is claimed that the Riesling planted extensively in the Soviet Union – 25,000 hectares (62,500 acres) in the Ukraine alone – is the noble white sort.)

Examined internationally, from a metaphorical satellite with a well-stocked cellar perhaps, Riesling is a puzzle. The Germans know the Riesling as a late budder, a late ripener and generous yielder. In the California climate, leafing is relatively early, ripening mid-season, and yields only average. In South Africa it is known as a shy bearer and early ripener, not just in isolation (one would expect any vine to ripen earlier in a warm climate than a cool one) but relative to other European grape varieties.

The easiest to explain of these apparent contradictions is that concerning yield. Perhaps the single most impressive long-term viticultural research programme the world has ever seen is Germany's dogged search for high-yielding clones of Riesling. Since the work of Georg Fröhlich in the 1870s, possibly stimulated in part by the Riesling's sensitivity to flowering in cool weather, successive generations of researchers have made increasingly rigorous selection of cuttings so that today nearly 50 Riesling clones are officially listed by the Bundessortenamt. Some of them are designed to leaf and flower earlier, many to escape *coulure*, some to drop fruit less, some to be more resistant to chlorosis, many to respond particularly well to the individual soils and climates of Germany's different wine regions, most to give a notably high yield, and all to maintain high must weights. Since the 1930s the average Riesling yield in Germany has increased fourfold, without any drop in average must weight, and without any discernible loss in quality. So much for the French maxim, which conveniently ignores the great control factor of foliage restriction, that quality and quantity can never commingle. Average German yields from Riesling today are between 70 and 110 hectolitres per hectare, about double what would be expected of good quality wine in France. It is significant that Appellation Contrôlée law allows Alsace winemakers higher yields than anywhere else in France – up to 100 hectolitres per hectare in some cases. The same high-yielding clones have clearly found their way across the Rhine. Why not outside Europe?

South Africa's markedly low Riesling yields are presumably a function of their vine virus problems and general ill-health in the vineyard. This may also be an explanation, at least in part, for Australian yields of only about two to five tons per acre. It is also possible in the warmer climates of California and Australia, where the vines show markedly less vigour than in northern Europe, that higher density plantings or careful trellising may improve yields.

This difference in yield is probably one of the more dramatic illustrations of the rude state of health of German vineyards. The Germans are dismissive of Riesling planted in warmer climates precisely because of its tendency to degenerate. But Australia and California are daily becoming more health conscious, viticulturally. Perhaps soon they will demonstrate quantity as well as quality in their already estimable Riesling production.

The disparity in relative leafing dates may partly be explained by the particular Riesling clones prevalent in "New World" vineyards, and, perhaps, because their Riesling microclimates are so much warmer than the

RIESLING

Leaf
length: 120mm (4½in)   width: 76mm (3in)

Grape Cluster
length: 152mm (6in)   width: 63.5mm (2½in)

*P*art of Riesling's thrall is its extraordinary versatility. It can thrive and produce soaringly beautiful wines as far north as here at Ockfen on the Saar, close to the Luxembourg border, as well as giving us the apricot-rich yet tangy Late-Harvest Johannisberg Rieslings of Santa Barbara in California, a good 15° closer to the equator. Only its late ripening precludes it from growing further north than the Saar.

German models. This particular disparity is even more puzzling than that concerning ripening dates.

The reason the Californians describe Riesling as early ripening, while the Germans consider it late ripening, is doubtless simply a question of philosophy. Riesling was traditionally grown in California to make dry, hence early picked, wine. Very few of the sites on which it was initially cultivated were cool enough to suggest that a long growing season would result in a well-balanced richer wine. This is changing slowly, as some of the finer California Late-Harvest Rieslings show.

Australian wine producers have also been seeking out cooler spots for the production of fine, elegant, sweeter Rieslings with notable success. While being responsible for one style of Riesling – dry and sappy – which is both highly successful and indisputably their own, the Australians have probably come closest to making another with the same sort of finesse and quality as a top German Riesling.

Because they are at the northern limit of vine cultivation, the Germans have to be very careful about where they plant Riesling. In their literature this is often couched in terms which suggest that the vine itself is particularly fastidious – that it will simply refuse to grow on sites which are less than ideal – but of course the reasons for choosing to plant a vine other than Riesling are often commercial. The Riesling is planted on the steep and awkward slatey banks of the Mosel because no other variety grown there could fetch prices to justify the high cost of working such sites.

Because the Mosel is so far north, the grapes need every ray of sunshine available to ripen them. Therefore, the sluggish ripener Riesling takes top priority on the south-facing slopes. Manfred Prüm, one of Bernkastel's most respected growers, has not a single Müller-Thurgau vine on his property, and favours southwest-facing vineyards for their exposure to maximum heat and light (southeast slopes can too easily be shrouded in early morning mist).

Riesling will rarely ripen more than 200 metres above the river, and the best wines are usually made from those vines on the first 100 metres up the hillside because of their lower temperatures.

Elsewhere in Germany, and the world, altitude and latitude are in less critical conjunction and the Riesling can be cultivated on a much wider range of sites. It is also happy on a variety of soils. Mosel slate helps heat retention, but elsewhere in warmer microclimates the Riesling can thrive on anything from shallow topsoil on rock to deep loam or clay. The resulting wine is affected by soil type, but in character rather than quality.

The Riesling is a very hardy vine. That it produces wine at all as far north as the Mosel and Rheingau proves that. The fact that it produces such good wine there tends to distract us from the number of interesting wines it can produce in more hospitable settings. It has good resistance to disease as well as weather – indeed, compared with our other great provider of sweet wines, Sémillon, it is inconveniently resistant to botrytis.

In Bordeaux Sémillon produces at least some "serious" sweet white wine every year. In Germany, the autumn is sufficiently warm and dry for Riesling to ripen to richness only about once every four years; and *Botrytis cinerea* or *Edelfäule*, the rot which nobly concentrates the flavour of sweet white wines, is even rarer in German vineyards. Riesling is much less susceptible to this fungus than many of the crossings that have been developed from it. Optima has been bred specifically to bow to botrytis, but the wine produced, no matter how high in Oechsle, is always notably less aristocratic than its Riesling counterpart. Although it will never achieve the must weights which varieties like Siegerrebe find so effortless, the Riesling has such good natural acid that it provides balance and ballast for a long life even in a comparatively ripe example.

The Riesling also shines at lower must weights, as the New Zealanders have found to their (and our) delight. Even with Oechsle readings in New Zealand as low as 50° (when acidity will often be so high in Germany that many wines have to be chemically deacidified), grapes can be transformed into a wine of delicacy and real character. The German Wine Law recognizes this, in setting lower Oechsle requirements for Rieslings than for wines made from other varieties. In the Mosel, for instance, a reading of 70° Oechsle on the refractometer is sufficient to qualify Riesling grapes as potential Kabinett material, whereas 73° is required of any other grape variety, and the gap widens, with levels of 83° and 88° respectively, for Auslesen.

All Germany's greatest wines are made from Riesling. This statement is guaranteed to rankle with Franconians, who are justly proud of their Silvaners, and with the many fans in Germany of her rosy Spätburgunders, but no impartial connoisseur would disagree.

Most expensive of these treasures are the super-ripe Beerenauslesen and Trockenbeerenauslesen. More fruit liquors than wines, they have prices which reflect their rarity, and the risks involved in making them. The grower who has succeeded in ripening his grapes to Auslese level has to gamble every day on the weather if he has higher aspirations. The Riesling is always the last variety to be picked, and is rarely harvested before mid-October, whatever the ripeness. Extensions of this phenomenon are the famous St-Nikolaus wine (harvested on 6 December), Christwein (24 December) and even Dreikönigswein (6 January of the year after the vintage).

These very late-picked Rieslings have enviable ageing ability because of their high acid levels and over the years deepen in colour as dramatically as their Sauternes counterparts. They, too, eventually dry out, but in their first two decades at least develop the most inspirational layers of flavour of any mature varietal. The freshness is always there and, unlike Sauternes, they are both high in acid and low in alcohol. Some only just reach the minimum legal alcoholic level, 5.5 percent, to qualify as wine.

The Rieslings probably most treasured by non-German connoisseurs are the slightly less precious Spätlesen, Auslesen and the finest Kabinetts, all of them capable of maturing into deep green-gold with a curious whiff of petrol or kerosene. Each region, each vineyard even, prints its own stamp on the Riesling pattern. There are the earthily straightforward country Rieslings of Württemberg; the heavily scented plumper versions from the best sites of the Mittelhaardt in Rheinpfalz; the crackling beauties of the Nahe; the sleek honeys of the Rheingau; the rather intellectual types from the Middle Mosel; and the lissom aristocrats of the Saar and Ruwer in the Upper Mosel. Beauties every one, whenever nature is sufficiently cooperative and man has the nous to take advantage of it. Sometimes he does not, and there are many examples of German Riesling, especially Mosel Riesling, which display few of the alluring characteristics of the varietal.

Outside Germany the debate continues over whether the Germans' current predilection for Trocken, or dry, Riesling is purist wisdom or modish folly. The nub of the matter, how much alcohol and body are needed to give a dry Riesling interest, is well illustrated in many of the Riesling's resting places outside Germany.

The enigmatic Soviet Union apart, the wine region with the most extensive plantings of Riesling outside Germany is California, where total plantings are about 4,400 hectares (11,000 acres). This makes the varietal about as important as Sauvignon Blanc, although nowhere near as fashionable. New plantings of Sauvignon Blanc were more than twice those of Riesling in 1983.

Until the seventies, Riesling (usually called Johannisberg Riesling) was invariably picked early and fermented out as a dry wine. The last 10 years or so have seen later-picked Rieslings emerge as one of California's most promising wine styles. That the wines obviously have much more flesh than their European models helps to establish them as something uniquely Californian in a more convincing way, for example, than the state's Cabernets and Chardonnays. This is reinforced by the ironic fact that probably more Riesling is treated to "traditional" oak ageing, albeit for a short time in most cases, in ultra-modern California than in the whole of Germany.

As an off-dry and even late-picked wine, California Riesling usually retains the relatively high acid but manages alcohol levels a good two degrees higher than in Germany, and much more extract. In examples where this has been kept in check, there is a luscious fruitiness suggestive of apricots or peaches that evades any German wine, although hinted at by a few of the riper Pfalz vintages. These West Coast examples have yet to show how they age, and one would expect their "cellar potential", as the neat – and surely California – phrase has it, to be considerably less than the great German wines.

We will not have to wait too long, for wineries such as Chateau St Jean and Joseph Phelps have been making top quality Late-Harvest Rieslings for well over a decade, usually blessed and concentrated by *Botrytis cinerea*. The misty moist Russian River area in northern Sonoma and the Bay-cooled southern end of the Napa Valley each provide with ease the perfect botrytis conditions of early morning humidity followed by sunshine which are so elusive in Germany. Felton-Empire Vineyards of Santa Cruz have also had great success with very rich Rieslings, and there are signs that great Riesling sites are being identified way south of San Francisco. In an area as cool as parts of Monterey, growers can keep Riesling on the vine

until well into November without risking any dangerous loss of acid.

The variety is planted throughout those California districts designated Region I and Region II where it can produce wines of real interest with residual sugars from zero to about 20 percent by weight. Grapes may be picked as early as mid-August, at well under 20° Brix for a specifically light early-harvest wine (whose closest German relative is probably a Spätlese Trocken from the Rheingau). The great majority of California Riesling grapes, however, are picked at Brix readings in the low to mid twenties to make medium-dry wines, many of them with great succulence and character.

As one might expect, Riesling has had considerable success on the West Coast north of California, notably in Oregon where the vibrancy of the wines produced on its 360 hectares (900 acres) make it, together with Chardonnay and Pinot Noir, one of the state's "big three" varieties, qualitatively as well as quantitatively.

Tualatin were perhaps the first to make a Riesling impression outside the state, but the dedicated are discovering the exciting later picked, and sometimes botrytised, Rieslings of Hillcrest. If California Rieslings are the West Coast's answer to hock, then these Oregon examples do the job for Mosel. In the Willamette Valley Riesling comes into its own with an ability to offer sufficient flavours for an interesting wine, even when technically underripe. The relatively high humidity of this region makes later harvesting risky, and therefore expensive. The world's wine drinkers must hope that Oregonians will persevere with the varietal, and must be prepared to pay the price for them.

Washington State's rather less gentle climate can also turn out some appetizing Rieslings. Chateau Ste-Michelle and Hinzerling have both had success with botrytised late-harvest versions. The German-owned Langguth winery is also expected to demonstrate that Riesling grown in the Columbia Basin can display the great floral aromas which characterize good German Riesling.

Riesling is also cultivated fairly successfully in Ontario, in New York State on Long Island (Bridgehampton) and at a number of Finger Lakes wineries, notably Heron Hill, Wagner and Dr Frank's defiantly named Vinifera Wine Cellars. There is a struggle here for flavour in some years, but without question this is a Riesling area to watch.

Slightly less in acreage than America's Riesling vineyards are the Australian plantings, usually called Rhine Riesling to distinguish them from many other "Rieslings". Riesling plays a much more important part in the Australian wine business than in California; with nearly 5,000 hectares (12,500 acres) it is Australia's most widely planted good quality white grape variety by far, beaten in size only by the 18,000 hectares (45,000 acres) of wine-producing Sultana still grown in Australia's irrigated areas.

The great majority of this Riesling is grown in South Australia, largely developed by the famous Silesian settlers in the Barossa Valley. The Rhine Rieslings made here define the Australian way with the grape: dry to off-dry but definitely fruity; relatively tart but often enhanced by slight

The nose is all with Riesling, one of the world's most gloriously aromatic grape varieties. The summery balance of fruits, flowers and honey so characteristic of a good Rheingau is savoured by Freiherr zu Knyphausen.

spritz; low on floral aroma but with a tangy citric, almost limey flavour. Such wines, made by the bucketful in the medium-climate areas of South Australia and sold under names such as Kaiser Stuhl, Hoffmanns, Henschke and even Bernkastel, form the backbone of the Australians' enthusiasm for white-wine drinking. The style, admirably suited to our times, is uniquely Australian and, some think, could become one of her most successful liquid exports.

Winemakers who have been impressed by Riesling's performance in the Barossa (which has an almost identical climate in terms of "degree days" as St Helena in the Napa Valley) have been tempted to see how the varietal would react in cooler areas. The results of this experimentation can now be tasted in some stunning Rieslings from the high altitude vineyards of the Eden Valley–Springton district, 240 metres above the Barossa Valley floor. The yield may be as little as two to three tons per acre in this non-irrigated area (as opposed to four or five in irrigated Clare vineyards), but the quality of such wines as those from Pewsey Vale vindicate the move uphill admirably. In these Rieslings there is the nervy elegance for which Germany's best are revered.

Leo Buring and Gramp's Orlando have the longest track record for great Rieslings, and older vintages from each show just how spectacularly the Riesling can age here. Ageing is still slightly faster than in northern Europe, but the same deep gamboge tints and oily kerosene flavours develop. These are great wines by any standards.

Rhine Riesling is now being cultivated all over Australia's vineland and has shown great delicacy and vivacity, particularly in the cooler areas of Western Australia. The varietal's greatest enemy in Australia, even greater than in most other parts of the world, is Chardonnay. Riesling is engaged in a constant struggle against what is fashionably dry, even if unfashionably alcoholic.

New Zealand is also producing some interesting Rhine Riesling, although it is less common than Chardonnay, accounting for only two percent of the total harvest. Winemakers are currently somewhat dazzled by the twin possibilities of the floral German and much weightier Australian styles, but they are lucky that both styles may be possible in time. Their Rieslings made from grapes grown in the long dry autumns of the Marlborough area at the north of the South Island look most promising, combining the delicacy found in Germany and the vibrancy of Australia's cooler-climate Rieslings. This southern area is probably New Zealand's most promising for botrytis. Alcohol content can vary between 9 and 13 percent and there is also wide disparity in residual sugar levels, although it is generally agreed that the varietal works best with at least some sweetness.

Riesling has fared much less successfully in South Africa where even the combined weight of all their Geisenheim-trained technicians has failed to solve the main problem: planting healthy vines in sufficiently cool sites. The varietal, or cultivar, is called Weisser Riesling here to distinguish it from the Paarl, Cape or South African Riesling, to which it is completely unrelated. It has been

used to greatest effect so far as an ingredient in Günter Brözel's luscious Nederburg Edelkeur, but many think there is great potential for the grape in dry and medium-dry wines. Doubtless when the twin problems of clone and climate are solved, we shall see some less vapid examples of Riesling from South Africa. At the moment, it provides the Germans with their most convincing evidence of Riesling's unsuitability for non-German territory.

Even the Germans find it hard to argue that Alsace is unsuitable for Riesling, especially since the German border has in its time been moved west to encompass it. What remains is a strong ideological difference between German and Alsace winemakers. Alsace Rieslings may share the heavenly perfume of their counterparts outre-Rhin (as evinced by the synonym Gentil-Aromatique), but on the palate they are full and dry whereas German Riesling is usually light and sweet. The Vosges-sheltered climate of Alsace is particularly warm and dry, but its winemakers ferment out all that extra ripeness into alcohol. Alsace Riesling has a steeliness that makes it quite impossible to confuse it with a German wine, even one designated Trocken. Everything about Alsace winemaking is determinedly different from the German way with the grape, and this has the inevitable effect on flavour and style. Wines

South Africa's Twee Jongegezellen Estate produces probably the finest Riesling on the Cape – as opposed to the distinctly inferior Cape Riesling, or Crouchen. They have planted the top clone and introduced night picking in 1982.

*T*he steely, scented Rieslings of Alsace hint at what else France might do with the great grape variety were she to allow it greater infiltration. Here at Ammerschwihr's world-class restaurant Aux Armes de France is ably demonstrated daily that Riesling is quite at home at the dining table.

are not usually released from Alsace until at least 18 months after the vintage, whereas many German wines are sold when only a few weeks old. Even the most basic Alsace Rieslings can age well, and the best can last for a decade or two. These are wines that, unlike German wines, seem made for the dining table.

Riesling is the uncontested queen of Alsace, although there is more Gewürztraminer planted. Gewürztraminer may be the blowsy village wench who catches the attention of the tourists, but Riesling is the aristocrat to which the region's winemakers remain faithful. Plantings of Riesling in the twin Alsace *départements* of Bas-Rhin and Haut-Rhin more than doubled in the seventies, and now total well over 2,000 hectares (5,000 acres). The greatest increase has come in the flatter vineyards of the Bas-Rhin where it has sensibly replaced much Silvaner, but the majority of Riesling vines are still planted in the Haut-Rhin where all the best sites are to be found. The great majority of the vineyards designated Grands Crus are planted with, and most suitable for, Riesling. On particularly rich soils, Gewürztraminer is allowed to wallow, but Riesling shows its thoroughbred best on the less fertile soils of such top vineyards as Clos Ste-Hune, Schoenenberg and Schlossberg.

In especially good years, some sweet late-harvest wines are made, called either Vendange Tardive or, even richer and botrytised, Sélection de Grains Nobles. These are much fuller-bodied than their German counterparts, can even be drunk with savoury food and are rarer (though perhaps less fine) than Germany's great sweet wines.

Much more like Alsace Riesling than German Rieslings are those of the Italian Tyrol or Alto Adige in northeast Italy. In these high sunny sub-Alpine valleys the grapes ripen well but keep their acid levels appetizingly high, making wines a bit like New Zealand Rieslings without the maritime influence. As in New Zealand, a little natural carbon dioxide is often retained in the wine and there is usually notably more extract than in the average German wine, especially in those Rieslings made close to the valley floor. Those from steeper and higher vineyards have in general the most pronounced acid and aroma, thereby providing a neat lesson in microcosm of the effect of site and climate on the variety. Minimum must weight is 80° Oechsle, about the same as for a Spätlese in Germany, while the maximum yield, 84 hectolitres per hectare, is much lower. In recognition of the fact that the Alto Adige is seen as the Italian home of the variety, EEC law permits the use of the name Rheinriesling solely for this region.

In Friuli-Venezia Giulia it is known as Riesling Renano to distinguish it from the infinitely inferior, yet more widely planted, Riesling Italico. Poorly made, the wines lack the exciting zip and aroma of those of Trentino-Alto Adige. The better-made examples inspire one to hope that Italian growers might replace one of their seas of Pinot Grigio with this exciting grape variety.

In the far north Riesling's domination of the upper Mosel spills over the border into Luxembourg where it constitutes 10 percent of vines planted, a flavoursome relief from the eye-watering Elbling and Rivaner. Here the

Riesling characteristics are reduced to skeletal form, but can also be classically beautiful. Some Riesling is also known, as Petracine, in the extremely light wines of the upper Moselle in France.

It is planted throughout central and eastern Europe though very little, curiously, in Switzerland where they presumably tire of waiting for it to ripen. In non-EEC Austria, which calls the Riesling Rheinriesling, the variety represents only about 2 percent of all plantings and does not generally respond so well to the warmer climate and fatter style of wine as do most other Germanic grapes.

Some attractive Rieslings are said to be made over the Czech border, the wines of Bohemia resembling those of the Palatinate, whose climate is similar. In the Soviet Union, Riesling is usually used as a base for sparkling wines, or blended into dessert wines with lower acid components.

Many of the vineyards in southeastern Europe are too warm for top quality Riesling, but there are some delicate examples from Slovenia up in the Lutomer hills and some rather less delicate ones from Slavonia to the east. This is the fief of the other, less noble, sort of Riesling. A small amount is planted in the Somló region of Hungary and, perhaps more successfully, 1,500 hectares (3,750 acres) in Bulgaria. In Romania the Italian Riesling reigns supreme, but Japan claims some true Riesling.

The vine is rarely encountered in either Spain or Portugal. Miguel Torres has some Riesling planted in the high Penedés, and some boosts Palomino in Arcos de la Frontera's Tierra Blanca in Andalucia.

In Portugal the Riesling has been cited in paternity cases for both Arinto and the Sercial of Madeira. Neither theory withstands ampelographical scrutiny, but their supposed historical backgrounds, involving Teutonic crusaders and Queen Victoria respectively, are great fun.

Synonyms:
Weisser Riesling, Rössling, Riesler, Rieslinger,
Rheinriesling, Moselriesling, Rheingauer,
Johannisberger, Hochheimer, Niederländer,
Klingelberger, Gräfenberger, Kastellberger,
Karbacher Riesling, Kleinriesling, Kleinriesler,
Weisser Kleiner Riesling, Gewürztraube,
Pfefferl (Germany);
Riesling Blanc, Petit Riesling,
Gentil(e)-Aromatique, Petracine (France);
Riesling Renano, Reno (Italy);
Petit Rhin, Johannisberger (Switzerland);
Rheinriesling, Weisser Riesling (Austria);
Rezlink, Starosvetske,
Reszlink Rynsky (Czechoslovakia);
Rajinski Rizling, Gras(ch)evina,
Rizling Rajinski Bijeli (Yugoslavia);
Rajnai Rizling (Hungary);
Riesling de Rhin, Rheinriesling, Reynai (Romania);
Rizling (Bulgaria); Risling, Rislig Rejnski (USSR);
Weisser Riesling (South Africa);
Johannisberg Riesling (J.R.), White Riesling (USA);
Rhine Riesling (Australia and New Zealand).

Vigour:
In Germany, relatively vigorous,
though in warmer climates less so.

Pruning:
Wide variety. Upright training on tall stakes
on hillsides as in Mosel or Alsace where
the *palissage* method of maximum foliage exposure
is also used. More standard trellising is
common elsewhere in Germany and abroad.
Clusters are small, so head training and
cane pruning are generally advised.

Susceptibility:
Very hardy vine with exceptional resistance
to low temperatures.

Rootstocks:
Dependent on soil fertility.
Coulure can be a problem with vigorous rootstocks
on fertile soils. 3309 is good on fertile soils,
5BB on very shallow, dry soils
and SO4, 125AA or 5C otherwise.

Soils:
Planted on and well adapted to a wide variety
but slate is classic,
sandy loams also traditional,
and well-drained poor fertility
generally agreed preferable.

Yields:
Variable, but potentially very high,
as the Germans have shown. Yields of over 100 hl/ha
are not uncommon in Germany, while in Australia
and California yields are between
two and six tons per acre, averaging around five.

Unbeatable quality; indisputably aristocratic. Ludicrously unfashionable.

Chardonnay

In Chardonnay is one of the happiest of all combinations: the grower loves to grow it; the winemaker loves to fashion it; and we all love to drink it. The result of this felicitous *cuvée* is that Chardonnay is, without question, the single most sought after varietal in the world today. This applies at each of the three levels. Viticulturists in all corners of the globe, and particularly in Australia and South Africa, are clamouring for cuttings to plant. So great is the demand from winemakers for Chardonnay grapes that in all lively markets, such as those on the West Coast, Chardonnay consistently fetches higher prices than any other varietal. Consumers are so enamoured of wines made from Chardonnay that examples as varied as Pouilly-Fuissé, Montrachet, Chardonnay di Miralduolo and varietals made by the likes of Stony Hill, Chalone, Acacia, Matanzas Creek, Petaluma and Leeuwin have to be allocated rather than sold.

First things first. Chardonnay is delightfully easy to grow. "The most forgiving variety of all" is how it is described by Australia's famous wine guru, Brian Croser, who trained in California and worked in France. Our expectations may have been fashioned by the styles of wine produced in its "homeland" of Burgundy, but it is quite happy to set down roots in a wide range of much warmer (and some cooler) climates all over the world.

Its major disadvantage is early budding, which makes it prone to spring frost damage. This can make the lives of Chablis vignerons a misery for days, or rather nights, at a time. Anti-frost measures are being refined constantly, notably in California where Chardonnay worship probably reaches its peak. In any case, the variety makes up for this by ripening early, just after Pinot Noir, and therefore usually before autumn rains can initiate rot. This makes it perfectly practicable in climates with only a short growing season, unlike that other great white grape variety, Riesling. It has good resistance to cold weather, which makes it yet more suitable for wine regions with harsh winters, such as Champagne and England.

The Chardonnay is a naturally vigorous vine and can easily dissipate the available energy and nutrients into foliage instead of grape-ripening. This can be combated, as in Champagne, by dense planting – up to 7,500 plants per hectare (3,000 per acre) – or by fierce pruning to restrict leaf growth as in areas of California and much of Australia where there may be as few as 1,000 plants per hectare (400 per acre). It seems likely that Chardonnay could be persuaded to ripen properly, and in sufficient quantity, as far north as southern England by a combination of dense planting and rigorous pruning.

A major boon for growers is that Chardonnay consistently produces relatively high sugars (and therefore alcohol) and yields quite generously and, most important, very consistently: 50 hectolitres per hectare with ease in Burgundy and 2.5 to 5 tons per acre in California. These West Coast yields are achieved without the benefit in most cases of strict pruning; and authorities admit that yield varies enormously with clone, soil fertility and vine health. In California, South Africa, Italy and Australia there are doubts whether the Chardonnay clones (which are either the only ones available or the only ones promulgated) are absolutely right. There are also virus problems, especially in South Africa, but also in California and Australia.

Chardonnay's popularity becomes more obvious when it is brought from vineyard to winery. It is difficult, although not impossible, to make a poor wine from it. The most common fault seems to be late picking. This is especially so with new plantings where the viticulturist may not be prepared for quite such quick and early ripening. It is also a problem in warmer climates where the picking time is critical. Acid levels fall so fast, and Chardonnay is so naturally high in extract, that flab can easily result. Provided this mistake is avoided, Chardonnay can be relied upon to produce a wide range of different, but decidedly high quality, styles of wine. The amount of extract compensates well for high acid in cooler climates and vintages, as witness Chablis and Champagne; and excellent ageing potential makes for many exciting bottlings in warmer climates, as with some of Australia's and California's best.

Chardonnay is probably the white grape whose wines have the greatest affinity with oak ageing. This, together with a naturally high level of pigmentation in the grape skins and the wide practice of skin contact, makes Chardonnay wines unusually easy to spot with the aid of the eye alone. Part of the winemaker's fascination with Chardonnay is its very malleability. It is unquestionably a very noble grape variety, but its wines are sturdy enough to withstand quite a bit of superimposed structure. (Robert Mondavi of California tested this to the limit in the seventies with his famous experiments on different oaks, chars and stavemaking techniques.) Chardonnay will happily respond to a variety of processes from super-centrifuged juice to week-long skin contact, from months of icebox fermentation to warm barrel fermentation, and from champenization to long oak maturation.

Partly because of this wide range of styles, it is difficult to pinpoint the flavour of Chardonnay, and its related appeal to wine drinkers. Chardonnay's varietal character is much more subdued than that of the Cabernets, Riesling and Sauvignon; in a high proportion of cases it is merely a very sound raw material ready to receive the stamp of soil, climate or winemaker. Chardonnay is not a strongly aromatic variety. Its impact on the nose is broad and muted rather than sharp and piercing. Some associate it with apples, barely ripe apples in Chablis. Others find melon flavours in Mâconnais Chardonnay, and more

CHARDONNAY

Leaf
length: 127mm (5in)   width: 127mm (5in)

Grape Cluster
length: 203mm (8in)   width: 120mm (4½in)

exotic fruits such as pineapple in Napa examples. To some blind tasters a certain smokiness is the Chardonnay giveaway. "Buttery" is a common tasting note for Meursault and other broader Chardonnays, "steely" for Montrachets and "nutty" for Corton-Charlemagne, but these often refer to texture and weight rather than flavour.

The reasons for Chardonnay's extraordinary international consumer appeal are more difficult to fathom than is its popularity with those who grow and make it. Its relatively high alcohol and extract put it out of line with today's supposed favour for the light and innocuous, though perhaps Chardonnay's appeal is to consumers more sophisticated than those at whom the likes of Liebfraumilch and "Lite" wine are so mercilessly aimed. The fact that in many cases it demands inconvenient and expensive ageing also militates against its popularity, yet it is the darling of every nascent connoisseur, as well as every sophisticated gastronome. Perhaps it is because Chardonnay's models, the great white burgundies, are so unquestionably aristocratic – the finest, subtlest, most complex dry white wines in existence – that their glamour rubs off on every little first-vintage Chardonnay from whatever corner of southern Europe or the "New World". Just as every winemaker who has tasted great claret wants to emulate it, every one whose palate is exposed to top quality white burgundy is inspired to find, or make, an equivalent of it.

Almost without geographical exception, wherever wine aspirations are high Chardonnay and Cabernet Sauvignon are cultivated in the hope of making the relevant regional variation on the white burgundy and claret themes. Australians have their very own rich and fruity, assertive though not necessarily alcoholic, style of Chardonnay. California on the other hand, where Chardonnay is arguably even more modish, has been going through an interesting identity crisis over the varietal. Throughout most of the seventies, the Brix levels became higher, the oak newer and more obvious, and some of the wines so big they were almost galumphing. Then came a single, seminal article by Frank Prial of the *New York Times* which questioned the desirability of a Chardonnay so massive that a second bottle was unthinkable. This defence of French subtlety merely crystallized something which had for some time been worrying many consumers and winemakers, and the subsequent vintages saw a distinct moderation in all aspects of the California Chardonnay style. Grapes were picked earlier, oak was used more sparingly. The curious phrase "food wine" evolved (Prial argued that the super-golden Chardonnays were too fat to sit comfortably at the dining table). Some curiously lean wines were released in the name of restraint. Critics and consumers objected to this filleting of their beloved Chardonnay, and the early eighties saw the California winemaker in search of a more suitable style. Today, it is relatively easy to mistake some top quality California Chardonnay for top quality white burgundy, especially if the influence of French oak is still detectable. It is much more difficult, curiously, to find the opulence of California in a white burgundy.

California has also been the last bastion of a common misconception about Chardonnay's origins. For years Pinot Chardonnay has been a common synonym for the varietal, resting upon the assumption that it belonged to the same basic Pinot family as the Pinots Noir and Blanc with which it is traditionally planted in northeastern France. There was quite good ampelographical evidence for this theory since the leaves of each plant have exactly the same shape, but arch-student Pierre Galet in his *Cépages et Vignobles de France* highlights three points of minute ampelographical detail which render the theory invalid.

The Chardonnay appears to be unrelated to any other major vine variety, although there is a pink version whose grapes blush when ripe, and an interesting Chardonnay Blanc Musqué which is currently under investigation. The general consensus among viticultural academics, such as Amerine and Olmo, is that all *Vitis vinifera* is descended from wild vines, white Muscat being the probable progenitor. It is also agreed that Chardonnay is a particularly ancient vine variety. Those who see some relationship between the fruit-salad flavours of Chardonnay and Muscat will be interested to know that the Chardonnay Blanc Musqué can be found in a nursery near the village of Chardonnay in the Mâconnais. Perhaps the clonal selection work currently under way on this subvariety will throw more light on Chardonnay's origins.

The Lebanese and Syrians claim original responsibility for nurturing the variety. There was certainly no shortage of through traffic in the Near and Middle East that could have transported the variety to Europe in a crusader's pannier. It is a relatively important white variety in the Lebanon today, called locally Meroué when cultivated in the valley, and Obaideh when mountain grown and producing wines more like Burgundian Chardonnays.

Today, Chardonnay has become so popular in France that between the two most recent agricultural censuses, in 1968 and 1979, it rose from eleventh to fourth most important white grape variety. Plantings now total more than 13,000 hectares (32,500 acres) – considerably less than France's 127,000 hectares (317,500 acres) of brandy-making Ugni Blanc admittedly, but nudging those of Sémillon and Grenache Blanc. Most of this increase has been in Champagne and Chablis country. It is in the champagne-producing *départements* of Marne and Aube that nearly half the French plantings are concentrated.

The Côte d'Or accounts for a relatively small area of Chardonnay, about 1,000 hectares (2,500 acres) as opposed to nearly 6,000 hectares (15,000 acres) of Pinot Noir and 600 hectares (1,500 acres) of Aligoté, but it has increased by about 20 percent in the last decade. Much more, over 3,000 hectares (7,500 acres), are planted in the Côte Chalonnaise and Mâconnais areas. This southern Burgundy total has hardly increased recently, in stark contrast to the 1,600 hectares (4,000 acres) of Chablis vineyards which covered less than 500 hectares (1,250 acres) at the end of the Second World War. It should be said, however, that the dramatic increase in Champagne and Chablis plantings is the result more of fashion and

Chateau St Jean winery in Sonoma County won early fame for its Chardonnays produced, unusually for California, from single, named vineyards – one of the first, brave attempts to link variety to geography here.

commerce than any intrinsic qualities in the Chardonnay grape itself, although it is a tribute to the vine's ability to withstand cold.

In Chablis, where the vine is known as Beaunois because initially it was associated with Beaune and the Côte d'Or, Chardonnay is encountered in perhaps its purest form. The vines are raised on the sort of calcareous soil which is supposed to underline the inherent qualities of any grape. They rarely run the risk of *surmaturité* (which sounds so much better than "overripeness"). Ambient temperatures are too low to allow any fermentation to run amok. Only a handful of producers use any oak at all today; and those who do will rapidly be in danger of being accused of making "atypical" Chablis. All these factors conspire together to produce unadorned Chardonnays of great simplicity and refinement. High acid is the keynote of any Chablis, with the better Premier Cru and longer-living Grand Cru wines exhibiting green-fruit flavours and an almost nostril-enlarging tartness. Chablis of any quality tends to be rather more aromatic than more southerly Chardonnay, while some young-vine examples can bear a disconcerting similarity to young Sauvignon.

It is much easier to confuse Chablis with a white Mâconnais Chardonnay than with one raised on the Côte d'Or. The "golden slope" may have only limited plantings of its most favoured white grape, but their liquid products vary enormously. Even at the most basic level, Bourgogne Blanc, Côte d'Or Chardonnay is able to produce everything from floweriness to a certain meatiness of flavour.

Higher up the quality scale oak is much more widely used, both for fermentation and ageing. The oak is rarely new, its provenance seldom an issue, and the geographical nuances of flavour allowed to sing out. In Corton-Charlemagne it takes on a nuttiness; in that rarity, Musigny Blanc, it can be almost honey rich; in Meursault brazenly buttery; and in the various Montrachets distinctly steely, with nuances of various fruits, many of them citric. With the various white wines of the Côte d'Or, it is arguable that the commune characteristics are much more distinct than in, for example, the red wines of the Médoc, although these distinctions are blunted with age.

In the south, in the Côte Chalonnaise and even Mâconnais, Chardonnay can be persuaded in a felicitious vintage to take on the mantle of Côte d'Or nobility by judicious winemaking, but most examples are rather simpler wines. Montagny and Rully can possess some of the attractive leanness of a fine Côte d'Or white, but in the Mâconnais, with appellations such as Mâcon Blanc, Pouilly-Fuissé, St-Véran and Beaujolais Blanc, Chardonnay puts on noticeably more weight. Here it becomes smooth, almost rounded, with flavours more reminiscent of melon than the tarter fruits of the Côte d'Or. Only rare examples from such southern Burgundian vineyards as Château Fuissé can develop with age, and this phenomenon is presumably a function of vinification techniques, average yields and the vine's venerability.

Almost every vintage Chardonnay is Burgundy's boon, grappling as the region does with the myriad problems of Pinot Noir. Chardonnay will ripen, achieving consistently higher alcohol levels than Pinot Noir wines; there are no problems of poor colour; and there is a ready market for Chardonnay wines at all price levels. All over Burgundy there are plots planted with truculent Pinot Noir which technically could be planted with the much more docile Chardonnay. One has the impression that were Burgundians more, shall we say, Californian in their outlook, Chardonnay would equal far more than a mere sixth of all Pinot plantings in the Côte d'Or.

Over the hills towards the Swiss border is Chardonnay's other French sphere of influence, the Jura. It is rare to taste a Palomino flavour in sherry; and for similar reasons freshness is not seen as a virtue in the Jura. Far more dominant than any varietal flavour, the influence of *flor* and controlled oxidation is everywhere present in the aroma of any Jura white, just as so many Greek whites have a whisper of resin whether sold as Retsina or not. Presumably proximity to Burgundy, and the vine's good cold weather resistance are the reasons for the Jura's faithfulness to Chardonnay. It is known as Melon d'Arbois in the northern part of the Jura and, even more oddly, as Gamay Blanc in the southern part. Unusually for Chardonnay it is often blended here with the oddly varnishy

Savagnin for the appellations L'Etoile, Arbois and Côtes du Jura, and even occasionally for the liquorous Vin de Paille which the ubiquitous Henri Maire makes with 100 percent Chardonnay.

The one region in which Chardonnay is blended more often than not is that capital of the art of blending, Champagne. In the Marne *département*, it is the second most important variety (after Pinot Meunier, not Pinot Noir) with nearly 6,000 hectares (15,000 acres), or 31 percent of all vineyard plantings. Pinot Meunier accounts for 45 percent and Pinot Noir 24 percent of the area which produces three out of every four bottles of champagne. In the outlying *département* of the Aube, Chardonnay is the least planted of the three (Pinot Noir being the most important) with only 300 hectares (750 acres), while Pinot Meunier is the only significant variety in the Aisne.

Whatever local deviations from the official recipe there may be in these lesser districts, Chardonnay is a vital ingredient. A few Blanc de Noirs champagnes are made without Chardonnay, and pretty coarse or massive they usually are, depending upon whether they are made predominantly with Pinot Meunier or Noir. Quite a lot of Blanc de Blancs champagne is made solely from Chardonnay, and can be attractively light and delicate. But the champagne purist wants the weight of Pinot Noir, and the fruitiness of Pinot Meunier, to be counterbalanced by the aristocratic vitality of Chardonnay.

In this, the chilliest and chalkiest wine region of France, the still wines produced by Chardonnay are even less generous than those made in Chablis, although only those brave enough to try a bottle of the still Coteaux Champenois ever taste them in this raw state; and most of those who have, understand well why champagne has bubbles in it. The wine is bone dry, searingly high in acidity, and not a great pleasure to drink. The famous body of Chardonnay is reduced to a skeleton, but what is left has the same nobility as any other well-brought-up Chardonnay.

The great majority of Chardonnay plantings are on the Côte des Blancs where each village has established a

*A*utumn foliage á la champenoise. The Champagne region is rare in having matched variety to district so relatively early in its history. The Côte des Blancs, Sparnacian wash over chalk, is the domain of Chardonnay, which will ripen reliably despite the eastern aspect.

reputation for the particular character of its wines: Avize for lightness, Cramant for perfume, and Mesnil for zip. Chardonnay wines from these top-rated communes are the most sought-after, and most expensive base wines for champenization. The early start to Chardonnay's growing cycle can be a problem as far north as this, and it is one of the preoccupations of viticultural research.

Small, often experimental, plantings of Chardonnay are cropping up in isolated pockets all over France. At one end of the scale there is the lean, "young vine", rather muted Chardonnay de Haut Poitou, and at the other, vintages of varietal Chardonnay made at the full-blooded Château-neuf property Château Rayas. Perhaps more successful have been the new plantings of Chardonnay in the Ardèche under the auspices of Louis Latour of Beaune, who has managed to make an open, almost California style of wine from this recently recovered vine territory.

The only French wine region where Chardonnay is showing major signs of taking hold is the middle Loire. Anjou growers have always been allowed to add up to 20 percent of other varieties to mitigate their late-ripening Chenin, and an increasing number of them are choosing to add the softening, early-ripening Chardonnay – some of them obviously unconstrained by the legal requirements. Chenin and Chardonnay make a surprisingly happy couple. Chardonnay tends to dominate, especially on the nose, but rounds out the sharp corners of Chenin on the palate. Chardonnay could be responsible for changing the shape of Anjou Blanc in years to come.

Unlikely as it may seem to the outsider, who sees the country as smoulderingly hot and suitable only for the richest of reds, Italy is a hotbed of Chardonnay innovation. This is doubtless, at least in part, a reflection of the very open love affair currently being conducted between that varietal and the most important importers of Italian wine, the Americans. It is also a very worthy reflection of the revolution which has been sweeping discreetly through the vineyards and cellars of Italy. Nor is Chardonnay experimentation limited to the coolest vineyards on Italy's alpine flanks. Good-quality Chardonnay can be found all over Italy, including Apulia where it is responsible for the much-vaunted white Favonio.

The arrival of good-quality Chardonnay cuttings has come at the right time for Italy's own rather more illicit

love affair with small oak maturation. The issue is so controversial in some quarters that *barrica* almost constitutes a swear word, but in Italy, as elsewhere, the varietal has proved itself ideal raw material for barrel maturation and, among the really avant-garde, barrel fermentation.

That said, Burton Anderson, an authority with whom few would venture to argue, maintains that the Alto Adige or South Tyrol, where Chardonnay receives not the slightest suggestion of oak, "may be the nation's most exciting Chardonnay source". Although the vine has been planted in this dynamic wine region for many years, the dangerously Gallic name was allowed to appear on labels, as mere *vino da tavola*, only in 1983. The authorities have been extraordinarily slow to accord DOC status to any Italian Chardonnay, although Alto Adige versions were at last allowed a DOC from the 1984 vintage, with Trentino Chardonnay next in line for the honour.

In the past, Alto Adige Chardonnay was blended with local Pinot Bianco, or Weissburgunder, and sold under that name. Even today much of Italy's northeastern Chardonnay is not sold as such. It leaves the region either as a wine labelled Weissburgunder/Pinot Bianco or as very early-picked raw material for the *spumante* industry. An increasing proportion is made, however, from better-flavoured grapes picked at full maturity into a varietal Chardonnay, with discernibly Chardonnay characteristics. There are also signs that plantings of Chardonnay on the more promising hillsides are increasing, their produce destined for this varietal DOC market.

In the adjacent province of Trentino, Chardonnay is rapidly making a name for itself, producing slightly fuller wines, but with the same smoky-appley perfume, refreshing tartness, often a spike of carbon dioxide and a gentle level of alcohol. These are not wines for ageing but, if well made, are very much Chardonnays for our times. Not all are well made, and the absence of DOC controls has fostered a wide variation in quality.

In Friuli-Venezia Giulia there has been a similar confusion between Pinot Bianco and Chardonnay, even though the two varieties look quite different at vintage time – Chardonnay grapes ripening to a much yellower glow than those of Pinot Bianco. It gradually became clear that a good half of all Friuli "Pinot Bianco" was Chardonnay and a separate DOC has duly been awarded. These wines are, if anything, rather more perfumed and substantial than those of Trentino-Alto Adige, although here again there is a wide variation in quality.

More surprisingly some producers in Alba, the heart of Piedmont's deepest red-wine country, have taken up this flighty pale French model. One might have expected it from someone as internationally minded as Gaja, but Pio Cesare? and with *barricas* too! These are just two neighbouring examples of how the great white French grape is being nurtured, virtually in secret, in Italy's most quality-conscious cellars. On the Vallania estate in the Colli Bolognesi, Chardonnay is transformed into the delicious Terre Rosse white, in defiance of EEC regulations which do not permit Chardonnay in Emilia-Romagna. In Umbria,

Lungarotti somehow circumvents this, and many other problems, in his single-vineyard Chardonnay di Miralduolo. Much further south, there are the drip-irrigated Favonio vineyards and a new entry, Villa Banfi's rich oaky Fontanelle, a California clone if ever there was one, from Brunello di Montalcino country. The Italian Chardonnay scene is changing in an exciting and thoroughly unexpected manner by the minute.

Chardonnay is now grown on the Grinzing hills overlooking Vienna. Even Germany has a little Chardonnay, although special government dispensation had to be sought for growing such an un-Teutonic vine. Some Chardonnay is grown on Schloss Rheinhartshausen's Mariannenau island in the Rheingau, but only the version blended with Weissburgunder is available commercially. The climate, however, is not sufficiently reliable to guarantee a successful flowering and ripening every year.

In Spain Chardonnay is encountered in some of its fullest, and not always successful, forms. Miguel Torres keeps it nicely in check by blending it with the local Parellada in his middle-quality version of Viña Sol (though not, curiously, in his top-quality oak-aged version). Also in Penedés, Jean León makes a really fat, oaky whopper of a Chardonnay, presumably designed for the customers of his Los Angeles restaurant. In neighbouring Lerida, Chardonnay styles are being refined on the extensive Raimat wine farm, and the vine is known in Portugal.

In eastern Europe there have been small plantings of Chardonnay in Slovenia, Romania, the USSR and even vinously introspective Hungary. The vine has been adopted most enthusiastically by the Bulgarians, who have planted about 1,000 hectares (2,500 acres), mainly in their eastern vineyards. High yields may explain the somewhat dilute character of Bulgarian Chardonnay, but acidity levels are good and some qualities are given oak ageing.

Outside Europe, California has embraced Chardonnay most heartily. American plantings of the varietal (or in some cases graftings on to other, less charismatic varieties rather than original plantings) now total more than 9,600 hectares (24,000 acres), of which an amazing quarter were plantings too new to be bearing commercially in 1983. California's stylistic dilemma over Chardonnay has already been outlined. Growers continue to seek out good microclimates for the varietal all over the state, but some of the finest Chardonnays to date have come from northern Sonoma and some of the cooler vineyards of the Napa Valley. At this level, California Chardonnay is a provocative rival to top-quality white burgundy, but there is no shortage of California wines labelled Chardonnay exhibiting either the clumsy use of oak or very few Chardonnay characteristics at all. They are tolerated presumably because of the intensity of consumer demand. Meanwhile, French coopers continue to give thanks for California's Chardonnay fixation.

The grapes can be badly affected by grey rot, but good-quality botrytised Chardonnay is by no means unknown. Pepperwood Springs of Mendocino have even "commercialized" one vintage and Jean Thévenet of Mâcon, among others, produced a botrytised *cuvée* of Chardonnay from Burgundy's super-ripe 1983 vintage.

Chardonnay is quality-conscious Oregon's most widely planted white variety, covering nearly 360 hectares (900 acres). These wines have rather more acid than most California examples and can, with good winemaking, be very subtle and appetizing. Positively Prial-pleasing, in fact. The variety has also performed quite well in Washington State, but there is a tendency to allow acid levels to fall too low for any staying power.

The variety is of particular interest in the very cool climates of New York State and Ontario, Canada. Good results have been achieved in their nascent *vinifera* industries such as at Hargrave on Long Island, Wagner in the Finger Lakes and Chateau des Charmes at Niagara. Restraint is the key here, but that is no bad thing and, as the vines gain maturity and the winemakers experience, the wines will presumably gain complexity.

In South America small amounts of Chardonnay are grown in Argentina, but tend to suffer from the heat. Chile's interest in Bordeaux white grapes is much greater than in their Burgundian counterpart.

While wanting to leap on to the Chardonnay bandwagon, South Africa has had severe problems in finding appropriate healthy stock. By 1981 there were still only 19 hectares (47½ acres) of official Chardonnay vineyard and since then much of it has been found to be Auxerrois.

The vine also produces surprisingly fine sparkling wine near Bombay.

Australians may have been held back by a shortage of good-quality Chardonnay cuttings, but have made light of the problem. They have been producing some absolutely stunning – and some shameful – Chardonnays for years. Plantings now total more than 1,600 hectares (4,000 acres), nearly half of which were too young to bear a commercial harvest in 1983. The vine is one of the best distributed in the country, with widely varying styles, including the vibrant citrus from Cowra, New South Wales; the smoky rich unctions from the Hunter; vapid overproduced specimens from the irrigated areas; almost Burgundian examples from the Yarra Valley in Victoria; and delicately crisp offerings from Mount Barker in Western Australia.

Geography is not necessarily the best key to understanding when one of the most revered and highly priced Chardonnays (Petaluma's) can consist of a blend from two vineyards more than 800 kilometres (500 miles) apart. Even more than in any other wine region the name of the winemaker is the telling clue. The most quality conscious are fiendishly active in their single-minded achievement of the goal (often a string of gold medals awarded at the state shows). The less scrupulous may simply blend in a 40 percent slug of cheaper wine and blast the mixture with new-oak character hoping to capitalize on Australia's undeniable Chardonnay boom.

Chardonnay-mania shows every sign of infiltrating New Zealand too, although it may well be more difficult to produce the exciting fruit-salad cocktail of flavours achieved in some of Australia's more favoured spots. There has been a tendency to smother the naturally rather muted fruit character with overemphasized oak.

Synonyms:
Pinot Chardonnay, Chardennet, Chardenai, Chardonnet, Chaudenay, Pinot Blanc à Cramant, Pinot Blanc Chardonnay, Epinette (Champagne); Arnaison (Touraine); Plant de Tonnerre, Morillon (Yonne); Rousseau, Roussot (Saône); Mâconnais (Isère); Petite Sainte-Marie (Savoie); Melon d'Arbois, Gamay Blanc, Petit Chatey (Jura); Beaunois (Chablis); Noirien Blanc, Arboisier, Aubaine, Auvernat (rest of France); Gelber Weissburgunder (Alto Adige); Weisser Clevner (Germany).

Soils:
Adapts well to all but the richest and wettest. Poor fertility calcareous soils rated highest. Can respond well to careful irrigation.

Vigour: Moderately vigorous.

Pruning:
Medium to long cane pruning.

Susceptibility:
Quite hardy but prone to powdery mildew and botrytis of both sorts.

Rootstocks: Vigorous but various.

Yields:
Moderate but consistent.
25 to about 60 hl/ha in France; two to five tons per acre on the West Coast of the USA and in Australia, sometimes substantially more when commercialism takes over.

Top quality. Very fashionable.

Sémillon

Sémillon is a very odd grape indeed. It is grown, often extensively, all over the world. In most of these vineyards it sits around sullenly like an overweight schoolgirl, showing awkward fatness or just plain dullness in the wines it produces. In odd places though, as if under the spell of a fairy godmother, it can be transformed into a raving beauty. Great white Bordeaux and mature Hunter Valley Sémillon prove that the grape can provide some of the world's finest wines.

Of course Sémillon alone is rarely responsible for great white Bordeaux. Whether dry as in the case of the top whites of Châteaux Haut-Brion and Laville-Haut-Brion or, more usually, sweet as in the case of the top Sauternes properties, it is in conjunction with Sauvignon Blanc that it displays its dazzling best. Sauvignon, with its irrepressible aroma and savage tartness, is the ideal soul mate for Sémillon in temperate climates such as that of Bordeaux, where it tends to lack both reek and vigour.

Fully ripe, sparsely cropped Sémillon, reared in not too hot a climate, produces a wine high in alcohol and extract but relatively low in aroma and acidity. Often lightly lemony when young, it responds extremely well to both oak *élevage* and ageing, attaining a rich lanolin flavour which some describe as "waxy", as well as a deep golden colour with hints of orange.

Much more than most other grapes in this collection of "greats", Sémillon is the victim of its environment. Cabernet, Riesling and Chardonnay from any but the youngest of vines are quite discernibly so, wherever they are planted. Sémillon planted in cool climates as found in New Zealand and Washington State, however, acquires an aroma intriguingly Sauvignon-like in its grassiness. In the hotter extremities of vine cultivation, such varietal character as there is becomes so diluted as to be scarcely distinguishable, and here Sémillon produces merely "white wine". This is certainly true of most of the produce of the extensive Sémillon plantings in the southern hemisphere: in Chile, Argentina, South Africa and Australia. The vine will produce a prodigious number of grapes unless curbed by either ultra-rigorous pruning or stress. Control over the sort of wine produced is, therefore, even more in the hands of the grower, sometimes dangerously so. It is this perhaps which is responsible for so much poor-quality high-yield Sémillon wine throughout the world.

There is considerable clonal variation between different Sémillon plantings: Galet notes an historical distinction between Gros Sémillon and Petit Sémillon. Even within Sauternes itself, thought to be the vine's real as well as its spiritual home, the most casual visitor can observe how Château d'Yquem seems to have exercised its own clonal selection by arriving at a much smaller-berried, looser bunch than is common elsewhere. The grapes are, more typically, quite large – certainly larger than those of Sauvignon Blanc – and are distinguished everywhere by their thinnish skins. It may be that the relatively deep colour of many Sémillon wines owes more to the must's tendency to oxidize than to grape pigmentation. It is almost certainly the same early to mid-season-ripening vine that is planted everywhere, with its distinctive rough-surfaced, undulating, bright green leaves; though some New Zealand viticulturists are perplexed by the similarity between their Sauvignon and "Sémillon" vines.

The world's most substantial plantings of Sémillon are in France, to be precise in Bordeaux and its eastern satellites. The variety's grip on the French *vignoble* is extremely localized but strong: Sémillon rates as France's second most important white-grape variety after the cognac grape Ugni Blanc (Trebbiano), despite a dramatic drop in total area from 34,000 to 23,000 hectares (85,000 to 57,500 acres) between the two agricultural censuses of 1968 and 1979.

The principal reason for the Girondin disaffection with the variety has, of course, been commercial. The price of Bordeaux Blanc, in which Sémillon is the dominant variety by far, has lagged further and further behind that of Bordeaux Rouge, so that replanting has commonly taken the ordinary Bordeaux vineyard (in Entre-Deux-Mers in particular) from white to red in interesting contraflow to the direction being taken by the world's newer vineyards.

In many cases this step is being resisted, not necessarily because the grower has a long and noble tradition of making Sémillon – the average Bordelais cooperative and small-scale *cave* has a poor understanding of white wine vinification – but for the simple reason that Sémillon is a relatively productive and reliable vine. This is especially so by comparison with Sauvignon, the grape variety which some of the more fashion-conscious merchants are urging upon growers of white grapes in Bordeaux.

Normal maximum yield for basic Bordeaux Blanc, in which Sémillon, Sauvignon and the declining Muscadelle may be, but rarely are, blended with up to 30 percent of Ugni Blanc, Merlot Blanc, Colombard and Ondenc, is 50 hectolitres per hectare. Bordeaux Supérieur, the appellation for many of the Gironde's better dry white wines, is allowed to make only 40 hectolitres of wine per hectare, and must use the three traditional varieties only.

There is probably a generation of wine drinkers unable to distinguish the aroma of Sémillon from that of sulphur dioxide, so unsubtle have techniques been at the most basic level of white winemaking in Bordeaux. Enthusiasts such as Pierre Coste of Langon and Peter Vinding-Diers of Château Rahoul, who are prepared to persevere at transforming the image of Bordeaux Blanc, have been doing their best recently to encourage clean, appetizing wines. Interestingly, both are great proponents of Sémillon over the more modish Sauvignon Blanc, because of its

SEMILLON

Leaf
length: 127mm (5in)   width: 121mm (4¾in)

Grape Cluster
length: 190mm (7½in)   width: 127mm (5in)

If ever a single property were associated with the fortunes of a single grape variety, it is Château d'Yquem with those of Sémillon. Sauternes' grandest "farm" is planted with nearly 80 percent Sémillon (most of the rest being Sauvignon). The reputation of its wine rests on a varietal characteristic cursed in other circumstances: Sémillon's thin skin and tendency to rot. Here it is the magic "noble" rot.

ability to develop complexity. Recent experiments have certainly demonstrated that Sémillon has an affinity with oak matched only by that of Chardonnay.

At the head of the ranks of dry white Bordeaux where oak ageing has been *de rigueur* for decades, in Château Laville-Haut-Brion, the proportion of Sémillon is being reduced to 50 percent, to match that of the rare Haut-Brion Blanc. That other much-respected white Graves, Domaine de Chevalier Blanc, has, sadly, even less faith in Sémillon.

The classic sweet white Bordeaux varietal recipe is roughly 80 percent Sémillon to 20 percent Sauvignon with perhaps a little Muscadelle. It is easy to see why the plumpness and longevity of Sémillon is favoured for sweet wines. Great Sauternes and Barsacs, though rarely wines from the lesser appellations such as Ste-Croix du Mont, Cérons and Loupiac, go through a fascinating and unique evolution in bottle. Depending on how much oxidation is allowed during vinification and *élevage*, the wine is bottled when a pale yellow to tawny gold, and gradually, and sometimes quite rapidly, deepens and takes on a fox-red tinge. It can eventually look more like a deep tawny port than any unfortified wine. Château Rieussec's wine, for instance, seems to colour very rapidly, while that of Lafaurie-Peyraguey deepens only slowly. During this entirely natural tinting process, the wine gradually loses apparent sweetness and accumulates the heady compounds of age. If left for several decades, it finally tastes almost dry but burnt. Butterscotch is a favourite tasting

note for great mature Sauternes; and certainly these wines seem closer to the confectionery counter, and further from the garden, than their German counterparts.

The common factor in the production of great natural sweet wine, whether in Germany or Bordeaux, is botrytis. It is Sémillon's thin skin and inherent physical propensity to "rot nobly" which, perhaps more than any other varietal characteristic, sets it apart. It would be impossible at any latitude to produce wines of such sweetness yet with such counterbalancing acidity without this curious fungus.

If, and only if, the weather conditions are right, will *Botrytis cinerea* ("noble rot" or *pourriture noble*) strike and Sauternes enjoy one of its really great vintages. If the autumn is hot, but not humid, the grapes are merely very ripe and the wine, as in 1976, very, very sweet but not necessarily very, very interesting. If the harvest time is too cold then botrytis will not develop. In order to produce wines with the richness and interest of botrytis-infected Sauternes, as a prerequisite the harvest temperatures must be fairly high. The mornings must be sufficiently humid to encourage the fungus to spread, yet the afternoons must be dry enough to prevent the ravages of the morning turning to the disastrous grey rot to which Sémillon is very prone. And, as if all these conditions were not difficult enough to fulfil, they have to last in order not to sacrifice too much of the paltry crop. Proprietors presumably try not to think of the maximum permitted Sauternes yield of 25 hectolitres per hectare as they send the pickers to the vineyard day after day to harvest only grapes that are fully botrytised.

The fungus looks quite disgusting, like a dusty grey mould, but it works the magic not just by concentrating the sugar and raising potential alcohol from, say, 13° to 21°, but, because of the complex reactions inside the grape, by increasing the total acidity. Botrytis adds a layer of extraordinary flavour too, a kind of vegetal honeyed quality which seems to complement Sémillon particularly, and you have a tiny quantity of very great wine indeed. Sémillon just loves to be ravaged.

Sémillon is also a significant ingredient in the increasingly fashionable dry wines of Sauternes, made when the grapes fail to ripen sufficiently for a sweet wine. Y or Ygrec is Château Yquem's candidate in this field. Both it and R (Château Rieussec) are the most blatantly Sémillon-based dry whites of the area. They are huge wines, Ygrec particularly so, and should be treated with great caution.

Although it is giving way to the less productive Sauvignon in many vineyards, more than 70 percent of all France's Sémillon plantings are in the Gironde, and more than 25 percent in the Dordogne. Sémillon continues to be the major variety in all the Gironde's white wine appellations such as Premières Côtes de Bordeaux and Côtes de Blaye. It is also valued enormously in the Dordogne *département* where it is responsible for earning Monbazillac its helpful comparisons with Sauternes. Sémillon is also an ingredient, usually a major one, in white Bergerac, Côtes de Bergerac Moelleux and Montravel (whose often rather oily texture presumably owes much to this grape).

The remaining 3 percent of French Sémillon is planted in the Lot-et-Garonne *département* where it is permitted as an ingredient, together with its usual travelling companions Sauvignon and Muscadelle, in Côtes de Buzet whites, and often with quite a bit of Ugni Blanc, Mauzac and Ondenc in white Côtes de Duras.

In these lesser appellations, where (with the often noble exception of Monbazillac) botrytis is rare and great sweet white wines are not a commercial possibility, Sémillon is largely used to give body and boost alcohol levels in the blended dry and medium-dry whites. Increasingly, growers are being schooled to emphasize the distinctive Sauvignon ingredient and we may well see a further decline in total plantings of Sémillon in France.

The biggest plantings of Sémillon outside France are in Chile where it is responsible for about three-quarters of all white wines produced, and covers an estimated 35,000 hectares (87,500 acres). Inspiration for Chile's whites as well as reds has been taken from Bordeaux and Sémillon/Sauvignon blends are far from uncommon among Chile's better whites. These tend to lack acidity, and there is still room for much progress in Chilean vinification techniques. Many of Chile's Sémillon plantings are quite cool enough to produce well-balanced wines, and there is an oak-ageing tradition of which advantage could well be taken. Currently, however, the ungrafted Sémillon tends to produce rather fat, oily wines which grow tired rather than mature.

These criticisms apply even more to Sémillon grown in the 5,500 hectares (13,750 acres) of hotter, often irrigated,

Argentine vineyards, where it is frequently blended with Sauvignon and sold as "Riesling".

Sémillon has played a major part in all the main wine-producing countries of the southern hemisphere, to an extent that hints more at the importance of trade routes than at coincidence. In 1822, 93 percent of all South African vineyards were planted with Sémillon. So common was it that it was called simply Wyndruif or "wine grape". More recently, as many other varieties have overtaken it in popularity, it has become known as Green Grape, because its foliage is so much brighter than the usually pallid leaves of Cape vines. In South Africa, as in Australia, a red-fruited Sémillon has been identified. At the Cape it is called, confusingly but perhaps inevitably, Red Green Grape.

Today Sémillon accounts for less than 4 percent of South Africa's vineyard, about 3,700 hectares (9,250 acres). Some of these vines are very old, with 80-year-olds still producing enough in some areas to warrant their existence. Even much younger vines produce higher yields than is usual for Bordeaux Sémillon which, together with the fact that bunches tend to be rather longer with slightly smaller grapes, indicates some clonal variation from French Sémillon in Green Grape, or Greengrape as some authorities have it.

Its cultivation is currently centred on the deep fertile soils of the Paarl, Wellington and Franschhoek valleys, particularly their more sheltered sites as young Sémillon is prone to wind damage. Almost alone among wine industry commentators, Graham Knox points out in his *Estate Wines of South Africa* that "Sémillon is an underrated variety in South Africa. It is capable of making high-quality wine in cooler areas, if grown prudently, without irrigation." It is used by the typical producer merely to add weight to blends of lighter, blander cultivars as, for example, the local Cape Riesling. Such is the Cape winemakers' current fascination with their new toys, Chardonnay and Sauvignon Blanc, it seems unlikely that their Sémillon heritage will be capitalized upon for some years yet.

The one country which has really made something exciting from the Sémillon cuttings taken there by the early settlers is Australia. Hunter Valley Sémillons may be great because of a conjunction of quirks of nature, but they do indisputably deserve a place in the wine world's top ranks. Sadly for the rest of us, the best Hunter Sémillons, which means mature bottles from exceptional vintages, are available in quantities so small as to hardly satisfy connoisseur demand in their own country. Exports are virtually unknown, and there seems little chance of exposing any significant proportion of the thousands of Sémillon growers around the world to the miracle achieved with the varietal in one corner of Australia.

Total Sémillon plantings in Australia are less than 3,000 hectares (7,500 acres), a figure that has remained fairly constant. Sémillon is sufficiently respected not to be subject to the rather frantic grubbing up of varietals such as Sultana and Pedro Ximénez. Yet it does not have the glamour of Chardonnay or even Rhine Riesling, and is therefore not increasing its hold on Australia's vine land. It will be some years, however, before it is tumbled from its place as the second most important noble white variety after Rhine Riesling.

Two-thirds of all Australian Sémillon plantings are in New South Wales, split almost equally between the wine-factory Murrumbidgee Irrigation Area and the cottage-industry Hunter Valley, in both of which it is the most important white grape. It is of their mature Sémillons that most Hunter winemakers are, justly, most proud.

The proof of Sémillon's star quality as a dry white varietal lies, more often than not, in a bottle of orange-golden liquid, labelled Lindemans. It both looks and tastes toasty rich, has high viscosity, fairly low acid, and yet is both venerable and lively. In very hot vintages, and there is no shortage of them in the Hunter, Sémillon can become simply fat, oily and confected. But in vintages such as 1961, 1964, 1968, 1974, 1979 and 1983 (which are by no means always regarded as good vintages for Hunter reds) the acid is sufficient to nurture the wines through to the state of maturity needed to show what they can do. Such wines deserve at least 10 years in bottle, and can happily take 20, but unfortunately are rarely allowed to.

Incarcerated in glass, they magically grow out of their green-gold, bland lemon-syrupy youth and achieve a complexity in middle age which can be rivalled only by absolutely top-quality white burgundy. A certain butter-scotch character, together with a suggestion of burnt toast characterizes the greats. The unique geological and clima-tological nature of the Hunter starts to show through.

There is great breadth of flavour and a definite hint of something mineral rather than fruity on the nose. Gentle they are not, and we may see more different styles of Hunter Sémillon, or Riesling as it has confusingly been known, than in the past.

In its home in western France, Sémillon is not at all accustomed to mixing with any but the top Bordeaux grape varieties. In New South Wales, however, it is asked to share a bottle and even vineyard with all sorts of unlikely mates. Its commingling with Chardonnay is trumpeted on many a wine label. Its other just as common blending partners, Trebbiano and Verdelho, are less well publicized but the success of such blends accounts for its popularity in the Murrumbidgee Irrigation Area. Sémillon is accommodat-ing in the amount of fruit it will yield, although in these irrigated vineyards its quality is usually but a very faint reflection of the concentration possible in a top Hunter vineyard. As in Chile, Argentina and South Africa, Sémillon is treasured as a relatively full-bodied and characterful ingredient in basic table-wine blends. The exceptions that so gloriously prove this rule, however, are the golden Late-Harvest Sémillons of De Bortoli, a Griffith firm who have the monopoly of a Sémillon vineyard which is naturally subject to "noble rot", and who turn out bottles of rich and increasingly subtle Sauternes-like wine that have won international acclaim.

South Australia's Barossa Valley is the only other Australian wine region to have any quantity of Sémillon, although here it will presumably always be overshadowed

Sémillon is taken seriously outside Sauternes only in Australia where it is particularly important in New South Wales, but also to a certain extent in South Australia and here in the Barossa Valley. The quality of the wine produced is almost always in strict, and inverse, proportion to the yield of the vines.

by Rhine Riesling. Local authority James Halliday reckons the varietal may enjoy a new lease of life here and quotes Basedow's White Burgundy and Orlando's Goldbeeren as evidence of the rich, buttery quality possible. Such is German influence here that late-harvest wines are called Spätlese Sémillon!

In Australia's coolest wine regions – Tasmania, Drumborg and the like – Sémillon can display an oddly grassy aroma which together with the higher acidity can suggest Sauvignon Blanc. In more pronounced cool-climate conditions, there is some Sémillon in New Zealand whose owners think it must be Sauvignon Blanc. Villa Maria have pioneered a "herbaceous" style, but New Zealand plantings of Sémillon have so far been very limited. Its good weather resistance has been noted, perhaps a reflection of its very late leafing. It is interesting that all over the world, and for various reasons, Sémillon and Sauvignon Blanc appear to be inseparable, even though they are ampelographically quite distinct.

Sémillon is not an important varietal in California. In quantitive terms there are more than 1,200 hectares (3,000 acres), about the same area as Emerald Riesling. There are signs, however, of a small cult following of Sémillon among devotees of Sauvignon–Sémillon blends both dry and sweet. As described on page 125, the Sémillon synonym Chevrier has been incorporated in the name of one well-received dry white blend; and it has its proponents as a "middle palate complement" for the much more modish Sauvignon Blanc.

More significantly for the varietal's long-term future worldwide, there has been considerable experimentation with laboratory culture of botrytis spores in California, starting as far back as the fifties at the University of California at Davis. Some of the more Euro-conditioned commercial winemakers on the West Coast are starting to experiment, using this technique on Sémillon to produce wines genuinely in the mould of Sauternes (as opposed to the sticky blends so cruelly labelled Sauternes). Genuine vineyard botrytis-affected late-harvest Sémillons are also being developed, as well as techniques involving drying grapes on mats after picking.

In California the varietal can display an aggressively green-grass character when grown in areas which are too cool (as it does in many Washington State examples); so Sémillon has been generally recommended for Regions II and III. It is grown in Region IV but is usually so flabby that it is not even particularly valued for jug wine. Sémillon needs a very delicate climatological balance.

Parts of eastern Europe can offer that balance, though winemaking techniques are not always designed to capitalize on this. Sémillon is planted in pockets throughout central Yugoslavia and around Lake Balaton in Hungary. R. E. H. Gunyon also located it, disguised as St-Emilion, as an ingredient in the sparkling wines made in Romania's Dealul Mare area, and it is generally agreed that Sémillon is an important, if rather furtive, white-grape variety in the Crimea. The variety is also grown in Catalonia, at Castell del Remei.

Synonyms:
Sémillon Blanc, Sémillon Muscat,
Sémillon Roux, Chevrier,
Malaga, Colombier, Blanc Doux (France);
St-Emilion (Romania);
Green Grape, Greengrape, Wine Grape or
Wyndruif (South Africa);
Hunter River Riesling (Australia though not,
confusingly, Western Australia).

Soils:
Grown on a wide variety worldwide,
but heavier soils favour botrytis in Bordeaux,
and overcropping in hotter climates.

Vigour: Vigorous growth.

Pruning:
Spur pruning, with additional summer pruning
necessary in some areas.

Susceptibility:
Very susceptible to rot – both grey rot and,
on very special occasions, *Botrytis cinerea*.
Good resistance to anthracnose.

Rootstocks:
Wide variety of rootstocks used, but care is needed
with their health because of fan-leaf virus.

Yields:
Moderately high (unless shrivelled by botrytis).
5–10 tons per acre in California.

**Potentially top quality in conjunction with noble rot (Sauternes)
or lean year maturity (Australia's Hunter Valley). Not very fashionable.**

Sauvignon Blanc

Sancerre and Fumé Blanc may be the most fashionable names on wine lists from San Francisco to South Kensington, but of the nine grape varieties included in this "Classic Varieties" section, Sauvignon Blanc's claim to classic status is perhaps the weakest.

Sauvignon Blanc produces wines for our times: white, dry, refreshingly zesty, aggressively recognizable and ready to drink almost before the presses have been hosed down after the vintage. The varietal has not proved, however, that unassisted it can produce wines for the future, and longevity is surely a component of greatness in wine.

It is Sauvignon Blanc's divine combination with Sémillon in parts of the Bordeaux region that earns it a place in this classic collection. The top châteaux of the Sauternes district produce luscious liquids which show how much greater is the blend than either variety in isolation. The vibrantly unctuous white wines of the great Graves properties, Châteaux Haut-Brion and La Mission Haut-Brion, demonstrate that the same can be true for dry wines. To be an essential ingredient in such vinous wonders, there must be something special about Sauvignon Blanc.

It is, strictly speaking, necessary to give Sauvignon Blanc its full name for there is a veritable rainbow of other Sauvignons – Jaune, Noir, Rosé, Rouge, Vert and Violet – of which only Jaune is identical.

It has been grown for centuries in those areas of France where the Cabernet family flourishes: the Gironde, the surrounding vineyards of the Dordogne, and the Loire valley. Only in the last couple of decades has it become popular in the newer wine regions, although it had already spread in Italy, eastern Europe and South America (though not so widely there as most wine drinkers suppose; see page 125). Sauvignon Blanc is encountered in its purest form, unblended and unsoftened, as Sancerre and Pouilly-Fumé, the twin appellations which face each other across the upper Loire. The grape produces wines which are typically very aromatic, with a smell suggestive of green, almost unripe, fruit. "Cat's pee on a gooseberry bush" is an oft-quoted description from an impeccable source. In the best chalky vineyards of Sancerre and Pouilly-Fumé, the Sauvignon essence is overlaid with an extra layer of flavour which has for long suggested gunsmoke, and therefore gunflint: the local name is "flinty". Certainly this is a cool, cool wine – both in ethos, and in the temperature at which it is best enjoyed.

Much more Sancerre is produced than Pouilly-Fumé. The character of the wines tends to vary rather more with vintage and producer than with appellation, but they are so easy to appreciate (no youthful shyness here) that the wines have become extremely popular with trend-conscious diners-out. They cost a bit more but not absurdly more than basic house wine. They are refreshing and do not feel too aggressively alcoholic. Dammit, they almost taste *slimming*! although in fact Sauvignon Blanc grapes are noted for their relatively high sugar content.

These are wines for early consumption and the great majority will be past their best a couple of years after the harvest. But the cellars of the Château de Nozet, where Patrick de Ladoucette so cleverly makes the most expensive Pouilly-Fumé, do contain older vintages which prove that the best can at least survive, if not actually improve. Those who have tasted examples of nineteenth century Pouilly-Fumé find little trace of evolution, but have been impressed by the grape's potential stamina.

Sauvignon Blanc produces a collection of much less famous dry whites in various corners of north-central France, of which Quincy, Reuilly and Ménétou-Salon are the most like Sancerre and Pouilly-Fumé in terms of fruit and weight. The others are relatively obscure outside France, although they have the idiosyncratic appeal of any rarity. To the south of the starry twins towards the northern Rhône is St-Pourçain-sur-Sioule, where Sauvignon Blanc is a significant ingredient with Tresallier in a tart light white. To the north, on the fringes of Chablis country, is another VDQS, Sauvignon de St-Bris, which is always regarded as a Burgundian oddity, but is merely a Loirish phenomenon a little far from home.

The area in which the Sauvignon Blanc grape has really gained ground in the last two decades is the eastern end of Touraine around Blois, so that there are now almost as many vines in the Loir-et-Cher *département* as in Cher, where Sancerre is produced (although not nearly so many as in the Gironde). These newer plantings have largely been directed towards Sauvignon de Touraine, a distinctly second-class appellation, but one thought sufficiently respectable to warrant considerable investment by Patrick de Ladoucette, for instance.

Sauvignon de Touraine rarely has the concentration of a good Sancerre/Pouilly-Fumé. If the varietal aroma seems to shriek rather than sing, and there's a distinctly unwelcoming "stoniness" to the flavour, then at least the Touraine wines are cheaper than the more renowned models upriver. Higher yields are allowed, as can be tasted in their rather dilute character.

Despite all this new planting in the Loire, the total area of French vineyard planted with Sauvignon Blanc declined quite considerably between the last two national vineyard surveys from 8,900 hectares in 1968 to 7,000 hectares in 1979 (22,250 to 17,500 acres), making it considerably less important than Chardonnay and significantly less widely planted than the Muscadet grape. This was because of the particularly dramatic disaffection with white wine production in Bordeaux. Whole vineyards were converted to producing more healthily priced red wine. Between 1968 and 1979, more than half the Sauvignon Blanc vines

SAUVIGNON BLANC

Leaf
length: 152mm (6in)   width: 190mm (7½in)

Grape cluster
length: 152mm (6in)   width: 120mm (4½in)

*T*his huddle of houses on a chalky hilltop represents nirvana to a generation of new wine drinkers in northern Europe. Sancerre (or Pouilly-Fumé in the US) is the *most famous, and felicitous, product of Sauvignon Blanc. With its easily recognizable aroma, high acid and no residual sugar, Sauvignon or Fumé Blanc is THE varietal of the eighties.*

planted in the Gironde were uprooted, leaving just 2,400 hectares (6,000 acres). Even more Sémillon was uprooted, 6,200 hectares (15,500 acres), presumably reflecting the local practice of growing, harvesting and vinifying the two grapes together, with Sémillon dominating the blend.

In very recent years news of the *succès d'estime* enjoyed by Sauvignon Blanc in other parts of the world has reached Bordeaux, and it is possible that some of those who pulled up their Sauvignon vines so enthusiastically may now regret it. It took a surprisingly long time for the Bordelais, traditionally makers of red and sweet white wines, to learn how to make crisp dry whites in the approved modern style: rapid crushing, sterile conditions, low temperature fermentation and stainless steel. For this Pierre Coste of Langon must take considerable credit.

Once the lessons had been learnt in the late seventies, and the necessary equipment bought, presumably on long-term loans from the Crédit Agricole, a "new generation" of Bordeaux Blanc started to appear, with Sauvignon often the dominant partner in the blend, and sometimes the only constituent. These wines prove what a treasure Sémillon can be. Grown in the rather milder climate of Bordeaux, on alluvial rather than chalky soil, the Sauvignon Blanc grape loses its fruitiness and much of its aroma. Less gooseberry bush, more cat's pee. If the fruit is picked early enough to capture the aroma, the wines are often horrifyingly acid. If acid levels are allowed to drop before picking, then the resulting wines can be too bland.

There are some very well-made examples which can give simple drinking pleasure, but white wine philosophers, such as Pierre Coste, are preaching more and more widely the benefits that Sémillon can bring to a blend, rounding out the weight and flavour. Dry white Bordeaux at its most simple level, as produced in quantity in the Entre-Deux-Mers and outlying Bordeaux districts, is still finding its way.

Few can afford to lavish the sort of attention on a dry

white wine which is possible at a château where a reputation for top quality in this field has been established, such as Châteaux La Mission Haut-Brion and Haut-Brion and Domaine de Chevalier in Graves. Here the Sauvignon is carefully blended with Sémillon and given the luxury of oak maturation to produce a rich, golden, lemony, lanolin-textured wine, high in alcohol, which can last for decades. It is perhaps significant that a blend of equal parts of the two complementary grapes is thought optimum both at the great Graves châteaux and at Château d'Yquem for their dry wine, Ygrec. The Sémillon gives guts and longevity, the Sauvignon Blanc aroma and *nervosité*.

This is the recipe used to make those dry white curiosities from the Médoc, Château Loudenne Blanc and Caillou Blanc de Château Talbot, but it has been ignored by the most exciting incursion into this rarefied field of activity, that of the new Pavillon Blanc de Château Margaux. Under orders from the new Mentzelopoulos régime to make a stunning white emissary, Professor Emile Peynaud is giving an all-Sauvignon wine a de-luxe education. Hyper-clean juice is fermented in oak and kept in barrels,

at least a third of them brand new, for up to six months. The wine is evidence of a respect for the varietal that is unequalled anywhere else in the world, although it mirrors Robert Mondavi's experimentation in California, and it will be fascinating to see how this undoubtedly "serious" wine ages. It is priced as though it has many years ahead of it. Like so many great wines, it goes through a petulant toddler stage at around two years old, but the results of this five-star treatment of what is possibly only a four-star grape cannot be certain before the turn of the century.

The most expensive, and in most years the most exciting, wine in which Sauvignon Blanc plays a minor but vital part is the great sweet wine of the Sauternes château, Yquem, famous from Texas to Tokyo. Sauvignon Blanc is planted all over the Sauternes district and the lesser outlying districts such as Ste-Croix-du-Mont and Loupiac, to add acid and aroma to Sémillon-based sweet wine. Each vineyard has its own chosen *encépagement*, often including a dash of the more obvious and less noble Muscadelle. Among the 11 Premiers Crus the proportion of Sauvignon planted can vary from 5 percent (Château Lafaurie-

Peyraguey) to more than 50 percent (Châteaux Guiraud and Rayne-Vigneau), but Comte Alexandre de Lur-Saluces at Yquem reckons that 20 percent is ideal for a wine expected to live some time. Many Sauternes vineyards still follow the old practice of planting one Sauvignon vine at regular intervals along the rows of Sémillon, but Yquem have been moving towards fully parcellated plantings so that picking at optimum ripeness for each variety is easier. The Sauvignon flowers about 10 days before the Sémillon and yields can be quite different, with the Sauvignon crop more at risk. Both varieties are prone to the intensifying effects of botrytis which, while concentrating the apparent sweetness, tends to dampen natural aroma. This is why the distinctive smell of Sauvignon can be hard to find in Sauternes from a great year. Quality-conscious producers try to harvest Sauvignon just a little earlier in its ripening cycle than Sémillon, to preserve a hint of its zestiness.

The appellations that skirt the eastern edge of the Bordeaux region are, as one might expect, planted with Bordelais grape varieties. This means that Sauvignon Blanc is part of the blend for the sweet, earthy Monbazillac and the rather less luscious Rosette and Montravel, as well as producing light, sometimes slightly coarse dry whites

In California, and a number of other newer wine regions, Sauvignon Blanc is often known as Fumé Blanc, often with no very clear distinction between the two. When vinified with maximum technological sophistication, including rapid grape reception, it tends to be called Sauvignon Blanc.

under such names as Bergerac and Côtes de Duras. It is planted all over southeast France, though rarely plays an important part in the local blended whites such as Béarn, Gaillac and the rare Côtes de Buzet Blanc.

Over the Pyrenees Sauvignon Blanc is rarely encountered, but it is on the increase in Rueda and Miguel Torres has planted it in his mountain vineyards of the Penedés. Like his Chardonnay, it is blended with the local Parellada grape for his Gran Viña Sol range, but it is the Sauvignon blend, with some oak ageing, which he designates the superior wine. Perhaps he too has been influenced by the success of Robert Mondavi with the combination of wood and Sauvignon Blanc.

Sauvignon Blanc is grown on a much wider scale in northeastern Italy where the best examples have an alluring combination of varietal character with delicacy, the appeal of Sancerre with the structure of a Mosel. It is planted in well-drained corners of the Veneto and is becoming increasingly popular in Alto Adige; examples in Terlan have hinted that the varietal aroma is at its most pronounced and enticing in wines from the region's steeper, warmer sites. On the gentle hills bordering Yugoslavia, Collio Sauvignons have more varietal character and substance than Colli Orientali del Friuli versions, with Eno'Friuli providing the yardstick. Enrico Vallania, with his Terre Rosse Sauvignons, has also proved that Sauvignon can succeed outside this northeast corner, in the Colli Bolognesi in Emilia-Romagna.

The variety is well-known in eastern Europe, but tends to produce progressively sweeter, heavier wines the further east it is planted. The most elegant fruit is grown in Slovenia, although the delicacy is not always preserved as far as the bottle. There are also good plantings in the Fruska Gora hills of Serbia and increasing experimentation with the variety in Czechoslovakia, Bulgaria, Romania and, it is rumoured, in the USSR. Austria cultivates a sturdy Sauvignon Blanc just over the border from Slovenia, in Steiermark, under its German name Muskat-Silvaner.

Of the newer wine regions, indeed of any wine region, California has taken Sauvignon Blanc most seriously. The story is by now a famous one of how one man can change the fortunes of a varietal, internationally. In the early seventies it was perceived by the American public as a distinctly unexciting variety. Then Robert Mondavi, Mr Napa Valley, observed how popular imported Pouilly-Fumé, made from the same grape, had become with his customers. Sauvignon Blanc, as grown in California, tends to have an extremely aggressive aroma, positively stinking. They call it "grassy". Why not tame that a little by putting the wine into oak for a while, and rename it Fumé Blanc? He did it, and they bought it, in millions of bottles. The varietal is now second in modishness only to Chardonnay. Plantings have increased extraordinarily fast to cover more than 5,200 hectares (13,000 acres) and there is now a trend away from the rather oily heavier style towards lighter, tarter, unoaked versions more genuinely in the mould of Pouilly-Fumé, often deliberately and confusingly called Sauvignon Blanc rather than Fumé Blanc.

Some exciting Sauvignon Blanc is produced from Livermore vines, and the varietal is cultivated all along the coastal wine regions, but Sonoma and Napa have so far set the standards. Producers such as Joseph Phelps believe that blending with a small proportion of Sémillon makes a better, if not more "typical", wine. Furthermore, the initial 1983 recipe for Vichon's masterfully named Chevrignon blend showed how blending almost as much Sémillon with Sauvignon Blanc could fashion a stylish liquid that is greater than the sum of its parts. Robert Mondavi even pioneered a botrytised Sauvignon Blanc in 1978 which certainly exhibited an impressive level of ripeness, but could have done with a bit more acidity. The Sauvignon Blanc grown in California seems relatively more productive than its European equivalents, with yields of around 6 tons per acre in Napa being far from unusual.

There are substantial plantings of Sauvignon Blanc in Argentina, but only some of Chile's "Sauvignon" is Sauvignon Blanc. In the past, most was the more ordinary Sauvignonasse or Sauvignon Vert, thought by the Australian A. J. Antcliff to be Italy's Tocai Friulano. Both Chilean variations on the Sauvignon theme have a marked sweetness, almost floral character, not associated with French Sauvignon Blanc.

This can also be tasted in some of South Africa's and Australia's Sauvignon Blanc. There are only about 300 hectares (750 acres) of the variety in Australia, mainly in South Australia. Cullens in Western Australia, Tisdall and Enterprise have had some success with the variety but the climate is probably slightly too hot in most vineyard areas

to preserve the freshness and aroma so essential for appetizing Sauvignon Blanc. Besides, who needs Sauvignon Blanc when they have succeeded so well with Rhine Riesling, and when New Zealand does so much better with the French variety?

Ironically, parts of New Zealand may be just slightly too *cool* for Sauvignon Blanc. There are some exciting examples, such as recent vintages from Selaks and Delegat's, but the overpoweringly simple varietal flavour of less ripe versions, such as Montana's made from South Island grapes, may need to be shaped into something more interesting – and put on the market earlier. Some producers are experimenting with oak ageing and, inevitably, the name Blanc Fumé.

In South Africa, Sauvignon Blanc, also sometimes named Blanc Fumé in West Coast style, is enjoying almost cult status among connoisseurs as they wait for Cape winemakers to get to grips with Chardonnay. It has a fine, distinctive aroma and in some examples, such as those of Lemberg and L'Ormarins, evidence of stylish oak treatment. Plantings are still tiny and centred on Paarl and Stellenbosch, but growing fast as the potential for this grape is recognized.

Sauvignon Blanc looks set to fall out of favour, so well is it doing in fashion-conscious corners of the globe. The great debate continues: does it age well? The wines of Sancerre and Pouilly-Fumé suggest not. The great wines of Bordeaux, in which it plays a role, have so far hidden the clues by blending. We shall have to inspect 1978 Pavillon Blanc de Château Margaux in 1998.

Synonyms:
Sauvignon Jaune, Blanc Fumé,
Surin, Fié dans le Neuvillois,
Punechon, Puiechou,
Gentin à Romorantin (France);
Muskat-Silvaner (Germany, Austria);
Savagnin Musqué (California);
Fumé Blanc (California, South Africa,
Australia and New Zealand).

Soils:
Chalk in middle Loire, elsewhere prefers
medium-yield gravelly or sandy loams.
Very prone to rot on fertile soils.

Vigour: Vigorous to very vigorous.

Pruning:
Summer pruning
can help ward off bunch rot
by increased air circulation
as bunches are
quite compact.

Susceptibility:
Very prone to botrytis, oidium and
black rot.

Rootstocks:
Low to moderate vigour preferred.

Yields:
Low to moderate.

Only moderate quality. Too fashionable.

Chenin Blanc

Chenin Blanc is a magical chameleon of a grape, although remarkably few of the thousands of growers who harvest it each year even realize that magic is there. It is used, in various and distant corners of the globe, to produce exquisite sweet whites so long-lived that few bottles survive to reach their peak; attractively nervy, medium-dry wines with one of the most curious bouquets know to wine tasting; basic table wine of the most ordinary off-dry sort; the spritzy, neutral white base of an entire nation's wine industry; fine sparkling wines ranging from austerely dry to stinking rich; and in South Africa, even as the raw material for sherry, port and brandy.

One of its caprices is that it undergoes a complete personality change on leaving its homeland, France (is it something to do with clones?). For more than 500 years production was concentrated on the Anjou-Touraine area, the heart of the Loire valley's tourist zone. But this century it has been losing ground there while becoming important in newer wine regions, notably those of South Africa and California. It is hard to believe, however, that the neutral everyday whites produced in these hotter climates, with about as much smell as a well chilled honeydew melon, have any connection at all with the strongly scented, searingly tart French prototypes made in appellations such as Vouvray and Coteaux du Layon.

The Chenin Blanc is a particularly venerable French vine, cultivated from the ninth century at the Abbaye de Glanfeuil in the Anjou region on the left bank of the river. In 1445 it was exported a few miles up river to the squire of Chenonceaux and his brother-in-law the Abbot of Cormery, on the banks of the Echaudon at Mont-Chenin just south of the Touraine countryside which now produces Vouvray and Montlouis. Hence the name, although there is a host of synonyms, of which Pineau de la Loire, and sometimes Pineau d'Anjou, are the most common. Its relationship to Pinot, however, is purely onomatopoeic.

The genealogical aspect of Chenin Blanc most relevant for today's wine drinker was the discovery in 1965 that Steen, one of the most popular cultivars planted in South Africa, was in fact Chenin Blanc. This variety was probably one of the original European cuttings brought to the Cape in 1655 by the industrious Jan Van Riebeeck of the Dutch East India Company. Its versatility, relatively high yields and good resistance to disease and wind made it South Africa's third most popular cultivar by 1965. Since its identification with Chenin Blanc it has become the Cape's most popular variety, accounting for a phenomenal 31 percent of the total vines planted by 1983. Amazingly, this South African area of nearly 30,000 hectares (75,000 acres) is more than three times the total vineyard area now planted with Chenin Blanc in France.

When, in the sixties, the South Africans discovered the wonders of cold fermentation for white wine production in a hot climate, the Chenin Blanc proved the ideal raw material. The grapes ripened moderately early in the season and could be fermented at low temperatures to produce a wine that was, if not overpowering in bouquet, at least refreshingly crisp. These medium-dry Chenins constituted what is affectionately known in the South African wine trade as "the Lieberstein revolution". Using this derivatively named new wine style as bait, an important new generation of Cape wine drinkers was hooked.

Cape winemakers remain masters of the cold fermentation technique to the extent that almost all South African Chenin Blancs, indeed a good number of South African whites, taste the same. The style is refreshing, thanks to relatively high acid and often a slight spritz, and so clean that there is virtually no varietal character left in the wine at all. Many of the varietal Chenin Blancs are still called Steen, or even Stein, though strictly speaking Stein relates to a medium-dry style of wine and not to the cultivar (often Chenin Blanc) from which it was made.

One of the few variables left to the Cape winemaker is sweetness. At the bottom end of the price range, where South African Chenins can offer such excellent value, there are now bone dry wines as well as those with a fair smack of residual sugar to choose from. Higher up the scale it has been proved, after some pioneering work by estates such as De Wetshof and Nederburg, that South African Chenin Blanc can make some exciting botrytised sweet wines. Nederburg's Paarl Edelkeur has so far been the finest of all, designed to keep South African winegrowers on their toes. This wonderfully rich blend of butterscotch and orange blossom, in which Chenin Blanc is sometimes bolstered by Paarl Riesling (Crouchen), is occasionally a bit short on acid – although magnificent.

As those who suffer from indigestion are only too well aware, the one sin of which no French Chenin Blanc can be accused is low acidity. The River Loire seems to wash the vineyards on its banks with a charge of tartaric acid which makes its impact on every wine from Sancerre and Pouilly-Fumé near Nevers to Gros Plant and Muscadet on the Atlantic. This includes the great mass of Loire wines made from the Chenin Blanc between these vineland limits in Anjou-Touraine.

The very acid that makes tasting young Vouvray such a taxing experience is capable of masking youthful sweetness and sustaining the wines into a very ripe old age. In specially favoured corners of the Loire vineyards, where the sun can take full advantage of the vine's propensity for vigorous growth and potentially good sugar levels, the Chenin Blanc can be coaxed into producing wine that is not just good, but very great. It is ironical, however, that so far north the most popular grape is such a late ripener. Picking in November is by no means uncommon; the vintage in Vouvray is one of the latest in France.

CHENIN BLANC

Leaf
length: 127mm (5in)   width: 127mm (5in)

Grape Cluster
length: 190mm (7½in)   width: 121mm (4¾in)

At its most basic level, Chenin is grown in the Loire to produce wines to be drunk young as basic Anjou Blanc or an inexpensive Saumur or Vouvray. Even these relatively lowly wines, if, as is decreasingly the case, made purely from Chenin, will exhibit the characteristic aroma of young Chenin as grown in France. So forceful is the stamp of Chenin that it makes itself obvious on the far side of the tortuous *méthode champenoise* sparkling wine process, so that any 100 percent Chenin Saumur or Vouvray Mousseux will be heady with the grape's very special fume.

The aroma does not exactly pierce the nostril with its purity unlike, for example, Sauvignon or Riesling, but is more of an intriguing vapour. There is something almost musty about it, whether, as is still too often the case, it has been oversulphured or not. Along with Gewürztraminer and Muscat, Chenin is one of those varieties that actually "smells sweet", although physiologists tell us this is impossible. Overlaying, almost blurring the impression of sweetness, is one of texture. Perhaps this is what Rabelais meant when he likened Vouvray to taffeta. There is weight there, too; a basic Loire Chenin Blanc may be sweetish and it may have marked acidity, but it is not light-bodied or simple. A high degree of extract is noticeable both in the mouth and in the trails of glycerine running down the side of a swirled glass. "Honey and flowers" is a classic tasting note for some, "damp straw" for others. Young Chenin is more floral than fruity, which is why parallels are drawn so readily with wines from the great German rivers.

As in Germany, the most prized Loire Chenins are late picked and high in residual sugar achieved by the natural sunny process of ripening. In certain favoured spots this is often further concentrated excitingly by botrytis. The "noble rot" works its magic in the sheltered countryside bounded by the superior Bonnezeaux and Quarts de Chaume sub-appellations within the more basic Demi-Sec Coteaux du Layon area, and in the particularly sheltered or well-inclined vineyards in the Anjou, Vouvray and Montlouis appellations.

Top quality late-harvest wines, that demonstrate the thrilling combination of raciness and richness of which Chenin Blanc is capable, are made by producers such as the Château de Fesles in Bonnezeaux and the Château de Belle Rive in Quarts de Chaume, where the more fastidious selection produces even richer wines. More flowery wines with perhaps enhanced bouquet and slightly less weight are to be found behind such Vouvray labels as Gaston Huet, Prince Poniatowski, A. Foreau and Marc Brédif. The acidity is so high in these wines when they are young, however, that even those given the richest accolade, *moelleux* (literally, full of marrow), may taste only very slightly sweet when young.

It takes time for these treasures to gain appreciable value. A *moelleux* from a good year can start to display its riches after about two decades, but is just coasting into the prime of life at six, as has been so pleasurably demonstrated by the Anjou Rablay wines dispersed from Madame

Château de la Bizolière, one of the best-known estates in the most curious enclave of Chenin Blanc vines in the Loire. Old vines give a low yield of concentrated wine with varying amounts of residual sugar and, most notably, seeringly high acidity that takes decades to soften. The ultimate illustration that acidity preserves.

Prunier's London cellars and the Anjou wines of the Moulin Touchais estate. The latter's cellar is said to contain vintages of the 1880s which are still entrancing.

A further but often ignored delight offered by the Chenin Blanc grape is that even drier versions, such as well-made Vouvray Sec, Coteaux de Loir, Jasnières, or the intriguing wines that are produced on the flinty soil of Savennières, are capable not just of lasting, but of maturing for decades. Many of those wine drinkers who dismiss young versions of such wines as facile and (cardinal sin) medium dry, would be amazed were they to cellar them for 10 years or more.

Like their South African counterparts, California Chenin Blancs have not so far shown any cellaring potential, rather the reverse. Most producers demand little of the varietal even though, or perhaps because, it is so widely planted. In the last decade, the total California acreage under Chenin Blanc more than doubled to over 17,600 hectares (44,000 acres), comfortably overtaking the total area of Chenin Blanc vineyards in France.

Cast in shadow by the spotlight of fashion in which bask Chardonnay and Sauvignon Blanc, Chenin Blanc is categorized as a supplier of everyday table wine, a little but not much above French Colombard in status. Most of these West Coast Chenin Blancs are vinified as fruity, medium-dry or semi-sweet wines often rather short on acid.

Dry Chenin Blancs from wineries such as Chappellet, Kenwood and Landmark show that early picking of good quality fruit can result in much crisper wines. These are like the more flavoursome versions of Cape Chenin Blanc, although any tastable relationship between California and Loire Chenins is yet to be demonstrated. Even botrytised California Chenin Blanc such as Callaway's "Sweet Nancy" is merely a very sweet white rather than an expression of varietal character. Climate is clearly a factor here, but even the Chenin Blanc produced in the cooler climes of Washington State gives no hint of the extraordinary bouquet which the Loire Chenins exhibit.

It would be fascinating to see what would result from more severely limiting yields. Even very ordinary Anjou Blanc must be produced from less than 50 hectolitres per hectare. In South Africa Chenin Blanc is prized for its generous production, while in California 10 tons per acre (about 130 hectolitres per hectare) in the Central Valley, and 6 tons per acre in Region II "quality" wine-producing zones, are common. Soil may also be an important factor in bringing out the best from the variety. Chenin is planted on a wide range of soils in South Africa and California, but there is some correlation between calcareous soils (e.g. the *tuffeau* of Touraine) and quality in France.

With scant regard for its noble roots, Chenin Blanc has established itself as a popular commoner in many of the world's newer wine regions. Australia is rapidly increasing her plantings of Chenin Blanc, having blithely called it Sémillon in Western Australia, Albillo or "Sherry" in South Australia and Chardonnay in Rutherglen, until the seminal visit in 1976 of French ampelographer Paul Truel to nose around Australia's vines.

*A*s Steen, Chenin Blanc is the single most important grape variety in South Africa, even on the relatively new Zevenwacht Estate. It seems to offer particularly malleable raw material for the Cape's cool-fermentation techniques.

Chenin Blanc seems naturally prone to this sort of confusion. For decades a white grape very common in Argentina and quite common in Chile was called Pinot Blanc or Pinot Blanco. It has now been established that this is really Chenin Blanc, which produces the same kind of soft, lightly fruity wines in South America as north of the Rio Grande.

Chenin Blanc seems to thrive best, and demonstrate its undoubted flair, in marginal climates. The Loire valley is the most obvious and established example, even if the grape's lack of modishness is causing many producers to replant with the more commercially viable Chardonnay, Sauvignon or even Cabernet Franc. The cool climate of New Zealand may well prove to have the most exciting potential outside France for Chenin Blanc. It is the islands' third most common grape variety, being particularly so in the Poverty Bay and Hawkes Bay areas. Acid levels are sometimes uncomfortably high, a refreshing change from most other non-French Chenins. Good fruit flavours have already been achieved with dry to semi-sweet styles and experiments are being made with late-harvest botrytised versions. In New Zealand and Australia short oak maturation has also been tried, although these experiments are too recent to have produced any prescription for winemakers.

Although often blended with other basic white grapes for ordinary table wine blends in California and Australia, Chenin Blanc has traditionally been used for 100 percent varietal wines in its homeland. In appellations such as Anjou and Savennières however, it is increasingly blended with up to 20 percent Chardonnay or Sauvignon Blanc to soften the acidity and make the wine fruity earlier. This tinkering tends to blur the bouquet, and the new blends are unlikely to have the extraordinary lasting qualities of pure Chenin wines.

The Chenin Blanc is one of the wine world's most undervalued treasures. The pricing of wines made from Chenin Blanc does little to suggest that Chenin is a great grape. Even the Quarts de Chaume and Savennières wines available in the most limited quantity are not expensive relative to other wines with half their ageing potential. It would be sad to see the remorseless march of Chardonnay and Sauvignon Blanc, so evident in newer wine regions, deprive us of some unique classics in the Loire. It is to be hoped that these will become more modish, better known, command a more viable price, and inspire the growing band who work with Chenin Blanc outside the middle Loire. Listel's experimental plot in the Midi has already shown great potential.

Synonyms:
Pineau de la Loire, Pineau d'Anjou,
Pineau de Savennières, Pineau de Briollay,
Gros-Pineau de Vouvray, Plant de Brèze,
Gout-Fort, Verdurant,
Blanc d'Anjou, Confort,
Cou-Fort, Quefort, Blanc d'Aunis,
Franc-Blanc, Franche (France);
Steen (South Africa).

Soils:
French growers
treasure calcarous soils,
the *tuffeau* of Touraine in particular.
In newer wine regions
it is planted on a wide variety of soils.

Vigour:
Very vigorous growth with particularly good wind resistance. Early bud burst exposing it to spring frosts; early-mid ripening.

Susceptibility:
Clonal variation in rot resistance (and bunch shape). Susceptible to botrytis on rich soils. Susceptible to oidium; medium resistant to downy mildew; very resistant to anthracnose.

Rootstocks:
Some clones have weak affinity with 101–14 and 143–B rootstock. Moderately vigorous rootstock preferred.

Yields: Moderate to high yield with spur pruning.

Very variable quality. Unfashionable.

Major Varieties

Cabernet Franc

Just as Pinot Meunier is regarded as a rather ignoble form of Pinot Noir, so Cabernet Franc languishes in the shadow of the much more revered Cabernet Sauvignon. This is considerably fairer to Pinot Meunier than it is to Cabernet Franc. No grape primarily responsible for Château Cheval Blanc can be dismissed so summarily. It is capable of producing truly great wines in St-Emilion and some very good ones in the middle Loire. It is also widely planted in Italy.

Typically, and Cheval Blanc is atypical, Cabernet Franc wines are rather more herbaceous than Cabernet Sauvignon, lower in tannins, acids and extract and therefore more approachable, with a distinctive aroma that reminds some of raspberries, others of violets and me of pencil shavings. When blended with Merlot as in St-Emilion, the Merlot fills in the holes of Cabernet Franc's rather lean structure and the blend magically makes a lush mouth-filler. When merely used as a seasoning for Cabernet Sauvignon and Merlot, as in the Médoc and Graves, Cabernet Franc is barely noticeable.

Cabernet Franc wines never taste like Cabernet Sauvignon, but Cabernet Sauvignon can taste very like Cabernet Franc when made in too cool a climate. This is demonstrated particularly in New Zealand and occasionally in Washington State, curiously mirroring the phenomenon concerning Bordeaux's two most important white grapes whereby cool-climate Sémillon takes on a grassiness very like Sauvignon Blanc.

The secret of cajoling the best from these two vines is to match the right one to the prevailing climate. Cabernet Franc is better suited to rather cooler climates. It buds considerably earlier than Cabernet Sauvignon, which is largely why it is a much less even cropper, but it also ripens rather earlier (mid-season rather than late mid-season) and will therefore ripen in areas, such as St-Emilion, where Cabernet Sauvignon is thought to succeed only in exceptionally warm years.

In France in the sixties, Cabernet Franc was a much more widely planted variety than Cabernet Sauvignon, but was overtaken in 1979 when each variety covered about 23,000 hectares (57,500 acres) and became France's eighth and ninth most popular red grape varieties. Although more recent totals are not available, both have become increasingly popular, but Cabernet Sauvignon has raced ahead because of its "ameliorating" progress through the Midi. Cabernet Franc's sphere of influence is more northern: the Anjou-Saumur region of the Loire valley, Bergerac and the right bank of the Gironde.

Cabernet Franc, known as Bouchet, was already recognized as particularly suitable for the Libournais vineyards by the end of the eighteenth century, as shown in the Subdelegate's appraisal of contemporary vine varieties dated 1784 and quoted by Enjalbert in his study of the wines of St-Emilion, Pomerol and Fronsac. It seems likely that it was exported from here to the Médoc where it now constitutes about 20 percent of the average property's *encépagement*.

It is reasonable to ask why the Médocains persist with Cabernet Franc. Their Merlot is an obviously different grape variety whose complementary qualities can easily be appreciated. If Cabernet Sauvignon is their truly great variety, why not more of it? This is like, and closely associated with, the canard that if a bit of tannin is good for a wine, then a lot of it will be very good. The Cabernet Franc gives the wine the same sort of flavour and structure as Cabernet Sauvignon, without as much of the uncompromisingly hard elements of acid and tannin, which must be a help in some vintages. The fact that Cabernet Franc is more productive than Cabernet Sauvignon should not be overlooked, and a bit of Cabernet Franc is also presumably a hedge against the vagaries of the weather. Both Cabernets are unlikely to suffer equally, and in a very cool year the Cabernet Franc does at least stand a chance of ripening. Perhaps best proof of the benefit of the muting qualities of Cabernet Franc are some of the 100 percent Cabernet Sauvignons made in California in the image of classed-growth claret. They show that you can, with wine as with everything else, have too much of a good thing.

One of the many delightful legacies left to discerning wine drinkers by the urbane and truly European Martin Bamford was evidence concerning just this aspect of claret doctrine. In the large and successful 1970 vintage, he had the obvious but iconoclastic notion of getting Château de Pez to vinify one cask of each of its four grape varieties separately so that the parts of the whole could be analysed. Fifteen years later, at a tasting in London, it was the Cabernet Franc that shone most radiantly. In cask, it had been the deepest coloured and least opulent on the nose, although, according to Michael Broadbent, it had gained a bit of flesh in bottle by 1976.

There is now about as much Cabernet Franc planted in the Loire as in Bordeaux: nearly 10,000 hectares (25,000 acres). In the Gironde total plantings of Cabernet Franc have been increasing gradually, while in the middle Loire the vine has been gaining ground rapidly as a popular alternative to Chenin Blanc. There is now no shortage of red wines labelled Anjou, Saumur and Touraine made substantially of Cabernet Franc, or Breton. The prototypes are Chinon, Bourgueil and the meatier St-Nicolas-de-Bourgueil, all made at the western end of the Touraine, bordering on Anjou-Saumur's red-wine capital, Champigny. In all but very exceptional vintages such Cabernet Franc wines are notably lighter in body and higher in acidity than wines based on Cabernet Franc grown further south – a sort of claret Beaujolais. Wines from the most fanatically quality-conscious growers can develop greater riches with the years, showing the pencil shavings when young but more layered fruitiness in maturity. The great majority of such wines are made, however, for less self-conscious enjoyment.

With their relatively high tannin content, Cabernets are not usually associated with rosé wines, but the Loire provides us with the exceptions to prove the rule: the luscious Cabernets d'Anjou. Some residual sugar is often used to overcome this disadvantage, and in any comparison with the ubiquitous Rosé d'Anjou, made usually of Gamay and Groslot, the firm fragrance of Cabernet seems dazzlingly aristocratic.

Galet thinks it highly probable that it was the Abbé Breton, Richelieu's intendant when he took over the Abbaye de St-Nicolas-de-Bourgueil, who was largely responsible for the export of the vine from Bordeaux to the Loire. If so, it provides earlier evidence than is available in Bordeaux of the vine's early establishment there, and it is an etymologically appealing theory. It was not until 200 years later, in the early nineteenth century, that the vine was recorded in northern Italy, having left little or no traces in the south of France.

Originally and erroneously the Italians called it Merlot (anticipating by a good 150 years the sort of difficulties Californians have had in differentiating the two vines); today it is still quite often called Bordo [*sic*] in the Veneto. It is one of the most widely planted red vine varieties in northeast Italy, which is also its most important territory outside France.

As with Pinot Bianco and Chardonnay, the Italians have not been obsessive about distinguishing the two Cabernets, even in DOC regulations, and so statistics on plantings of each are even more difficult to extract than most concerning Italy's vineyards. It is clear, however, that Cabernet Franc has been much more widely planted than Cabernet Sauvignon. On the face of it, this may seem at odds with the observation that Cabernet Sauvignon can withstand a warmer climate better than Cabernet Franc – even though parts of the northeast such as Trentino-Alto Adige can be pretty chilly.

The explanation lies in the sort of wines for which Cabernet is primarily being raised. Although there has been a very noticeable increase in interest in wines made with Cabernet Sauvignon and the life expectency of a good claret, most Italian "Cabernet" is fairly simple stuff intended for early consumption, for which purpose Cabernet Franc is, of course, much more suitable. This is certainly the case in both Friuli-Venezia Giulia and the Veneto where Cabernet is the most popular red varietal wine. Either or both Cabernets may be allowed, but the relatively light-bodied, soft structure of most demonstrates clearly that high-yielding clones of Cabernet Franc must be responsible (and it would be fair to say that the northeast of Italy provides some of the very few slurs on the good name of

*C*abernet Franc constitutes on average only 8 percent of the encépagement in the Médoc, although it can account for as much as 35 percent as here at Château Poujeaux in Moulis. One Cabernet Franc in five red vines is the average in St-Emilion and Pomerol, on the other hand, and that proportion is increasing as the poor Cabernet Sauvignon clone promulgated there by the authorities in the sixties is replaced.

CABERNET
FRANC

to the north. Probably the best Italian Cabernet Franc is produced, extraordinarily, on the heel of Italy, from Simonini's Favonio vineyards in Apulia, proving what can be done by warming up Cabernet Franc to give it flesh.

It would be interesting to compare a varietal Cabernet Franc from California or Australia, but such wines hardly exist. The Californians reckoned they had more than 160 hectares (400 acres) of Cabernet Franc planted by 1983 (120 hectares (300 acres) since 1977) mostly in Napa and Sonoma, where they are used almost exclusively as ballast for Cabernet Sauvignon and Merlot as winemakers get closer to the holy grail of Médocain practice.

Although Merlot is a more obliging producer, it seems likely that plantings of Cabernet Franc will increase perceptibly in California as the need for a suitable complement to Cabernet Sauvignon in top quality wines is recognized. In Australia, however, that need has been met surprisingly successfully by their ubiquitous Shiraz. Until recently Cabernet Franc was encountered in Australia as an old misfit vine in a parcel of Cabernet Sauvignon vines. Some growers, however, have been experimenting with Cabernet Franc, notably in Clare where the climate is just on the cusp, qualifying as a "cooler hot area" in which fully ripe Cabernet Franc can add a herbaceousness to balance the sometimes porty character of their Sauvignon.

There are no official records of Cabernet Franc in New Zealand although one might expect it to ripen more easily than Cabernet Sauvignon, their chief red grape variety which so often produces wines that taste as cool and leafy as Cabernet Franc. Plantings in South Africa total only a few hectares, but there are considerable plantings of Cabernet Franc in the southern hemisphere in Chile where they are often vintaged and vinified with the more prevalent Cabernet Sauvignon.

Cabernet Franc also appears to be widely planted throughout eastern Europe, in Yugoslavia particularly but also in Hungary, Romania and Bulgaria. This is a development of the northeastern Italian theme, but the wines are rarely sold as varietals so assessment is difficult.

Cabernet). Most of these wines are at their best within two or three years of the vintage, although there are some "serious" blends of the two Cabernets and sometimes even with Merlot. There are higher acid levels and sometimes more character in Cabernets produced in the upper vineyards of the South Tyrol and Trentino, though here again the two varieties are not distinguished.

According to Burton Anderson, Cabernet was the red grape of Emilia-Romagna's Colli Piacentini in the last century and there is now an increase in plantings of both kinds for more full-blooded wines than many of those made

---

Synonyms:
Breton (Loire); Carmenet (Médoc); Bouchet, Gros-Bouchet, Grosse-Vidure (St-Emilion and Pomerol); Véron, Bouchy, Noir-Dur, Méssange Rouge, Trouchet Noir (rest of France); Bordo, Cabernet Frank (Italy).

Soils:
Can withstand markedly wetter soils than Cabernet Sauvignon, e.g. clay or even volcanic soils.

Vigour:
More vigorous than Cabernet Sauvignon.

Pruning: Long cane pruning. Guyot commonly.

Susceptibility:
Good resistance to infections, but some susceptibility to downy and powdery mildews.

Rootstocks:
SO4, 5BB, 3309, Gloire de Riparia and 420A depending on soil type.

Yields:
Moderate; slightly higher than Cabernet Sauvignon.

High quality sought after in Italy and by those outside France trying to emulate Bordeaux most closely.

Gamay

In wine quality terms, the Gamay (or Gamay Noir à Jus Blanc, to give it its full name) is perhaps the Sauvignon Blanc of red grape varieties. It is vinified, using a special express route more often than not, specifically to produce light, fruity, uncomplicated wines for early consumption. Who wants or can afford to drink serious wines of venerable age all the time? What price Château Lafite in high summer? Gamay earns its place in this collection of major grape varieties with ease on the strength of the sheer quantity of good, if not great, wine it produces each year in a single region, Beaujolais.

No French wine region shows such devotion to a single grape variety as Beaujolais, where more than 98 percent of vines planted are Gamay. And these Gamay plantings, grown to produce France's most popular red wine, represent nearly 60 percent of France's 34,000 hectare (85,000 acre) total. Because the widespread plantings of Gamay outside Beaujolais and the eastern end of Touraine have declined quite substantially in the last 20 years, total plantings in France have decreased, but Gamay is still France's sixth most common red grape variety, rather less popular than Merlot, but more important than Cabernet Sauvignon.

Perhaps more than any other internationally known grape variety, Gamay is associated with a single wine region and a single wine type. A Gamay wine is expected to be just like the typical Beaujolais: light purple, with notably high acid, low tannin, no more than medium weight and an intense aroma suggestive of rather inky fruit juice. Equally cosmopolitan grape types have by now shaken off the dust of their home patch; but those who tinker away on their versions of Gamay, even in distant California, work with the Beaujolais manual very close by their side.

Gamay may well have originated a little to the north of the region it now so happily dominates. A huddle of Burgundian farm buildings near Chassagne-Montrachet rejoices in the name, and it is well known that, much to the disgust of the authorities, "Gamet" was extensively planted in the Côte d'Or in the nineteenth century and as far back as the fourteenth. It is a productive plant, much more so than the Pinot Noir, which it was thought to be ousting so dangerously on the Côte d'Or; and it is not difficult to understand its popularity with growers in a region such as Burgundy where the correlation between quality and reward has always been unreliable. Gamay was even widely planted in the Yonne in the last century, and it has only been the formulation and enforcement of the Appellation Contrôlée laws that have restricted it firmly and almost exclusively to the southerly region in which it performs best.

Less than 6 percent of all Côte d'Or vineyard is now planted with Gamay, although the variety is still the most popular in that buffer state between Burgundy proper and Beaujolais, the Mâconnais. But Chardonnay plantings are rapidly catching up here; and many vineyards are also being switched from Gamay, which here produces a thin, dull wine, to Pinot Noir which can be sold much more profitably as Bourgogne Rouge.

The more lowly *appellation* Bourgogne Passe-Tout-Grains, which sanctions a blend of not more than two-thirds Gamay with Pinot Noir, is a common product of the nearby Côte Chalonnaise, although the best versions, in which Pinot can start to dominate after five years or so, come from the Côte d'Or.

In his splendidly iconoclastic book *Burgundy*, Anthony Hanson argues that the Gamay is an inherently inferior grape variety that has been lucky enough to have been rescued from complete opprobrium by the application of a particularly felicitous vinification technique in Beaujolais. The grapes are fermented whole, fast and relatively warm, with some pumping over and a high proportion of added press wine, in a modified version of *macération carbonique*, except that the maceration is only about three (for Nouveaux) to eight days in total, and no carbonic gas is added. This helps to maximize the pigments and minimize

GAMAY

and longevity. The single most significant indicator that Gamay is capable of greater things than, for example, Sauvignon Blanc, is what happens to the best of these Crus Beaujolais with time. It is by now a common tenet of wine lore that a Moulin-à-Vent from a ripe vintage starts to taste like a mature Côte d'Or Pinot Noir after eight years or so. The same sort of mysterious transformation can happen to wines from other *crus*, and the innumerable, although not necessarily revered, caches of nineteenth-century bottles to be found in Beaujolais growers' cellars testify to the Gamay's ability not only to survive, but to mature.

On the flatter, more clayey vineyards of the Bas-Beaujolais, straightforward AC Beaujolais is produced, for which the official maximum yield is 55 hectolitres per hectare, as opposed to 48 hectolitres for the *crus* and 50 hectolitres for AC Beaujolais-Villages. This is usually jacked up by the annual petition of mitigating circumstances presented by the growers to the authorities, just as minimum alcohol levels of 9 and 10 percent are often wildly surpassed by overenthusiastic chaptalization. The Gamay attains relatively low sugar levels, but few bottles of the cheapest Beaujolais give any hint of that fact.

Another characteristic of the Haut-Beaujolais is its special training method, the *gobelet*, whereby up to five branches, each with only two buds from the current year, are tied up in a goblet shape to a stake, or in a fan shape to a wire. In the Bas-Beaujolais the Guyot method, common-place in Burgundy and Bordeaux, is allowed, and accelerates the growing process somewhat. Throughout the region the density of vines is laid down at between 9,000 and 13,000 per hectare (3,600 to 5,200 per acre).

According to Anthony Hanson, by 1977 the research station in Villefranche had identified five clones of Gamay as suitably resistant to grey rot and poor flowering, yet giving good yield, sugars and acids in fairly small grapes. It is planned to propagate these throughout the Gamay vineyards of France.

About 15 percent of all French Gamay is planted in the Loire, mainly in the Touraine, where it produces wines labelled Gamay de Touraine (one of the few instances of varietal labelling in France) varying from very dilute ink to mouthwatering reds every bit as juicy as a good Beaujolais. Gamay is grown all over the Loire valley and can be found in many an Anjou Rosé. Anjou Gamay red has an *appellation* all to itself, although Cabernet Franc seems to work better here. Gamay is also a common ingredient in most northern *vins rouges de pays* (it can flourish and produce quite appetizing wine as far north as the Marches de Bretagne), and in many Loire satellite reds such as Coteaux d'Ancenis, Coteaux de l'Aubance and the wines of Haut-Poitou.

East of Anjou, Gamay (supported by Pinot Noir) takes over from Cabernet Franc as the predominant red grape variety. It crops up in that outer group of VDQS wine districts such as Châteaumeillant, St-Pourçain-sur-Sioule (where Pinot influence is clear in the better wines), Côtes d'Auvergne, Côtes du Forez and, even more successfully in the Beaujolais tradition, as Côte Roannaise. The Gamay is

*T*he human face of Beaujolais. Few of these men will be aware of how unusual they are in the wine world to work exclusively with one vine variety.

the tannins extracted from the skins, and makes long-term evolution of the wine unlikely. But if the method is so effective at transforming a mediocre grape variety into the succulent and stimulating fruit juices that epitomize good Beaujolais, why is it not practised more widely elsewhere?

A further counterargument to the widely held theory that rotten old Gamay is saved only by vinification technique is that many of the finest wines of the Beaujolais region are not made in this speedily efficient way at all, but by traditional red-winemaking methods involving long fermentation of pressed, destalked grapes, practised by *all* Beaujolais growers until the sixties.

It is certainly true that much of the Gamay planted outside the Beaujolais region produces wine that is simply *too* thin and acid, although the quality of Ardèche and some Touraine examples has improved considerably in recent years. Part of the explanation for Gamay's superior performance in Beaujolais may lie in the soil and in particular the vines' interaction with the granite base of the Haut-Beaujolais where all the finest wines are produced.

It is beyond dispute that Gamay is at its finest on the rolling hillsides of the Haut-Beaujolais, in the nine Crus of Beaujolais: Chiroubles, St-Amour, Brouilly, Côte de Brouilly, Fleurie, Juliénas, Chénas, Morgon and Moulin-à-Vent, in very approximately ascending order of richness

*T*he Château de St-Amour is distinctly grander than the typical peasant farmhouse of the Beaujolais region, just as the wines of the ten Beaujolais crus, including St-Amour, are grander – more concentrated and longer-lived – than the typical basic Beaujolais. The crus tend to have particularly pretty names; it is easy to confuse them with their wines' supposed characteristics.

also planted in fringe vine areas of the northern Rhône and is particularly successful in some years as Gamay de l'Ardèchc. There still, curiously, a few Gamay plantings in Champagne, mostly in the Aube.

All these wines are made from the grape called Gamay Noir à Jus Blanc to distinguish it from the less noble family of Gamays Teinturiers, which have that mark of ill-breeding, red pulp, sometimes used to add colour to *vin de table*, but less and less commonly.

Gamay vines can perform well at high altitudes: they are grown, again in conjunction with Pinot Noir, in both the Vaud and Valais cantons of Switzerland, and are often a major ingredient in the ubiquitous Dôle, although apparently heavily chaptalized, or even cut with the ordinary reds Switzerland imports in such quantity. Just over the Pass, Gamay has recently been planted in the Valle d'Aosta and has resulted in the eminently gulpable Vin des Chanoines.

Apart from some tiny experimental plantings noted by Ian Read in Bairrada, Gamay is not encountered in the Iberian peninsula, nor indeed anywhere else in Europe.

The newer wine regions have on the whole ignored Gamay, though many California growers have been under the erroneous impression that they were growing it for some years. The grape they call Gamay Beaujolais, producing a heavy, rich, deep-coloured wine, has been identified by Davis's Professor H. Olmo as a fairly inferior clone of Pinot Noir. More recently, Montpellier's Professor P. Galet has

suggested that the more productive, lighter grape called Napa Gamay, and sometimes just Gamay to distinguish it from Gamay Beaujolais, is Valdiguié, the rudely productive but declining grape of the Midi and southwest France. Both grapes are vinified in traditional and current Beaujolais techniques, producing a wide range of different styles of wine, few of them of great quality.

Charles F. Shaw was a pioneer in making "serious" wine in the Beaujolais mould at his eponymous winery at St Helena in Napa. Since then full-bodied, wood-aged wines supposedly modelled on ultra-traditional Beaujolais have appeared under the Verité label. Unsurprisingly, the California wines that have come closest to current Beaujolais as produced in France appeared under the label of the self-appointed "Prince de Beaujolais", Georges Duboeuf, using a blend of Gamay Beaujolais and Napa Gamay grapes.

Even more misleading – and common – is the long-standing confusion of Gamay with the quite distinct variety known as Blauer Limberger in Germany, Blaufränkisch and Limberger in Austria, Kékfrankos in Hungary and so on. Indeed so well entrenched is the theory that these two varieties are closely related that the Bulgarian synonym for Blaufränkisch is Gamé.

A quite remarkably small proportion of wine drinkers and vine growers are aware of the extent to which true Gamay is geographically concentrated: in Beaujolais and, to a lesser extent, in the Loire valley.

Synonyms: Gamay Noir à Jus Blanc, Petit Gamai, Gamay Rond, Bourguignon Noir.	*Pruning:* Classically *gobelet*, but Guyot is also common.
Soils: Responds best to the high schistous granite hills covered with sandy clay of the Haut-Beaujolais.	*Susceptibility:* Grey rot. *Rootstocks:* Vialla in the Haut-Beaujolais, otherwise 3309C and SO4.
Vigour: Relatively vigorous.	*Yields:* Quite productive.

Medium to good quality. Not fashionable outside Beaujolais.

Garnacha (Grenache)

The quality of the wines this hot-climate vine produces may not always dazzle, but their sheer quantity, whether as Garnacha, Grenache or even Cannonau, earns it a place in this section. Indeed the quality of its wines can only be guessed at since this is a vine designed for blending rather than varietals. That in itself is a fair indication that most of the wine lacks something; colour and tannin, for instance. Garnacha is noted for brawn rather than beauty.

The Spanish spelling is only proper for a vine variety now dispersed the wine world over, but Spanish in origin and widely planted in Spain. It was probably first identified in the northern province of Aragón, whence it spread without too much difficulty to Rioja, and later across the Pyrenees to Roussillon and beyond into what is now Grenacheland in the south of France.

As Garnacha Tinta, and often Garnacho Tinto, it is Spain's most widely planted dark vine, covering about 15 percent of Spain's uniquely extensive vineyards. This reflects in part Garnacha's great viticultural strength: it is one of the comparatively rare vines that thrives in very arid, rather windy conditions. Its upright growth and particularly strong wood help in these respects, and those cultivating Garnacha in irrigated vineyards take care to stop irrigation sooner than for most other varieties so as to simulate the conditions in Spain and the Midi, for which the vine seems to have been naturally selected.

The vine buds relatively early but needs a long growing cycle to ripen, during which sugar levels are often built up to readings unparalleled in any other variety. Varietal Garnacha with an alcohol level of 15 or even 16 percent is by no means unknown in Spain. The musts, notably low in malic acid, can be difficult to ferment fully; they also have an inconvenient habit of oxidizing easily, which means that they are rarely good candidates for long ageing.

Standard wine lore has it that Garnacha grapes are thin-skinned, low in pigments and therefore ideal for rosé production. It is true that Garnacha makes some very pretty rosés all over the world, but this may have as much to do with the rather sweet, very fruity flavour, markedly low in tannin, as with the quality of the colouring matter. Certainly the colour of Garnacha grapes when ripe varies enormously according to how severely the vine was pruned and in what microclimate and soil it was grown. On flat fertile plains the vine can easily produce lots of pale pink, thin-skinned grapes, but on land too inhospitable for any crop other than vines or olives, the grapes can ripen to a deep purplish crimson producing a wine to match. To retain its exuberant character, Garnacha's yield should be kept low, certainly below 50 hectolitres per hectare unless very carefully trained.

Although it is commonly used as sole progenitor of rosés, Garnacha is usually blended with other, rather less blowsy grape varieties in red wine production. This is true in its adopted principal Spanish wine region Rioja. Like the much leaner Tempranillo with which it is usually blended, Garnacha occupies 40 percent of total vineyard land in Rioja, although its influence shows signs of decline. Unlike Tempranillo it is concentrated very much at the hotter, eastern end of the region, comprising Rioja Baja's most important grape variety by far, though Jan Read notes extensive plantings around San Asensio and Mormejilla in Rioja Alta. Garnacha's traditionally pallid grapes are sometimes picked specially early here (although Rioja's early is late for most of France) to produce *rosados* or the region's light red *claretes*. Some of Rioja's full-blooded *tintos* are the product of Garnacha alone, and rather oppressively rumbustious they can be. Alcohol without elegance is the hallmark of much of Rioja's Garnacha, but when well vinified (and there have been some interesting carbonic maceration wines) it can provide a velvety wine with a voluptuousness quite impossible from the angular Tempranillo.

Just to the north, Navarra is the Garnacha region par excellence, showing how a lower yield can be a good thing. Most reds here are based on or exclusively made from Garnacha, as indicated by their relatively light colour. They tend to be higher in acid and lower in alcohol than their counterparts from Rioja. Garnacha is also a customary ingredient in Catalonia's wide range of blended reds, adding its particularly casual note of ripe fruitiness in an area which is perhaps in no great need of it.

Garnacha has the distinction of being one of the ingredients in Spain's most revered wine, Vega Sicilia produced near Valladolid. It achieves lesser heights in the rest of Spain's vineland.

The grape has become increasingly important in the south of France where it has decisively overtaken the high-yielding, low-quality Aramon to become France's second most widely planted dark grape after Carignan. The agricultural census of 1979 notes 78,000 hectares (195,000 acres) of Grenache, 27,000 (67,500 acres) more than a decade earlier.

GARNACHA (GRENACHE)

Grenache is concentrated very positively around the south and particularly southeast of France. Although Grenache Noir is usually the fourth or fifth most important vine variety in each of the four *départements* that go to make up the vast and basic Languedoc-Roussillon wine region of the Midi, it is most important in Tavel, Châteauneuf-du-Pape and Côtes-du-Rhône country. More than a third of all French plantings of Grenache are in the neighbouring *départements* of Gard and Vaucluse. Here, especially in Châteauneuf-du-Pape, is the large-pebbled terrain subject to the merciless mistral where Grenache flourishes above all other varieties. This is presumably a major factor in its popularity here.

This is blending-vat territory where, ever since the Châteauneuf-du-Pape recipe was drawn up with its 13 possible ingredients, all local vintners have fashioned wines in this image. As well as being the major ingredient in this, the most reputed wine of the southern Rhône, it is also the major contributor to the reds and rosés, especially rosés, of Tavel, Lirac, Gigondas, Côtes du Ventoux, Coteaux du Tricastin and Côtes-du-Rhône wines of all ranks. In the most *sérieux* examples of these southern Rhône wines, the complex Syrah can dominate the blend, turning it into a deep-coloured, positively perfumed, dry and tough brute when young, the antithesis of a predominantly Grenache blend. The lesser appellations provide perhaps the best example of the simple, openly fruity style of mainly Grenache wines, with the less common varieties such as Mourvèdre often adding notes of interest.

Tavel rosé, whose glory has rather faded now, is the wine most commonly associated with Grenache, and certainly those who have succumbed know that it amply demonstrates the variety's high alcohol level. Like its lesser cousin Lirac rosé, it can often show the must's tendency to oxidize, although this is helped by the practice of including white varieties in the blend.

The variety is also part of the make-up of just about every Provençal red and certainly of the dry salmon-pink wines so popular in this *coin de vacances*.

Around the coast towards Spain Grenache Noir makes a major contribution, with Grenaches Gris and Blanc, to the rich and robust *vins doux naturels* such as Banyuls, Rivesaltes (a synonym) and Rasteau – all the local sweet fortified wines except for the Muscats.

Grenache is also important in Corsica where it blends commonly with local varieties, just as it does, under the name of Cannonau, in Sardinia. Some have advanced the theory that Cannonau is the Canocazo of Andalucia, but ampelographical evidence points to the link with Garnacha. With this vine, too, sugar levels are particularly high, grape flavour is fairly simple, and the major problem is one of colour extraction. Garnacha Blanca is also probably present on the island as Cannonau appears in all colours between red and white, as well as all degrees of sweetness up to a sort of countrified port.

Regulations for the very common DOC Cannonau di Sardegna require the wine to be at least 13.5 percent alcohol for the basic dry red, and a fearsome 15 percent for the *superiore*. The wines are given at least a year in wood here, as of course are the Châteauneuf-du-Pape models, but they are not considered wines for long ageing. Here the varietals take on an earthiness but the typically simple sweet fruitiness underlies it. The grape is also occasionally encountered in Sicily and the deep south of Italy.

The vine should be extremely well suited to other Mediterranean vineyards and has perhaps been prevented from an assault on Greece, for instance, by that country's viticultural insularity. It is grown quite extensively in Israel, and was one of the more successful vines in the Algerian wine industry in its heyday, and still makes a significant contribution to the surprisingly alluring rosés of Morocco.

The vine's ability to withstand dry heat and produce fairly generously has been recognized in the major newer wine regions, notably Australia, South Africa and particularly California. Grenache is the state's fourth most common red-wine grape, with 7,200 hectares (18,000 acres) planted mainly in the Central Valley, but also in the rather more temperate Mendocino area. It is used mainly for slightly sweet pink or porty wines and may account for some of the rather light colour and jammy character of so many California ports. Since neither rosé nor dessert wines are exactly the most modish wines in the United States, one might expect total Grenache plantings to decline, but there has been a steady increase. This may not continue as the vine with its strong stems is difficult to machine harvest.

The vine is expected to earn its keep here by producing huge quantities of wine, up to 15 tons per acre from 14 to 18 two- to four-bud spurs. It would be interesting to see whether restricting yields in a medium-hot area such as Mendocino could produce wines with the character of some of the best (mainly Grenache) Châteauneufs such as Château Rayas.

Grenache is Australia's best kept secret. It constitutes the country's second most widely planted red-wine grape, after Shiraz, yet is hardly ever encountered on a wine label. The 4,000 hectares (10,000 acres) are scattered over the irrigated areas of New South Wales and Victoria but the great majority are in the non-irrigated vineyards in the Southern Vales and Barossa Valley of South Australia. Here especially, Grenache's lack of colour, tannin and longevity could be a problem in unblended wines, so it typically forms part of a blend for a cheap dry red or fast-maturing dessert wine. (And if the Australians describe Grenache as a rapid developer, it must practically brown before one's eyes.)

The Australian experience underlines the observation that crop levels determine quality with this variety more than most, and that there is a very marked relationship between expected crop level and foliage.

Grenache has a long history in South Africa: in 1910 the vitculturist A. Perold could gleefully demonstrate that South African Grenache, Grenache cuttings from Montpellier and Garnacha cuttings from Rioja were one

*O*ak barrels are fundamental to both of Garnacha's most famous liquid manifestations, Châteauneuf-du-Pape and Rioja. The Muga bodega in Haro is one of the most traditional in its methods of making Rioja, and Garnacha is bought in to flesh out the Tempranillo backbone.

and the same cultivar. It has dipped in favour there, however, and now represents a tiny proportion of the country's vintage.

Grenache Blanc is also well known, especially in the south of France where its profusion makes it France's third most important white-wine grape.

Synonyms:
Garnacho, Lladoner, Tinto, Tinta,
Tinto Aragones, Granaccia, Carignan Rosso,
Roussillon Tinto, Uva di Spagna,
Tintilo de Rota, Tinto Menudo,
Tinta Mencida, Tentillo (Spain);
Grenache Noir, Granacha, Alicante,
Bois Jaune, Carignane Rousse,
Sans Pareil, Roussillon, Rivesaltes,
Redondal, Rouvaillard,
Aragonais, Ranconnat (France);
Cannonau (Sardinia);
Granaccia (Sicily).

Soils:
Produces best quality on dry, rocky slopes.
In California it is best adapted to deep loamy sands or fine sandy loams.

Vigour:
Very vigorous, upright growth.

Pruning:
In Spain and France both long and short spur pruning with *gobelet* training are employed. It has performed well as head-trained spur-pruned vines in Australia. Spur pruning and cordon training are used in California.

Susceptibility:
Very susceptible to downy mildew, as well as anthracnose, bunch rot, grape berry moth and a wide range of insect predators. On very vigorous vines there is a tendency to berry shatter. Virus-infected vines suffer from *coulure*.

Rootstocks:
No affinity problems. Chiefly Rupestris St George, 99R, 44-53M, 110R, 41B and 3309C.

Yields:
Productive, and one of the best producers in dry and windy conditions.

Quality depends on yield, but generally only moderate. Useful, not fashionable.

Cinsaut

Like some cleverly marketed tonic, Cinsaut has been successfully sold to the vignerons of the south of France on the basis that it is good for them. The most widely planted of the replacements for the likes of Aramon and Alicante Bouschet, vaunted as a saviour of wine from the Midi, Cinsaut trebled its territory in the seventies to become France's fourth most common red-wine grape variety with well over 50,000 hectares (125,000 acres) planted by 1979. At its peak as a wine producer, Algeria used to have even more than this, but today most of these plantings are but memories or neglected stumps.

The vine owed its popularity in North and South Africa to its ability to withstand very hot conditions. It also shares with Grenache an attractively high (to vine growers at least) level of productivity. Cinsaut has the advantages of ripening earlier and having distinctly more acidity, colour and even a bit of character. Like Grenache, however, its intensity of colour and flavour are inversely proportional to the yield, which means that Cinsaut is capable of producing styles of wine encompassing everything from delicate rosé to fiery port.

Its character, a rather meaty, chunky sort of flavour, uncomfortably suggestive of dogfood to some, is highly individual but can add real substance to a blend that is primarily Grenache and/or Carignan. Like them, it produces wines low in tannin; Syrah or Cabernet Sauvignon is needed to give a Midi blend life expectancy.

Unlike the strong-stemmed Grenache, Cinsaut has that highly desirable modern attribute, the ability to be machine harvested with ease. And it has thick grapeskins, which give it useful botrytis resistance. It is not surprising that it has enjoyed such popularity and may just be one of the varieties with which we become more familiar as a single varietal wine over the next decade or two, although we should not be persuaded it is a variety with the individuality or class of Syrah.

While France's Grenache plantings are concentrated in the eastern half of the southern vineyard sweep, those of Cinsaut are mostly in the west. The three "problem" (problem = wine lake) *départements* of the Languedoc-Roussillon – Aude, Hérault and Gard – accounted for well over a third of all French Cinsaut plantings at the 1979

CINSAUT

agricultural census. Provence is the other important grower of Cinsaut as is northern Corsica.

Although it can make excellent rosé, Cinsaut is usually used either as an improving ballast for the oceans of ordinary table wines produced in the west of the Midi, or as just one ingredient in the varietal cocktail characteristic of the better-quality wines from the eastern Midi. In Châteauneuf-du-Pape it is not as widely planted as Syrah, nor even as much as Mourvèdre, and throughout this corner of rather recherché little appellations, it usually plays third or fourth fiddle. Experiments in the Midi also show it blends well with Cabernet Sauvignon.

To taste Cinsaut pure and simple it is necessary to go to South Africa – and even there it is a rarity. The variety was imported from the south of France in the mid-nineteenth century and until the mid-sixties Cinsaut was the single most widely planted cultivar, occupying nearly 30 percent of Cape vineyards at one stage. Ironically, it began to be known as Cinsaut only in the early seventies when its star was waning. Until then, when trading agreements with France made certain, perhaps understandable, demands concerning nomenclature, it was known as Hermitage. This was not only naughty but confusing, since Cinsaut is neither grown in northern Rhône nor allowed in this great wine. Perhaps the Boerisation of the word which transformed it into "Hermitake" excuses this liberty.

Cinsaut's position in South Africa is similar to that occupied by Shiraz in Australia and Zinfandel in California. Its popularity was due to its productivity and sugar levels. But such high yields are expected of the vine that much of the wine produced is fairly thin stuff. It is clearly difficult for a nation's winemakers to even consider how to make interesting wine from their most widely planted red grape variety: the answer is, in part, by much stricter pruning. Fairly predictably, Cinsaut is used chiefly as blending material, but the exceptionally high sugar levels attained in some areas make it a good base for port-style wines. Much of the less concentrated Cinsaut is distilled under the terms of South Africa's alcohol regime.

In lighter wines, though light is only a relative term here, it also makes a fine complement for the much harder Cabernet Sauvignon and some producers blend it with Shiraz to produce a rather looser-textured red. Extreme care is needed in site selection, pruning and training for the vine to succeed as a varietal wine, and such wines are not noted for their longevity, though they can be fruitily charming with better structure than a Grenache.

Total South African vineyard planted to Cinsaut is declining but the variety is still the Cape's third favourite, behind Chenin Blanc and Palomino, accounting for well over 10 percent of all vines planted. Whatever happens to the popularity of Cinsaut, it still lives on as parent of South Africa's gift to the world, Pinotage. Their Professor A. Perold crossed Pinot and "Hermitage" in 1925, but it was only in the early sixties that it was acclaimed and popularized. A Cinsaut Blanc or Albatros has also been developed on a small scale in South Africa.

In Australia too, it is not one of those varieties nurtured by the warmth of fashion: there are fewer than 200 hectares (500 acres) planted, mainly old vines in the Barossa Valley with some irrigated area plantings used chiefly for blending with Cabernet or Shiraz. Certainly there seems little point in continuing with Cinsaut (or Oeillade with which it used to be confused) when Shiraz is such an obliging and noble alternative. In the meantime, it has been noted that those Cinsaut grapes still harvested in Australia make notably better table grapes than most other grapes used more usually to make red wine. The low tannin level helps.

Like Grenache, Cinsaut seems ideally suited to the eastern Mediterranean and has been the most popular variety in Lebanese vineyards. There is also an island of Cinsaut in the far south of Italy round Brindisi where the vine is known as Ottavianello and the best-known wine produced from it, distinguished by Burton Anderson as "subtly flavoured", is Ostuni Ottavianello. Some estimates put plantings of the vine in Apulia as high as 3,000 hectares (7,500 acres).

Cinsaut, often spelt Cinsault, is still found in many North African vineyards. Algerian reds owe much to it, usually blended with Carignan and Alicante. It is worth ruminating on just how much Cinsaut (and Grenache) "old-fashioned burgundy" may have contained. Perhaps it can develop quite well when blended with Pinot Noir!

Synonyms:
Cinsault, Cinq-saou, Plant d'Arles, Bourdales,
Milhau, Morterille Noire, Prunelas, Picardan Noir,
Espagne, Ulliaou, Passerille, Papdou,
Poupe de Crabe, Prunella, Calabre,
Cuviller, Petaire, Salerne, Malaga (France);
Ottavianello (Italy); Hermitage (South Africa);
Oeillade, Blue Imperial (Australia).

Soils: Adaptable.

Vigour: Low to moderate.

Pruning:
Spur pruning necessary.
Head pruning yields best quality results.

Susceptibility:
High and varied. It is sensitive to both downy and
powdery mildew and sometimes drops its berries just
before picking. Tough skins give it good
resistance to rain damage.

Rootstocks:
Less vigorous rootstocks such as 3309C recommended
for hillside vineyards and quality; berlandieri-rupestris
rootstocks are so vigorous that grapes will not darken
sufficiently.

Yields:
Potentially high. Can vary (as does quality)
between 30 hl/ha and 100 depending on
how and where grown.

Medium quality; good blending material. Not fashionable.

Carignan

Although it is grown in quantity only in France and California, Carignan probably produces more red wine than any other vine variety in the world. The much more widely dispersed Trebbiano is its only serious rival as the most productive vine in the world.

It was first isolated around the town of Cariñena in the province of Aragón in northeast Spain. The wine Cariñena is still that region's most famous, but the eponymous vine is only its third most important ingredient after Grenache and Bobal. Not even among the country's top twenty vines, Cariñena has never caught on in Spain the way it has over the Pyrenees and across the Atlantic (which is why it has not been honoured with its Spanish name).

Carignan was already known in southwest France in the twelfth century and from its base in the Pyrenées Orientales and Aude has spread all over the Midi. In the sixties it replaced and overtook the much less substantial Aramon as most common producer of *vin ordinaire* from the Languedoc-Roussillon, which made it France's most widely planted grape variety by far. In the seventies plantings levelled off and by 1979, the last agricultural census, there were 207,000 hectares (517,500 acres), nearly treble the total plantings of France's second most important red-wine grape variety, Grenache.

Today in the Languedoc-Roussillon region there is a perceptible diminution in Carignan's popularity as the nobler varieties slowly gain ground, and as the Carignan grapes' tenacious hold on the vine and the tendency to produce a second crop of hard green berries are recognized

CARIGNAN

as disadvantages in the age of the mechanical harvester.

Carignan's great viticultural advantage over Aramon is that it buds late and is therefore rarely prey to spring frosts. Flowering is usually in warmer, settled weather and, therefore, much more successful. Perhaps the great catalyst to replacing Aramon with Carignan was the damage suffered by Aramon after the winter frosts of 1956 and 1963.

Carignan shares with Aramon extraordinarily bountiful yields, but the quality of the wine produced is very obviously higher. The thick-skinned Carignan produces deep-coloured wines, relatively high in alcohol, extract and tannin. These qualities are more pronounced in wines made from hillside vines grown on poor soils with fairly strict pruning, but even on the more fertile plains, some shadow of these characteristics is apparent. For this reason, Carignan is officially classified as a vine "recommended" for the Midi as opposed to the Aramon which is merely "authorized".

It may come as a surprise to learn that this extremely popular vine is not all that easy to raise to healthy ripeness. It is so sensitive to powdery mildew that it needs considerably more sprayings than most other vines. It is also susceptible to downy mildew, and rot can be a problem on higher-yielding vines. In these circumstances, the thicker skins are not always sufficient compensation for the compactness of the bunches. Were the French anything like as enthusiastic nurserymen as the Germans, one feels sure that such a vine, or at least such clones of the vine, would not have been allowed to spread so widely. The producers of agricultural chemicals at least have good reason to be grateful for official vine policy in the Midi.

The vine is hardly found north of the Mediterranean *départements* as it is very late ripening as well as late budding, and so needs an area which permits a long growing season. Two-thirds of French plantings of Carignan are in the Aude and the Hérault, the biggest of the big Languedoc-Roussillon wine *départements*, in which it represents a staggering 65 percent of total plantings of wine grapes.

No wine in France is ever sold as a varietal Carignan, but a considerable proportion of red *vin de table* must be just that. Better, more fleshy and interesting wines result from blending in a bit of Cinsaut and/or Grenache (Cinsaut being more likely in the west and Grenache in the east of the Midi). Worse, coarser, thinner wines result from blending with Aramon. More alcoholic, deeper coloured, though not necessarily more interesting wines result from blending with the huge quantities of *rosso* imported into southern France from Sicily and Apulia. It seems odd that such an astringent grape should have been promulgated for cheap wines that no one would dream of ageing. A considerable and increasing proportion of southern French reds are now made by some sort of carbonic maceration rather than traditional vinification methods in an effort to produce softer Carignan. Tannin is usually seen as an advantage in a young red wine, but since so much Carignan is produced to be drunk young, and at a yield so high that the compensating fruitiness level is low, its

astringency is ironically a disadvantage, although it provides a good foil for the much softer grapes Cinsaut and Grenache. A maximum of 60 percent Carignan blended with equal parts of these two varieties is the approved recipe for the Midi red of the future.

In California, gaining a vowel in mid-Atlantic, the Carignane is the state's third most widely planted red-wine grape variety, having been overtaken by the much more aristocratic Cabernet Sauvignon in 1976. Although the rate of new planting has slowed dramatically, there are still about 8,000 hectares (20,000 acres) of Carignane in California. The majority are in the Central Valley as much of the cooler areas is unsuitable for such a late-ripener and anywhere affected by coastal fog encourages powdery mildew. Much of the plant material is virus infected, which reduces sugar levels and colour in many instances.

It is still possible to find a varietal Carignane so labelled in California, but the great majority of the wine disappears into blends for cheap jug wines, reds and rosés. Home winemakers represent another major market for this grape, sometimes called "the grower's grape" in California because it grows so vigorously and yields so productively, not qualities that would ever qualify it as "the wine drinker's grape". Californians have also noticed very marked differences in quality according to the fertility of the soil, weather and pruning technique.

Carignan is also a considerable variety in South America. There is nearly as much Carignan produced in Chile as Merlot, and it is also known in both Argentina and Mexico.

There are some plantings in South Africa and even China, though probably none in Australia although there are varieties called Carignan and (another synonym) Mataro. Their "Mataro" is definitely Mourvèdre, while "Carignan" is a disease-prone variety called Bonvedro.

Like Cinsaut and Grenache, it has possibilities all around the Mediterranean, and like them was cultivated extensively in Algeria and to a much more limited extent in Morocco and Tunisia. Carignan has also been the mainstay of the Israeli wine industry, though it is being gradually replaced by nobler grape varieties.

As Carignano, the vine is also known in Italy. Some is grown in Latium just south of Rome, but it is most common in Sardinia as a robust red which is occasionally accorded the compliment of ageing. There is even a relatively new DOC, Carignano del Sulcis for red and rosé wines made chiefly of grapes grown on the islands of Sant'Antioco and San Pietro in the corner of Sardinia closest to Spain.

And finally, back to the birthplace of the vine. Cariñena, so sought after in the last century, is still made near Zaragoza today for those who have the head for it. Most of the rest of the vines called Cariñena in Spain are grown in Catalonia. Along with Garnacha Tinta, Monastrell and Tempranillo, it is one of the selection of local red wine varieties from which the sturdy blends are made. As in the Midi, its deep colour and astringency is a particularly apt foil for the soft, fairly pale, fruitiness of Grenache.

A vine called Mazuelo is one of the Rioja region's oldest, now falling into disfavour because of its susceptibility to powdery mildew but still constituting 10 percent of the average red Rioja blend. The EEC allows Mazuelo to be used as a synonym for Cariñena and the varieties seem to be viticulturally and vinously identical. The Rioja producers acknowledge the very useful deep colour of the musts produced but deplore the coarseness of the wine.

The Carignan will never be great and, productivity apart, its chief characteristics – disease-prone vines producing wines high in colour and tannin – are not what one would expect of the most common wine producer today.

Synonyms:
Carignan Noir, Bois Dur, Catalan, Roussillonen, Monestel, Plant de Lédenon (France); Cariñena, Mazuelo, Tinto Mazuelo, Crujillon, Samsó (Spain); Pinot Evara (Portugal); Carignano, Uva di Spagna (Italy); Carignane (California).

Soils:
Performs relatively well on very fine and poor soils.

Vigour:
Very high on very fertile soils.

Pruning:
Usually very generous. Its upright growth precludes the need for trellising. Cane pruning may lead to overcropping. Secondary crops are common on shoots.

Susceptibility:
High, especially to fungus diseases. Very susceptible to both sorts of mildew, especially powdery mildew, and to grey rot and grape berry moth.

Rootstocks:
Wide range; no affinity problems. Rupestris St George, 99R and 110R have most commonly been used.

Yields:
Very high. Up to 150 hl/ha or 12 tons per acre.

Low-mid quality. Not fashionable but very popular.

Barbera

Barbera is one of the world's most widely planted grape varieties. It is agreed that it beats Sangiovese as Italy's most common red-wine grape and, unlike Sangiovese, it has been embraced outside Italy, particularly in the Americas and notably in California where it is responsible for something like 12 percent of the state's red wine production.

With this impressive diffusion, it could do with better public relations; its image is in need of a polish. In both Italy and California it is generally regarded as a useful vine that thrives in warm to hot climates, producing wine usefully high in acid both reliably and copiously. In the last few decades, thanks to this reputation as the grape of expediency, Barbera has spread all over southern Italy and even to the islands, not short of volume-producing vines of their own. Meanwhile, as American demand for table wine grew, the California wine industry collectively planted 4,000 hectares (10,000 acres) of Barbera in one two-year span alone. And most of this planting has been in the sort of soils and microclimates designed to bring out the worst of the variety.

Unlike most other grape varieties employed in this workhorse role, Barbera does have thoroughbred potential, although only in areas cooler than those so enthusiastically planted in recent decades. At its best, in northwest Italy, Barbera can produce wines genuinely thrilling in their combination of deep purple with an almost shocking pink rim, pricklingly high acid, mouthfilling fruit and bone-dry finish. For all these elements to be realized, the grape's ripening must not be hurried, as it so often is in the Mezzogiorno and San Joaquin Valley; this results in much duller, almost "cooked" wines with few characteristics other than alcohol, a tendency to oxidize and an acid level higher than it deserves to be. Barbera is a relatively late ripener – a week or so earlier than the mighty Nebbiolo, it is true, but nearly two weeks after Piedmont's other "cheap and cheerful" grape, Dolcetto, distinguished from Barbera by being an even less suitable candidate for ageing.

Opinions vary on the merits of ageing Barbera. Some Piedmontese see Barbera as standing in the same sort of relation to Nebbiolo as does the Gamay of Moulin-à-Vent to the great Pinot Noir of the Côte d'Or: that with time, a well-made Barbera, from a good year, can evolve into something solid and very similar to the great wine that traditionally overshadows it. Other Piedmont palates cherish Barbera for those qualities that distinguish it from Nebbiolo: its easy, early drinkability. Its tannin level, usually higher than Dolcetto's, is considerably lower than Nebbiolo's. This helps make it the favourite drink by far of the typical, wine-drinking northwest Italian (although beer and cola continue their inexorable campaign south of the Alps). The great Nebbiolo wines are for marvelling at, and gently sipping after meals; Barbera is what lubricates the daily bread.

The vine probably originated around Monferrato and there were certainly references to grapes called Barbero and Barberi in the thirteenth century. The vine is gradually losing ground in its native Piedmont region but still accounts for an estimated 52 percent of all vine plantings there. Newcomers such as Cabernet Sauvignon may well annex some of its territory over the next few years. In his *Life Beyond Lambrusco*, Nicolas Belfrage points out that even Angelo Gaja, whose Vignarey is arguably the best Barbera of all, has been toying with the idea of uprooting all his Barbera in favour of Cabernet simply because Barbera's image is not sufficiently good to command high prices. At every vintage in the Albese grape market, Nebbiolo regularly fetches twice the price of Barbera, and Dolcetto about a third more.

Huge quantities of Barbera are vinified outside the DOC regime and enjoyed as simple *vini da tavola*. Among those relatively few DOC Barberas of Piedmont (Barbera

BARBERA

accounts for only 13 of more than 200 Italian DOCs), only Barbera d'Alba and Barbera d'Asti must be made solely of Barbera. The other well-known DOC Barbera, from Monferrato, contains 10–15 percent of Freisa, Grignolino and/or Dolcetto, and the more obscure Colli Tortonesi Barbera and Rubino di Cantavenna may be lightened by an even higher proportion of gentler grape varieties. The relative merits of the top three Piedmont Barberas are hotly disputed, but those from Alba and Asti usually fetch a higher price than the lighter wines of Monferrato.

Viala cites Pavia as Barbera's oldest known stamping ground and today Barbera is the major ingredient in a number of Oltrepò Pavese reds, including the region's straight DOC Rosso in which the acid of Barbera is muted by up to 45 percent of other grapes. Barbera is also well established in the neighbouring Piacenza hills in Emilia-Romagna where the local speciality, Gutturnio dei Colli Piacentini, has 60 percent Barbera blended with 40 percent Bonarda. Good Barbera, often slightly *frizzante* and sometimes even with the impression of sweetness, is also made in the hills around Bologna and Parma.

The variety has also played a major part in the struggle for postwar economic survival in the intensively agricultural regions of Italy's south, with Apulia and Campania having planted great swathes of Barbera across their arid land. It is perhaps significant that Barbera is particularly easy to machine harvest. Its noblest appearance this far south is in the DOC regulations for permitted commingling with the local Aglianico in Campania's great Taurasi but, significantly, the top producer Mastroberardino scorns the northern interloper. Offshore manifestations of the grape include a Barbera di Sardegna from around Cagliari and an experimental blend from Agrigento in southern Sicily.

By 1970, exasperatingly the last year for which official statistics on Italian vineyards are available, land producing nothing but Barbera grapes totalled 73,000 hectares (182,500 acres), representing 6 percent of all Italian vineyard land and about the same as plantings of Grenache in France. Barbera also played a part in a further 17,000 hectares (42,500 acres) of mixed cultivation. Today, Italy's Barbera vintage averages 5 million hectolitres, most of it in Piedmont, Oltrepò Pavese and the Piacentino.

There is considerable clonal variation in Barbera, notably in size of grape cluster. Generally speaking, the smaller the cluster, the better the resulting wine. Current Italian viticultural research is also concerned with improving the health of the Barbera, much of which is subject to leafroll virus.

This is also a problem in California's San Joaquin Valley where the vast majority of California's 6,800 hectares (17,000 acres) of Barbera are planted. Authorities as respected as Bob Thompson can cite occasional examples from the vineyards of Napa and Sonoma showing that brilliance is possible in cooler areas. In the main, however, Californians encounter Barbera merely as an ingredient in a cheap blended red, usually included to write off flab rather than contribute any specific flavour of its own.

Thanks to the strong Italian accent in the vineyards of

South America, Barbera is planted in Argentina, Brazil and even Uruguay. It is planted in Dalmatia, too.

The variety's importance in the world's vineyards is perhaps out of proportion to the relatively unimportant place it has in the heart of today's wine consumer. One wonders whether Barbera would occupy half the space it does today were it not for the fact that a high-acid grape makes useful blending material.

Synonyms:
Usually only geographical qualifications such as d'Asti and del Monferrato.

Soils:
Responds best to poor, calcareous soils and fairly well to sandy and clay loams. Vigour declines on sandier soils and poor performance on alkaline or saline soils.

Vigour: Quite vigorous.

Pruning: Generous spur pruning is customary.

Susceptibility:
Older vines very susceptible to leafroll virus both in Italy and California. Some problems with rot and with Pierce's disease too.

Yields:
High. 6–9 tons per acre in California. 70 hl/ha the norm for DOC Barbera in Italy.

Low to medium quality with isolated exceptions. Not fashionable.

Nebbiolo

Italians believe firmly in keeping their treasures to themselves. This applies as much to their best vine varieties as to their artistic and gastronomic heritage. Nebbiolo produces some of the greatest wines of the world, and yet is hardly planted outside one very specific corner of northwest Italy. It uniquely combines top quality and almost total isolation.

Nebbiolo produces excellent wine wherever it is grown here, whether on Lombardy's interface with the thirsty Swiss or in the higher reaches of the alpine foothills to the northwest. It has a concentration of non-fruity but complex, sometimes bitter flavour and a unique combination of extract, tannin and acid that, *in the right hands*, can be fashioned into a glorious liquid of awesome longevity.

It is generally agreed that Nebbiolo conveniently reaches its peak of quality in the hills to the southwest that supply Turin with its gastronomic delicacies, around the prosperous and historic truffle town of Alba. Flanking the town are Piedmont's twin stars of wine, Barolo and Barbaresco, the former conventionally masculine and imperiously long-lived, the latter gentler and more feminine. (As in Burgundy, the producer is no less important than the provenance of the grapes, but it is still easy to see how the stereotypes evolved.) So revered are these wines throughout the major population centres of Italy that they were the natural first candidates for elevation to the newly created rank of DOCG, though the wine-drinking public had to wait during their customary lengthy maturation period before inspecting these glamorous new creatures.

NEBBIOLO

*T*he Langhe hills of Barolo and Barbaresco country are so steep that matching exposure to variety is vital. Nebbiolo ripens last, sometimes not until well into November, and needs every ray of midday sunshine. Here Nebbiolo vines are trained high to minimize the effects of the autumn mist, or nebbia, from which the variety takes its name.

Italian viticulturists claim that wines made from what little Nebbiolo has been experimentally planted elsewhere in Italy show nothing like the intensity and class of these wines. And almost everywhere else in the world the most Nebbiolo can hope for is a row or two in an experimental nursery plantation. Alexis Lichine's researches managed to run some to earth in commercial production in Uruguay and there are a few isolated old plantings in California. Poor Nebbiolo is even at risk of losing ground in its homeland as an ever-increasing number of growers are swept away by enthusiasm for Cabernet Sauvignon and, yet more surprisingly, Chardonnay.

Everything about the vine suggests venerability: the ancient history of Alba at the heart of Piedmont's Nebbiolo country; local folklore; and the very character of the wines themselves. It is almost certainly the oldest of the Piedmontese varieties and doubtless evolved by natural selection as has most suitable genetic material for the region. A grape called "Nebiolium" is cited as early as 1512 in the records for the commune of La Morra, in the middle of what is today the Barolo district. Other hints at Nebbiolo's presence as an already recognized entity can be dated two centuries earlier, and some local historians are quite convinced that the Romans knew and loved the grape, to the extent of tarring the inside of barrels for other wines in the hope of giving them some Nebbiolo character.

The name is supposed to be derived from the word "nebbia", Italian for the fog that often rises out of the warmer valleys to enshroud the Albese hills in late October when the grapes are picked. There are a number of quite dissimilar local synonyms in different corners of Piedmont and those parts of the Valle d'Aosta and Lombardy in which the vine is cultivated. Most common, to non-Italians

at least, is Spanna (probably spelt Spana originally) under which name considerable quantities of non-DOC Nebbiolo are sold. The Nebbiolo-Spanna subvariety forms the base for most of Piedmont's DOC blends.

Today several subvarieties of Nebbiolo have been identified, the most highly respected, and those sanctioned by the DOCG regulations for Barolo and Barbaresco, being Michet, Lampia and Rosé. Picotener, Pugnet and Nebbiolo-Spanna are specified for that other highly regarded 100 percent Nebbiolo wine Carema produced from higher vineyards way to the north. Nebbiolo d'Alba and the fairly recent Roero, made from grapes grown in the lighter soils of the land between the Barolo and Barbaresco zones, are the only other DOC wines made exclusively from Nebbiolo unblended and untamed by any other variety.

Careful selection of vineyard sites is more important for Nebbiolo than for most other vines, and such is Nebbiolo's significance in terms of both price and prestige to the Piedmontese growers that it tends to get the very best land. This means that the late-ripening Nebbiolo is planted on the south-facing slopes of Piedmont's hilly vine country.

The altitude of the vineyards, and their distance from the sea, means that conditions are relatively cool for Italy. The snow-covered Alps are always in the background, winters can be very hard, and summers are never sweltering. The long autumns are a boon to Nebbiolo, whose naturally high levels of acid need to be abated by as much ripeness as possible. It rarely ripens much less than two weeks after Barbera and sometimes four weeks after Dolcetto. The additional sunlight of a south-facing slope is absolutely crucial to Nebbiolo, and very useful for the Cabernet Sauvignon being tried out in the Piedmontese hills – growers are having to make some tough decisions.

Toughness is indeed the essence of Nebbiolo. There is no other grape that is quite so cussedly high in tannin, acid, and dry extract, and which needs very careful winemaking to tame it into drinkability. Fermentation can last up to two weeks, often with the skins submerged to make the resultant wine even more tannic and deeply coloured than it would be otherwise. The wines need extensive ageing in most years, certainly as long as top-quality claret in many vintages. Large old wood, usually Slovenian oak, has been used traditionally so as not to add wood tannins to the already high level of fruit tannins. There has been something of a modernist movement recently to treat the wine to the refinement of some bottle ageing, resulting in rather less brutish liquids.

Nebbiolo wine has typically, as might be expected, a very deep colour. The only exception to this might be a straight Nebbiolo or Spanna in a poor vintage. Many of the wines are still black, with a notably orange rim through slight oxidation in cask, at 10 years old. They look "thick" in the glass and taste enormous. There is always lots of acid, usually discernible tannin even in older vintages, but in the best bottles there is fruit and, the real allure of Nebbiolo, a most wonderful scent.

The Romans might have been reminded of tar. The modern taster can certainly detect a certain dark grittiness. But, more attractively, there are violets there, and in Barolo and Barbaresco, to the fancifully minded at least, a hint of Alba's great delicacy, truffles. Such wines are liquids to linger over, both because of their high alcohol content (Barolo's minimum of 13 percent is higher than for any other table wine) and the complexity of their bouquet. They also seem to benefit from considerable aeration before serving.

Annual production of Nebbiolo in Italy averages only about 160,000 hectolitres, or about a quarter percent of all the wine produced by Italy each year. Less than a quarter of this goes into *vino da tavola*, most of it labelled Spanna and grown in the north of Piedmont. Unusually, the biggest production of Nebbiolo is also its most prestigious: Barolo, of which more than 50,000 hectolitres is made in an average vintage, and – after Nebbiolo *vino da tavola* – Barbaresco is the third most important manifestation of this great grape. This doubtless reflects Nebbiolo's limited yield, and uncooperative performance in the vineyard.

Gattinara and Ghemme are the most commonly encountered Piedmontese DOCs in which Nebbiolo may be blended with Bonarda and, in the latter case, with Vespolina. Others include Lessona (75 percent Nebbiolo), Boca (40 percent), Sizzano (40 percent), Bramaterra (50–70 percent) and Fara (30 percent).

Nebbiolo also has a strong presence in neighbouring Lombardy (it is likely that in the last century it was grown all over northern Italy). The Valtellina region way up on the Swiss border is a major stronghold of Nebbiolo, here called Chiavennasca. Each year up to 60,000 hectolitres are produced as Sassella, Grumello, Valgella and the wonderfully named Inferno containing at least 95 percent Nebbiolo, and ordinary Valtellina Rosso with at least 70 percent Nebbiolo. A local speciality is the concentrated Sfursat, Sfurzat or Sforzato, the method by which straight Valtellina grapes are semi-dried before being fermented up to 14.5 percent and beyond. Much of the wine is absorbed into Switzerland, which is a pity for the rest of us.

Nebbiolo is planted further south near Brescia where, with Cabernet Franc, Barbera and Merlot, it is one of the ingredients in the extraordinary Franco-Italian blend that constitutes Franciacorta Rosso. There is also Nebbiolo in the high altitude vineyards of the Valle d'Aosta, which produces small quantities of Donnaz, just across the regional boundary from the Carema vineyards.

Even the noble Nebbiolo is not immune from the plague of fashion, however. There is now a vogue in Italy for *vino novello* in the image of Beaujolais Nouveau. Oddly fruity young Nebbiolos following the Vinòt launched by Gaja in 1975 are now quite commonplace.

Some Nebbiolo is cultivated in Switzerland. In California Nebbiolo's influence is only the faintest shadow of that other vine import from Piedmont, the much more common or garden Barbera. All but half a hectare of the 154 hectares (385 acres) of Nebbiolo are in the San Joaquin Valley, which must put some heat stress on the poor old aristocrat more used to its sub-alpine hideaway.

*T*he great barrel debate affects Nebbiolo more than any other grape variety. At issue currently is not only the age and provenance of the wood, but also how long the wine should stay in it and what size the optimum cask should be.

Synonyms: Spanna, Spana, Picotener, Pugnet, Chiavennasca, Nebbiolo Canavesano.	*Susceptibility:* Susceptible to oidium, but resistant to all parasitic infections.
Soils: Mainly calcareous in Piedmont.	*Rootstocks:* 420A and Kober 5BB most commonly used in Piedmont.
Vigour: Vigorous; some tying up of the longer shoots is often necessary.	*Yields:* Only moderate. Between 50 to 60 hl/ha in general.
Pruning: Mostly Guyot, vines trained relatively high.	

Top quality. Shamefully underrated.

Sangiovese

Perhaps more than any other grape variety, Sangiovese has demonstrated to wine lovers the virtues of clonal selection. Central Italy's vineyards are littered with different clones of various subvarieties of this ancient vine. The wines that they produce range from near-undrinkable thin, inky mouthwash, to essences of fermented grape juice that can keep their concentration and beauty for a century. In between are some of the world's most vibrant lighter-bodied wines, as well as blends more reminiscent of top-quality claret than anything else.

In the original, Biondi-Santi Brunello di Montalcino, one carefully selected clone of Sangiovese produces Italy's most expensive wine, while on the low fertile plains of Emilia-Romagna and Latium the carelessly bred Sangiovese vines that proliferate are responsible for some of Italy's cheapest reds, just one step above the oceans of wine-lake *rosso* produced expressly for compulsory EEC distillation. The poor quality of so much of the Chianti made in the Tuscan hills, in much more suitable soils and weather conditions than these lowland vineyards but again with low-quality Sangiovese plant material, demonstrates quite clearly, if shamefully, how clones can be even more important than climate.

Today Sangiovese in its various forms is cultivated all over Italy, being officially recommended in 58 provinces and authorized in another seven. Indeed its influence is so great that it rivals Barbera as Italy's most-planted dark grape. Its origins are firmly Tuscan, however, and most authorities agree that it was probably known in its original, wild form by the Etruscans in the area around what is now Florence. It is documented as far back as the sixteenth century as Sangiovese di Lamole or Sangiovese Grosso.

The name is credited with an etymology far more robust than most of the wine itself: blood of Jupiter or *sanguis Jovis*. Perhaps the vine stock was such that it produced a more powerful wine three hundred years ago?

Most ampelographers agree that by the early nineteenth century when Sangiovese had spread, particularly to Emilia-Romagna, two subvarieties had emerged: Sangiovese Grosso and Sangiovese Piccolo. Sangiovese Grosso is more widely planted, generally more productive, ripens earlier – in the second as opposed to third epoch – with a looser bunch of bigger, thicker-skinned grapes. A gamut of different clones of Sangiovese Grosso is planted all over Tuscany, while various clones of Sangiovese Piccolo, itself putatively imported from Tuscany as early as the fifteenth century, are cultivated in Emilia-Romagna.

Study of the two subvarieties as separate entities is necessarily confused because for each there is such variation in clones, microclimates and methods of both viticulture and vinification. The Sangiovese Grosso may, for example, be in general the more productive vine, but the particular clone isolated by Biondi-Santi for his Montalcino vineyards has been "educated" to produce small quantities of extremely concentrated wine. A considerable proportion of the Sangiovese di Romagna currently produced, on the other hand, is made from Sangiovese Piccolo vines that have wearily become accustomed to fecundity. It is this variation that makes it so difficult to generalize about the characteristics of wine made from Sangiovese. The problem is compounded by the fact that it is so often blended with other grape varieties – indeed is one of the very few red grapes whose most important manifestation, Chianti, sanctions the addition of white grapes in the winemaking process. In very general terms, Sangiovese grapes are not particularly well pigmented and the resulting wines are not usually noted for their intensity of colour, nor for their ability to withstand oxidation. An orange rim can be a Sangiovese giveaway. The exact Sangiovese flavour varies enormously, but usually has at least a hint of something very earthily rural, perhaps even suggestive of farmyards. Acidity is noticeably high, extract is fairly low, alcohol is moderate, there is not a hint of sweetness, and tannin can often be quite marked. Brunello di Montalcino is the exceptional case that ostentatiously proves the rule that 100 percent Sangiovese rarely lives more than a decade.

Sangiovese is the mainstay of perhaps Italy's most famous wine, Chianti, whose formula has always specified the blending of white grapes – some Malvasia but usually the dreary Trebbiano – and local red ones such as Canaiolo, Colorino and Mammolo. After much wrangling, a new recipe has emerged, with the high-ranking official sanction of the DOCG regulations no less. The proportion of white grapes allowed has been dramatically reduced, although some are still supposedly required, much to the disgust of most of the more quality-conscious producers. What horrifies them still further is that in some zones it is still allowed to add 15 percent of wine or must imported into the region, usually from the south. It is hardly surprising that different Chiantis vary so much.

It is perhaps most appropriate, and certainly least depressing, to consider only the top wines called Chianti. Typically they are made almost exclusively of Sangiovese (the law stipulates 75–90 percent), preferably from one of the better clones, supplemented by 5 percent of Canaiolo and up to 10 percent of "other grapes" which in practice often means a fortifying dollop of Cabernet Sauvignon.

The marriage of Sangiovese and Cabernet Sauvignon, the great red grapes of western France and western Italy respectively, has proved to be sublime. The banns were read in the late sixties by Count Ugo Contini Bonacossi who successfully campaigned to have some Cabernet allowed into his local, chiefly Sangiovese, DOC Carmignano, just west of Florence. In the mid-seventies Antinori confirmed the felicity of the match with their "Superchianti" Tignanello, the wine that showed every other Chianti producer how a wine that qualified only as *vino da tavola* could earn ten times more money and prestige than their world-famous DOC product. Now almost every respectable Chianti producer, and several less scrupulous ones, have their de luxe blend of Sangiovese given stuffing, backbone, longevity and bouquet by a bit of Cabernet Sauvignon.

This eulogy of what Cabernet brings to Sangiovese may lead some Francophiles to wonder exactly what Sangiovese contributes to the blend. Would not unadulterated Cabernet Sauvignon be the desirable logical conclusion? New examples of such wines are appearing each year in the image of the much-admired Sassicaia, but they are not necessarily better than the Sangiovese/Cabernet cocktail, just different and distinctly "international" in flavour. The exciting feature of the Sangiovese/Cabernet wines on the other hand is that, provided the Cabernet element is kept at

SANGIOVESE

around 10 percent, it merely serves to show the principal Sangiovese in the most flattering, and distinctly Tuscan, light. Some producers blend with Cabernet Franc rather than Cabernet Sauvignon but this leaner grape is less good at filling in the holes in what might rather pompously be called the "palate profile" of Sangiovese.

Brunello di Montalcino is, in a very different style, the other great star of Tuscany. The Biondi-Santi family isolated a clone of Sangiovese Grosso producing particularly concentrated, tannic wine a full century ago, calling it Brunello, or "little dark one". There is nothing remotely little about the wines. Virtually unbroachable in the first decade of their life, Biondi-Santi Brunellos have demonstrably survived, nay flourished, for a century. Few other producers of Brunello di Montalcino achieve such power, but some can manage the quality.

Vino Nobile di Montepulciano is another, rather less obvious recruit to the ranks of DOCG from Tuscany and it too relies heavily, though not exclusively, on Sangiovese, or the similar Prugnolo clone that is common here. The varietal mix is very similar to that for Chianti, but in better examples such as those of Avignonesi there is a tenacity, slightly burnt flavour and firm structure that are lacking in the standard Tuscan red, whether Chianti or one of the many others fashioned in its image.

Neighbouring Umbria has its own variation on this

theme: Torgiano, of which Lungarotti is undisputed king. He too has been mixing experimental tones from a palette of imported and local grape varieties including Montepulciano and Ciliegiolo, the "cherry grape".

Sangiovese plantings are far more extensive in Emilia-Romagna to the north, where about 20 million litres of DOC Sangiovese di Romagna alone are produced each year. Like Sangiovese di Aprilia produced on the plains south of Rome, and Sangiovese dei Colli Pesari in the Marche's holiday land on the east coast, much of this wine is, to put it politely, designed for very early consumption. Recently, some Sangiovese, notably in Tuscany, has been persuaded to produce a wine for very early consumption

indeed: a *vino novello*, or Italy's answer to Beaujolais Nouveau. The leanness of Sangiovese is often accentuated in these double-quick ferments and provide further evidence that the rest of the world may eventually simply let the Beaujolais farmers get on with it.

Less than Nebbiolo, and considerably less than Barbera, has Sangiovese been exported to vineyards outside Italy; its rather blurred quality profile may be a factor. There are small plantings of Sangioveto [*sic*] in California and of a vine called locally Sangiavettoe in Argentina. Davis viticulturists rate their Sangioveto as one of the "pippiest" grapes, which may help to explain the uncompromising hardness in so many examples.

Sangiovese Grosso
Synonyms:
Sangiovese Dolce, Sangiovese Gentile, Sangiovese Toscano, Sangiovese di Lamole, Morellino, Calabrese, Nerino, Sanvicetro, Prugnolo (Montepulciano); Brunello (Montalcino).

Soils:
Calcareous preferably, particularly well-drained.

Vigour: Average.

Pruning:
Wide variety of methods, though Guyot or *tendone* seem to work best.

Susceptibility:
Good resistance to most infections.

Rootstocks: Wide range.

Yields:
Variable but moderate to high in general. 70 hl/ha is the usual DOC maximum.

Sangiovese Piccolo
Synonyms:
Sangiovese Forte, Sangiovese di Romagna, Sangiovese del Verrucchio, Sangioveto, San Gioveto.

Soils:
Well-drained clay, calcareous.

Vigour: Low.

Pruning: Variable.

Susceptibility:
Thinner skins can mean that rot is a problem.

Rootstocks: Wide range.

Yields:
Naturally moderate, but much of the Sangiovese Piccolo currently cultivated is forced to be more productive.

Very variable quality. Not fashionable.

Tempranillo

I f the Rioja region is Spain's Bordeaux and Burgundy in one, then its famous Tempranillo should be the unity of Cabernet and Pinot Noir: her most noble red-grape variety, capable of producing dry, scented wines worth ageing. This neat aphorism is even given a factual basis by some historians, who consider that Tempranillo vines

were originally brought to Spain, as variants of Pinot Noir or Cabernet Franc, from monasteries in northern France by French pilgrims on their wellworn route to Santiago de Compostela.

It is certainly possible to taste a similarity between mature, good-quality Rioja and burgundy of old-fashioned richness, thus supporting the Tempranillo-Pinot Noir hypothesis; and the Tempranillo is unusual among Spanish grape varieties for its Pinot-like ability to withstand low temperatures. Throughout Rioja, on the other hand, Tempranillo is known for its thick-skinned grapes and deep-coloured wines that are not too high in alcohol (as little as 10.5 percent, a very claret-like strength) and can age, just like Cabernet, without losing colour.

Tasters and winemakers may find these similarities obvious, but ampelographers can find no relationship between Tempranillo and either of the classic French varieties. The vine is probably northern Spanish in origin, and takes its name from *temprana*, Spanish for "early", because it usually ripens in late September, a good two weeks before Rioja's other important grape variety Garnacha (although it tends to foliate after it). It should also be pointed out that old-fashioned Rioja probably contained much less Tempranillo and more of the richer traditional varieties such as Graciano.

Today Tempranillo and Garnacha each accounts for about 40 percent of all plantings in Rioja, but Tempranillo is virtually confined to the more highly regarded western Rioja Alta and Rioja Alavesa subregions, while the hotter, drier Rioja Baja is the domain of the rather more earthy and alcoholic Garnacha. The Tempranillo needs most of the 450 mm of rain that falls in western Rioja in an average year. It thrives particularly in the Rioja Alavesa (where it constitutes 70 percent of all vines planted) and in the northern half of Rioja Alta. Its relatively short annual growth cycle needs the tempering influence of the Atlantic rather than any Mediterranean acceleration.

Because of its dominance in the most highly regarded parts of the area, Tempranillo tends to be cast as the hero of the Rioja region to casual enthusiasts of its wines. It certainly constitutes the major part of any self-respecting blend designed for ageing, with the balance made up substantially by Garnacha and seasoned with Mazuelo, and perhaps a little Graciano. It is this last, subtle grape variety that is probably the highest-quality ingredient in the red Rioja blend, however. Tempranillo is not nearly as noble or as interesting.

Garnacha can be loose and jammy, Mazuelo a bit coarse in a tannic sort of way, but Graciano is delicate, aromatic, flavourful and long-lived. It has lost ground to Tempranillo because it is so much less productive.

Apart from producing rather characterless wines, Tempranillo has one serious disadvantage: it is relatively low in acidity. The musts tend to have a markedly high pH, and a good half of their acidity is malic. This means that an all-Tempranillo wine, while keeping its colour well, would lose its fruit and liveliness after a few years. Blending of different grape varieties grown in different parts of the Rioja region is an important part of the winemaking art, but some growers mix the different grape varieties as far back in the production process as the vineyard.

Marqués de Riscal, one of the oldest bodegas in Rioja and one of the original importers of techniques from Bordeaux. Although 85 percent of their blend is made up of Tempranillo they, unusually, spice it with Cabernet Sauvignon as well as with Graciano and Viura. Of their 300 hectares (750 acres) of vineyards around Elciego, 20 hectares (50 acres) are Cabernet, although the Tempranillo is much more prolific.

junior partner to Garnacha and is hardly discernible to the taster. Only in Valdepeñas, where it is known as Cencibel, is it important in terms of acreage, making it the fourth most planted red-grape variety in Spain, after Garnacha, Monastrell and Bobal, with about 2.5 percent of all vineyard land, or about 40,000 hectares (100,000 acres). Here its musts can reach much higher alcoholic strengths of impenetrably deep colour, often lightened considerably by blending with the white Airén to produce *claretes* as opposed to *tintos*.

Even though it is neither recommended nor authorized, plantings of the variety increased considerably in France in the seventies, but there were still only about 600 hectares (1,500 acres) by 1979. Its lack of acidity is less of a problem north of the Pyrenees, but plans to replace Carignan with Tempranillo have been dropped because the wine produced in the Midi has colour but no character.

As Aragonez and Tinta Roriz respectively, Tempranillo is grown in the Alentejo and Douro regions of Portugal, thus being one of the very few Spanish varieties that is grown in any quantity at all over the Portuguese border. It is considered useful in port production though it is lighter than most of the top varieties.

In Argentina Tempranillo is an important grape variety covering some 11,000 hectares (27,500 acres) of vineyard land, but producing a much less lean style of red wine than in Europe.

There are strong ampelographical and oenological similarities between Tempranillo and the variety known as Valdepeñas grown in California's hot San Joaquin Valley, though some authorities believe it to be related to Carignane. Total California area of Valdepeñas is about 480 hectares (1,200 acres), but there have been few new plantings in the last two decades. The grape is used to produce ordinary jug wines in which low acidity is an expected characteristic rather than a problem.

TEMPRANILLO

Elsewhere in Spain the Tempranillo is not so highly regarded, although Miguel Torres of Penedés blends it with Monastrell for Coronas, his claret-like basic red, and adds a bit of Cabernet Sauvignon to make a Reserva version that can age gracefully. In Navarre it is a very

---

Synonyms.
Ull de Llebre, Ojo de Liebre (Catalonia); Cencibel (La Mancha); Tinto Fino (Ribero del Duero); Tinto Madrid (Arganda); Tempranilla, Tempranillo de la Rioja, Tinto de la Rioja, Grenache de Logrono, Tinto del Pais, Jacivera, Tinto de Toro (rest of Spain); Aragonez, Tinta Roriz (Portugal); may be Valdepeñas of California.

Soils:
Prefers deep soil of calcareous or sandy clay and does markedly better on slopes. Soils in the Rioja tend to be low in phosphorus.

Vigour:
Vigorous shoots with upright growth.

Pruning:
Traditionally trained in goblet, *en vaso*, in Rioja, but yields well with spur pruning on wires.

Susceptibility:
Susceptible to powdery mildew, downy mildew, anthracnose.

Rootstocks:
41-B and Rupestris du Lot commonly used.

Yields:
Relatively productive, though probably could be more so in many Rioja vineyards. 4,500 kg of grapes per hectare is the maximum allowed in Rioja.

Medium quality. Not fashionable.

Zinfandel

Zinfandel, California's very own "European" varietal, is thrilling, not just because of the exciting air of mystery surrounding its origins, but because of the potential quality of the wine made from it. Yet, just as most Australians ignore the greatness of their Shiraz simply because it is their most widely planted red-wine grape, so most Californians treat Zinfandel as little more than jug wine material simply because it is *their* most common red-wine grape.

With about 10,800 hectares (27,000 acres) planted all over the state, "Zin" has steadily increased its hold on the California *vignoble* – even capitalizing on the nation's preoccupation with white wine. Remarkably few wineries treat the varietal with anything like the respect given to Cabernet Sauvignon, Pinot Noir and, more recently, Merlot. A "Zinfandel Guild" formed in California in 1983 to promote the varietal ignominiously folded two years later owing to lack of interest and financial support.

Ridge Vineyards have earned the title of post-Prohibition patron saint of Zinfandel, seeking out plots of ancient, low-yielding vines all over the state and fashioning them into the most stylish, concentrated essences by treating them to prolonged fermentation and painstaking *élevage* in small oak barrels. Ridge truck in grapes to their ramshackle winery high in the mountains above Palo Alto from plots as far apart as San Luis Obispo on the south California coast and Amador county in the Sierra foothills. The separate Ridge bottlings prove what different and exciting wines can be produced by this grape in different settings.

One of their original sites, Lytton Springs just north of Healdsburg in Sonoma, a particularly reputable locale for Zinfandel, went solo with a small shed of a winery in 1976, and is now one of the world's handful of Zinfandel specialists, producing inky, tannic, heady deep reds. Even earlier, Bob Trinchero kindled the flames of the cult of Amador Zins from the sunbaked Shenandoah Valley, old prospecting country, with varied but noble examples made at his Napa winery, Sutter Home. He has even won acclaim for his "white" Zins which somehow manage to inject an element of freshness into this galumphing great grape.

The most common description of Zinfandel is that "it produces a wide range of different styles of wine" and it is certainly true that in terms of the number of jobs asked of it, it is California's jack-of-all-trades. It comes out red, white and rosé; light(ish), full and fortified; bone dry to teeth-rotting sweet; *nouveau* to *cru classé* in style; still wine and even as a base for sparklers. This is more because it is seen as a biddable lapdog than for the pedigree chum it really is. The vine obligingly turns out all these different wine types because it is so widely planted, produces lots of grapes with reliably high sugars, and there is, therefore, ample raw Zinfandel material.

What it is probably best at is producing still, dry, bright red wines with relatively high alcohol content, lots of extract, reasonable acid, and a great noseful of brambly fruit flavours that can develop into a rich spicy stew with time. This it can achieve when treated properly, and when grown in the right places. Zinfandel has a nasty habit of uneven ripening; the same bunch can sport hard green pellets and luscious fully ripe berries. If it is grown in conditions that are too hot it can easily start to shrivel and raisin, so fast do the sugar levels shoot up towards the end of the growing cycle.

Ideal conditions are fairly cool, say Region I or II, with lots of sunshine; many high altitude sites work well. At Paso Robles it can be herby, in the Amador Sierra foothills very intense, and in its best Sonoma sites around Dry Creek and Geyserville it can be found at its most rich and complex.

A good 40 percent of California Zinfandel plantings, however, are in the Lodi district of the hot Central Valley where the problems of excessive heat are exacerbated by the high yields growers have come to demand and expect of this particular vine. It is this sort of wine made from such grapes, and those grown further south in the Central Valley, that have given Zinfandel a bad name. Jammy, loose-textured, often raisiny, short on acid and extract but

ZINFANDEL

*A*s Ridge Vineyards have demonstrated so eloquently, the key to Zinfandel quality is the age of the vines. "White" and light cherry-red specimens can be made from the rest, but mature plants are needed for classic Zin.

high in alcohol, these wines, which can come in any style from fast-fermented to relatively long-macerated, have the distinguishing mark of an aroma suggestive of "berries" which is the Zin callsign. Rather than suggesting something alluringly like blackberries or deep-scented strawberries, these basic Zins are just vaguely fruity – like the difference between Swiss black cherry jam and a catering pack red jelly.

In addition to responding well to careful pruning, producing ideally three or perhaps as little as one ton per acre, Zinfandel thrives best in climates no hotter than California's Region III because of the grape's tendency to shrivel. Although some years it ripens irregularly, it is generally harvested in early mid-season, not long after Pinot Noir. Richard Peterson harvested it as late as December (with 25.2 degrees of sugar and 0.9 percent acid) in the cool Gonzales region of Monterey way back in 1974, thereby helping to create the late-harvest Zin market.

Zinfandel has for decades been a major ingredient in California's port-style wines and continues to make an important contribution to their increasing respectability. In addition to these fortified wines a number of naturally very heady, usually sweet Zinfandels have been made, vaguely suggestive of the Recioto wines of Valpolicella.

Like Recioto, they are an acquired taste, in some instances serving only to show that you can have too much of the good things that Zin can offer.

Apart from ports and jug wines, Zinfandel is rarely blended. The thought of mixing it with the more refined character of Cabernet Sauvignon strikes the wine lover as unlikely as shaking a claret and burgundy cocktail. Paul Draper of Ridge is a committed, if unique, believer in the efficacy of a shot of Petite Sirah backbone "if the Zinfandel is to last two decades".

Zinfandel can age extremely well, though it is rarely given the opportunity. Louis Martini, whose Zins are some of the best to be found in economy class, has said they are at their best at between six and 10 years, while others have seen evidence that they can last as single varietal wines for two or even three decades. Paul Draper reckons they reach an initial peak at around five years, and then continue to develop but much more slowly.

Good Zinfandel is still a bargain, chiefly because so much less cachet attaches to it than to Cabernet and Pinot. The Reserve Cabernet is supposedly the collector's item; the Zin is priced low enough to move off the shelf fast. Just as American connoisseurs have cottoned on to the pleasures of vintage port, there are signs of a small resurgence of interest in the grape that plays such an important part in California's fine wine heritage – even if as a result of the bizarre popularity of "White" Zinfandel.

Zinfandel almost certainly made its way to America in the baggage of an early nineteenth-century settler on the East Coast of America. Historian Charles Sullivan has traced its passage from Long Island to Boston in the early 1820s and points out that it could, possibly would, have been brought to California in any collection of vine cuttings trekked across the Rockies for the emerging thousands west of them. It – or at least a clone of it called Black St Peters – was definitely planted by nurseryman Antoine Delmas of San Jose as early as 1859.

By the 1880s Zinfandel was starting to take over from the familiar and productive Mission grape. At that time, those who were interested in wine were interested in profits rather than ampelography, or even semantics. The precise background to Zinfandel was lost in the rush for gold, both bankable and drinkable, of that era.

It was assumed for some time that Zinfandel was a Hungarian grape variety, but ampelographers have now established that the Primitivo of Apulia (and possibly the Plavać Mali of Dalmatia across the Adriatic) is Zinfandel – although, interestingly, no reference to Primitivo in southern Italy has been found earlier than the late 1860s.

Mysterious indeed – but there are certainly strong similarities. Apulian Primitivo, reared in very hot sunshine, tempered by some marine influence, is very dark, concentrated and high in alcohol. Much of the wine was traditionally used for blending, adding colour and strength to many an anaemic *vin de table*, but Burton Anderson reports a noticeable increase in refinement as gentler fermentation techniques are employed.

Primitivo di Manduria has a DOC of its own, which

Zinfandel's route to California and the reasons for its success there remain one of the wine world's great mysteries. Even the derivation of its name is an enigma as, to this day, is the style of the definitive Zinfandel.

may be a robust dry wine, with Zinfandel-like blackberry flavours, or an *amabile* with 16 percent natural strength and a bit of sugar to boot, or a fortified *liquoroso dolce* or *secco* with up to 18 percent alcohol which, according to the American expert on matters Italian and vinous, "can last almost indefinitely". Primitivo di Gioia is produced on the other, eastern, side of the peninsula south of Bari. Sometimes known as Gioia del Colle, it is not exactly a "hillside wine" with its 14–16 percent alcohol, but then such strengths are by no means exceptional for California Zinfandel. Interestingly, a number of Italian Primitivo producers have started to label their wines Zinfandel for export to the United States. Some Californians got very hoity-toity about it,

conveniently ignoring their own infamous tradition of "California Burgundy" and "California Chablis".

Far western United States and deep southern Italy apart, the grape is rarely seen outside experimental stations – except that some South African growers have taken a recent shine to it, and there are isolated plantings in Australia. One Southern Vales winemaker has even blended it with both Pinot Noir and Cabernet Sauvignon to produce a sort of liquid United Nations. Cape Mentelle's Western variations on the theme are the most exciting and owe much to the winemaker's Davis education. Interestingly, he is one of the few Australian growers to accord Shiraz the respect it deserves, too.

Synonyms:
Probably Primitivo, Primativo (Italy)

Soils:
Because of its California base, this question is rarely considered!

Vigour:
Moderately vigorous growth.

Pruning:
Cordon training with spur or cane pruning is recommended.

Susceptibility:
Susceptible to bunch rot in irrigated vineyards, also tends to raisin.

Yields: Can be very productive.

Potentially pretty high quality. Not at all fashionable.

Pinot Gris

Pinot Noir is a notoriously degenerate vine variety, prone to mutate at the drop of a gene, as any Burgundian grower can testify. Galet records Pinots Blanc, Rosé, Violet, Tête de Negre, Teinturier and Cioutat before listing a further 11 strains isolated by individuals, some as long ago as the mid-eighteenth century. It is a wonder that Pinot Gris ever managed to establish itself, let alone spread so widely with such a very positive character.

This mutation of the Pinot Noir hardly knows whether it is a dark or a light grape. The grape skins can be anything from greyish blue to brownish pink; sometimes they look closer to black, sometimes white. The wine produced from them is usually a notably deep-coloured white, but in Italy and Switzerland for instance, it is sometimes a delicate pink. It is planted all over central Europe and has an almost chameleon-like ability to adapt the style of wine it produces to each different environment. It is difficult to believe that the rich, almost oily Tokays produced in Alsace bear any relation whatever to the light, spritzy Pinot Grigios of northern Italy. All they seem to have in common is that characteristic common to members of the white Pinot family, a notable lack of aroma.

The key to understanding the link is perhaps provided by the manifestations of Pinot Gris in Germany, usually called Ruländer. Certainly Germany has more of the vine planted, nearly 3,300 hectares (8,250 acres), than any other country, but it reached the fatherland by a markedly circuitous route.

This mutation, along with Pinot Noir, reached Switzerland from Burgundy probably in the Middle Ages, an amazing thought. Around 1375 Emperor Charles IV took Pinot Gris cuttings to Hungary and the Cistercians planted them on the warm, mineral-rich slopes of Badascony near Lake Balaton. Even today the vine is known in Hungary as Szürkebarat, or "grey monk", though this may owe more to a direct translation of its old Burgundian name Pinot Beurot or Burot after the *bure*, or rough serge, of a monk's habit. In 1568 a colonel in the imperial army, one Baron Lazare de Schwendi, is supposed to have brought back the vine to his properties in Alsace (today the headquarters of the Confrérie St-Etienne) and to the Kaiserstuhl region in Baden, southern Germany. Since he fought the Turks over the town of Tokay, it seems quite understandable, if slightly muddleheaded, that the vine is known as Tokay in Alsace (a practice that EEC bureaucrats have elected for some reason to stamp out). However the vine reached Alsace, "Tokay" was recorded there as early as 1750.

In 1711 in the Palatinate, then Germany's second most important wine region, a merchant, Johann Seger Ruland, discovered an unfamiliar vine growing in a semiwild state. He found that the blue-grey berries produced wine that was not bad at all and he propagated the vine, known commercially as Ruländer.

Eventually, it was noted that this was none other than the Pinot Gris which was at that time relatively common in both Burgundy and Champagne. In the eighteenth and nineteenth centuries the vine fell into disfavour in Germany as well as in Burgundy and Champagne, because of its tendency to degenerate and unwillingness to produce a reliable crop. Twentieth-century German vine breeders soon sorted this problem out and, thanks to clonal selection in the 1950s, a grower can expect anything from 80 to 120 hectolitres per hectare of his Ruländer. It is an illuminating sign of the productivity of other varieties in Germany that even with such high yields Ruländer, covering 3.5 percent of the vineyard land in Germany, produces less than 2 percent of the average crop.

Pinot Gris is characterized by relatively high extract, slightly low acidity and, in good examples, a certain spiciness of aroma. These characteristics are most pronounced in Germany and Alsace, and the full-bodied nature of the wines makes them particularly noticeable in Germany, land of the feather light. Ruländer achieves must weight levels on average 10° Oechsle higher than Riesling grown in similar circumstances. The vine is certainly highly regarded there, though its more modest production compared with the new crossings and its need for relatively warm soils precludes it from being planted much more widely. German Ruländers are atypical of

PINOT
GRIS

German wine, just as the Tokays are the least typical wines of Alsace. The wines are reminiscent of white burgundy. Only in years that are too hot does their naturally low acid level tip them over the threshold into clumsiness.

In Germany the Ruländer makes fairly high demands in terms of site and microclimate, but not quite so high as Riesling. Soils need to be deep and heavy to maximize the extract of the wine. Its growth cycle is very similar to that of Silvaner, and they tend to be picked at the same time, although Ruländer grapes lose their acidity much earlier.

In Italy most growers of Pinot Grigio are so frightened of this phenomenon that they pick the grapes long before they have absorbed any flavour. Fear of autumn rains is invoked to explain this unseemly haste. Pinot Grigio is currently much sought after by drinkers of dry white wine in Italy, which certainly provides the most eloquent evidence of the theory that the Italians do not like their white wines to be smelly. No wine producer or connoisseur can explain why such cachet attaches to Pinot Grigio when Pinot Bianco is capable of producing wines of so much greater interest.

Pinot Grigio is planted all over northeastern Italy, chiefly in Friuli-Venezia Giulia and often alongside a quite separate variety called Tocai, confusingly similar sounding to the Alsace synonym for Pinot Gris. Much Pinot Grigio makes pretty dreary drinking, its only distinguishing mark being a relatively full body. The best examples, and there are many ordinary ones sold off as spurious Pinot Grigio delle Venezie, come from Friuli, especially from some of the best producers near the Yugoslav border in the Collio and Colli Orientali districts.

Lombardy also produces a notable amount of Pinot Grigio, but rarely distinguishes between the various Pinots of Oltrepò Pavese, and even more rarely exports its wines further than Milan. Such is the popularity of Pinot Grigio that it has now marched as far south as the Colli Piacentini in Emilia-Romagna. Growers appear to be undaunted by Italian Pinot Grigio's rather unreliable cropping levels.

The vine is also cultivated in Alto Adige, though here they very sensibly produce much more Pinot Bianco. These sub-alpine Pinot Grigios often have a certain smoky aroma, and provide varietal examples higher in acid than any-where else in the world (although appropriately enough some Swiss wines rival them). Many are labelled Ruländer in this German-speaking region.

Pinot Gris is grown on an increasing number of sites in eastern Switzerland, where the microclimate is kind enough to allow the grapes to reach *surmaturité*, possibly even leading to "noble rot". Such wines may be slightly sweet and/or slightly tinted, and represent some of Switzer-land's most unexpected gifts to wine drinkers. Much of this is called Malvoisie de Valais, although Pinot Gris has nothing to do with any Malvasia and is known in France as Malvoisie only in Ain, Savoie and the Loire.

There are tiny plantings of Pinot Gris in Luxembourg, Austria, Moravia (just over the Austrian border) and Eastern Germany where the vine also produces wines notable, in the local setting, for their weight. As Rulandac Sivi it is cultivated in northern Yugoslavia, in both Slovenia and Slavonia, but is particularly important in Romania. Called both Ruländer and Pinot Gris, the vine produces particularly valued wines in Transylvania.

The vine is also grown in the Soviet Union but it is in Hungary that it is perhaps revered most in the world – by the locals anyway. Three subvarieties of Szürkebarát have been identified: the excellent, large-fruited Nemes or noble kind; the useful smaller-fruited but quite difficult to fertilize Kozönseges or common sort; and the Oreg or old type that rots too easily to make it useful. The wine produced by the first two is one of Hungary's great wine treasures. The grapes are left on the vine so long that the wines are deep coloured, often with a slightly coppery tinge, and so high in extract that they taste sweet, just like many Tokays d'Alsace. An official guide to Hungarian wines counsels of their Szürkebarát, "It is recommended to be drunk with pork fried in breadcrumbs if served with compote, cakes and with noodles and sweet cakes."

In Alsace they are even more conscious of the role of Pinot Gris in gastronomy. Indeed of all their varietals, most of them Germanic, it is Pinot Gris or Tokay d'Alsace that they recommend most fervently as an accompaniment to food. The wine stands out in this region of powerful wines, for its sturdiness, its lack of distractingly floral bouquet, and its alcohol content. Along with Riesling and Gewürztraminer it is regarded as one of the region's finest grape varieties and one of the few that can be persuaded to make late-harvest wines. The 1976 Vendange Tardive Tokays are monumental, like the best of California's Chardonnays of the rich, buttery school. There has been a perceptible increase in plantings of the variety in Alsace recently, but its 600 hectares (1,500 acres) represent less than 5 percent of the total. Four times as much Tokay is planted in the higher, more promising slopes of the Haut-Rhin than on the plains of the Bas-Rhin.

There are still small amounts of Pinot Gris scattered around the rest of France. It is a possible ingredient, often called Malvoisie, in Bugey made between Beaujolais and Savoie. The vine was at one time commonly intermingled with other varieties in the vineyards of Burgundy and even quite recently, according to Anthony Hanson, constituted 5 percent of the Corton vineyard to soften the red wine. There are still some vines, called Pinot Beurot, to be found in well-reputed vineyards on the Côte d'Or.

The vine has not spread in any quantity to the newer wine regions except logically to the coolest, New Zealand. There have been small plantings of it in Australia, but the low acid level has prevented it from developing a following. In California, life with Pinot Blanc is already complicated enough. In New Zealand it fell from favour because the growers there, like the Italians, were exasperated by its irregular yields. Since new clones such as Klosterneuberg and Hauser H-1 have been developed, it may blossom again. There are great hopes of extending its area – fewer than 30 hectares (75 acres) in 1983 – especially in the Canterbury area in the South Island. It produces a firm, full-bodied wine here that at least one producer cannot resist but, sadly, labels it Tokay d'Alsace.

Synonyms:
Pinot Beurot or Burot (Burgundy); Tokay d'Alsace (Alsace); Malvoisie (Ain, Savoie, Loire); Gris Cordelier, Fauvet, Auvernat Gris, Petit Gris, Fromentot (rest of France); Ruländer, Grauer Burgunder, Grauklevner, Grauer Riesling, Tokayer (Germany); Pinot Grigio (Italy); Malvoisie, Tokayer (Switzerland); Rulandac Sivi, Crvena Klevanjka (Yugoslavia); Szürkebarat, Grauer Mönch (Hungary); Rulanda (Romania); Cervena Klevanjka, Rouci Sedive (Czechoslovakia).

Soils:
Responds best to deep soils with a high mineral content. High extract is required to make an interesting wine in cooler regions.

Vigour: Medium.

Pruning:
Guyot training so as to suit the soil type. Also well suited to high trellising.

Susceptibility:
Relatively good resistance to most pests and diseases.

Rootstocks:
Fairly vigorous rootstocks are best, especially 125AA and SO4.

Yields:
Newer clones very good; old stocks variable. Medium quality.

Very fashionable in Italy, practically ignored in the "New World".

Pinot Blanc

Pinot Blanc is a contentious vine. Is it descended from Pinot Gris, itself a mutation of Pinot Noir? It sounds a logical bleaching process. Are its wines better than those produced from Pinot Gris? Some Germans and Californians think yes, the Italians and French no. Is it related to Chardonnay, for long called Pinot Chardonnay?

Pinot Blanc is indeed a true Pinot. Its leaves really are identical to those of Pinot Noir (and Pinot Gris) and it is clearly a mutation of Pinot Noir, very possibly a descendant of Pinot Gris. Alsace has a long tradition of growing Pinot Blanc and plantings of "Clevner" were noted there as early as the mid-sixteenth century by Jerome Bock. Clevner is the Alsace name for Pinot in general, so there is no clear indication that this was specifically Pinot Blanc as opposed to Pinot Noir, although Pinot Blanc is manifestly one of Alsace's most established varieties. The quite distinct variety most commonly known as Auxerrois, which is still planted widely in Alsace (as well as in pockets elsewhere in France), is usually blended into Alsace's Pinot Blanc, the blend sold as Pinot Blanc, Clevner or Klevner.

In answering the second question it is significant that the Pinot Blanc grown in Alsace is a selected strain known as Gros Pinot Blanc with notably higher yields than the true Pinot Blanc of the Côte d'Or, or even the very early ripening, medium quality selection of Pinot Blanc made by the viticulturist Bronner. In French vineyards at least fecundity is not usually associated with nobility. It is not surprising, therefore, that the Pinot Blanc is not exactly revered in Alsace. The average Alsace yield of Pinot Gris on the other hand is relatively low, thus helping to maintain the variety's reputation for quality there.

The Germans also rate Pinot Gris above Pinot Blanc because they reckon it has more aroma which, perversely, may well be partly why the Italians prefer Pinot Bianco. One suspects that in both Italy and California, the high reputation enjoyed by Pinot Bianco/Blanc is helped by the general impression that it is as close as a favoured stepsister to their favourite princess, Chardonnay.

The last, genealogical question is easiest to answer. Pinot Blanc is a member of the extremely ramified Pinot family; Chardonnay is not. Chardonnay leaves have an almost identical shape to Pinot leaves, it is true, but they are naked where the stem meets the leaf, which Pinot leaves never are. Pinot Blanc tends to be more productive, with rather lower sugar levels than Chardonnay, and less varietal definition; this makes Pinot Blanc a rather good candidate for sparkling wine production. World plantings of Pinot Blanc are expected to increase to meet the world's apparently insatiable desire for carbon dioxide mixed in with its wine.

France, including Alsace of course, with about 1,300 hectares (3,250 acres), has rather more vineyard planted with Pinot Blanc than Germany. (Italy may well have even more, but is not statistically well-equipped.) There are small parcels of Pinot Blanc vines still planted in some of the Côte d'Or's most reputable corners. Most of their produce is blended with Chardonnay, but the few varietal Pinot Blanc burgundies that are produced are notable for their

A wide range of grape varieties cling to the slopes of the Colli Euganei just south of Padua, but Pinot Bianco is thought to have particular potential. It is sometimes vinified sweet, as an Abboccato.

weight and attractive appley aroma, which is not as complex as that of Chardonnay but has some similarities. Perhaps the single most telling distinction between Pinot Blanc and Chardonnay wines is that the latter are so obviously built to last in a way that is rare for a Pinot Blanc.

Plantings of the high-yielding Gros Pinot Blanc have been increasing in Alsace and, with Auxerrois, now total well over 2,000 hectares (5,000 acres), mainly on the plain where they produce a soft, relatively heavy wine that blends well with high-acid grapes such as Sylvaner and Chasselas in bottles labelled Edelzwicker. Pinot Blanc of Alsace is specifically not for ageing, and is notably low in aroma; but it can often exhibit a whiff of the spiciness typical of Alsace, as though there were a few Gewürztraminer or Muscat grapes in the bottom of the press.

Pinot Blanc is called Weissburgunder in Germany. Total plantings have increased to more than 900 hectares (2,250 acres) chiefly, like Pinot Gris or Ruländer, in the southern wine regions Baden and Rheinpfalz. Where it has been added to the repertoire of an estate, it has often replaced Silvaner whose wines are notably more acid. Weissburgunder is appreciated by growers for its ability to register high Oechsle levels even at high yields, although it has to reach a reading of 85° Oechsle to produce a wine with much interest.

Being relatively non-aromatic, the wines can be useful as foils for some of the smellier crossings – a role fulfilled adequately, if without much style or body, by Müller-Thurgau. Very ripe Weissburgunder is also used as a relatively versatile sweetening (*Süssreserve*), although its future may lie at the other end of the hydrometer, in the dry Trocken and Halbtrocken wines that are so popular with Germany's new generation of gastronomes. Its relatively high level of extract and moderate acidity makes it ideal for the dining table, or at least much closer to ideal than the much more fragrant Germanic varietals.

Although some plantings of the vine may have been encouraged in Tuscany by the House of Lorraine at the end of the eighteenth century, Italy's first records of Pinot Blanc plantings date back to the 1820s. One General Emilio di Sambuy's experiments with the vine in Piedmont showed that it thrived best on cooler hillside sites. Throughout the last century, Pinot grew increasingly desirable as the Italians noted the international success of champagne and burgundy, and it became the most widely planted "foreign" grape variety, concentrated in the north.

It has been only remarkably recently that the Italians have sorted out the distinction between Pinot Bianco and Chardonnay, both in theory and in the vineyard. It was not until 1984 that a DOC was granted for any Chardonnay, in recognition of its existence as a separate variety from the ubiquitous Pinot Bianco, even though many an Italian vineyard had been planted with a casual mixture of Pinot Bianco and Chardonnay for years. No one thought to consider that there might be two varieties and therefore never bothered to distinguish between them. Even now, as the leaves are very similar, it is only towards vintage time that it becomes obvious which has looser bunches of round

PINOT BLANC

viticultural research centre at Conegliano, called after Manzoni, a professor there.

It is in Italy in particular, that Pinot's advantages as base wine for sparkling wines are being recognized and exploited: high acid, fairly neutral character, not too much sugar, and the advantage that early picking obviates the rot potential of the tight bunches. There is also the nicely vague term Pinot to flaunt on the label of this or that fancy *spumante*. This is particularly true of the Pinot Bianco grown in Lombardy's Oltrepò Pavese, though further north there is also a veritable ferment of champenization of the variety.

Over the eastern frontier Pinot Blanc, often called Beli (white) Pinot, is grown in Slovenia and Slavonia and increasingly further south in the Serbian province of Vojvodina. The variety's stronghold in Hungary is in the Mecsek area of Transdanubia, but it is not so highly regarded as the Pinot Gris grown exclusively at Badacsony. Pinot Blanc accounts for a substantial proportion (16 percent) of wine grape plantings in East Germany. With about 2,000 hectares (5,000 acres) – much more than in West Germany – it is the fourth most popular white grape in Austria. As one might expect, the vine's influence is particularly strong in Styria near the Yugoslav border, but there are also significant plantings around Vienna and in Gumpoldskirchen. It often reaches the must weights required by the relatively liberal Austrian wine laws for Auslese and even richer wines, though it lacks the acidity of some of the country's more Germanic grape varieties. Some of the wines have a richness and bouquet more reminiscent of Chardonnay than anything else, although they can taste disconcertingly sweet, and true Austrian Chardonnay (still often called Pinot Chardonnay here) has more finesse. Presence these Austrian Weissburgunders do not lack.

In Chile white "Pinot" is one of the better-known grape varieties, but there is great confusion about exactly what it is. Almost everything labelled Pinot Blanc in Australia is Chardonnay. The only newer wine region with a substantial area of genuine Pinot Blanc is California where plantings have been increasing at a steady rate with 880 hectares (2,200 acres) planted in 1983. More than half this total is in the cool, late-harvested vineyards of Monterey.

Leafroll virus has dampened yields in California, but the variety is still popular for varietal wines, as bolster for Chardonnay and as base wines for the increasing production of good quality sparkling wine in the Golden State. Premature browning of the wine has been noted here and attributed to high tannin content of the skins, but in the state's beloved blind taste-offs many Pinot Blancs have performed extremely well "against" Chardonnays. Perhaps this is because they are inherently much more neutral in flavour, a disadvantage in cool-climate Europe but an advantage that can be labelled subtlety in this land of the big, oaky Chardonnay. The lofty Chalone Vineyards have done Pinot Blanc one of the greatest favours by treating it as a very serious varietal wine. Like others since, they have accorded Pinot Blanc the compliment of wood-ageing, an unheard-of luxury elsewhere in the world.

Pinot Blanc remains an enigma.

yellow grapes (Chardonnay, or Gelber Weissburgunder in Alto Adige) and which tighter bunches of oval green ones (Pinot Blanc or Grüner Weissburgunder).

Most of the Pinot Bianco DOCs, of which there are many, may be in Trentino-Alto Adige, Veneto, Friuli and Lombardy, but today the vine is grown all over Italy, even as far south as Apulia where Castel del Monte vineyards are capable of producing something really appetizing. In Trentino-Alto Adige there is still much confusion over it and Chardonnay, not to mention the linguistic confusions in a region in which both Italian and German are regarded as the native tongue. Pinot Blanc wines made here are apple-crisp but with more body than most local whites, often spritzy, and often sold as Weissburgunder, with or without some Chardonnay. Yields may be as high as 90 hectolitres per hectare.

In the Veneto these qualities are also apparent, though acidity is slightly more muted and, as in Friuli, there are producers who bother to make it into a "serious" wine: the DOCs Collio, Colli Orientali del Friuli and Breganze spring to mind. In Emilia-Romagna some sweetish wines are made from the grape. It seems highly likely that, with so much Pinot Bianco planted, Italy will be producing some very substantial wines in the future, perhaps experimenting with conscious Chardonnay blending. So interesting are the possibilities for the variety, that a successful crossing of White Riesling and Pinot Bianco has been developed at the

Synonyms:
Weisser Burgunder, Weissburgunder,
Weisser Klevner, Clevner, Clävner,
Weisser Ruländer, Weisser Arbst (Germany);
Pinot Bianco, Borgogna Bianco, Pineau
Blanc, Chasselas Dorato (Italy);
Weissburgunder (Austria);
Beli Pinot, Biela Klevanjka (Yugoslavia);
Feherburgundi (Hungary);
Rouci Bile (Czechoslovakia).

Soils:
Relatively deep and damp are preferable.
Chalky soils intensify aroma.

Vigour: Low to medium.

Pruning:
Guyot is normal but cordon training is also possible.

Susceptibility:
Good resistance to most pests and diseases, but a
tendency to rot because of compactness of bunches.

Rootstocks:
Should promote growth. SO4 and 5C suitable for deep
soils; 125AA and 5BB otherwise.

Yields:
Regular and quite high, using the right clones,
without deleterious effect on quality.
Three to five tons an acre in California;
70 hl/ha in Alsace.

Moderately high quality. Overlooked (often in favour of Pinot Gris) in many regions.

Welschriesling

WELSCHRIESLING

Most serious wine drinkers have been taught to despise this Middle European variety utterly, not so much because of the variable quality of its wine, but simply because of its name. So effective has the German propaganda machine been against any variety whose name incorporates that of their most revered grape that we tend to forget that no blame should be attached to the variety itself – only to those who saddled it with such an ambitious name. Our reactions are about as justified as penalizing the child who bears the newly, and questionably, hyphenated surname.

It is true that a high proportion of the Welschriesling traded around the world is of uninspiring quality, but this is more a reflection of what the vine is made to do rather than what it can do in a more sympathetic context. Some examples of the varietal's faintly floral, zesty, almost dry style in northeast Italy and late-harvest wonders from Romania show that the vine deserves better than opprobrium.

Because this is not a variety cultivated in the world's better documented and ampelographically sophisticated wine countries, hard facts about Welschriesling's origins and genealogy are thin on the ground. Etymology, fanned by history, provides the most helpful clues.

Since apparently no one in the modern wine world has had the inclination to study this variety in any detail, we must be grateful to the ampelographer R. Goethe for at least giving one quotable (and oft-quoted) opinion: that

Jeruzalem in Slovenia, northwestern Yugoslavia, is close to Ljutomer, the fount of one of the world's most enthusiastically exported Welschrieslings, the "Laski Rizling" or "Laskiriesling" (or many a variation on that theme). Jeruzalem was a popular Crusader staging post: hence the name.

Welschriesling's origins are French, probably in the Champagne district, and that it migrated to Austro-Hungary via Heidelberg.

If this were true, it is interesting that not a single Welschriesling vine appears to have survived west or north of the Alps. Even at the turn of the century when Viala was compiling his great ampelographical register, there was no evidence of any variety known in France or Germany related to the Welschriesling of Austria and Romania, the Riesling Italico of Italy, the Olaszriesling of Hungary, the Vlassky Riesling of Czechoslovakia and the Laskiriesling or Graševina of Yugoslavia.

The vine has poor resistance to wet weather, prefers warmer soils and can produce wines excessively high in acidity in cooler climates: these facts suggest that the variety is ideally suited to central Europe but not at all to northern France or Germany. Even if the vine had originated as hypothesized by Goethe, then surely its exceptionally high productivity would have been enough to ensure that it left some tracks?

"Welsch", sometimes written Wälsch, comes from the same proto-Germanic root Walhaz as our word Welsh, meaning foreign, which does not get us very far in sniffing out Welschriesling's origins, except in confirming that it is very unlikely that they lie in a German-speaking country. (The main synonym – Riesling Italico – is doubtless a result of the evolution of the term Welsch in German because to

the Germans Italy was the epitome of a foreign country.)

The variety does perform extremely well, and importantly, in Romania, however. Could "Welsch" be a corruption of "Wallachian", from the province of Wallachia in southern Romania? The Czech and some Yugoslav evidence certainly supports this. In Slovene Vlassky means "from Vlaska", the Slav name for Wallachia; and it is not difficult to see how Vlassky became Laskiriesling, Welschriesling's most famous synonym. I am indebted to Cornelia Smith-Bauer and her late husband Hugh for this ingenious theory.

Viticulture was certainly well established in Romania by the time the Romans conquered Dacia in 101. They could either have brought the Welschriesling vine with them or, if it were already established in what is now Romania, then they helped to diffuse it westwards. The Wallachians have certainly been known as such since the ninth century and the Vlachs are still a distinct people with which the variety may have originally been associated.

There is little resemblance between the Welschriesling vine and that of true Riesling. Even as early as spring, Riesling's shoots are distinctively crimson-tipped while Welschriesling's are tipped with pale green. Like Riesling, however, "the upstart" is a very late ripener, is only moderately vigorous, maintains high acidity in the grapes and produces wines that are light in body and high in aroma. Those, and only those, are the similarities.

Welschriesling is notable for its high yield, provided it is not highjacked by botrytis, powdery mildew or shoot necrosis – a problem in parts of Italy.

In Italy it is grown chiefly in the northeast, Friuli-Venezia Giulia bordering on Yugoslavia, around Bologna and in Lombardy, though there are still a few hectares in the Alto Adige. Often blended with the real McCoy, known in Italy as Riesling Renano, these blends of very different wines sold simply as "Riesling" do little for the reputation of either. It thrives on flat land and its performance in Alto Adige, especially in comparison with the local Riesling Renano, demonstrates powerfully that it needs a relatively warm climate.

On lower land Riesling Italico is, as almost everywhere, treasured for its high yield. Collio in Friuli is one of the very few DOCs in which 100 percent Riesling Italico grapes are specified. Both this and, even more so, that of Colli Bolognesi prove that the variety can produce very delicate, sprightly wines – admittedly not for keeping but for very enthusiastic sipping.

Such wines are quite easy to find on the other side of Trieste, provided one takes the trouble to go to Yugoslavia oneself. The typical export model of Laskiriesling is heavy, sweetened stuff, so weighted down by residual sugar that it must plod rather than skip. The variety grows in, and seems well adapted to, most of the north and central part of this vast country, playing a significant role in the republics of Croatia, Serbia, Vojvodina, even Kosovo and especially Slovenia. The high Fruska Gora vineyards of Vojvodina can rival Slovenia for the raciness of its relatively dry domestic consumption version of Laskiriesling or Graševina (a term also used for proper Riesling).

Bulgaria has 4,000 hectares (10,000 acres) of Welschriesling, making it the country's fifth most important white grape variety. It is particularly important in the Shumen region in the east of the country, where the other sort of Riesling is also being groomed for stardom. Such is the Bulgarian wine Kombinat's single-mindedness about the fashionable varieties that Welschriesling's future here seems uncertain.

As Olaszriesling, the variety is extremely well entrenched in Hungary, even though it has been known in the country for little more than a century. After phylloxera, the variety became very popular, at least partly because of its reassuringly high yield. Total Hungarian plantings are nearly 20,000 hectares (50,000 acres), a total bettered only by the very ordinary Kövidinka. It is planted in every one of the country's very varied wine districts other than Tokajhegyalja, which has other preoccupations. Olaszriesling from three wine districts on the north shore of Lake Balaton – Balatonfüred, Badacsony and Csopak – are particularly prized and show that the variety can struggle very valiantly against flabbiness even in such warm, sunny conditions.

There is probably still some Vlassky Riesling in Czechoslovakia but the Russians claim that all their Riesling is the Rhine and Mosel rather than Danube variety. It is on the Danube that the seminal Welschriesling of Romania

flourishes. It is highly regarded as a noble grape here and does particularly well around Arges (in Wallachia). In nearby Dealul Mare some of the Welschriesling is used in sparkling wine production. It thrives on the flat Dobrogeia vineyards in the hinterland of the Black Sea coast; and it is also grown in the Transylvanian hills. The wines, often sold simply as "Riesling" (no wonder the Germans get so upset), vary enormously in quality and often show signs of needing more sympathetic vinification. With the Feteascăs, arguably varieties with a more forceful personality, this is still a variety of enormous importance in Romania.

It is in Austria, however, that evidence of Welschriesling's potential is easiest to find. With nearly 5,000 hectares (12,500 acres) planted, the variety is the third most important in Austria, after Grüner Veltliner and Müller-Thurgau. It is particularly important in late-harvest country, Burgenland, and in the south of the country, although there are notable plantings in Falkenstein, Lower Austria.

There are two distinct styles, both of them successful. Welschriesling can be a relatively light (for Austria) fruity-flowery wine with a distinct crackle of carbon dioxide that

After Grüner Veltliner, Welschriesling is the most planted grape variety in Burgenland, whose romance and chequered history is more than hinted at by Burg Schlaining. The grapes here can reach higher sugar levels than anywhere else the variety is grown, producing rich, if fast-maturing, dessert wines.

cries out to be gulped immediately. In the warm microclimate of Burgenland where "noble rot" develops nicely, Welschriesling grapes may be left on the vine until snow is on the ground. Welschriesling Trockenbeerenauslesen are by no means uncommon. They lack the steely purity that rebukes the drinker of a proper late-harvest Riesling for broaching it before the end of its first decade. These wines are softer and are best drunk between five and ten years, but they can be marvels of richness and – let us not overlook this facet of wine drinking – pleasure.

Under pressure from the Germans, the EEC is trying to exert the influence of a major customer in discouraging the Welschriesling producers of eastern Europe from using the word "Riesling" in any form to describe it. They like to see it either incorporated as a suffix, as in Welschriesling or, preferably, written in unmistakably Slav versions such as Rizling.

Perhaps if the variety could be divested of its apparently social-climbing nomenclature, we could all settle down and enjoy its produce more. The Chinese are prepared to.

Synonyms:
Wälschriesling (German-speaking countries);
Riesling Italico, Rismi (Italy);
Laskiriesling, Laski Rizling, Graševina, Grasica,
Italianski Rizling, Talijanski Rizling,
Biela Sladka Grasica (Yugoslavia);
Riesling Italianski, Rizling Vlassky (Czechoslovakia);
Olaszriesling, Olasz Rizling (Hungary);
Riesling Italien (Romania);
Italiansky Rizling (Bulgaria).

Soils:
Not fussy; it can tolerate poor soils as well as relatively rich alluvial flats.

Vigour: Medium.

Pruning:
Medium to long canes.

Susceptibility:
Fairly susceptible to both oidium and botrytis.

Rootstocks:
Vigorous rootstocks needed.
Some success with 5BB and 125AA.

Yields:
Very high.

Medium quality. Very unfashionable.

Gewürztraminer

Gewürztraminer has the dubious dual distinction of being the easiest grape variety to recognize and the most difficult to spell. It comes from a large, ramified family and is cultivated in almost all of the world's wine-producing countries. Its story is a complicated one.

The headily scented wine made from Gewürztraminer has many fans, the majority of them wooed by examples from Alsace. By and large they are exactly those wine drinkers who scorn Italian white wines for their lack of character and body, so they might well be surprised to learn that Gewürztraminer's origins are almost certainly Italian, or at least what we call Italy today.

The grape Traminer was first mentioned as growing in the village of Tramin, or Termeno, in the higher reaches of the Etsch valley in what is now the Italian Tyrol, around the year 1000. It was widely cultivated in the Alto Adige until the middle of the sixteenth century when it was ousted by the much more heavily cropping Vernatsch or Trollinger still so popular there today. Even earlier, the grape may have been a descendent of the *uva Aminea* from Thessalia in northern Greece according to a number of seventeenth-century ampelographers, some of whom attribute its dissemination northwards and Rhinewards to the Romans.

Traminer has been a popular variety in Rheinpfalz for more than 150 years, and there was a time when Traminer from the Palatinate was popular with Rheingau growers for adding richness to their Rieslings.

The relationship between Traminer and Gewürztraminer has been much discussed and much misunderstood. The prefix Gewürz means "spice" in German, and in international winespeak spicy has come to be synonymous with the characteristic aroma of Gewürztraminer. This is perhaps one of the best examples of wine tasters' straw-clutching abilities. It is difficult to think of a single ingredient on the spice rack that resembles the almost fetid aroma of Gewürztraminer. The smell is closer to tropical fruits or highly perfumed flowers. Lychees and roses are some of the most commonly used tasting notes: cold cream, the cosmetic sort, has been heard in unrelated instances on both sides of the Atlantic. Gewürz in this context should probably be understood to mean simply "perfumed", like *musqué* in French.

In the last century they were relatively untroubled by these problems of semantics. The variety was known simply as Traminer, of which there were many forms, including red, white and blue versions. Today the red, or rather pinkish form, also known as Traminer Musqué, Traminer Aromatico or Gewürztraminer, is by far the best known. Gewürztraminer just happens to be the most widely accepted synonym, and the one required by law in Alsace since 1973. In many other regions, Traminer is preferred, although it denotes exactly the same variety, ampelographically "red" Traminer producing predominantly pink but occasionally yellow fruit, even on the same bunch.

In Alsace, for instance, where more of the vine is grown than anywhere else, there is hardly any of the less aromatic "white" Traminer left. Incidentally it is the white Traminer which bears the closest resemblance to the Savagnin Blanc of the Jura. The Gewürztraminer common today is Savagnin Rosé and was acknowledged so as early as 1909 by Viala.

The well-pigmented colour of the skins of Gewürztraminer means that the wines are some of the deepest coloured whites. An Alsace Gewürztraminer is usually mid-gold, sometimes with a slightly peachy glow, especially since some skin contact is beneficial for maximum aroma, provided that the ambient temperature is not so high that oxidation is a problem. Along with Cabernet Sauvignon and Syrah, Gewürztraminer is one of the few varieties that can be identified by sight alone (although this exceptionally deep colour worries some winemakers in the newer regions and they occasionally carbon treat the wines, thereby losing some of the flavour as well). Although its aroma is overwhelming, it is in practice easy to confuse Gewürztraminer with Muscat, at least in the context of Alsace. Both are grapey and intense.

Another of Gewürztraminer's hallmarks is a high level of alcohol, up to 14 percent, often coupled with dangerously low acids. The wines tend to have considerable extract as well as alcohol, which can accentuate this shortcoming. Malolactic fermentation tends to be suppressed wherever the variety is grown. Conditions in which long-lasting Gewürztraminer can be made are much more exceptional than those producing Rieslings that can last. Great Gewürztraminer, wines that are capable of interesting maturity, are produced in Alsace perhaps only once in a decade.

In Alsace it is officially designated a "noble" grape variety and is regarded along with Riesling and Pinot Gris as one of the region's greats (albeit rather scorned by the winemakers themselves as being too obvious and ever so slightly too much of a good thing – one has to suffer for one's pleasures, after all). In northern Italy, Germany and Austria it makes equally distinctive, if very different wines. It is presumably this very distinctive quality that has made

GEWÜRZTRAMINER

it so popular in the newer wine regions, even though many of them are too warm for the resulting wines to escape a certain oiliness and bitter finish. Of these new habitats, only in New Zealand does Gewürztraminer seem really very comfortable. One of the wine world's more bizarre manifestations of fashion over sense must be the current vogue for planting Gewürztraminer in northeast Victoria, home of Australia's amazing liqueur Muscats. In this sweltering climate, perfect for the production of these intense traditional "stickies", Gewürztraminer ripens so fast that the grapes have to be harvested far too early for any character to develop.

This popularity owes nothing to Gewürztraminer's viticultural characteristics. It is a relatively low and erratic yielder (although the Germans have developed some higher-yielding clones, specifically in Baden). In Alsace average annual yields can vary between less than 40 and more than 100 hectolitres per hectare. The variety is very prone to virus diseases and to degeneration on certain sites. It leafs early and can therefore suffer from spring frosts, after which its recovery rate is low. Gewürztraminer ripens in early mid-season, being harvested before Riesling wherever it is grown.

French Gewürztraminer effectively means Alsace Gewürztraminer, a sizeable planting of more than 2,500 hectares (6,250 acres). This substantial increase over the last two decades makes it the region's most planted noble grape variety, with vineyards as extensive as those of

Sylvaner. More than two-thirds of Alsace plantings are in the Haut-Rhin where it is particularly selected for richer soils. Sporen at Riquewihr, Kitterlé at Guebwiller and Eichberg at Turckheim are some of the most famous individual Gewürztraminer vineyards.

In Alsace all Gewürztraminer is fermented out to dryness: the classic "smells sweet, tastes dry" wines. The exception to this rule are the very exceptional Vendange Tardive and, even richer, Sélection de Grains Nobles wines. Gewürztraminer musts for these can reach a potential alcohol level of more than 20 percent, certainly more than Riesling and usually more than Pinot Gris. Although Alsace winemakers could never be accused of hastening their wines on to the marketplace, these sweeter wines are their only offerings designed for really long maturation. They are too new to have established a track record of longevity, but one imagines that a late-harvest Gewürztraminer of the 1976 or 1983 vintages will still be hale and hearty at the turn of the century. Léon Béyer have a particularly well sung reputation for Gewürztraminer, epitomizing the strong, sturdy style beloved in Alsace.

German Gewürztraminers, often called Traminer, are as different from the Alsace model as their Rieslings. Gewürztraminer vines total less than 1,000 hectares (2,500 acres) representing less than 1 percent of total vineyard in Germany, and are most common in the southerly regions of Rheinpfalz and Baden. This is partly because Gewürztraminer requires sites that further north can be more profitably planted with Riesling, and also because it needs sufficient warmth to promote good flowering and to set fruit for adequately high must weights to result.

Some of these German Gewürztraminers can seem flabby, doubtless a reflection of the German winemaking style, which also serves to dampen the aroma. The Germans have found the variety cussedly difficult to tame, so much does it vary from site to site. Often the wine is used in blends, though some of the top producers in the Mittelhaardt have a great reputation for their varietal Gewürztraminers. The variety also flourishes on the volcanic tufa and loess of Baden's Kaiserstuhl area.

There is as much Gewürztraminer planted in Austria as in Germany, but the wines too often demonstrate the oiliness lurking there. South and east Styria on the Yugoslav border are the grape's strongholds and it is not too difficult to persuade it to ripen into a Beerenauslese as officially designated by the Austrians. Such wines can be impressively rich and smooth as syrup, but need to be consumed within a few years of the vintage.

Just over the border in northern Slovenia, and in the hills of Fruska Gora, the variety surfaces as Traminac, with the breadth of an Austrian example but often not much more weight than a German one. Most eastern European Traminers are sweetish, and are certainly the cheapest versions on offer. Hungary is proudest of the full-bodied Tramini grown on the southern shores of Lake Balaton at Balatonboglar. Romania has some planted in Transylvania. Bulgaria's Traminer vineyards are mainly in the east and at Karlovo in the south. The variety is known in

Young vines at Turckheim are in the very heart of geographical Alsace, just as Gewürztraminer represents the very heart of vinous Alsace. Indeed, to many of the world's wine drinkers (though few of the region's winemakers), Gewürztraminer IS Alsace. It has long been the region's most planted variety, though the subtler Riesling is now catching up.

Bohemia in Czechoslovakia where the climate is not unlike that of Rheinpfalz; and it is also treasured in the USSR, in Moldavia and the Ukraine in particular, as a ripe ingredient in sparkling wine and in sweet varietals.

Although there are isolated plantings of Gewürztraminer in the rest of Europe, as in the high Penedés for Miguel Torres' Viña Esmeralda Muscat blend and in Luxembourg and Switzerland, it is in the Italian Tyrol that it is most at home. Today there are only about 150 hectares (375 acres) of Gewürztraminer vines in this cool northerly region. Plantings have been declining chiefly because of the Italians' distrust of strongly aromatic wines. Indeed the Alto Adige winemaker specifically tries to restrain the perfume of his Gewürztraminer by keeping skin contact to a minimum; he wants to make a wine that is fuller than most from his area with just a suggestion of floweriness and sufficient acid to stop it becoming flabby after a year in bottle. This is done by relatively early picking in September when temperatures can still be so high as to cause problems with hotheaded fermentations and the proliferation of bacteria. It is curious that those in the traditional birthplace of the variety are so unenthusiastic about it.

Not so the Californians, whose perseverance with what on the face of it is probably not a particularly suitable grape variety is reminiscent of their persistence with Pinot Noir. Much of California is too warm for Gewürztraminer; acids fall below acceptable levels long before any varietal character has been developed. Plantings have doubled to 1,800 hectares (4,500 acres) in the last decade, notably thanks to 240 hectares (600 acres) planted in Santa Barbara in 1980. Monterey and Sonoma are Gewürztraminer's other strongholds.

California's great problem, as in all warmer wine regions with low-acid grapes, is judging the optimum picking date. It is one of the first varieties to be picked there, with Gewürz fermentations already over in August being by no means unknown. The trouble is that such concern for natural acidity levels (acidification being quite legal) diminishes flavour, often resulting in facile, rather confected wines. To achieve anything like the depth of flavour of an Alsace wine, on the other hand, vineyard sites have to be chosen very carefully. To avoid coarseness, extreme care has to be taken to keep oxygen out of the process and to ferment only carefully cleaned juice.

Wineries such as Joseph Phelps, Chateau St Jean and Grand Cru have managed to produce sweet Gewürztraminers with impressive balance and even potential (it is a characteristic of good Gewürztraminer made anywhere that it often needs months in bottle before showing its best). Botrytization, either naturally or by cultivation of spores, has occasionally played a part in such wines.

Dry California Gewürztraminer is a more versatile wine, and here the battle is to avoid the fat oiliness and the bitter note which can be masked by sweetness. Delicacy is all, as Stony Hill showed way back.

The vineyards to the north of California in Oregon and Washington are better suited to the variety. With nearly 160 hectares (400 acres), it is the fourth most planted

*G*ewürztraminer is one of New Zealand's smarter wines, thriving best in the Gisborne area of the North Island. Like all varieties there, however, much of it is trucked to the older wineries in and around Auckland as here at Nobilo's.

variety in Oregon, although, as in northern Germany and indeed in any cool climate, *coulure* is a problem, as it is in the United States' eastern vineyards and Canada.

Winemakers elsewhere have found their fancy tickled by this flirtatious grape variety. The South Africans are wrestling with it, though short of moving the whole country several hundred miles south, it seems unlikely that they will achieve any satisfactory result.

Gewürztraminer is a relatively recent import into Australia, its proliferation hampered by ultrafastidious quarantine requirements for cuttings. There are more than 300 hectares (750 acres) each in South Australia and New South Wales, most of them very young vines; and many plantings in warmer areas, whose output is yet to impress. Added acid is a useful ingredient in such wines, and some residual sweetness is usual. The Australian solution to counteracting the rather galumphing nature of their Traminer is to blend in a bit of their enviably large Rhine Riesling harvest. Their Traminer-Rieslings, of which McWilliam's Bin 77 made from Riverina Traminer is probably the best known, have a crisp, clean finish and a good dose of fruity acid.

Along with Sauvignon Blanc, Gewürztraminer is one of those varieties the Australians should concede to their trans-Tasman neighbours. New Zealand has nearly 300 hectares (750 acres) of Gewürztraminer and the variety has the singular distinction of giving the impression that it has already found its New Zealand home: the Gisborne area where approximately half of all such vines are to be found. This is due in no small part to a single, very singular man, Denis Irwin of Matawhero, whose Gewürztraminers (inspired, according to him, by Germany not Alsace) were winning international acclaim as early as 1978. No hint of oiliness here, but an aromatic nerviness, occasionally dampened by a bit of "back blended" sweet grape must. In the Australian image, Gewürztraminer is also occasionally blended with Riesling here, but there is not the same need. Along with Alsace, New Zealand ranks as one of Gewürztraminer's ideal spots. The cooler vineyards of the United States show potential too.

Synonyms:
Traminer, Rotclevner, Rousselet, Frenscher, Edeltraube (Alsace); Traminer Musqué, Traminer Parfumé, Traminer Aromatique, Savagnin Rosé, Fromenteau Rouge, Fermin Rouge, Gentil-Duret Rouge, Gris Rouge (rest of France); Roter Traminer, Clevner, Klavner, Dreimanner, Christkindltraube, Rotedel, Rotfranke, Frankisch, Kleinweiner (Germany); Traminer Aromatico, Termeno Aromatico, Traminer Rosé, Traminer Rosso, Flaischweiner (Italy); Roter Nurnberger, Ranfoliza (Austria); Tramini, Tramini Piros, Fuszeres (Hungary); Traminer Rozovy (USSR); Traminac, Traminac Creveni, Rdeci Traminac (Yugoslavia); Drumin, Ptinc Cerveny, Pinat Cervena, Liwora (Czechoslovakia); Traminer Roz, Rusa (Romania); Mala Dinka (Bulgaria); Haiden, Heida (Switzerland).

Soils:
Fairly deep fertile soils of a loamy texture are good. Heavy soils with some clay produce the most aromatic wines. Chlorosis is a problem in chalky soils.

Vigour: Moderate.

Pruning:
Head training and cane pruning is recommended. Careful spacing can combat *coulure.*

Susceptibility:
Some clones are known for their tough skins, though rot, sometimes noble, has been known in many regions. Oidium is a problem in South Africa and *coulure* is a problem everywhere.

Rootstocks:
Low to moderate vigour is best; good affinity with SO4, 5C, 26G and 3309.

Yields:
Low to moderate. Interestingly, most satisfactory yields are achieved where quality is universally acknowledged best: Alsace. Six tons per acre have been managed in California but half this is more common.

Good quality. Quite fashionable.

Silvaner

I t would not be surprising if the world's Silvaner plantings dwindled to nought over the next half-century, although it would be a shame. The varietal may be capable of presenting wine drinkers with just the same sort of palate profile as the beloved Sauvignon Blanc (and vine growers with a much higher yield), but it loses by a nose – or lack of it. Because of this, Silvaner has been noticeably low on the shopping lists of those establishing experimental vine plantings outside Germany.

The chief characteristic of wine made from Silvaner is high acid. The grapes ripen between Müller-Thurgau and Riesling and have no problems in achieving respectable must weights, so the wines have sufficient body. They are not vapid in structure, just short on discernible character. After all, Sauvignon Blanc is simply tart and medium-bodied on the palate, its only distinction being its powerful aroma (it is easy to see why the Germans call that variety Muskat-Silvaner). The nose of a Silvaner is, in all but a handful of isolated bottles, best described as neutral. Silvaner is not a wine for our times.

Just occasionally, as in some of the best vineyards of its spiritual home Franken or in odd sites in the north of Rheinhessen, Silvaner wines can excite with their combination of dry tingle and substance, so rare in Germany.

And in Alsace, ultrafastidious producers such as Trimbach are sometimes capable of coaxing some (Alsace) Riesling characteristics out of Sylvaner, as it is spelt on that side of the Rhine. A 30-year-old example from Faller of Kaysersberg was in tremendous shape in 1977.

Silvaner's heyday was in the first half of this century when it replaced Elbling to become Germany's most important grape variety. Until the late fifties, it was the variety most commonly chosen by growers replanting vineyards. Today its place in Germany has been taken by the earlier ripening, even higher yielding Müller-Thurgau, but its total area of just over 8,000 hectares (20,000 acres) still constitutes by far the largest planting of Silvaner worldwide.

Even the Germans admit that the vine came via, and probably from, Austria, as suggested by its Rheingau synonym Osterreicher, although some theories attribute its more common name to Transylvanian origins. Either way, wild vines cultivated on the banks of the Danube were almost certainly the precursors of this vine variety which is still commonly, if not prolifically, found throughout central Europe.

Its progress through Germany was definitely westward, with evidence of its introduction in Würzburg and Heilbronn as early as the seventeenth century. Today, 40 percent of all German Silvaner plantings are in Rheinhessen, 25 percent in Rheinpfalz and 13 percent in Franken. It is accorded most respect in the last of these where Riesling is difficult to ripen in many years. Indeed some impressive Silvaner Beerenauslese wines have been produced there.

Rieslaner is a crossing of Silvaner and Riesling, which has been particularly suitable for Franken. Practically all of Germany's many successful crossings owe some parentage to Silvaner, from Müller-Thurgau through Scheurebe, Morio Muskat, Bacchus, Optima and Ehrenfelser on. Blauer Silvaner, a light red distant relative, is known around Württemberg. Grüner Silvaner is the proper name of the white variety, whose acid levels are in fact slightly below those of the Riesling but which seem so much higher because there is no great aroma and fruit to compensate. Late harvesting Silvaner can mute the tartness, but rarely results in rewardingly high must weights.

Outside Germany, Silvaner is probably best known to the world's wine lovers as one of Alsace's more basic varietals. Even here it is being replaced, by the softer Pinot Blanc (though there has recently been evidence that some producers are becoming dissatisfied with this grape's low acid levels). There have been roughly 2,500 hectares (6,125 acres) of vineyard planted to Sylvaner in Alsace for many years, but this represents a decreasing proportion of the total. By 1982, Riesling and Gewürztraminer had all but matched Sylvaner's 20 percent and Pinot Blanc was catching up fast.

It is *the* grape of the lower, flatter, more fertile vineyards of the Bas-Rhin, representing half of all plantings there. Those familiar with Sylvaner's inherent neutrality can only marvel at Alsace's ability to make its spicy mark even on this raw material, albeit faintly. That it is, on the right site, possible to make wines of truly exciting quality is evinced by some exceptional bottles. Pamela Vandyke Price in her *Alsace Wines* cites the growers Boeckel and Seltz and the Zotzenberg vineyard in Mittelbergheim.

Despite the vine's original route west, there is today very little Silvaner in Austria. There are isolated tiny pockets in Slovenia in northern Yugoslavia, about 250 hectares (625 acres) at Badacsony on Hungary's Lake Balaton and elsewhere in eastern Europe. Silvaner's high acid makes it an ideal blending material for this part of the world. The variety is regarded with some respect in the Soviet Union.

Throughout the rest of the world, Silvaner is accorded scant attention except in the South Tyrol, where it is regarded as an almost-noble grape variety. Examples with a year or two of bottle age can please with the same sort of firm, dry steeliness enjoyed in a good Franken Silvaner. Plantings of Silvaner here total more than those of Rheinriesling and Müller-Thurgau put together.

The only other place where it attains respectability is Switzerland where it is often called Johannisberger and, compared to the prevalent Chasselas, looks positively rich.

Elsewhere Silvaner is planted but little, though its high acid and good yields could presumably make it a useful ingredient in blends in warmer climates. Brown Bros of northeast Victoria in Australia chose it as one of the best-performing of the 40-odd vines they experimented with in the late seventies. The Californians have, perhaps

SILVANER

*T*his old wine press at Nordheim in Franken represents ancient German winemaking just as Silvaner represents ancient German viticulture. Silvaner was Germany's most planted variety as recently as 1964 but only in Franken is it still, rightly, taken seriously as fine wine material. Riesling was overtaken in number one spot by Müller-Thurgau by 1969.

surprisingly, more than 480 hectares (1,200 acres) of the variety, most of it in Monterey County. Many of these plants suffer from virus infections, but its prevalance is perhaps a hangover from the official Davis view that it withstands heat better than proper Riesling. Much to the disgust of the Germans, Californians have been known to call Silvaner Franken Riesling, Monterey Riesling and Sonoma Riesling.

Synonyms:
Grüner Silvaner, Sylvaner, Osterreicher, Franken, Frankenriesling, Grünfränkisch, Salviner, Salvaner, Grünedel, Schönfeilner, Scharvaner, Bötzinger (Germany); Sylvaner, Silvain Vert, Gentil Vert, Picardon Blanc, Gamay Blanc, Clozier (France); Grüner Zierfandl, Fliegentraube (Austria); Johannisberger, Gros-Rhin (Switzerland); Silvania, Silvaner Bianco (Italy); Zelena Sedmogradka, Silvanai Zelini (Yugoslavia); Zöldsilváni (Hungary); Cynifal, Zeleny, Moravka, Silvanske (Czechoslovakia); Monterey Riesling, Sonoma Riesling, Franken Riesling (California).

Soils:
Fussier than Riesling, Silvaner likes fairly moist, deep soils but can overcrop on clay in warmer climates.

Vigour: Medium.

Pruning: Very versatile.

Susceptibility:
Frosts (for wood), oidium to some extent.
Less susceptible to rot than Müller-Thurgau.

Rootstocks:
Very important; Silvaner is chlorosis-sensitive, therefore choice of rootstock is governed by chalk content of soil.
5BB can compensate for dry gravels;
SO4 or 5C are good on fertile soils.

Yields:
Reliable and higher than most other German varieties, though lower than Müller-Thurgau. 150 hl/ha is possible, though poor soils may average 80 hl/ha.

Fair quality. Not modish.

Müller-Thurgau

Müller-Thurgau is the wine world's most famous, most established crossing, at least of the present generation of vine varieties used for wine. Who knows what permutations of earlier vine types were originally responsible for the varieties that are so familiar today? It is Germany's most widely planted grape variety. It forms the basis of New Zealand's burgeoning wine industry and is a major variety all over what was the Austro-Hungarian empire. It is even the most important grape variety under commercial cultivation in England. And these territorial conquests have all been made in a remarkably short time.

There is more than a touch of Frankenstein in the tale of Müller-Thurgau, although the crossing itself is less monstrous than simply drearily mousy (as many familiar with its flavour will agree). It was the creation of a Dr Müller, born in the Swiss canton of Thurgau but working at the Geisenheim viticultural station in 1882 when he wrote in a trade magazine: "Who is there who has not already noticed that in all descriptions of the best vine varieties, there is a 'but' which makes mention of at least one disadvantageous characteristic? How useful it would be therefore if one could combine the advantages of two vine varieties to the exclusion of their disadvantages! How

important the result of such a union, combining the superb characteristics of the Riesling grape with the reliable early maturing qualities of the Silvaner, could be for some wine producing areas."

Like any new product launch, the arrival of the Doctor's crossing in 1883 was trumpeted the year before by its creator. He seems to have been a better technical director than public relations man, however, for the German wine industry all but ignored this strange new "Müller-Thurgau" vine at first, and continued to depend predominantly on Silvaner for everyday wines and Riesling for special treats until well into the twentieth century. There was even a movement which tried to have the mousy new monster banned altogether.

Those concerned only with top quality German wine were undoubtedly right to distrust Dr Müller's attempt to give them their cake and let them eat it. It by no means lived up to its pre-publicity. The new creation could not provide anything more than a pale shadow of what gave Germany's top grape variety greatness. Moderate yields, the attendant risks of a late ripener and a certain fastidiousness about location were, and still are, quite simply the price that has to be paid for the magnificence of Riesling. Müller-Thurgau was certainly earlier ripening than

If only Müller-Thurgau wines were as durable as the paniers still used occasionally to harvest the grapes! For all the technological wizardry employed in Germany's larger wineries today, many of the small-holdings are worked with almost archaic methods. The dearth of vineyard workers has been a major factor in the literal reshaping of the vineyards.

much more anonymous blends marketed as QbA wines and Tafelwein. Most importantly, Müller-Thurgau provides the volume for the ocean of Liebfraumilch and the like that every year washes over thousands of nascent wine drinkers in northern Europe and North America. For this reason, perhaps, we should be grateful for the crossing, although in most such cases it is merely a neutral base for the more aromatic grape(s) that give the wine its character.

It is still a subject for discussion whether Switzerland's most bizarre gift to Germany was a crossing of Riesling and Silvaner, as Dr Müller clearly intended, or of two different Rieslings. What is certain is that while Germany's thriving wine business is dependent on downmarket wines, Müller-Thurgau is likely to remain the German grower's most popular variety, but there are signs that Riesling is slowly regaining ground. Müller-Thurgau, with that other grandfather of the vineyard Scheurebe, showed the way towards the myriad more recent crossings, of which a little usually goes a long way. Müller-Thurgau itself is even part of the genetic make-up of more than 10 successful subsequent crossings, including such popular varieties as Bacchus, Ortega and Optima.

In Germany the regions with the largest area of Müller-Thurgau are Rheinhessen, Baden and Rheinpfalz, with nearly 17,000 hectares (42,500 acres) between them, slightly more than an equal share in that home of Liebfraumilch, Rheinhessen. Mosel-Saar-Ruwer, to the chagrin of many, now has Germany's fourth biggest plantation of the crossing: nearly 3,000 hectares (7,500 acres) which constitute nearly a quarter of total plantings in the region. Riesling may prevail on the steepest sites, but Müller-Thurgau is planted just about everywhere else. The Rheingau retains its probity and its Riesling, with a mere 200 hectares (500 acres) of Müller-Thurgau, while the variety now constitutes almost one half of all vines in Franken, a region once so proud of its Silvaner.

Müller-Thurgau is not even particularly easy to grow. It may ripen early and therefore reliably, but it is very susceptible to peronospera, blackrot and even has its own special plague, Roter Brenner. Rot of a very ignoble sort is a special problem, too. It can take hold so suddenly that a grower can find his entire crop attacked overnight, which is one reason why no vine grower is keen to grow only Müller-Thurgau. Indeed growers are advised not to plant more than 30 percent of the variety, but the recommendation is robustly ignored by many. Wide spacing and sprays can help combat rot, as does the German habit of picking at the earliest possible moment. It is little wonder that few complex flavours can be found in Müller-Thurgau.

The vines' wood is not at all hardy – in comparison with Riesling it looks positively puny – and young vines can suffer terribly in winter frosts. Even two or three winter days with temperatures below −15°C can leave Müller-Thurgau buds reeling from the shock. The vine recovers fast from spring frosts, however, its auxiliary buds being particularly fertile, and incidence of *coulure* is very rare.

It would be unfair to say that Müller-Thurgau has no flavour. It does have a flavour, which the Germans describe

MÜLLER-THURGAU

Silvaner, and was much less liable to chlorosis, leaf yellowing and stunted growth, in richer soils. But the price paid for that was a loss in acidity and ageing potential. All in all, the crossing's chief advantage appeared to be productivity, but at a notable cost in quality.

Müller-Thurgau entered the well-kept records of Germany's vineyards in 1921 (almost 40 years after its launch!), but it was not until a major symposium on the crossing was held at Alzey in 1938 that it gained any widespread acceptance. The upheaval of the war years left its future in the balance, but its solid commercial attractions for an industry rebuilding itself after the war were too strong to resist. Since then Müller-Thurgau plantings have increased dramatically, so that in the early seventies it finally overtook Riesling to become Germany's most popular variety. Today its 25,500 hectares (63,750 acres) constitute 26 percent of Germany's vineyard area, and a considerably higher proportion of the amount of wine produced in an average year. Müller-Thurgau's productivity is famous, or notorious: between 100 and sometimes even 200 hectolitres per hectare, as opposed to Riesling's usual range between 80 and 110. It would not be an exaggeration to say that Germany owes the enormous commercial success of its wine industry (the word is used advisedly) to Müller-Thurgau.

Relatively few German wine labels at the elevated level of QmP announce the presence of any Müller-Thurgau, which shows just how important the grape must be to the

*M*üller-Thurgau (or "Riesling-Sylvaner") dominates the New Zealand wine industry and is the most important white variety here. Mission Vineyards at Hawke's Bay has the longest tradition of under-same-management vine cultivation in New Zealand. It was founded by the French Marist order in the last century and originally may well have produced wine from imported French vine cuttings.

as "a pleasant note of Muscat". Cat maybe, turning to positively mousy in some less favoured years. What is particularly curious is that much of the wine made from Müller-Thurgau cultivated outside Germany manages to taste so much more attractive. The German bill for fertilizing Müller-Thurgau must be substantial. Is greed, translated into force-fed crops, the explanation?

In New Zealand, for example, where the variety accounts for about 45 percent of each year's total vintage, it is not difficult to find examples that have a fresh, appetizingly floral aroma and sufficient acidity to keep them lively. The New Zealand *Wine & Food Annual*, an excellent publication written with balance rather than hyperbole, begins its section on the grape thus: "Müller-Thurgau epitomises the Riesling-style wines that are light, fresh, fragrant, and fruity." Yields here can vary between 55 and 200 hectolitres per hectare, depending on the fertility of the soil. Like the Germans, the New Zealanders rely heavily on the practice of adding *Süssreserve* (or "back-blending", as they call it) and often beef up the flavour of their Müller-Thurgau with a sweet reserve of another, more aromatic variety. The results are noticeably more alluring than most German equivalents.

Much of the wine produced on New Zealand's 1,800 hectares (4,500 acres) of vines is, confusingly, labelled Riesling-Sylvaner. It is thought, quite rightly, that this conjunction of possible antecedents has a racier ring to it than the less misleading combination of the good doctor's

name and provenance. The wines are made from bone dry to positively unctuous, but the majority of examples by far are exactly like most German Müller-Thurgau: medium dry. The varietal looks set for an exciting future here.

The EEC's two smallest wine-producing countries also share a predilection for this variety. Müller-Thurgau responds well to the "marginal" climate of England: the vine is planted on 150 hectares (375 acres) of rolling English countryside, 100 hectares (250 acres) more than England's second most popular variety, Reichensteiner, and about 149 hectares more than total plantings of its great progenitor Riesling which ripens impossibly late for commercial production so far north. It has been markedly more popular as Rivaner in Luxembourg. It constitutes about 50 percent of Luxembourg's wine production and nicely complements the searingly tart Elbling which is its second most prolific grape variety.

Perhaps the best European Müller-Thurgaus come from northern Italy, where the vine responds well to high altitudes, particularly in the mountains of the South Tyrol, or Alto Adige. Maximum yield on these steep slopes is about 90 hectolitres per hectare and the cool ambient temperatures delay this usually early-ripening grape so that it is actually one of the last varieties to be picked, and it manages to soak up enough fruit flavours to make the wine one of the most modish whites in Italy. It may not be Wehlener Sonnenuhr, but it is indisputably better than most German Müller-Thurgaus. The vine is also cultivated as far south as the Colli Piacentini in Emilia-Romagna.

Also in mountain country, Switzerland has about 500 hectares (1,250 acres) of "Riesling-Sylvaner" (not for them a reminder that Müller was an expatriate) mainly in the east, much of it lightly *pétillant* and some even late harvested. At rather lower altitudes, Austria has about 6,000 hectares (15,000 acres) constituting 10 percent of all vineyard plantings and making it Austria's most popular grape variety after Grüner Veltliner. It is grown all over the country's wine regions, as well as spilling over into Slovenia in northern Yugoslavia.

Across the border, Czechoslovakia's Moravian vineyards are populated with Müller-Thurgau in a similarly dominant role; and there are even about 200 hectares (500 acres) of the crossing in East Germany to the north. Relative to other grape varieties, its role may be slightly less important in Slovakia, eastern Czechoslovakia's main wine country across the border from Hungary, but in terms of area it is very important, bringing the Czech total under Müller-Thurgau to over 5,000 hectares (12,500 acres). It would be surprising, therefore, if the crossing were not known in Hungary and indeed it is – as Rizlingszilvani.

Hungary is the world's second largest cultivator of the vine, with nearly 8,000 hectares (20,000 acres). Many of them are around Lake Balaton in the northeast, producing Badacsonyi Rizlingszilvani in huge quantity, and another significant, and perhaps surprising, area of cultivation is way down on the southern border in the warm, sandy Kunbaja region. The Hungarians themselves seem to be far more tolerant of flabbiness in their wine than most of their export customers.

Müller-Thurgau's characteristically low acid levels are seen as a positive boon in some other, very different parts of the world. In Oregon, for example, the area planted with Müller-Thurgau is still minuscule, but local viticultural sages reckon that the varietal could produce very agreeable jug wine in this cool climate for the simple reason that it would be less tart than most other varieties. (Oregonians would also be more modest in their productivity requirements than most growers.)

Elsewhere, either the climate tends to be too warm and the market too fastidious for such a low-acid varietal (vide California and Australia) or they simply have better things to grow (Alsace).

Synonyms:
Riesling-Sylvaner (Switzerland and New Zealand);
Rivaner (Luxembourg and Yugoslavia);
Rizlingszilvani (Hungary).

Soils:
Deep, cool, moist soils. It can take heavy chalk and loam, but not shallow sandy or rocky soils.

Vigour: Vigorous.

Pruning:
Needs a roomy training system. Wide spacing: perhaps 1.5 metres (4.9 feet) between vines and 2 metres (6.5 feet) between rows. Summer pruning may be necessary for quality.

Susceptibility:
Generally quite high.
It is most susceptible to peronospera and is also very susceptible to ordinary botrytis, blackrot and Roter Brenner (literally "red scorcher"). Low incidence of *coulure*.

Rootstocks:
These must be vigorous because of the vine's own vigorous growth. In low fertility soils, 5BB and 125AA, or 5C in more fertile soils. Soil must be very fertile for SO4.

Yields:
Very high indeed. Low to medium quality.

Ordinary. Fashionable only (temporarily?) in Italy.

Melon de Bourgogne (Muscadet)

The key to this surprisingly well-travelled vine variety is in its most common synonym, Muscadet. Although its origins are thought to lie in Burgundy, where it is still found at least in theory if not in practice, it is now almost exclusively used for the production of Muscadet at the mouth of the river Loire. Californians were also amazed to learn in the 1970s, after Pierre Galet's inspection of the experimental vineyard at Davis, that the varietal they call Pinot Blanc is in fact Melon de Bourgogne.

Total French plantings have remained remarkably steady over the last 20 years, and 8,900 of the 9,500 hectares (22,250 out of 23,750 acres) planted in France in 1979 were in the Loire Atlantique *département*, most of the rest in neighbouring Maine-et-Loire, practically all used to produce tart, dry, limpid Muscadet. This unprepossessing vine region was known chiefly for thin red wines until the seventeenth century, when Dutch traders exerted their influence on producers to change to more exportable (and distillable) whites. The switch was accelerated by the extraordinary winter of 1709 which is reputed to have frozen not just the vines but the sea itself.

Members of the Burgundian Pinot family were commonly planted in the Muscadet region well before this particular big chill, and Hubrecht Duijker even argues that "experts from Burgundy helped with the planting – there is a hamlet named Bourguignon in the Vallet district". But it is a mystery exactly why this variety came to dominate the *vignoble* so effectively, accounting for half of all the varied plantings in the Loire Atlantique today. The vine's good resistance to cold weather was presumably a factor – the vines withstood better than most the notorious winter of 1956. It may well have been those Dutch traders, who especially valued the Melon's early ripening and commercially attractive combination of reliable high yields and early maturing wine. Perhaps it was they who influenced the selection of this vine above others which they saw as less marketable.

In the Muscadet region the wine produced is a real maritime drink; bone dry, even sometimes slightly salty, almost bubbling with neutral-flavoured fruit at best, dull and flavourless at worst. With its singular lack of distinguishing marks, Muscadet is the blind taster's *bête noire*. It is exceptional in that appellation laws set a maximum alcohol content, 12 percent, in recognition of the growers' tendency to overchaptalize. The wine needs to be light to keep its appetizing quality, and is at its best bottled off the lees, *sur lie*, a much-traduced description. This practice evolved partly in an understandable effort to extract maximum flavour from the grapes, and also importantly to minimize its tendency to oxidation.

The grape rarely shows much ageing potential in France. Several 1976 Muscadets were almost reminiscent of English wines in their steely fruitiness in 1982, but did not appear to have achieved great complexity. And in Burgundy, Melon's homeland, it is allowed to contribute only to the lowly Bourgogne Grand Ordinaire appellation, which suggests they do not think much of its longevity either.

In California on the other hand, the grape called Pinot Blanc is accorded quite considerable respect, as a sort of muted, countrified Chardonnay. A hotter climate, more varied soils, and oak ageing in many cases produce wines so extraordinarily different from lean little Muscadet that one wonders whether the Davis sample vines as inspected by Professor Galet are truly representative of the state's increasing area of well over 800 hectares (2,000 acres).

*T*he countryside around the mouth of the Loire is as flat and densely planted with vines as its Girondin equivalent to the south. Some older vineyards are still planted with Gros Plant rather than the Muscadet grape Melon de Bourgogne, but most new plantings sanction the better-quality variety.

Certainly California growers note that their Pinot Blanc wine is prone to oxidation, and that the vines producing the small round berries recover well from spring frosts. It has been recommended only for the cooler Region I vineyards, where it is rated as a mid-season ripener, whereas early ripening is seen as one of Melon's characteristics. It would be fascinating to see how Melon would perform in the south of France. Perhaps Professor Galet is testing his hypothesis with a few rows of Melon in Montpellier?

Chalone, high in the Pinnacles district of Monterey County, where half of all California's Pinot Blanc is to be found, were one of the first to treat the varietal seriously. Alongside their often stunning Chardonnay, a lower-priced alternative was needed. They have applied the same peasant-farmer techniques to Pinot Blanc as to their Chardonnay and Pinot Noir and come up with rich wines capable of medium-term development. Up in Sonoma, Chateau St Jean have emulated the Chalone style and also produced extremely noble examples of the varietal, whatever it may be. A wide range of earlier maturing styles such as Fetzer's are also available.

MELON DE BOURGOGNE (MUSCADET)

Synonyms: Muscadet (Loire); Melon (Burgundy); Gamay Blanc à Feuilles Rondes, Gros Auxerrois, Lyonnaise Blanche (France); Weisserburgunder (Germany); Pinot Blanc (California).	*Pruning:* Messy in Muscadet, where a form of *gobelet* was commonly practised in the last century. Needs spur pruning. Up to 20 buds now allowed.
Soils: Thin topsoil on stony ground in the Muscadet region, best when schistous or granitic. Often deep fertile loam in California.	*Susceptibility:* Very good resistance to cold, but susceptible to downy mildew, powdery mildew and botrytis.
	Rootstocks: 3309C is by far the most common in Muscadet.
Vigour: Moderate.	*Yields:* Good, up to 70 hl/ha is possible in Muscadet, though the official maximum is 40 hl/ha. 3 to 5 tons per acre in north coast regions of California.

Low to medium quality. Virtually a one-region grape.

Aligoté

Aligoté is to Chardonnay what Silvaner is to Riesling: a poor copy of its native region's noble grape, with notably more acid, less body and much less ageing capacity. That said, just as exceptionally fine Silvaners can be found in Germany, so Burgundy occasionally yields up a genuinely toothsome Aligoté.

The vine has been cultivated in and around Burgundy for centuries and was considerably more popular than it is today when the higher yield of Aligoté was more important than the *réclame* of Chardonnay (indubitably the most powerful brand name in today's wine market). Aligoté's sphere of influence continues to shrink, in France at least, where total plantings had fallen by more than a third to just over 1,000 hectares (2,500 acres) by 1979.

About two-thirds of all of France's Aligoté is still planted on the Côte d'Or, but it is hardly surprising that it is losing ground each year to Chardonnay. Indeed, what *is* surprising, in view of the wildly better price that a grower can get for his Chardonnay, is that there is still so much of the lesser vine planted. In the last agricultural census of 1979, Aligoté plantings on the Côte d'Or were more than half those of Chardonnay. While this proportion has doubtless declined since then, there are clearly still a huge number of growers to whom their Aligoté tradition is more important than current market forces.

In the old days, many a white wine from Burgundy was a blend of Aligoté, Chardonnay and perhaps some Pinot Blanc and Melon. Since the introduction of Appellation Contrôlée laws, such commingling is not allowed and wine made from Aligoté must be sold (and ostracized) as Bourgogne Aligoté, at around half the price of a Bourgogne Blanc made from Chardonnay. The yield of Aligoté may be better than that of Chardonnay but it certainly is not the double needed to compensate financially. The Aligoté that

remains on the Côte d'Or is relegated to the outer edges of that precious region: the Arrières Côtes and the flatter land on the wrong side of Route Nationale 74.

Most of the rest of France's Aligoté is planted around the Mâconnais and Côte Chalonnaise vineyards, although there are still isolated plantings in the Yonne, around Chablis, where together with Sacy its high acid and low alcohol attracts makers of sparkling wines based further south who ship it out of the region.

It is unfair to dismiss all Aligoté as tart and vapid. It has the same broad structure as Chardonnay, and top quality examples such as those of Bouzeron's Pierre Cogny and Aubert de Villaine have sufficient weight to make the acid seem more like exciting *nervosité* than meanness.

The vine has spread to some surprising corners of the world and is notably popular in eastern Europe. Bulgaria has 2,500 hectares (6,250 acres) of Aligoté, well over twice as much as France, a statistic which would doubtless amaze many a Burgundian. It seems to be prized especially as blending material, because of the relatively high acid, and is particularly cultivated in the Chirpan region in the central south.

ALIGOTÉ

*A*ligoté does particularly well on the higher slopes of the Côte d'Or, though few accountants allow it to prove this nowadays on land that could be more profitably employed producing Chardonnay. Pernand-Vergelesses, famous for Aligoté, also has access to the fabulous Corton-Charlemagne appellation.

In Romania where it is also relatively popular, varietal Aligotés are produced from grapes that have obviously been exceptionally well ripened, to the limits of sufficiently high acidity. Some of these display a nuttiness of bouquet and most impressive body and length. It is also widely cultivated in the most northern vineyards of the Soviet Union, where it is treasured both as base for sparkling wine and as a pretty good table wine with slight bitterness.

Synonyms:
Chaudenet Gras (Côte Chalonnaise), Giboudot Blanc (Rully), Griset Blanc (Beaune), Plant Gris (Meursault), Troyen Blanc or Blanc de Troyes (Yonne).

Soils: Apparently fairly adaptable.

Vigour: Average vigour.

Pruning: Spur pruning.

Susceptibility: Relatively hardy.

Yields:
Moderately good.
50 hl/ha in Burgundy and about 4.5 tons per acre in experimental plantings in California.

Lower middle quality. Not at all fashionable.

Viognier

Quantitatively, the Viognier vine hardly deserves a mention in this book. Any qualitative assessment of the world's wines, on the other hand, tends to linger over the intriguing Viognier, even though little more than 32 hectares (80 acres) of it are planted anywhere in the world. Almost all of these are in France, producing some of her most expensive white wines at the top end of the Rhône valley, and yet Viognier does not even feature by name in the French Agricultural Census, being wildly outplanted by the obscure likes of Monbadon and Corbeau.

Viognier produces full-bodied, golden wines with a haunting and tantalizingly elusive bouquet. Some say may blossom, others apricots; others musky peaches, one authority, John Livingstone-Learmonth, even ripe pears just below the skin. Whatever it tastes like, enthusiasts are so smitten that they can even convince themselves of a wonderfully onomatopaeic quality in the word Viognier itself. Soft yet strong (it sounds dangerously like a brand of toilet paper), Viognier works a magic of its own.

Its rarity doubtless increases its allure for connoisseurs. If we had the opportunity to taste Viognier grown on less than suitable land and made carelessly into wine, then the grape might seem less of a star. As it is, the vine's character is preserved exclusively in bottles carrying some of the top *appellations* of France: Condrieu, Château-Grillet and Côte Rôtie.

Viognier used to be cultivated fairly widely in and around the farmland south of Lyon, but its capricious nature made it unpopular with vine growers who were not rewarded for their persistence by the price of an Appellation Contrôlée wine. Since then, even within the carefully delineated vineyards of Côte Rôtie and Condrieu, plantings have been grubbed up or, even sadder, left to go to seed. With its tiny yields and unreliable ripening, the vine was simply not profitable. Now that prices for Condrieu have risen there have been new plantings – 6 hectares (15 acres) in the early eighties – but even the resulting Condrieu total of 23 hectares (57 acres) is a telling fraction of the 200 hectares (500 acres) which can legally be planted.

Those who do cultivate Viognier among the fruit trees of Condrieu, on its dusty narrow terraces on the west bank of the Rhône, can find their efforts churlishly rewarded. One vintage produced a grand total of 19 hectolitres of wine in the entire *appellation*, and in the sixties and seventies the vine rarely gave much more than half the legal maximum yield of 30 hectolitres per hectare. A factor here may be the advanced age of many of the vines, for the new plantings have helped increase the average yield to 20 hectolitres per hectare. The oval grapes are small but deep coloured which, together with a tendency to lengthy fermentations, gives a considerable golden glow to most Viognier wines.

This is even more noticeable in Château-Grillet, made on a single wine farm just south of Condrieu and given the luxury of 18 months in oak before being put into its distinctive, if ungenerous, bottle, apparently modelled on a hock bottle. Château-Grillet tends to be rather softer and often less vibrant than Condrieu, and of course deepens more dramatically with age. Most Condrieu growers reckon their wines are at their best when two to four years

Château-Grillet is Viognier's most famous incarnation, with the added ingredient of eighteen months in oak. It seems almost perverse to persist with such an obscure and ungenerous vine – until one tastes the wine. The ungenerous standard bottle size of 70cl underlines the wine's scarcity.

old, and Château-Grillet policy is to sell the wine, after just a few months in bottle, very definitely *à boire.*

Consumption after eight years old is officially proscribed, although a 50-year-old example opened by Robin Yapp for a Tippett and a couple of Grigsons in 1976 was much appreciated by this palate. It had perhaps been one of the sweeter styles of wine no longer in favour in Condrieu (although still possible to find in the village itself). The wine was certainly magnificently dry by the time we tried it, with a peculiarly concentrated bouquet that was still discernibly Viognier. French vine growers are, quite understandably, greater proponents of youthful grapiness than their eventual customers.

It is some of these growers whom Livingstone-Learmonth credits with the most elaborate theory about the origins of this unusual grape, which tastes like no other in France – though it does perhaps have a hint of the heady muskiness of Gewürztraminer about it, as well as the sweet-sour apricot flavour of Portugal's Alvarinho. The theory is that the Emperor Probus brought Viognier to the Condrieu area from Dalmatia in AD 281; the area was certainly producing wine during the Roman occupation, but its vines may have been uprooted by Probus' predecessor, Vespasian. A grape called Vugava survives, chiefly on the island of Vis off the Dalmatian coast, and is distinguished by highish alcohol, remarkable dry extract and a very particular aroma. Any keen ampelographer to whom a Yugoslavian seaside holiday would appeal might give Vis serious consideration.

Not only is its flavour so particular, the Viognier is also

unique in France because it is a white that is sanctioned by Appellation Contrôlée laws as an ingredient in a top quality red wine, Côte Rôtie. Côte Rôtie is the red version of Condrieu: a very close neighbour, where the steep vineyards can be as difficult to work, producing small quantities of mainly Syrah wine. It now attracts sufficiently high prices so that plantings have increased, possibly to the detriment of future quality.

The laws allow the addition of anything from 0 to 20 percent of Viognier grapes to the Syrah in Côte Rôtie, but the white vine is so fickle that it accounts for only 5 percent of the total vintage today. Max Chapoutier reports that raising Viognier is almost an act of charity here.

Almost all of Côte Rôtie's 6 hectares (15 acres) of Viognier vines are on the lighter Côte Blonde, and the grapes must be fermented with the Syrah, to soften the wine slightly, but more importantly to add an extra dimension to its bouquet, which can evolve over 20 years to something more subtle, a hint of violets perhaps, than the all-Syrah Hermitage can ever manage. All too few Côte Rôties are worth maturing this long, but Guigal's La Mouline is a paradigm.

Outside this brave corner of vineland, French cultivation of Viognier is limited to some experimental plots much further down the Rhône, for example at the Domaine Ste-Anne at St-Gervais and the Château de St-Estève. The only other patch of Viognier vines exists in California's Napa Valley, under the auspices of Joseph Phelps, whose passion for the wines of northern Rhône has encouraged him to add cuttings of Viognier to his plantings

VIOGNIER

of true Syrah. After waiting eight years for Davis to remove the virus in their Viognier budwood, he finally imported enough virus-free Viognier budwood from New York State in 1985 for a 1.2 to 2 hectare (3 to 5 acre) plot.

Synonym: Vionnier

Pruning:
Guyot at Château-Grillet,
one long *archet* in Condrieu and Côte Rôtie

Soils:
Light, sandy with decomposed
mica particles (arzelle).
Limestone of Cote Blonde better than
clay of Cote Brune.

Yields: Tiny, barely 20 hl/ha.

**Top quality.
Very gradually gaining modishness.**

The Muscat Family

Perhaps it is not surprising that every wine-producing country makes a wine that actually tastes like ripe grapes. Perhaps too, in view of how headily, muskily overpowering that flavour can be, it is not surprising that it rarely features among a country's most important wines. Muscat-based wine may be ubiquitous, can be delicious, but it is not very quantitatively significant.

Although the majority of wine experts quite understandably choose to skirt round it, there is a jungle of different sorts of Muscat vine, often related only by the approximate taste of their produce. Viala alone lists well over 200 different sorts of Muscat and derivatives. The grapes themselves can be anything from palest yellow to blackest black. When picked, they may be used for eating fresh or dried, as grape concentrate or for wine. The wines produced can vary from delicate and often fizzy white to sweet and often fortified dark. Some, such as Australia's liqueur Muscats, constitute some of the finest wines in the world, others – some Spanish Moscatel springs to mind – represent the other end of the quality spectrum.

Muscat of Alexandria, one of the least exciting qualitatively, is undoubtedly the most widely planted worldwide, a very high proportion of the grapes being destined for the table or dried fruit market. Muscat Blanc à Petits Grains, or Muscat de Frontignan, produces probably the finest wines and is gratifyingly widely dispersed.

Muscat Blanc à Petits Grains

This is the real goody of the Muscat family, known by so many names around the world that it can be difficult to identify in a local setting. Its chief viticultural characteristic, other than the small grapes of the name, is the paucity of its yield, and certainly in its best manifestations it does taste sufficiently concentrated to support the theory that there is a necessary connection between yield and quality (Germany has so little Muscat planted that it cannot legitimately take part in this particular argument).

Vines with exactly the same ampelographical profile as Muscat Blanc à Petits Grains produce grapes that may be pink or fairly dark reddish brown (but not dark enough to produce a properly red wine). There are thought to be two strains – one of which mutates to pink and red and back to white again, the other remaining stable. Most of what is planted in Europe is stable and white, but in Australia in particular there are vineyards the colour of whose Muscat à Petits Grains, or Frontignan, grapes cannot be forecast by vine or year. Much of what they count as their Frontignan plantings is called Brown Muscat because of the high proportion of darker grapes. A high proportion of South Africa's Muskadel population is dark too, providing further proof of the historico-viticultural links between the two countries.

Muscat vines are thought to be the oldest known to and recognized by man. There is even the theory that the Pinot family is descended from Muscat – indeed that all *Vitis vinifera* vines are mutations and strains of Muscat. There is still a strong tradition of Muscat cultivation in Greece, with both the noble variety and Muscat of Alexandria present, and indeed all Muscats are grown round the Mediterranean. It is thought to have been Muscat vines that the Phoenicians, Greeks and then Romans most commonly dispersed around southern Europe. The Greeks are supposed to have taken Muscat beyond the Crimea, and the first vineyards planted in the south of France are thought to have been stocked with Muscat. The vine was certainly a very early arrival in the vineyards of Languedoc-Roussillon and especially of Frontignan. There is evidence of Muskateller cultivation in Germany as early as the twelfth century, and the grape also has the distinction of being the earliest recorded in Alsace, in the mid-sixteenth century. It seems certain that Pliny the Elder's *uva Apiana* or "grape of the bees", so attractive to insects because of its sweetness and strong aroma, was Muscat. There is an obvious link between the word Muscat and musk, and there are even linguistic theories linking Muscat with *mosca* and *mouche*, Italian and French for fly.

Like the Alexandrian version, Muscat à Petits Grains is not extensively planted in any wine region. France and Italy probably have about the same amount: 3,000 hectares (7,500 acres). Nearly half the French total is to be found in the area around Frontignan in the Pyrénées Orientales *département* where its influence has always been strong (but it has now been decisively overtaken by the inferior Muscat of Alexandria). Here it is the top quality ingredient, with Grenache Blanc and Muscat of Alexandria, in the strong dark *vins doux naturels* such as Banyuls, Côtes d'Agly, Maury, Grand Roussillon, Rivesaltes and the Muscats of Mireval, Rivesaltes, St-Jean de Minervois, and of course Frontignan.

Muscat à Petits Grains plays the title role in the much more fashionable Muscat de Beaumes-de-Venise, both light and dark versions, and gives the wine its unusually deep hue. It is also a major factor in giving this eastern Muscat more finesse than its western counterparts. The variety also plays an important supporting role in the Clairette de Die where it is blended with Clairette up to 50 percent to make the recherché sparkling wine called Tradition, so much more interesting than the Diois wines made only from Clairette. One wonders how long it will be before the producers in these two specialist areas discover they can make a poorer wine more economically from a more productive sort of Muscat.

The wine growers of Alsace found out well over a century ago when the vine-breeder Moreau-Robert created a variety he called Muscat Ottonel. It is conveniently earlier maturing and bigger yielding than Muscat à Petits Grains which, usually in its red form, can still be found in isolated spots on the vine-covered slopes of the Haut-Rhin though the berries shatter, and then rot easily.

Wines of varying quality carrying the name Moscatel constitute one of the mainstays of Spain's wine industry, but it is doubtful that much of the Spanish version of Muscat à Petits Grains (presumably the same as Moscatel de Grano Menudo) is still cultivated.

The white form of Muscat à Petits Grains, alias Moscato Bianco, is the most widely planted Muscat in Italy. It forms the base for the important sparkling Moscato industry of whose products the much reviled Asti is the best known. Moscato is the oldest known variety grown in Piedmont. It is cultivated in all sorts of wayward spots, all the way down to Calabria and the islands – especially the islands, though Sicily's Pantelleria is made from Muscat of Alexandria. Like Malvasia, this ancient vine, with strong dessert wine associations, is still cherished today, and expected to produce a wide variety of sweet wines, including fortified and *frizzante*.

MUSCAT BLANC A PETITS GRAINS

Trentino-Alto Adige is exceptional in its Moscato as it is in so much else, growing tiny but much sought after quantities of low-yielding vines called Goldenmuskateller and Rosenmuskateller, which must be coloured variants of Muscat à Petits Grains. These produce extraordinary light-bodied, richly scented wines, gold and pink respectively, which are the only wines of the region that may be vinified dry or sweet. The sweet ones have assumed almost cult status.

The Germans also call their tiny quantities of Muscat gold and red (Gelber Muskateller and Roter Muskateller) and in Baden and Württemberg produce rather earthier versions than the Tyrolean Italians. They have less than 10 hectares (25 acres) of Roter Muskateller and about 300 hectares (750 acres) of Gelber Muskateller, as well as about 25 hectares (63 acres) of the less fine Muscat Ottonel – though the most important contributor of Muscat flavour to their blends is the crossing Morio-Muskat which, almost incredibly, has not a single Muscat gene.

The finest sort of Muscat was known in Greece centuries before any of these other manifestations became apparent. Both Muscat à Petits Grains and Muscat of Alexandria are widely cultivated here but it is the former that has the unique honour of producing four dessert wines under their own carefully controlled regime: the famous naturally sweet and strong wine of Samos, Muscat of Patras, Muscat Rion of Patras and Muscat of Cephalonia.

The island of Samos is the Muscat headquarters of the world, or at least its holiday home. Fine white Muscat is still the most important grape variety on the island and produces golden-syrup wines of real elegance as well as dry wines and fortified sweet wines. This kind of Muscat is also grown in fairly high proportions in the vineyards of the Peloponnese and there are substantial plantings of red Muscat as well.

Because it produces such a full-flavoured wine, the vine is ideal for relatively hot vineyards. Just as with Malvasia, Muscat and Greece seem an entirely suitable marriage of elements. Further north, the wines produced can be simply a bit coarse. Much of the Muscat produced in eastern Europe is now made from Muscat Ottonel, but about 150 hectares (375 acres) of Muscat Blanc, as (Gelber) Muskateller, is planted in Austria, particularly in Styria in the southeast, and Slovenia's Muscat is also yellow.

There are still some plantings of Yellow Muscat (sometimes called Muscat Lunel) in Hungary as opposed to the much more common Muscat Ottonel. It comprises about 5 percent of total vine plantings, or more than 300 hectares (750 acres), in the intriguing Tokay region (the rest of the *vignoble* being shared equally by Furmint and Hárslevelü). Most of the wine produced is sold as a single varietal, occasionally of sweet Aszú quality, rather than blunting the extraordinary flavours of the Tokay Two with its more obvious sweetness. The wines made from this grape have great roundness of flavour and more than a hint of burnt caramel. There are also plantings of some white and, particularly, pink versions in the USSR, where it is used to produce sweet dessert wines with great character and ageing ability in the south, and more ordinary table wines in the north.

Although Muscat of Alexandria and Orange Muscat, the Moscato Fior d'Arancio of Italy, are grown in California, it is White Muscat or Muscat Canelli that is most widely planted. Plantings have nearly trebled in the last decade to 680 hectares (1,700 acres), quite widely spread around the North Coast and Central Valley vineyards. Some interesting sweet red or black muscats are produced, but in sufficiently cool locations Muscat Blanc can turn out very pretty wines, faintly reminiscent of Asti Spumante in their fresh, grapey aroma, lightness of touch and slight tingle of *pétillance*.

The Californians – Mondavi's Moscato d'Oro springs to palate memory – have undoubtedly led the way towards a modern treatment of Muscat. Low temperature fermentation, minimal skin contact and early consumption seem to be the answer here.

In Australia similar conditions prevail and, with one notable exception, a similar style of wine is produced from their Muscat, unless it is used for blending. Although Muscat of Alexandria, also known as Gordo Blanco, is much more common in the land of Liqueur Muscat, there are nearly 700 hectares (1,750 acres) of Muscat Blanc. The grape, often called Frontignan, occupies more than 400 hectares (1,000 acres) in South Australia's Barossa Valley, and produces light, grapey, off-dry wines as well as counterparts of Australia's most famous dessert wine type.

The grapes that produce the Liqueur Muscats of northeast Victoria are locally called Brown Muscat and seem to produce wines which are distinctly fuller flavoured than so-called White Muscat. The ampelographer Truel on his historic visit in 1976 demonstrated that all of the colour gradations, many of them encountered in the same vineyard in Australia, are in fact different strains of Muscat à Petits Grains. By maximizing sugar levels in these Brown Muscat grapes and maturing the resulting wine in a semi-*solera* system in old oak barrels stacked in exceptionally hot conditions, the dessert winemakers of Rutherglen manage to make treacly wines with the concentration of port and the tang of madeira, all overlaid with essence of grapiness.

In South Africa this fine sort of Muscat, known here as Muskadel (as opposed to the less noble Hanepoot or Muscat of Alexandria) is most often encountered in red form. There is a substantial area of about 1,000 hectares (2,500 acres) of red Muskadel, many of them in the Robertson area. The grape was an important ingredient in the famous sweet wine of Constantia, once the country's best-known wine, but today is used for rather curious sweet reds with a shorter life expectancy.

It seems likely that the Moscatel that forms an important part of the South American wine industry is also of this sort. Argentina calls its many-hued vines Moscatel Rosé, or Moscatel d'Asti, and the strong viticultural connections between that country and Italy strengthen the hypothesis. They are one of the most widely planted grape varieties in Argentina, especially in the south, and cover almost 10 percent of Argentina's total vineyard.

Synonyms:

Muscat Blanc, Muscat de Frontignan, Muscat d'Alsace, Frontignac (France); Muskateller, Gelber Muskateller, Weisse Muskettraube (Germany); Moscata Bianca, Moscato Bianco, Moscato d'Asti, Moscato di Canelli, Moscatello Bianco (Italy); Moscatel de Grano Menudo, Moscatel Menudo Bianco, Moscatel Dorado (Spain); Muscatel Branco (Portugal); Muskateller, Schmeckende, Katzendreckler, Gelber Weihrauch (Austria); Sargamuskotaly (Hungary); Tamyanka (USSR); Zutimuscat, Beli Muscat (Yugoslavia); Muskuti (Greece); White Muscat, Muscat Canelli, Muscat Frontignan, Muscat Blanc (California); Moscatel Rosé (Argentina); Muskadel (South Africa); White Frontignan, Frontignac, Brown Muscat (Australia).

Soils:
Responds well to fairly fertile soils; very low vigour on sand.

Vigour:
Variable depending on soil type and vine stock but usually fairly vigorous.

Pruning:
Vines may be head-trained or trained using bilateral cordon training.

Susceptibility:
Very susceptible to downy and powdery mildew, and to grape berry moth. Its grapey smell attracts insects. Fruit may brown and shrivel if left on the vine too long.

Rootstocks: Moderately vigorous.

Yields:
Fairly low: 20 hl/ha in some older plantings, though Californians have managed to get 12 tons per acre on fertile Central Valley soils (6 to 8 is the norm there).

Very good quality. Not at all modish.

Muscat of Alexandria

Like the much more respectable Muscat Blanc à Petits Grains, this Muscat is an exceedingly ancient vine, one of the most ancient cultivated plants we know. Cuttings rather than seeds were used to propagate it and it is probably one of our oldest genetically unchanged plants still thriving today. The vine is presumed, by no great leap of imagination, to be of North African origin, perhaps even first associated with the ancient Egyptians whose plantings demonstrate such admirable grasp of winemaking techniques. It is also known as Zibibbo in southern Italy, supposedly after a North African Cape Zibibb.

Perhaps the most convincing demonstration of its lack of class is that it has traditionally been more widely grown as a table or raisin grape than as a wine grape. It has even been grown in English greenhouses, for heaven's sake.

This isolated exception apart, the vine has to be cultivated in a fairly hot climate because it is extremely sensitive to cool weather during flowering, which can decimate the potential crop, and needs quite a bit of heat to ripen fully. Within this constraint, it is grown in a very wide variety of countries: southern France, Spain, Portugal, Italy, Greece, Cyprus, eastern Mediterranean, California and all but the coolest of southern hemisphere vineyards. Only in Australia and South Africa, however, is it quantitatively important to the local wine industry, but is gradually losing favour there as almost everywhere else.

As well as being a fairly cussed, weak plant to grow, the wine produced from the Muscat of Alexandria vine often lacks the complexity and depth of flavour of wine made from the superior Muscat Blanc à Petits Grains. It may be fine for producing high yields of grapes with impressively high sugar levels, but the wine's aroma is too often more reminiscent of raisins than of anything grapily fresh. Muscat of Alexandria wine is, typically, merely very sweet and slightly earthy. The contrast between the best Moscatel de Setúbal and the best Muscat de Beaumes-de-Venise nicely demonstrates the point (though some of the poorer sweet wines produced in the name of Beaumes belie it). Attractively robust though the best Moscatel de Setúbal can be, it will never have the refinement of its Vauclusien counterpart. Muscat of Alexandria wine is used chiefly to make very sweet wines of the Spanish Moscatel school or as fairly low-acid blending material.

The country with the greatest area of Muscat of Alexandria is Spain, with about 20,000 hectares (50,000 acres), though they represent less than 1.5 percent of that country's sprawling vineland. It is the principal grape variety around Alicante and Valencia on the Mediterranean coast as well as in the much-depleted vineyards of Málaga and on the Canary Islands. Because of Spain's jumble of vine varieties it does not necessarily represent a very high proportion of total vineyard in each of these areas: 10 percent in Alicante for instance, and a minute proportion of the Jerez vineyard. As a wine grape it is usually known as Moscatel de Málaga and produces sweet, strong wines called Moscatel, of which the Málaga version is probably the best. Only Moscatel and Pedro Ximénez grapes are allowed into Málaga and many wines are made solely of the former, varying in colour from gold to almost impenetrable black. As in northeast Victoria, a sort of *solera* system is employed, although the addition of Pedro Ximénez makes Málaga a less luscious, higher acid wine. It can be very, very good, however, with great length of flavour, and can vary considerably in sweetness. Other Spanish Moscatels often lack acid and ageing potential.

Portugal's preponderant Muscat is also the Alexandrian variety, and Moscatel de Setúbal, already described, its most famous product. Like so many of the southern French Muscats, the wine is produced by stopping fermentation with neutral grape spirit and then gaining extra flavour by macerating on the pungent Muscat skins. It is difficult to quantify the amount of Muscat grown in the famous sandy soil of Setúbal (or "Shtoobal", as it sounds to foreign ears) as the good sturdy red for which Portugal is well known is also increasingly produced on its 20,000 hectares (50,000 acres). Jan Read also notes that there are 2 hectares (5 acres) of a black variety, Moscatel Roxo, which have been vinified and marketed separately within Portugal. J. M. da Fonseca, who have a virtual monopoly on production of Moscatel de Setúbal, also make a very stylish off-dry light table wine from just such Muscat grapes, João Pires. Significantly, the winemaker is Australian. The Australians above all others know how to produce delicate gulpable light wines from baked Muscat grapes.

MUSCAT OF ALEXANDRIA

France's total of just over 3,000 hectares (7,500 acres) of Muscat of Alexandria has remained fairly constant, almost all of them in the Pyrenées Orientales where there is almost three times more of it than of the Muscat Blanc. With its much higher yields, it is chiefly responsible for the family of robust sweet dark Muscats of southwest France like those of Lunel, Rivesaltes and Mireval, though not Frontignan which is made with the eponymous and finer grape. Like Moscatel de Setúbal, they are *vins doux naturels* whose sweet or *doux* quality owes all to the not entirely *naturel* process of arresting fermentation with alcohol.

Italy's most respected version of such wines is Moscato di Pantelleria made from Muscat of Alexandria grapes, here known as Zibibbo, grown on the volcanic island of Pantelleria off Tunisia but administered from Sicily. (Not surprisingly, Tunisia also makes strong rich Muscats.)

In Greece as in Italy, the Muscat Blanc is more common than Muscat of Alexandria, but Muscat of Lemnos is made from the coarser variety. It is presumably this sort that was once widely planted in Turkey and Israel. Moscatel de Alejandria is Chile's most important Muscat, used mainly for dessert wines.

There are a further 3,600 hectares (9,000 acres) of Muscat of Alexandria planted in California. Most of them serve the raisin industry, but some are used to produce Muscat wines with rather less finesse than those made from Muscat Blanc or the Orange Muscat, made modish by Quady and which is also produced by Brown Brothers in Australia, being originally an Italian variety.

The Australian wine industry is still heavily dependent on Gordo Blanco, which literally means fat and white in Spanish and the grapes are indeed fairly big. It is amazingly the single most important contributor to the wine business there and only about 10 percent of the grapes produced on the 4,500 hectares (11,250 acres) of Gordo is used for anything other than wine.

Most of the grapes are planted in the irrigated river regions that pour forth neutral but full-bodied wines for Australia's cardboard "wine casks". In the past Gordo Blanco, together with Sultana and some Pedro Ximénez and Palomino, underpinned the huge fortified Australian wine industry and it is still used to give a curious Muscat character to the "cream sherries" of Australia today.

Brown Brothers' Spätlese Lexia, sold as Late-Harvest Muscat inside the EEC, epitomizes the clever Australian way of persuading Muscat of Alexandria to produce a well-balanced flavoursome table wine. The grapes are grown on relatively high ground and acid levels carefully maintained, perhaps even chemically ameliorated after a prolonged ripening. Very cool fermentation retaining some sugar results in a very frisky medium-sweet wine of 10 or 11 percent alcohol with a clean floral finish.

The South Africans are now trying out these techniques on their White Muscat or Muskadel grapes, but their Muscat of Alexandria, called here Hanepoot, is used for everything from raisining and grape syrup and even jam through to table wines of dubious interest and quality. Its best manifestation is as a base for sweet fortified wines.

Hanepoot now constitutes just under 10 percent of all South African vines and is the fourth most planted grape variety there, though it is falling from favour while plantings of Sultana, curiously, rise. While Muscat of Alexandria will doubtless flourish in those corners of the world such as Setúbal and Pantelleria where some reputation has been built up, it seems likely that its importance as a workhorse grape will continue to decline. In the dried fruit context it has varieties such as Thompson Seedless to blame; in the wine context the trend towards lower alcohol.

Synonyms:
Muscat Roumain, Panse Musquée (France); Moscatel, Moscatel Samsó, Moscatel de Málaga, Moscatel Gordo, Moscatel Gordo Blanco, Moscatel Romano (Spain); Moscatel de Setúbal (Portugal); Zibibbo (Italy); Moscatel de Alejandria (Chile); Muscat Gordo Blanco, Gordo Blanco, Muscatel, Lexia (Australia); Hanepoot (South Africa); Iskendiriye Misketi (Turkey).

Soils:
Relatively fussy. The damper the better. Only sandy soils not recommended.

Vigour:
Not very vigorous; careful shading, through close planting usually, can be necessary in hot areas.

Pruning:
Short spurs with one or two buds most recommended.

Susceptibility:
Inconsistent fruit set because sensitive to cool weather during flowering and suffers from zinc deficiency. Sensitive to most cryptogamic diseases. Tendency to raisin.

Rootstocks:
Poor affinity with the likes of 101–14 and 143–B, but fine, if loose-bunched, on 3309 and Richter 99.

Yields:
Very high. 7 to 10 tons per acre in California's Central Valley.

Not very good quality wine or table grapes or raisins. Losing ground.

Muscat Ottonel

This is a real upstart in Muscat terms, bred only in the middle of the last century by the Loire vine breeder Moreau-Robert. Galet reckons that Chasselas was one parent and that probably some sort of inferior Loire Muscat, such as Muscat de Saumur, the other. It was cultivated in Alsace from 1852 and has virtually elbowed the poor-yielding Muscat Blanc à Petits Grains, once known as Muscat d'Alsace, out of Rhineside.

The wine produced has a Muscaty aroma, to be sure, but it is usually much lighter than the other Muscats, and often has a rather mousy overtone which is particularly evident in the many eastern European Muscats for which Muscat Ottonel is responsible. Its advantage is that it can be grown in relatively cool latitudes, but it produces much more vapid (delicate when they work) wines than the more widely planted Muscats of Alexandria and à Petits Grains.

Of the three types of Muscat grown reasonably extensively in France, Muscat Ottonel is the least important, covering barely more than 400 hectares (1,000 acres), almost all of them in Alsace. There were fewer than 200 hectares (500 acres) in 1968 and this usurping of Muscat Blanc's role in Alsace has been relatively recent. This may account for the lack of definitive Muscat flavour in many

MUSCAT OTTONEL

so-labelled offerings from Alsace today. In others it can be difficult to distinguish one man's Muscat from his Gewürztraminer. Perhaps some producers even give fillip to the aroma of their weaker Muscats by adding a measure of strongly scented Gewürz.

It is notable that until winemakers in the newer wine regions applied cold fermentation technology to their widely planted Muscat grapes, Alsace was the only area producing dry Muscats. The hallmark of the wines should be a pure, grapey perfume suggestive of roses followed by a firm dry impact on the palate – just like the dry Muscats made in the fashion-conscious Alto Adige nowadays. In Alsace Muscat is classified as one of the four noble grape varieties but is very much an also-ran, constituting less than 4 percent of total plantings. It is technically possible to produce a Vendange Tardive wine from Muscat grapes, but in practice just about every drop of Muscat Ottonel produced in Alsace is drunk as a light, dry aperitif.

There is much more of the vine planted in Austria than in Alsace: well over 1,000 hectares (2,500 acres), 10 times more than of the noble Muskateller. Although some is planted in Wachau, it makes its most individual wines in the Rust/Neusiedlersee region where it can produce very rich dessert wines that may not improve with age but can dazzle in their youth. The vine is said to flourish also in Czechoslovakia and the Moldavian part of the USSR.

The yellow version of the Muscat Blanc à Petits Grains is more common in northern Yugoslavia, but further south, as in Vojdovina just over the border from another Muscat Ottonel stronghold in Hungary, the grape produces slightly flabby sweetish wines. In Hungary Muscat Ottonel or Muskotaly is much appreciated – it is one of the relatively few non-Hungarian grape varieties to be accorded this compliment. Akali on the north shore of Lake Balaton and the wonderfully named Balatonboglari Muskotaly from the south are well known, but most other prized Hungarian Muscats are produced in the northeast. Abasar, Domoszloi and Kompolti are all known Muscats from locations around Eger of Bulls Blood fame.

In Romania's Transylvania vineyards the Muscat Ottonel of Tirnave is among their most treasured wines and certainly a 1969 Edelauslese, in blue-green bottle, was a wonder of rich survival in 1985. The deep apricot gold just hinted at the lovely development of the bouquet in this toasty sweet wine which needed just the slightest bit more acid to make it great. Perhaps Muscat Ottonel's strength lies in late-harvest wines.

Synonyms:
Muskotaly (Hungary);
Muscadel Ottonel (South Africa).

Soils:
Likes deep, fertile, fairly damp soils best.
One of the least happy vines on calcareous soil.

Vigour: Low to moderate.

Pruning: Short canes.

Susceptibility:
Quite susceptible to wet weather and oidium,
slightly susceptible to downy mildew and rot.

Rootstocks: Moderate to vigorous.

Yields:
Moderate to good. 50–100 hl/ha in Alsace.

Medium quality. Not particularly modish.

Muscat Hamburg

This incontrovertibly black Muscat (as opposed to the many-hued Muscat à Petits Grains) is grown chiefly as a table grape, but in various less quality-conscious corners of the world is also asked to produce wine. In France about 7,000 hectares (17,500 acres) of Muscat Hamburg are grown, chiefly in Vaucluse and solely for the fruit basket. In California there are a couple of small plantings in the hotter regions that are classified as wine producers; and in Australia it is used a great deal but only for the table.

In eastern Europe, however, Muscat Hamburg makes rather thin red wines with a light Muscat aroma. Since the grape is relatively late ripening, these Serbian and Macedonian wines are usually dry. The grape is also cultivated in the USSR where market forces are presumably now turning it from table to wine grape use, and in China.

Synonyms:
Muscat de Hambourg,
Muscat de Hamburgh (France);
Moscato di Amburgo (Italy);
Muscat Gamburgskiy (USSR);
Black Muscat (Australia).

Very low quality.

Aleatico

This venerable red grape is sometimes thought to be a red mutation of Muscat Blanc à Petits Grains, or Moscato Bianco so widely planted in Italy. In support of this theory the wines produced are very fine, long lived and have an intensely flowery "Muscat" perfume; against is the fact that Aleatico wines made in Italy are extremely deep in colour, an asset shared by no other dark mutation of Muscat Blanc. They are usually very sweet, often very alcoholic and have a velvety texture.

As Aleatico, its sadly waning influence is strongest in Apulia and Latium; it can also make fine sweet grapey red wines in Tuscany and Umbria. The Aleatico di Portoferraio made on Elba is a cult wine for Italian oenophiles. Aleatico di Puglia from the deep south and Aleatico di Gradoli produced in the northwestern hills of Latium have been awarded DOC status; both are rare, sweetly fragrant and come in natural and fortified versions. The vine has been cultivated in Tuscany since the fourteenth century and Alessandrio in Piedmont still has some Aleatico. Also, strongly under the influence of Enotria, Corsica has some Aleatico vines. "Aleatica" is important in Chile as a producer of "red Moscatel". It has been planted at Mudgèe in New South Wales. The small plantings in California have been sufficiently promising to excite attention from the Davis viticultural mafia. They cite low colour and acid as problems in the hotter regions, but have perhaps less than perfect plant material so far.

Aleatico is a grape capable of making really fine, individual wine.

Synonyms:
Agliano, Allianico, Leatico, Liatica, Livatica,
Moscatello, Livatische,
Muscateller, Occhio di Pernice.

High quality.

Trebbiano (Ugni Blanc)

Yes, this is it: the world's most prolific wine producer. In its combined but universally productive guises as the Trebbiano of Italy, the Ugni Blanc of the French Midi and the St-Emilion of Cognac, and its many other manifestations all over the world, the vine may not cover the largest total of vineyard land (Airén, Garnacha and Rkatsiteli beat it in that respect), but it probably produces more wine each year than any other.

In its homeland Italy, the various strains of Trebbiano together constitute by far the most common white vine, planted on an estimated 130,000 hectares (325,000 acres). Thanks to the extraordinary expansion of vineyard in the Charentes, Ugni Blanc is France's most important white variety by far, with 127,000 hectares (317,500 acres) planted at the last agricultural census in 1979, a figure bettered only by Carignan's 207,000 hectares (517,500 acres). Good heavens, as recently as 1979 there was considerably more Ugni Blanc planted in the Gironde than Sauvignon Blanc! Put this supremacy in the world's top two wine-producing countries together with substantial plantings in both North and South America, South Africa and Australia and you have a virtual Big Brother of a vine variety. Wherever a vine is grown, there doubtless lurks a Trebbiano plant not far behind it.

The picture is not so much sinister as depressing. Trebbiano, to call it by its original name, produces a very characterless wine indeed. As a vine, its twin virtues are the tenacity with which it keeps its acid right up to a late ripening (except in very warm climates) and, of course, its extraordinary high yields. The vine is absurdly easy to grow and when it gives a yield of 150 hectolitres per hectare, for instance, this is considered not a generous freak of nature but entirely normal.

It should be made clear that a very high proportion of the Trebbiano cultivated in France, perhaps as much as 80 percent, is not finally consumed as wine, but as distilled wine or brandy. The tenet of brandy production is that the worse the base wine tastes, the better the resulting spirit will be. That the vineyards of the Charentes (95 percent of which are planted with Trebbiano) produce what is universally acclaimed as the finest brandy is testament enough to the drinking qualities of Trebbiano wine. The fact that in the Gironde it is known as Muscadet Aigre or "sour Muscadet" says it all.

A typical tasting note on a varietal Trebbiano is characterized by its brevity: pale lemon, little nose, notably high acid, medium alcohol and body, short. And that, I am afraid, is it. One wonders whether the whole risky business

TREBBIANO

of nurturing a vine vintage after vintage could not more conveniently be circumvented by a simple laboratory mix of ethyl alcohol, tartaric acid and H_2O.

A historical perspective is necessary to understand the extent of Trebbiano's influence today. There is no shortage of possible derivations for Trebbiano's name, and no dissension from the theory that its origins are central Italian. The vine may indeed be the Trebulanum mentioned in Pliny's tract on natural history. He associated this vine with Campania and it might well have been dispersed throughout Italy by Roman legionaries. On the other hand, Andrea Bacci, doctor to Pope Sisto V and a famous botanist, assumed that the vine originated from the village of the same name in Tuscany. Others attribute it to the Trebbia river in Emilia-Romagna or perhaps even to Trebbiano Nizza near Pavia in Lombardy (Barbera's putative birthplace). "Trebbiare" means to thresh and it is hardly surprising that a wide range of place names incorporate words like Trebbiano. What is certain is that, as Trebbiano, the vine was first described by the Bolognese agronomist Pier de'Crescenzi in 1302.

The removal of the papal establishment from Rome to Avignon encouraged popular vines such as the Trebbiano to voyage north and west out of Italy and into southern France. Indeed Trebbiano, as Ugni Blanc and Clairette Ronde, is still widely planted in the Midi and especially in Provence. From here it has had five centuries to spread deeper into France and much further afield.

The various Italian subvarieties are different in name, but not always so very different in characteristics. All have approximately the same ampelographical profile. All but the large-leaved Trebbiano Toscano, admittedly one of the most common, have a medium-sized trapezoidal, five-lobed leaf. Most Trebbianos mature very late, not until the first half of October in Italy, although the Trebbiano Toscano and Trebbiano Giallo ripen earlier. The Tuscan version also has larger clusters than most Trebbiano, but its berries are always fairly deeply coloured when ripe – a definite amber and sometimes even light red (hence the synonym Clairette Rosé). In all Trebbiano, the vine's natural productivity is underscored by the fact that it buds late and therefore usually manages to avoid the decimating ravages of spring frosts.

Within Italy Trebbiano is the *éminence grise* of *vino bianco*. There are a few interesting Italian white oddities that do not contain a drop of Trebbiano intentionally, but they are very few. In the north Soave is composed primarily of Garganega but is laced with Trebbiano Toscano and up to 30 percent of Trebbiano di Soave. (Soave's DOC regulations allow a yield of more than 100 hectolitres per hectare.) There is Trebbiano di Soave in Gambellara and Trebbiano Toscano in Bianco di Custoza. Nearby Lugana is made from Trebbiano di Lugana. And so on. Only the staunchly varietally minded northeastern corner of Italy is to all practical purposes a Trebbiano-free zone.

Trebbiano is widely cultivated all over the south of Italy and is known on Sicily and even on Sardinia, which is otherwise an island viticulturally as well as geographically. (There are also about 600 hectares/1,500 acres of it on Corsica.) The great majority goes to make very ordinary *vino da tavola*, although there is the odd DOC or more inspired table wine such as Apulia's San Severo and the Trebbiano di Serra Meccaglia of Molise respectively.

Trebbiano's real stronghold is central Italy. Trebbiano di Romagna is virtually Emilia-Romagnan for white wine, and is made chiefly from the Trebbiano Romagnolo or Trebbiano della Fiama (because the ripe grapes are flame-coloured). Tons of these same grapes also go into the white table wine made here. Further down the east coast, the ubiquitous vine is an ingredient in Verdicchio, along with the eponymous grape, and it also contributes to Bianco dei Colli Maceratesi and Falerio. (Even further down, the so-called Trebbiano Abruzzo is not in fact Trebbiano but Bombino Bianco.)

Trebbiano's grip on central western Italy is so strong that these are just some of the better-known white examples: Orvieto (with up to 50 percent of Verdello, Grechetto and others); Frascati and Marino; Bianco Vergine della Valdichiana; the oceans of rather dreary Trebbiano di Aprilia produced on the plains south of Rome; Montecarlo Bianco (with, of all unholy mixtures, Sémillon, Sauvignon, Chardonnay, Pinot Grigio and Pinot Bianco); Est! Est!! Est!!! (with up to 35 percent of Malvasia); and in Umbria Colli Altotiberini, Perugini and del Trasimeno as well as Torre di Giano.

There is worse though. So entrenched was Trebbiano in the vineyards of Tuscany when the laws governing Chianti (and hence Vino Nobile di Montepulciano) were drawn up that it, together with the much nobler white grape Malvasia, was enshrined in the production of this potentially great *red* wine. Throughout central Italy, Trebbiano is the bad guy and Malvasia the good guy. The most quality-conscious Chianti estates have either maximized the Malvasia content of the white part of their Chianti blend, or ignored the laws altogether. The proportion of white grapes allowed has now been reduced and a suitable use for the vast tracts of Trebbiano has had to be found.

The answer has been the family of Tuscan dry white *vini da tavola* such as Galestro and Bianco della Lega, low-alcohol, ultra-crisp dry whites in the modern vinification style. This suits Trebbiano better than most grape varieties; the complaint that low temperatures deprive us of the grape's interest cannot be true of a grape with so little character. These newish wines prove that even the noblest attempts must fail to make a silk purse out of a sow's ear, though some cold maceration of fruit before fermentation may help a little. It is notable that although a number of producers of that great central Italian dessert wine Vin Santo use Trebbiano, the most quality-conscious concentrate on Malvasia.

France's total of this characterless but useful vine increased by more than 30,000 hectares (75,000 acres), or one-third, in the seventies, thanks almost exclusively to the rationalization and extension of the cognac vineyards in the Charentes on the western seaboard. The total vineyard in cognac country increased by about 16,000 hectares (40,000 acres) but the number of varieties occupying more than 200 hectares (500 acres) each declined from a dozen in 1968 to just two (95,000 hectares/237,500 acres of Ugni Blanc, 800 hectares/2,000 acres of Colombard!) by 1979. Ugni Blanc, or St-Emilion as it is commonly known here, is treasured specifically for its high acid and frost resistance. It is often picked before it is fully ripe, at under 8 percent alcohol, and pretty searing it tastes too; but it does make wonderful brandy.

Perhaps not surprisingly, Ugni Blanc's second most important region is that which produces armagnac where it is replacing Baco 22A. It covers well over a third of the vineyard land and is the most important ingredient in this more rustic brandy.

Outside the south and west, Ugni Blanc is also quite prominent throughout the Languedoc-Roussillon and especially Provence. It is rarely vinified separately, certainly never labelled thus, but must be a major ingredient in many French *vins de table* as well as in some of the nobler offerings such as white Bandol and Palette. Part of the difficulty in identifying exactly what goes into what here is that Ugni Blanc's local synonym, Clairette of various sorts, is so confusingly like other, unrelated local varieties called Clairette, with which it is often blended.

As Thalia, the variety is one of the few "internationals" to have infiltrated the vineyards of Portugal. It is relatively common in eastern Europe. Trebbiano is also cultivated on

*T*rebbiano is grown all over central Italy but is most controversial in Tuscany. Until recently, it has made an important contribution to the red Chianti of the region, but quality-conscious producers have increasingly found other, more suitable uses for it – notably in dry white wines such as Galestro, named after the local rocky white soil.

a fairly major scale in the world's important newer wine regions. Relatively speaking, the vine is most important in Australia where there are about 1,600 hectares (4,000 acres). It is typically planted in the irrigated regions, Australia's answer to the Languedoc-Roussillon, where it is sometimes used for brandy and valued as neutral blending material with fairly high acid for table and dessert wines. There are more than 400 hectares (1,000 acres) of "St-Emilion" planted in California, mainly in the central San Joaquin Valley. It is so hot here that, harvesting in September, there have been problems keeping acidity

levels high enough for the brandy production which seems its chief use. Only in cooler areas can it produce wine with sufficient bite, and there the list of more desirable grape varieties is endless. The Trebbiano known in California is particularly large-leaved and is therefore probably Trebbiano Toscano. It is known but not important in South Africa.

Some cuttings have also found their way to South America, notably to Argentina and Brazil. It will be a sad reflection on the evolution of consumer taste in wine if Trebbiano's world supremacy were to continue unabated.

Synonyms:
Turbiano, Lugana, Greco, Rossola, Rossetto, Rusciola, Trebbianello, Perugino, Buzzetto, Trebbiano della Fiamma, Spoletino, Albano, Procanico, Santoro, Bobiano (Italy); Ugni Blanc (Midi); St-Emilion (Charentes); Clairette Ronde, Clairette de Vence, Clairette Rosé, Gredelin, Roussan (Provence); Muscadet Aigre (Gironde); Thalia (Portugal); St-Emilion (California); White Shiraz, White Hermitage (Australia). The six most important Italian clones are Trebbiano Toscano, Trebbiano Romagnolo, Trebbiano Giallo (or Greco), Trebbiano di Soave, Trebbiano Perugino and Trebbiano Spoletino.

Soils:
A necessarily wide range, though sand does not work well.

Vigour: Very vigorous.

Pruning:
Wide systems of training work well. In California 14 to 16 two- to three-bud spurs are commonly retained.

Susceptibility:
Young shoots are particularly prone to wind damage. Downy mildew is a special problem and there have been viral diseases, although careful selection of nursery material has helped eliminate this. The thick grapeskins make it very rot resistant.

Rootstocks:
Rupestris, 41–B and 161–49 have all worked well on various soils.

Yields:
Very high indeed. 200 hl/ha is possible in Italy; 13 tons per acre in California is normal.

Low quality. Not modish but very important.

Palomino

The grape that is revered by sherry producers and aficionados as almost solely responsible for their chosen livelihood and preferred libation respectively is considered distinctly infra dig elsewhere. Palomino, for all its equine connotations of pale, pleasure-giving pedigree, turns out dull, flabby wines wherever it is planted outside the Jerez region.

Much of the Palomino planted in South Africa, California and Australia is baked by the same sort of climate as prevails in Jerez, and some is subjected to similiar sherry-making magic (for example, the careful *flor* cultivation at Penfolds for what they call their Mantillo Dry Sherry).

Since the best "proper" sherry is so discernibly superior to any of its imitators, this suggests that either the soils of Jerez are very special, or even perhaps that the grape is less flavour forming and quality determining than the sherry-making process. It is also perhaps significant that South African sherry producers increasingly prefer to work on a Chenin Blanc base as it has a higher fixed acidity.

To paraphrase, Palomino happens to produce a potentially great style of wine, but is not an inherently great grape. The 25 percent of Spain's 30,000 hectares (75,000 acres) of Palomino vines outside sherry country certainly seem unable to produce wines of any great finesse.

*W*here else but a
bodega in Jerez? A
cathedral devoted to
the worship of the holy mixture of
Palomino and air (oloroso
sherries) or Palomino and flor
(finos). Young table wines,
varietal Palomino, are now also
exported from Jerez but give
few hints as to the essential
Palominoness of the variety.

Palomino's origins are essentially Andalucian, supposedly named for one of Alfonso X's knights. The Palomino Fino now preferred in the Jerez region is distinct from the Palomino Basto or Palomino de Jerez which used to prevail. As Julian Jeffs points out, Palomino Fino has been found to offer that happy combination, quality and quantity. Considerable work has been done, notably by Gonzalez Byass, on clonal selection to give good nematode resistance. The Palomino can easily be distinguished from the Pedro Ximénez which it is fast replacing in the vineyard because it sprouts laterally rather than vertically, with large, loose bunches. Palomino now accounts for well over 90 percent of all Jerez vines.

Palomino must tends to be low in sugar as well as in acid, although the variety is traditionally picked early and reckoned to be ripe at as little as 19° Brix. The flat, slightly decayed flavour which results from the must's tendency to oxidize and from its low acidity (as little as 3.5 grammes per litre expressed as tartaric) is particularly evident in the dry white table wines of the deep south of Spain and the Canaries. It can even be tasted in the increasing number of Jerez table wines now exported from the region.

The grape is known as Perrum in Portugal and has produced wines of some respectability in the south.

As Listan, Palomino is cultivated in pockets of Midi vineyard, but many are being grubbed up and the French total is now well under 1,000 hectares (2,500 acres).

After Spain, South Africa is the country that cultivates most Palomino, about 12,000 hectares (30,000 acres), although it is now a very poor second to Chenin Blanc in terms of both area and popularity. Cape Palomino tends to be particularly low in acid and sugar; work with increased leaf cover, however, has helped to slow ripening and increase sugars. This has also decreased the musts' susceptibility to oxidation. The Cape's best Palomino wine is produced well away from coastal regions. Nearer the coast anthracnose is a problem and heavy pruning concentrates the fruit. Lacking aroma, the wine tends to be used for brandy or as a softening ingredient in blended table wine.

In California the grape has wrongly been called Golden Chasselas in its time (although nurseryman Thompson, of Seedless fame, listed Palomino among his imported cuttings as early as 1861). There have been few new plantings in the last decade and total acreage is stable at around 1,320 hectares (3,300 acres), most of the vines being harvested in the hotter regions for sherry styles and table wines. There are more than 100 hectares (250 acres) of Palomino in Argentina, but Pedro Ximénez is far more widely planted there.

In contrast to the California attitude, Australians see Palomino as unsuitable for table wine; they make sherry-style wines from it, often adding a good dollop of Pedro Ximénez. Official statistics, and possibly many an individual winemaker, fail to distinguish between Palomino and

Pedro Ximénez, and the two varieties between them cover about 2,000 hectares (5,000 acres) in Australia, most of them in South Australia. In the Langhorne Creek district it has been known as Paulo.

True Palomino should not be confused with the grape called Common Palomino in Australia, which is actually Cañocazo, a Jerezano vine which combines some of the characteristics of both the Palomino and Pedro Ximénez.

PALOMINO

Synonyms:
Palomino Fino, Palomina, Palomino del Pinchite, Palomino de Chipiona, Tempranilla, Temprana, Horgazuela (in Puerto de Santa Maria), Alban, Listan (Spain); Perrum (Portugal); Listan (France); White French, Fransdruif (South Africa); Sweetwater, Paulo (Australia).

Soils:
Most revered when planted on albariza compacted chalk (north and west of Jerez) because it performs best in high pH soil. Planted on fertile land in South Africa and deep sandy loam for maximum production in California.

Vigour: Vigorous and versatile.

Pruning:
Wide variety, from classic Jerezano short cane plus a spur to trellising on the Cape.

Susceptibility:
Susceptible to anthracnose and downy mildew but quite resistant to oidium.

Rootstocks:
Wide affinity though some poor results on 101–14 reported by C. J. Orffer.

Yields:
Potentially very good, varying upwards from Jerez legal maximum of 80 hl/ha for better quality wines to 13 tons/acre on fertile California land.

Low to medium quality. Not fashionable.

Malvasia

Poor Malvasia. There is not a thing wrong with it. It produces fairly good quantities of wine with real character without too many viticultural problems. The catastrophe for all of us is that in two of its important strongholds this antique vine happens to be planted alongside the neutral, much higher-yielding whipper-snappers, Trebbiano and Viura, which are currently ousting Malvasia from central Italy and Rioja respectively. Malvasia might easily become extinct as the wine world conspires to produce ever higher quantities of anodyne but conveniently fast-maturing wine.

Along with Muscat, the vine is one of our most ancient, thought to have originated in Asia Minor but taking its name from a corruption of Monemvasia, the southern Greek port. Wine, probably strong and fairly sweet, shipped from this busy harbour came to be known as Monemvasia, later Malvasia, even though it was not made there but on various islands of the Cyclades like Naxos and also importantly on Crete, whence it would probably have been shipped from Heraklion (or Candia). Today, Malvasia di Candia is an important ingredient in Frascati; and the chief variety of Malvasia grown on Madeira is called Malvasia Candida, a corruption of Candia.

Malvasia is one of the world's most widely travelled names, though hardly one of its most widely planted grape varieties. Most wine-producing countries know a vine, a wine or a wine style incorporating the name Malvasia or some derivation of it. Not all of these, however, are true Malvasia.

Proper ancient Malvasia or its direct descendants are now to be found, in ever-shrinking quantity, in Spain, Portugal, Italy, Yugoslavia, Austria and Germany. France has 800 hectares (2,000 acres) planted with proper Malvasia vines, most of them on Corsica. But there are also many non-Malvasias called Malvoisie. In the Loire and Switzerland, for example, Malvoisie is used as a synonym for Pinot Gris; in Limoux, Maccabeu is called Malvoisie; in the Languedoc it can be used as a synonym for Bourboulenc; in Roussillon once for the Tourbat; in Savoie for the Veltliner; and even in Corsica, confusingly, for the Vermentino.

Like Muscat, the grapes can vary enormously in colour, although there is no distinctly dark subvariety of Malvasia. It can be vinified to produce a fairly deep-coloured rosé, however, and any untreated Malvasia wine is notable for its relatively deep colour, which can occasionally topple over into oxidation if care is not taken. The wine is also notably full-bodied, high in extract and strongly scented with an almost musky perfume that can have overtones of almond nuttiness with a twist of acidity at the end. Malvasia is well capable of producing a forceful wine which is worth ageing, and it can also stamp its very strong, spicy identity on a lighter wine. Traditionally it has been used for rich and powerful dessert wines such as those Greece still produces, although today they are more commonly made from various sorts of Muscat.

Malvasia shows its character most forcefully and most often in Italy where many different subvarieties are grown, from Basilicata to Trentino-Alto Adige, to produce both varietal and blended wines of all degrees of sweetness, alcohol and fizziness. The Venetian Republic imported Malvasia wines in such quantity from Crete in the fourteenth century that wine shops in Venice were even called *malvasie*. The vines themselves may well have been brought from Greece long before this, for in Italy today there are more than 10 different identifiable strains of Malvasia, of several hues and varying quality.

Malvasia Nera, or Roter Malvasier as it is known by the German-speakers of Alto Adige, is grown in Piedmont and the South Tyrol, but rather damp conditions in the north mean that rot can be a problem and there are a mere 10 hectares (25 acres) left in Alto Adige. The highly perfumed Malvasia Nera is quite common in Apulia.

Much more widely planted are Malvasia Bianca del Chianti, Malvasia di Candia and Malvasia del Lazio which can still be found in some quantity in central Italy. Malvasia Bianca del Chianti is the Malvasia which is technically allowed in the Chianti blend to add fragrance (and danger of oxidation), but which is being so forcefully elbowed out by the much more expedient Trebbiano in the

vineyards of Tuscany. There are some fascinating all-Malvasia wines made in Tuscany, of which the best, Vin Santo made from dried grapes, is a fine example.

A judicious blend of Trebbiano and Malvasia can satisfactorily cover up Malvasia's slight tendency to flabbiness, and it is this classic central Italian combination that is technically responsible for wines such as Frascati, Marino, Est! Est!! Est!!! and Galestro, although one suspects that Trebbiano is becoming an ever more powerful component. The commonest Malvasia used in these Latium wines is Malvasia di Candia, sometimes called Malvasia Rosso because of the pinkness of the vine's flowers, which produces a distinctly nutty wine. Rather finer but producing less wine is Malvasia del Lazio, or Malvasia Puntinata because of its speckled berries.

In this region more than any other, the deep-coloured grape skins are hardly allowed to leave their traces in the final wine. Modern Italian winemakers have their sometimes overenthusiastic ways of bleaching white wines to a watery hue.

The fourth easily identifiable strain of Malvasia is the least exciting. Malvasia Friulana or Istriana with its distinctly greener berries is grown in Friuli, where it produces wines such as Malvasia del Collio and Malvasia dell'Isonzo which are much less aromatic and luscious than mainstream Malvasia; it is thought possible that it may not even be related. It is also encountered in Yugoslavia's coastal wine regions; as Malvazija it is grown on the Istrian coast.

Perhaps not surprisingly, the Malvasia made on the Italian islands is much closer to the original Greek model.

MALVASIA

Malvasia delle Lipari is made to dazzle on the rocky islands to the north of Sicily, while Malvasia di Sardegna is vinified dry or sweet but always fairly strong all over Sardinia, with Cagliari and Bosa versions being most esteemed. It is regarded as a distinct subvariety and is thought to have come from Spain, which is perfectly possible if slightly circuitous.

Malvasia is still relatively important in Spain though it accounts for not much more than 1 percent of Spanish vineyard land, rather less than Moscatel. It is common in the Canary Islands and in mainland Spain its cultivation is concentrated in Rioja and neighbouring Navarra. It is the heavyweight foil for Viura in white Rioja blends. Traditionalists favour a 50:50 mix, but Malvasia is declining in popularity as "crispness" takes on the mantle of ultimate virtue. Less than 5 percent of all white vines planted in Rioja now are Malvasia, almost all of them close to the river in Rioja Alta. Malvasia used to be added to red Rioja to give it body and fragrance.

Of all the vines used in the production of the great fortified wine madeira the *vinifera* crossing Tinta Negra Mole constitutes well over half, while Malvasia, which has given its name to Malmsey, is only the third most important ingredient, Verdelho being the second. The commonest subvariety is known in Madeira as Malvasia Candida but some Malvasia Babosa ("lazy") and Malvasião (imported from Genoa in the sixteenth century) are also grown. Malvasia is also treasured here for its fragrance, infused into the wine from the grape skins and even, in cooler years, by the inclusion of some usefully yeasty leaves in the fermentation vat. (Malvasia's leaves are notably big.) The extreme sweetness and strength of flavour of the late-ripening grapes led the madeira producers to associate the name Malmsey with their sweetest wine, and this practice continues even though, as a result of phylloxera, its most famous exports are very far from varietal wines.

On the Portuguese mainland Malvasia is found in wine regions as widespread as Beiras, Torres Vedras and Colares, and Taylor for one claim it as principal ingredient in their white port. It is one of the white grapes that makes up the blend for the rare white cult wine Buçaco.

There is a tiny amount of Früher Roter Malvasier in Germany. Enthusiastic planting of "Malvasia Bianca" in California in 1982 brought the state's total of this varietal (Pinot Gris?) to over 520 hectares (1,300 acres).

Synonyms:
Malmsey (British arch.);
Malvoisie (limited use, France);
Malvasier, Früher Roter Malvasier (Germany);
Malvasia Bianca del Chianti, Malvasia di Candia,
Malvasia Rosso, Malvasia del Lazio,
Malvasia Puntinata, Uva Greca (Italy);
Malvasia Fina, Rojal, Subirat,
Blanquirroja, Blancarroga, Tobia, Cagazal,
Blanca-Roja (Spain); Malvasia Fina (Portugal);
Malvasia Candida (Madeira);
Malvazija (Yugoslavia); Monemvasia (Greece);
Malvasia Bianca (California).

Soils:
Grows well in dry climates and well-drained soils,
prefers upland and slopes.

Vigour: Vigorous.

Pruning:
Gobelet training and spur pruning
is most common.

Susceptibility:
This dry-weather grape
is relatively sensitive to damp-condition problems
such as mildew and rot,
especially on damp soils.

Rootstocks:
Moderate vigour.

Yields:
Variable but relatively productive.

Fine quality. Fading fast.

Other
Varieties

Red-wine Varieties

France
Bordeaux

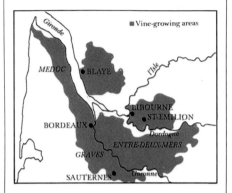

COT

In the Gironde Cot, or Malbec as it is more often known by wine drinkers, produces a sort of watered-down rustic version of Merlot, mouthfilling and vaguely reminiscent of blackberries in youth but soft and fairly low in acid, and, therefore, early maturing. It is relatively unimportant in the Médoc but still fairly popular with growers in Bourg and Blaye. Such a pedigree does nothing to enhance its status in the eyes of the world's connoisseurs, but they would do better to examine the reputation of the wines of Cahors.

On the higher rugged limestone vineyards of Cahors, Cot, or Auxerrois as they so confusingly call it, once produced small quantities of thick-skinned grapes so full of colour, tannin and flavour that one suspects a different original genetic material from that found in Bordeaux. Wines made only from these vineyards, pre-phylloxera, made Cahors' reputation as "the black wine". Today, the wine comes mainly from the richer vineyard land down by the river Lot; it consists of a minimum of 70 percent Cot blended chiefly with Merlot and Tannat, and is closer to a slightly more fiery Côtes de Blaye than the prototype Cahors.

Although the Cahors *vignoble* has been steadily increased since the wipeout by the 1956 frosts, France's total plantings of the notably warm-sapped Cot have declined to less than 5,000 hectares (12,500 acres). Cot has been losing ground both in the Gironde, its chief sphere of influence, and in the Loire where it has traditionally been blended with Gamay and Cabernet Franc.

A major reason for Cot's fall from favour is its strong tendency to *coulure*. It is a tribute to the attachment of Cahors growers to tradition (and of course to the power of Appellation Contrôlée laws) that they are prepared to persevere. At least when the flowering is successful, the crop is relatively abundant.

This is presumably one reason why it is so popular in Argentina where it is the third most widely planted grape variety, with about 30,000 hectares (75,000 acres). In these much hotter and usually irrigated vineyards, the wines produced are loose-textured but definitely bear the stamp of Bordeaux. Chile's Cot has more structure and staying power and is usually blended with Merlot and Petit Verdot.

Australia has about 500 hectares (1,250 acres) producing a distinctive if unsubtle full-flavoured wine, a fairly lightweight foil for Cabernet Sauvignon, notably in South Australia's cooler Keppoch vineyards. California has few Malbec vines so far and it is to be hoped that growers do not get too carried away with the authenticity of their copies of claret. Merlot, Cabernet Franc and Petit Verdot are much more likely to make interesting blending partners for Cabernet Sauvignon.

Cot

Synonyms:
Malbec, Malbeck (Médoc);
Noir de Pressac, Pressac (St-Emilion);
Auxerrois (Cahors); Cahors, Pied Rouge,
Jacobain, Grifforin (rest of France).

Medium quality.

PETIT VERDOT

Petit Verdot

This excellent variety has long been established in the Médoc, probably considerably longer than Cabernet Sauvignon, and at one time was much more important. Its very dark, thick-skinned grapes produce wine as deep as Syrah and, like Syrah, peppery, spicy and fragrant. Indeed Petit Verdot is not unlike a seasoning for the usual Médoc *encépagement*, adding extra flavour and interest as well as alcohol, tannin and colour. For this reason it has traditionally been planted in the southern Médoc where the soils and therefore wines are lighter, and more in need of the deep, dark Petit Verdot.

The trouble is that it is a very late ripener and in poorer years simply refuses to ripen at all, although grafting on to early maturing rootstock such as Riparia de Gloire can help. It is also an irregular cropper and therefore very expensive to produce. Many châteaux have been quietly abandoning Petit Verdot, although among the more quality conscious there is a perceptible swing back in its favour. The long-lived and much admired Château Léoville-Las-Cases, for example, is one of its exponents, and Petit Verdot plantings are planned to add substance to Château Lascombes.

Verdot is one of Chile's minor grape varieties, and some of California's more cosmopolitan producers of Cabernet Sauvignon blends have started to experiment with small plantings of the vine.

Synonyms:
Petit Verdau, Verdot Rouge,
Carmelin (France); Verdot (Chile).

Very good quality.

GROS VERDOT

The French agricultural census of 1979 found 400 hectares (1,000 acres) of "Verdot" in the Gironde, but some of them must have been Gros Verdot, another old Girondin vine that is traditionally planted on damper, less promising *palus* land and produces thin tart wine of low quality. According to Galet it is probably not even related to Petit Verdot.

Synonyms:
Verdot-Colon, Colon, Plant de Palus.

Poor quality.

CARMENERE

This variety was very important in the Médoc and Graves before oidium and phylloxera. Growers took these twin disasters as signs from nature that they should give up trying to cultivate such a low-yielding vine so subject to *coulure*. But today there are signs that one or two properties plan to include it in their *encépagement* for its roundness, colour and additional character.

Synonyms:
Carmenelle, Cabarnelle, Grande Vidure, Grand Carmenet, Carbouet.

Fine quality.

Other red varieties more readily associated with the Médoc than anywhere else include the very rare and rather ordinary St-Macaire (or Bouton Blanc), also known in California, and Pardotte (or Pignon) and the Cot-like Mancin. Only relatively tiny traces remain today.

The Loire

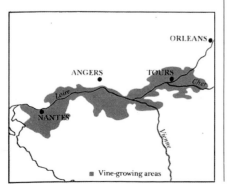

GROLLEAU

Grolleau

The very common synonym Groslot is apt: this is the Loire valley's most basic dark vine producing huge quantities of rather ordinary grapes and thin wine. With yields of up to 120 hectolitres per hectare, it is seen as the Loire's own equivalent of the Aramon. It is strictly of local interest.

Grolleau was first recorded at the beginning of the last century in Touraine. It can legally be planted all over the west of France, but in practice is encountered only in and around the vineyards at the western end of the Loire. Total French plantings are declining markedly, mainly in favour of Gamay and Cabernet Franc, and were fewer than 6,000 hectares (15,000 acres) in 1979. Of these, two-thirds were in the Anjou district and nearly a fifth in Touraine. The agricultural census draws a happy picture in which quality is being recognized by the vine growers of the Loire, with hybrids such as Plantet, Villard and Rayon d'Or in retreat.

Today's wine drinker never knowingly encounters a varietal Grolleau, but may taste it as the major ingredient in the red and, particularly, the rosé of Anjou. The vine ripens just after Gamay, with which it is often mixed, and produces wines low in alcohol, relatively high in acid and without much colour or character. Grolleau can be expected to decline further.

White and *gris* forms are also known on a very limited scale.

Synonyms:
Groslot, Plant Boisnard.

Very ordinary.

PLANTET

This is one of the most widely planted hybrid direct producers (HDP) in France although total plantings of Plantet, as of Baco, Villard and Couderc, have been shrinking rapidly as official disapproval takes effect. At the last count (1979) France's Plantet vineyards covered only 4,000 hectares (10,000 acres), as compared with more than 26,000 hectares (65,000 acres) a decade previously.

Nearly three-quarters of these Plantet vines were in the Loire valley, especially in the vineyards of Anjou and in the Muscadet *département*, Loire-Atlantique. (In 1968, Plantet was planted in no fewer than 20 *départements* in France, from Ain to the Yonne.)

Two possible sets of parents have been posited for the hybrid: Seibel 867 × Seibel 2524 and Seibel 4461 × Berlandieri-Jacquez. Lucie T. Morton points out that the second of these would explain the Plantet's difficulty in rooting and the frangibility of its shoots. The berries are also relatively difficult to crush. Set against these disadvantages are the very high yields that Plantet can achieve. It is also a reliable cropper and will even produce some useable fruit after severe spring frosts, hence its popularity as far north as the Loire, although the winters of New York State have proved too severe for it.

The variety has good disease resistance but is bad at keeping mature fruit on the vine, and loses shoots in high winds. The wine itself is least offensive if the fruit is picked just before maturity.

Synonyms:
Seibel 5455, Plantet Noir.

Hybrid, low quality.

PINEAU D'AUNIS

No more a member of the Pinot family than Chenin Blanc (also known as Pineau de la Loire), Pineau d'Aunis is another Loire original and was at one time the most admired red-wine grape there. According to some authorities, it was wine from this grape, much enjoyed by the Plantagenet Henry III, which was exported to England as early as the thirteenth century. It would certainly be difficult to refute this.

Pineau seemed to be a portmanteau word for better quality grapes in the Middle Ages, and this particular one was probably associated with the Prieuré d'Aunis near Saumur. Today it is chiefly cultivated at the eastern end of Anjou-Touraine along with the white Arbois as a complement to the Gamays and Sauvignons de Touraine which are the principal products of the vineyards of Loir-et-Cher. It is most usually encountered as a relatively neutral ingredient in Touraine Rouge or in the reds and often the rosés of Cheverny and Coteaux du Vendômois.

Alcohol levels are closely related to yield (the higher the latter, the lower the former), but Pineau d'Aunis can produce very attractive if fairly simple wines provided yields are kept below 50 hectolitres per hectare and the vines are grown preferably in calcareous soils. The vine has been gradually losing ground because, although it is usefully vigorous when young, its productive life is very short. Cabernet Franc has been seen as a more viable alternative to many growers, especially to those in the heart of Anjou-Touraine.

Synonyms:
Chenin Noir, Plant d'Aunis,
Pineau Rouge, Cot à Queue Rouge,
Cot à Bourgeons Blancs.

Moderate quality.

CHAMBOURCIN

Countering the withering antihybrid winds current in France today, which have blown such old faithfuls as Baco, Villard, Couderc and Plantet all but out of the *vignoble*, is this new hybrid of Joannes Seyve of which total French plantings have actually been increasing.

The vine, thoroughly approved by Galet, has been commercially available only since 1963 but more than doubled its territory to 3,400 hectares (8,500 acres) in the decade between the agricultural censuses of 1968 and 1979. More than half of the Chambourcin planted is in the Loire and, after Melon and Folle Blanche, it is the third most planted variety in the Loire-Atlantique where its good crimson colour and fairly full flavour must provide welcome relief.

The vine is extremely vigorous and high-yielding except during the first few seasons. It has good disease resistance and is generally healthy apart from being sensitive to lime. Galet reports an assertive aroma and herbaceous flavour. While some producers vinify it as a rosé, there has even been praise for the ageing potential of red Chambourcin.

Synonym:
Joannes Seyve 26.205.

One of the better hybrids.

Other minor red varieties that are most commonly associated with the Loire are the disease-prone hybrid Seinoir, which has hardly been planted for the last 30 years, and the almost forgotten Lignage.

Northeast France

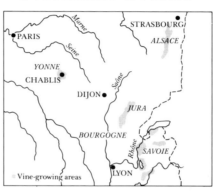

Chablis and the Yonne

CESAR

No prizes for guessing the putative origins of this grape, often called Romain in the Yonne where it is still cultivated, although it is giving way to the finer and arguably more suitable Pinot Noir. (To judge from the combined ampelographical works available, the Roman legionaries must have been positively weighed down by vine cuttings on their travels.)

Although the vine is sensitive to frosts and ripens rather less readily than Pinot Noir, it can still be found in some bottles of Irancy, but it is almost always blended with the region's most noble red grape. Its high level of tannin and colour can endow longevity on the wines of some vintages. With Tressot, it is permitted in the Seine et Marne *département* for those few vineyards to have escaped the depredations of urbanization there.

Synonyms:
Céear, Célar, Romain,
Rončain, Picargneau, Gros Monsieur,
Gros Noir.

Medium quality; very hard.

TRESSOT

Traditionally grown and vinified with César, Tressot has all but disappeared

---

since it never responded well to the grafting necessary after phylloxera. The grapes register impressive sugar levels for this latitude and the wines can last well.

Synonyms:
Tresseau, Tréceau, Vérot.

Moderate quality; useful alcohol.

Jura

Often regarded as a mere country cousin of Burgundy, the Jura has its own grape varieties as well as its own landscape, geology and *spécialités de la cave*.

POULSARD

Delicate, pink, rather finicky, but with undoubted talent, Poulsard has a very distinct, perhaps humanly recognizable to many, identity. The vine buds early and is therefore very sensitive to spring frost. *Coulure* can be a problem, and the vine is susceptible to a wide variety of later seasonal ailments. Its thin-skinned grapes produce pale red wines very prone to oxidation which means that they turn swiftly to a salmon colour or *vins gris*. Average yields are only about 40 or 50 hectolitres per hectare.

Nevertheless, because the bouquet of such wines is sufficiently perfumed and "pretty", Poulsard is still the most planted grape variety for Jura's red wines. Arbois and Côtes de Jura are usually made from a blend of Poulsard, Trousseau and, increasingly, Pinot Noir.

Poulsard's versatility is demonstrated by its occasional manifestation as a Jura white wine, L'Etoile.

With Gamay, Pinot Noir and Mondeuse, Poulsard is also a contributor to the renaissance of the light red wines of Bugey, in the Ain *département* (01) between Beaujolais and the Jura.

Synonyms:
Plousard, Peloussard, Pleusart,
Pulceau, Mieckle, Mescle.

Very light – almost rosé – but fine.

Other dark varieties associated particularly with Jura include Trousseau (see Bastardo) and, in their heyday, the productive but good Argant, the productive but poor Valais Noir, Dameron, Gueuche Noir, Enfarine and Petit Béclan.

Savoie

——— MONDEUSE NOIRE ———

The House of Savoy appears to have left its visiting card in northeastern Italy in the form of this vigorous and widely planted vine variety. Friuli's Refosco is none other than the Mondeuse Noire, responsible for some of Savoie's best, if little-known reds.

The wine varies considerably with site and yield. On a hillside vineyard well exposed to sunlight, the grapes should ripen (they don't always) and produce between 40 and 60 hectolitres per hectare of dense, deep, strong, chewy wine that is serious stuff indeed. On an alluvial valley floor the yield may be more than 100 hectolitres per hectare and the wine is more likely to be thin and tart.

Before phylloxera struck, the vine was grown extensively all over eastern France: in Isère, Jura, Doubs, the Haute-Saône, Allier, Nièvre and even as far north as the Yonne. Today, its sphere of influence in France is Savoie, where it may be found in wines made in such villages as Chautagne and Montmélian, and in the wines of Bugey in Ain. It is lightened and perfumed by blending with Pinot Noir and Gamay and, in Bugey (where Mondeuse Blanche is still known), with Poulsard.

In Italy it is known almost exclusively in Friuli where its slight obduracy is seen as no disadvantage. Almost invariably sold as varietal wines and usually labelled simply Refosco, they may be DOC Grave del Friuli or Latisana, or simply table wines from several corners of the region – each with definite colour and sometimes just too much acidity. The best clone is Refosco del Peduncolo Rosso, also known in northern Yugoslavia as Terrano. Refosco Nostrano is a speciality of the Carso area. As in France, the grape shows itself well able, if not always encouraged, to produce wines worth ageing.

Refosco has proved itself vigorous and robust in California, but despite approval for "standard wines" from Davis, total plantings have declined to fewer than 40 hectares (100 acres) on the West Coast, most of them in Napa.

The vine has also been planted in that other American sphere of Italian viticultural influence, Argentina. It is also grown in northeast Victoria in Australia where it is a valued ingredient in port-style wines; they presumably have little problem in fully ripening their Mondeuse.

With its good colour, high acid, alcohol and extract, it could probably perform even more consistently and better in a number of warmer regions than the two in which it is mainly planted at the moment.

Synonyms:
Grand Chétuan, Savoyanche, Molette Noire, Grand Picot, Grosse Syrah (France); Gros Rouge du Pays (Switzerland); Refosco (Italy, Argentina, California); Terran, Terrano (Yugoslavia).

Good quality; tart but can age.

Other dark grapes grown in the Savoie include the rather ordinary Corbesse, Grosse Rogettaz, Hibou Noir and Hibou Rouge.

Rather surprisingly, the hybrid Oberlin Noir, as well as Baco Noir, were planted in considerable quantities in the Greater Burgundy region as recently as the 1960s.

Southeast France

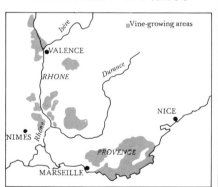

——— AUBUN ———

A sort of sub-Carignan, Aubun is puzzlingly being planted more and more in the southern Rhône valley. When last counted in 1979, total plantings had reached nearly 6,000 hectares (15,000 acres), most of them in the Vaucluse, Var, Gard and Bouches-du-Rhône *départements*. The wine is produced in rather the same style, and with the same impressive yield, as Carignan, but with less tannin.

It achieved some recognition because it seemed at one time to have good resistance to phylloxera (its home ground is in the sandy soils of Gigondas and the environs of Mont Ventoux) and to downy and powdery mildews. It also buds late, which gives it very good armour against spring frosts. Its grapes are much more prone to heat stress than those of Carignan, and the wine it produces is not even as good, being less deep-coloured and lively. The wines tend to be a bit fat with a slightly bitter finish. Aubun, in sum, is suitable only for those areas very prone to spring frosts.

According to Galet, Aubun is identical, both as a vine and a wine, to the variety Counoise, which is a permitted though not often used ingredient in Châteauneuf-du-Pape. It is also identical to Moutardier. French statistics still list Counoise as a separate variety with 660 hectares (1,650 acres) in 1979 and, according to John Livingstone-Learmonth, no less an authority than Baron Le Roy considers it one of the best of the Châteauneuf varieties. This enthusiasm may just be attributable to the very best effects of subconscious clonal selection; the Baron's "Counoise" is probably Aubun at its most glorious in his corner of Châteauneuf.

Aubun has nothing to do with the similarly named Aubin that is grown in the Côtes de Toul area of Lorraine.

Particularly healthy examples of Aubun and Counoise were found, to everyone's surprise, in an ancient and isolated planting in the Great Western district of Australia. They are doubtless direct descendants of Busby's cuttings in which they or their synonyms were listed.

Synonyms:
Counoise, Quenoise, Moustardier, Moutardier, Carignan de Bedoin, Carignan de Gigondas.

Medium-quality wine.

——— MOURVEDRE ———

Mourvèdre is one of the better travelled of France's more obscure wine vines, though it often travels under an assumed name, Mataro. In Australia, for instance, Mataro is the fifth most popular red-wine grape, covering a vineyard area of 1,200 hectares (3,000 acres), and California has nearly 800 hectares (2,000 acres).

The Spanish towns of Murviedro and Mataro, near Valencia and in Catalonia respectively, have each been posited as the original home base for this vine, which has nevertheless been known in the south of France for at least four centuries. Although the vine tolerates very hot conditions slightly less well than Garnacha or Grenache, it would be quite suitable for much of Spain in that its wine is markedly high in acidity and often astringency. A definite link with any vine currently grown in Spain on any scale is yet to be established.

Mourvèdre

In terms of the wine it produces, Mourvedre has a considerable image problem. In France Mourvèdre is considered an improving structural ingredient in a blend – a sort of vinous RSJ with the perfume of blackberries thrown in for good measure. The rules for making Bandol have been amended to increase the minimum proportion of Mourvèdre required to 50 percent, as it is considered that the much lighter, looser and softer Grenache and Cinsaut can benefit from its strength. In Australia it is seen as useful if rather hard blending material, often combined with Shiraz, and a possible ingredient in port-style wines, but without individual distinction. In California it is dismissed as useful only in areas at risk from spring frosts because of its propensity to bud late.

It should be pointed out, however, that the Californians complain that their Mataro has low acidity and colour, whereas it is precisely these attributes that are treasured in France. It seems highly likely that the plant material available in California is of particularly low quality.

What is agreed is that the vine buds and ripens late (thus needing quite a bit of heat), grows relatively vigorously and particularly upright, and produces a not enormous quantity of very thick-skinned berries that are most unlikely to rot. It is less susceptible than Carignan to powdery mildew but is a rather reluctant grafter.

France's total plantings of Mourvèdre, at one time scattered all over the Midi, shrank considerably, usually in favour of Grenache, in the first half of this century.

Its fortunes have since been reversed and its domain increased from 860 to 3,100 hectares (2,150 to 7,750 acres) in the seventies, but it remains a Provençal phenomenon. Like the bougainvillaea on the coast, it needs the full force of the sunshine of Provence to ripen it.

It is most common in the Var and Vaucluse *départements*, in superior Côtes de Provence and Côtes du Rhône vineyards respectively. It is one of the four most common red grape varieties allowed in Châteauneuf-du-Pape, but is not nearly so widely planted as Grenache, Cinsaut and Syrah. It is particularly complementary to these varieties, and this is underlined by the regulations for the production of Côtes-du-Rhône-Villages. Mourvèdre crops up in all manner of appellation descriptions, from Coteaux du Tricastin to Tavel, and Côtes de Provence to Palette.

In Australia it is grown chiefly in the south and principally in the Barossa Valley. Some winemakers object to the relatively high tannin levels that result from such thick-skinned grapes and most find it lacking in individual flavour. One clone of the vine is confusingly known as Morrastel in South Australia although it has nothing to do with the Spanish and French vine of the same name.

California's plantings of Mataro are concentrated in southern coastal districts but have been slowly declining.

Synonyms: Mataro, Balzac, Esparte.

Sturdily good, deserves more attention.

TERRET NOIR

The progenitor of the much more widely planted Terret Gris is one of several permitted varieties for Châteauneuf-du-Pape, but it does not play a significant part today. Someone somewhere loves it, however, since total French plantings increased from 151 to 1,150 hectares (377 to 2,875 acres) in the seventies.

Terrets Noir, Gris and Blanc bud extremely late, sharing that favourite attribute of the vines of southeast France. They also grow vigorously and upright and are fairly productive, although the Noir is less so than the Gris, producing in the range of 50 to 80 hectolitres per hectare. The resulting wine is light in both senses, rather tart and strongly perfumed, adding a welcome touch of *nervosité* to the more customary southern Rhône *cépages* where allowed.

Synonyms: Tarret, Terrain.

Tartness can be useful.

PIQUEPOUL NOIR

Whether Piquepoul, Picpoul or Picapulla, this variety has a name that once heard is never forgotten. Perhaps this is why it seems so oddly difficult to locate, the very obverse of ubiquitous. The agricultural census of 1979 counted 334 hectares (835 acres) of Piquepoul Noir, and 592 hectares (1,480 acres) of Piquepoul Gris, but no single *département* is willing to admit to even 100 of them. Along with Clairette and Cinsaut it is almost certainly one of the Midi's oldest domestic varieties, preceding such Spanish parvenus as Grenache and Carignan. Its name is repeated dutifully whenever the list of 13 Châteauneuf-du-Pape varieties is extolled, but its part must be a very minor one now.

Like so many of those associated with this part of the world, the vine buds late and is relatively sensitive to oidium but can easily manage a yield of between 50 and 80 hectolitres per hectare.

Synonyms:
Picpoul, Picpoule, Picpouille, Picapulla, Picapouya, Languedocien, Avillo.

Quality almost impossible to assess nowadays.

VACCARESE

Like Counoise and Muscardin, Vaccarèse is a Châteauneuf variety that seems to be indigenous to this corner of France and to have remained rooted there rather than gently sidling towards the Italian frontier over the centuries. It is rarely cultivated in isolation, let alone vinified as a varietal. To François Perrin of Château de Beaucastel the world is indebted for as close an encounter with these more rarefied varieties as is possible today. He is able to provide interested visitors with tasting samples of most traditional Châteauneuf varieties vinified separately (shades of Château de Pez 1970). His Vaccarèse has an almost rubbery, hot nose with a peppery, tannic character on the palate. Not dissimilar, in short, from Syrah.

The vine is yet another late budder and is particularly sensitive to downy mildew.

Synonyms:
Camarèse, Vaccareso, Brun Argente.

Rather Syrah-like wine.

MUSCARDIN

The wines produced by those few Muscardin vines that survive in the southern Rhône are low in output per vine, high in acid, low in alcohol and unusually light in colour for this region, with a tendency to oxidize. Galet considers this is a local variant of Mondeuse, the plants being identical except that Muscardin buds are less downy. Beaucastel's Muscardin sample tasted in 1984 had the "farmyardy" fruit so typical of Châteauneuf-du-Pape, but noticeably more perfume and lighter tannins than most other varieties.

Synonyms: None.

Useful "lightener" in
Châteauneuf-du-Pape.

FUELLA

The tiny appellation of Bellet perches on steep terraces above Nice and commands equally steep prices from such a well-heeled local market. It is distinguished for drawing on several grape varieties unknown elsewhere in France; Braquet, Italy's Brachetto, is one and Fuelle Noir the other for reds and rosés.

Fuella is an ancient vine for long associated with this corner of France; it produces limited quantities of deep-coloured wines which can sometimes be slightly flabby.

Synonyms:
Fuelle Noir, Folle, Fuola, Beletto Nero.

Characterful wines.

TIBOUREN

The ever-questing Domaines des Salins du Midi have been experimenting with various traditional Provençal varieties of which Tibouren is the most promising. (Its leaf structure suggests to Galet that Tibouren's origins are Greek or Middle Eastern.) Its strongest point is its unique and intensely Provençal aroma, most pronounced when the vines are grown on schist. Varietal Tibouren virtually smells of the *garrigue* itself and is particularly successful as a well-macerated rosé.

Its disadvantage is that *coulure* can sometimes be a problem so that yields are variable and occasionally quite low, although in this respect it is no less satisfactory than the current mainstay of Provençal rosé, Grenache Noir.

The variety is grown in small quantities on a large number of Provençal properties.

Synonyms:
Tiboulen, Antiboulen,
Antibouren, Antibois, Gaysserin.

A possible saviour for
Rosé de Provence.

Other red varieties that are or have been more associated with southeast France than anywhere else include the rather common Calitor, or Pecoui-Touar, Brun-Fourca, Mourvaison, Bouteillan, Teoulier, Plant Droit, an intriguing Grec Rouge and Négrette de Nice (unrelated to the Négret of Gaillac).

Southwest France

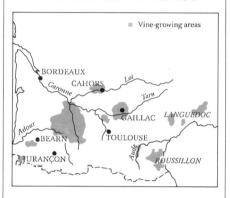

■ Vine-growing areas

BORDEAUX
CAHORS
Garonne
Lot
Tarn
GAILLAC
LANGUEDOC
Adour
BEARN
TOULOUSE
JURANÇON
Aude
ROUSSILLON

This region of France, like the other side of the Pyrenees, has its own very distinctive grape varieties, usually blended with each other and often with the classic Bordeaux varieties. Vine varieties are listed here in approximate order of current importance.

JURANÇON

Although according to many authorities on wines rather than vines, this variety plays at best a supporting role in the vineyards of the southwest, the last French agricultural census counted more than 7,000 hectares (17,500 acres) of "dark" Jurançon, more than twice as much as total plantings of the much more distinctive Tannat.

The variety is slowly declining but is planted all over the southwest, in virtually every wine district apart from that of Jurançon itself. Jurançon Noir and Jurançon Rouge, very closely related, are distinguished by Galet; but he pays them scant attention; they are in fact so popular that some vines have even been planted in the northern Rhône valley.

According to some authorities, the vine is descended from the bountiful though not beautiful Aramon. It is certainly both vigorous and very productive, which doubtless accounts for its popularity. It

---

resists disease well, although in its tight-bunched form it is easy prey to botrytis.

The wine is hardly ever left unblended. Alcohol levels are good; colour intensity is usually not. As Jurançon Noir it contributes about 10 percent to the Malbec-dominated blend of Cahors. The wines of Lavilledieu (between Cahors and Gaillac) have their Fer peppered with a mix of varieties including Jurançon Noir, and Jurançon Rouge is a permitted ingredient in Gaillac. The Noir version is also important in the light rustic reds of Aveyron, the wines whose names are so much less simple: Vins d'Estaing, d'Entraygues et du Fel and de Marcillac. It would appear that however minor Jurançon's role in the rulebook, growers must like its productivity sufficiently to push it as close to the centre stage as they are allowed to.

Only moderately good.

TANNAT

This is the variety that wine lovers would associate much more readily than Jurançon with the highly individual red wines of the southwest, and it is often Tannat that gives them their firm structure, long life and raspberry-like perfume. Young wine made from Tannat is a force to be reckoned with: almost Piedmontese in its deep colour, high alcohol and extremely high level of tannin.

In its most widely available form Tannat contributes between 40 and 60 percent to the blend for Madiran, the house wine of the armagnac producers, which also includes Fer and the two

Tannat

Cabernets. With such ingredients, it is hardly surprising that the recipe calls for nearly two years in wood before bottling. Because the southwest of France is associated with "country" (which is taken to mean simple) wines, these are liquid treasures that are rarely given the time they need to develop.

Madiran's kid brother, red Tursan, is a bit more approachable and made of the same varietal mix. The VDQS Côtes de Mont is to Madiran just what Bergerac is to claret, with 70 percent of Tannat. The fourth wine made from roughly the same mix is Irouléguy, most famous for its rosé. As one might expect, these Tannat-based rosés are very full-flavoured and fruity. Presumably skin contact has to be kept to a minimum to stop them tasting too harsh.

Also from the very far south and west of France, the red and pink wines of Béarn have to contain at least 60 percent of Tannat, but here with a blend of the province's other specialities such as Manseng Noir, Pinenc and Courbu Noir.

It seems highly likely that there are some of these vigorous Tannat vines south of the Pyrenees, too.

Synonyms:
Tanat, Moustrou, Moustroun,
Madiran (France);
Bordeleza Belcha (Spain);
Harriague (Uruguay).

Very good; worth ageing.

GRAPPUT

There were still more than 1,000 hectares (2,500 acres) of Grapput, or Bouchales, planted in France in 1979, two-thirds of them in the Lot-et-Garonne and one third in the Gironde. This made it one of the Lot-et-Garonne's top three varieties along with Ugni Blanc and Merlot. Since Côtes de Buzet has sidled into the spotlight of international attention, *département* plantings of the two Cabernets have doubtless risen, but Grapput must be responsible for a high proportion of its more basic red wine. It is not officially listed as an approved vine for its other "name" wine Côtes du Marmandais.

The vine is often difficult to graft because the wood is especially sappy and it suffers easily from the two mildews and black rot. Plantings are, perhaps not surprisingly, on the decline.

Synonyms:
Bouchales, Grappu,
Prolongeau, Gros de Judith.

Ordinary.

NEGRETTE

Négrette grows almost exclusively in the hills between the beautiful Albi and Toulouse, contributing to red Gaillac, Côtes du Frontonnais and Vins de Lavilledieu.

It is easiest to taste in the somewhat recherché wines of the Côtes du Frontonnais in which it must constitute 70 percent of the blend, supplemented by several of the Bordeaux and southern Rhône grape varieties or, more usually, Gamay. These wines demonstrate the versatility of Négrette. It has the suppleness to be drunk young (unlike Tannat), but the potential for medium-term ageing.

The Petit Noir which was once quite prevalent in the Charentes was demonstrated as identical to Négrette by Vidal in 1910. According to Galet, this vine was deemed to produce the cognac region's best and much needed red. Unfortunately the Négrette's susceptibility to oidium and grey rot have precipitated its gentle but notable decline.

The mysterious "Pinot St-George" of California, so stubbornly not of Pinot Noir quality, has also been shown to be Négrette. It is grown on about 80 hectares (200 acres), producing vaguely sweet but inconsequential wine.

Synonyms:
Négret, Négret de Gaillac,
Morillon, Morelet,
Petit Noir des Charentes (France);
Pinot St-George (California).

Good quality wine but unhealthy vines.

VALDIGUIE

Plantings of this, "the Aramon of the southwest", were at one time well spread out over the southern half of France, including some as far west as Bordeaux and as far east as Bandol. During the seventies, total plantings fell from more than 4,000 to 840 hectares (10,000 to 2,100 acres) and the total is likely to be considerably less now, its wines in all probability fodder for the EEC's distilleries.

It came to the fore in the last century, from the Lot, because of its extremely high productivity and relative resistance to the oidium which devastated so many French vineyards at that time. Like those of Aramon, its wines are fairly well coloured but notably low in alcohol and indeed any other property. It is grown in small quantities in Gaillac where it is called Brocol.

As Napa Gamay it causes confusion in California, especially as the characteristics of Valdiguié wine are so unlike those of true Gamay. California has more than 1,200 hectares (3,000 acres) of this still contentious variety, more recently referred to as "Gamay 15", all over the state but primarily in Monterey and, of course, Napa. It produces a fairly light-coloured wine vinified in a wide variety of styles, from carbonic maceration to wood aged. It rarely merits the latter.

Synonyms:
Valdiguer, Brocol, Gros Auxerrois,
Jean-Pierrou à Sauzet (France);
Napa Gamay, Gamay 15 (California).

Very ordinary indeed.

MERILLE

France still has several hundred hectares planted with this rather ordinary grape, almost all in the reaches of the Garonne. It produces fairly coarse *vins de table* in the less reputable vineyards that surround Buzet and Côtes du Marmandais.

Synonyms:
Grosse Mérille, Bordelais,
Plant de Bordeaux, Périgord, Pica,
Picard, Piquat, Pouchou.

Basic table wines.

ABOURIOU

This vine sounds much more *sauvage* and characterful than it is. Along with Fer, Malbec, Gamay, Merlot, the two Cabernets and Syrah it is a permitted ingredient for the light rustic reds of Côtes du Marmandais, but Galet dismisses the wine of Abouriou alone as "coloré, plat, mou, sans caractère".

The vine itself is both vigorous and fertile, budding and ripening conveniently early and it has particularly good disease resistance. Plantings fell, however, from 800 to 500 hectares (2,000 to 1,250 acres) during the seventies. The close link with Gamay suggested by many of its synonyms is confusingly erroneous.

Truel's examination of cuttings despatched to Australia from California in 1976 suggested that the blending variety called Early Burgundy in California coastal vineyards is in fact Abouriou. There are currently only 120 hectares (300 acres) and it is declining. Early yes, Burgundy no.

Synonyms:
Beaujolais, Gamay du Rhône,
Gamay St-Laurent, Précoce Nauge,
Malbec Argente (France);
Early Burgundy (California).

Good colour but little flavour.

DURAS

Readers of this section will not be surprised to learn that the Duras vine has nothing to do with the wine from Duras in the Dordogne. It is today almost exclusively linked with the Tarn *département* and its best known red wine, Gaillac Rouge; together with Fer and Négrette, Duras is one of the local varieties in that fruity but undistinguished wine.

Duras is one of the very few obscure varieties that has been gaining popularity in France: plantings increased by 600 percent to nearly 500 hectares (1,250 acres) in the decade to 1979. This is unexpected in view of the vine's tendency to bud too early to escape spring frosts and its susceptibility to oidium and black rot.

Synonyms:
Duras Mâle, Duras Femelle,
Duraze, Durade.

Moderately good quality.

FER

The hardness suggested by the name is more in the vine's wood than in the wine, though the wine itself is well coloured and well constituted. In the past Fer has helped to add to the reputation of such wines as Madiran, Gaillac and the esoteric country wines of Aveyron. In 1979 there were still more than 300 hectares (750 acres) of the vine, used mainly for Gaillac, Madiran and the wines of Béarn where it is sometimes called Pinenc. The real Fer should not be confused with the Argentinian clone of Malbec with the same name.

Synonyms:
Fer Noir, Fer-Servadou, Pinenc, Hère.

Good quality.

Other varieties still grown in the southwest are Courbu Noir and Mansenc or Manseng Noir which are specialities of Béarn way down in the far southwest corner.

"*Workhorse*" *Grapes*

ARAMON

Aramon! The very word sounds like a curse over the ocean of vines that constitute the Languedoc-Roussillon, France's

Aramon

contribution to the headache that is the European wine lake. Whispers of witchery involving yields as high as 300 hectolitres per hectare do nothing for the reputation of this variety, planted far and wide by greedy Midi farmers in the second half of the last century.

The twin catastrophes of oidium and phylloxera paved the way for the influx of vines that would guarantee their cultivators some financial return: the ludicrously generous Aramon and hybrids such as Villard and Couderc. So closely have the respective histories of Aramon and France's hybrids followed each other that many a well-informed commentator accuses Aramon itself of hybridity.

Those who have tasted the wine produced by Aramon, at its most rampant on the plains of Hérault, may feel that the distinction is somewhat academic. A poor wine is a poor wine whoever its parents. The vast majority of all Aramon grown produces very pale reds with a distinct blue-black tinge which are notably low in alcohol, dry extract and character. Because they are so pale, they have traditionally been cultivated alongside the red-fleshed Teinturier, or "dyer" vines such as Alicante Bouschet and Grand Noir de la Calmette, though neither is able to transform the base Aramon into a wine of real quality. These wines, whether blended with Teinturier vines or not, are the stuff of which the European wine lake is made. The produce of today's Aramon typically finds its way either into the cheapest of the *rouge* sold by French supermarkets or into the stills administered from Brussels.

There is, however, a slightly brighter side to the picture of Aramon. When it is cultivated on well-drained, hillside vineyards with a much reduced yield, it is

capable of making quite respectably tinted wines with a decent alcohol level and a certain amount of fruitiness. At the Salins du Midi experimental station Aramon has been persuaded, by dint of sophisticated modern winemaking technology, to produce a most attractive rosé, especially when yields are controlled.

The tide began to turn against Aramon in 1949 when many blenders passed over Aramon-based *vin de table* for the much stronger, deeper reds of Algeria. The frosts of 1956 and 1963 wiped out a number of vines, and now the French government is effectively bribing wine farmers to replace their Aramon (and indeed all the varieties mentioned in this section) with something a bit more respectable.

Significantly, Grenache Noir overtook Aramon between the agricultural censuses of 1968 and 1979 to become France's second most popular red wine grape after Carignan (whose wines are, mercifully, perceptibly better than those of Aramon). By 1979 France had 63,000 hectares (157,500 acres) of Aramon, almost half of which were in the Hérault *département* and the rest in the various surrounding vineyard regions. There were also nearly 400 hectares (1,000 acres) of a white version, doubtless impossible to distinguish from Aramon proper when tasted blindfold.

Viticulturally, Aramon's only advantage, yield apart, is a reasonable resistance to powdery mildew. It suffers the twin disadvantages of budding early and ripening late; it is sensitive to most major vineyard ailments, particularly grey rot because of its puny thin skins, and can even suffer *coulure* if grafted on to too vigorous a rootstock in the fertile soils of the plain.

It is not surprising, therefore, that Aramon is not widely cultivated outside France, but it is depressing that in France the authorities allowed such large tracts of totally unsuitable land to be planted with it earlier this century. A *gris* version is also known.

Synonyms:
Ugni Noir, Plante Riche,
Rabalaire, Revalaire, Gros Bouteillan,
Burkhardt, Pisse-vin.

Very thin stuff usually, though low yields improve quality.

ALICANTE BOUSCHET

Wherever Aramon goes, there has to go a red-fleshed Teinturier, and this one is statistically the most likely. It is France's most-planted Teinturier vine and ninth most popular red-wine variety overall, as well as being found in five continents.

We have Bouschet Père et Fils to thank for this much-needed prop to the less distinguished side of the French wine business. Louis Bouschet de Bernard decided as early as 1824 to try to breed vines that produced not just grapes with deep-coloured red flesh, but lots of them, or at least more of them than had been customary with Teinturiers. His first attempt, a fairly obvious 1828 crossing of Aramon and Teinturier du Cher, resulted in Petit Bouschet which was very popular in the last century.

Alicante Bouschet

His son Henri carried on the work and came up with several notable successes of which the 1886 Alicante Bouschet, a crossing of Petit Bouschet and Grenache, was most outstanding. Cuttings of Alicante Bouschet were soon in great demand from all over the world and commanded the dizzy price of two golden francs a metre according to Galet.

Alicante Bouschet succeeded quite spectacularly in both the chosen fields of colour and productivity. Its colour intensity is 15 times that of Aramon, and more than twice that of Grand Noir de la Calmette. It can easily produce 80 hectolitres per hectare of wine that has 12° of alcohol, and is of little interest to connoisseurs. The wine is basically characterless, slightly flabby, and the deep colour is a short-term phenomenon.

Alicante Bouschet is not just a tinter of thin *vinifera* wines, but has spawned all of the French hybrid Teinturiers.

Unfortunately the vine's active life can be short in poor soil without careful pruning. The vine buds and ripens early and is usually the first to be picked in the Midi, often in August. It is sensitive to downy mildew and anthracnose, and there have been problems with diseased cuttings.

Because of all Teinturiers in France this is the only one recommended, it has been gradually and rather frighteningly increasing its territory: nearly 22,000 hectares (55,000 acres) in 1979, all of it in the Midi, while the likes of Grand Noir are on the decline. Presumably, and suitably, it will eventually follow Aramon out of the vineyards of France, as it was conceived as a prop for it. There were still 2,500 hectares (6,250 acres) of Alicante Bouschet in Corsica in 1979. It is also grown in Calabria in southern Italy, and to a limited extent in Yugoslavia.

The variety was most popular in California with home winemakers during the Prohibition era. There are still more than 1,440 hectares (3,600 acres) of Alicante Bouschet vines in the state, the majority of them in the Central Valley where it is still popular with those who believe winemaking belongs in the home, and with more commercial outfits in other states whose local produce lacks the dramatic purple, if fast-fading, tints of this grape.

Alicante Bouschet is sold as a varietal by a handful of California wineries, notably Angelo Papagni whose Alicante Bouschet was once accorded the singular distinction of being house wine at London's Tate Gallery restaurant.

There are a few Alicante Bouschet vines in South Africa where it is prized for its almost rude productivity. The vine has also been planted quite widely in North Africa, which is odd since vineyards there produce some of the world's deepest-coloured wines without any help at all. The same could be said of Alicante planted in Calabria.

Synonyms:
Alicante Henri Bouschet,
Alicante, Alicante Bouschet No 2.

Teinturier useful only to add colour to basic wines drunk young.

VILLARD NOIR

Villard Noir is France's most widely planted hybrid direct producer. Total plantings fell quite dramatically between the two most recent agricultural censuses: from 30,000 hectares (75,000 acres) in 1968 to fewer than 8,000 (20,000 acres) in 1979, but this hybrid ne'er-do-well was still France's thirteenth most commonly planted red-wine grape variety. In addition to this staggering total, there were a further 2,800 hectares (7,000 acres) planted with the many dark Seyval Villards. This aspect of the French wine scene is not exactly trumpeted in the literature.

To be fair, attempts are being made to suppress these hybrid varieties. New plantings have been forbidden since 1977 and subsidies are paid to those who grub them up. The problem is widespread however, since the last agricultural census revealed that Villard Noir was still planted in 15 *départements*, including those most famous for Muscadet, Hermitage and even – horror of horrors – Bordeaux. There were 300 hectares (750 acres) of Villard Noir and 100 (250 acres) of Villard Blanc in the Gironde in 1979.

The vine is concentrated not in the Midi as one might expect, but in the southwest, with Tarn having the highest proportion, 28 percent of total plantings.

The encroachment of the hybrids on to French territory is described elsewhere (see page 35). Villard subsequently replaced one of its parents, Chancellor (or Seibel 7053) in France when Chancellor, still planted quite widely in the eastern United States, was banned from France. The other parent was Seibel 6905, the resulting hybrid being very productive, of medium vigour, mid-season budding and ripening cycle. The wine is said to have fairly good colour and alcohol but some astringency and too much of an American vine taste to remain unblended. Few wine drinkers will ever have the chance to taste Villard Noir as a varietal wine; a very high proportion of what is now made must be trundled straight to the distillery.

Villard's advantage is that it is all but immune to downy mildew, although it is sensitive to powdery mildew and botrytis. According to Lucie T. Morton, it is usually grafted on to Berlandieri hybrids.

Synonyms:
Seyve Villard 18.315, Villard.

Hybrid. Fit only for the worst table wine.

COUDERC NOIR

This natural hybrid of *Rupestris-Lincecumii* and *vinifera* was in the vanguard of the army of hybrid direct producers, which marched across the plains of the Midi in the early years of this century. Named after the propagator Couderc, whose name survives as does Baco's, Seyve's and Seibel's in the names of many a hybrid variety, it was actually bred by a baker called Contassot according to the American expert Lucie T. Morton.

The vine is productive and vigorous

and ripens so late that it is chiefly a Midi variety, with the Gard *département* harbouring 36 percent of the Couderc in the region. The resulting wine is deep-coloured with a very definite flavour of its less noble ancestor, and must be muted for commercial consumption. Although it is a hybrid, it does not even have very good resistance to phylloxera, so it has to be grafted on to a vigorous rootstock.

In 1979 there was almost as much Couderc as Villard: 7,700 hectares (19,250 acres) mainly in the southeast of France. It ripens too late to be suitable for the eastern states of North America.

Synonyms:
Couderc 7120, Couderc.

Hybrid. *Vin de table* and wine lake only.

GRAND NOIR DE LA CALMETTE

Grand Noir de la Calmette

Henri Bouschet named this crossing of his father's Petit Bouschet (Aramon × Teinturier du Cher) with Aramon after his breeding station, Domaine de la Calmette at Mauguio. Perhaps he suspected its true worth and was unwilling to have the family name associated with it.

This particular red-fleshed grapevine's sole advantage is productivity. Budding late and escaping spring frost damage, it can easily produce 100 hectolitres per hectare of vapid wine, without alcohol, acidity or even half as much colour as

Alicante Bouschet. The sins of the parents were indeed visited on this infelicitous crossing. The high productivity of the vine ensured that it was planted widely in the 1920s, and it was not until a decade or two later that it became embarrassingly plain that the vine suffers badly from powdery mildew and winter cold. Understandably, total French plantings fell from 23,000 to 2,700 hectares (57,500 to 6,750 acres) between 1968 and 1979 and there are strong efforts to rout it out of the most famous national *vignoble* in the world. Most of it is planted in the Midi, but there were still 300 hectares (750 acres) of Grand Noir in Cognac country, which made it the region's second most-planted variety, although admittedly much in the shadow of Ugni Blanc. It is also grown, to a limited extent, in northeast Victoria in Australia where it is blended with (overwhelmed by, one hopes) gutsier ingredients in port-style wines.

Synonym: Grand Noir.

Teinturier, even worse than Alicante Bouschet.

SEIBEL

The hybridizer Seibel gave his name to an enormous array of hybrids, including the Plantet, Rayon d'Or and Seinoir described in the Loire sections. The French agricultural census groups together all other red "Seibel" hybrids, showing that between 1968 and 1979 their combined territory fell from 70,600 to 4,500 hectares (176,500 to 11,250 acres), a more dramatic reduction than that affecting any other variety.

Red Seibels were particularly widely grown in France in the 1950s but the wines produced never managed to achieve sufficient quality. Seibels of various sorts have been grown in cooler climates, notably New Zealand, Canada and England.

Poor quality hybrids.

Other Teinturiers which have been planted in France at some time include the father of them all, Petit Bouschet, together with Morrastel Bouschet and Carignan Bouschet as well as the 300 hectares (750 acres) of Gamay Teinturiers mentioned on page 137. For other hybrids see the Loire (red and white) and white workhorse varieties.

Mainly for Sparkling Wines

MEUNIER

If ever a variety lived its life in the shade of another it is the (Pinot) Meunier. Cabernet Franc may be patronized by many as a mere country cousin of the aristocratic Cabernet Sauvignon, but it does at least lead an independent existence in all corners of the globe. It plays a leading role not only in St-Emilion but also in the Loire and northern Italy, and is planted and valued in places as far apart as California and South Africa. Poor old Meunier has to resign itself to playing an entirely secondary role to the more reputable Pinot Noir in just one corner of France.

Of course, the not widely disseminated

Meunier

truth is that in quantitative terms at least, Meunier's role in Champagne is far from secondary. Meunier is, in fact, the most extensively planted grape variety in the Champagne region, its 10,400 hectares (26,000 acres) covering 44 percent of planted vineyard in the Marne, Aube and Aisne *départements*. This compares with Pinot Noir's and Chardonnay's 30 percent and 26 percent respectively.

Ask champagne makers what ingredients are in their *cuvée* and most will be very coy about Meunier, ever conscious of the noble reputation built up for Pinot Noir and Chardonnay to the south. Only a handful of those who can afford to, Henri Krug, for example, will extol the virtues of this grape.

Meunier's chief attribute is fruitiness, something in which Chardonnay and often Pinot Noir are notably low. A preponderantly Meunier champagne may not age as well as one with more Pinot Noir, but it will have lots of youthful vivacity. Meunier also tends to be rather higher in acid, and slightly lower in alcohol, than Pinot Noir and so can bring useful crispness to a blend in a very ripe year such as 1976. In some years, Meunier wine can take on almost too much flavour for a fine champagne. Certainly champagnes from areas known to grow a very high proportion of Meunier are relatively light and tart, and are rarely capable of great development.

Viticulturally, Meunier's strong suit is its ability to withstand spring frosts. It buds rather later than Pinot Noir and Chardonnay and the wood's lower sap content makes it less vulnerable to frost damage. Meunier is therefore the obvious choice for those parts of the Champagne *vignoble* particularly vulnerable to frost, such as the Vallée de la Marne. This also explains why practically all of the chilly valleys that make up Champagne's most northerly vineyards in the Aisne are almost exclusively devoted to Meunier.

Meunier is a member of the Pinot family that was originally distinguished from Pinot Noir by being much more villous (hairy). Today it is characterized by the downiness of its leaves which look as though they have been sprayed with flour, hence its main names in both French and German. Meunier is susceptible to oidium and the compactness of its bunches makes rot a problem in damper years. Meunier flowers later than the less vigorous Pinot Noir (and is therefore less subject to *coulure*) but ripens before it, suddenly gaining sugar at a great rate just before harvest. Average yield (which is much less variable than Pinot Noir's) is 10 to 15 percent higher than that of Champagne's best publicized Pinot.

Thanks to careful clonal selection, there are 1,000 hectares (2,500 acres) of Meunier – "Schwarzriesling" – in Germany, most of them in Württemberg, where it is one of that region's light red specialities, and some in northern Baden.

Wines that included Meunier were entitled to the Alsace Appellation Contrôlée until 1979, and there are still some Meunier vines there. It has also been encountered around Beaugency in the Loire, in Styria and in Yugoslavia.

Today, however, Meunier is cultivated only in Australia in any quantity; and it is probably only in Australia that Pinot Meunier is sold as a still, varietal wine, albeit fairly undistinguished. Best's have for long marketed a Great Western Pinot Meunier in which the great Len Evans managed to find a "distinctive 'dusty' middle-palate" flavour.

California's rush into champagne apeing will presumably involve planting Meunier as soon as healthy cuttings are available.

Synonyms:
Pinot Meunier, Plant Meunier, Gris Meunier, Auvergnat Gris, Munier, Blanche Feuille, Farineux Noir, Morillon Taconé, Plant de Brie (France); Müllerrebe, Schwarzriesling (Germany); Blaue Postitschtraube (Austria); Rana Modra Mlinaria (Yugoslavia); Miller's Burgundy (Australia).

Vivacious in youth.

Other red varieties once associated with the Champagne region include Bachet and Beaunoir, specialities of the Aube, and the odd Gamay that lingers on.

Corsica

——— *NIELLUCCIO* ———

Nielluccio's 3,600 hectares (9,000 acres) make it Corsica's most planted native grape variety, although the imports from France (Carignan, Cinsaut and Grenache) beat it into fourth place overall. This particularly early budding vine is regarded as a Corsican speciality, but is said to be related to Tuscany's Sangiovese. It produces quite alcoholic wines which lack colour and can lack guts – not unlike Sangiovese. And, like Grenache, they are usually best vinified as a fairly formidable rosé. Patrimonio's Nielluccio-based rosés (and some of the reds) constitute one of the few Corsican wines regularly to impress non-Corsicans.

Synonyms:
Niellucio, Niella, Nielluccia, Negretta.

Moderately good quality.

——— *SCIACARELLO* ———

It is perhaps significant that even the French authorities do not know how to spell Sciacarello, Corsica's most revered grape variety. The cultural distance between this very Italian influenced island and the mainland is much greater than the 170 kilometres shown on the map.

Sciacarello is admired for its intense perfume of the herby scrub that constitutes much of the Corsican landscape (in which respect it is reminiscent of the Tibouren of Provence). It buds and ripens late – Galet reports that at one time it was mistaken for Piedmont's Barbera – and is planted particularly around Ajaccio whence, general opinion has it, the best wines come.

Sciacarello is rarely sold unblended as it is naturally lean and relatively astringent. Provided it is given suitable substance, Sciacarello can develop genuine complexity of bouquet over the years.

Synonym:
Sciaccarello.

Scented, light but interesting.

Italy

While the Germans can give planted areas for each of their vine varieties down to a single hectare, by district, the Italians present a less well-marshalled appearance to the outside world.

The many instances of brilliance in Italian wine are intensely individual affairs. One feels that any government statistician would be roundly sent off the premises of most *cantine* and *tenute*, even in the unlikely event that he was sent there to try to measure some dimensions of the exciting Italian winescape.

All of which is a lengthy way of excusing any discrepancies between the order in which varieties are listed and their comparative importance in each region.

Northwest Italy

DOLCETTO

Dolcetto

"The little sweet one" does taste notably sweet, and lusciously gulpable because of it, but chemical analysis of the grapes' composition stubbornly refuses to yield an explanation. Their sugar and acid levels are very much on a par with those of other red Piedmont grapes, although total tannin is very low indeed. This means that Dolcetto is extremely useful in this, the homeland of the intractable Nebbiolo, in that its wines are ideal for early consumption. They are deep purple, often have a very slight prickle, and taste so thick with fruit that the acid is hardly perceptible. Victor Hazan finds quince in the riper examples, bitter almonds in the coarser ones. Looking at the wine, it is easy to find mulberries too, often with a slightly bitter aftertaste. With Barbera, Dolcetto is what the Piedmontese drink; Nebbiolo is what they sell and occasionally use as a postprandial treat.

The vine is, unfortunately, relatively prone to fungus diseases, especially peronospera. Since phylloxera the vine has also shown a disturbing tendency after grafting to drop its fruit before they are fully ripe, especially in vineyards outside its ideal production zone. Dolcetto will produce well only on suitable sites and has seven DOCs all its own and all in Piedmont: Dolcettos di Diano d'Alba, d'Alba, delle Langhe Monregalesi, di Dogliani, d'Asti, d'Acqui and di Ovada, in approximately decreasing order of sophistication. Some theories have the vine originating

in France, but it has probably been cultivated in the Monferrato region of Piedmont since the eleventh century. Today it is useful to the vine growers in the Langhe hills because it can thrive on exposed sites where Nebbiolo would never ripen. Nebbiolo ripens on average three to four weeks later than Dolcetto, anyway.

Synonyms:
Dolsin, Dolsin Nero.

Good quality but not for keeping.

GRIGNOLINO

Grignolino is even more specifically Piedmontese than Dolcetto, growing successfully only in sparkling-wine country, the provinces of Asti and Alessandria. Although red, it is a rather frothy little number, and is too delicate to drink with many foods. There is something almost alpine about the aroma of a good Grignolino with its gentle suggestion of herbs and flowers. The wines are notably light in body and most are best drunk young. The best Grignolino is a wine for which the adjective charming was designed.

The name of the variety has evolved from a local term describing the particularly pippy nature of the grapes. They also have some difficulty in ripening and the same vine can have clusters at completely different stages of ripeness. This means that yields can vary considerably from year to year.

Grignolino

Synonyms:
Barbesino, Verbesino,
Balestra, Arlandino.

Light but not inconsequential.

CROATINA

This rather confusing variety is also thought to have its origins in Alessandria. Today it is grown around Pavia on the borders of Piedmont and Lombardy, and its most famous and only DOC wine (making use of its common but probably mistakenly applied synonym) is called Bonarda dell'Oltrepò Pavese. The picture is confused by the fact that Bonarda Piemontese is the proper name of another, less common, related but quite distinct variety (see below). Nowadays both Croatina and Bonarda Piemontese are commonly known as Bonarda, but it is the Croatina that blends so well and often with Barbera, notably in the Gutturnio of Emilia-Romagna.

Croatina, like Dolcetto, is a good if late yielder of early-maturing, roundly fruity, deep-coloured wine, except that it is distinctly bitter, sometimes noticeably tannic and can benefit from a couple of years in bottle. The wine is made to be gulped fairly early; the vine buds and ripens late.

Synonyms:
Bonarda, Croattina, Crovattina, Croata,
Crovettino, Neretto, Uva Vermiglia

Very Italian; good potential.

BONARDA PIEMONTESE

True Bonarda at one time represented 30 percent of all dark grapes planted in Piedmont, but post-phylloxera times saw a decrease of interest in wines as easy to drink as this in favour of Freisa and, especially, Barbera. Today there are signs that like Dolcetto, Bonarda is becoming more popular. The light, easy, fruity wines are the sort that can happily be drunk chilled. The variety is now grown particularly on the hills around Turin.

Synonyms:
Bonarda di Chieri, Bonarda di Gattinara,
Balsamina.

Lighter and suppler than Croatina.

FREISA

There are records of this curious variety growing in Piedmont as early as 1799. Today there are two slightly different clones, Freisa Piccola grown usually in the hills and Freisa Grossa producing less sprightly wines on the flat.

Its curiosity lies in what Burton Anderson describes as a "unique sweet-acidic flavour (something like lightly salted raspberries)". It is made into cherry-red wines

Freisa

of all degrees of sweetness and fizziness and fell from fashion when dry, still Nebbiolomania was at its height, but is enjoying a gentle resurgence of popularity.

The vine is usefully resistant to peronospera, less to oidium, and its ideal site is not only at some altitude but in some dry, sunny, well-exposed positions. The grapes are high in acid and often relatively high in tannin, though without very much colouring matter for this corner of Italy.

Synonyms:
No correct ones.

Interesting and versatile.

—— *BRAQUET/BRACHETTO* ——

Brachetto is one of the few Italian grapes found outside Italy, admittedly only to a very limited extent, as Braquet, in pockets of vines that still exist around Nice. Its origins are almost certainly French since it is considered an ancient Bellet variety in France, whereas it was first noted in Piedmont only in the nineteenth century (an 1869 Brachetto showing the vitality of a healthily rustic great-grandfather when tasted in 1985 must have been a relatively early model).

Today it is more widely cultivated in Italy than France and can be found in Piedmont, notably as Brachetto d'Acqui, a *frizzante* rather strawberry-like in both colour and flavour. As Brachetto it is considered a fairly early ripener, as Braquet fairly late, which is more a comment on the other varieties planted in Piedmont and Provence respectively than on Braquet itself.

Synonym: Bracchetto (Italy).

Grapey fizz.

Rossese (di Albenga) is the alluring red grape of Liguria at its best around Dolceacqua. It produces scented red wines that are fairly low in acid and can be drunk either very young or after two or three years, when they develop rather Fleurie-like interest.

The low-yielding Vespolina is grown especially in Novara and often blended with Nebbiolo in wines such as Fara, Sizzano, Boca and Ghemme. The ancient Uva Rara was also grown in this zone but is associated today with Oltrepò Pavese reds. Petit Rouge is the red variety of the Aosta valley, ripening fairly late to produce deep-coloured flowery wines without too much acid. The variety has small grapes which are so dark and dusty they are almost grey. According to Viala it is the same variety as the near-extinct Swiss Rouge de Valais. Other varieties that have been associated with the northwest include Avana, Avarengo, Barsalinga, Caloria, Groppello, Neretto di Bairo, Pignola Valtellinese, Plassa, Pollera Nera, Rossola Nera, Vien de Nus.

Northeast Italy

—— *CORVINA* ——

With Rondinella, Molinara and occasionally Negrara, this is the most important ingredient in Valpolicella and neighbouring reds, making up to 70 percent of the blend. There can be few wine drinkers in Britain and the United States who are unfamiliar with the light crimson colour, light to medium body, fairly tart, soft, bitter almonds character of the variety. Some producers even take the trouble to show us that this blend can be a complex marvel. It ripens late and quality is clearly dependent on yield.

Synonyms:
Corvina Veronese, Cruina.

Light.

—— *RABOSO* ——

Here is a grape that makes Cabernet Sauvignon look rather a softie in some important respects. While Cabernet's average tannin level is about 4.7 percent, Raboso's is 5.4, and comparison of total acidity levels shows even more markedly how Raboso is even less compromising than the supposedly tough Cabernet of the Médoc.

Raboso, too, is deep-coloured, but the one dimension in which it is lacking is alcohol, which makes it extremely difficult to drink (chewing is easier) when young, but quite useful for blending with softer wines. Some DOC Raboso from the Veneto can even start to show charm after some years in bottle.

The vine is widely planted on both sides of the Piave river flats. The Raboso Veronese clone, actually from Treviso and named after a Signor Veronese, is the more planted, although the Raboso del Piave clone can also be found. It is a very good yielder, ripens late and has excellent resistance to rot and most fungus diseases.

Raboso

Synonyms:
Rabosa, Friulara, Negron.

Eye-stingingly tough.

—— *SCHIAVA GROSSA* ——

Although few of its names are ever seen on a wine label, this is one of the world's better travelled grape varieties. As Black Hamburg it is quite well known as a table grape in Britain and Benelux countries. As

Trollinger it is *the* red grape variety of Württemburg, – *the* red wine region in Germany. But it is perhaps most readily associated with the Trentino-Alto Adige region in the far north of Italy, where it is the most planted variety by far, being grown on nearly 3,500 hilly hectares (8,750 acres) of South Tyrol alone.

The variety has clearly long been well adapted to this region and it is easy, therefore, to see why the Germans call it Trollinger, an easy corruption of Tirolinger. Its Italian name Schiava suggests perhaps Slavonic origins (from Slava), or its slave girl connotation may be a reference to the ease with which the vine will thrive with scant attention or comfort. It has certainly been grown in northern Italy since the fifteenth century and perhaps very much longer, whereas it was known in Germany only from the seventeenth century when the Swabians brought it from the Tyrol.

There are several very distinct clones of Schiava or Vernatsch as it is called in the northern, German-speaking part of South Tyrol, of which Grossvernatsch or Schiava Grossa is the most important. Grossvernatsch owes its popularity to its hardiness and productivity. On the flat land of the South Tyrol it could happily yield nearly 10 tons per acre unless pruned strictly within the limits of DOC regulations, and not even two-thirds of this is permitted for St Magdalener. It is only when so pruned and grown to full ripeness on the hillsides that it produces wine of any constitution at all in South Tyrol. Left to its own devices it can produce lovely table grapes, but the wine does a veritable disappearing trick lacking colour, acid, alcohol, body and tannin. At its best, the wine can be attractively fruity though surprisingly characterless for a red wine, and it cries out to be drunk that instant.

Grossvernatsch is the clone most planted among Württemberg's 2,200 hectares (5,500 acres) of Trollinger. As one might expect of the Germans, yields are even higher with 100 to 150 hectolitres per hectare a happy average. The vines retain their susceptibility to oidium but are otherwise hardy except that they ripen very late indeed, after Riesling (producing wines notably higher in acid than their Italian counterparts). It was this risky characteristic that led to Trollinger's disappearance in all other regions of Germany. Grape pigmentation is a problem and many wines are made into Weissherbst or rosé.

Other clones include Grauvernatsch or Schiava Grigio, which makes much more distinguished wines but ripens inconveniently earlier and suffers stalk necrosis; the even earlier ripening but unhealthy Kleinvernatsch; and the low-yielding Tschaggelevernatsch. Very little of these is planted. A little Lagrein may be blended into the local *vino da tavola* made principally from Schiava.

Synonyms:
Raisin Bleu (France); Vernatsch (Tyrol); Trollinger, Fleischtraube, Bockstraube, Schwarzälscher (Germany); Grosser Burgunder, Aegypter (Austria); Black Hamburg (England).

Table grape; pretty ordinary.

—— *LAGREIN* ——

With Schiava, this variety is almost exclusively associated with the light reds and rosés of Trentino-Alto Adige, although it is probably a much more recent arrival and is much less important. It is made both in a delicate rosé style as Lagrein Kretzer or, especially around Bolzano, as the dark velvety Lagrein Dunkel. There is a suggestion of sweetness in each style and much more character than in Schiava. The vine ripens generously but late and, therefore, needs fairly warm sites. It can cope well with sand as well as gravel.

Synonyms:
Lagrain, Lagarino.

Medium quality, lightish.

—— *TEROLDEGO* ——

Teroldego is Trentino's speciality and grows nowhere else. In its geographical concentration it is like Gamay, thriving only in one very specific area. The Campo Rotaliano plain north of Trento is Teroldego's very flat answer to the Gamay's Beaujolais and is planted with virtually nothing else. Like Gamay, Teroldego is low in tannin, but unlike Gamay it is high in just about everything else. It is substantial, slightly rasping, definitely bitter and designed to be drunk in its first five years. This is just the sort of local, supremely self-confident speciality in which Italy excels.

Synonyms:
Teroldigo, Tiraldega, Tiroldola.

Sturdy, good quality.

—— *MARZEMINO* ——

This other local speciality was once internationally acclaimed, and its name lives romantically on at Don Giovanni's last supper. It is still possible in very isolated examples to see the riches that were presumably offered by earlier, more concentrated versions. Today, this late-ripening variety is mainly grown in the south of Trentino around Isera and the wine is, typically, a lightly plummy offering whose most distinguished feature is its dark tint. The vine is susceptible to oidium and has perhaps degenerated post-phylloxera to the extent that it is incapable of reproducing its past glories.

Synonym:
Marzemino Gentile.

Tantalizingly average quality.

Other varieties associated most readily with northeast Italy include the newly resurrected Schioppettino of Friuli and the American hybrid Clinton (parent with Schiava of Othello) which is officially prohibited. Also grown in tiny quantity are Parana (Nera Gentile di Fonzaso), Rossignola, Tocai Rosso, Trevisana Nera and Turca.

Central West Italy

—— *CANAIOLO NERO* ——

Canaiolo is known by name to any student of the regulations for the production of Italy's most famous wine, Chianti. With Sangiovese and the headily scented, very local Mammolo, it is one of the red grapes allowed into the blend, but in reality has been declining in importance in Tuscany.

Part of the reason lies in the difficulties experienced when trying to graft Canaiolo after phylloxera. Today Chasselas × Berlandieri 41B and Aramon × Rupestris G1 give best results with this medium-productive, otherwise fairly healthy vine.

Another factor has been the decline in popularity of the *governo* system of adding dried grapes to Chianti after fermentation for which Canaiolo was ideal. The rather neutral, slightly bitter but robust grapes could be dried for several weeks after picking without harm. Much less characterful than Mammolo and much less tannic and acid than Sangiovese, Canaiolo is most treasured for its colour, and "*governo*bility".

It is now grown in Umbria, Latium, the Marche, Sardinia and Emilia-Romagna where small quantities of gulpably grapey red dessert wine, called after its local synonym Cagnina, are made.

Synonyms:
Caccione Nero, Cagnina, Calabrese, Canaivola, Uva Canina, Tindilloro, Uva dei Cani, Uva Donna, Uva Marchigiana, Uva Merla and many more.

Medium quality.

CILIEGOLO

This variety grows all over central Italy, but is perhaps best known in Tuscany where it is thought to have originated. The wines it produces tend to be light, inconsequential and, as the name suggests, cherry-like, at least in colour, and sometimes even in flavour. DOC regulations allow it as an ingredient as far south as Velletri in the Alban hills, and with Montepulciano it is an ingredient in Torgiano, thought by Burton Anderson to provide the clue to the wine's unique character.

Moderate quality.

CESANESE COMUNE

This is Latium's bid for red wine respectability, though rarely a very exciting one. It is grown all over south-central Italy and is distinct from Cesanese di Affile.
Synonym: Bonvino Nero.

Ordinary.

SAGRANTINO

This is a strictly local but much more exciting phenomenon. Grown strictly around Perugia, especially in the Montefalco zone, it produces wines of great concentration and, usually, liveliness with deep ruby colour and some bitterness. It was traditionally partly dried before fermentation to produce sweet wine, but more dry styles are emerging now. The grape has in its time even been given the compliment of association with St Francis of Assisi.

Good quality.

Other varieties associated with pockets of the central west include Abbuoto, Canina Nera, Olivella Nera and Nero Buono di Coro.

Central East Italy

MONTEPULCIANO

After Sangiovese, Montepulciano is Italy's most widely dispersed native red grape variety. It is recommended in about 20 of the 95 Italian provinces although it is most common in central Italy, especially along the eastern coast where it is planted from the Marche down to Apulia. It originated in Tuscany and has often been confused with the quite similar Sangiovese.

Today it is most closely associated with Abruzzi where it is the principal red-wine grape. More than 20 million litres of Montepulciano d'Abruzzo are made in an average year, either as a robustly mouth-filling red with only enough tannin to keep it three or four years, or as the pink Cerasuolo. The vine's connection with the much more intense Vino Nobile di Montepulciano is merely linguistic. Montepulciano produces wines that deserve attention for their smooth drinkability but not for any complex nuances of flavour.

Other wines it produces or shapes include Rosso Cònero and Rosso Piceno of the Marche, the *vino da tavola* Rosso della Bissera of Emilia-Romagna, Cori Rosso of Latium and, its finest incarnation, the splendidly named Riserva Il Falcone made at Castel del Monte by Rivera in Apulia in which it stamps its character on the local varieties, Bombino Nero and Uva di Troia.

Montepulciano, with its dependably high yield of late-ripened grapes, could well become internationally appreciated as a source of individualistic yet supple reds from central Italy.
Synonyms:
Cordisco, Cordisio, Morellone, Primaticcio, Uva Abruzzi.

Promising.

LAMBRUSCO

The connotations of this name are not necessarily the noblest in an age when Lambrusco is used as a standard weaning mixture for cola drinkers on their way to wine, but Lambrusco has a very respectably ancient history. It originated in Emilia Romagna – where its extraordinary influence is still strongest today, particularly in the provinces of Modena and Reggio Emilia – and was known to the Etruscans as Lambrusca (not to be confused with *Vitis labrusca* wild vines). It is still trained high on trellises as in ancient times, and total production is about as awe-inspiring as that of Montepulciano in some vintages.

Today there are more than 60 members of the Lambrusco family, dispersed over all Italy, from Sicily to Piedmont and the Veneto. The most important are Lambrusco Salamino, Lambrusco Marani, Lambrusco Maestri, Lambrusco Montericco, and Lambrusco di Sorbara whose yield is much reduced by its tendency to drop its flowers. The four DOC wines produced from Lambrusco, all in Emilia-Romagna, are in approximate descending order of respectability, Lambrusco di Sorbara, Lambrusco Grasparossa di Castelvetro, Lambrusco Salamino di Santa Croce and the less specific Lambrusco Reggiano, which can be made from a blend of Lambrusco subvarieties grown around Reggio Emilia, and is the lightest.

The subvarieties share the Lambrusco distinguishing marks of vines with nearly circular medium-sized leaves, sometimes with three lobes, and the medium-sized clusters that take the form of elongated pyramids. The vines are productive and have good disease resistance. The grapes mature between the third and fourth epoch, with Lambrusco Maestri being one of the last to ripen. Lambrusco Grasparossa is notably higher in tannin than the others, an asset rarely associated with the gulpable Lambrusco wine stereotype. The Lambrusco di Sorbara and Lambrusco Salamino have considerably higher acidity than most.

The average Lambrusco wine is light to medium bodied with fairly low alcohol, considerable residual sugar, sufficient fizz to make it *frizzante* and not too distractingly vinous a flavour. So popular has it been, especially in the United States, that it now comes in all three colours, the white version being produced by separating the juice from the skins at the earliest possible opportunity. Just as every action produces a reaction, so the true cognoscenti profess a love for the atypical but "genuine" Lambrusco, juicy, usually off-dry, clean and very obviously made from grapes.
Synonyms:
None, but many subvarieties.

Medium quality for early drinking.

Other varieties once associated with the central east include the traditional Barbarossa and the red Lacrima, as well as Maiolica, Notardomenico and Sgaretta.

Southern Italy

GAGLIOPPO

Six out of every 10 red vines grown in Calabria are Gaglioppo; the vine is also grown in Abruzzi, Campania, Umbria and Marche. Its origins are thought to be Greek but it is also called Uva Navarra outside Calabria.

It is very good at resisting drought and is, therefore, ideal for the Calabrian climate, but there can be problems with both peronospera and oidium. It performs best on silicious or clay soils and the grapes ripen fairly early.

The wines are high in alcohol, full-bodied and, like the other Greek import Aglianico (see below), need time in bottle to show their form. Best known is Cirò, which sounds inappropriately frivolous to the English ear. Gaglioppo is usually blended with 10 percent white grapes to make this very considerable wine, usually 13.5 percent alcohol.

Synonyms:
Galaffa, Uva Navarra, Gaioppo.

Concentrated and serious.

AGLIANICO

This is the very exciting inspiration of such top quality reds of the deep south as Taurasi and Aglianico del Vulture. It was brought to southern Italy, and especially Campania, by the Ancient Greeks and its name is even said to be a corruption of *Vitis hellenica* or Greek vine. As principal ingredient in Falernum (now Falerno) it was known to the Romans.

The early-budding vine performs best in dry, sunny conditions – as one might expect from its origins – and has good resistance to oidium, though less so to peronospera and botrytis. It reaches its apogee in the cool microclimate of the high vineyards of Taurasi in Campania. The wine is very concentrated and impenetrably tannic in youth so that many years in bottle are needed before the Aglianico starts to yield its tarry, subtly fruity and, eventually, nobly balanced flavours.

Most other examples of Aglianico wines are uninspiring though some of Basilicata's Aglianico del Vulture can be stunning, with real vibrancy shining out beneath the concentration. A healthy deep garnet is the hallmark of Aglianico.

Synonyms:
Uva Aglianica, Gnanico, Ellenico.

Top quality.

Other varieties of the deep south, apart from the Primitivo which is thought to be an ancestor of the California Zinfandel, include the Bombino Nero of Castel del Monte, the Negroamaro of Salento, the Piedirosso (or Per'e Palummo) and Guarnaccia of Campania, the excellent Uva di Troia of Apulia as well as Agliancone, Caddiu, Cagnulari, Caricagiola, Castiglione, Nocera, Sciascinoso, Magliocco Canino and Marsigliana Nera.

Sicily and Sardinia

NERELLO

This important Sicilian variety is actually two varieties that originated on the island: the Nerello Mascalese which can add alcohol and colour to overproduced table wine blends, and the distinctly superior Nerello Cappuccio, concentrated on the northeast of the island, which can produce fine varietals.

Nerello Mascalese takes its name from the Mascari plain in Catania and its most respectable wine is the DOC Etna Rosso, produced on vineyards sufficiently high to protract the ripening season and add some depth to the wine. It is also one of the three grapes that make up the best-selling Corvo Rosso. Both Nerello wines are high in alcohol and, if well-made, can age well.

Synonyms: (of Nerello Mascalese)
Nireddu, Nirello, Niereddu.

Medium quality.

Other Sicilian red varieties include the excellent Nero d'Avola (or Calabrese), Frappato (di Vittoria), Bovale (di Spagna and Sardo), Catanese, Perricone (Pignatello).

MONICA

This is one of the few red Sardinian grapes whose name is allowed to grace a label. Like several other Sardinian varieties, its origins are Spanish, although it is not known in Spain's vineyards today.

It is grown all over the island and produces fairly nondescript reds designed

---

for early consumption. Monica di Sardegna is dry and can develop a little, while Monica di Cagliari is usually a rather more slightly sweet wine.

Synonyms:
Monaca, Munica, Niedda, Pascall.

Basic quality.

Fast disappearing is the Giro of Sardinia, probably another Spanish import, which produces a port-like *vino liquoroso*, and the Albaranzeuli Nero, Nièddera, Nieddu Mannu and Pascale di Cagliari.

Spain

MONASTRELL

After Garnacha Tinta, Monastrell is Spain's most planted red grape variety, with 113,000 hectares (282,000 acres). It

Monastrell

should be distinguished from the variety called Morrastel in southern France which is, in fact, Graciano.

In warm climates Monastrell is a dream to grow. It adapts well to almost any soil type, and recovers very well from spring frost. It has excellent resistance to disease, even to phylloxera, and most growers do not bother to use American rootstocks. The leaves of ungrafted vines in an old vineyard were observed to have been ravaged by phylloxera as recently as 1984 without any evidence of resulting damage to fruit or vine potential. Put this together with the fact that by Spanish standards the yields are moderately good and its popularity is not surprising.

The vine is late budding and late ripening, often not until mid-October. The wine produced from its small, very sweet berries is alcoholic, slightly flabby, and not very deeply coloured, not dissimilar, in fact, to Garnacha. Where Garnacha wine is sweet and scented, however, that of Monastrell is much drier and meatier, and well capable of ageing, provided oxidation has been avoided in the winery. It is chiefly used for *rosados*, light red *claretes* and some sweet dessert wines.

Alicante is great Monastrell country; the variety covers nearly 70 percent of vineyard land there, though the average vine density, owing to the arid conditions, is just 1,500 vines per hectare. It is grown all over the Levante in both Valencia and Murcia provinces (it is almost the sole ingredient in the sturdy Yecla and Jumilla) as well as in Aragón, Rioja Baja and in Catalonia where it can add real savour to Tempranillo in blends such as Torres Coronas.

Synonyms:
Morastel, Moristel, Monastel, Morrastal, Moraster, Ministral, Alcayata, Valcarcelia.

Interesting, very big and distinctively Spanish.

BOBAL

Bobal is one of Spain's most important red varieties – it is planted on almost as much land as Monastrell – yet the wine it produces is not in the heady, almost soupy Spanish mould. Bobal is almost lean. In Utiel-Requena where it is planted on 95 percent of the 50,000 hectares (125,000 acres) of vineyard it produces wines of only about 11.5 percent alcohol, with a fair degree of acidity. This distinguishes the wines of this region at the western limit of Valencia very clearly from the gargantuan

reds of Jumilla and Yecla to the south. Jan Read recommends the *rosados* from Utiel-Requena's Bobal. It is also grown in Alicante in a supporting role with Garnacha to Monastrell and is encountered in Aragón wines such as Cariñena.

Synonym: Tinto de Requena.

More acid and less alcohol than the Spanish norm.

TINTO DE MADRID

This is a very ordinary variety still widely planted, with Garnacha, in the undistinguished vine country just south of Madrid. The authorities are trying to encourage replacement with Tempranillo or Tinto Fino, especially in Méntrida which has its own denomination of origin for its 32,800 hectares (82,000 acres). The *Annuario del Vino 1984* put plantings of Tinto de Madrid as high as 30,000 hectares (75,000 acres) in total. The wines are very alcoholic and undistinguished.

Synonym: Tinto Basto.

Common and commonplace.

MENCIA

Mencía is probably the finest of the many grape varieties cultivated in Galicia, although sadly it is giving way to the much less subtle Garnacha and the much lower quality Alicante Bouschet. In Valdeorras it is even called Cabernet or Médoc though there is no ampelographical evidence for a relationship between Mencía and the great Bordeaux varieties.

Because winemaking is so unsophisticated in this northwestern corner of Spain, and stretching with other varieties is so commonplace, it is difficult for the outsider knowingly to taste varietal Mencía, but the grapes are said to be delicate, sweet and aromatic, the wine correspondingly delicate, alcoholic and aromatic with fairly light colour (which militates against any connection with Cabernet Sauvignon at least). The vine is also grown in neighbouring León where, with Tempranillo, it lends support to Prieto Picudo.

Very good quality, delicate wines.

PRIETO PICUDO

The twentieth most common grape variety cultivated in Spain is this black-skinned variety of León. It produces wines not unlike those of Tempranillo, with which it is sometimes blended along with Mencía.

GRACIANO

Graciano

It is to the Riojanos' shame that so little Graciano survives in their vineyards today. This delicately scented, subtle grape variety persists as an ingredient in red Rioja more in the literature than in reality. There are just a few hundred hectares of Graciano left, all of them in the oldest vineyards of Rioja Alta.

Undoubtedly the low yield of the Graciano is the major reason why plantings have declined, but the vine also requires some spraying to keep healthy during the late growing season. It is usually picked well into October when the leaves have started turning even redder.

The low yield has also been a factor in France where the "Morrastel" has been fiercely uprooted in those *départements* closest to the Mediterranean Spanish border in which it was once quite popular. By 1979 total plantings in the Languedoc-Roussillon were just 1,600 hectares (4,000 acres), as compared with the 8,900 hectares (22,250 acres) which had been cultivated 10 years earlier. There have been very few plantings in the last 50 years.

Graciano wine is characterized by a very strong aroma and good lasting ability and colour. Its absence in modern Rioja blends helps to explain some of the qualitative difference between the great Riojas of then and now. The vine has also traditionally been cultivated in Navarra.

There are very limited plantings in Australia, though those vines called Morrastel there have been demonstrated to be Mourvèdre.

Synonyms:
Morrastel, Perpignanou Bois Dur, Courouillade, Couthurier (France); Xeres (California).

Aromatic, high quality.

The following vine types are the principal Spanish red varieties which have been officially selected from the many hundreds cultivated there for future encouragement: Brancellao – traditional Galician variety common around Orense; Caiño Tinto – traditional Galician; Garnacha Tintorera (Teinturier) – a red-fleshed teinturier traditional in Alicante, Toledo and Ciudad Real; Listan Negra – black version of Palomino; Manto Negro – Majorcan variety; Pansa Negra – very ordinary northeastern variety; Pansa Valenciana (Vinater, Vinyater) – basic Valencian grape; Sonsón – good quality traditional Galician variety.

Others of the many hundreds of traditional but fading red grape varieties of Spain include the Juan Ibanez of Cariñena, the Moravia of La Mancha and the Sumoll of Alella.

Portugal

Because Portugal's vineyards are in a state of flux, and constitute *terra incognita* to any statistician, the following varieties are not listed in strict order of area planted.

General Good Quality

———— *TOURIGA NACIONAL* ————

In Touriga Nacional we have, the Lord be praised, an aspect of Portuguese viticulture about which there is universal agreement: it is the finest variety for making red port. Murmurs of assent can be heard from as far away as Australia.

The variety grows vigorously but produces very, very little fruit: perhaps 300 grams per vine as opposed to the two kilos more usual in the Alto Douro. It is usefully resistant to fungus diseases, such as the oidium which blights the Douro, which somewhat makes up for its low yield and helps to account for its relatively high level of plantings. A 15-year programme of clonal selection was initiated in 1979 with the aim of increasing average yields by 15 percent and average sugar levels, already high, by 10 percent.

The wine produced by Touriga Nacional is very dark indeed (the berries are notably small) with a powerful aroma suggestive of the most highly perfumed fruit syrup, mulberries perhaps. The scale of the wine is vast but perfectly balanced, with great reserves of fruit to counterbalance the high extract and tannin in youth. This is the variety on which most of the finest vintage ports have been based.

Touriga was described at great length and with much admiration by Villa Maior in 1875, with its subvarieties Touriga Fina, Touriga Foiufeira and, surely the one used for port today, Touriga Macho. He compared Touriga closely with Cabernet.

Touriga Nacional was the most prized ingredient in red Dão. By law it should

Touriga Nacional

make up at least 20 percent of the blend, but the region's total plantings of this noble variety have declined by 95 percent in the last 50 years.

The variety is also much appreciated as a port ingredient in Australia in that dessert-wine enclave on the borders of northeast Victoria and New South Wales.

Synonym: Touriga.

Superb quality, low yield.

———— *ALVARELHAO* ————

Alvarelhão

Alvarelhão's inclusion under this heading is much more contentious. Where Touriga Nacional is full, rich and deep-coloured, Alvarelhão produces wine that is fairly, light in every respect, but sufficiently well-balanced that some think it has great potential as a producer of red table wine in Portugal.

It is grown chiefly in the wild northern Tras-os-Montes and Douro districts, but is also authorized in the Minho and Dão. Despite its Alto Douro origins, it is not highly regarded as a port ingredient.

Villa Maior describes Alvarelhão as one of the best varieties in Portugal, deserving much more vineyard space. He cites in particular the good acid levels of the grapes and resulting delicious wine flavour when picked at the end of August. The grapes are tough skinned but red rather than black in colour.

It is also grown to a limited extent over the Spanish border in Galicia, and a few vines survive in South Africa.

Synonyms: Locaio, Pilongo (Dão).

Fine, not at all hefty.

TINTA MIUDA

This variety, the "small red one", is grown chiefly in the Estremadura, now officially called Oeste, and in the Ribatejo region in the south of the country and often used as an ingredient in ordinary bulk wines. It has shown itself capable of producing varietal wines of real distinction and character, and its reputation and even acreage may increase as a result.

Promising.

TOURIGA FRANCESA

Quite unconnected with the more ordinary Tinta Francisca, this is one of the most respected port varieties, slightly lighter in colour and weight than Touriga Nacional but more productive, very heavily scented and capable of giving very fine perfume to a blend. In these two senses, Touriga Francesa plays Cabernet Franc to Touriga Nacional's Cabernet Sauvignon.

Experiments with rosés indicate that the Touriga Francesa is the better suited, producing a fruity, well-balanced wine.

A "Touriga" has also been planted in California on a small scale, known there as moderately productive with yields of 8 tons per acre. The leaves, furthermore, are described as moderately rough whereas Touriga Nacional's leaves are smooth, so this is probably Touriga Francesa.

Good quality, aromatic.

Mainly Minho

The varieties used for the light, bitingly tart red Vinhos Verdes are, so far, of little more than local interest, as these wines are so rarely exported. Espadeiro, grown all over the Minho, is also known in Galicia, in the north of the Bairrada, in the Tomar district, in Carcavelos, and is an ingredient in the red wines of Setúbal. Others include Azal, Borraçal, Brancelho, the dark Rabo de Ovelha and Vinhão and the less good Labrusco and Samarim.

Mainly Douro

TINTA CAO

Tinta Cão has been growing in the Douro at least since the sixteenth century but total plantings have dwindled almost to

nought because of its very low yield. The wine produced is very fine and complex and there are now moves afoot to revive the variety, involving promising experimental work with bilateral cordon training rather than the Guyot system that is traditional in the Douro. It is also recommended for Dão.

Tinta Cão

There have been some very successful experiments with it at the University of California at Davis where good quality and yields of almost five tons per acre have been achieved.

Top quality, almost extinct.

TINTA BARROCA

Tinta Barroca is still regarded as one of the "new" varieties in the Douro – because it has been there only a century. It can withstand cool conditions well and is usually planted on the north-facing slopes. The vines are very vigorous and healthy, providing a relatively high yield.

The wines are robust and are sometimes used by the port producers as softeners of a blend. Even shrivelled Tinta Barroca grapes make good port.

This variety has been the most successful "port sort" in South African conditions. There are more Tinta Barroca vines than the rest of the Douro varieties put together in South Africa, where earthily

robust deep-tinted varietal table wines are now regularly produced from it as well.

Earthy and robust.

MOURISCO TINTO

Another of the favoured few for quality in the Douro, Mourisco is less deeply tinted than the rest, but keeps its colour well with age. It produces a very well-balanced wine with good, firm tannic structure in youth. It would be much more popular were it not for its very poor flower set, which diminishes its otherwise excellent yield in many years. Mourisco de Semente is less distinguished.

Very firm, though lighter than most.

TINTA AMARELLA

Although this is one of the "top nine" for red port, it is not as highly regarded as the Tourigas, Tinta Barroca, Tinta Cão and Roriz (Tempranillo). It is very productive and its strong suit is colour rather than flavour. This is another port variety recommended to a limited extent for Dão table wines.

Trincadeira is its common synonym in the south of Portugal. Villa Maior suggested that Trincadeira and Periquita were the same variety but today the two are grown side by side, especially in Estremadura, the Alentejo and more ordinary Ribatejo. They are discernibly different. Trincadeira is also one of the lesser Bairrada varieties.

In South Australia, where it is still grown on a small scale and was probably part of James Busby's initial vine import shipment, it is thought that it may be the French variety Amarot of the Landes. It has been commonly confused in Australia with Malbec.

Synonyms:
Trincadeira Preta,
Espadeira (Portugal);
Portugal (Australia).

Medium quality, a bit neutral.

BASTARDO

Although this, one of the world's better travelled vines, is one of the nine varieties recommended for constituting at least 60 percent of red port, it is not one of the most highly regarded. Its chief contribution can be measured in quantity and sugar rather than colour or character. It ripens early, but even higher sugar levels can be achieved by leaving the berries on the vine till the leaves wilt.

It is also allowed up to 80 percent in red Dão and throughout Bairrada, although it is not widely cultivated in this Baga stronghold.

The variety is also grown and respected in Madeira, though some ampelographers reckon Madeira's Bastardo is not the same as that grown on the mainland, and, like the Terrantez with which it is linked there, it is now a rarity.

With such sugar levels, the variety's value is clearly as a dessert wine ingredient and the produce of the few plantings to be found in Australia are used as such. It has been a rather irregular yielder because of rain damage but its high sugar levels may encourage further plantings for Australia's port-style wines. In Australia it has been known, confusingly, as Cabernet Gros and, erroneously, as Touriga. Truel put the record straight in 1976.

Perhaps its most curious incarnation is in the Jura where there are still more than 100 hectares (250 acres) locally called Trousseau. Trousseau provides the iron fist for Poulsard's velvet glove. Provided that it is strictly pruned (it is quite capable of providing 100 hectolitres per hectare), the Trousseau vine can produce wines of great colour and body which are capable of a long life. However it suffers in severe winter weather and is susceptible to anthracnose. It is difficult to understand how this unusual interloper in France made such a long pilgrimage. It is extraordinary to think that the variety can thrive in conditions as dissimilar as those in the Douro and South Australia on the one hand and the Jura on the other.

It is also called Trousseau in California where it has not performed well, but see Trousseau Gris (page 264).

Synonyms:
Trousseau, Triffault, Toussot,
Trousse (Jura);
Trousseau (California);
Cabernet Gros (Australia).

Moderate quality, high sugars.

TINTA FRANCISCA

This is the Douro variety that for long has erroneously been linked with Pinot Noir. The wine produced shares a certain sweet perfume but no ampelographical link can be established. Tinta Francisca, different from Touriga Francesa, is not one of the most respected of the top nine.

Sweet but less concentration than most.

SOUSAO

Sousão or Souzão has travelled far from its native north Portugal where it is authorized for both Minho and Dão. Not particularly highly regarded in the Douro, it is today used to make port in both South Africa and California where it is accorded the respect thought due to such an authentically "porty" vine.

The colour is high but the taste is often very coarse and raisiny with a slight lack of acidity, although it is well thought of in California where there are about 120 hectares (300 acres), mainly in the very hot regions. They have managed yields of nearly 7 tons per acre there.

Productive but coarse.

Other varieties recommended as ingredients in up to 40 percent of the blend of a red port are Cornifesto, Donzelinho (of which there is also a white version), Malvasia, Periquita, Rufete (which is also found in Spain) and Tinta Barca.

The list of other authorized red port varieties is daunting: Alicante Bouschet, Alvarelhão, Aramont (presumably the coarse French Aramon), Carinhana, Carrega Tinto, Casculho, Castela, Concieira, Goncalo Pires, the French Grand Noir, Grangeal, Mondet, Moreto, Mourisco de Semente, Nevoeira, Patorra, Petit Bouschet, Portugues Azul, Preto Martinho, Santarem, São Saul, Sevilhão, Sousão, Tinta Aguiar, Tinta da Bairrada, Tinta Carvalha, Tinta Lameira, Tinta Martins, Tinta Mesquita, Tinta Miúda de Fontes, Tinta Pereira, Tinta Pomar, Tinta Roseira, Tinta Valdosa, Tinta Varejoa and Touriga Brasileira.

Mainly Bairrada

BAGA

The vineyards of Bairrada are dominated by Baga, which accounts for 85 percent of the red-wine output of this red-wine region. It is almost certainly Portugal's most widely planted red grape variety.

It is a very productive but not particularly fine variety. Wine made from the thick-skinned Baga grapes is dense in colour and often very astringent as the custom has been to ferment on the skins, without destalking, for more than a week. The region is going through a period of transition in which vinification methods and perhaps even *encépagement* may be modified to bring Bairrada wines more into line with conventional international consumer tastes, though it would be sad to see this go too far towards that scourge of modern life, the "international" way of doing things.

Baga is also planted in the Minho and Dão, where it is responsible for perhaps half of all red Dão produced today, and in many of the districts surrounding Bairrada that have not officially been classified.

No better than medium quality, often astringent.

Castelhão, Preto de Mortágua, Agua Santa and Trincadeira have largely been squeezed out of the Bairrada vineyards by Baga, as have a number of red Dão varieties.

Mainly Dão

The fruity Jaen, Alfrocheiro Preto and Tinta Pinheira are planted in Bairrada as well as in Dão. Tinta Pinheira is the oldest and was thought at one time to harbour Pinot genes. There are some vines called Tinta Pinheira in California but they are not thought to be the same as the Portuguese original.

Mainly the South

PERIQUITA

Periquita (parakeet) and the rather less common Camarate are both names of vine varieties found particularly in the traditional coastal wine regions, which have been chosen as names for the branded red blends for which Portugal is justly famous. The J.M. da Fonseca Periquita produced at Azeitão, just south of Lisbon is not necessarily made exclusively from that vine variety, however.

Periquita is grown all over southern Portugal, both inland and, especially, on the coast, where it can thrive in sandy soils.

The wine is very full but quite harsh in youth and softens convincingly in bottle. It has real grip and staying power and seems well suited to a wide range of Portuguese conditions. Periquita wine ages well and has the ability to appeal to non-Portuguese palates. In the Algarve it is much diluted with Negra Mole to produce a lighter wine less worthy of ageing.

Synonyms:
Santarem, João de Santarem,
Castelhão Frances.

Fairly good, robust wine.

RAMISCO

This curious variety responsible for one of Portugal's most famous wines, Colares, has all but disappeared from its traditional territory on the Atlantic coast near Lisbon. Housing prices have forced vineyard shrinkage though the vines may not disappear altogether.

The small thick-skinned grapes traditionally gave top-quality wines as demanding of time as top-quality claret. Ramisco is exclusive to the sandy vineyards of Colares and is probably, therefore, the only *vinifera* variety in the world that has never been grafted.

Top-quality wines for ageing.

MURETO DO ALENTEJO

This variety, particularly popular in the Alentejo, is distinct from Mureto do Douro, thought at one time to have sired Portugieser, the important red German variety. It is also grown in the Algarve.

The vine is very productive but its produce is quite highly regarded in Portugal. To outsiders, its wine has a very curious, nutty flavour.

Synonym: Moreto.

Local interest.

Other varieties planted in the south include Tinta Carvalha, Tinta Mole, Sumo Tinto, Tintinha, Alva, Castelhão, Parreira Matias, Preto Martinho, Tinto de Pegoes, Molar, Tinta Caiada, Abundante and in the Algarve Castelhão Nacional, Mortágua, Aragonez (Tempranillo), Monvedro, Crato-Preto (of which there is a white version), Pau-Ferro and Pexem.

Madeira

BLACK SPANISH

Black Spanish or Jacquet, as it is called in Madeira, is the most widely planted direct producer there. It probably means that this particularly red-juiced hybrid is more widely spread than any other variety on an island which wine drinkers most readily associate with white varieties of the classic sort – though Negra Mole, another dark variety, is fast catching up.

Its exact origins are unknown but, like several of the hybrids known at one time on Madeira, it is probably a crossing of *Vitis vinifera* with *Vitis aestivalis*, itself similar to *Vitis labrusca*. It is treasured for its deep colour and fairly high sugar levels, which have helped some growers overcome their dislike of its relatively small juice yield.

As Jacquet, it was already established on Madeira by the end of the last century when it was well placed to surge into pre-eminence in the wake of phylloxera's depredations in the island's vineyards. The hybrid has in its time, and in various places, been used both as rootstock and direct producer. Throughout the twentieth century the robust wines produced by Jacquet have been used as a major ingredient in cheap "cooking" madeira exported in quantity to northern Europe, and they were particularly useful in adding body to thinner base wines.

EEC policy demanded as a precondition of Portuguese entry that not a drop of hybrid wine be included in any madeira exported to their sensitive populace. The produce of the direct producers of the island is now meant to be drunk as local unfortified rustic red. In 1984 only 2 million litres of the 6 million litres of wine produced on Madeira was *not* made from hybrids. Total exports of madeira in 1984 were just under 4 million litres. In his book on Madeira, Noel Cossart describes a 60-year-old straight Jacquet madeira as "a typical old madeira, although rather a heavy peasant wine". Old Jacquet is, typically, rather thin, with a herbal nose.

The hybrid was once grown near Perpignan in France, and it is grown commercially in Texas at the Val Verde winery almost on the Mexican border.

A white version is also known on Madeira.

Synonyms:
Jacquez, Jacquet, Lenoir,
El Paso, Blue French.

Hybrid. Lowish yield,
relatively concentrated.

NEGRA MOLE

The "soft black" grape is by far the most important *vinifera* ingredient in modern madeira. It accounts for just over 60 percent of all *vinifera* plantings on the island.

It is claimed that Tinta Negra Mole was the result of crossing Pinot Noir and Grenache. Neither antecedent flourishes on the island today, though there are some Pinot Noir-like vines around Calheta. The subvarieties Negra, Maroto, Castelhão and the Porto Santo speciality, Tinto Molar, have all been identified, but are not vinified separately.

In addition to registering high must weights, the grapes are small and their skins can impart considerable colour and tannin to the must if left in, though this is customary only for colouring wines and for the richer qualities. However it is vinified, all Negra Mole base wine has at least a reddish tinge in youth, which ages to the gamboge-tinged tawny colour associated by the connoisseur with the wonderfully long-lived fortified wines of Madeira. Much of the madeira on sale today will have been made substantially from Negra Mole, whatever the label says. It would be safe, therefore, to assert that Negra Mole wine is naturally high in acidity, which increases considerably with the altitude of the vineyard.

The Negra Mole vine is officially classified as "good" rather than "noble" in Madeira, although one school of thought argues that it can, uniquely, acquire the character of the traditional noble Madeira varieties Malvasia, Bual, Verdelho and Sercial depending on the altitude at which it is planted.

It is grown more than is realized on the Portuguese mainland, especially in the Algarve where it is recommended as an ingredient in local reds up to 60 percent. It is known in Spain as Negramoll.

Synonyms:
Tinta Negra Mole, Tintiha (Madeira);
Negramoll (Spain).

Workmanlike, good juice yield.

Complexa is a newly developed substitute for Negra Mole with the advantages of the same organoleptic characteristics but at lower altitudes and without such aggressive tannins. The larger berries ripen early and have good resistance to powdery mildew and grey rot.

Cunningham is the second most prolific hybrid on the island, another crossing of *Vitis aestivalis* with *Vitis vinifera* more often known as Canica. It is very much paler than Jacquet and was used as a base for the lighter madeiras such as Rainwater, often called poor man's Verdelho. It is on the wane in Madeira but can still be found in Canada as a basis for pale rosé.

The hybrid Isabella (see page 224) was imported as a rootstock and is used to produce rough, pink, very "foxy" *vinho americano* for local consumption. It is also known as Isabellinha or Bellina.

Tinto da Madeira is on the increase but it is still a very minor variety on Madeira, even though it is now appreciated for its disease resistance. Ironically, there is much more Tinta Madeira grown in California where plantings total 80 hectares (200 acres), almost all in the Central Valley and used for "port". Some Portuguese authorities question whether this is the true Madeira variety.

Triunfo is a productive but not very good permitted variety also grown in very limited quantity in the Algarve and southeast Portugal as a table grape.

Barrete de Padre (padre's hat) is also cultivated but in minuscule quantities. Feral thrives as a table-wine producer in Porto Santo.

Germany

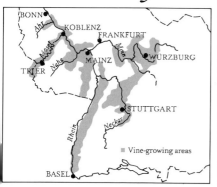

■ Vine-growing areas

—— BLAUER PORTUGIESER ——

Portugieser may be the variety on which Germany so much depends for her oft-ridiculed reds, but it is Austria's most planted red-wine grape, and France has more than 1,000 hectares (2,500 acres) of Portugais Bleu. Put that together with the extent of eastern European vineyards in which Oporto or Portugaljka can be found, and the variety begins to emerge as of considerable importance in one extensive geographical area.

How it got its determinedly Portuguese name is a mystery for, despite ingenious

Blauer Portugieser

attempts to link it with native Portuguese varieties, the vine's origins seem decidedly Austrian – not that the quality of Portugieser wine is such that these origins seem worth disputing. The vine is extraordinarily prolific, even by the standards currently prevailing in Germany, where yields of 160 hectolitres per hectare are by no means unusual, helped partly by the vine's good resistance to *coulure*. The wine is characteristically rather light in colour, slightly flabby and, often because of overzealous chaptalization, curiously sweet.

The exceptionally vigorous vine, susceptible to oidium as well as rot, both buds and ripens early. In Germany it is often picked even before Müller-Thurgau, partly to get it out of the way and partly to avoid the ravages of rot. This means that the wine is even less distinguished than it need be; relatively firm, sturdy Portugieser wine can be made by harvesting closer to the Silvaner epoch when Oechsle readings may climb towards a respectable 80° rather than the more usual 55° or 60°. Portugieser is material for Tafelwein or ordinary Qualitätswein at best.

A good half of Germany's Portugieser – 3,200 hectares (8,000 acres) in 1984 as compared with 4,300 hectares (10,750 acres) of the red burgundy grape – is planted in Rheinpfalz where it is most popular as the off-dry pink Weissherbst. It also helps to bolster up the rather more noble Spätburgunder in the Ahr. One wonders whether the variety would be so popular in a country which found it easier to produce red wine.

The same could be said of Austria where there were 3,000 hectares (7,500 acres) of Portugieser in 1983, producing about 5 percent of the country's wine, for strictly local delectation. Almost all of the vines are in Lower Austria, especially in

the Vöslau area just south of Vienna where 40 percent of the vineyard is planted with this dreary variety. *Offene Weine* material through and through.

Across the border in Hungary it is presumably this variety which imaginatively pops up as Oporto, a minor ingredient in Bulls Blood among other backstage roles. In Yugoslavia it is grown chiefly in northern Croatia and can produce a relatively toothsome *nouveau*.

Although they were once much more widespread, French plantings of Portugais Bleu are practically limited to the Tarn *département*, where the total actually increased between 1968 and 1979. It is one of those allowed in Gaillac Rouge but does little for its quality.

There are grey, green, red and white variations, but only the Grüner has any currency at all in Austria.

Synonyms:
Portugieser; Portugais Bleu (France); Oporto (Hungary); Portugaljka, Portugizac Crni (Yugoslavia).

Very ordinary.

New Crossings

—— DORNFELDER ——

This is perhaps Germany's most promising "new" red crossing, bred by August Herold in 1956 at Weinsberg and now planted on more than 400 hectares (1,000 acres), chiefly in the Rheinpfalz and Rheinhessen. Its forebears include just about every established German red-wine grape variety for it is the rather bovine-sounding crossing of Helfensteiner (Frühburgunder × Trollinger) and Heroldrebe (Portugieser × Limberger). The founding father of the Württemberg viticultural school in the mid-nineteenth century lives on in the grape's name.

Most obligingly, the crossing is in many ways better than the sum of the parts. It does not rot easily (as Portugieser does), is naturally healthy and very easy to grow (as most Pinot relatives are not), its stalks are much more robust than Trollinger, and it is considerably easier to ripen than Limberger. The wine produced has a healthy, relatively deep colour, interestingly flowery/fruity nose and better Oechsle levels than Portugieser and Trollinger, with a good balance of acidity in most vintages. The wines have also shown some evidence of being able to withstand cellaring. The vine has the additional advantage of a high yield: often 120 hectolitres per hectare.

Dornfelder demonstrates most eloquently the advantages of the German approach to plant breeding.

Very promising.

HEROLDREBE

Herold's eponymous crossing of Portugieser × Limberger ripens relatively late and is therefore suitable only for more southerly wine districts. The resulting wines tend to have more character than those made from Portugieser – not a difficult achievement – and their earthy flavour is particularly treasured in the Württemberg area. Viticulturally, Heroldrebe's great advantage is the reliability of its yields, usually around 140 hectolitres per hectare.

There were 245 hectares (600 acres) of the variety in 1983, more than half of them in Rheinpfalz.

Low-key, rustic wines. Inconveniently late-ripening vines.

HELFENSTEINER

This crossing may be remembered more as a necessary intermediate step towards Dornfelder than as a very useful plant in its own right. Herold bred it from Frühburgunder and Trollinger and it has remained a distinctly local speciality. There were 61 hectares (152 acres) of it planted in Germany in 1983, of which 60 hectares (150 acres) were in Württemberg. Its chief advantage is that it ripens early, two to three weeks before Trollinger, but the yield is very unreliable because of its susceptibility to *coulure*. The wine is marginally better than that of Portugieser.

Limited use.

DOMINA

Portugieser and Spätburgunder were obvious candidates for a crossing, and this result, from the Geilweilerhof viticultural research station in Rheinpfalz, is eminently respectable. So far only 25 hectares (62 acres) have been planted with Domina, 10 (25 acres) of them in the Ahr and 7 (17 acres) in Franken.

The crossing yields as generously as Portugieser, ripens slightly after it but is noticeably less fussy than Pinot Noir about where it is planted, which makes it of real potential in Germany's more northerly red-wine districts. The resulting wine is also noticeably better than that of Portugieser, having a deeper colour and on average 10 more degrees Oechsle and 2 more degrees of acidity. Most of the wine produced easily reaches QmP status, though it should be said that this is at best a vine of expediency because, where it can be grown, Spätburgunder probably produces a better wine.

Very useful for difficult sites.

ROTBERGER

This Geisenheim crossing of Trollinger × Riesling has proved very useful indeed. Some of the most promising very recent crossings developed at Geisenheim for white wines which can outperform Riesling have, perhaps surprisingly, been those of Rotberger × Reichensteiner. Some of these have been planted on an experimental basis at Lamberhurst Priory in southeast England. Rotberger itself produces red and especially rosé wines of real character not unlike that of Trollinger, but the vines ripen earlier and are hardier. Rotberger is delightfully easy to grow. There were only 20 hectares (50 acres) planted in 1983, mainly in Baden, Württemberg and the Ahr regions.

Very good wines and vines.

Other Red Crossings

Kolor was bred from Spätburgunder and the Teinturier Färbertraube in 1938 and is still grown (just) as a colour-intensifying vine. There are still almost 20 hectares (50 acres) of Deckrot, the crossing of Pinot Gris and the Teinturier Färbertraube bred at Freiburg in 1938. Its function is, like Kolor, to add colour to either Portugieser or Pinot Noir. Carmina, a Portugieser × Spätburgunder crossing, has not found commercial favour, being markedly high in acid. Sulmer is a Limberger × Schwarzer Elbling (possibly a Trollinger mutation). Origins of the usefully deep-coloured Dunkelfelder are not known.

Declining Old Faithfuls

Blauer Frühburgunder (also variously known as Augusttraube, Jacobstraube, Magdalentraube, Madeleine Noir) is an old mutation of Pinot Noir and is very similar to it, although it ripens even earlier and produces less distinguished wine on the whole. A little Samtrot ("red velvet") is still cultivated in Germany, but this Meunier mutation is dogged by its very low yield. The Blauer Arbst form of Pinot Noir is almost extinct, as are the Blauer Affentaler and Bodenseeburgunder.

Switzerland

A dark version of the very traditional Valais variety Humagne, Humagne Rouge, produces a drink described by Hugh Johnson as "simple, pleasantly tannic and appetizing country wine".

Cornalin is another old Swiss variety known also in the Aosta valley.

Austria

BLAUFRÄNKISCH

This middle European variety is occasionally and mistakenly thought to be Gamay. Although both have very similar leaves, Blaufränkisch is a distinct variety, most commonly associated with Austria. With more than 2,500 hectares (6,250 acres) it is Austria's second most planted red variety and is considerably more important there than in any other wine region. Despite its name, it is extremely unlikely to have originated in Franken, where the climate is too cool for the variety to flourish.

Blaufränkisch buds very early but ripens late and therefore needs a relatively warm climate. Its wood is winter hardy, but spring frosts can harm fruit, so sheltered sites are needed. It adapts well to different soil types and its growth is so vigorous that it is especially suitable for wide spacing. It is not particularly susceptible to disease so a moderately good quantity, about 75 hectolitres per hectare, of healthy grapes can be harvested.

The wine is characterized by colour that is deep by Austrian and German standards (if not by those of Bordeaux or the Rhône) and by discernible levels of tannin. Although locally put between the qualitatively distinguished Pinot Noir and quantitatively distinguished Portugieser in terms of the calibre of the wine produced, Blaufränkisch wine has a style of its own. The often sweet earthiness is counterbalanced by a relatively high level of acidity (fuelling the argument that the variety is Gamay). The Austrians consider this a variety worth maturing, but many such examples seem slightly oxidized to a non-Austrian palate. Of the young wine, German-speakers can use their favourite complimentary tasting note *rassig*.

The warmish climate of Burgenland provides an Austrian home for Blaufränkisch, with most of the vines planted on the warm shores of Neusiedler See. This area even produces the awesome sounding Blaufränkischer Bismarkwein, so named in memory of the Chancellor's partiality for Limberger from Pöttelsdorf. Those with an eye on posterity should clearly publicize their wine preferences.

Most of Germany is too cool for this late-ripening variety, but there are about 470 hectares (1,175 acres) planted with what they call Blauer Limberger (never Blaufränkisch). They are almost exclusively in Württemberg where red (and pink) oddities are tolerated, even relished.

On the other side of the Hungarian border from Burgenland, where it is known as Kékfrankos, the variety produces a rather soupier red than would find favour with Beaujolais enthusiasts. But the Sopron district enjoys the reputation of producing the best of this wine, chronicled by Napoleon, no less. (This is clearly the wine of expansionism.) Köröshegyi Kékfrankos is regarded as Hungary's answer to vintage port. On the other side of the country in the vineyards of Eger, Kékfrankos provides an important, if slightly anaemic, ingredient in the export blend of Bulls Blood. The variety is also grown in parts of Yugoslavia.

Synonyms:
Blauer Limberger, Lemberger (Germany); Gamé (Bulgaria); Schwarze Frankische (Austria); Crna Moravka (Yugoslavia); Kékfrankos (Hungary).

Undistinguished, fairly tart wine.

ZWEIGELT BLAU

After Portugieser and Blaufränkisch, the relatively new Zweigelt is already Austria's third red-grape variety, with 2,400 hectares (6,000 acres). It is a Blaufränkisch × St-Laurent crossing by Dr Zweigelt of the Klosterneuburg research station.

It ripens early and has good disease resistance. The wines it produces are more like St-Laurent than its other parent, but are designed to appeal to the Austrian palate. Its yield is designed to appeal to the Austrian grower. It is popular both in Lower Austria (especially Krems, Klosterneuburg, Vöslau) and to a lesser extent in Burgenland.

Synonyms:
Rotburger, Blauer Zweigelt, Zweigeltrebe.

Rather hollow wine.

ST-LAURENT

Although it was first identified as a variety grown in land long since abandoned by the vine growers of Alsace, St-Laurent is today almost exclusively grown in Austria – to good effect, it would seem, to judge by some of the smoothest, deep-coloured, velvety versions produced in the vineyards of the Vöslau district of Lower Austria.

It is commonly thought to be a mutation of Pinot Noir, but Galet refutes this, and the leaves are certainly quite distinct. St-Laurent would have been cultivated in its Haut-Rhin base with Pinot Noir and indeed its deep colour led authorities then to counsel blending Pinot Noir with St-Laurent. The variety ripens a good 10 days earlier than Pinot Noir (although later than the precocious Portugieser) and is considerably less fussy about site than the minx from Burgundy. St-Laurent's grape skins are much tougher than those of Pinot Noir and rarely suffer attack from botrytis.

St-Laurent's main viticultural disadvantage is its fairly early budding which leaves it prey to spring frosts. This is doubtless what helped its disappearance from the vineyards of Alsace, but it rarely causes problems in Austria where yields are around 75 hectolitres per hectare.

There are still about 15 hectares (37 acres) of St-Laurent in Germany, mainly in the south, but no current plantings are recorded in France and the variety is no longer officially sanctioned there.

Synonyms:
Pinot St-Laurent, Sankt Lorenztraube.

Soft, sweet and scented.

BLAUER WILDBACHER

There are scarcely more than 140 hectares (350 acres) of Blauer Wildbacher in Austria, almost all in Weststeiermark.

The wines, characterized by relatively high acid and an almost overpowering spicy aroma, almost all qualify as Schilcher wine, a Styrian variant on the pink Württemberg theme of Schillerwein. They vary in colour from palest pink to pale ruby and are usually drunk young.

The variety ripens late and is susceptible to mildew. Subvarieties are Spätblauer and Schlehenbeeriger Wildbacher.

A local rosé speciality.

Blauburger, like the Zweigelt, is a Klosterneuburg crossing, of Portugieser × Blaufränkisch.

Hungary

KADARKA

Kadarka

This variety, Hungary's most widely planted, has an intriguing history. It is thought to have been first identified near the Albanian town of Skadarsko on the sea-like lake that divides Albania from Yugoslavia; its name certainly suggests this. Yugoslavian settlers probably brought it to Hungary during the Turkish occupation and, since it was more obliging than any other red variety then planted there, it caught on. Producing a wine of formidable character, it is now grown all over eastern Europe.

It covers 17 percent of total Hungarian vineyard land, and is particularly popular on the plains. It is surprising that, in this land which can boast a dazzling range of proudly Hungarian white grape varieties, Kadarka so dominates the vinescape. Kadarka is grown in every Hungarian wine region apart from Sopron which is, viticulturally at least, Austria anyway.

One of Kadarka's great advantages is

that it has very good disease resistance. As a vine it also reaches the most productive part of its life early and both its bearing period and effective lifespan are long. The vine is quite productive and, although its flowers are not particularly easy to fertilize, it regenerates quickly.

Must weights at ripening are usually medium, but the berries have occasionally been left on beyond conventional harvest time in good years to produce very rare and much-prized red Aszú wines from shrivelled berries. Not really so noble, Nemes Kadar (meaning "noble Kadarka") can be medium sweet. Csongrad, Szekszárd and Villány are officially recognized as producing the best dry table wines from the grape.

Kadarka has noticeably more guts than the acidic Kékfrankos (Blaufränkisch) which has taken its place in Bulls Blood and is gaining ground in parts of Hungary. Kadarka also has a fair amount of tannin. In the best examples it has its own spicy fieriness but is rarely very deep in colour. Kadarka Vörös is the wine at its most concentrated, but the grape can turn out very charming pink wines, too.

The variety is still grown to a limited extent in the Burgenland region of Austria on the Hungarian border, where late-harvest versions have been a speciality. Some good Kadarka is still produced in Yugoslavia, including fairly sweet versions in Macedonia. It is also made into basic table wine, often known as Cadarca in the Banat region of Romania along the Hungarian border; and who knows, perhaps the odd Kadarka vine survives behind the near-impenetrable Albanian frontier.

In Bulgaria it is known as Gamza and covers 2,000 hectares (5,000 acres), making it the third most popular "eastern European" red variety, although way behind Cabernet Sauvignon and Merlot. The wine it produces in Bulgaria is well-scented, meaty and it can age well.
Synonyms:
Kadarkska, Skadarska (Yugoslavia); Gamza (Bulgaria); Cadarca (Romania).

Good chunky stuff with positive character.

Other red varieties, more Magyar than anything else, include the very ancient and confusingly named Oporto, which may be Portugieser of Germany, and a colouring grape Titian that is blended with the relatively pale Kékfrankos.

Yugoslavia

PLAVAC MALI

Plavać Mali ("small") is probably the most highly regarded red-wine grape variety native to Yugoslavia. The wines produced are high in alcohol, extract and, unusually, tannin which gives them a life expectancy rare in Yugoslav cellars. Many have a suggestion of sweetness on the nose but finish dry and firm.

Plavać is grown all down the Dalmatian coast and on many an island; it thrives in sandy soil. The wines in which Plavać is the major, often sole, ingredient have names that almost seem designed to confuse the foreigner: Pelješac, Dingač, Postup, Marjan and Faros from the island of Hvar are robust reds which may be kept for up to a decade.

Plavać also makes attractive rosés, notably those labelled Opol.

Good wines for keeping.

PROKUPAC

Prokupac vies with Plavać and may still be Yugoslavia's single most planted grape variety. Prokupac Crni ("black") used to account for by far the majority of vines in Serbia south of the Smederevka white-wine belt. Much of its produce was drunk as a dark rosé Ružica, often with soda. It was also important in Kosovo. Classic European varieties have been encroaching on its territory, but it is still the most likely ingredient in any blended sturdy red from middle to southern Yugoslavia.

Subtlety is not the strong point of the variety, but it does not lack strength. It can produce very dark red wines, but is at its most appetizing as Ružica.
Synonym: Rskavac.

Rustic.

VRANAC

Vranac is the Plavać of Montenegro and Macedonia producing, hardly surprisingly in their climate, alcoholic, dry wines that are usually well-balanced and have an almost Italianate twist of bitterness on the finish. Vranac is very deep coloured but does not usually age as well as Plavać.

The variety is quite often blended with the other good quality Macedonian variety Kratosija or the region's less exciting Stanusina and Ohridsko Crno.

Good, dark robust wine.

Blatina is the top quality variety of Herzegovina; Trnjak is planted around Mostar. Kadarun and Plavka are grown in the tiny republic of Crna Gora. Babic and the rather more ordinary Lasina (Lelekuša) and Plavina (Brajdica) are Dalmatian specialities. Zametovka (otherwise known as Zametna Crnina, Kavzina and Blauer Kölner) is one of the few truly Yugoslav varieties that is given vineyard space in Slovenia; it is usually used to produce the light rosé Cvićek. Other varieties still grown in Yugoslavia are the quite highly regarded Tikvesko Crno and Arhivisko as well as Koncina, the Zacinka of Timok and the Plovdina of Macedonia. Yugoslavia deserves greater attention from the ampelographers.

Romania

FETEASCA NEAGRA

Romania's best-known native red grape variety makes wines for early consumption, often pink and sometimes apparently made by the carbonic maceration method.

The vines are grown all over the country but particularly in the Odobesti region on the eastern slopes of the Carpathians.
Synonym: Schwarze Mädchentraube.

Light, fruity but inconsequential wines.

BABEASCA NEAGRA

Odobesti is also the region producing the best wines from this traditional Romanian grape variety. They luxuriate in the reputation of being well balanced, full of flavour and savoury. A connection between Băbească and Dalmatia's Babic would not be far-fetched.

Good, mouth-filling stuff.

Negru Virtos is an old Romanian variety still found in some vineyards in the Dragasani region.

Bulgaria

PAMID

Pamid is Bulgaria's most planted native red grape variety, although its 9,000 hectares (22,500 acres) now represent just half of total Cabernet Sauvignon plantings and even Merlot beats it into third place.

This is the Bulgarians' answer to Plovdina of Serbia. It produces large quantities of rather thin, early-maturing red wine, with little acid or tannin but often with a touch of sweetness.

Low quality, basic soft table wine.

SHIROKA MELNISHKA LOSA

Bulgaria has 2,500 hectares (6,250 acres) of this cumbersomely named native variety. Its full name means "broad vine of Melnik", but it is often called simply by the name of this town in the southwest of the country almost on the Greek border.

The wine has a very distinctive flavour that is vaguely reminiscent of some of Greece's better reds. Melnik wine is high in tannin, colour, alcohol, extract and flavour when young and handsomely repays ageing. After five years or so its edges have been softened and it resembles nothing so much as a Châteauneuf-du-Pape of the old school, with a definite suggestion of middle-aged oak on the nose and a hint of sweetness on finish, but there is power and balance throughout. Most of Bulgaria's Melnik is given the oak ageing it deserves.

The berries are very blue for Bulgarian varieties, thick-skinned and relatively small, but yield almost as well as Merlot. *Synonym:* Melnik.

Very good, concentrated.

MAVRUD

Mavrud is Asenovgrad's answer to Melnik: a fairly productive robust local variety whose wines repay ageing in wood and bottle. For many Bulgarians, Mavrud is the finest wine the country can produce.

It tends to oxidize fairly easily and the wines take on a tawny tinge relatively young. The wines epitomize plumminess, but can be a bit short on aroma and have less acid and tannin than those of Melnik. Mavrud wines in general lose their bite rather earlier than Melnik, and smooth out to a rather dull and dusty middle age.

The variety is grown exclusively in the south, around Haskovo, Pazardjik and, most reputed of all, Asenovgrad.

Synonym: Marvud.

Good sturdy stuff, highly regarded.

> Other reds traditional to Bulgaria include Senzo and Saperavi.

USSR

SAPERAVI

Saperavi means "dyer" and the juice of these grapes is light pink: this is the Soviet equivalent of a Teinturier grape. It does seem, however, to have qualities unknown in the commonplace colour-enhancing varieties of western Europe, and it is widely cultivated within the USSR and, more recently, Bulgaria.

Although it brings colour to any blend, Saperavi is known more for its ability to age, up to 50 years in bottle, and is said to be at its distinctively plummy best for an impressively long span between four and 30 years. A late ripener, it achieves high sugar levels very easily but the wine is usually well balanced and has the ability to develop extra nuances with age.

One of its more famous incarnations is the concentrated Yuzhnoberezhny red table wine made on the Crimean coast, with potential alcohol as high as 28 percent. In higher Crimean vineyards and in central Moldavia the acidity can be too pronounced and the wine used only for blending, although Purkara in Moldavia makes a good, sufficiently ripe Saperavi table wine. It is also planted in Azerbaijan, Uzbekistan, Dagestan, Stavropol and Krasnodar where it may be used for anything from sparkling wine to very sweet fortified wines, a speciality of Uzbekistan where the pulp may be heat-treated.

The variety has also been successful in Bulgaria, especially in blends with Gamza (Kadarka of Hungary). The Saperavi manages to achieve high sugars and acids at ripeness, as well as developing its characteristic plummy aroma. Very young Saperavi can be rather coarse and harsh, but a Gamza blend will eventually soften and take on mature Saperavi taste characteristics. A 10 percent dose of Saperavi is recommended to boost colour and alcohol, 20 to 40 percent for long ageing with eventual Saperavi flavour.

Demands ageing.

KHINDOGNY

This is the most important variety in the Nagorno-Karabakh district of the Azerbaijan Republic in the deep south, covering 70 percent of the vineyard there, and it is widely planted elsewhere.

The vine is medium ripening and achieves medium sugar levels, but yields notably more than the other thick-skinned red variety, Cabernet Sauvignon. The chief characteristics of Khindogny are its colour and tannin levels, producing deep, sometimes astringent wines that are often very useful, full-bodied ingredients in blends for table and fortified wines. In the Crimea they are also used, surprisingly, in sparkling-wine production. Up to 25 percent of Khindogny leaves the *cuvée* sufficiently sprightly to sparkle prettily.

Winemakers have learnt to be wary of Khindogny fermentations in cooler autumns; they can be difficult to complete. Provided the must is not subjected to heat treatment, the variety produces wines that are capable of keeping their deep colour for many years, and they are said to soften eventually.

Somewhat harsh.

BLACK TSIMLYANSKY

This is the main variety in the Don region, famous for Tsimlyanskoe sparkling red, made with the help of the local Plechistik. Although it can reach high sugar levels, Tsimlyansky is better blended because it can easily be flabby, and varietal examples oxidize easily. In the middle ripening period, acid levels fall fast though potential alcohol levels can be 25 percent or more. High acid varieties such as Saperavi, Maysky and Cherny are obvious blending partners for Tsimlyansky.

This is perhaps the Soviet Union's most famous red sparkling-wine variety, which gives it real status in a country so devoted to sparkling wine of all hues. The Crimean sparkling Sevastopolskoye has now earned a reputation almost as high as the Don region's original.

The wine produced by the variety has some tannin and fairly good colour in youth, with a distinctive bitter cherry aroma. Sweet red table wines are made from Black Tsimlyansky in the Don region but they mature rapidly and are probably kept too long in barrel.

Synonym: Tsimlyansky Cherny.

Chiefly for sparkling wines, ages fast.

MAGARATCH RUBY

Just as the University of California at Davis came up with Ruby Cabernet by crossing Carignan with Cabernet Sauvignon, so the Institute Magaratch has produced Magaratch Ruby by crossing Cabernet Sauvignon with the interesting native Saperavi. The Soviet attempt to combine the quality and subtlety of Cabernet Sauvignon with a deeper coloured, higher yielding variety seems to have been rather more successful, however. The crossing has performed well in the Crimea and is recommended for extensive further planting. Even in the higher vineyards of the Crimean steppe, it can produce wines with good colour when Cabernet Sauvignon starts to look and taste rather weedily like Cabernet Franc. Sugar and acid levels are good, and the Cabernet genes fill in the flavour hollow.

The resulting wines have apparently been useful for both the firm-structured red table wines the Russians call "Cahorstype" and for sweet dessert wines. The stability of the pigments give this variety useful resistance to heat treatment.
Synonyms:
Rubinovy Magaracha, Crossing 56.

Very promising crossing.

MATRASSA

This is a speciality of the hot Azerbaijan Republic and is used extensively to produce sweet and very sweet wines, both natural and fortified. It is traditionally associated with the Matrassa settlement in the Shemakhinsk region.

The vines ripen medium late and the grapes achieve high sugar levels. The wines are deep coloured although actual flavour is not very pronounced.
Synonyms: Shirey, Kara Shirey.

Useful for dessert wines.

ISABELLA

The USSR's most widely planted hybrid is known also in Switzerland, Madeira, New York State, Brazil, Uruguay and at one time in France. It was one of the first known hybrids and is the result of a natural hybridization between *Vitis labrusca* and *Vitis vinifera*.

In the Soviet Union it is grown near the coast in Georgia, in Azerbaijan, Dagestan, Krasnodar and in Moldavia. The wine suffers from a very pronounced *labrusca* flavour, like an artificial strawberry drink.

The grape must is inconveniently slimy and difficult to ferment, though the addition of pectolytic enzymes can help the process along. This also has the effect of reducing the yield of finished wine, even though Isabella produces a very high yield of grapes. It seems unlikely that the variety will continue to be so popular. It is no longer very favoured in New York State.

In the USSR it is used to produce grape juice and pink wine. The red Isabella wine ages very fast.
Synonyms: Americano (Switzerland); Isabellinha, Bellina (Madeira).

Hybrid, very "foxy".

MAGARATCH BASTARDO

A crossing of the Portuguese Bastardo and Saperavi, it combines some of the concentrated flavour of the port variety with the high acid, colour and yield of Saperavi.

It ripens medium late and is not very widely planted as yet.

Medium quality.

Greece

XYNOMAVRO

Greece's most respected indigenous vine variety is also, happily, fairly widely planted and covers a high proportion of vineyard in the northern half of the country.

"Xyno" means acid, "mavro" black, and Xynomavro does indeed produce wines as black as pitch when young, with a remarkably high level of total acids for the latitude at which it is grown. Naoussa is perhaps the best-known of these, made from vines grown on the southern slopes of Mount Velia sheltered from the cold winds which can make the Macedonian climate so harsh. The best Naoussa is well capable of demonstrating the class of this variety. If the tannic concentration of young Naoussa brings to mind the Grange Hermitage of South Australia, then Amynteon is its St Henri, a rather leaner, faster-maturing version produced in vineyards as high as 650 metres.

Xynomavro is distinguished among Greek red varieties in its deep and stable pigmentation and in its capacity to age into relatively complex maturity. It would be interesting to see more examples from better equipped cellars. It seems rather perverse, therefore, that the Greeks treasure it also as a base for sparkling wine,

rather like choosing to produce a sparkling Châteauneuf-du-Pape, though presumably the acid comes in very useful.

Xynomavro is blended with Krassato and Stayroto in Rapsani, the curious tawny wine produced on the slopes of Mount Olympus. It also constitutes up to 80 percent of the blend, with Negoska, for the local wine Goumenissa.

Good, concentrated wine.

AGIORGITIKO

The St-George vine is grown almost exclusively in Greece's largest wine region, the valley of Nemea in the Peloponnese, at such varying altitudes that these determine the quality and style of the wine.

Below 300 metres the vines mature relatively fast, acid levels plummet, and the grapes are used to produce a sweet red dessert wine. Between 300 and 650 metres the Agiorgitiko vineyards are at their most extensive and their produce is known simply as Nemea, as opposed to the much rarer High Nemea made from vines grown even higher up the mountains – even then they can suffer a lack of acidity. Standard Nemea is much as one might expect from its nickname, "blood of Hercules".

Good quality, can be slightly flabby.

MANDILARIA

This variety is widely planted on the islands, including Crete. Varietal Mandilaria is not one of the world's greatest wine treats, but the variety makes excellent *mistelle* for local vermouth production.

It is characterized by its deep and stable colour but is distinctly lacking in alcohol. It makes a good balancing blend, therefore, with local, even more traditional varieties such as the red Monemvasia and the characterful Kotsifali grown around Heraklion for Cretan reds like Peza and Archanes.

Light in body, dark in colour.

LIATIKO

Amazing as it may seem to vine growers further from the equator, Liatiko takes its name from the Greek for July, Iouliatiko, because that is when it ripens.

Liatiko is another Cretan grape variety, seen by many as a direct descendant of the great Malvasia. It is grown in the Sitia vineyards in the extreme eastern corner of the island. The vines, planted up to 600 metres, produce a tiny yield of wine that is extremely high in natural alcohol – up to 16 percent. This is used for the Sitia and Daphnes aperitif wines of the island and can develop real interest with age.

Ancient, strong and curious.

ROMEIKO

Romeiko is the vine of the west of Crete and dominates the Khania vineyards. It produces very old-fashioned heavy reds, sometimes blended with the local very ordinary Tsardana. Romeiko produces its most elegant dry reds on dry, pebbly soils.

Respected locally.

LIMNIO

This is the "Limnia" mentioned by Aristotle and is a speciality of Limnos. Unknown outside Greece, it is also cultivated in Chaldiki and on Mount Athos.

MAVRODAPHNE

Mavrodaphne

Like Portugal's Loureiro, the name of this variety incorporates laurel, black laurel this time. The old-fashioned, full-bodied wine made from Mavrodaphne certainly has a very individual aroma, which is almost always allowed to develop into an even more arresting bouquet.

The lightly fortified red wines that Mavrodaphne produces today need several years to soften into an approachable dessert wine. The most common softening technique is reminiscent of traditional sherry-making, barrels of wine being left outside for a bake in the sunshine during the first summer.

Mavrodaphne territory is concentrated to the southwest of Patras in the northern Peloponnese, but it also grows on the island of Cephalonia.

At the beginning of this century, Viala postulated a close connection between the Mavrodaphne of Greece and the Mavrud of Bulgaria, though of course Mavrud could merely be a corruption of any grape known in Greece as Mavro.

Aromatic, good for liqueur wine.

VERTZAMI

Vertzami is grown on the Ionian islands, sometimes at altitudes so high that some years it refuses to ripen before the cold winds of winter arrive. In warmer autumns it can produce attractive light rosés with 8 or 9 percent alcohol. Grown on vineyards up to 500 metres, however, the wine can be high in extract, reach 13.5 percent natural alcohol, and have a deeper colour than any other *Vitis vinifera* varietal.

Very, very deep in colour.

> Messenikola is grown in Thessaly, mainly as a table grape. Amorgiano is a speciality of Rhodes.

Cyprus

Perhaps more than any other, Cyprus is an island viticulturally. Having escaped the ravages of phylloxera, vine growers have been unwilling to tempt fate by importing vine cuttings. A consignment of specimens imported from Montpellier as early as 1959 were largely ignored until recent experimentation by The Model Winery at Limassol. The industry is still concentrated on just two native grape varieties, Mavron and the white Xynisteri, supplemented by a small quantity of indigenous Muscat of Alexandria.

MAVRON

Since it covers something like 80 percent of Cyprus's vineyard, or about 40,000 hectares (100,000 acres), Mavron ("mavro" is simply Greek for black) has to be versatile. It produces virtually all of the island's sturdy dry and off-dry reds, as well as all the less rarefied Commandaria dessert wine from grapes allowed to dry in the sun for a week or so.

As any visitor to the island or occasional drinker of the brand Othello will know, Mavron produces a very Mediterranean sort of red wine with lots of tannin and alcohol but no great finesse. Early picked, the grapes can produce fruity well-balanced wines, but grape prices tied to sugar levels (more sugar equals more cash) ensure that the average wine is too low in acids to be really appetizing, and average yields are so high – around 100 hectolitres per hectare – that it is difficult to get sufficient colour into the must. However, supposedly ancient vintages of the island's rather derivatively named blends suggest that Mavron is capable of ageing into robust middle age, and that with lower yields and earlier picking it could produce much better wine.

Sturdy but overproduced.

OPTHALMO

Small quantities of this ancient variety can also be found in the island's vineyards, but the wine it produces is considerably lighter and more acidic than Mavron. Blended with Mavron, it can add complexity to a Commandaria.

Light seasoning.

MARATHEFTICON

This superior local variety is found interspersed with Mavron vines in many older vineyards. It produces wines with real concentration. Aroma, tannin, colour and structure are all positively Cabernet-like.

Very promising and perhaps should be more planted.

Turkey

Turkey presents the wine drinker with an exotic cocktail of local varieties, and the viticultural student with an impenetrable enigma. Some of the most reputable red varieties are Papazharasi of Kirklareli, Sergikarasi and Okuz Gozu of southeastern Anatolia and Kalecik and Cubuk grown around Ankara. Others include the Karalahna, Kuntra, Adakarasi and Karasakiz grown in Thrace and Marmara, the Horozkarasi and Bogazkere of southeastern Anatolia and a grape variety that seems all too appropriate to this section, Dimrit of central Anatolia.

Japan
—— CAMPBELL'S EARLY ——

With the other American hybrid Delaware, this accounts for more than 50 percent of the total Japanese vineyard. It is also grown in Washington State but is not highly regarded there.
Synonym: Island Belle.

Ordinary.

China
—— BEICHUN ——

Low winter temperatures are the most severe problem in China's northern vineyards. The native wild *Vitis amurensis* is well able to cope and crossings with *vinifera* have therefore been attempted by Chinese plant breeders (and by Professor Helmut Becker in Germany).

Beichun is one of the more successful of these hybrids, developed by Peking viticulturists. It combines cold-hardiness with good resistance to the fungus diseases that plague *vinifera* vines in the humid southern vineyards of China and is, therefore, widely planted. In the winery its uses are either for dessert wines or for adding extra colour to blended dry wines. Productivity is very high, almost 10 tons per acre or over 100 hectolitres per hectare.

Very versatile.

California

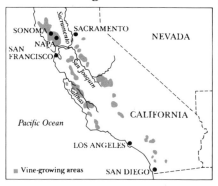

—— RUBY CABERNET ——

Ruby Cabernet is the oldest and, in terms of acreage planted, the most successful of the crossings that emerged from Davis in the middle years of this century. Dr H. P. Olmo's aim in crossing Carignan with Cabernet Sauvignon in 1948 to combine the productivity of the former with the distinction of the latter is not difficult to comprehend. What is extraordinary, however, is that almost exactly the same scheme was being hatched at the Russian equivalent of Davis, the Institut Magaratch. Their crossing of Cabernet Sauvignon with the native Saperavi is called Magaratch Ruby.

Ruby Cabernet

Unfortunately, Ruby Cabernet is a bit more Ruby than Cabernet. The better examples have good young Cabernet Sauvignon aroma and good Carignan colour which is both deep and stable, but start to disappoint on the palate. The wines tend to lack body and structure and are simply lightly tart and vaguely vinous. Although they can pick up some flattering extra flavour from a short stay in oak, they are not worth ageing.

There were more than 4,800 hectares (12,000 acres) of Ruby Cabernet in California in 1983, the vast majority of them in the Central Valley, which may in part explain why the flavour has apparently been baked out of so many varietal examples. The variety is used both to improve

the quality of the Central Valley's most basic blends and in varietals. The Cabernet name has a certain magic after all.

The crossing usually yields between 6 and 9 tons per acre although on sandy and very hard soils vigour has been too low to scale such heights. Both leaf roll and fan-leaf virus also took their toll in the early days but the propagating wood is heat-treated now. Ruby Cabernet has, unfortunately, inherited Carignan's susceptibility to powdery mildew. The vine buds and ripens late and is relatively difficult to pick by hand or machine because of its tough stems. It has been planted in Australia.

Not a stunner.

—— RUBIRED ——

Rubired is a hybrid, Alicante Ganzin × Tinta Cão, offered up for those in need of wine colour by Davis in 1958. Alicante Ganzin (Aramon Rupestris Ganzin No 4 × Alicante Bouschet) is the progenitor of all the French Teinturier varieties, while Tinta Cão is a much-respected port variety that has all but disappeared in Portugal because of its low yield. The result is an unusually productive vine yielding between 8 and 10 tons per acre of red-juiced grapes that provide the rouge in the makeup of both wine blenders and grape-juice manufacturers.

By 1983 there were well over 3,200 hectares (8,000 acres) of Rubired in California, all of them in the hotter areas and many of them planted in the late seventies by Central Valley wineries in need of deeper tints in their jug reds and port-style wines. The vine is adaptable and has no major health problems. The Australians have been experimenting with it.

Teinturier – easy to grow.

—— DURIF ——

The name Durif means nothing to most wine drinkers, but its California synonym Petite Sirah is known to millions. The mystery about Petite Sirah is how it got its name. There is nothing particularly petite about it, and it has no connection whatsoever with the noble Syrah of the Rhône valley, except that its home ground is in the southeastern quarter of France.

The variety takes its name from a nurseryman Dr Durif who propagated it around 1880. By the middle of the twentieth century it was tolerated, though never encouraged, in such regions as Isère and Ardèche in the Rhône valley. Despite a

Durif

couple of its French synonyms, it was quite clear that it had none of the *noblesse* of the Pinot family and was always regarded as a rather ordinary variety, producing wine to match. Its attraction lay purely in its resistance to mildew.

France harbours hardly a Durif vine today, but California has been consistently increasing its plantings so that by 1983 there were 2,920 hectares (7,300 acres) all over the state, notably in Monterey and San Joaquin. It is probably most suitable for the cooler vineyards of the generally warmer, less fashionable regions, or those parts of the likes of Napa that are too hot to produce top quality Cabernet Sauvignon. Here it can produce deep-coloured, fairly tart wines that are relatively tannic in youth and, if allowed to, could probably age rather better than most.

Its attraction is slightly puzzling as it is not stunningly productive, giving between 5 and 8 tons per acre, and in hot vineyards the berries tend to raisin quickly. Paul Draper of Ridge Vineyards is an exponent of the variety as good, rigorous blending material for blowsier Zinfandels, but his is a keener appreciation than most. Perhaps it is simply, as so often the American case, a question of skilful marketing of the name.

It is cultivated in Israel and, in Australia, the excellent Alan Antcliff has spotted the odd Durif vine among the related Peloursin, also from the Isère, in northeast Victoria.

Synonyms:
Dure, Duret, Plant Durif,
Pinot de Romans, Pinot de l'Ermitage,
Nérin, Bas Plant, Plant Fourchu,
Sirane Fourchue (France);
Petite Sirah, Serine (California).

Rigorous though unsubtle.

GAMAY BEAUJOLAIS

The tale of California Gamay is a convoluted one, and one that hardly involves the real Gamay of Beaujolais at all. Viticulturists were aware for some time that there was a considerable difference between what was called Gamay Beaujolais and another variety they had been taught to call Napa Gamay, but they thought Gamay Beaujolais was the real thing. The varieties have finally been identified as a rather uninspiring clone of Pinot Noir and the productive Valdiguié of the Midi respectively, although these facts are not widely known among ordinary wine drinkers. In 1983 there were just over 1,200 hectares (3,000 acres) of Gamay Beaujolais planted in the state to about 1,360 hectares (3,400 acres) of Napa Gamay. Almost all of these are in the coastal counties.

Little of the nobility of Pinot Noir is apparent in the wines produced by California's Gamay Beaujolais (which now may also be labelled Pinot Noir) which tend to be fairly high in acid and simply fruity in flavour. For viticultural information, see Pinot Noir. This particular strain is also cultivated, as Gamay Beaujolais, in New Zealand where there were more than 150 hectares (375 acres) in 1983.

Synonym: Pinot Noir.

Poor quality Pinot Noir.

MISSION

Mission

The historic grape known as Mission in California is probably a subvariety of Chile's Pais, even closer to it ampelographically than Argentina's Criolla. It was this subvariety which was the first *vinifera* wine grape planted in North America by the Jesuit priest Father Juan Ugarte at the Mission San Francisco Xavier in southern California in 1697. Over the next century the Mission grape proliferated up the West Coast along the developing Mission Trail so that it became the dominant California grape until about 1870. It is still cultivated, although not exactly revered, throughout California today. In 1983 there were more than 1,200 hectares (3,000 acres) of it, mainly in southern California and nearly half of them in San Bernardino county.

Rustic, light wine.

CARNELIAN

This complex crossing was let out of Professor Olmo's nursery only in 1972, but already covered nearly 640 hectares (1,600 acres) by 1974, since which time plantings have hardly increased. It was the result of crossing the 1936 Carignan × Cabernet Sauvignon crossing called F2-7 with Grenache, and represented an attempt to produce a hot-climate variety with some Cabernet class.

The results have not dazzled, though yields have been as high as 13 tons per acre in the Central Valley where it is planted. In fact, the young vines had to be restrained from rampant overproduction, and the light bodied, rather neutral wines which result may simply be the product of too much irrigation and too little pruning. The wines do at least have good colour and can be useful for blending in *nouveaux* and in rosés.

The Grenache genes predominate in vine character, including the toughness of its stalks and resulting poor relationship with pickers of all sorts.

Quality potential may not yet be realized.

SALVADOR

The development of Rubired has put paid to this *rupestris-vinifera* hybrid. Its only suit was its deep colour, and it was only ever planted in the Central Valley as a useful tinter of cheap blends. New plantings have been virtually nil in the last 15 years and 520 hectares (1,300 acres) of its state total of 630 hectares (1,575 acres) were in Kern County in 1983. Its juice is inconveniently gelatinous and the small bunches make it suitable only for machine harvesting.

Hybrid Teinturier.

ROYALTY 1390

Royalty was released with Rubired in 1958, although with Trousseau rather than Tinta Cão cited as co-respondent.

It has been considerably less successful, producing less overall from vines which need careful management to keep their health and strength. Its total 1983 plantings of 560 hectares (1,400 acres) were spread through several Central Valley counties, but the variety is on the decline.

Less-than-popular Teinturier.

CENTURION

Centurion has exactly the same parents as Carnelian, but was released three years later in 1975 and has accordingly been less widely planted. The state total was 345 hectares (886 acres) in 1983. It is as productive, marginally easier to harvest, and, unlike Carnelian, has not inherited Grenache's delayed bud-break problem. The wine is a long way from Cabernet Sauvignon, however, and it is difficult to see a future for this new crossing.

Lots of rather ordinary wine.

> Other red varieties planted in very small quantities in California are Black Malvoisie, presumably a dark member of the mainstream Malvasia family, as in Italy's Malvasia Nera; Charbono, which is probably the same as the nearly extinct Corbeau or Charbonneau of France; the minor Girondin variety St-Macaire; and the very minor Jura variety Béclan.

The Eastern USA

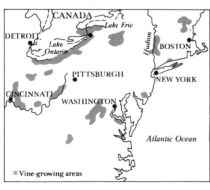
Vine-growing areas

East of the Rockies is the territory of American wild vines and hybrids, whose produce is of interest in the same naturally limited way as the wines of other fruits less complex than *vinifera* grapes. The wines rarely rivet and the vines themselves, grown in fairly limited quantity compared to most of California's *viniferas*, have not been deemed sufficiently interesting for detailed study.

CONCORD

Concord is *the* grape of New York State, which is great for grape jelly fans though less so for connoisseurs. Concord is also *the* *labrusca* grape variety, oozing the musky smell of a wet and rather cheap fur coat which wine tasters have agreed to call "foxy" in their tasting notes on wines made from members of the *Vitis labrusca* species.

The vine was named after Concord, Massachusetts by Ephraim W. Bull who planted the seeds of a wild *labrusca* grape there in 1843.

Only about a fifth of all the 11,600 hectares (29,000 acres) of Concord grown in New York State is made into wine, but

Concord

that is enough to make it the state's most important single wine-grape variety. The resulting wine is a rather lurid deep pink, is usually quite sweet, sometimes bubbly and has helped wean many an American, via cheap Lambrusco, on to wine drinking. It is also grown in Brazil.

CATAWBA

Catawba is eastern America's second most popular variety, a hybrid of *labrusca* and another native species. It produces wines of all shades of pink and is even older than Concord.

OTHER HYBRIDS

De Chaunac (Seibel 9549) is the most widely planted French hybrid in America: about 400 hectares (1,000 acres). It ripens very early and is particularly vigorous.

Baco Noir (Baco 1) is a crossing of the cognac grape Folle Blanche with a *riparia* and is distributed widely throughout the wine-producing states of the eastern United States even though the total area planted is barely 400 hectares (1,000 acres). Its fairly fruity wines have a certain leafy appeal and are mercifully untainted by the mark of *labrusca*.

Maréchal Foch (Kuhlmann 188.2) is much less widely planted but is considered usefully winter-hardy and is grown in Canada. It is a crossing of a *riparia-rupestris* American vine with Goldriesling and is almost extinct in France today, despite its name.

Chancellor (Seibel 7053) was the most widely planted hybrid in France before the 1940s but has now all but disappeared. It produces a relatively innocuous fruity red all over the eastern states.

Chelois (Seibel 10.878) was also grown in France at one time. It ripens early, buds late and is well adapted to cool climates.

Cascade (Seibel 13.053) suffers virus infections to such an extent that it is likely to dwindle despite its convenient early ripening.

Leon Millot (Kuhlmann 194.2) has the same progenitors as Maréchal Foch, is vigorous and manages high sugar and colour levels despite its very early ripening. It is also grown by a handful of English wineries to add colour to punier but nobler red varieties.

Other red hybrids grown in the United States and occasionally encountered as varietals include Cynthiana (Norton), Landots and Ravats of various sorts, the Rosette (Seibel 1000) and Rougeon (Seibel 5898).

South America

LIMA
PERU
LA PAZ
BOLIVIA
BRASIL
CHILE
RIO DE
JANEIRO
SANTIAGO
URUGUAY
BUENOS AIRES
ARGENTINA

■ Vine-growing areas

Chile

PAIS

Pais is Chile's version of Criolla and Chile's version of its history also involves the Jesuits in the mid-sixteenth century. They probably brought cuttings direct from Spain, or perhaps the Canaries, though it is puzzling that no variety like the Pais is known today in the Canaries or mainland Spain. One theory has the Pais springing up when the seeds of the Spanish sailors' raisin ration fell or were planted.

Whatever its origins, it is still the most important wine-grape variety in Chile, producing 35 percent of all Chile's vintage, especially the rough and ready *vino pipeno*. It is particularly productive in irrigated vineyards when the wines produced are particularly light in colour and extract and so fast maturing that they seem to brown before one's very eyes. On non-irrigated, less fertile land such as that of the Cordillera de la Costa, the quality of the resulting wine is better, but Pais is gradually being replaced by better quality *vinifera* vines. However, the vine's healthiness, the ease with which it can be harvested and its productivity (8 to 13 tons per acre) are enough to sustain interest in it as a dessert-wine ingredient.

See also Mission page 227.

Very rustic, thin wine.

Argentina

CRIOLLA

The Argentine wine industry can trace its roots back to 1556 when the Jesuits planted the first vineyard in the Cuyo region with the forebear of the "native"

varieties that still play such an important part. Criolla Grande and Cereza are the two most important by far, accounting for nearly 30 and 10 percent respectively of Argentina's particularly productive vineyard. Criolla is thought, in fact, to be the Pais of Chile.

Criolla and Cereza are both *vinifera* varieties which have adapted over the centuries to the local conditions, particularly to the hot, irrigated, flat vineyards around Mendoza where yields of 200 hectolitres per hectare are not uncommon. They are gradually being replaced with more desirable, profitable imported varieties.

Fairly basic, rustic table wine.

Fer is a local clone of the very popular Malbec of which about 5,000 hectares (12,500 acres) are planted. A new and cleverly named variety Caberinta (C G 14892) has been developed by the National Institute of Agricultural Technology to achieve rewarding yields of musts high in both sugar and acid.

South Africa

PINOTAGE

This is perhaps South Africa's most famous wine – and vine – export, although its popularity is relatively recent. It was bred by Professor A. I. Perold in 1925 from Pinot Noir × Cinsaut, and Cinsaut's common, if misleading, Cape synonym Hermitage inspired the third syllable.

Professor C. J. Theron nurtured it on an experimental basis at Elsenburg. It gained general recognition only after an example from the Bellevue estate of Stellenbosch, made from some of the first vines to be grown commercially, waltzed off with top prize at the 1959 Cape young wine show. Not every example has been worthy of the compliment. The vine is easy to grow, achieving high sugars very easily and relatively early, and thrives without disease in all sorts of conditions.

It is only a medium cropper, however, and the temptation has been to over-produce, resulting in rather hollow wines that have a fairly good, if often unstable, colour in youth and a quite intense aroma, but which taste as though the flavour has

Pinotage

been literally baked out. The best examples are those produced from well-pruned vines allowed to ripen well. They are still only medium bodied but have good colour and can age, demonstrating a rather more subtle variation on the theme of the very distinct Pinotage flavour. Some describe it rather unkindly as "drains", and there is certainly something reminiscent of disinfectant in youth.

There are about 5,000 hectares (12,500 acres) of Pinotage in South Africa, and the vine has excited enough interest to be exported to California, New Zealand, Zimbabwe and even Germany.

Very individual, potentially fairly good quality.

PONTAC

Pontac sounds wonderfully archaic, and indeed it is, though it is worthy of more detailed contemporary scrutiny. The vine was already producing one of the first varietal wines in the eighteenth century; the vessel *De Hoop* returned to the Netherlands with some Cape-produced Pontac aboard in 1772.

It seems quite possible that Pontac was a vine that had been imported by the Huguenots and named after the Pontac family who were such important vineyard owners in the Médoc. We may never know exactly which of the early Médocain vine varieties they chose to bring with them, however, as Pontac is rapidly being grubbed up from Cape vineyards because of its low yield and poor vine health. All who have tasted the Pontac wines in the past agree that they were deep coloured, tannic, subtly flavoured, distinguished and had great ageing ability. Perhaps it was Petit Verdot.

Top quality wine.

Australia

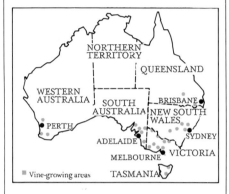

NORTHERN TERRITORY

QUEENSLAND

WESTERN AUSTRALIA

SOUTH AUSTRALIA

BRISBANE

NEW SOUTH WALES

PERTH

ADELAIDE

SYDNEY

MELBOURNE

VICTORIA

TASMANIA

■ Vine-growing areas

——— BOMVEDRO ———

The main interest of this variety in Australia concerns its identification rather than the quality of its wines. It was probably imported into Australia, like so many other Portuguese varieties, in a jumble of early cuttings. It was blithely called Carignan until in 1976 Truel identified it as the once widely planted Portuguese variety, Bomvedro.

There are scarcely 200 hectares (500 acres) of it in Australia, mainly in South Australia, although the variety thought to be the Spanish variety Miguel de Arco at Barooga is probably Bomvedro, too.

The vine's problems are caused by drought and frost and it does not have particularly good disease resistance, but the wine produced in ideal conditions is self-confidently light, fruity and fashionable.

Synonyms: Bonvedro, False Carignan.

Attractive wine from finicky vine.

——— TARRANGO ———

Tarrango

This Touriga × Sultana crossing bred at Merbein in 1965 and released in 1975 was designed specifically for the hot irrigated inland vineyards of Australia. It is a relatively successful attempt at what might be called Gamay de Murray et Murrumbidgee, producing a light-bodied, well-coloured, low-tannin, low-pH, fruity, very early-maturing wine.

The vine ripens very late and is, therefore, unsuitable for cooler vineyards. Its yield is very high, about 10 tons per acre, and the popularity of such wines as Hickinbotham "Cab Mac", in which Tarrango has been an important ingredient, may do much to increase plantings.

Light and fruity.

> Tiny quantities of Currant, including Carina, are used for wine-making in Australia.

New Zealand

——— HYBRIDS ———

Black hybrid grape varieties were at one time relatively important to the New Zealand wine industry and in 1983 still constituted 3.6 percent of the harvest. Plantet (see page 199) is slightly more planted than the "foxy" Teinturier Seibel 5437, also known as Siebouchet and Tintara, of which New Zealand has about 60 hectares (150 acres). Other hybrids include Albany Surprise, used chiefly for grape juice, Seibel 4643 and Seibel 5455. The Italian *vinifera* Melascone Nera has also been experimented with.

The Levant and North Africa

It seems both tactless and hopeless even to enquire about the *encépagement* of Syria, Iran, Iraq, Jordan and Afghanistan, each of which have several thousand hectares of vineyards making wine for local consumption.

In the Lebanon the Bekaa Valley's vineyards presumably continue to produce some very respectable wines, of which Château Musar has become the most internationally famous. Varieties imported from France have all but replaced the local *vinifera* progenitors. Before the arrival of Cinsaut, Cabernet Sauvignon and Syrah, the vineyards were planted principally with white varieties, of which the low-yielding Meroué and Obaideh are said to be closely related to Chardonnay.

Israel's vineyards have been even more deliberately and systematically Frenchified, though the local Dabuki is still grown on a small scale. The white "Claret Egreneuse" is none other than the Clairette Egrainée of Algeria.

The revival of Ancient Egypt's well-documented viticultural activities by Nestor Gianaclis at the beginning of this century included the importation of more than 70 likely grape varieties and development of 20 of them.

In Tunisia the white grapes Beldi and Muscat de Terracina persist, to no great effect, as does the red Nocera.

In Algeria Farranah or Ferrana is an indigenous white still grown in the Coteaux de Tlemcen. Other Algerian white varieties are Tizourine, Bouafrara and El Maoui.

In Morocco's red varieties, French influence is all-pervasive, but the white Rasafi and mysteriously named Plant X are still grown to a limited extent, the latter having even found its way to Cyprus for experimental plantings.

White-wine Varieties

France
Bordeaux

(See map page 198)

MUSCADELLE

Although it shares a strong grapey aroma with members of the Muscat family, Muscadelle is a distinctly Bordelais variation on the theme. It buds late and ripens early and this shortness of growing season has the effect of producing rather simplistic wines in the sweet-wine areas of Bordeaux, where about 2,000 hectares (5,000 acres) of it are grown.

It is regarded there as a very poor third to the classic Sauternes mix of Sémillon spiked with Sauvignon Blanc. At a classed growth château a mere 5 percent is considered quite enough to give extra perfume to a sweet wine, although the vine's attractively high productivity means that it may constitute a considerably higher proportion of the *encépagement* in, for example, a generic Premières Côtes de Bordeaux. Muscadelle has been an obvious first casualty of the swing away from sweet wines and total French plantings are falling, but it can still be found in the satellite wine regions of Dordogne and Lot-et-Garonne as well as in the Gironde.

Muscadelle's most exciting incarnation by far is in the form of Australia's Liqueur Tokays, dessert wines as rich, dark and strong as the famous Liqueur Muscats. Australians believed for a long time that their "Tokay" grape was perhaps the Hárslevelü that goes into Hungary's most famous dessert wine. Some of them still think it must be connected in some way with Pinot Gris (or Tokay d'Alsace). The clever French ampelographer Professor Truel was able to tell them in 1976 that it is none other than Muscadelle, as were some cuttings thought to be Sauvignon Vert imported from California. Some enthusiasts for Australian dessert wines prefer the more subtle, slightly "cough sweets" and rarer Liqueur Tokay to a Liqueur Muscat. Most of Australia's few hundred hectares of Muscadelle are planted in South Australia, but there are some old and treasured plantings around Rutherglen.

South Africa's Muskadel or Muscadel is nothing to do with this variety, but some of the Muscat-type vines in eastern Europe may well be Muscadelle.

Muscadelle

California's 120 hectares (300 acres) of "Sauvignon Vert" are almost certainly Muscadelle, which has a leaf very similar in shape to Sauvignonasse. The "Sauvignon Vert" also has many loose bunches of small, thin-skinned grapes which ripen early and are subject to insect attack and subsequently to rot.

Synonyms:
Muscade, Musquette, Muscadet Doux,
Guillan, Muscat Fou, Angelico,
Raisinotte (southwest France);
Tokay (Australia);
Sauvignon Vert (California).

Moderate grapey quality.

MERLOT BLANC

There are still nearly 2,000 hectares (5,000 acres) of this productive vine which is quite unrelated to Merlot Noir. According to Galet, the vine was probably brought to Fronsac from deep in southwest France and, at the end of the last century, having caught the attention of the nurseryman Jean Elie, it was propagated and spread all over the north bank of the Gironde. It was called Merlot Blanc because the leaves look quite similar to "proper" Merlot.

Today most of the world's Merlot Blanc is still to be found in Fronsac, Bourg and especially Blaye. It is losing popularity because it is very sensitive to frost, rots easily and the wine it produces so copiously is rather boring.

Synonym: Merlau Blanc.

Poor quality.

The Loire

(See map page 199)

ARBOIS

Arbois has nothing whatever to do with the Jura (although its leaf has something in common with Sávagnin). Its most common Loire synonym Menu Pineau establishes it as a distinctly Loire variety. Its home territory is on the principal bend westwards of the river Loire, in the now largely abandoned vineyards around Orléans.

There are still about 1,000 hectares (2,500 acres) of Arbois in the Loir-et-Cher *département* as well as a few hectares in the Indre for the production of Valençay Blanc in which Arbois or Menu Pineau is the main component. Cheverny and *vins de pays* are the chief outlet for Arbois wines, which are usually blended with Chenin Blanc and possibly with Sauvignon and Romorantin.

This vigorous variety produces a fairly good quantity of wine notably lower in acid than Chenin Blanc, for which reason it was traditionally valued at the easternmost end of the main Loire vineyards as a "softener". This is a very local variety, officially recommended for Indre, Indre-et-Loire, Loiret and Loir-et-Cher.

Synonyms:
Menu Pineau, Petit Pineau,
Herbois, Orbois, Verdet.

Moderately good quality.

ROMORANTIN

Like Arbois, this variety is specific to the coolest end of the main Loire vineyards although it is much less planted. There were about 300 hectares (750 acres) in Loir-et-Cher in 1979 and no sizeable plantings elsewhere. The wine has less alcohol and character than Arbois but the vine can produce between 50 and 100 hectolitres per hectare.

Galet, contradicting Viala, maintains that the vine is identical to the Loire variety Dannery.

Synonyms:
Dannery, Petit Dannezy,
Verneuil, St-Amand,
Gros Blanc de Villefranche.

Moderate quality.

RAYON D'OR

Rayon d'Or has all but disappeared in Loire vineyards, where it was popular in the fifties, except for those of Loir-et-Cher where there is still as much of this hybrid planted as of Romorantin.

It is a crossing of Seibels 405 and 2007 which has the advantage of budding so late that it usually misses spring frosts but, even if it does not, it can recover well from them. It ripens early and has good disease resistance, although it can rot at vintage time.
Synonym: Seibel 4986.

Low-quality hybrid.

MESLIER ST-FRANCOIS

This is another white variety most commonly associated with the Loir-et-Cher where 400 of the 600 hectares (1,000 of the 1,500 acres) planted in France are located. It is also an auxiliary variety in the production of cognac and, especially, armagnac; in those regions it is less susceptible to black rot than Folle Blanche.

The vine can be very productive, up to 200 hectolitres per hectare of very neutral wine which is ideal for distillation. Unlike Rayon d'Or, the vine buds very early and is therefore open to attack from frost, but it can produce a satisfactory second crop.
Synonyms:
Gros Meslier, Meslier Blanc,
Meslier d'Orléans.

Thin, ordinary wine.

St-Pierre Doré is another white variety at one time chiefly associated with the Loire.

Northeast France

(See map page 200)

Chablis and the Yonne

SACY

This pushy little number was cast as possible usurper of Chardonnay from its rightful place as queen of Chablis. In the twenties plantings of Sacy in the Yonne were so high they motivated the Chablis producers proper to protect their name.

(Their success was geographically limited, as is so evident in America today.)

Current total French plantings of Sacy are sufficiently low to have escaped official notice in the last national agricultural census, but the vine is still planted in the Yonne and considered a useful ingredient in sparkling wine production. Contemporary wine drinkers are most likely to encounter the rather thin, low-alcohol and extremely tart wine produced with Sacy in bottles labelled Crémant de Bourgogne (particularly those filled by the Auxerrois SICA agricultural collective) and in branded sparkling wines made in eastern France, particularly Kriter.

According to Galet, Sacy is supposed to have been brought from Italy in the thirteenth century and cultivated at the Abbaye de Reigny near Vermonton. At one point it was planted as far south as the Jura, as well as in the lower reaches of Burgundy, and its productivity made it so popular that in 1732 an official ban had to be imposed by the Parliament of Besançon, followed by another issued at Vermonton. Such is the impact on agriculture of legislation that it has been cultivated in the Yonne continuously. Growers there who appreciate it as a booster of the Aligoté, which is often cultivated alongside, and a stretcher of Chardonnay character, are clearly prepared to forgive the vine's proneness to both sorts of mildew in exchange for its high yields.

The only other incarnation of Sacy known to modern wine drinkers is in that cussedly unspellable country wine from the dead centre of France, St-Pourçain-sur-Sioule Blanc. Its tartness is due to the inclusion of Sacy, known here as Tresallier, in the blend, along with such unlikely co-stars as Sauvignon *and* Chardonnay, as well as Sacy's habitual partner Aligoté.

One wonders whether Sacy's forebears can still be identified in the vineyards of Italy, though not being a top quality variety it is unlikely to have attracted any attention.
Synonyms:
Tresallier (Allier); Gros Blanc,
Blanc Vert (Yonne);
Farine (Doubs).

Low quality; thin.

The good quality Roublot and very ordinary Plant Vert were once important in the Yonne, too.

Alsace

AUXERROIS BLANC

The important role of Auxerrois Blanc is one of Alsace's better-kept secrets. Little is ever said or written about it. Yet this variety, as distinct from Pinot Blanc or Pinot Gris, was the region's fourth most widely planted vine according to the last French agricultural census which found 1,100 hectares (2,750 acres), mostly in the higher, Haut-Rhin vineyards.

The situation is confused because the variety is usually called simply "Auxerrois". Auxerrois Gris is a common synonym for Pinot Gris, another important variety in Alsace; Auxerrois Blanc is a synonym for Chardonnay in nearby Lorraine; through the town of Auxerre, the name erroneously suggests some connection with the Yonne; and to crown it all the "black-wine" grape Malbec is called Auxerrois in Cahors.

Even within Alsace itself, many believe the true Auxerrois to be related to Sylvaner, Chardonnay, Melon or even one of the Mesliers. It is occasionally referred to as Pinot Auxerrois even though it is not related to the Pinot family. Galet identifies it as a quite separate plant which can provide moderately high yields of rather dull wine high in acid and fairly high in alcohol. Most of the wine produced from Auxerrois Blanc in Alsace is blended into Edelzwickers. Its place on the ladder of quality in Alsace is one rung below Pinot Blanc, but above Chasselas. It is also grown in South Africa where, until 1986, it was thought to be Chardonnay.
Synonym:
Auxerrois Blanc de Laquenexy.

Low to medium quality.

KNIPPERLE

This dark-berried vine, vinified to produce thin white wine, is fast disappearing from the Alsace winescape but it enjoyed a great vogue at the end of the last century. By the turn of the century it was planted on nearly a quarter of the region's admittedly much more extensive *vignoble*. As one of its synonyms indicates, its chief promoter was the nurseryman Ortlieb who made much of the vine's high production and conveniently early ripening.

What he was less forthcoming about was the vine's disastrous propensity to rot. Even in the arid climate of Alsace this has been a sufficient problem to see total plantings of Knipperlé dwindle almost to nothing, although one or two producers still produce varietals from it.

Synonyms:
Kipperlé, Ortlieber, Kleinergelber, Kleiner Rauschling, Eltinger, Petit Mielleux, Reichenweierer.

Fair quality.

Goldriesling, or Riesling Doré, supposedly a cross between White Riesling and Muscat, is another variety tolerated but not officially encouraged in Alsace. Very early ripening, it is most often encountered in the dangerous milky cocktail of esters sold as new season's wine in the cafés of Riquewihr. Other old varieties associated primarily with Alsace include Bouquettraube and Putscheere which may well be of Hungarian origin.

Jura

—— SAVAGNIN ——

Rather like Viognier, Savagnin Blanc is an indisputably noble vine that is cultivated on a very limited scale in just one corner of France. This is the grape that underpins the unique and most exciting wines made in the Jura. Today it is hardly cultivated elsewhere in the world, presumably because it is so subject to *coulure*. In the Jura such a reputation has been built for its *vins jaunes*, which can be made only from the extraordinary Savagnin grape, that producers there are still prepared to cope with this viticultural inconvenience, and price them accordingly.

Savagnin Blanc reaches its apotheosis on the gravelly soils around Château-Chalon where the naturally late-ripening vine may not be picked until December. In some years the grapes do not ripen at all and the wine has to be declassified.

The grapes are small and the wine high in colour and extract with a peculiar nuttiness. This is accentuated in the special oxidation-defying production process for *vin jaune*, sherry-like wines that can live a very full and vivacious life for more than a century.

Even to more basic white wines of the Jura such as Arbois, Côtes de Jura Blanc and L'Etoile, in which Savagnin is blended with increasing proportions of Chardonnay, the variety brings a very definite aroma, also suggestive of nuttiness or perhaps some rather delicious polish.

The leaves of Savagnin Blanc are very similar to but not identical with those of the vines once called Traminer in Alsace and a relationship was therefore assumed. Today hardly any Savagnin Blanc is cultivated in Alsace, but a pink form, Savagnin Rosé, is encountered, often called Clevner d'Heiligenstein or Heiligensteiner Klevner, and the full-bodied wine produced is generally admired. Savagnin Noir is a synonym for Pinot Noir.

Synonyms:
Savagnin Blanc, Savagnin Jaune, Salvagnin, Nature, Fromente, Gringet, Gentile Blanc (France); Edeltraube (Germany); Formentin (Hungary).

Very good quality and very good keeping qualities.

Other white grape varieties once primarily associated with the Jura or Franche-Comté were Gouais Blanc, Peurion and Cinquien.

Savoie

—— JACQUERE ——

This is Savoie's basic white-wine grape. Almost by definition, therefore, its wines characterize those of the whole region – dry, light, tart and halfway between smokey and low-key. The vine is very productive and can yield 100 hectolitres per hectare without difficulty. It is late budding and prefers gravelly or limey soils. Rain at vintage time, usually the first half of October, can cause rot problems but Jacquère's usual strong suit is blameless neutrality. Total plantings in France, which effectively means in Savoie, were still more than 800 hectares (2,000 acres) in 1979.

Synonyms:
Jacquerre, Jacquière, Cugnette, Plant des Abymes de Myans, Buisserate.

Moderate quality.

—— ALTESSE ——

The wines of Altesse are full-bodied, full of flavour and spicily aromatic. As befits such an interesting variety, Altesse has an interesting history. The exact cast involved is disputed, but what is sure is that the vine was brought to Savoie from Cyprus at the end of the Middle Ages, when the House of Savoy was at its most globetrotting.

Galet has found strong similarities between it and the famous Furmint of Hungary's Tokay. He postulates that Furmint could well have been taken to Cyprus by the Knights Templar and all traces of the vine could then have been destroyed by the Turks. This theory would certainly account for the strong character and weight of the wines made from Altesse even in this relatively cool region. Galet also notes that in the last century rich *vins liquoreux* were produced around St-Gilles near Arles that were distinctly reminiscent of good Hungarian Tokay.

Today, most of the wine produced by Altesse is dry, relatively full-bodied and ripely scented, and a considerable proportion of it is sparkling. Sparkling Seyssel, for instance, is built on Altesse together with the much less substantial Molette, while the rare but delicious still Seyssel can be made only from Altesse. Such wines do not taste like the shy retiring flowers one might expect to find in this subalpine region -- and all because of the political past of its most famous dynasty.

Often called Roussette, it has nothing to do with the Roussanne grown much further down the Rhône valley. Altesse produces grapes that will happily stay on the vine until they are fully ripe without rotting, but is notably low-yielding. Twenty-five hectolitres per hectare is considered high, and a fast-maturing rootstock such as 41B can encourage full maturation.

Along with a cocktail of Burgundian and other Savoie varieties, Altesse is one of the grapes responsible for the white, and sometimes even reds, of Bugey between the Jura and Beaujolais. It deserves much wider distribution, although until higher-yielding clones are found it is unlikely to get it.

Synonyms:
Roussette, Roussette Haute, Mâconnais, Altesse Vert.

Inspiring quality.

—— MOLETTE ——

This rather common variety is especially planted around Seyssel where it contributes to the sparkling wine industry. It is high yielding but the wine produced is at best characterless, at worst bitter and coarse. A similar vine called Roussette Basse is very closely related to Molette.

Synonym: Molette de Seyssel.

Other varieties associated chiefly with Savoie include the Mondeuse Blanche, Cacaboué, Hibou Rosé.

Southeast France

(See map page 201)

—— CLAIRETTE BLANC ——

Rather out of step with today's fashion in white wine, Clairette is fast losing the influence it once had in abundance all over southern France. The trouble is that wine made from Clairette tends to be very high in alcohol, a little low in acid and to oxidize dangerously fast – rather like the Italian whites pre-*pasteurizzato*. Treated with care, Clairette grapes can be turned into a wine with an attractively fruity aroma, which soon goes stale.

At one time Clairette was just what the vermouth producers of southern France wanted. Today white vermouth is much more likely to have originated in the vineyards of southern Italy, and Clairette is more usually blended into basic *vin de table* and those appellations for which the variety is still prescribed. Plantings are spread fairly evenly over Var, Vaucluse, Gard, Hérault and Drôme. Total French plantings were down to 5,300 hectares (13,250 acres) in 1979 and are doubtless much less than this now.

Clairette is one of the Châteauneuf and Côtes-du-Rhône-Villages varieties, contributing to the ponderousness of some of these whites. It is also an ingredient in most Provençal whites, including the highly priced Cassis and Palette although, perhaps significantly, not Coteaux d'Aix-en-Provence. Unless vinified with extreme care, as at Château Simone, for example, Clairette desperately needs the additional acidity that Ugni Blanc (Trebbiano) can bring to it in many appellations, although not officially in the Côtes-du-Rhône.

Clairette's name is enshrined in several appellations, but Clairettes de Bellegarde and Languedoc are rarely a good advertisement for the variety and should, like almost all wines made from this variety, be drunk almost before they are bottled. Clairette de Die, the unexpectedly flavoursome sparkling wine of the Drôme *département* halfway between Hermitage and Châteauneuf, is perhaps the grape's most noble incarnation. In this area alone

are plantings of Clairette increasing, although it should be said that, despite the name, it is the fine Muscat à Petits Grains that is chiefly responsible for the flavour and class of the best *mousseux* labelled Clairette de Die. Although Blanquette is a common synonym, Clairette is quite unrelated to Blanquette (or Mauzac), which it supplements in small quantities in the production of Blanquette de Limoux.

Cultivation of this vine is not without its problems. It has to be grafted to a low-vigour rootstock to avoid serious *coulure*, and the grapes are so thin-skinned that they are very prone to rot, a problem exacerbated by the vine's late ripening. It shows its ancient Mediterranean pedigree, however, in the ease with which it adapts to very poor, dry soils.

Clairette is quite widely cultivated outside France. Nowhere is it particularly important, but in the middle of this century it became relatively popular in South Africa, especially for their sparkling wines, *vonkelwyn*. The cultivar was one of the most obvious first recruits to South Africa's new programme of vinification in stainless steel. There are still 3,600 hectares (9,000 acres) of Cape vineyard planted in Clairette Blanche.

As in a number of other cases, the vine's appearance in South Africa is matched by one in Australia. Most of it is planted in the Hunter Valley where there are probably fewer than 100 hectares (250 acres) of "Blanquette".

The variety is also planted in Sardinia, where it is the major perfumer of Nuraghe Majore, and in Algeria and Israel.

Synonyms:
Blanquette (Aude);
Clairette Blanche (South Africa);
Blanquette (Australia).

Overweight and therefore tires easily.

—— ROUSSANNE ——

Marsanne and Roussanne are the two varieties traditionally associated with the white wines of the northern Rhône, south of the tiny Viognier zone which encompasses only Condrieu and Château-Grillet. Marsanne is the big fat one, Roussanne the elegant, delicate one. After a perky youth, Roussanne wine often goes through a slightly maderized stage in middle age, and can emerge as a well-preserved 10 or even 20 year-old.

By the early 1950s, plantings of Roussanne around Hermitage had been almost entirely supplanted by the much higher-yielding Marsanne owing to the

fragility of the vine, which is particularly susceptible to oidium. Selected clones of Roussanne specially suited to these steep northern vineyards have recently been developed, however, notably at the Domaine de l'Espiguette on the Mediterranean coast, and Roussanne plantings are increasing in the northern Rhône, though admittedly from a tiny base.

In the top white wines of Paul Jaboulet Aîné there are equal proportions of Roussanne and Marsanne, which result in much more scented, lively wines than those made exclusively or almost exclusively from Marsanne. Roussanne has always been planted to some extent in St-Péray, whose sparkling wines are greatly in need of it to add zest and delicacy to the Marsanne that covers about 80 percent of the *vignoble* there. In some years Roussanne's later ripening can be disastrous this far north.

Further south there have been fewer problems, and the French agricultural census of 1979 found about 1,000 hectares (2,500 acres) of Roussanne in the Var *département*. A pink subvariety, Roussanne du Var, is said to go into many a lesser local wine. If so, it must be a good deal easier to grow than the Roussanne known to growers in the Rhône valley.

Roussanne is one of the four permitted white grape varieties in Châteauneuf-du-Pape and, bolstered by Grenache Blanc, it constitutes an unusually high 80 percent of the white wines of the idiosyncratic Château de Beaucastel. Roussanne is also cultivated in limited quantities on superior estates in the Côtes-du-Rhône.

The grape crops up in the list of permitted grape varieties in Montecarlo Bianco, the well-balanced dry white made near Lucca in Italy. One Australian grower of Marsanne, Yeringberg in Victoria, has even started to grow some Roussanne to add vivacity. And as early as 1882, notes on early vine varieties grown in Australia include a reference to Roussanne.

A note on Roussette: There is considerable confusion about the name Roussette as applied to vine varieties in this area of France. In some northeastern districts – Savoie and Bugey, for instance – Roussette is a synonym for the Altesse that is grown there (but it is quite unrelated to Roussanne). Some northern Rhône growers also refer to their vines, or some of their vines, as Roussette, and Galet is able to give two sources who have cited a variety very like Marsanne called Roussette which at one time constituted a high proportion of plantings around Hermitage. This may well have been Roussanne misnamed; but since Marsanne plantings in the northern Rhône have risen so dramatically close to 100 percent of the *vignoble*, it can safely be said that there is no longer any question of a puzzling third variety called Roussette.

Synonyms:
Bergeron (Savoie),
Barbin, Rebelot, Greffou,
Picotin Blanc (rest of France).

Fine wine capable of development.

MARSANNE

A virtual takeover in the northern Rhône does not make Marsanne a widely planted vine on a national scale. The French agricultural census of 1979 could locate only one *département* with as many as 100 hectares (250 acres): the Drôme of Hermitage and St-Joseph fame.

The vigorous Marsanne vine produces substantial quantities of deep-coloured, almost brown-tinged wine high in extract and alcohol with a very definite smell, slightly but not unpleasantly reminiscent of glue of the same sort of hue. It is simply too heavy to produce a wine capable of

Marsanne

ageing well, unless it is picked very early as in some Australian examples.

Up to 15 percent of white grapes, which has effectively meant Marsanne, may be added in theory during vinification of red Hermitage, but this rarely happens now that white Hermitage has a ready market. White St-Joseph is made almost exclusively from Marsanne planted at the north of the appellation where it overlaps with land technically allowed to grow the churlish yielder, Viognier. Marsanne, alas, seems to be winning that territorial dispute. As

well as producing white St-Joseph virtually single-handed, it is chiefly responsible for white Crozes-Hermitage and is the principal component in St-Péray both still and sparkling. Almost all these wines should be drunk in the first few years after the vintage, but the newer style Hermitage Blanc in which Roussanne plays a perceptible part can age well.

Although Marsanne is not in the Thirteen Elect of Châteauneuf, it is planted on one or two of the more enterprising Côtes-du-Rhône estates such as at the Château du Trignon at Sablet, and it is permitted, though rarely included, in Cassis.

Rather surprisingly, Marsanne is cultivated in small quantities in the Valais in Switzerland, where it is known as Ermitage Blanc, and can reach extremely high alcohol levels in a good year.

Marsanne's route to Australia is even more puzzling, although, of course, that country's most important grape variety has for years been the red-wine grape of Hermitage. Today there are fewer than 100 hectares (250 acres) of Marsanne in Australia, most of them in Victoria where it has been grown continuously since the 1860s. Old-fashioned examples such as Chateau Tahbilk have shown the ability to age in bottle, although this may have been because in older plantings Marsanne is pre-blended in the vineyard with other, perhaps more interesting varieties. Today there is a tendency to ferment a much cleaner and thus faster-maturing must.

This is a variety that is still oak aged in some cases, both in France and Australia.

Synonyms:
Avilleran, Grosse Roussette (Savoie);
Ermitage Blanc,
Hermitage Blanc (Valais).

Wines of perhaps too much substance.

PIQUEPOUL GRIS

The grapes permitted by law in Châteauneuf-du-Pape include Piquepoul, without specifying whether the dark or lighter Gris version. Most assume it is Piquepoul Gris because this is the more widely planted, if genetically more recent, variety, although very little is grown in the southern Rhône today. Total French plantings have been declining, but there were still nearly 600 hectares (1,500 acres) in 1979 scattered fairly widely over the south of France.

Piquepoul Gris buds late and is sensitive to oidium. Since phylloxera, it has enjoyed a certain success in the sandy vineyards of the Camargue and on the flat

vineyard land west of the blending capital Sète. Together with Clairette and Terret Gris, it provides the majority of the grapes for the rather flabby Picpoul de Pinet.

It is grown in small quantities in northeast Spain.

Synonyms:
Picpoul, Picpoule, Picapulla,
Picapouya, Languedocien, Avillo.

Medium quality wine.

BOURBOULENC

This ancient vine is thought by Viala to be the Asprokondoura of Greece and at one time was widely dispersed throughout the vineyards of the Midi. Today there are just a few hundred hectares left, fewer even than that of the other elusive white Châteauneuf ingredient, Piquepoul Gris. These are mainly small and ancient plantings on estates in Châteauneuf-du-Pape, Côtes-du-Rhône, Tavel, Lirac and Bellet.

It has few champions, producing a rather thin neutral wine, though Galet puts in a plea for leaving it on the vine until October when it is capable of producing a strong, rustically characterful wine.

Synonyms:
Bourbolenco, Clairette Rousse,
Clairette Dorée, Grosse Clairette,
Roussaou, Clairette à Grains Ronds.

Usually mediocre.

Oeillade is a largely southeastern low-quality white French grape that is hardly used at all for wine today. Picardan is quite similar and is the last of the Châteuneuf-du-Pape permitted varieties to be mentioned here. One must assume that the inclusion of varieties such as this and the equally less than inspiring Bourboulenc, the Piquepoul(s), Clairette and, for red wine, Counoise and Terret Noir, was simply a reflection of what was commonly grown in the southern Rhône early in this century when the famous rules were drawn up.

Other white varieties almost exclusively associated, on however small a scale, with southeast France include Pascal Blanc (still particularly suitable for the dry soils of Cassis), Rolle (an interesting exclusivity for Bellet), Colombaud, Mayorquin and Valentin.

Southwest France

(See map page 203)

These grape varieties, all of them virtually exclusive to this corner of France, are listed in the approximate order of their importance by vineyard area.

MAUZAC BLANC

Many Francophiles would be astounded to learn that almost as much Mauzac Blanc is planted as Sauvignon Blanc: well over 6,000 hectares (15,000 acres) at the last agricultural census, two-thirds of them in the Tarn *département*. According to Galet, this "white" version, whose grapes can vary between greyish white and pink, is not genetically related to the Mauzac Noir, which is also associated more with Gaillac than with any other region.

Total plantings appeared to reach a peak of 9,000 hectares (22,500 acres) in the sixties, but a decline in Gaillac has been compensated for by the vine's increased popularity just to the south, in the Midi's Aude *département* where it is also known as Blanquette (de Limoux). Steven Spurrier attributes the local nickname to the fine white dust on the underside of Mauzac leaves. The unexpectedly and delightfully delicate sparkling wines of Limoux must be at least 80 percent of Mauzac grapes, supplemented by Clairette and/or Chardonnay. The crisp, green, almost cidery flavour of Mauzac is perfectly suited to *vins mousseux*. Its characteristically high acidity, which can be detrimental to some Gaillac whites, is a positive advantage to the *champenisateurs* of Limoux.

Mauzac Blanc is an important ingredient in the white wines of Gaillac of whatever sweetness and fizziness, and it is also one of the permitted varieties in Côtes de Duras Blanc.

The vine ripens relatively late and can achieve remarkable sugar levels, which endanger the resulting wines' stability. Yields vary enormously according to vineyard site but the vine is generally healthy.

Synonyms:
Blanquette, Maussac, Mauza, Moisac, Moysac, Sudunais.

Good base wine for *vin mousseux*; bit tart otherwise.

BAROQUE

This wonderfully named vine is the speciality of Tursan, indeed Tursan Blanc must contain at least 90 percent of the variety. But as the producers of Tursan have increasingly switched from white to red, Baroque has lost ground to Tannat. Total French plantings of Baroque fell from 5,300 to 1,600 hectares (13,250 to 4,000 acres) in the seventies.

Unlike Tannat, Baroque has shown itself a particularly good grafter, and has useful resistance to oidium, mildew and blackrot. After the onslaught of oidium and then phylloxera in the last century Baroque, with its good resistance to disease, was planted on a large scale to replace the previous good quality white grape, Claverie.

The wine produced is strong, up to 13 percent, and full of flavour in a countrified rather than elegant way. Its weight tends to dampen any natural aroma.

Baroque is, after Armagnac's Baco Blanc, the most widely planted variety in the Landes *département* and, further south, one of many permitted ingredients in the rare white wines of Béarn.

The vine's origins are disputed. Some claim it was brought by pilgrims returning from Santiago de Campostela in Galicia. Certainly to judge from its synonyms, and to leap conceptually just a little, this could be the white version of Portugal's Tinta Barroca. One authority posited Baroque as a crossing of Folle Blanche and Sauvignon Blanc, while another suggests that it must be an old vine native to the far southwest of France where it has been spotted growing wild. Whatever its history, it is certain that Baroque was identified only relatively recently by ampelographical students north and east of Tursan. Galet cites 1894 as the date its separate and distinct existence in the vineyard was acknowledged.

Synonyms:
Barroque, Baroca, Bordelais (France); Bordeleza Zuria (Spain).

Good, strong wines.

PETIT AND GROS MANSENG

Manseng means Jurançon means sex, if its producers' promotional literature is to be believed. Billed variously as *viril* and *puissant*, the wines claim the slogan *séduction du vert galant*. Colette's warning salvo to all wine writers, "I was a girl when I met this prince; aroused, imperious, treacherous, as all great seducers are – Jurançon", has clearly left its mark.

Petit Manseng is the vine primarily responsible for the truly great wines of Jurançon, one of France's unusually underrated treasures, Jurançon Moelleux. It has conveniently loose bunches of extraordinarily tiny berries with very thick skins that nevertheless can be persuaded to rot nobly in some vintages. Even when *Botrytis cinerea* fails to take effect, wonderfully strong (minimum alcohol 12.5 percent), concentrated, honeyed wines are made from these vines, usually trained well off the ground. They can develop for years, and yet in youth have more enticing aroma, almost entirely attributable to Manseng, than any other sweet French wine. The flavour is an exciting cocktail of fruit and spices, very ripe peaches with cinnamon toast, although always with very high acidity to keep such flights of fancy in check. The grapes are left on the vine till deep into November and are often shrivelled and concentrated by cold as in Eiswein. The yield is therefore tiny – perhaps 15 hectolitres per hectare even though 28 is technically allowed.

Gros Manseng is also trained high, and is added to Petit Manseng and the other local variety Courbu to produce Jurançon Moelleux, although it is mainly used to make the increasingly popular Jurançon Sec. The berries are noticeably larger than those of Petit Manseng but the vines are clearly very closely related. There is also a Gros Manseng that has very downy buds like Meunier. Average yields are much higher, but a wine no less distinctively flavoured results. Even Gros Manseng is highly aromatic and mouthfilling with lots of acid and alcohol and a texture that is almost "gummy".

Total plantings of Manseng have, encouragingly, been increasing considerably, from 90 to nearly 600 hectares (225 to 1,500 acres) in the seventies. Like Courbu (also known as Sarreat), the Mansengs contribute to the rather less distinguished Pacherenc du Vic Bihl and white Béarn wines as well as to Jurançon. It would be very sad if Petit Manseng were to be overtaken by Gros Manseng, and the methods of making Jurançon Moelleux were to become less fastidious. The wine drinkers of the world would surely pay the price for such a seductive wine.

Synonyms of Petit Manseng:
Manseng Blanc, Petit Mansenc, Mansegnou (France); Ichirota Zuria Tipia (Spain).

Petit Manseng excellent quality; Gros Manseng very good.

LEN DE L'ELH

Like Manseng, this southwestern variety has been enjoying a revival and total

French plantings were nearly 500 hectares (1,250 acres) by 1979. With Mauzac Blánc it is one of the main varieties in Gaillac Blanc, in which it must constitute at least 15 percent of the grapes used. Its arresting name is local patois for *loin de l'oeil*, or far from sight, but in exactly which direction is not clear.

In pre-phylloxera vintages, the variety used to constitute 30 percent of Gaillac Blanc, but Mauzac with its higher yield has been encroaching on this share. The wines produced by Len de l'Elh are often of great character and can be very high in alcohol, if a bit flabby, in which case the tartness of Mauzac is sorely needed.

This vigorous vine matures two weeks before Mauzac and can be prone to rot unless planted on a hillside site well exposed to sunshine.

Synonyms:
Len de L'El, Len del El, Cavalier.

Moderately good quality.

———— ONDENC ————

While Manseng and Len de l'Elh have gained ground, Ondenc, the producer of robust and perfumed wines, has been losing it. Total plantings fell from 1,200 to a mere 160 hectares (3,000 to 400 acres) in the seventies, even though the variety is permitted in a wide range of wines due east of Bordeaux as well as in Gaillac. The white wines of Bergerac, Côtes de Duras and Montravel may all contain some Ondenc, though few now do.

At one time it was planted as far north as the Côtes de Blaye and as far south as the foothills of the Pyrenees, but today it is mostly encountered in Gaillac. The vine degenerates easily, lacks vigour and produces relatively few grapes. For good measure, it is sensitive to oidium and grey rot, the latter being a particular problem because the vine also ripens earlier than most of the other varieties with which it is planted. Perhaps its decline is not too surprising.

Ondenc has had a colourful international history. In the early nineteenth century when it was planted quite widely in the Bordeaux region, a collection of Ondenc vines was taken to Cognac as Blanc Sélection Carrière, under which name it travelled as far as Portugal and California. One of the many varieties taken to Australia by the pioneer viticulturist James Busby in 1832 was called Blanc Select.

The other important date in this cosmopolitan saga is 1976, when the French ampelographer Paul Truel explained to the Australians that the variety grown by Joseph Irvine at the Great Western Champagne Cellars, called Irvine's White, so usefully high in acid, was none other than Ondenc. He also pointed out that the variety called Sercial in South Australia was Ondenc too. The explanation of some of this confusion may well lie in the fact that true Sercial and Blanc Select were originally imported from Portugal in the same batch and were somehow mislabelled. There is a total of about 300 hectares (750 acres) in Australia, mainly in Victoria. Cultivation of Ondenc in Portugal and California seems to have ceased (as has that in Bordeaux and Cognac).

Probably Ondenc's most successful modern manifestation is as a sparkling wine ingredient.

Ondenc

Synonyms:
Ondin, Oundenc, Ondent, Béquin, Primai, Chalosse, Sensit Blanc (France); Irvine's White, Blanc Select, Sercial (Australia).

Good wines, unhealthy vines.

Other vines planted either now in small quantities or traditionally in the southwest include the Lauzet and Camaralet of Béarn and Jurançon, as well as Ahumat, Clairette de Gascogne, Guillemot, Courbu Blanc (see Petit and Gros Manseng), Palougue, Raffiat de Moncade and Arrufiat or Ruffiac, which is still an ingredient in Pacherenc du Vic Bihl.

"*Workhorse*" *Grapes*
— TERRETS BLANC AND GRIS —

These little-heard-of sister varieties together cover 9,000 hectares (22,500 acres) in France constituting its eighth most-planted white-wine grape. Terret Blanc is planted exclusively in the Hérault (86 percent) and Aude (14 percent).

The viticultural characteristics of the Terret family are given on page 202. It is possible to find Terret vines carrying bunches of grapes that are black, white and "grey".

Both light Terrets were particularly cultivated along the Mediterranean coast, close to Sète and other vermouth centres where the crisp, light wines would be blended with Clairette and Piquepoul. Demand for French raw materials for wine aperitifs has shrunk since European agricultural policy has provided a cheaper source in southern Italy. Today Terrets Gris and Blanc with their light, crisp, modern dimensions are important contributors to standard white *vin de table*, and plantings in the Hérault have actually been increasing, despite their proneness to both sorts of mildew.

It is worth remembering that in these days when inexpensive white wine is very popular in many important consumer markets, France has few sources of cheap white grapes. In the three major Languedoc-Roussillon *départements*, for instance, no white variety has a higher proportion of the total *vignoble* than the 7.7 percent of Terret in the Hérault.

Synonyms:
Tarret, Tarrain. Terret Gris is also known as Terret Bourret, and Terret Blanc as Bourret Blanc.

Fashionably light and crisp, though very simple.

VILLARD BLANC

The French authorities are trying to eradicate Villard Blanc, a hybrid of Seibel 6468 × Seibel 6905, but farmers are resisting the uprooting of such a productive vine. Besides, along with Terret Gris and Grenache Blanc, it is one of the very few white varieties of the all-important Midi.

Total French plantings of Villard fell from 21,400 hectares (53,500 acres) in 1968 to 5,800 hectares (14,500 acres) in 1979, but it is still France's most widely planted white hybrid; 44 percent was planted in the Hérault. It ripens fairly late with a crop that is definitely worth waiting for, though the wine itself is often bitter and so high in iron that it may be difficult to clarify. It should ideally be blended with wines of a less pronounced flavour – Terret, for example. In France Villard Blanc is planted all over the south, almost as widely as Villard Noir. Most of the vines were planted in the 1950s and many more have presumably been grubbed up since 1979. It will be interesting to see whether the Midi vignerons can be persuaded to substitute a rather more distinguished white vine.

Synonym: Seyve Villard 12.375.

Hybrid of medium quality.

CARIGNAN BLANC

This white mutation of France's most popular grape variety is becoming a considerable force in its own right. Total plantings increased from 1,950 hectares (4,875 acres) in 1968 to 2,300 hectares (5,750 acres) in 1979, just below those of Gewürztraminer, for example. There has been experimentation with it in the Languedoc-Roussillon to replace Terret Gris. The southernmost vineyards of the Pyrenées Orientales seem to have embraced it most enthusiastically. It is used principally for *vins de table*.

Basic quality.

Mainly for Sparkling Wines

PETIT MESLIER

This local speciality is grown only in the Aube *département* but only a few hectares remain, and they are expected to be replanted with one of the three classic grape varieties when the last of these old vines are eventually pulled up. Since the reformation of the Champagne vineyards in the twenties, Petit Meslier has fallen from grace, at least partly because it is sensitive to *coulure*, downy mildew and rot. To make matters worse, its early budding can mean that spring frosts are a problem.

Even as far south as the Aube it is difficult to ripen the Petit Meslier and the wines produced by it, therefore, tend to be very high in acid and relatively low in alcohol but with an attractively fruity nose à la Meunier.

The vine seems to have its origins in the far northeast of France and can still be found in the vineyards of Berry. It is related to a little seen variety called Meslier Violet, but is unrelated to either Meslier Vert or Meslier St-François, otherwise known as Gros Meslier.

Synonyms:
Meslier Doré, Maille, Bernet, Hennequin.

Thin and tart.

ARBANE

Arbane is even rarer in Champagne today than Petit Meslier, although in the last century it was quite commonly cultivated in the Aube, and Galet gives at least one source for the variety's long history in Bar-sur-Aube.

Unlike Petit Meslier, Arbane is a very low-yielding variety, but its wines are full of character, fairly alcoholic and distinguished by their almost floral aroma. Unfortunately, its sensitivity to both sorts of mildew precludes its future here.

Synonyms:
Arbanne, Albane, Arbenne, Crène.

Good quality wine; frail vine.

Mainly for Spirits

BACO BLANC

Baco Blanc, hybridized four years earlier than Baco Noir, is the vine largely responsible for armagnac. Presumably because it plays such a vital role in the spirit of Gascony, it is the only hybrid that is actually recommended in France. The resulting wine is even tarter than that of Ugni Blanc, and the official recommendation limits it to those vineyards drawn on for armagnac and cognac production.

It was created in 1898 when Baco crossed Folle Blanche with Noah, itself a *labrusca × riparia* direct producer. At that stage Folle Blanche was the prime ingredient in France's most esteemed eaux-de-vie, but Cognac needed something (Ugni Blanc, as it turned out) less prone to grey rot, and Armagnac needed a vine less sensitive to black rot. Baco Blanc provided the answer for the Armagnac region where more than 84 percent of Baco Blanc's French total of 10,700 hectares (26,750 acres) were planted in 1979. However, Gascon plantings are decreasing slowly, and the Ugni Blanc has overtaken Baco Blanc to become the region's most planted grape variety.

A little Baco Blanc is also found in the Charente-Maritime, in the Middle Loire, the Gironde, and the wasteland between Cognac and Muscadet districts.

The vine is both vigorous and very productive. It buds early but it ripens late to produce just the sort of low-alcohol, high-acid wine that is perfect for distilling, although it produces a less fine spirit than either Folle Blanche or Ugni Blanc. This late ripening would be more of a disadvantage if the vine showed less tenacity in hanging on to its berries. Baco spirit ages fast, and Baco vines are susceptible to powdery mildew.

The emerging New Zealand wine industry showed an unseemly interest in Baco Blanc at one stage and there are still about 100 hectares (250 acres) of it today. Before Müller-Thurgau was available in such supply there, it formed the basis of some very crisp white table wines. New Zealanders have also experimented with making brandy from their Baco Blanc, with good results.

Synonyms:
Baco 22A, Maurice Baco,
Piquepoul de Pays.

Poor for wine;
fine for spirits to be drunk young.

FOLLE BLANCHE

At one time this must have been one of the most widely cultivated varieties in France, being largely responsible for both cognac and armagnac. It did not take kindly to being grafted after the phylloxera epidemic and has been gradually supplanted by Ugni Blanc and, to a lesser extent, by Baco Blanc. It was particularly difficult to establish on rootstocks in the very calcareous soils of Cognac country. Now there are fewer than 4,000 hectares (10,000 acres) of Folle Blanche in France, the vast majority of them completely unrelated to spirit production.

Today nearly three-quarters of all Folle Blanche (Gros Plant) is grown in Muscadet country, to produce the almost painfully tart, dry Gros Plant Nantais. Here yields are kept much lower than the plant will happily provide for the distillers (about 50 hectolitres per hectare) and neither black nor grey rot seems to pose a problem. The average Gros Plant can make Muscadet seem a lush, opulent sort of wine, yet a youthful, carefully vinified Gros Plant can genuinely titillate with its green freshness. The Muscadet and Gros Plant vines are easily distinguished in the vineyard by the much more indented leaves of the latter. It is odd that this popular wine region at the mouth of the Loire should have its vineyards stocked with two varieties, one all the way from Burgundy (now virtually extinct there), the other an import from the brandy regions to the south.

The wine is very thin and light, and Galet reports that even in Montpellier acid levels are eye-watering. The only French *département* to have substantial quantities of Folle Blanche planted, other than Loire Atlantique, is Vienne where it flanks the nobler *cépages* popularized under the name of Haut-Poitou.

Picpoule, the variety's most common synonym in Gers, the Armagnac *département*, is confusing, as Folle Blanche is not related to either the red or the white varieties more commonly called Piquepoul, although more than any other grape Folle Blanche merits the description "lip stinger" (the literal translation of this common term).

California has about 112 hectares (280 acres) of Folle Blanche, the largest planting being in San Benito County. It is chiefly used there for adding useful acidity to blends for jug wines, but it has also been used, with some logic, in sparkling wine production. Davis viticulturists would like to see more of this variety planted in California, where natural acidity is at such a premium. Folle Blanche wine may not have much character, but it is entirely without the whiff of *labrusca* that taints some Baco. And unlike Ugni Blanc, it does seem well capable of hanging on to its acidity even in the fairly hot regions of California.

With its naturally high yield and acidity, Folle Blanche is a variety which could well be more widely planted in the world's hotter wine regions, where the vine's sensitivity to grey rot would rarely be a problem.

Synonyms:
Gros Plant (Nantais);
Picpoule, Picpout (Gers);
Enragé, Chalosse, Rochelle Blanc,
Mendik, Amounedat,
Camobraque (rest of France).

Deserves more attention in hot regions.

JURANÇON BLANC

There were still about 600 hectares (1,500 acres) of Jurançon Blanc in Armagnac at the census of 1979. The variety hasn't anything to do with the white wine of the same name produced nearby. It was once cultivated all down the western wine regions of France, from the Charentes southwards. The vine is very vigorous and can produce large quantities of fairly characterless wine.

Synonyms:
Quillat, Plant Dressé, Dame Blanc.

Unexciting.

PLANT DE GRAISSE

Like Jurançon Blanc this is a variety that is fading fast in Armagnac. Unlike Jurançon Blanc, however, the variety is a particularly interesting one. It takes its name from the almost oily consistency of the grape must, and this name has been through many transmogrifications, including the confusing "Plant de Grèce". It is often called simply "Graisse". Little more than 400 hectares (1,000 acres) of Graisse remained in Gers at the last census.

This is another productive, vigorous vine, but its wine is relatively high in alcohol and can much more happily be drunk as a wine, provided it is well clarified. It seems likely, however, that it will eventually disappear.

Synonyms:
Blanquette, Gras, Taloche,
Plant de Mun, Président, Gros-Blanc.

Definitely drinkable as wine.

Corsica

VERMENTINO

Vermentino is grown relatively widely for a variety most often associated with Corsica. There were 1,300 hectares (3,250 acres) on the island in 1979, considerably less than those listed in the French agricultural census as "Malvoisie". Whether this indicates confusion in Paris or Corsica is difficult to assess by the overwhelming proportion of wine lovers who have no first-hand knowledge of that wild island. Galet suggests that Vermentino is indeed a Malvasia that has been grown on Madeira and has been transported directly to Corsica from the Spanish mainland. In line with the putative Malvasia link, Vermentino produces relatively deep-coloured wine.

Much of the Vermentino grown on Corsica is blended with the Ugni Blanc, also grown there and the only other important white variety left; but those who have tasted varietal Vermentino know that the wines are big and ripe-fruit flavoured with genuine interest – rather like the most serious white wines of the Rhône.

Similar wines are made on neighbouring Sardinia where there has been a perceptible movement towards earlier picking to retain acid levels, sometimes at the expense of flavour and richness. Vermentino di Gallura has its own DOC. On the northwestern coast of Italy in Liguria, the staging post for these Mediterranean islands, Vermentino is widely cultivated and can produce table wines of real character. This is a variety that deserves more attention. Careful winemaking could bring out flavours to be treasured more than the slightly hard, characterless whites typical of the variety today.

Synonyms:
Vennentino, Varresana Bianca,
Malvoisie, Malvasia.

Full and interesting.

> Other white varieties that were once considered Corsican specialities include Garbesso, Riminese and the high-yielding Biancone.

Italy
(See map page 208)
Northwest Italy

CORTESE

Cortese has the dubious distinction of producing Italy's most expensive dry white wine, Gavi dei Gavi. To many this accolade is a little difficult to understand, although Cortese wine certainly conforms to the Italian ideal for a *bianco*: low in aroma, high in acid and fairly neutral in character.

The vine has been known in Piedmont since the eighteenth century; it is now concentrated on the southeastern corner where temperatures are high enough to bring the grapes to their relatively early ripeness. The grapes' susceptibility to rot leads some growers to pick even earlier, and others to forfeit part of the crop to botrytis, thereby helping to boost the price of Cortese grapes.

In Piedmont its most famous wine is Gavi, of which Gavi dei Gavi uniquely achieves weight as well as crispness, while nearby Cortese dei Colli Tortonesi is rather thinner and Cortese dell'Alto Monferrato slightly coarser.

Cortese is also an Oltrepò Pavese grape and adds some refinement to the Garganega which is the principal ingredient in Bianco di Custoza.

Good quality.

Erbaluce is quite a widely planted Piedmontese variety with similar dimensions but perhaps rather less impact than Cortese. Arneis has been saved from near extinction by a local appreciation of the international demand for dry white wines. It produces full-bodied wines with crispness and a distinctive flavour that Victor Hazan likens to ripe pears. Favorita is grown around Alba as an inconsequential companion for the local potentate, Nebbiolo. There is also Bosco of Liguria and Blanc de Valdigne from which Italy's "highest" wines Blanc de Morgex and Blanc de La Salle are made in the Valle d'Aosta.

Other varieties associated with the northwest include Bianchetti Genovese, Buonamico, Lumassina, Pigato, Rollo, Veroga (Colombana), and Carica l'Asino, or Karija l'Osü, grown by Giuseppe Poggio to produce an odd, traditional, sedimented *frizzante*.

Northeast Italy

TOCAI FRIULANO

Tocai is one of the world's most interesting varieties to students of interrelationships between the plants and names of the vine world. The false clues let slip by Tocai seem almost calculated to confuse.

Its domain, as the name suggests, is Friuli where Pinot Grigio also holds sway. In Alsace, there is the Tokay d'Alsace which is actually a synonym for Pinot Gris or Pinot Grigio. Are then Tocai and Pinot Grigio the same? Not at all. The name Tocai, of course, brings Hungary to the mind of any wine enthusiast, but the most any Italian ampelographer will allow is that the variety was taken to Hungary in the seventeenth century by followers of Princess Aurora Formentini when she married a Hungarian Count Batthujany. Tocai's origins are Venetian – though its popularity in Friuli-Venezia Giulia is encouraging plantings elsewhere in Italy at the moment, especially Veneto and Lombardy.

A further twist to the Tocai story has been added by the Frenchman Paul Truel and other modern ampelographers, who have pronounced Tocai Friulano one and the same as Sauvignonasse or Sauvignon Vert, the variety which has leaves somewhat similar to Sauvignon Blanc and which probably constitutes about one in four or five of all "Sauvignon" vines in Chile (while, just to set the head spinning even faster, California's "Sauvignon Vert" is actually Muscadelle).

In Italy, Tocai is regarded as a fairly late-budding, high-yielding vine that has normal resistance to downy mildew and is rather susceptible to oidium. Galet on the other hand cites sensitivity to downy mildew as a characteristic of Sauvignonasse. Puzzling indeed, though it is agreed that both as Tocai Friulano and Sauvignonasse, the vine is prey to botrytis.

The wine produced by Tocai is more appreciated by the Italians than Sauvignonasse is by the rest of the world, being fairly full-bodied but not too strongly flavoured, with something very vaguely floral and with just about enough acidity to keep it lively. This is Friuli's most planted white and, it must be admitted, makes a wide range of rather similar wines designed for early consumption.

Synonyms:
Sauvignonasse, Sauvignon Vert (France);
Toca, Tokai (Italy).

Medium quality.

GARGANEGA

The most important subvariety of the Soave variety is Garganega di Gambellara or Garganega Comune. The wines it produces – well, few readers of this book will be unfamiliar with the typically bland Soave blend. Superior versions show the almond character with which the grape is theoretically credited, even though the Garganega is usually bolstered by about 20 percent of Trebbiano di Soave. Another subvariety, Grossa or Dorona di Venezia, is mainly used as a table grape.

The vine is very vigorous indeed, as summer visitors to the Veneto can easily see, and produces large quantities of rather irregular bunches of juicy grapes.

The Garganega family has been established in the Veneto for centuries, and is still most firmly rooted in the beautiful Palladian country of the provinces of Verona, Vicenza and Padua, but it is also now cultivated on the Lombardy/Veneto border where it is an important ingredient in Colli Morenici Mantovani del Garda Bianco, a wine far outweighed by its name. Its best-known Veneto wines are Soave, together with Gambellara, Colli Berici, Colli Euganei and the neat and relatively fruity Bianco di Custoza. It has also been grown successfully in Umbria, where it can achieve notably higher sugar levels than in its northern homeland.

Synonyms:
Gargana, Lizzana, Ostesona.

Everyday quality.

RIBOLLA GIALLA

Ribolla is intriguingly well-travelled for a variety now thought of as essentially Italian. It is grown, as Rebula, in Slovenia where it is a speciality of Brda. In Greece, the Robola of Cephalonia is regarded by many as the nation's most presentable dry white and may well be the same variety. In Italy it grows only in Friuli.

As Ribolla it has been known in Friuli since the twelfth century, but it is still not clear whether its origins lie in Greece or Italy. The tide of history suggests Greece but the connection between Robola and Ribolla, via Yugoslavia, has not been established.

The wines are fairly deep-coloured, dry, crisp, lemony and increasingly full-bodied towards the south. The vines are late budding and relatively productive. Ribolla's ancient travels deserve further investigation.

Synonyms:
Rebolla, Raibola (Italy);
Rebula (Yugoslavia);
Robola (Greece)?

Moderately good quality.

Picolit is Friuli's dessert wine treasure now enjoying a revival and the audacious pricing policy the Italians associate so readily with what they perceive as glamour. The vine has a long growing season but a very low yield owing to poor pollination of the flowers. The grapes are almost exclusively made into a sweet, rather dark and often astringent dessert wine.

Prosecco (otherwise known as Glera or Serprina) is the inspiration of some light, appley varietal *frizzante* which may be sold with either the name of Conegliano or of Valdobbiadene attached, though the best is Superiore di Cartizze within Valdobbiadene.

Verduzzo Friulano produces wines in the Veneto which are similar to Soave but have more character of a rather nutty nature.

Incrocio Manzoni 6–0–13 is a new Riesling × Pinot Bianco crossing that has performed well in Friuli. Incrocio Manzoni 2–15 has already established itself in the province of Treviso. Other varieties grown almost exclusively in the northeast include Veneto's Vespaiolo, which gets its name from the wasps that devour it towards vintage time; Nosiola of Trentino, Benedino, Bianchetta Trevigiana, Durella, Pinella and Verdiso.

Central West Italy

VERNACCIA DI SAN GIMIGNANO

There are several different white Vernaccias in Italy as well as Vernaccia Nera which grows in the Marche. The only other white of much importance is the exclusively Sardinian variety Vernaccia di Oristano, which produces a sherry-like varietal on the island and is quite unrelated to the fairly widely planted Tuscan Vernaccia di San Gimignano. The name Vernaccia is thought to come from the Latin *vernaculus*, meaning "native" or "of this place", which would explain its popularity as a vine name.

Vernaccia di San Gimignano is indisputably ancient though whether its origins are Greek, eastern European or Roman remains obscure. The wine, as Vernage,

was already known in the wine shops of medieval London.

The variety, which is grown almost exclusively around the tourists' favourite hilltop town, is moderately productive and covers about 400 hectares (1,000 acres), producing about 26,000 hectolitres. The grapes are high in total acids and the resulting wine is one of very positive character, if made in the old, fully ripe, full-bodied, dry and slightly bitter style.

Vernaccia di San Gimignano

To some palates the suggestion of varnish was sometimes more than simply onomatopaeic. There have been steadfast attempts, however, to get this ancient variety to conform to the paradigm of modern dry white wine in recent years.

Good quality, interesting wine.

GRECHETTO

Grechetto is the Umbrian vine of Orvieto and of the whites of Torgiano. Quite distinct from any Greco, it is often blended with Trebbiano Toscano, sometimes with Malvasia, occasionally with Verdello (in Orvieto).

The Grechetto is a particularly savoury grape variety whose varietal wines such as Grechetto di Todi show its distinctly nutty character. Along with Malvasia, the variety has enough character and body to make excellent Vin Santo. The vine has very good resistance to peronospera and production is medium.

Synonyms:
Greco Spoletino,
Greco Bianco di Perugia,
Stroppa Volpe.

Good sturdy quality.

Other central west varieties include Bellone, Canaiolo Bianco and Verdello (unrelated to the Verdelho of Portugal) used in Bianco di Pitigliano, Orvieto and Torgiano.

Central East Italy

VERDICCHIO

Verdicchio is the Marche grape which has been grown there since the fourteenth century but does not manifest any particularly exciting distinguishing features. The wines it produces are clean and crisp enough, often virtually colourless thanks to modern Italian wine treatments.

The vine is vigorous but its yield is so variable that the outsider wonders at the variety's continued popularity. "Verdicchio" refers to the yellowish-green skin of the grapes. It is cultivated chiefly around Ancona and in Macerata province. Verdicchio dei Castelli di Jesi is perhaps the best-known Verdicchio, though Verdicchio di Matelica has its supporters. The very high total acidity of the grapes makes them good raw material for Italy's burgeoning *spumante* industry.

Synonyms:
Verdone, Marchigiano, Uva Marana.

Medium quality.

ALBANA

This is the white grape of Romagna (other than the ubiquitous Trebbiano, of course). It was cited in the thirteenth century in Pier de' Crescenzi's work on Italian wines. Today it is also cultivated in La Spezia in Liguria, in Mantova in Lombardy and in Pistoia and Arezzo in Tuscany. About 30 million kilos are harvested each year.

Several discernible clones of this ancient variety have evolved over the centuries, of which Albana Gentile di Bertinoro is the most widely planted. The grapeskins are thick, producing fairly astringent, quite deep-coloured white wines.

Albana di Romagna, produced in huge quantity in varying degrees of sweetness, is its chief varietal. Despite its synonyms the variety is unrelated to Greco di Tufo.

Synonyms:
Greco, Greco di Ancona, Biancame.

Medium quality.

Other white grape varieties that are chiefly associated with the central east are Bianchello, Maceratino, Montu, Pagedebit, Passerina and Pecorino (Vissanello).

Southern Italy

—— BOMBINO BIANCO ——

Bombino may not be a name on the lips of the wine drinkers of the world, but its production is enormous – about a million hectolitres a year – and the wine makes its way by the devious routes of the wine trade into all the well-known vermouths and many Sekts and EEC table wines. Behind many a Gothic label lurks a well-travelled Bombino Bianco, Germanized, of course, by a dose of Morio-Muskat or some such.

The variety is grown all around the southeast coast of Italy being probably the main white grape of both Apulia and Abruzzi and it is also cultivated in Marche and Latium. So important is it in Abruzzi, for instance, that it is likened to Italy's most important white grape overall and called Trebbiano d'Abruzzo. Bombino may be quite unrelated to Trebbiano, but there is a certain similarity in the wine produced: low in alcohol and fairly neutral, making it ideal base material for blenders further north, though Bombino has rather less acidity than the merciless true Trebbiano. The wine called Trebbiano d'Abruzzo may be made from Bombino or Trebbiano or a blend of the two. This sort of blend makes other southern whites such as the whites of San Severo and Castel del Monte in Apulia.

The vine's origins are unknown but one theory holds that they are Spanish. The vine's vigour is medium and it responds best to fairly short training systems, it ripens late but can hang on to its grapes for some time without damage. Production is high, as suggested by its first synonym which means something like "tear up IOUs". Bombino grapes are sometimes sold for the table.

Synonyms:
Straccia Cambale, Trebbiano d'Abruzzo, Calpolese, Bammino, Buttspezzante, Colatamburo, Zapponara Bianca, Marese.

Basic quality. Wine canvas on which to paint a more interesting blend.

—— GRECO ——

The origins of this noble variety are, of course, Greek and it may well have been this which provided the ancients with their Falernian and Aminean tonic draughts. It is known as Greco di Tufo in Campania where the grapes grown around the village of Tufo, almost exclusively for Mastroberardino, produce a deep-coloured wine that can develop herby notes after several years in bottle. There is nothing opulent about the wine produced; it manages dry richness.

Greco adds substance to a wide variety of southern whites including Lacryma Christi del Vesuvio, Apulia's Torre Quarto Bianco, the lesser white version of Calabria's Cirò, and the cult sweet white wine made from shrivelled Greco grapes around the town of Bianco on the little toe of Italy, Greco di Bianco.

The vine matures late, is susceptible to mildew, and produces grey-golden berries on distinctively winged clusters.

Synonyms:
Greco di Tufo, Greco del Vesuvio, Greco delle Torre.

Classic quality.

Fiano provides the latterday incarnation of the wine known as Apianum to the Romans and makes a splendid, very individual dry white in the hills above Avellino. Revived by Mastroberardino, it is grown in the hazelnut plantations for which Avellino is famous and to some seems to impart a hazelnut flavour to the wine (just like the famous eucalyptus of Martha's Vineyard in Napa Valley).

Falaghina is the variety responsible for the revival of the ancient Falernum, while Forestera is more widely known, by tourists at least, as the inspiration of the whites of Ischia and Capri. It is often blended with Biancolella. Verdeca is very important in Apulia where it ripens early with average yields to produce, with Bianco d'Alessano, whites such as those of Locorotondo in the Mezzogiorno. Other deep southern white grapes include Asprinio Bianco, Pallagrello (or Coda di Volpa, which goes into Greco di Tufo), Francavida, Pampanuto and Prunesta.

Sicily

Most of Sicily's white varieties are exclusive to the island and Inzolia is perhaps the widest planted. It manages to sustain acid levels even at this latitude, though it is helped by an increasing tendency to pick very early. Catarratto Bianco Comune is the extremely healthy white vine of western Sicily and plays an important part in Marsala, as does Grillo. Catarratto Bianco Lucido is another, distinct Sicilian variety.

Grillo

Others, declining, include Albanello, Albarola, Damaschino, Minnella Bianca and Montonico Bianco (or Chiapparone).

Sardinia

Sardinia boasts quite an array of white varieties, including the Vermentino of Corsica and, originally, Spain. Nuragus is the most widely planted, although its produce rarely excites. It was brought to the island by the Phoenicians and takes its name from the local stone towers, the "nuraghe" (the wine named after them is, perversely, made from Clairette). Torbato, also Spanish, is at the other end of the quality scale and now produces table wines with real zest as well as considerable body. Nasco is the island's most curious, and apparently indigenous, variety producing rather nutty wines of all sweetnesses and strengths.

Other more effete Sardinian whites include Albaranzeuli Bianco, Arvesiniadu, Regina (or Pergolina), Retagliado Bianco, Anghelo Ruju and Semidano.

Spain

(See map page 213)

AIRÉN

It will surprise many who associate Spain with the reddest of red wine to learn that this white grape is the country's most common variety, accounting for almost 30 percent of all plantings, red and white. Airén, or Lairén, attains this importance mainly because it dominates its native region, La Mancha, where it constitutes nine vines out of every ten. La Mancha, Don Quixote country, is the Spanish answer to France's vast vineyard plain in Languedoc-Roussillon, producing nearly a third of Spain's vintage each year.

Airén, which is used in both red and white wine production, is particularly well suited to the harsh climate and arid conditions on this plain south of Madrid. Although Pardilla and Macabeo are officially tolerated as well, Airén is virtually the only white vine variety cultivated, with Tempranillo (called Cencibel here) taking up most of the rest of the vineyard. The summers are dry and hot, the winters dry and cold on this limy plateau 700 metres above sea level. Temperatures can vary throughout the year from $-22.5°$ C to $44°$ C. The vineyards receive an average of just 350 millimetres of rain a year, a puny total which growers are not allowed to supplement.

Viticultural disease is virtually unknown in this dry atmosphere, and in those rare growing seasons when rain falls near vintage time, growers have to rely solely on the thickness of Airén skins to ward off rot, so little experience do they have of vineyard preparations.

Spain is well known for her low yields, and nowhere is this more marked than in La Mancha where the average is still around 21 hectolitres per hectare (and Airén is considered productive compared with Cencibel). This is due to one of the lowest vine densities in the world: 1,600 vines per hectare (2.5 acres) in most parts and as low as 1,200 per hectare in the province of Toledo. Vines are head pruned to just two buds and grow in low bushes so as to make the most of what little moisture is available. Were irrigation allowed, Airén would doubtless produce an even higher proportion of Spain's annual crop of wine.

For decades the wine produced by Airén was of strictly local interest: high in alcohol, extract and, often in the high temperatures in which it was produced, off-odours. The wine was traditionally fermented in earthernware *tinajas*, as it was in ancient times, and most of it went to other regions for blending or distilling. The eighties have seen the advent of the modern white winemaking revolution in La Mancha, however. Temperature control during fermentation has resulted in clean, crisp, fruity, medium-bodied wines tailor-made for the international wine market. Airén may now be picked as early as the end of August so that potential alcohol levels are reduced a degree or two from the normal $13°$ or $14°$, and it has been successfully introduced to stainless steel.

A major use for Airén has been as a blending ingredient to lighten the heady, soupy reds produced in central Spain by the Cencibel. Valdepeñas to the south of La Mancha has 25,000 hectares (62,250 acres) of Airén planted to 4,000 hectares (10,000 acres) of Cencibel, yet it is much better known for its red wines than white.

Small quantities of Airén are also cultivated in Montilla-Moriles and in other corners of southwestern Spain.

Synonyms:
Lairén, Manchega, Valdepeñera Blanca.

Basic quality but promising raw material.

MACABEO

Those who believe that mature white oak-aged Rioja was one of Spain's great gifts to the wine-drinking world have every reason to curse Macabeo, or Viura as it is known in the Rioja region. Such is the popularity of this variety and the "modern", early maturing whites it produces that it has almost ousted every other white variety in Rioja and made traditional white Rioja little more than a richly flavoured memory.

Macabeo represents more than 90 percent of all white varieties planted in Rioja, with about 6,000 hectares (15,000 acres), most of them in Rioja Alta and a few hundred over the river Ebro in the Alavesa province. That it is now so much more popular than the more interesting Malvasia as well as the unfashionably hefty Garnacha Blanca is, fairly predictably, a result of its more generous yield. It is not a particularly disease-resistant vine, being susceptible to both downy mildew and grey rot. However, it does produce a fairly good quantity of relatively fruity, aromatic must that, unlike Malvasia's, does not oxidize easily.

Wine made from Macabeo in Rioja tends to be fairly light, relatively high in acid, almost florally perfumed in youth, and yet loses its freshness fairly early. In Rioja Alavesa, Macabeo grapes are often added to Tempranillo musts to lighten and perfume them. There have been recent signs from one or two *bodegas* that attempts are being made, either by blending with Malvasia or by using more extractive vinification techniques, to make more interesting white Rioja from Macabeo.

In Spain overall there are more than 50,000 hectares (125,000 acres) of Macabeo, the total being so high because it is the most common white grape variety of northern Spain. It is found in Catalonia, Navarra, Aragón and Penedés; throughout this corner of Spain it tends to be even more widely planted than its traditional blending partners, Xarel-lo and Parellada. This trio form the base for the flourishing sparkling wine industry of northeastern Spain, though Macabeo is not the most noble member.

Tarragona is the southern limit of Macabeo country, but its sphere of influence spreads quite far west. It is planted in small quantities in both the Ribera del Duero district and to a small but limited extent in the vineyards of Rueda. Its obvious current attraction is as a suitable ingredient for crisp, coolly vinified whites for early consumption. Catalonia's José Alegret and Navarra's Gran Feudo are typical of the current attempts to make more interesting varietal Macabeo, though neither this name nor Viura are much trumpeted on wine labels.

The same is true across the Pyrenees where there was a dramatic increase in the amount of Macabeo planted between 1968 and 1979; its 7,000 hectares (17,500

Macabeo

acres) made it France's ninth most popular white-wine grape variety in 1979. Almost 90 percent of French plantings are in the Pyrénées Orientales *département* where it is solely responsible for Côtes de Roussillon Blanc, is an ingredient in the local *vins de pays* and, to a certain extent, in the sweet wines of this corner of France. To avoid what to French palates is its relatively low acid, the trend is towards early picking; such is the difference in climates on either side of the Pyrenees.

According to Jan Read, the vine was first introduced to Rioja from Aragón in 1859, but Galet quotes Odart's theory that Macabeo's origins are Middle Eastern. It has certainly proved resistant to very dry conditions in Algeria and Morocco.

Synonyms:
Maccabeu, Lardot (France);
Viura (Rioja); Maccabeo, Maccabeu, Alacanon, Alcanol (rest of Spain).

Medium quality.

XAREL-LO

It is a sign of the importance of the sparkling wine industry to Spain that this variety, exclusive to Catalonia and used especially in and around the Cava capital of San Sadurní de Noya, is the country's sixth most important grape variety, only just behind Macabeo. Xarel-lo is a native of Catalonia; it represents 60 percent of white grape planting around Barcelona and nearly 30 percent in Penedés.

Xarel-lo is usually planted on the lower, more fertile soils of the Penedés and produces robust, slightly coarse but fairly acidic wines with rather less elegance than Parellada and less aroma than Macabeo, although it is customarily blended with those two varieties whether the end result is to be still or sparkling. The same basic formula is used to produce the still wines of Tarragona whose quality is gradually improving. In Alella Xarel-lo may be called Pansa Blanca and have some Pansa Roja, Malvasia or Picpoul blended in. The most quality-minded producers of this northeastern corner of Spain often overlook Xarel-lo in favour of Parellada. Galet wrongly suggests that Xarel-lo is a synonym of Macabeo.

The vine buds relatively early and ripens in mid-season in early September. Its yield is restricted by the size of the cluster, and sometimes by the vine's susceptibility to downy mildew.

Synonyms: Xarello, Pansa Blanca.

Low to medium quality.

CAYETANA BLANCA

This is the grape of the very dry Extremadura vineyards along the Portuguese border. Growers in this rather forgotten corner of Spain are so fond of Cayetana Blanca because of its average yield, at 36 hectolitres per hectare quite remarkably high for Spain.

To compensate for this the wines produced are quite remarkably low in both alcohol and character and a considerable proportion of them are distilled. The major part, however, is shipped to other wine regions – Jerez to the south and Galicia and Asturias to the north – for blending.

Synonyms:
Calegrano, Naves, Cazagal (Rioja).

Low alcohol, very neutral, best distilled.

PEDRO XIMÉNEZ

Pedro Ximénez

Although traditionally associated with sherry, "PX" is planted extensively all over southern Spain to produce neutral, dry white table wine – so extensively that its total plantings in Spain, about 35,000 hectares (87,500 acres), are greater than those of the more important sherry grape, Palomino.

Today, only a tiny proportion of Pedro Ximénez plantings are in the Jerez area where it is much more difficult to cultivate and more prone to disease than Palomino. It was traditionally prized there for sweet and sweetening wines, but the higher yielding Palomino is supplanting it even in this role.

Allegiance to Pedro Ximénez is one of several ways in which the producers of Montilla-Moriles in the province of Córdoba differentiate themselves very positively from their counterparts in Jerez. The variety constitutes 95 percent of plantings there and seems to thrive in these, the hottest vineyards of Spain, although average yields are considerably lower than those of the Palomino grown in Jerez. The vine's sensitivity to drought may be a factor, though the Córdobans are prepared to tolerate this since they so rarely have to cope with the tendency of the thin-skinned Pedro Ximénez grapes to shatter and rot after late-season rain.

It is curious that a variety which likes neither drought nor rain is so popular in so many corners of the world. It is also quite susceptible to powdery mildew, recovers poorly from spring frost damage, and suffers occasionally from black rot. In Australian experiments with trellissing and cane pruning, the rot problem has been successfully contained as the resulting bunches are much looser and better aerated. In Spain it tends to be short cane pruned in the classic Jerezano manner, or goblet trained and spur pruned. It buds mid-season and ripens early.

The vine is planted all over Extremadura and Levante as well as Andalucia where it produces not only Montilla but, with Moscatel, the very sweet Málaga as well. This is one of the varieties that, traditionally at least, has most often been left lying in the sunshine for sweet wine production. Its thin skins accelerate this process.

Outside the regions demarcated for dessert and apertif wines, Pedro Ximénez is used to provide large quantities of fairly neutral, high-alcohol table wine that is often blended.

Pedro Ximénez still constitutes about 5 percent of all vine plantings in the Canaries where, according to a wonderfully detailed and lovingly embellished legend, it originated. It was supposed to have been somehow taken from the Canaries to the Rhine and then brought back to Spain, and eventually to Jerez, by Peter Siemens (also known as Pedro Ximénez), a soldier in Charles V's army who visited Spain for rest and recuperation. Some theories even have the Elbling of the Mosel a descendant of Pedro Ximénez, which seems highly improbable since their leaves are three- and five-lobed respectively.

The vine, sad to say, is not really noble enough to be worth all this international jetsetting. It is a workhorse grape that tends to be grown where workhorses are best tolerated. It is, for instance, the most planted white variety in Argentina where it accounts for 8 percent or well over 20,000 hectares (50,000 acres) of the country's vineyard and produces flabby, often oxidized top-heavy wine. A little "Pedro Jiménez" is grown in Chile too, though its produce is used mainly in the production of *pisco*.

Australia has probably the world's third largest national collection of Pedro Ximénez vines: nearly 1,500 hectares (3,750 acres) of "Pedro". Like "False Pedro" (recently distinguished as Cañocazo, a minor Jerez variety), it is mainly grown in the irrigated areas where almost unparalleled yields of 50 tons per hectare have been reported, provided there has been no rain at or just before vintage time. As in Jerez, however, Palomino has been replacing Pedro as Australia's authentically Spanish ingredient in sherry-style wines because it suffers less from berry shatter in wet weather. Some Pedro also finds its way into Australia's ubiquitous cardboard wine "casks".

In 1958 McWilliam's produced an exceptional botrytized Pedro Sauterne [sic] in the irrigated Riverina area of New South Wales, a portent of the excellent botrytized wines such as De Bortoli now make there. The McWilliam's wine was very alcoholic and *liquoreux*, almost burnt, but had many layers of botrytis and caramel flavour with almost enough acidity to make it one of the world's greatest.

In New Zealand Palomino is the favoured Andalucian import, as it is in South Africa where False Pedro was thought to be Pedro Ximénez until relatively recently.

At one time California had significant plantings of Pedro Ximénez but there have been no new plantings for a decade and the state total is way below 80 hectares (200 acres); its wine is used, with a nice sense of tradition, as an ingredient in sweet sherry-style wines. In the Soviet Union, Muscadelle is sometimes called Pedro Ximenez Krimsky (Crimean).

Synonyms:
Pedro Jiménez, Pero Ximen,
Ximénez, Ximénes,
Pedro, Jerez.

Very high yields
and alcohol levels possible.

MESEGUERA

This is the most characteristic white variety of Valencia and in the higher, more interesting vineyards of Alto Turia they are extremely proud of the delicacy and aroma of the officially denominated white wines produced from this, the most planted variety of the subregion. It is also an ingredient in less distinguished white blends from vines grown all along the Levante, especially around Alicante. Many a northern European has been persuaded to become something of a wine drinker on the strength (literally, sometimes) of his holiday bottle of Meseguera and Verdil.

The vine ripens early mid-season with fairly compact bunches of large oval grapes. Although it is little-known outside Spain's coastal strip, the country has more than 30,000 hectares (75,000 acres) of Meseguera.

Synonyms:
Merseguera, Merzeguera, Exquitxagos.

Well-perfumed if grown on rocky soil.

PARDINA

Pardina is another of Spain's better-kept secrets. Although the total area planted with it is almost 30,000 hectares (75,000 acres), the rainfall is so meagre that it keeps yields deceptively low.

Along with Monastrell and Tintorera it is one of the authorized varieties for the denomination Almansa southeast of Madrid, and it is planted all over the arid plains of south-central Spain. The provinces of Albacete, Cuenca and Guadalajara just east of Airén country have for long cultivated this variety.

Viala suggests that Pardillo is a synonym for Albillo, the white variety grown in the Valladolid area and used in limited quantity to add scent to reds such as the famed Vega Sicilia. Albillo Castellana is also grown to a limited extent in Andalucia and the Canaries.

Synonyms:
Pardilla, Pardillo, Pardino, Albillo.

Quality of wine not known.

GARNACHA BLANCA

Grenache Blanc is France's third most popular white-wine grape variety. It is Spain's ninth. Yet Spain still has nearly 10,000 more hectares planted with it than France. Such is the contrast between these two wine superpowers.

Spain has nearly 25,000 hectares (72,500 acres) of Garnacha Blanca but because they are statistically lumped together with the considerably more common red version it is difficult to pinpoint their exact location. It is a permitted white variety in Rioja but is not widely cultivated, as the musts oxidize easily.

It is a relatively healthy vine – indeed it is much less prone to *coulure* and therefore more productive than Garnacha Tinta. It is most popular in the northeast of Spain and goes into Priorato, Alella and the white wines of Navarra (where it is really quite important), and Aragón.

The wines are high in alcohol and extract though low in acid. It is curious, therefore, that France increased her total plantings to more than 16,000 hectares (40,000 acres) between 1968 and 1979. As with Macabeo, that other "Spanish" white variety popular in France, plantings are concentrated in that corner closest to Catalonia, the *département* of Pyrénées-Orientales in particular. It should be said, however, that Grenache Blanc is gradually marching eastward and there were already 3,200 hectares (8,000 acres) in the Aude by 1979. It has presumably been taking over from Terrets Gris and Blanc.

The variety known as White Grenache in Australia was identified as Biancone by Truel in 1976.

Synonyms:
Garnacho Blanco, Garnatxa, Silla Blanc.

Heavy wine, good yield.

ZALEMA

This is the traditional grape variety of Huelva province in the far southwest, where it has accounted for 90 percent of all plantings, but Jan Read points out that it is being replaced with higher quality varieties – Palomino, Pedro Ximénez, Mantua and Garrido.

Coarse.

VERDEJO

Of all the white varieties among Spain's official top twenty, Verdejo is probably the one with the most discernibly aristocratic character. It is a native of Rueda just south of Valladolid in the northwest, where the vineyards are high, up to 900 metres, often calcareous and, more unusually for Spain, relatively cool and damp. These factors probably help to add a certain nobility to the variety's intrinsic worth.

Rueda has been famous for white wines

since the seventeenth century when they were pale (literally) imitations of Spain's most famous wine export, sherry. Today a significant proportion of Rueda's wine is crisp, light and has only about 12 percent alcohol (though the variety naturally attains anything from 11.5 percent to 14 percent). The best of them, such as that of Marqués de Griñon, is ultraclean and well-balanced but with an underlying almost nutty character.

The best dry whites of Rueda, Rueda Superior, must contain at least 60 percent of Verdejo, but may be supplemented by the Palomino Fino and Macabeo also grown there. Total Spanish plantings of Verdejo are said to be about 16,000 hectares (40,000 acres), although since the delimited area for Rueda is little more than 4,000 hectares (10,000 acres) and Verdejo Blanco is barely known elsewhere, the more widely dispersed Verdejo Tinto is presumably included in this total.

Synonym: Verdejo Palido.

Scented, crisp, very promising.

PARELLADA

This is the finest of the three grapes used as a basis for Catalonia's still and sparkling white wine production.

Parellada is the local grape whose appetizingly fruity potential has been so ably demonstrated in the best-selling Torres Viña Sol. It is also an improver of Macabeo, Xarel-lo and sometimes black Sumoll and Monastrell grapes that go into the *cuvées* of San Sadurní de Noya. The wines have high acid and good fruit when young but have shown no great ageing capacity. (For the better quality levels of Viña Sol, Torres blends in Chardonnay or, puzzlingly, Sauvignon Blanc, and seasons with oak.) Parellada grows best in the higher cooler vineyards of Penedés and is the last white grape to ripen. The yield is moderately high although the vines are fairly susceptible to both downy and powdery mildew. It is also grown in Tarragona and Conca de Barbera.

Parellada may be one of the Spanish varieties best suited to today's white-wine drinkers, but its potential is not limitless. Torres' experiments comparing the aromagraph of Parellada and Chardonnay by gas chromatography show many more peaks, and therefore nuances of interest, in the Chardonnay.

Synonym: Montonec.

A good local variety
for early-consumption wines.

Other primarily Spanish white varieties from among the hundreds grown there, both knowingly and not, that are officially encouraged are: Caiño Blanco – traditional Galician; Espadeiro – traditional Galician; Garrido Fino – replacing Zalema in Huelva; Godello – traditional and very good quality Galician; Malvasia Riojana (Rojal Blanco, Subirat) – the "Malvasia" of Rioja which some sources say is not related to the main Malvasia family; Pansa Blanca – prolific coarse commoner grown especially in Catalonia; Planta Fina de Pedrabla – grown in the Valencia province; Torrontes – Galician variety also grown in a relatively minor way in the Pisco region of Chile as Torontel Verdil, and grown in fairly large quantities in the Alicante and Yecla regions.

A number of Galician varieties are also listed with Portuguese white varieties on page 247.

Other traditional white Spanish varieties still grown to a certain extent include Marfil of Cáceres and Subirat Parent of Penedés.

Portugal

(See map page 215)

Most of the crossings which currently proliferate in Portugal are omitted here as they are notable more for productivity than quality, are of purely local interest and, it is hoped, their days are numbered. Because the Portuguese vineyards are in such a state of flux, varieties are listed in their different categories rather than in order of area planted.

Good-quality "National" Variety

ARINTO

Those who ever consider the matter believe that this traditional variety could be Portugal's saviour. It is remarkable for its capacity to hang on to its acidity however hot the prevailing climate. It can produce wine at 8 grammes per litre acidity in 40°C with ease, and the wine has both character and ageing capacity. While many other warmer wine-producing regions continue to churn out robust reds but vapid whites, or whites that are not particularly appropriate versions of varietals such as Chardonnay or Riesling, Portugal could be an important source of good-quality white wine, provided Arinto plantings are dramatically increased. So goes, at least, one of the creeds actively being pursued.

The sad truth is that while Arinto is a recommended variety for practically every wine region apart from Dão and the Algarve in the far south (it is even allowed into Moscatel de Setúbal), it has substantially lost ground to much more productive varieties. Typical, for instance, are the twin facts that it is the principal variety in Bucellas, in which it should constitute at least 75 percent, and that other varieties have been encroaching on its territory because of the low yields produced by run-down Arinto plant material. Yields should improve with improved vine breeding.

There are two subvarieties of Arinto Branco: Arinto Cachudo which is potentially a good yielder of fine wine and the much more ancient and less common Arinto Miúdo.

Bucellas probably provides the easiest manifestation of Arinto available to today's wine drinkers, though vinification techniques for this wine do not always make the most of its inherent qualities. Well made, Arinto wine is aromatic, aggressively crisp and can attain a curious lemony resinous quality with age.

The notably high acidity of the variety, together with its intense aroma, has led some tasters in the last century to conjecture a link with Riesling. Two theories about its import into Portugal concern Teutonic crusaders and the eighteenth century Marqués de Ompbal; ampelography lends little support to either.

Synonyms:
Arintho, Arinto-Cercial,
Pedernão.

Top quality, refreshingly crisp wine
worth ageing.

Mainly Vinho Verde

ALVARINHO

This productive variety, known as Albariño over the border in Spain's Galicia, is authorized only in and around Monção where Vinho Verde's only white varietal wines are made of it. These are commonly agreed to be among the best, though not necessarily most typical wines of the region. Most famous, and most expensive, is the wine from the Palacio de Brejoeira.

Alvarinho wines have about 2 percent more alcohol, more fruit, longevity and scent than other Minho varieties and noticeably less natural sparkle. Varietal Albariño is also produced in Spain and the variety has been tried elsewhere without success. The vines yield relatively little juice because they are thick skinned and many pipped.

Synonym: Albariño (Spain).

More character and body than most Minho varieties.

Loureiro is also known in Spain and is so called because it is supposed to give the wine a smell of "louro", or laurel. It is grown chiefly in the Lima valley and is highly regarded. Portugal's Trajadura, known as Treixadura in Galicia, is one of the Minho's better quality varieties, although it will always be a low yielder. Asal, as opposed to the local black Azal, and also grown in the north of the Bairrada region, is another variety which contributes flavour and structure to some of the better Vinhos Verdes.

Like Galicia, the Minho region houses a host of varieties little known elsewhere. Others, usually less reputable, include Avesso, Lameiro, Pintosa, Batoca, Casal and Douradinha.

Mainly Douro

The six varieties particularly recommended for white port production, and therefore required in at least 60 percent of the blend, are the very tart Esgana-Cão, the rather flat-tasting Folgasão, Verdelho, Malvasia Fina, Rabigato and Viosinho.

Of these Esgana-Cão (as Esganoso) and Rabigato are also known in the Minho. Esgana-Cão is closely related to Cercial or Sercial and is a speciality of the Penafiel region of the Minho. Folgasão is also known as Folgozão. Viosinho is more exclusive to the Douro and is also known as Veosinho Verdeal.

RABIGATO

Of the better quality Douro white varieties, Rabigato is most widely planted throughout the rest of Portugal, both as Rabigato and Rabo de Ovelha or "ewe's tail", a name that immediately calls to mind the Hungarian Juhfark. Indeed there are enough similarities between the varieties to suggest a relationship, although this is difficult to establish given the distances both actual and cultural between Portugal and Hungary. Caution is needed, however, since there is another variety called Rabo de Ovelha do Sul, which is known as Médoc in the Douro!

It is not generally regarded as a top-quality variety. It produces excellent table grapes and is more productive than any other traditional variety. The vigorous, healthy, strong-wooded vines ripen towards the end of September and the wine produced is usually quite high in alcohol.

Synonyms:
Rabo de Ovelha do Minho; Estreito (Tras-os-Montes); Moscatel Bravo (Minho).

Ordinary variety, sturdy wine.

Among the hundreds of varieties in the Douro which are considered in the second league and recommended for up to 40 percent of a blend are Arinto, Bual, Cercial do Douro (not the same as Madeira's Sercial and possibly a very good variety for table wines throughout Portugal), Codega, Donzelinho Branco, Malvasia Corada, Moscatel Galego and Samarinho. Codega is related to the Vermentino of Corsica according to Comte Odart and is also known as Malvasia Grosso in the Douro and Roupeiro in the south. Donzelinho Branco yields quite a lot of fairly good-quality wine.

Other varieties authorized, though not recommended, for white port production are Alvaraca, Avesso, Borrado das Moscas, Branco Especial, Branco Sem Nome [sic], Branco Valente, Caramela, Carrega Branco, Chasselas, Dona Branca, Fernão Pires, Formosa, Jampal, Malvasia Parda, Malvasia Rei, Medock [sic], Moscadet, Mourisco Branco, Praca, Rabigato Frances, Sarigo, Touriga Branca and Trincadeira.

Mainly Beira

DONA BRANCA

This is one of the Douro's less noble varieties and is also planted, usually as Dona Blanca, over the Spanish border in Galicia. In the Lafões vineyards between the Dão and Douro, however, it is a required ingredient, with Arinto, in the local rather Vinho Verde-like white, produced in very small quantities. It was at one time more important than now.

Synonyms:
Jampal (southwest Portugal); Dona Blanca, Moza Frésca (Spain).

Fading fast.

White wines represent only 5 percent of Bairrada wine output and a tiny proportion of the total Beira vintage. Bical (Barada da Mosca), Maria Gomez (Fernão Pires) and Tamarez are perhaps more readily associated with these newly demarcated vineyards than any others.

Mainly Dão

The varieties recommended for white Dão are Encruzado and Assario Branco described below, Barcelo, the rather oily Borrado das Moscas, Cercial, Verdelho, Rabo de Ovelha, Terrantez (the same as Torrontel in Spain) and Uva Cão.

It is recommended that at least 20 percent of Encruzado is included in the heavy, often almost oxidized white wines of Portugal's most famous table wine region. Carefully vinified, Encruzado can produce well-balanced, full-flavoured, rather nutty wine.

ASSARIO BRANCO

Assario is also quite common further south in the Alentejo and historically even in the Algarve. It is moderately productive, with short fragile shoots, ripening late at the end of September. It responds best to fairly damp conditions on lowish land, which may account for its decline in Dão.

Synonyms:
Arinto do Dão, Sarilho, Malvasia Esfarrapada.

Moderate quality.

Mainly the South
—— FERNAO PIRES ——

This variety is widely distributed throughout Portugal, if not in quantity at the moment. Its wines have the curious distinction of both smelling and tasting of pepper. It is quite productive and matures relatively early, from mid-August to mid-September depending on vineyard site. According to Villa Maior there are three subvarieties of Fernão Pires, the best being the most heavily fruited and perfumed, the others being known as Beco and Fernão Pirão. He also, intriguingly, gives one source citing Camarate as a synonym in Estremadura, though Villa Maior himself describes the white Camarate as a separate traditional white variety. In a rare instance of globetrotting for a Portuguese white variety, Fernão Pires has done well in tests in South Africa.
Synonyms: Fernam Pires, Maria Gomez.

Aromatic.

Jampal and Vital have official sanction in the much neglected Estremadura. The quite promising Antão Vaz, Alva (Elbling), Manteudo and the rather lemony Roupeiro (or Roupeiro Cachudo) are specialities of the Alentejo much further inland. Boais and Galego Dourado are allowed in many of the coastal denominations, especially Carcavelos.

"Workhorse" Grapes
—— SEMINARIO ——

Despite its fancy Douro synonym Malvasia Rei, the variety has nothing whatever to do with the noble Malvasia. (The Portuguese have a propensity for calling any white variety a Malvasia of some sort.)

This variety and some new crossings have been designed specifically for high yields in the first few years of the vines' life, although they may rapidly decline as Portugal's fan-leaf virus takes its toll. It is particularly popular in the neglected vineyards of the Oeste, as the once-revered Estremadura region is now known.
Synonym: Malvasia Rei (Douro).

Very ordinary wine in great quantity.

Alicante Branco and crossings developed at the Oeiras research institute – EAN numbers 2, 4 and 7 – are other signs of the short-term expediency that has taken over the choice of vines in the western vineyards.

—— DIAGALVES ——

This table grape has long been grown all over Portugal. Today it constitutes half of all vines grown in the Alentejo wine region, whose production is fairly evenly split between red and white. This explains the flabbiness of most of the Alentejo whites. The variety is very productive and produces heavy bunches of very large, thin-skinned grapes.

Table grape; very ordinary wine.

Madeira
—— VERDELHO ——

The much-travelled Verdelho is, contrary to many outsiders' impressions, Madeira's most-planted white variety. It was promoted to the Nobre (noble) class from merely Boa (good) early this century, when it was still more important than either Negra Mole or the hybrids.

Verdelho is moderately vigorous and productive with a spreading growth habit. Both bunches and berries are small, the berries being oval and notably hard. It

Verdelho

ripens particularly early but recovers poorly after spring frost damage. Cool humid nights can spread powdery mildew.

The name is used on madeira labels to indicate a medium-dry style somewhere between Sercial and Bual, with nuttiness and a just discernible amount of sweetness. The law currently requires 60 percent of Verdelho grapes in the blend.

A relatively rare Tinto version is also allowed into madeira but classified as good rather than noble. The Madeira Verdelho is not related to the (black) Verdelho Feijão of the Minho.

Verdelho is a recommended white Dão variety, and is also highly recommended as an ingredient in white port production; with the high alcohol and relatively high colour of its wines it seems well-suited to fortified winemaking.

In Australia, however, it is used to produce table wines of real character such as that unlikely beast Houghton's rich, nutty, almost varnishy version from Moondah Brook in Western Australia. Australia's total plantings are less than 100 hectares (250 acres), but the quality of some of the produce suggests there should be more. Verdelho obviously copes well with heat, managing to maintain acidity levels well.

The variety was also known in the Crimea by the end of the last century. Italy's Verdello is not related to Verdelho.
Synonyms:
Vidonia, Gouveio (Douro);
Madeira (New South Wales).

Good, characterful, nutty wines
with longevity.

—— BUAL ——

Even Bual, from which madeira's richest wine style other than Malmsey takes its name, is becoming rare in the island's vineyards. It is recommended or authorized throughout the mainland vineyards of southern Portugal and is considered one of the more suitable varieties for white port, but its small hairy leaves are hardly to be seen today, giving the wine great commercial value.

In Villa Maior's time, at the end of the last century, Bual was so common that he could describe it as *mais vulgarisadas*. He distinguishes several subvarieties of which Bual Branca was of good quality but the least productive, low yields being a general characteristic of the variety. Bual Cachudo is, today, the most common, producing more wine of higher quality than most.

Bual

Synonyms:
Boal, Boal de Madeira,
Boal de Porto Santo.

Good sugar levels,
rich and very rare

SERCIAL

On Madeira at least Sercial is perhaps even more difficult to find today than Bual. The vine is exceptionally fussy about its site and is particularly late-ripening, but thrives at relatively high altitudes.

The wine produced from the well-perfumed grapes is said to be almost unpleasant when young, but after seven or eight years its astringency is mellowed into a most subtle wine with nuances of flavour heralded by its curiously intricately shaded luminosity. The driest, lightest madeiras are called after Sercial and the variety is probably the most esteemed on the island.

It is cited in many a list of authorized grape varieties in mainland Portugal, but today it is probably only in the Dão region that it is much cultivated, even though it is sometimes used for superior Bairrada whites. Despite some of its synonyms, it should be distinguished from the Esgana-Cão of the Douro.

Synonyms:
Esgana, Esganinho, Esganiso.

Delicate and long-lived.

TERRANTEZ

This historic variety has all but disappeared from the vineyards of Madeira, where a black version was once known. It was not much replanted after phylloxera, but there is now a programme of gradual establishment of some Terrantez vines. They are still remembered for the sweetness, and slight astringency, of their must.

Listrão and Carão de Moca have also been known on Madeira. Today Listrão is quite common as a producer of rather flabby table wine in Porto Santo.

Germany

(See map page 219)

KERNER

The plant breeders of Weinsberg, Württemberg's viticultural institute, must be kicking themselves that, unlike Messrs Müller, Morio and Scheu, none of them managed to get his name attached to this, Germany's most successful recent vine crossing. Instead, a local nineteenth-century drinking song librettist, Justinus Kerner, is supposed to have provided name as well as inspiration and to him goes the honour of seeing an eponymous variety, launched only in 1969, become Germany's fourth most popular grape.

There were nearly 6,700 hectares (16,750 acres) of Kerner in Germany in 1984, represented in each of the 11 wine regions (though primarily in Rheinpfalz and Rheinhessen).

It is unusual not only in the enthusiasm with which the German wine grower and consumer have embraced it, but also because it is a crossing of a red with a white variety: Trollinger (Schiava Grossa) × Riesling. It is heartening to report that a major part of the success of this crossing of an earthy Tyrolean speciality with Germany's noblest is that the wine actually tastes rather delicious. Kerner yields reliably and about 10 percent more than the Riesling, and has particularly good frost resistance owing to a tendency to bud late inherited from its red parent, but its popularity is largely a result of its distinctive flavour and indubitable quality.

It is said that, the slightly fussier Ehrenfelser apart, Kerner is the crossing that tastes most like Riesling. While this is true, it is quite easy to find in Kerner qualities that make it distinctive in its own right. As well as all that acid, it has an appetizingly leafy aroma and often a less silky-smooth texture than Riesling. It shares with Riesling, however, the capacity to mature.

The variety ripens at about the same time as Silvaner, has low soil requirements and can be planted in almost any conditions other than in cool, moist valley sites. In general, it has good disease resistance, but is susceptible to oidium, *coulure* on windy sites and can also suffer vine apoplexy – perhaps at seeing itself passed over by some growers in favour of the still higher yielding Müller-Thurgau? Study of the two between 1973 and 1976 at Bad Kreuznach showed that Kerner consistently achieved must weights and acidity levels about 10 and 20 percent higher respectively than Müller-Thurgau.

Kerner's success in Germany is laudable. It should be pointed out, however, that its chief advantages over the king are

Kerner

that it is rather less fussy about site, can achieve higher must weights and is slightly more productive.

Along with Bukettraube, Kerner is one of the few recent crossings that has been adopted by the South Africans, with surprisingly good results when grown in the Cape's coolest vineyards.

Very good quality.

BACCHUS

The crossing of a Silvaner × Riesling crossing with a Müller-Thurgau which is named after the god of wine is almost as popular as Kerner. It covered more than 3,500 hectares (8,750 acres) of German vineyard in 1983, of which nearly two-thirds were in Rheinhessen. As its genealogy suggests, Bacchus is by no means as aristocratic as Kerner, but its dramatic increase in popularity suggests that it is extremely useful.

Bacchus

The main attributes of Dr Husfeld's Geilweilerhof crossing are that it can be grown successfully on much worse vineyard land than Riesling or even Silvaner, and that the wine produced is generally high in body and character. Ideal for blending with Müller-Thurgau, in fact. Rheinhessen rears even more Bacchus than Morio-Muskat to pep up its produce – so much of it Liebfraumilch; and both the Nahe and Mosel valleys significantly harbour more than 200 hectares (500 acres) of Bacchus apiece.

The disadvantage of Bacchus wine is that it tends to be low in acidity, especially if the grower is lured by the promise of its reliably high must weights at full ripeness to leave the grapes on the vine till he has picked his Müller-Thurgau. Bacchus buds just before Germany's most planted variety, which makes it susceptible to spring frosts, but ripens at the same time and in even greater quantity. Rot can sometimes be a problem, however.

One might naturally assume that Bacchus would be most useful in poor years, when its lack of acid would be less of a disadvantage, but unfortunately its high extract and strong, almost Muscat flavour evolve only in good years. A poor summer leaves it unripe and unclean, with none of the properties for which it is prized. Nevertheless, the variety is expected to gain ground in Germany's northern wine regions as an acceptable alternative to Riesling on less fine sites.

Usefully blowsy in good years.

MORIO-MUSKAT

One wonders whether Peter Morio had any inkling when he crossed Silvaner and Pinot Blanc that such restrained parents would beget such an extravagantly exhibitionist offspring. The low-key charms of Silvaner and Pinot Blanc are most unlike the almost sickly perfume of Morio-Muskat, a grape that proves you can have too much of a good thing: grapey aroma in this case.

The variety became very popular in the seventies, particularly in those regions so keen on varietal blending, the Rheinpfalz and Rheinhessen. There were still nearly 2,800 hectares (7,000 acres) of it planted in 1983, but there have been healthy signs that there is a limit to the amount of Morio-Muskat that German vine growers can stand, even when it presents them with 200 hectolitres per hectare. It is so useful, of course, because just a small dose of Morio-Muskat can spice up a very bland Müller-Thurgau or, even more suitably, Silvaner, giving it a Germanic (a scented, sort of poor man's Riesling) nose. Varietal Morio-Muskat is also sold, but the grapes have to be very ripe to avoid a coarse, mousey flavour and too much acidity.

Acid levels in Morio-Muskat are naturally medium to high, and must weights are low, usually 60° to 70° Oechsle even on a fairly good site. To make a good quality wine, the vine has to reach 80°, which means that it demands better vineyard sites than Silvaner. The vine is also very vigorous and needs fairly rich fertile soil if it is not to exhaust itself too early in life.

The grapes, which ripen about a week after Müller-Thurgau, often have to be picked early to avoid rot, which means that they still have an unpleasantly mousey character. (Bacchus is much more suitable for Germany's more northerly wine regions because it ripens so early.)

It is to be hoped that this variety will fade graciously into the background.

Very blowsy indeed.

SCHEUREBE

Like Kerner, Scheurebe is one of the goodies among Germany's newer varieties; though in this case, "new" means 1916 when Georg Scheu crossed a Silvaner and a Riesling at Alzey in Rheinpfalz and produced this very respectably Riesling-like vine, particularly good at producing Auslesen and even sweeter wines.

Like wine made from so many crossings, that from Scheurebe is not particularly appetizing when the grapes are less than fully ripe. Otherwise it has all the race and breed of Riesling with a distinctive blackcurranty sort of aroma. Scheurebe is characterized by extremely high must weights: a good 10° Oechsle above Riesling grown on the same site. Acidity will not usually be quite so high, but it is still high enough to preserve the wine for many years in bottle. Furthermore the average yield is markedly higher than Riesling and can often nudge 100 hectolitres per hectare, although it is significantly lower than the three more popular crossings Kerner, Bacchus and Morio-Muskat.

Scheurebe's chief disadvantages are that it needs to be fully ripe to produce a palatable wine (which is certainly not the case with Riesling); that it needs a fairly well-sited vineyard, thereby using up potential Riesling-producing territory; and when the vine is very young it is relatively susceptible to frost.

The mature vine, which is late budding, withstands frost well and has good resistance to chlorosis. It ripens just before Riesling, rots ignobly only when the foliage has been allowed to become extremely jungly, and encourages "noble rot" to spread rather faster than it does on Riesling grapes – another advantage in a producer of dessert wines.

There were nearly 5,000 hectares (12,500 acres) of Scheurebe planted in Germany in 1984, more than half of them in Rheinhessen and most of the rest in

Scheurebe

Rheinpfalz. Such is the undoubted quality of Scheurebe that it is now produced as a varietal wine in California.

Very good quality wines when fully ripe.

FABER

This is another of Scheu's Alzey creations, dated 1929, which is distinguished more by its quality than the quantity of wine produced. A crossing of Weissburgunder or Pinot Blanc and Müller-Thurgau, it is already Germany's ninth most popular variety, with 2,300 hectares (5,750 acres) planted in 1984; more than 1,700 (4,250 acres) of them are in Rheinhessen, and it is also relatively popular in the Nahe.

Faber's strong points are its must weight and acidity, usefully higher in both cases than Müller-Thurgau. The wine is, as in all these crossings, recognizably Germanic, but is agreeably fruitier and racier than most. The Germans think of Faber as a traditional (very Riesling-like) variety. Acid levels are higher even than for Silvaner and must weights are 8° to 10° Oechsle above those of Müller-Thurgau. Wines of Spätlese quality can be made successfully from Faber alone, though it is often also used for blending. Higher Prädikats are possible in some riper years.

Faber's chief disadvantage is that like Bacchus it is susceptible to stalk necrosis, and like Kerner its axial shoots grow so vigorously that trimming them is relatively labour intensive. It buds fairly late and ripens even earlier, by two to four days, than Müller-Thurgau, although it stands up well to being left on the vine until the Silvaner harvest to develop even higher must weights.

The variety is useful because it can thrive in almost any soil and on sites that are not quite good enough to fully ripen Riesling, and in predominantly Riesling wine districts it makes a good, fruitier substitute for Silvaner. Its average yield of around 90 hectolitres per hectare makes it slightly less productive – though much more interesting – than Müller-Thurgau. *Synonyms:* Faberrebe, Az 10375 (till 1967).

Good Riesling-like characteristics.

HUXELREBE

The variety named after Fritz Huxel is a crossing of Gutedel (Chasselas) and Courtillier Musque, the co-parent with Riesling of the Goldriesling of Alsace and an antecedent of the hybrid Maréchal Foch. Another product of George Scheu's work at Alzey, this crossing emerged in 1927 and was widely propagated by the vine grower Huxel.

It has emerged as one of the more popular crossings on two fronts. Some growers simply allow it to follow its head and produce huge quantities of fairly ordinary wine, while others prune carefully and persuade it to reach singularly impressive must weights. This is not, as its parentage suggests, one of the finer, more elegant crossings. The flavour is rather more blowsily Muscat-like than racily Riesling-like, but it can provide useful blending material as well as turning out rich if rather obvious varietal wines.

There were more than 1,700 hectares (4,250 acres) of Huxelrebe in 1983, almost exclusively in Rheinhessen and Rheinpfalz. The variety is usually planted on average to good sites where higher quality levels, quite often Auslese and even above, are a realistic target.

In years when the flowering goes well, so many flowers may form on the vine that the wood literally collapses under the strain of the fruit and may fail to bud completely the next year. Care has to be taken to prune carefully, especially when the vines are young. Because the vine is so vigorous, it demands strong rootstocks.

The vine should normally be harvested at about the same time as Müller-Thurgau, but the grapes are particularly good at keeping their acids when left on the vine to ripen into something a little bit richer. Nor do the grapes lose as much bulk as Müller-Thurgau in a similar situation. There is much room for manoeuvre with must weights, but the optimum level is agreed to be over 90 degrees.

Huxelrebe's great advantage is that, provided pruning is strict enough, it can provide QmP wines even in a poor year. But if asked to produce high yields, it can make very coarse wines.

It is also grown in England where it rarely produces very sweet wines but can provide rounded, gently Germanic wines with a fair amount of body and extract.

Usefully high must weights.

ORTEGA

Official German wine literature states blandly that this fairly recent Würzburg crossing of Müller-Thurgau and Siegerrebe is named after "the Spanish philosopher José Ortega y Gasset". One wonders why. Perhaps the scholar was given to particularly florid thoughts, for certainly Ortega, like Huxelrebe and Siegerrebe, can be relied upon to notch up high scores on the refractometer, even in bad vintages.

Oechsle levels may be on average slightly lower than those of Optima, but they are still a good 20° higher than Müller-Thurgau's and can often be 100°, or 80° in a poor year. The wines are very full and flowery, almost peachy, and share with Gewürztraminer the quality of being more suitable for occasional sipping than regular gulping. The Germans claim that it keeps quite well in bottle provided the wine is bottled relatively young. Less partisan tasters find the low acid a problem, especially in very late-picked examples. Ortega is probably most suitable as an enricher of lower Oechsle blends.

The crossing ripens early, before Müller-Thurgau but after Siegerrebe, and produces rather unpleasant, bitter wine if picked a minute too soon. If picked late, QmP wines can easily be produced even after dull, cool summers, though acidity levels are not as refreshingly high as for Huxelrebe or Faber.

Ortega's major problem is its susceptibility to fungal diseases, rot and *coulure*. Provided flowering takes place in settled weather, yields are between 80 and 100 hectolitres per hectare, but the *coulure* makes it unsuitable for cooler sites.

The appeal of Ortega is limited, especially when there are similar, less sensitive, high must-weight varieties available. In 1983 there were nearly 1,200 hectares (3,000 acres) in the Mosel, and more than 50 hectares (125 acres) in Franken where it originated.

Rich but too often flabby.

ELBLING

Elbling can offer two things: great productivity and even greater antiquity. Some authorities credit the Romans with bringing Elbling to Germany either as the *Vitis albuelis* mentioned by Columella or the *Vitis alba* of Pliny. Others say that the variety may well have been known in both Gaul and Germania before the Romans arrived. What is certain is that Elbling was already a well-established vine in what is now Germany even before the Middle Ages, when it rose to real prominence.

Today, Elbling is at all important only in one very small area, the upper reaches of the valley of the Mosel and nearby Luxembourg. All but 3 hectares of Germany's total Elbling plantings of more than 1,100 hectares (2,750 acres) are in the Mosel where the vine was important in Sekt production. Its high acid content and neutrality of flavour make it a suitable base for sparkling wine, but today it plays a relatively minor role in Sekt output.

In 1984, Elbling still accounted for nearly 10 percent of all Mosel vineyards, however, and showed no signs of relinquishing its hold on land unsuitable for the much more rewarding Riesling. This is concentrated in the Obermosel on those cooler vineyard sites where Riesling cannot be persuaded to ripen. The wine is mostly thin and rather Gutedel-like, though one or two estates such as that of Freiherr von Hobe-Gelting at Schloss Thorn have managed to earn a reputation for the definition of their still, varietal Elbling.

The vine is not fussy about site (even though it does not warrant a good one) and on almost any sort of soil will produce yields of up to 200 hectolitres per hectare. There is considerable yearly variation in yield, however, since Elbling is prone to *coulure*, and to oidium and botrytis as the grapes have very thin skins. As well as ripening early it buds early which can cause problems with spring frosts. It is difficult to see quite why growers in this northerly wine district persist with Elbling when the vine breeders could presumably provide them with much more flavoursome alternatives. Must weight levels are usually around 60° Oechsle, at least 10° lower than Riesling, while acidity levels are about the same.

In Luxembourg, Elbling with about a quarter of all vineyard land, or about 250 hectares (625 acres), is the country's second most planted vine variety and makes rather thin, almost unimaginably tart wine, much of it muted by the addition of carbon dioxide.

Synonyms:
Weisser Elbling, Kleinberger, Grobriesling, Alben, Albig, Weissable, Elben, Süssgrober, Rheinelbe, Weisser Silvaner (Germany); Burger (Alsace and Switzerland); Grossriesling, Kurzstingel (Austria); Pezhech, Blesez, Morawvka, Seretonina (Yugoslavia); Allemand, Bourgeois, Mouillet (France); Alva (Portugal).

Ancient but ordinary.

EHRENFELSER

This is one of the stars of Germany's new vine firmament. A crossing of Riesling × Silvaner developed at Geisenheim in 1929, Ehrenfelser tastes like a very slightly flabby Riesling, ripens better and slightly earlier than Riesling, and produces about 10 percent more than Riesling. It will also ripen on less favoured sites than Riesling and has such strong stalks and healthy if compact fruit that the berries can easily be left on the vine for a later harvest. Its only real disadvantage is that, largely because of its slight lack of acidity, wine made from Ehrenfelser does not age as magnificently as that from Riesling.

As Professor Helmut Becker of Geisenheim does not tire of pointing out, the chief disadvantage of Riesling-like crossings that can even outperform Riesling is that they are not called Riesling, or rather that the consumer finds it difficult to accept a usurper with a different name. Ehrenfelser is better than most, deriving its name from the romantic ruined Schloss Ehrenfels by the Rhine at Rüdesheim.

The variety is particularly useful in Germany's northern wine regions as it will ripen where Riesling will not. We may well see an increase in plantings in the Rheingau and Mosel. There were 538 hectares (1,345 acres) planted in 1983, of which 278 hectares (695 acres) were in the Rheinpfalz, 103 hectares (257 acres) in Rheinhessen and 82 hectares (205 acres) in Rheingau. Must weights are regularly between 5° and 10° Oechsle above those of Riesling, and Ehrenfelser rarely fails to produce a wine that is at least of Kabinett quality and often well above.

Adaptable, better than Riesling in some circumstances.

OPTIMA

This relatively recent (1970) crossing from Geilweilerhof resembles the more widely planted Ortega in more than name. It is early ripening – sometimes more than 10 days before Müller-Thurgau – and achieves high must weights without necessarily great elegance or raciness.

Optima's mother was a Silvaner × Riesling crossing and its father Müller-Thurgau. The result is even lower in acid than this last antecedent, but Optima finds it easy to reach must weights of around 98° Oechsle. This means that the wine can be rather oppressively heavy and generally no more than 20 percent is recommended in a blend. The variety is, therefore, useful on those properties in need of Oechsle-boosters, and Optima will grow in most sorts of soil, on sites that are even too poor for Müller-Thurgau. If the berries fail to ripen properly, however, the resulting wine may have a rather coarse, off-flavour. In 1983 there were just over 500 hectares (1,250 acres) of Optima, of which 200 (500 acres) were in the Mosel and most of the rest were in Rheinhessen.

Optima's popularity in the Mosel valley is both puzzling and worrying. The variety is not one of the better yielding of the newer crossings; others can reach slightly higher must weights, and the variety is not one to add any finesse to a Riesling. Because of late budding, Optima's good resistance to spring frost is doubtless a factor as are its obvious Prädikat-boosting powers.

Optima does have the disadvantage of being a prey to rot, which can be noble in ideal conditions but is more often less exciting. Yields are only around 75 hectolitres per hectare.

Very popular in Mosel as Oechsle-scorer.

REICHENSTEINER

As its creator Helmut Becker has pointed out, this is the first "EEC crossing", with antecedents from France, Italy and Germany. It has made steady progress since 1978 when it was issued from Geisenheim, out of Müller-Thurgau and a crossing of the (female) French table grape Madeleine Angevine and the Italian Early Calabrese. Germany had 349 hectares (870 acres) planted by 1983 (largely in Rheinhessen, but also in the Mosel and Rheinpfalz), and the variety has also made considerable progress in English vineyards. Like Ehrenfelser, Reichensteiner takes its name from a castle, Schloss Reichenstein near Trechtingshausen in that tiny wine region, the Mittelrhein, where 1 hectare (2.5 acres) of vineyard was planted with Reichensteiner in 1983.

As one might expect from its genealogy, the wine is not the noblest but Reichensteiner is a very useful plant. As a vine and wine it perhaps most closely resembles Müller-Thurgau. It is no less susceptible to disease, but because of the looseness of its bunches it does not rot quite so easily, and produces about the same amount of similarly neutral wine. Must weights and acid levels tend to be slightly higher than those of Müller-Thurgau, however, and late-harvest wines are at least a possibility, especially if the grower is prepared to prune quite heavily.

The chief use of the crossing is on poor sites where it can be planted in the hope that it will achieve fairly high must weights. The wine has few distinguishing marks, but on some soils in England has achieved a certain distinction.

Neutral wine, fairly fussy vine.

PERLE

Gewürztraminer × Müller-Thurgau is an obvious crossing to develop and Perle, originally called Perle of Alzey, was the result of such experimentation at Alzey in the time of George Scheu. It was subsequently refined by Dr Breider at Würzburg using clonal selection.

The resulting wine is flowery, but not as extravagantly perfumed as one might expect from a child of Gewürztraminer. Only in Franken is the Perle treasured. Most of the rest of the German plantings – 281 hectares (700 acres) in 1983 – are in Rheinhessen.

The light pink grapes ripen between Müller-Thurgau and Silvaner; they are so compact on the bunch that rot is often a problem and care is needed in training to keep the vines well ventilated. The vine's strength is that its late budding gives it extremely good resistance to spring frost and it can therefore be planted on frost-prone sites with equanimity, a useful attribute in Germany.

Lightly floral; not particularly useful.

SIEGERREBE

The highest must weight ever achieved in Germany was in a parcel of Siegerrebe grown at Nussdorf in the Rheinpfalz which was harvested in 1971, as a Trockenbeerenauslese, of course, at 326° Oechsle, more than five times sweeter, for instance, than the average Liebfraumilch ingredient, or more than twice as ripe as necessary to qualify as a TBA. It is probably fermenting still and will never technically reach the alcohol level required for wine. The 1971 vintage may not have been the ripest ever for Germany, but it was the ripest in which these high-achieving new crossings were widely cultivated.

As well as being richer than any other German variety, it is also one of the most strongly flavoured. Indeed, so strong is its character that it is almost overpowering. Although a few producers make a varietal Siegerrebe, most of the Siegerrebe grown is used, in tiny proportions, to add richness to a blend. Riesling in particular can find itself completely subdued by the addition of just 10 percent Siegerrebe. Curiously, Gewürztraminer, which can seem rather muted when grown in Germany, produces a more pronounced variety by its crossing with a table grape.

There were only 270 hectares (675 acres) of the variety planted in 1983, mainly in Rheinhessen and Rheinpfalz.

The almost stultifying strength of its flavour effectively limits the potential growth of the crossing in Germany. Another disadvantage is that it is very susceptible to *coulure* and so average yields are very low for Germany, between 40 and 50 hectolitres per hectare.

The grapes need to ripen to above 100° Oechsle to give of their amazing all, and should, even though they ripen very early, be picked after Müller-Thurgau, thereby resisting disease (although not always the wasps). The vine buds early which can pose problems in years of spring frosts, so that Siegerrebe is not a viable proposition just any old where.

Like Gewürztraminer, Siegerrebe produces wines fairly low in acid, which means that they do not keep particularly well. They are a force to be reckoned with in youth, however, and make a useful blending ingredient in both Germany and England.

Very high must weights, very strong character.

Other Crossings

Fashions come and go in crossings and it would take but one really enthusiastic promulgator to lift a crossing into a much more important bracket. Fewer than 200 hectares (500 acres) of German vineyard were planted in 1983 with each of the following; they are listed in decreasing order of importance.

NOBLING

Silvaner × Gutedel (Freiburg 1939). 172 hectares (430 acres), mainly in Baden. Late budding and ripening. Relatively fussy about both site and soil. Good resistance to everything apart from botrytis. Average yield, about 90 hectolitres per hectare. Good must weights, Auslese no problem. Fresher and livelier than Silvaner but other crossings have overtaken it in popularity.

NOBLESSA

Madeleine Angevine × Silvaner Geilweilerhof 1975). 171 hectares (428 acres), 85 percent of them in Baden. Early budding and very early ripening. Not fussy about site or soil. Very susceptible to spring frost. Low yields, 40 to 50 hectolitres per hectare. High must weights. Too shy-bearing to gain ground.

REGNER

Luglienca Bianca (the white table grape Seidentraube) × Gamay (Alzey 1929). 147 hectares (367 acres) mainly in Rheinhessen. Early budding and very early ripening. No dry or calcareous soils, no great site requirements. Aeration needed to guard against oidium and rot. Yields slightly lower than Müller-Thurgau. Goodish must weights with slightly low acid. Not tiptop quality but reliable even in poor years, slightly better wines than Müller-Thurgau. Has performed very well in trials in England.

KANZLER ("Chancellor")

Müller-Thurgau × Silvaner (Alzey 1927). 114 hectares (285 acres), mainly in Rheinhessen but some in Rheinpfalz. Early budding and very early ripening. Poor wood quality necessitates fairly warm sites; soil requirements are high. Susceptible to spring frosts and peronospera. Lowish yield, about 65 hectolitres per hectare. High must weights even when the yield is relatively high.

Very good quality wine but low yields and fussiness about site militate against increase in popularity.

WÜRZER

Gewürztraminer × Müller-Thurgau (Alzey 1932). 113 hectares (283 acres), mainly in Rheinhessen. Medium-late budding, early ripening. Quite fussy about soil type. Loess/clay perfect. Medium hardiness and susceptibility. High yield, 80 to 120 hectolitres per hectare. Fairly high must weights.

Very dominating "spicy" aroma from Gewürztraminer; difficult to regulate yield to produce wines of any real quality in Germany. Possibly more successful in England.

FREISAMER

Silvaner × Pinot Gris (Freiburg 1916 and originally called Freiburger). 74 hectares (185 acres), mainly in Baden. Medium-early budding, medium-late ripening. Medium site requirements. Spring frosts a problem and oidium to a certain extent. Low to medium yield, usually less than Silvaner. Good rot resistance allows late harvesting and high must weights.

Relatively low yield usually of full-bodied but neutral wines. Intended as improvement on Silvaner, but overtaken by Müller-Thurgau fever.

SCHÖNBURGER

Pinot Noir × IP1 or Pirovano 1, itself Chasselas Rosé × Muscat of Hamburg (Geisenheim 1979). 69 hectares (172 acres), quite widely distributed in Germany, plus a notable presence in Somerset and Kent in England. Medium-late budding, early ripening. Medium soil and site requirements. Wood can cause problems in severe winters but good disease resistance. Medium yield; lower than Würzer, Kerner and Bacchus. Very good Oechsle, 10–15° higher than Riesling.

Slightly flabby wine, sometimes with odd off-flavour in Germany, where the lowish yield argues against wider cultivation. Some notable success in Britain despite its table grape antecedent. The grapes are pink, the wines white.

ALBALONGA

Rieslaner × Silvaner (Würzburg). 44 hectares (110 acres), mainly in Rheinhessen. Late budding, fairly early ripening. Medium to high soil and site requirements. Susceptible to botrytis. Yields just below Müller-Thurgau. Must weights just above Müller-Thurgau with good acid.

Good, vivacious, fruity wines, especially if absence of rot allows the grapes to reach Auslese level.

FINDLING

Müller-Thurgau mutation. 43 hectares (107 acres), mainly in Mosel. Medium-early budding, very early ripening. Medium site requirements. Very susceptible to botrytis. Yields 30 percent lower than Müller-Thurgau, but must weights higher, acidity at Müller-Thurgau level.

Produces even more neutral wines than Müller-Thurgau.

RIESLANER

Silvaner × Riesling (Würzburg 1921). 41 hectares (102 acres) mainly in Franken. Late budding and ripening. Fairly fussy about site, though not quite so much as Riesling. Susceptible to rot of both berries and stalks and to oidium. *Coulure* often ravages potential Riesling-like yield. High must weights.

This variety is most valued in Franken; barely accepted elsewhere, having been overtaken by its progeny Albalonga. Above 80° Oechsle, good, racy if slightly earthy wines, but high site requirement suggests expansion is limited.

SEPTIMER

Gewürztraminer × Müller-Thurgau (Alzey 1927). 31 hectares (77 acres), mainly in Rheinhessen. Late budding, early ripening. Needs slightly warmer sites than Müller-Thurgau, prefers sandy loam or clay. Can suffer from winter frosts and has poor disease resistance. Lowish yields, though higher than Siegerrebe. Highish must weights, best is 90° Oechsle.

This is Alzey's "seventh" (after Scheurebe, Siegerrebe, Perle, Huxelrebe, Kanzler and Faber) but is not as successful as its sister Perle, chiefly because of poor disease resistance. Its must weights can make it useful in English blends.

MARIENSTEINER

Silvaner × Rieslaner (Würzburg 1971). 31 hectares (77 acres) in Rheinpfalz, Rheinhessen and Franken. Late budding and ripening. Needs a fairly good site. Healthy vines. Good and reliable yields. High must weights. Promising wines whose only disadvantage is too much acidity in poor years. This is one to watch.

GUTENBORNER

Müller-Thurgau × Chasselas Napoleon (Geisenheim). 17 hectares (42 acres) mainly in Germany (unusually, in Mosel and Rheingau) and some sheltered territory in southern England. Medium-late budding, early ripening. Needs frost-free site and fairly damp soils. Healthy vines which need training to encourage air circulation. Quite high but very variable yields. Good must weights but not quite as good as Kerner in most regions.

In early stages of experimentation, but best results on Upper Mosel and, to a lesser extent, in England. In the Nahe, wines can be too neutral. Variability of yields probably a problem for the future.

FORTA

Madeleine Angevine × Silvaner (Geilweilerhof). 11 hectares (27 acres). Early budding and ripening. Relatively fussy about site but not about soil. Good disease resistance. Yield about the same as Riesling, 60 to 80 hectolitres per hectare. High must weights and good acid. Good quality wine, low yields.

Other varieties, most still at an experimental stage, of which no more than 10 hectares (25 acres) were counted in Germany in 1983, were Thurling, formerly

Aurea (Müller-Thurgau × Riesling); Hölder (Riesling × Pinot Gris); the Silvaner-like Gloria (Silvaner × Müller-Thurgau); Fontanara (Rieslaner × Müller-Thurgau); Ruling (Pinot Gris × Riesling); Cantaro (< Riesling × Silvaner> × Müller-Thurgau); Osteiner (Riesling × Silvaner); Oraniensteiner (Riesling × Silvaner). Fontanara, Cantaro and Hölder seem quite promising.

Other crossings that are even more experimental include Comtessa (Madeleine Angevine × Traminer); Aris (716 Oberlin × Riesling clone 91); Rabaner (Riesling clone 88Gm × Riesling clone 64Gm); Edelsteiner (Smederevka × Bouvier); Muscabona (Siegerrebe × Müller-Thurgau); Sisi (Silvaner × Siegerrebe); Tamara (Müller-Thurgau × Siegerrebe); Witberger (Trollinger × Riesling); and Arnsburger (Riesling clone 88 × Riesling clone 64). This last can, according to Becker, outperform Riesling in every way apart from consumer acceptance.

Crossings which seem to have dropped out of the race for the affections of German growers include Diana (Silvaner × Müller-Thurgau); Zähringer (Traminer × Riesling); and Multaner (Riesling × Silvaner).

Senator is the name given to what is supposedly a Silvaner mutation, of which there is a tiny plot at Langenlonsheim. Dalkauer is a crossing based on an unknown Veltliner mutation and unlikely to receive commercial recognition. Traditional white varieties that have all but died out include Früher Gelber Malinger which originated in the nursery of Malingre near Paris in the last century and was used to make Rheinpfalz primeur. The Alsace variety Früher Gelber Ortlieber was at one time cultivated in several southern German wine regions, but it has been abandoned in favour of varieties with more botrytis resistance and some discernible flavour.

Switzerland

CHASSELAS

For a vine that produces such generally unremarkable wine, Chasselas has a remarkable history. It may well be the oldest known vine variety cultivated by man. The leaves, red-veined and emphatically five lobed, bear a strong resemblance to those painted on the walls of the burial grounds at Luxor, and similar vines are said to thrive in Egypt today. The vine may well have been disseminated by the Phoenicians from this North African base, itself perhaps just a staging post from putative origins in what is now southern Lebanon. In theory at least, they could have taken it to Spain, to Italy and up the Rhône valley to France and Germany.

It is known that Chasselas flourished at Fontainebleau, producing popular grapes and wine for the royal court. Some say the Chasselas cuttings came from around Cahors, others that the ambassador Vicomte d'Auban brought them back from Constantinople in the time of François I. Ampelographer Babo, however, had the king bringing the cuttings back from Cyprus (a great wine breeding ground, according to many theories on the history of the vine). His counterpart Bronner cites Spanish origins. What is certain is that the Swiss owe their most important grape variety to a general of Louis XV, Courten, who took Chasselas cuttings from Fontainebleau to Valais.

Nowadays, the vine is important as a wine producer only in Switzerland, where more than 6,000 hectares (15,000 acres) are planted in the French-speaking cantons alone, compared with just over 1,000 hectares (2,500 acres) in France and 1,250 hectares (3,125 acres) in Germany. In the Valais it is called Fendant and sold as such: a soft, invariably dry, intriguingly alcoholic wine low in aroma and character and often enlivened by a little spritz to lubricate many a tourist meal. Dorin is the Vaud equivalent and it is on the higher slopes here, round Dézaley in the subregion Lavaux in particular, that the variety can be persuaded to show some real character: a smokiness of aroma and flinty delicacy. Other subregions of Vaud are La Côte and Chablais. In the canton of Geneva, the variety is known as Perlan, often a cleverly onomatopaeic name, as it would be in Neuchâtel where the local very dry Chasselas are often almost fizzy.

As one might imagine from the fact that the Swiss are so keen on it, Chasselas can be persuaded to be quite productive (50 to 150 hectolitres per hectare), provided it is given a site protected from wind for it can suffer from *coulure*. The grapes usually ripen just after Müller-Thurgau (or Riesling-Sylvaner as the Swiss insist on calling it) with fairly low levels of both sugar and acid. On the other hand, the naturally low potential alcohol levels mean that very cool vineyards are unsuitable. In Germany, for instance, it is cultivated almost exclusively in an enclave in the Markgräflerland district of Baden just north of Basel. Most of the wine produced

is café or Weinstube stuff to be drunk young and often by the jug rather than bottle. There are also about 30 hectares (75 acres) in East Germany planted with "Gutedel". Between the sixteenth and nineteenth centuries Gutedel was a relatively important and respectable variety in Germany, especially in Rheinpfalz.

As Chasselas it has also been a great deal more important in France than it is today. At one time it was cultivated all over eastern France, but is now of importance only in Alsace where its territory is shrinking. There were barely 400 hectares (1,000 acres) planted with it in Alsace in 1982, as opposed to more than 1,000 hectares (2,500 acres) in 1969. There are about 100 hectares (250 acres) planted in Haute Savoie close to the Swiss border producing fairly appetizing if neutral wines at Douvaine, Ballaison and Loisin. And, as every wine examinee knows, it is the variety responsible for the lesser and eponymous wine of Pouilly-sur-Loire.

There is said to be a small enclave of Chasselas vines in Cinqueterre in northwestern Italy; Viala certainly cites Marzemina Bianca as a synonym for Chasselas Doré but it is unrelated to Marzemino. The variety's role in eastern Europe today seems to be strictly as table grape supplier, although at one time it was grown for wine in Hungary and known as Fabian after its importer.

A very few acres of the related Chasselas Doré are still cultivated in California. The variety is relatively important in New Zealand where there are more than 230 hectares (575 acres) and in the 1983 vintage it produced more wine than all but three other varieties. After an attempt at varietal incarnation, it is chiefly used as blending material and, as in Switzerland, treasured for its low acidity.

Synonyms:
Chasselas Blanc, Chasselas Doré, Chasselas Croquant, Mornen Blanc, Viala, Valais (France);
Gutedel, Weisser Gutedel, Moster, Junker, Süssling, Silberling, Silberwissling, Süsstraube, Grossblättrige, Schönedel, Krachmost, Doppelte Spanische (Germany);
Marzemina Bianca, Tribianco Tedesco (Italy);
Fendant, Dorin, Rosmarintraube, Terravin, Perlan (Switzerland);
Moster, Wälscher (Austria);
Zupljanka (Yugoslavia).

Important table grape.
Wine is mostly thin, soft and insipid except in some Swiss locations.

Other specifically Swiss white varieties include the Valais' Amigne, Arvine and Humagne, traditional, very particular and progressively richer "oddities" which sound like synonyms for a single variety. Paien (also known as Heida) is a local variant of Gewürztraminer cultivated on some of the highest vineyards of Valais. Another Valais speciality Rèze, also available in Noir and Rosé versions, provides the little-known *vin du glacier* made tart and light tawny using the *solera* system. Completer was also grown at one time.

The Zurich speciality is Rauschling, a variety that was once planted in Alsace and Baden. Also known as Zürirebe, Thuner Rebe, Tuner and Welsche, its wine is about as distinguished as Müller-Thurgau but the Zurichers appreciate it as a local gulp.

Austria

GRÜNER VELTLINER

This, *the* grape of Austria, is a charming variety, producing wines of real interest to wine drinkers in quantities of interest to vine growers: an unusual combination. At first glance, it is puzzling that Grüner Veltliner is grown only in central Europe. This is partly because it ripens fairly late and therefore needs milder autumns than can be offered further north; and partly, one suspects, because the wine it produces is almost always good, but never great. It is almost incapable of *not* giving great pleasure and delight, but would never warrant intellectual study. Producing a wine for quaffers rather than connoisseurs, it was apparently designed specifically for the casual *heurigen* wine-cafés in the hillside villages around Vienna.

Typical Grüner Veltliner is pale green, fruity and dry, fairly high in acid, medium in body, often has a slight prickle of gas and always a spicy, almost musky aroma that is faintly reminiscent of the pungency that is common to all Alsace wines. Grüner Veltliner is best enjoyed when the bloom of youth is still on it.

Austria's 19,000 hectares (47,500 acres) of Grüner Veltliner constitute 32 percent of her total vine plantings, and the variety is the most planted vine in almost all wine districts apart from those in Styria. It is very important in Lower Austria where it responded particularly well to the famous Hochkultur high trellising introduced by Lenz Moser in the thirties.

The vine is generally healthy, and can well withstand chilly winters. It is slightly susceptible to peronospera and ripens middle to late in the season, producing yields of 100 hectolitres per hectare without difficulty. It is the Müller-Thurgau of Austria, but so much more exciting.

The variety is also cultivated just over the Czech border in Moravia, over the Yugoslav border in the reclaimed sandy plain between the Danube and Tisza rivers and over the Hungarian border in that nick out of Austrian territory Sopron, as the slightly flabby Soproni Veltlini. The Grüner Veltliner, also well known in Romania, blithely and understandably ignores border controls.

There are also the minor Brauner

Gruner Veltliner

Veltliner and Roter Veltliner (as distinct from the Frühroter Veltliner described below) which are popular in Lower Austria and produce very fruity whites on heavy soils. The Roter Veltliner, which Georg Scheu considered suitable for Germany, is also grown in California where there are still about 20 hectares (50 acres),

mainly in Monterey and San Benito counties.

Synonyms:
Grüner, Grünmuskateller, Weissgipfler, Mouhardrebe, Manhardsrebe (Austria); Zleni Veltinac (Yugoslavia); Veltlini (Hungary).

Crisp, lightly spiced wines.

NEUBURGER

Austria has nearly 2,000 hectares (5,000 acres) of Neuburger, a Weissburgunder × Silvaner crossing probably developed in the Wachau district of Lower Austria but its exact origins are unknown. The wine is full bodied but not as distinctively flavoured as most Austrian varieties, although the official literature endows it with nuttiness. The vine ripens early with a fairly good yield and higher must weights than Grüner Veltliner. It is virtually unknown outside Austria apart from some plantings in Transylvania.

Full, slightly flat.

FRÜHROTER VELTLINER

This variety is the cause of much confusion involving Veltliner with the completely unrelated Malvasia of southern Europe, and the Valtellina region of northern Italy. It was grown in the hills of Savoie in France and Switzerland as Malvoisie Rosé (distinct from their "Malvoisie" which was Pinot Gris). It was known in Germany at one time as Frühroter Malvasier, or Roter Malvasier. And it is but a slip of the tongue from Veltliner to Valteliner and thence to Valtellina, one of the few wine regions of Italy where Malvasia of some sort is not known today.

It is in Austria that most of today's plantings are to be found: more than 1,200 hectares (3,000 acres), chiefly in northern Lower Austria. As the name suggests, it ripens early. Yields are only moderate. The wine produced, while high in extract, is rather low in acid.

The variety is grown to a very limited extent in the South Tyrol (Alto Adige) and may still be found in older plantings in Switzerland and Savoie, but has virtually disappeared in Germany.

Synonyms:
Malvoisie Rosé, Valteliner Précoce, Malvoisie Rouge d'Italie (France); Roter Malvasier, Frühroter Malvasier (Germany); Veltliner (Italy).

Bit overweight.

BOUVIER

This table grape bred at Radkersburg is used for wine chiefly in Burgenland and to a certain extent in Styria where there is a total of 600 hectares (1,500 acres) planted. Significantly, the name is rarely found on wine labels. The vines ripen very early and have such good must weights that Spätlese wines are possible in Burgenland, but the wine is sufficiently ordinary for most to be used for blending.

As Ranina it is cultivated in Slovenia and Fruska Gora in Yugoslavia. The Ranina of Radgona is a sweetish Slovenian speciality marketed as "Tiger's Milk". Bouvier can also be found in Hungary.

Synonyms:
Ranina (Yugoslavia); Bouviertraube (Austria).

Table grape; very basic.

ROTGIPFLER

Like Rosencrantz without Guildenstern, Rotgipfler is nothing without Zierfandler. These are the wonderfully idiosyncratic vines responsible for a wine that manages to match them in tongue-twisting ability, Gumpoldskirchner, perhaps Austria's single most famous wine. The score is Rotgipfler 190 hectares (475 acres), Zierfandler 140 hectares (350 acres).

Rotgipfler is the slightly more ponderous of the two varieties. It ripens late but before Zierfandler, and is planted only in the best, south-facing sites. It is today a local speciality, although at one stage it was known in Württemberg, Baden and Alsace and is mentioned in several international ampelographies of the 1800s.

The wine produced is very rich but fermented out dry to produce the ultra-spicy, very heady Gumpoldskirchner – another wine that suggests Alsace, almost of Vendange Tardive level.

Synonyms:
Rotreifler, Reifler (Germany); Zelen, Slatki Zelenac (Yugoslavia).

Heady.

ZIERFANDLER

A particularly late-ripening variety, Zierfandler is Rotgipfler's "other half" in Gumpoldskirchen. Its wine is notably more perfumed than Rotgipfler and has a bit more acidity, although it is just as full-bodied. Unblended, Zierfandler can produce late-harvest wines that can take ageing. Late ripening apart, the variety is relatively easy to grow and it is a mystery why Rotgipfler is more popular.

As Cirfandli, it is cultivated quite widely on the Great Hungarian Plain and the wine, especially that produced in the sandy vineyards around Kecskemet, is heady even in the Hungarian context.

Synonyms:
Cirfandli (Hungary);
Spätrot, Roter Zierfandler (Austria).

Heady and flavourful.

Other white varieties associated most readily with Austria include Jubilaumsrebe developed at Klosterneuburg from Portugieser and Blaufränkisch for white wine production and Goldburger, a crossing of Welschriesling with Orangetraube still grown (just) as a colour-intensifying vine.

Hungary

EZERJO

Like so many of Hungary's intriguingly wide range of native white vine varieties, Ezerjó owes its name not to tame geography or physical characteristics, but to romance: Ezerjó means "a thousand boons". Many growers have taken its name literally and it is planted all over the country, constituting Hungary's third most planted white grape variety with 14,200 hectares (35,500 acres).

Much of the wine produced by these vines is turgid stuff but there is a very honourable exception. Best known and best quality is the Móri Ezerjó made in the district of Mór where it covers a good 90 percent of all vineyard land. The extensive vineyards to the northeast of Mór between the Danube and Lake Balaton manage to keep acidity levels in the Ezerjó grapes appetizingly high. The resulting wines are usually dry, light and clean and have a freshness all too rare in Hungarian whites. They may sometimes be slightly spritzy and have a finish whose slight lack of fruit suggests that the Móri custom is to pick the grapes early. Móri Ezerjó is perhaps Hungary's nearest answer to the fragile charms of Muscadet.

Synonym: Tausendgut.

Fairly basic but crisp.

MEZESFEHER

The literal translation of this varietal name gives a good indication of the wine it produces: "white honey". It is an important white vine grown on the Great Plain, around Balaton, in Eger, Bulls Blood country, and on the foothills of the Matra mountains, although it is rarely trumpeted on wine labels seen abroad. Perhaps this is because Hungarians are conscious that their appreciation of sweet wines is unusual today. The wines vary from flabby table wines to rich dessert wines of real quality. The best provenances are Eger and the Gyöngyös district of Mátravidék. No connection has ever been established between this variety and any vine grown outside Hungary.

Sweet and variable.

FURMINT

This is the white variety which international wine drinkers associate most readily with Hungary, chiefly because it is the predominant variety in Tokay, one of the few wines that could justifiably be described as legendary.

Furmint

The variety may well be Hungarian in origin and certainly reaches its apogee there, though R. E. H. Gunyon suggests a more exotic past in his *Wines of Central and South-eastern Europe.* According to him it was imported into the Tokay district in the thirteenth century by Walloon vine growers invited there by King Bela IV in the wake of the Tartar invasion. The wine

was called "froment" after its wheat-gold colour and the rest of the story is obvious.

Furmint is quite widely planted, covering nearly 5,000 hectares (12,500 acres) in total, and red mutations are by no means uncommon. Most of Hungary's Furmint vines are in the Tokay region, but there are substantial plantings in Balatonfüred-Csopak, Mecsek and Sopron.

The wine it produces is distinctly Magyar: sturdy with real fire, though more acid and rather less subtle in flavour than the Hárslevelü with which it is blended to produce Tokay. Natural alcohol strengths of 14 percent are by no means uncommon. Furmint used to be the dominant variety in the Tokay blend, but the state wine cellarmaster has been moving towards an almost equal mix, with up to 5 percent of Yellow Muscat in some vintages to give Tokay more apparent lusciousness. Its most common manifestation is as a strong, dryish varietal table wine produced all over Hungary and in much of the rest of eastern Europe.

Furmint is early budding and medium flowering but its vegetative cycle starts to slow up as ripening approaches and the famous shrivelled Aszú berries may not be picked until well into the autumn. The thin-skinned grapes rot nobly and easily and are particularly useful as an Aszú ingredient in dry weather.

A little Furmint is doubtless grown across the Czech border from Tokay, as it is across the Austrian border from Sopron. The Sipon, and almost certainly Pošip, of Yugoslavia are thought to be none other than Furmint, and Grasa of Romania may be a distant relative too. Sipon is considered one of Yugoslavia's better white varieties and is grown in Slovenia, though it rarely reminds the drinker of the great wines of Tokay. As Pošip, it is highly regarded on the Dalmatian coast where it produces strong, dark golden wines of varying degrees of sweetness. Some Furmint is also grown in the USSR.

For obvious reasons, Furmint is sometimes wrongly associated with the Italian variety Tocai, and sometimes even with Pinot Gris or Tokay d'Alsace.

Synonyms:
Sipon, Moslavac Bijeli (Yugoslavia).

Strong and tart. Has produced one of the world's great sweet wines.

HARSLEVELU

This is the variety that gives smoothness and spicy character to the famous Tokay. A few vines over the Czech border apart, the "lime leaf" variety is exclusively Hungarian and is today a major shaper of the flavour of Tokay.

The grapes have less acid and lower must weights than those of Furmint, but are more aromatic. They are much larger, thicker skinned grapes which do not respond well to the depredations of "noble rot", but "cover" for Furmint by providing useful material for Tokay Aszú in wetter vintages.

The vine is grown all over Hungary with the best-known varietal wines produced from grapes grown around Kunbaja on the Yugoslav border, at nearby Baja on the Danube, and in the prolific vineyards of Vilány; the relatively sweet and pungent Debroi Hárslevelü comes from the foothills of the Matra mountains. Its almost sweet perfume and spicy flavour is much prized by Hungarians.

Powerfully scented.

JUHFARK

The "sheep's tail" variety was at one time grown all over Hungary. It took the ravages of phylloxera and, in particular, oidium to purge the plains of it, but it can still be found in old plantations on the north side of Lake Balaton around Zánka and Köveskal and in the vineyards of Györ. Today plantings are probably not more than 100 hectares (250 acres).

The variety's chief disadvantage is its extreme sensitivity to spring frost and to disease, especially peronospera. The green-tinged wine is notably aromatic with acidity that is relatively discernible for a Hungarian white.

Difficult vines.

KEKNYELU

The "blue-stalked" variety is a great deal more famous in Hungary than it perhaps deserves to be now that its area is so reduced: today there are only about 10 hectares (25 acres) in an all-Kéknyelü plantation in Badacsony.

It is commonly thought to be another ancient Hungarian variety, though some ampelographers have seen similarities between it and the little-known Italian variety Picoletto Bianco. Badacsony Kéknyelü, which seems to be made in greater quantity than one would think 10 hectares allowed, is spicy in flavour, relatively high in alcohol and extract, but just off-dry with lots of acid and often a fairly deep colour, although this may be due

Kéknyelü

more to vinification techniques than to the inherent properties of the grape.

Probably Balaton's best.

> Other white varieties planted chiefly in Hungary include Kövidinka (or Dinka), a traditional but very ordinary vine that is also grown in Yugoslavia, the equally uninspiring Sahfeher and Szlankamenka that are grown on the Great Plain, and Irsayi Oliver, a new sort of Muscat which is being developed at Eger.

Yugoslavia

It is almost as difficult to penetrate Yugoslavia's viticultural labyrinth as to understand the complex administrative make-up of what many outsiders believe is a single nation. The following highlights the best-known and/or most important varieties, and lists other specifically Yugoslavian varieties which are likely to withstand longest the onward march of Rieslings, Merlot, Cabernets and the like.

PLAVAC

Plavać of several sorts, either Beli (white) or Zuti (yellow), is perhaps the nearest Yugoslavia has to a national basic white grape variety, although it is rarely found outside Slovenia and the coastal vineyards. (Plavać Mali is its red counterpart.)

It thrives on sandy soils and is commonly grown on the islands that occlude the Dalmatian coastline as well as on the marl of the Sava area of Slovenia. The wine produced is often blended with other, more powerfully flavoured varieties. These include Welschriesling, which gives some idea of the lack of character of Plavać solo. Alcohol it can produce, however, and wines up to 14 percent are commonplace.

Basic but sturdy.

SMEDEREVKA

This is Serbia's answer to white Plavać and is of notably better quality for wine, although it is also grown as a table grape. It takes its name from the town of Smederevo just south of Belgrade where until recently it constituted 80 percent of all wine-grape plantings, though plantings of Welschriesling, with which it is often blended, have been increasing.

On the higher vineyards of the autonomous republic of Kosovo between Belgrade and Albania, Smederevka is reckoned to produce a varietal good enough to qualify as a quality wine, but it is more usually blended and sold with less honour. The variety is moderately high in natural acids and is usually vinified dry.

Widely grown in southern Yugoslavia, Smederevka is also encountered occasionally in Hungary and was a parent, with the Austrian Bouvier, of a newish Baden crossing, Edelsteiner.

Synonyms:
Belina, Szemendrianer, Grobweisse.

Light but crisp; above average.

MARASTINA

This essentially Yugoslavian variety is much planted in Dalmatia, especially in the south and on the wine-producing islands. Some quite crisp dry varietals are made from the grape around Dubrovnik, although it is also commonly blended with other, even more intriguing local varieties such as the "island varieties" of Grk and Vugava. Perhaps the most exciting manifestation of such a blend is in the fiery dessert wine Prošek Dioklecijan produced near Split. It is nutty, long, very sweet but well-balanced and has a natural strength of 16 percent.

Its most prized and protected form is as the Dalmatian Maraština Smokvica Cara.

Synonym: Rukatac.

Very good quality.

ZILAVKA

This is a speciality even within this country of specialities. Zilavka is the white grape of Herzegovina in Muslim Bosnia where only about 2 percent of the country's wine is made. This is white-wine territory, centred on the town of Mostar, and such is the quality of the Zilavka grape that even at this latitude it manages to produce a fullish, dry wine of almost nerve-tingling freshness and intriguing nutty fragrance. This may also have something to do with the valley's limestone subsoil, because Zilavka planted further inland seems much heavier.

Zilavka Mostar, made from Zilavka blended with Krkosija and Bena, is one of Yugoslavia's most fiercely protected wine names and its exotic label proclaims its *grand cru* status.

Unique.

Other varieties regarded as definitely superior in Yugoslavia are Grk and Vugava, most popular on the islands. Grk, much grown on Korcula, is relatively easy to find as a dry lightish white varietal (sometimes the permitted 15 percent fillip is Maraština), although it is also responsible for some heavier sherry-like wines. Vugava is a speciality of the island of Vis but seems to be on the decline; it is not even included in the list of varieties accepted by the EEC authorities. A connection between it and Viognier makes for interesting speculation.

Also Dalmatian and much more important are the rather ordinary Debit and the better quality Bogdanuša, a specialty of Hvar. Belan is Macedonia's equivalent of Debit while Krstac is a Montenegro speciality.

Pinela and Zlatina are the native varieties of Istria which appear, despite the name of the first, to have no connection with any vine now grown in nearby Italy. Zlatina is also known as Zlahtnina, Zlatitnina and Salsa Bela.

Other goodish quality Yugoslavian white varieties are Kujundzusa and Moslavac, while Kraljevina of Croatia, Ranfol of Slovenia, Plavaline and Slankamenka are also grown.

Romania

FETEASCA ALBA

This variety, identical to Hungary's Leányka, has almost as strong a character as Gewürztraminer, and if more examples had just a bit more acidity, might well be almost as popular. The wine produced is very aromatic in a peachy, sometimes apricoty, way suggestive of a Muscat gene.

There must be something feminine about the variety for both its Hungarian name Leányka and Mädchentraube its common synonym in Romania, especially for German-speaking markets, translate into something young, girlish, almost virginal.

The Hungarians and Romanians view this variety as one of their whites worth ageing. It is true that it has so much flavour that it does not pale into insignificance with age, a common characteristic in eastern European white wines. With only moderate acidity, however, the older examples can be obtrusive rather than impressive. An Egri Leányka 1969 tasted at 10 years old was fiery but flabby. Unusually, the red version, Feteascǎ Neagrǎ, ages considerably faster.

Feteascǎ Albǎ

Leányka is one of Hungary's more important white grapes and is widely grown on the Great Plain and, especially, on the vineyard slopes of northeastern Hungary. Most of the wine made from the

variety whether in Hungary, Romania or the USSR is off-dry to medium sweet.

In Romania, two subvarieties have been identified, Feteascǎ Albǎ and Feteascǎ Regalǎ (which is also known as Königliche and Königsast in Germany). The Romanians are particularly proud of this, exclusively Romanian "royal" subvariety. Feteascǎ is probably still Romania's most planted white grape and is grown in Transylvania, Banat, Odobesti and the ancient wine district of Cotnari, famous for very rich white dessert wines.

There are about 1,000 hectares (2,500 acres) of Fetiaska in Bulgaria and it is also grown in Zakarpatye in the USSR, where it is used in sparkling-wine production.

Synonyms:
Leányka (Hungary); Mädchentraube (Germany and Romania); Fetiaska (Bulgaria).

Very perfumed.

GRASA

Grasǎ's most glorious role is as major ingredient in the sweet wines of Cotnari in Moldavia, with Feteascǎ and the minor variety Frincusa in the supporting cast. Such is the staying power and evolution of mature Cotnari that varietal Grasǎ would seem to be well worth ageing. The Romanians have evolved strains of this variety variously called Coarna and Som in different regions. They all produce very alcoholic, rich, but not necessarily sweet, wines with a fairly deep colour which have led some authorities to suggest a close connection with Furmint.

Grasǎ is an important variety in the extensive Dealul Mare region, especially in the Petroasa district.

Synonyms:
Coarna, Som (Romania); Dicktraube (Germany).

Good quality; can age.

TAMIIOASA ROMANEASCA

This, the "frankincense grape", has the most extraordinary aroma, reminiscent in its acrid quality of freshly ground coffee beans. Tǎmiîoasǎ is a true original whose grape can be ripened up to very high must weights in some years, and whose wines can have enough acidity to make extremely good, if slightly rustic, sweet wines – at absurdly low prices.

Tǎmiîoasǎ is one of the few survivors among Romania's ancient varieties and is grown in the Dragasani region, in Arges,

Dealul Mare and to a very limited extent in Cotnari. It is also grown, as Tamianka, in parts of Bulgaria, but its odd and very positive character is out of step with that country's policy on viticulture.

Synonyms:
Weihrauchtraube (Germany);
Tamianka (Bulgaria).

Very individual – sweet wines especially.

BANAT RIESLING

This rather neutral variety is grown in the Banat region of Romania as well as over the border in Yugoslavia. The wines are rather flabby and age at lightning speed.

Synonyms:
Creata, Zackelweiss,
Kreaka (Yugoslavia).

Dull.

Bulgaria

DIMIAT

Dimiat, Bulgaria's own version of the Yugoslavian Smederevka of Serbia, is highly regarded as a common grape of better than average quality within Bulgaria, even if its name is less familiar on the international market than that of many other varieties grown there.

Bulgaria grows more than 8,000 hectares (20,000 acres) of Dimiat, making it the country's most planted white grape variety after Rkatsiteli. It is a speciality of Chirpan and Haskovo in the south and of Shumen and Varna in the east.

The grapes are large and copper coloured and the variety is capable of relatively high yields. The wines produced vary enormously in sweetness, and Dimiat is quite commonly used for dessert wines as well as for light table wines. What characterizes it is its aroma suggestive of sweet, ripe fruit. It can produce very attractive wines for early consumption.

High yields of soft, gently perfumed wine.

RED MISKET

Despite the name, and the rather grapey flavour, this is a traditional Bulgarian variety, unrelated to the major Muscat Blanc à Petits Grains family, which has several red members. The quality of Bulgarian Misket exported is not usually such as to inspire comparison with this, the noblest form of Muscat. It is also distinct from Muscat Ottonel, planted all over eastern Europe.

The grapes are used chiefly to produce fairly light white wines, as are those of the red Muscat grown in Alsace. The resulting wines have a certain grapiness but they are often stale and musky rather than glorious and aromatic. The variety is relatively productive and is particularly successful in Karlovo in the southern Valley of Roses. It is also grown at Sungurlare in the east, and in Pleven and Varna on the coast as Varnenski Misket. The variety is very well established in Bulgaria and subvarieties are often called after the region to which they have become acclimatized.

The variety is quite a high yielder and ripens early. It can be found around the Black Sea coast in the Soviet Union.

Synonym: Misket de Sliven.

Moderate quality. Muscat flavour but not genealogy.

USSR

RKATSITELI

Despite its origins in that most impenetrable of wine superpowers, Rkatsiteli is an international variety, grown in New York State, California and China as well as in eastern Europe. Translated from the local dialect, its name means simply "red vine".

Not only does the variety enjoy wide distribution, it is the Soviet Union's most planted wine grape, covering more than 18 percent of the Soviet vineyard or some 248,000 hectares (620,000 acres) and increasing fast. It has by now in fact overtaken Trebbiano in area planted (though it probably still produces less wine) to become the world's second most planted white grape variety.

Rkatsiteli was first recognized in Georgia and accounts for well over half of all wine production there, but it has spread to prominence in all other vine-growing Soviet republics. It is heartening that a grape so important quantitatively should also be of fairly good quality. It can produce wines of real style. Acidity levels are refreshingly high and yet there is character there, too: a pure, spicy yet almost floral aroma as well as good sugar levels. In this respect the sprightly table wines are distinctly reminiscent of Alsace.

Within the Soviet Union it is highly regarded as useful, productive and versatile, providing the raw material for many

Rkatsiteli

different wine types in Georgia. Its main use, however, is in what they call "European" table wines. In Kakhetia and Kartalinia it is also used for very sweet dessert wines inventively sold as "Krardanakhi port", "Khirsa madeira" and "Saamo liqueur wine". And while they are about it, they also use Rkatsiteli to produce sherry-like and cognac-like liquids, for the wine reacts well to intentional oxidation and oak maturation.

In the south of the Ukraine Rkatsiteli wines retain their aroma, but can be harsh and too tart. The grapes are best picked when the potential alcohol is almost 20 percent in mid-October. The acidity then is usually still more than 9 grammes per litre but can be tamed by modern vinification methods of extracting maximum fruit flavours. The only respect in which Rkatsiteli lets the Soviet wine industry down is in its imperfections as a base wine for their extraordinarily popular sparkling wines; it has too much alcohol.

Rkatsiteli is also the most planted variety in Bulgaria; its 19,000 hectares (47,500 acres) just beat Cabernet Sauvignon's 18,000 hectares (45,000 acres). It is used there almost exclusively for dryish white table wines.

The variety is cultivated only on a very small scale in the United States, but varietal bottlings have been seen.

Very important and quite high quality.

MTSVANE

In the Soviet Union this is regarded as one of the finest native varieties, producing very fresh aromatic fruity wines designed for early consumption when vinified at fairly low temperatures with extended skin contact. Its home is the Kakhetia region of Georgia but it has also been cultivated in the Crimea. It has an attractive floweriness in young table wines. Test bottlings of dessert wines with Mtsvane as base have also been promising, retaining some of the perfume in a well-balanced richer wine.

Good quality.

TERBASH

Terbash is a very traditional Turkmenian variety which is now also grown in Tadzhikistan, Uzbekistan and the Crimea. It generally ripens late and in the most southern wine regions loses acidity fast as it ripens, making it unsuitable for top-quality table wine. It is used there for raisining, as a table grape, for grape juice and as base for sweet dessert wines.

In the cooler vineyards in more northern regions it is used for ordinary table wines. It is relatively important for this purpose in the Crimea.

Ancient but usually flabby.

BAYAN SHIREY

Bayan Shirey is also widely cultivated in the wine regions of the Soviet Union, although it takes its name from the Bayan area in Azerbaijan, the most southerly vine-growing republic. It is losing ground, however, as its heavy, easily oxidized style is not in tune with national wine policy.

It ripens late and yields very well to produce base wine for ordinary blended table wines, unexceptional sparkling wines and also for grape juice.

Greece
SAVATIANO

Greece's most planted vine variety is chiefly responsible for her best-known wine, retsina. Savatiano, with Rhoditis and Assyrtiko, is responsible for the oceans of resinated, alcoholic, light golden liquid swilled in tavernas all over the world.

It dominates the vinescape in the most important wine regions, Central Greece and the island of Euboea, and is almost the only variety planted in the Attica vineyards around Athens which constitute the Greek centre of white wine production.

Total plantings are around 32,000 hectares (80,000 acres).

It owes its popularity in this, Greece's hottest and driest wine region, to its good drought resistance. Indeed conditions are so arid that the incidence of vine disease is negligible. The chief disadvantage of Savatiano wine is that it is very low in natural acid. The high-acid wine of Assyrtiko grapes is used as a corrective in Attica, while Rhoditis is the traditional blending partner in Euboea and Anchialos. However, the very process of adding Aleppo pine resin seems to make the result rather less of a wine, with the concomitant need for "balance", and rather more of a drink. Who needs acidity when they have something as overpowering as resin?

Kantza is the best-known wine made (solely) of Savatiano.

The retsina grape; flabby.

RHODITIS

Before the vineyard plagues of the end of the last century, Rhoditis was widely grown in Greece, but it has not recovered this position in the post-phylloxera era, as the vine is particularly susceptible to the oidium which was in many ways a more serious problem. Its current cultivation is restricted to the area from Anchialos to Magnesie near Volos, and it is especially popular in the Peloponnese.

This pink-berried vine is medium-late ripening, fairly high in acidity and can cope well at high altitudes. The produce of Rhoditis vines grown around Patras between 200 and 450 metres are responsible for the relatively delicate and prized wines bearing the name of the city. Anchialos wine is also made of Rhoditis, most of it used for nothing grander than ordinary, nameless table wine, both resinated and not, and usually blended with the much flabbier Savatiano.

Synonym: Roditis.

Moderate quality.

ASSYRTIKO

Like the Arinto of Portugal, this is a high quality variety designed to keep its acid well when grown in hot conditions. It is a speciality of the island of Santorini in the Aegean and is one of the main ingredients in the dry white wine of that name.

It is also used as an acid corrector for the Savatiano grown around Athens and has produced the extraordinary *liastos* wines reminiscent of Italy's nutty-sweet

vino passito and indeed often labelled, like the Tuscan version, Vin Santo.

Good quality, good acid.

MOSCOPHILERO

This family of vines – white, yellow and pink – is the speciality of the high Mantinian plateau in the middle of the Peloponnese. The altitude does a great deal to compensate for the latitude of these vineyards and some rather elegant wines can result. The grapes are not usually picked until the end of October and their produce used either to make light, dry, fragrant whites or, unusually, sparkling wines. Although all the grapes are capable of producing a fruity, well-balanced wine, only the pink Moscophilero grapes have a distinctly muscaty aroma. A relationship with the Muscat family seems likely, though the variety is clearly distinguished within Greece from its many members.

Aromatic, relatively delicate.

DEBINA

Debina is grown in the Epirus region just south of Albania and its best-known wine takes the name of the northern town Zitsa. It is unique to six villages, all around 600 metres above sea level on very dry, hillside terrain. The wine, like that from Moscophilero, is lighter than one normally associates with Greece, varies in sweetness and is often the lightly sparkling Perle.

Light, crisp.

ROBOLA

Robola completes the trio of Greek light whites and produces the most reliably appetizing wine. It is grown exclusively on the island of Cephalonia off the northwest coast of the Peloponnese and produces a wine with considerable body, quite enough acidity and a lemony, very slightly floral flavour. The grapes may be picked as early as the third week in August.

Much admired by sophisticated Greeks, Robola is a curiously isolated vine, both literally and metaphorically. It would help to explain this mystery if it were related to the Ribolla of Udine in northeast Italy and/or the Rebula of Slovenia in northwest Yugoslavia. Robola may have travelled along the same trade routes as Malvasia did from Crete.

Good; full but balanced.

Athiri is an ancient vine grown in small quantities on many of the islands. It is allowed exclusive rights to the name Rhodes on a wine label. In other wines it may be blended with the likes of Vilana and Ladikino.

Aidani brings a slight Muscat flavour to some island wines, while Batiki is grown in Thessalonia mainly as a table grape; various subvarieties of Verdea can also be found.

Comforting evidence of conventional vine wisdom can be seen in the odd example of Greece's most famous vine Monemvasia (surely our old friend Malvasia?) which survive on the island of Paros in the Cyclades, where Malvasia is thought to have originated.

Cyprus

XYNISTERI

This is Cyprus's native white variety, accounting for most of the vineyard not planted with the red Mavron; about 500 hectares (1,250 acres). The vineyards high up on the southern slopes of the Troodos mountains above Limassol are most respected as yielders of delicate Commandaria dessert wine, a marked contrast to the more sugary charms of the commercial blends based on Mavron.

Xynisteri produces table wine that is rather neutral, which is perhaps hardly surprising since yields are expected to average 100 hectolitres per hectare. Aroma has to be coaxed out of it by fastidious fermentation, which also helps to guard against its natural tendency to oxidize in the prevailing climate.

Experiments with August-picked, cool-fermented Xynisteri have produced fragrant, crisp table wines. October-picked, overripe grapes turned into fairly flabby, flat, deep-coloured whites may be a caricature but are nearer the current norm.

Medium quality, neutral.

Nave can produce light, fruity wines but is much less widely planted.

Turkey

Some of Turkey's most admired white varieties are Hasandede, Emir and Nerince from central Anatolia; Emir makes the best dry whites. The Beylerce of Bilecik is also respected. Other varieties in this truly exotic wineland are Yapincak, Atlintas and the Kabarcik and Dobulgen from Anatolia bordering on that tantalizingly impenetrable wine country Syria.

Japan

With the red Campbell's Early, the following four varieties account for 90 percent of Japan's total vineyard of more than 30,000 hectares (75,000 acres). The other 10 percent is planted chiefly with small plots of varieties imported from Europe such as Sémillon, Riesling, Chardonnay, Cabernet Sauvignon and Merlot. Unusually, each of the three vine families – European, American and Asian – will grow in Japan. Unfortunately the climate is so wet and the soil either so waterlogged or so acid, that it is difficult for any of these vines to produce top-quality wine. American hybrids seem to cope the best. Local hazards can include landslides, typhoons and salt winds, but work continues on developing varieties best adapted to the conditions that prevail in each of the very different wine regions.

DELAWARE

Together Delaware and Campbell's Early cover more than half of Japan's vineyard land. Delaware is also grown in North America and Brazil, although it is by no means one of the most popular hybrids either north or south of the Mexican border. Its popularity in Japan is something of a mystery.

The variety with its sharply pointed and indented leaf was first taken in 1849 from the nursery of Paul Provost of Frenchtown, New Jersey, to be propagated in Delaware, Ohio. It is thought to be a *labrusca-aestivalis-vinifera* hybrid. The wines it produces are less aggressively "foxy" or *labrusca*-tasting than many other hybrids (which has helped to promote the *vinifera* connection thesis) and are usually high in acid, making them suitable base material for sparkling wines. The dark pink grapes are also popular table grapes.

Like its postulated *vinifera* antecedent, the vine is susceptible to phylloxera, and to fungus diseases, so that it does not have one of the major advantages of a hybrid. This is

presumably a factor in making it so much less popular in New York State than, say, Concord of which there are over 10 times more plantings in the United States even though Delaware is almost as productive and ripens more than two weeks earlier. It is thought of as a distinctly superior hybrid in the States where it is prized for the delicacy and slight spiciness of its wines, many of them sparkling.

In Japan growers at the beginning of the century, whose vineyards had been devastated by phylloxera, were presumably prepared to persevere with Delaware simply because it was the best white hybrid that they knew, and therefore offered reasonably high yields of wine suited to consumers more familiar with pale drinks such as sake. Early ripening also helps protect it from Japan's September rains. The Japanese solution to Delaware's sensitivity to rainfall in July before picking is individual wrapping of vines with waxed paper or plastic parasols.

Delicate wine for a hybrid.

KOSHU

Koshu is the nearest the Japanese have to a national grape variety and, surprisingly, it is a member of the *vinifera* family rather than of the *amurensis*, *coignetiae*, *Thunbergii* or *flexuosa* species native to the Far East.

The first records of Koshu's successful cultivation in Japan are dated 1186, although it was not until the last century that it was asked to produce wine. It is now an important ingredient in many blended whites, and has sired another important Japanese variety, Muscat Bailey A.

Synonym: Konshu.

Fruity wines.

MUSCAT BAILEY A

This variety does not exactly lend itself to varietal labelling. Its Koshu genes must endow it with some suitability for Japanese conditions; it is a hybrid of *labrusca* and Koshu. Muscat Bailey A is grown particularly on the southern coast and is sometimes even given barrel ageing. The wines it produces can be quite a deep pink.

Useful rosé material.

NEO MUSCAT

This is grown extensively in the San Yo coastal region but is more often eaten than drunk. It is also grown in China.

China

Scores – though significantly not hundreds – of traditional Chinese grape varieties are grown in China today, many of them for the table only, none exclusively for wine. Local varieties have names which translate into the likes of Cow's Nipple, Dragon's Eye and Cock's Heart. Imported varieties which have flourished as wine producers include Cabernet Sauvignon, Merlot, Pinot Noir, Carignan, Saperavi, Gamay, Welschriesling, Gewürztraminer, Muscat de Frontignan and Rkatsiteli. Muscat Hamburg is extensively used in China's nascent wine industry, too.

——— LONGYAN ———

The Dragon's Eye grape is widely cultivated over northern China and southern Manchuria, especially on higher land. It copes well in very dry conditions and is a formidable yielder.

Although it was considered a table grape initially, Longyan has produced wines, such as the exported Great Wall, of real distinction with considerable extract, good balance and an aroma perhaps more reminiscent of lacquer than wine but by no means unpleasant.

Good balance.

India

Vines have been grown and wines have been made in this country of abstinence at various times during the last 350 years. Today the Indian wine industry is gently expanding, though not to the extent of yielding information to any but the most dogged personal callers. Portuguese grape varieties still flourish on Goa.

California

(See map page 226)

SULTANA

For many of today's children Sultana is almost certainly the first grape they encounter, and the odds are that it will have been in a packet of raisins. Being seedless, abundant and very sweet, Sultana is primarily a grape for drying, and California plantings supply more than half the world's and 95 percent of California's raisins. Secondly, it is a table grape, and only thirdly of interest to winemakers.

In some years more wine has been made from Sultana than from California's most-planted white-wine grape French Colombard. In 1983 there were 112,000 hectares (280,000 acres) of Sultana (representing nearly 40 percent of all California grape plantings) compared with 29,200 hectares (73,000 acres) of French Colombard. Sultana was particularly important to the California wine industry in the early and mid-seventies when there was a severe shortage of material with which to satisfy the new American craving for white wine.

Sultana is known as Thompson Seedless in California, thus named after William Thompson who first grew it commercially in the state, near Yuba City.

It is not ideal for winemaking because its seedless state does nothing to conduct the rather slippery juice from the firm, dense flesh once the grapes have been crushed to a pulp. Sultana does, however, have usefully high natural acidity, is extremely productive and its wine is at least neutral in flavour, so that it provides a suitable base for cheap sparkling wine or as an addition to a more strongly flavoured variety in everyday blends.

Sultana

Viticulturally it demands hot, dry conditions for it is considerably more susceptible to both powdery and downy mildew than the average wine grape, has fairly thin-skinned grapes which can easily suffer rain damage, and it can be devastated by black spot. Sultana thrives in the San Joaquin Valley and more than half the state's plantings are in the sunbaked raisin county of Fresno.

The vine's origins lie in Asia Minor, and it is an important table and drying grape especially around the eastern Mediterranean and eastern Black Sea coasts. Even today it is used for wine on some Mediterranean islands; it is the chief grape, for instance, in one of Cyprus's fresher whites, their perlant Bellapais.

In Australia barely a sixth of the country's 18,000 hectares (45,000 acres) of Sultana vines were used by winemakers in 1983, but it was still the country's second most important wine grape after Muscat of Alexandria or Muscat Gordo Blanco. Two-thirds of all Australia's Sultana is grown in the irrigated Sunraysia vineyards in the Murray basin in Victoria.

South Africa's plantings have been gradually increasing and now total about 5,000 hectares, but most of their wine produce goes straight to the distillery.

Sultana has not been planted to any extent in France where wet autumns preclude raisin production.

Synonyms:
Sultanina, Sultanine Blanche (France); Oval Kishmish (Middle East); Kismis (USSR); Feherszultan (Hungary); Thompson Seedless (California).

Excellent raisins, good table grapes, neutral wine.

——— COLOMBARD ———

Originally a Charentais variety for long regarded a poor third to Ugni Blanc and Folle Blanche as an ingredient in French alembics, Colombard must still be reeling from the impact of such sudden popularity in the California of the eighties. It is now California's most planted wine grape, almost twice as popular as Chenin Blanc, the state's second most planted wine grape. One wonders how many other vines, spurned in their homeland, could be given such a glamorous new lease of life in some completely different setting.

The environment of California in the decade between 1973 and 1983 was absolutely perfect for Colombard. Here was the vineyard of a major nation, crying out for a vine that could supply huge quantities of fairly crisp wine in warm to hot conditions. Colombard fitted the bill, and in that time plantings rose from an already notable 9,600 hectares (24,000 acres) to more than 29,200 hectares (73,000 acres), 11,200 hectares (28,000 acres) of them still not bearing by 1983. Ironically, the only variety which has experienced a quantitatively similar increase in plantings in Europe recently is Ugni Blanc, which has largely displaced Colombard and Folle Blanche in France.

As the producer of a varietal wine, Colombard is several notches above either of its traditional distillery companions in Cognac and Armagnac. The high acidity is complemented by a distinctly flowery perfume making a well-balanced and genuinely appetizing young wine, provided the vines are grown with sufficient care in one of California's medium-cool regions such as Mendocino or Lake County. Even the wine produced from the vast majority of Colombard vines which are reared in the much hotter San Joaquin Valley is self-confident stuff, with sufficient acid to keep it crisp and a certain perfume to make it useful in medium-dry blends. Colombard wine is not for ageing.

The vine is very vigorous, and very easy to grow in the warm, dry vineyards of California. It buds fairly early, which can be a problem in cooler locations, but suffers from no serious diseases or susceptibilities, except for the California phenomenon of "spindle shoot" whereby the leaves on some shoots are stunted, puckered up and yellowish. A medium-late ripener, Colombard is well able to hold its fruit in good condition for up to a week extra, which helps to spread the picking schedule. It is one of California's most productive vines giving 6 to 9 tons per acre in coastal counties and up to 13 tons per acre in the Central Valley.

Yields of 100 hectolitres per hectare are common in France where today it is mainly cultivated in the Gironde, being considered not sufficiently neutral to play a major role in the eau-de-vie production in the Charentes and Gers. In 1984, there were still about 3,300 hectares (8,250 acres) of Colombard in Bordeaux, the majority of them in the Bourg and Blaye northern fringes. The dry and medium-dry white wine produced here rarely has the fruit that can so happily soften Colombard's high natural acidity in California. The explanation for this probably

lies more in the cellar than in the climate, as recent varietal Colombards emerging as carefully vinified Côtes de Gascogne have testified. These crisp yet fruity wines from Gascony demonstrate eloquently that transatlantic traffic in oenological expertise is without doubt two-way.

In South Africa, as Colombar, the variety has enjoyed the same sort of recent success as in California. In a similar climate, the variety's high acid and suitability to cool temperature fermentation have resulted in a discernible increase in plantings since 1970. With Chenin Blanc it can often be found in blends labelled Stein. So prized is its fruity aroma that one authority has managed to find in it the scent of the local keokamakranka flower.

Synonyms:
Colombar, Colombier,
Pied Tendre, Queue Tendre,
Queue Verte (France);
French Colombard,
West's White Prolific (California);
Colombar (South Africa).

Good, crisp everyday whites,
even in hot climates.

Colombard

—— EMERALD RIESLING ——

The artfully named Emerald Riesling is the white counterpart to Professor H. P. Olmo's red Ruby Cabernet, also released in 1948 and also a fairly ordinary grape crossed with a noble one, Muscadelle × Riesling in this case. It was useless, of course, to try any of the many Riesling crossings tested in Germany as these were specifically developed for cool climates.

Happily, Emerald Riesling seems to have inherited much more Riesling character than Muscadelle and is well capable of producing wines as vital and attractively aromatic, in youth at least, as its more aristocratic progenitor. The state's total plantings, after nearly four decades, are still well under 1,600 hectares (4,000 acres), much less than a third of the area planted with what many consider is the distinctly less successful Ruby Cabernet. Such is the awkwardness of a plant that requires long-term planning.

About half of all California's Emerald Riesling is planted at the south of the San Joaquin Valley in Kern County where it produces fairly full-bodied, though always fairly high-acid, aromatic wines without too much flavour definition. In some of the cooler locations in which it has been tried, as in Monterey, it can have all the raciness of proper Riesling in its first year or so in bottle, with slightly more body.

It may be the fact that its perfumed style is out of favour in a market besotted by Chardonnay and Fumé Blanc which accounts for Emerald Riesling's not being more widely planted. A subsidiary reason is probably that it is extremely difficult to machine harvest, a difficulty that is easy to compound by its tendency to brown if picked by hands in anything other than sulphur-doused kid gloves.

Emerald Riesling

The late-ripening vine is susceptible to powdery mildew but can yield between 9 and 13 tons per acre without too much loss of character. It has also been tried out, with some success, in South Africa but the Australians have found it harder to extract any varietal definition.

A slightly broad version of Riesling.

—— TROUSSEAU GRIS ——

The average American wine drinker may never have heard of the traditional and near-extinct black Jura variety Trousseau, but even if he hasn't, a few vine growers will know the Trousseau × Rubired crossing Royalty. He will, however, almost certainly have heard of Gray Riesling, which is the adoptive name of a grey mutation of Trousseau, Trousseau Gris, occasionally encountered in the Jura and widely planted in California.

Plantings of this rather undistinguished variety have been increasing steadily so that there were nearly 1,080 hectares (2,700 acres) by 1983, spread all over the state but mainly in coastal regions. Gray Riesling is used largely for varietal bottlings and, to damn with faint praise, the wine is characterized by the word "pleasant". It is well-balanced, usually just off-dry, muted in aroma, and can be flabby if the grapes are left on the vine a minute too long. The vine is prone to botrytis, ripens very early and can be embarrassingly and inconveniently vigorous. Its popularity is puzzling, though the average yield at 5–7 tons per acre is relatively high.

There are about 50 hectares (125 acres) of it in New Zealand. More flavour seems to be extracted in this cooler climate.

Synonyms:
Gray Riesling, Chauche Gris (California); Grey Riesling (New Zealand).

Unremarkable and very un-Riesling-like.

MONBADON

Another unfamiliar name masks California's drinkable sort of Burger, a warm-climate variety whose neutral wine is used chiefly in blends.

This variety, of which there were still more than 100 hectares (250 acres) in the Midi in 1979, was also declining dramatically in California where it was once the most-planted *vinifera* grape variety. Between the mid-seventies and mid-eighties, however, there has been a slight resurgence of Burger whose total California plantings were back to 800 hectares (2,000 acres) in 1983, most of them in the San Joaquin Valley with some in Napa and Sonoma. Yields average between 8 and 11 tons per acre; some older plants are seriously infected with leafroll virus.

Synonyms:
Castillone à Montendre, Caoba, Grand Blanc, Meslier d'Orléans (France); Burger (California).

Productive.

GREEN HUNGARIAN

An odd grape this, Green Hungarian's origins remain obscure although a subconscious and rather satisfying link with the father of California viticulture, Agoston Haraszthy, is surely suggested by the name. The name is probably the most interesting thing about the variety, whose wines are merely vaguely fruity and often hefty. Its 188 hectares (470 acres) are well distributed over the state. There may be a Hungarian connection, but the wine lacks Magyar fire. It would be Superpalate indeed who could pick this varietal blind.

Plodding.

Other varieties include the hot-climate, undistinguished Peverella (Pfeffertraube), almost all of whose 160 hectares (400 acres) are in Kern County (it is also grown in Brazil); Flora, the Sémillon × Gewürztraminer crossing released by Olmo in 1958, which has met with some success in Mendocino and New Zealand, but produces flabby wine anywhere warmer; the Hungarian dessert-wine grape Feher Szagos; the hot-climate Mantuo Pilas; and the cooler, crisper Helena and Symphony (Grenache × Muscat of Alexandria).

The Eastern USA

(See map page 228)

Niagara is an all-American crossing of Concord × Cassady and has inherited extreme "foxiness" of flavour. It is popular throughout the eastern and even midwestern states in many styles of white wine. It is also grown in Brazil and in a very limited way in New Zealand.

Aurore (Aurora, Seibel 5279) is a French hybrid and vies with Niagara as the eastern states' most planted white-wine grape variety. There are about 800 hectares (2,000 acres) planted.

Vidal Blanc (Vidal 256) is an Ugni Blanc × Seibel 4986 crossing that manages quite high sugar levels in cool climates. Acid levels are also agreeably high and the flavour is sufficiently neutral and gently fruity to make one hope that the variety will prove increasingly popular.

Dutchess is a *labrusca* × *vinifera* hybrid which tastes like it and is produced, usually as a fairly sweet wine, by nearly 20 eastern US wineries as well as in Brazil.

Cayuga is an exception to this list of well-established French hybrids or crossings of all-American species in that it was developed only recently at the Geneva experimental station in New York State. It takes its name from one of the nearby Finger Lakes and has been embraced enthusiastically.

The avid wine producers of America also use some varieties from the Muscadine subgenus, as opposed to the subgenus *Euvites* to which *vinifera*, *labrusca*, *riparia*, *rupestris* and all American and Asian species belong. Best known is Scuppernong.

Other varieties commercially cultivated in the eastern states to a limited extent include Ravat (Vignoles), Carlos, Diamond, Magnolia and Elvira.

South Africa

CRUCHEN BLANC

Though rather naughty, those who decided to tag the magic word Riesling on to a local name for this curiously well-travelled variety were very sensible really. South African Riesling, Cape Riesling, Paarl Riesling, Clare Riesling all sound so much more attractive than "Cruchen" The variety's real name must have come as rather a shock to those hundreds of growers in Australia, who were happily growing something as saleable as Clare Riesling, when told in 1976 by the visiting official French ampelographer that it was in fact a dreary Gascon grape with an even drearier name.

The news has since been washed across the Indian Ocean to the vineyards of the Cape where Cruchen is even more widely planted. South Africa's total plantings were over 2,000 hectares (5,000 acres) and still increasing in 1980, while Australia had only about 1,000 hectares (2,500 acres) in 1983.

Cruchen Blanc

The variety was a speciality of the Landes region in the far southwest of France, and the *vin de sable* it once produced may give the clue to the identity of the "Sales Blanc" in one of Australia's first shipments of imported vine cuttings. Plantings in France have now dwindled to extinction as it was much affected by *court-noué* and has shown great susceptibility to both sorts of mildew. It was thought for some time to be the table grape Teneron, which gives some idea of its quality.

Its wines are flabby in too hot a climate and tartly neutral in one that is too cool. In the medium cool vineyards of hot wine-making countries such as Paarl/Stellenbosch and Barossa/Clare Valley in South Africa and Australia respectively, it seems capable of making easy, if not exactly distinguished, gently aromatic wines, often with a little residual sugar. The South Africans believe it is best made steely-dry and at least one example, Nederburg 1974, has demonstrated the ability to age.

The South Africans genuinely thought the variety was Riesling, while the Australians for long confused it with Sémillon.

Synonyms:
Crouchen, Cruchenton Blanc,
Trouchet Blanc, Méssange Blanc,
Cougnet, Navarre Blanc (France);
South African Riesling, Cape Riesling,
Paarl Riesling (South Africa);
Clare Riesling (Australia).

Medium, mildly aromatic.

PEDRO LUIS

Viala identified this as a variety distinct from, though commonly grown with, Pedro Ximénez in Andalucia. It is being planted, with Pedro Ximénez, to replace the ubiquitous Zalema in Huelva to the north and west of the sherry region.

The South Africans reckon that they have more than 2,000 hectares (5,000 acres) of this variety, imported originally as Pedro Ximénez. They have found it particularly useful in the sandy soils of the very dry Paarl and Malmesbury districts. Its produce is used chiefly in sherry styles, but some is blended into table wines.

Synonym: False Pedro (South Africa).

More interesting viticulturally
than oenologically.

BUKETTRAUBE

This variety, which the South Africans have taken to their hearts as a recent import from Germany, is curiously difficult to identify in the meticulous annals of German viticulture. Galet notes an Alsace variety, Bouquettraube, said to have originated in Würzburg, whose leaves resemble those of Elbling and whose grapes are lightly Muscat-scented.

This may well be the variety of which several hundred hectares are planted on the Cape, especially in cooler coastal regions. Relatively early maturing with good sugar and acid levels, it is prized for the aromatic note it can bring to blends and it makes well-balanced medium-dry varietals. Some dessert versions have also done well.

Synonym: Bouquettraube (Alsace).

Aromatic.

CHENEL

This crossing of Chenin Blanc with Ugni Blanc was developed by Professor Chris Orffer specifically for South African conditions. It is reliably vigorous and productive, does not rot or split and can be cultivated in warm regions with a minimum of vineyard treatments.

It was named after the first syllables of its nobler parent and the Elsenburg research station, whence it was released in the early seventies. It has been grown successfully on all sorts of soils and seems to cope well with both the hot Karoo region and the cooler coastal vineyards.

The wine produced is light, crisp and presumably cheap. The only problem is that the consumer is still unfamiliar with it.

From the same parents, Orffer has also developed Weldra which is at an even more experimental stage.

Viticulturally expedient,
if oenologically unexciting.

SERVIN BLANC

This rather ordinary Midi grape variety is probably the vine that still makes such a significant contribution to Cape spirit. About 6.5 million Raisin Blanc vines (about a tenth of the nation's tally of Chenin Blanc) are cultivated for this purpose. The vines are not very healthy.

Synonym: Raisin Blanc

Poor quality wine.

CANAAN

There are 5 million vines of this equally uninspiring wine grape in South Africa. Their produce is also consigned to the distillery. It has a long Cape history although its susceptibility to rot and disease makes its produce unacceptable to modern winemakers. Orffer thinks it may be the same as the Macedonia of Sicily.

Synonyms:
Kanaan, Belies (South Africa);
Macedonia (Sicily).

Poor quality wine.

Australia

(See map page 230)

DORADILLO

This variety sounds like a particularly colourful Gilbert and Sullivan character. Its curiosity value lies in the fact that it is impossible to find in its native Spain today, but there were 1,600 hectares (4,000 acres) of it in Australia in 1983, about the same as the area planted with Chardonnay.

Undoubtedly a hot-climate variety, Doradillo is planted chiefly in the Murray irrigated vineyards of northern South Australia. It is notable more for quantity than quality or character. Most goes to the distillery, though it is prized by some as an ingredient in dry sherry-style wines.

At one stage it was erroneously thought to be identical with the Spanish Jaen and it has also, equally erroneously, been called Blanquette in parts of South Australia.

Neutral wine in great quantity.

CANOCAZO

Cañocazo is another white Spanish variety now more commonly encountered in Australia. There are about 300 hectares (750 acres) of it in Australia, mainly in South Australia where it produces grapes rather similar to those of Doradillo, but ripens earlier and not in such quantity. It was traditionally grown in the Jerez area and is still used as a parent in breeding programmes there, with Palomino, Pedro Ximénez and Garrido which, unlike Cañocazo, are authorized for wine production.

Easier to grow than Pedro Ximénez.

BIANCONE

Only Biancone can beat Doradillo for productivity but it does so resoundingly: an average of 30 tons per hectare in the irrigated Riverland of South Australia where its mere 44 hectares (110 acres) are concentrated. The rather characterless wine is used mainly for distillation.

It is probably the same as the Biancone

of Elba and Corsica but is not known elsewhere. It was thought to be Grenache Blanc until Truel's visit in 1976.

Very productive indeed.

Two varieties designed to put quality into Australia's famous wine casks have also been developed by the official research station at Merbein, South Australia, both named after places near (by Australian standards) Merbein. Goyura is Muscat of Alexandria × Sultana and has a vaguely Muscat flavour but is most useful for its high levels of natural acid. Tulillah, which is Macabeo × Sultana, is more neutral although it yields very well and has fairly high acid. Neither has so far been welcomed as heartily as the red Tarrango. Waltham Cross is primarily a table grape but is sometimes used for brandy.

New Zealand

—— BREIDECKER ——

This hybrid of Müller-Thurgau × Seibel 7053 was specially developed for New Zealand at Geisenheim. It "graduated" at the same time as Reichensteiner and Ehrenfelser and has been grown in New Zealand since 1962. It has the advantages of wild vine resistance to rot and downy mildew without too aggressively savage a flavour. About 130 tons of fruit were harvested in 1983, constituting 0.2 percent of the vintage. The wine tastes much more like Müller-Thurgau than anything else and is useful for blending. The variety has already been used for further breeding at Geisenheim so perhaps even more suitable hybrids will emerge for New Zealand. This one is named after a German viticulturist who helped the nascent New Zealand wine industry. The next successful new hybrid is expected to be called Becker.

—— DR HOGG MUSCAT ——

This is New Zealand's "own" Muscat, used nowhere else to produce wine. There are 90 hectares (225 acres) planted with it, chiefly in the Poverty Bay area. It was originally a table grape imported from the greenhouses of Victorian England. It can produce quite palatable, strongly flavoured table wines in New Zealand. It has good resistance to wet weather, ripens late and is not at all vigorous.

July Muscat is an import from California and hybrids other than Baco 22A include Gaillard Girerd 157 and Muscat St-Vaillard 20743.

England

No wonder English wine has to fight so hard to be noticed; the vineyards are so tiny. The average holding is less than half a hectare (1 acre). The total area planted in 1984 was less than 450 hectares (1,125 acres). The most planted variety, Müller-Thurgau, covers barely 150 hectares (375 acres). Reichensteiner is second most popular, covering less than 50 hectares (125 acres), with Seyval Blanc not far behind. The next three most-planted varieties – Madeleine Angevine, Huxelrebe and the very successful Schönburger – cover just over 65 hectares (162 acres).

That a total of 35 varieties have been tried on at least three holdings is testimony both to the youth and enthusiasm of the English wine industry. The majority of them are new German crossings designed to ripen in dull summers (the noble Riesling cannot, alas, be persuaded to ripen in England). The Pinot family and Chardonnay are all being given an English footing, however, and other non-German varieties include the Austrian Rotburger (as Zweigeltrebe) and Wrotham Pinot and Triomphe d'Alsace.

—— SEYVAL BLANC ——

If ever evidence were needed that in certain conditions French hybrids are a Jolly Good Thing, it is in the great number of bottles of Seyval Blanc produced in England. There is simply no difference in quality between the wines produced from this hardy vine, well-suited to low temperatures, and those made from 100 percent *vinifera* varieties. There is, of course, a difference in wine character. Seyval wines tend to be high in acidity, more etheric and a little bit leaner than, say, Müller-Thurgau, and many winemakers give them stuffing in the form of sweet reserve made from another, more characterful variety. On its own, it can

Seyval Blanc

have a certain grapefruit quality. There is no hint of "foxy" flavour.

It was produced by crossing Seibel 5656 with Seibel 4986 (Rayon d'Or) which has in the past done quite well in both northern France and New York State. It probably owes its exceptional popularity in England to the English pioneer, Major-General Sir Guy Salisbury-Jones, who was advised to plant it in the early 1950s by friends in France. It thrived and has since spread from his Hambledon vineyard in West Sussex all over southern England.

The vine is vigorous, productive and has good disease resistance. It buds and ripens early and pruning has to be done carefully to avoid overcropping at one extreme and poor fruit at the other.

Synonym: Seyve-Villard 5276.

Useful, medium quality.

—— MADELEINE ANGEVINE ——

This variety, of which 26 hectares (65 acres) were planted in England in 1984 with some degree of success, has excited controversy and detailed analysis. The original Madeleine Angevine was a crossing of Madeleine Royale and Précoce de Malingre made by Vibert in, as the name suggests, Angers in 1857 to produce a female table grape. Most of the Madeleine Angevine now planted in England, however, seems to have come from a vine imported by Ray Barrington Brock, called after him and by the number 7972. The origins of this hermaphrodite variety are thought to be German and work is under way to unravel them. The wine produced in England has a fairly strong Muscat aroma but *coulure* can be a problem.

Glossary and Bibliography

A boire Ready to drink.

AC Appellation Contrôlée. French designation with official guarantee of the source and production method of wine.

Acidity Natural tartness in grapes, essential ingredient in wine.

Alembic A still, usually a pot still.

Amabile Semi-sweet.

Ampelography The science of describing, and therefore identifying, the different vine varieties.

Anthocyanins Colouring matter, concentrated just under the grape's skin.

Anthracnose Fungus disease, unusually, of European origin, encouraged by rain. It attacks both vine and fruit producing cankers all over the vine, leading to holes in the leaves.

Aszú Hungarian term for grapes infected with "noble rot". Applies to Tokay.

Auslese Selected, i.e. German quality wine (QmP) made from selected bunches of particularly ripe grapes and usually naturally sweet.

Back blending New Zealand term for adding Süssreserve.

Barrique Standard Bordeaux barrel of 225 litres.

Beerenauslese Selected grapes, i.e. German quality wine (QmP) made from individually selected over-ripe grapes, high in both sugar and price.

Black rot Fungus disease of both vine and fruit encouraged by hot, damp weather. Initial symptoms resemble those of anthracnose but result in tiny, hard black berries.

Blanc de blancs White wine made only from white grapes, especially champagne.

Blanc de noirs White wine made from black grapes, especially champagne.

Bodega In Spain, a firm making wine and/or shipping it; a wine shop.

Botrytis Rot, fungus attacking fruit, not vine, encouraged by humidity. Causes red grapes to lose their colour and quality. Adversely affects white grapes if they are already damaged (e.g. by rain) but if the grapes are ripe and healthy, and the ambient conditions are alternately damp (not rainy) and sunny, the rot is deemed "noble". Noble rot shrivels the grapes and concentrates the sugar so that top-quality sweet wines can be made.

Botrytis cinerea Noble rot.

Brix A scale for measuring the sugar content of grape juice, used in the United States and Australia.

Bunch rot *See* botrytis.

Cane Woody, mature stage reached by the shoot after leaf fall.

Carbonic maceration *See macération carbonique.*

Cépage Vine variety.

Cépage améliorateur "Improver" vine, used in France to boost the quality of *vins de pays*, etc.

Chaptalization Addition of sugar during fermentation to increase alcohol level.

Chlorosis Yellowing of vine foliage due to lack of usable iron in the soil, often because of high lime content.

Chromatography Liquid- or gas-based method of analysing the chemical constituents of, for example, a wine.

Clarete Light red (Spain).

Clonal selection Deliberate programme of selecting clones according to some preordained criteria.

Clone Member of a group of plants propagated asexually from a single source.

Cluster Bunch, of grapes.

Coulure Failure of vine flowers to develop.

Court-noué *See* fan-leaf.

Crossing A crossbreed produced by members of the same species of vine.

Cru classé Classed growth; applied in particular to the 1855 classification of Médoc châteaux.

Cultivar Grape variety (South Africa).

Cuve Vat.

Cuvée A blend of wines; a special selection.

Département French administrative region, similar to a UK or US county.

Direct producer Ungrafted vine.

DOC Denominazione di Origine Controllata. Italian designation indicating official regulation of the geographical origin, grape type, etc., of wine.

DOCG Denominazione di Origine Controllata e Garantita. Italian designation of origin of wine officially regulated and guaranteed.

Downy mildew Winter-dormant fungus disease of the vine, one of whose symptoms is a white mildew on the underside of leaves.

Edelfäule German for "noble rot". *See* botrytis.

EEC European Economic Community.

Eiswein "Ice Wine" made to strict specifications in Germany from grapes frozen on the vine. As sweet, though not so long-lasting, as a Beerenauslese.

Elevage Attention to making of wine between fermentation and bottling.

Encépagement The varietal make-up of a vineyard.

Epoch One of the four periods into which the ripening span of all vines is arbitrarily divided, fourth epoch being the latest. Used particularly in Italy.

Fan-leaf Virus disease spread through the soil which stunts vine growth and shortens the vine's life.

Flor The yeast which grows on fino and amontillado sherry in barrel and protects it from oxidation.

Geneva Double Curtain A three-dimensional vine trellis.

Genus Botanical group of different species.

Gobelet Method of training the vine in a goblet shape.

Governo Traditional practice of adding dried grapes to Chianti after fermentation to provoke a second fermentation and soften the wine.

Grafted Usually of vinifera vine, growing on non-vinifera (phylloxera-resistant) rootstock.

Grand cru Top-quality French wine; specific and different meanings in Bordeaux, Burgundy, Champagne and Alsace.

Grey rot *See* botrytis.

Guyot Method of training the vine on a single vertical axis.

Halbtrocken Half-dry, containing less than 18 grams per litre of unfermented sugar (German).

Hectare 10,000 square metres, 2.471 acres.

Hectolitre 100 litres, 21.998 Imperial gallons, 26.418 US gallons.

Hybrid A cross between different species of vine.

Kabinett The most basic category of quality wine (QmP) in Germany.

Late harvest Of wines, produced from very ripe grapes and usually sweet.

Leafroll Airborne virus disease causing leaf edges to curl under and vigour and yield to diminish.

Lyre Three-dimensional vine trellis system developed in Bordeaux.

Macération carbonique Fermentation technique using whole bunches of unbroken grapes in an atmosphere saturated with carbon dioxide. Associated first with Beaujolais; now also used in the Midi and elsewhere.

Maderized Well on the way to being oxidized, used usually for white wines.

Malic acid Particularly raw, "appley" acid in grapes. The level falls as grapes ripen.

Malolactic fermentation A fermentation in which harsh malic acids are converted into gentler lactic acids. It is secondary and usually subsequent to the principal alcoholic fermentation and in hotter wine regions may be suppressed, but is usually encouraged in cooler regions.

Méthode champenoise Traditional method of putting bubbles in champagne by refermenting the wine in its bottle.

Metodo champenois (Italian.) *See méthode champenoise.*

Millerandage The phenomenon of unevenly sized berries on a single bunch. Often follows *coulure*.

Mistelle Mixture of unfermented grape juice and alcohol.

Moelleux Literally full of marrow, soft and mellow, used of sweet wines.

Mousseux Sparkling.

Musqué Heavily perfumed, often some suggestion of Muscat.

Must Unfermented grape juice and solids.

Must weight   Amount of sugar in ripe grapes or must.

Mutation   Changing of biological characteristics, sometimes sufficiently to produce a new variety.

Nervosité   French tasting term meaning raciness, liveliness, usually associated with well-balanced, high acidity.

Noble rot   *See* botrytis.

Nouveau   Wine made to be drunk in the months immediately after the vintage.

Oechsle   A scale for measuring the sugar content of grape juice, used in Germany (*see* Brix).

Oidium   Powdery mildew, a fungus disease of vines.

Oloroso   Rich, nutty sherry style.

Oxidized   Of wine that has gone stale and flat from over-exposure to air.

Peronospera   *See* downy mildew.

Pétillant   Slightly sparkling.

pH   Measure of strength of acidity/alkalinity. Water is 7; the pH of wine (always acid) varies between 2.8 and 3.9. The higher the pH, the weaker the acids.

Phylloxera   *See* pages 10–11.

Pied   (French) individual vine plant.

Pourriture noble   *See* botrytis.

Premier cru   First growth in Bordeaux, but second rank in Burgundy.

QbA   Qualitätswein eines bestimmten Anbaugebietes. A German quality wine of a designated region and made from authorized grapes. Between Tafelwein and QmP in quality.

QmP   Qualitätswein mit Prädikat. A German quality wine with special attributes; the top category of wines, from Kabinett to Trockenbeerenauslese.

Rootstock   The lower, rooting part of a grafted vine, designed to be phylloxera-resistant.

Secco   Dry (Italian).

Sélection des Grains Nobles   Selected individual grapes with "noble rot" (Alsace).

Shoot   Green leafy growth from bud in growing season.

Shoot necrosis   Rare virus disease killing young shoots and, eventually, the vine.

Solera   Fractional blending system used particularly in Jerez where old wine drawn off a barrel is replaced by young wine.

Spätlese   Late-gathered German quality wine (QmP), the rank above Kabinett.

Species   Member of a botanical genus.

Spritz   A slight prickle of gas in a wine.

Spumante   Sparkling (Italian).

Sur lie   Literally "on the lees". Used especially of Muscadets which are bottled straight from the fermentation vat so as to retain some carbon dioxide and add flavour by lees contact.

Surmaturité   Over-ripeness.

Süssreserve   Sweet reserve – unfermented grape juice added to wine, usually German, English and New Zealand, before bottling to achieve a required level of sweetness.

Tafelwein   Table wine as defined by EEC regulations. Not of German origin unless prefexed by Deutscher.

Tartaric acid   Most important grape (and wine) acid, especially in ripe vintages.

Teinturier   Red-fleshed vine variety.

Tendone   Italian system of training vines high and maximizing yield.

Tinto   Deep red (Spain).

Trocken   Dry, containing less than 9 grams per litre of unfermented sugar (German).

Trockenbeerenauslese (TBA)   Selected very sweet grapes, often infected with "noble rot", used in making the sweetest and most expensive German wine.

Varietal   Technically, "concerning varieties"; popularly, a wine made

principally from a single variety.

VDQS   Vin Délimité de Qualité Supérieure. French wines of lesser quality than Appellation Contrôlée wines and made under less strict laws. Between AC and *vin de pays* in quality.

Vendange tardive   Late harvest (especially Alsace).

Veraison   Stage at which the grapes start to take on colour and begin to ripen.

Vigneron   Grape grower (French).

Vignoble   Vineyard.

Vin de pays   Superior table wine, French country wine made to a minimum standard and in regulated quantities laid down by official decree.

Vin de sable   Wine produced from grapes grown in sandy soil.

Vin de table   Table wine not subject to particular regulations about grapes and origin.

Vin doux naturel (VDN)   Fortified sweet wine.

Vinification   The process of making wine.

Vin jaune   Jura sherry-like speciality made of late-picked Savagnin grapes aged in barrel for at least six years.

Vino da tavola   Table wine; Italian wine not produced to DOC rules.

Vino novello   Nouveau (Italian).

Vin ordinaire   Ordinary wine not subject to regulation.

Vins liquoreux   Sweet wines.

Viticulture   The process of growing grapes.

Vonkelwyn   Sparkling wine (South African).

Weight   The body and alcoholic strength of a wine.

Weissherbst   German QbA pink wine, especially popular in Baden.

Wine Lake   EEC surplus of low-quality table wine.

BIBLIOGRAPHY

Leon D. Adams, *The Wines of America*, McGraw-Hill, New York, 1985; Sidgwick & Jackson, London, 1984

Burton Anderson, *The Mitchell Beazley Pocket Guide to Italian Wines*, Mitchell Beazley, London, 1984; *Vino*, Atlantic-Little, Brown, Boston and Toronto, 1980; Papermac, London, 1980

A. J. Antcliff, *Major Wine Grape Varieties of Australia*, Commonwealth Scientific and Industrial Research Organization (CSIRO), Australia, 1979

Anuario del Vino Espanol, Sucro (Spain), 1984

Nicolas Belfrage, *Life Beyond Lambrusco*, Sidgwick & Jackson, London, 1985

Michael Cooper, *The Wines and Vineyards of New Zealand*, Hodder and Stoughton, Auckland, 1984

Noel Cossart, *Madeira, The Island Vineyard*, Christie's Wine Publications, London, 1984

Antonio Xavier Pereira Coutinho, *Cultura da Vinha*, Livraria Nacional e Estrangeira (Portugal), 1895

Hubrecht Duijker, *The Wines of the Loire, Alsace and Champagne*, Mitchell Beazley, London, 1983

Henri Enjalbert, *Les Grands Vins de Saint Emilion, Pomerol et Fronsac*, Editions Bardi, Paris, 1983

Len Evans (ed), *Complete Book of Australian Wine*, Lansdowne, Sydney, 1984

Nicholas Faith, *Château Margaux*, Christie's Wine Publications, London, 1980

Pierre Galet, *Cépages et Vignobles de France*, Vols II and III, Galet, Montpellier,

1958 and 1962

P. G. Garoglio, *Enciclopedia Vitivinicola Mondiale*, Vol I, Edizioni Schientifiche UIV, Milan, 1973

Rosemary George, *The Wines of Chablis*, Sotheby/Philip Wilson, London, 1984

Francisco Esteves Gonçalves, *Portugal, A Wine Country*, Editora Portuguesa de Livros Técnicos e Científicos, Lisbon, 1983

R. E. H. Gunyon, *The Wines of Central and South-eastern Europe*, Duckworth, London, 1971

James Halliday and Ray Jarratt, *The Wines & History of The Hunter Valley*, McGraw-Hill, New York, 1979

Anthony Hanson, *Burgundy*, Faber, London, 1982

Victor Hazan, *Italian Wine*, Alfred A. Knopf, New York, 1982

Charles Higounet (ed), *La Seigneurie et Le Vignoble du Château Latour* (2 vols), Fédération Historique du Sud-Ouest, Bordeaux, 1974

Walter Hillebrand, *Taschenbuch der Rebsorten*, Dr Blitz & Dr Fraund KG, Wiesbaden, 1972

Edward Hyams, *Dionysus, A Social History of Wine*, Thames & Hudson, London, 1965

David Jackson and Danny Schuster, *Grape Growing & Wine Making*, Alister Taylor, Martinborough, New Zealand and Prism Press, Dorchester, England, 1981

Ian Jamieson, *The Mitchell Beazley Pocket Guide to German Wines*, Mitchell Beazley, London, 1984

Julian Jeffs, *Sherry*, Faber, London, 1982

Hugh Johnson, *The World Atlas of Wine*, Mitchell Beazley, London, 1985; Simon & Schuster, New York, 1985; *Wine Companion (Modern Encyclopedia of Wine)*, Mitchell Beazley, London, 1983; Simon & Schuster, New York, 1983

A. N. Kasimatis and others, *Wine Grape Varieties in the North Coast Counties of California*, University of California, 1981; *Wine Grape Varieties in the San Joaquin Valley*, University of California, 1980

Graham Knox, *Estate Wines of South Africa*, David Philip, Capetown and Johannesburg, 1982

Max Lake, *Cabernet*, Rigby (Australia), 1977

Alexis Lichine's Encyclopedia of Wines & Spirits, Cassell, London, 1985; Alfred A. Knopf, New York, 1985

John Livingstone-Learmouth and Melvyn Master, *The Wines of the Rhône*, Faber, London, 1983

Lucie T. Morton (trans) and Pierre Galet, *A Practical Ampelography*, Cornell University Press, 1979

New Zealand Wine & Food Annual, Burnham House Publishing, Auckland, 1985

Charles Olken, Earl Singer and Norman Roby, *The Connoisseurs' Handbook of California Wines*, Alfred A. Knopf, New York, 1984

George Ordish, *The Great Wine Blight*, Dent, London, 1972

C. J. Orffer, *Wine Grape Cultivars in South Africa*, Human & Rousseau (S. Africa), 1979

Tom O'Toole, *South Tyrol Wine Guide*, Bozen Chamber of Commerce, 1985

Edmund Penning-Rowsell, *The Wines of Bordeaux*, Penguin, London, 1985

David Peppercorn, *Bordeaux*, Faber, London, 1982

Petit-Lafitte, *La Vigne en Bordelais*, 1868

Emile Peynaud, *Connaissance et Travail du Vin*, Dunod, Paris, 1981

George Rainbird, *Sherry and the Wines of Spain*, Michael Joseph, London, 1966

Jan Read, *The Mitchell Beazley Pocket Guide to Spanish Wines*, Mitchell Beazley, London, 1983; *The Wines of Portugal*, Faber, London, 1982; *Wines of the Rioja*, Sotheby/Philip Wilson, London, 1984; *The Wines of Spain*, Faber, London, 1982

Jancis Robinson, *The Great Wine Book*, Sidgwick & Jackson/William Morrow, London, 1982

Steven Spurrier, *French Country Wines*, Collins Willow, London, 1984

M. J. L. Stoltz, *Ampélographie Rhénane*, Strasbourg, 1852

Bob Thompson, *The Pocket Encyclopedia of California Wines*, Simon & Schuster, New York, 1980

G. G. Valinko, *Vinographie Vina*, Moscow, 1978

Pamela Vandyke Price with Christopher Fielden, *Alsace Wines*, Sotheby/Philip Wilson, London, 1984

P. Viala, *Traité Général d'Ampélographie*, Vol VII, Masson, 1909

Villa Maior, *Manual de Viticultura Practica*, Imprensa da Universidade, Coimbra, 1875

Jack Ward, *The Complete Book of Vine Growing in the British Isles*, Faber, London, 1984

A. J. Winkler, James A. Cook, W. M. Kliewer, Lloyd A. Lider, *General Viticulture*, University of California Press, 1974

Index